PREACHING CHRIST FROM PSALMS

*Foundations for Expository Sermons
in the Christian Year*

SIDNEY GREIDANUS

WILLIAM B. EERDMANS PUBLISHING COMPANY

GRAND RAPIDS, MICHIGAN

Wm. B. Eerdmans Publishing Co.
2140 Oak Industrial Drive N.E., Grand Rapids, Michigan 49505
www.eerdmans.com

22 21 20 19 18 17 16   1 2 3 4 5 6 7

ISBN 978-0-8028-7366-8

Library of Congress Cataloging-in-Publication Data

Names: Greidanus, Sidney, 1935- author.
Title: Preaching Christ from Psalms: foundations for expository sermons
in the Christian year / Sidney Greidanus.
Description: Grand Rapids : Eerdmans Publishing Company, 2016. |
includes bibliographical references and index.
Identifiers: LCCN 2016009761 | ISBN 9780802873668 (pbk.: alk. paper)
Subjects: LCSH: Bible. Psalms — Sermons. | Jesus Christ — Sermons. |
Typology (Theology) — Sermons.
Classification: LCC BS1430.54 .G74 2016 | DDC 251 — dc23
LC record available at https://lccn.loc.gov/2016009761

PREACHING CHRIST FROM PSALMS

This book is dedicated to
all preachers and student preachers
serving the Church of Jesus Christ.

How beautiful upon the mountains
are the feet of the messenger who announces peace,
who brings good news,
who announces salvation,
who says to Zion, "Your God reigns."

Isaiah 52:7 (NRSV)

Preach the word;
be prepared in season and out of season;
correct, rebuke and encourage —
with great patience and careful instruction.

2 Timothy 4:2 (NIV)

Contents

Contents

Contents

Contents

Contents

APPENDIXES

Table of Psalms Studied

Preface

I am deeply indebted to my first three proofreaders for the final shape of this book. Since I could not cover all 150 psalms, I was looking for a variety of psalms that could be preached as one or more series of sermons. Also, since I wished to demonstrate that there are ways to preach Christ from every psalm, I did not want to select psalms that made that task fairly easy — such as selecting the messianic psalms or the royal psalms. Therefore my first inclination was to help preachers with especially difficult psalms such as the imprecatory psalms. But, on second thought, what pastor would want to preach a series of sermons on the imprecatory psalms?

Next I considered a series on the Songs of Ascents (Psalms 120–134), but these would all be rather similar. Most helpful, I thought, would be a series that had a good mix of the different forms (types) of psalms: lament, hymn, thanksgiving, royal psalm, etc. But what topic would make this a meaningful series? I decided that it would be good to reinforce for the congregation the most foundational theme in the Bible: Creation–Fall–Redemption–New Creation. I selected twenty-some Psalms that could be arranged in different ways to preach one or more series on this biblical story-line. I submitted this plan to my proofreaders. John Witvliet, being the first to respond, suggested a shorter series on Creation–Fall–Redemption–New Creation and adding a second part with a series on the Christian feasts. I worked that out, passed it around, and my brother Morris responded that it would be good to add a series of psalms for Advent and Lent, as in the Lectionary. Finally Ryan Faber proposed that I follow *The Revised Common Lectionary*,[1] Year A, and offer the series on the biblical story-line in an Appendix.

---

1. *The Revised Common Lectionary* was published in 1992. Though it "is a widely accepted ecumenical text, there are still minor differences between *The Revised Common Lectionary* and

Consequently I have selected twenty-two psalms that *The Revised Common Lectionary* assigns for reading in Year A of the Christian year. It should be noted that these psalms (or parts thereof) were selected by a task force not to function as preaching texts, nor for their messianic content,[2] but "as the liturgical response to the first reading."[3] This selection of psalms consists of a good mix of forms:[4] eight hymns, four laments, three songs of thanksgiving, three royal psalms, two songs of trust, one song of Zion, and I have added the introductory Psalm 1, a torah (wisdom) psalm. This mixture of psalms will provide a good test for applying the redemptive-historical christocentric method also to the genre of psalms.

More importantly, this selection of psalms will help lectionary preachers to select as their preaching texts for the Christian year not the usual gospel readings but the psalms. This will provide fascinating new biblical angles on the Christian feast days. For example, preaching Psalm 96 on Christmas Day will provide the congregation with a wonderfully new perspective on Jesus' birth, a surprising historical panorama of the impact of Jesus' birth on Israel, the nations, and all of creation (see Chapter 7 below). When Jesus used Psalm 22:1 to cry out on Good Friday, "My God, my God, why have you forsaken me?" not many hearers will know that Jesus had in mind not only his present suffering but also his Easter victory (see Chapter 18 below). For Ascension Day, how many hearers will know that this feast day is more significant for the church than is Christmas and even Easter? (see Chapter 20 below). For Pentecost, not many hearers will know that God's Spirit was at work in Old Testament times not only in empowering kings and prophets but also in creating the material world and even *re-creating* it. Also for Pentecost, how many hearers will know that the imprecatory prayer in Psalm 104:35a, "Let sinners be consumed from the earth, and let the wicked be no more," which *The Revised Common Commentary* skips for the reading, is actually a very hopeful prayer for a world without evil? (see Chapter 21 below).

---

the actual lectionary systems that prevail among Roman Catholics, Anglicans, Lutherans, Presbyterians, and Methodists." Bert Polman, "The Liturgical Use of Psalm 29," *Psalm 29 through Time and Tradition* (Eugene, OR: Wipf & Stock, 2009; pp. 90–98), 97.

2. The task force did select some traditional messianic psalms for certain Christian feast days.

3. In *The Revised Common Lectionary*, "the Psalm is explicitly regarded as 'a congregational response and meditation on the first reading and is not intended as another reading.' . . . In revising the *Common Lectionary* '. . . the task force affirmed that the psalm (or scriptural canticle) should be chosen as the liturgical response to the first reading. . . .'" Howard N. Wallace, *Words to God*, 138, quoting "The Consultation on Common Texts" (1992), *The Revised Common Lectionary* (Nashville: Abingdon, 1992), 11 and 77.

4. As identified by Bernard W. Anderson, *Out of the Depths*, 173–77.

This selection of psalms will also help nonlectionary preachers preach series of sermons on the psalms for Advent, Lent, the Christian feast days, as well as on the biblical story-line and other possible series (see Appendix 6).

This book follows the method laid out in my *Preaching Christ from the Old Testament*. But in contrast to my books on Genesis, Ecclesiastes, and Daniel, I will not seek to trace all possible ways from the preaching text to Christ. I intend to be more direct by suggesting primarily the most solid ways from each psalm to Christ in the New Testament. Also, in formulating the theme and the goal of each psalm and the sermon, I intend to limit the discussion of various options and be more direct in suggesting how I would formulate these themes and goals.

As in the other books, I follow for each psalm the pattern of the ten steps from text to sermon I developed for first-year seminary students (see Appendix 1). The resulting repetition in each chapter is intended to inculcate a basic hermeneutical-homiletical approach to the biblical text.

Except for Chapter 1, each chapter concludes with a major section of "Sermon Exposition." These sections not only explain the meaning of all the verses but also (often in footnotes) quote many commentators whose valuable insights preachers may want to incorporate into their sermons. These "Sermon Exposition" sections are not sermons but the final instalment of "Foundations for Expository Sermons." Especially with lengthy texts, preachers will have to select key verses and add illustrations and applications relevant for their particular congregations. For immediate (aural) understanding, I will seek to model the sermon's oral style as much as possible, that is, short sentences, simple, vivid words, verse references *before* quotations, and forward movement (most quotations, complex arguments, and technical details are relegated to the footnotes). In these sections I will also show where and how in the sermon I would make the move(s) to Christ.

Appendix 2 provides the expository sermon model I developed for first-year seminary students. This model aims for sermons that are biblical, relevant, and well organized. As witness to the transforming power of the psalms, I have included in Appendix 3 a very personal meditation on Psalm 23, which I wrote years ago for our local church. My former seminary student, Ryan Faber, combined the proofreading of this book with the preparation and preaching of a series of sermons on the psalms. With his permission, I have included in Appendix 4 two of these sermons. Appendix 5 contains a New Testament sermon by my former student Roy Berkenbosch to provide a New Testament perspective on the cosmic Christ. Appendix 6 contains suggestions for preaching series of sermons on the psalms.

In the numbering of the psalms I have followed the Hebrew Bible and English versions. For those churches that use the Septuagint and Vulgate numbering, I have included the Greek number in parentheses.[5] Unless otherwise noted, the Bible version quoted is the NRSV. When the NIV is cited, it is the latest version (2011). Italics in biblical quotations indicate the word(s) I consider important for interpretation and/or would emphasize in reading. For the sake of consistency, the pointing in all Hebrew words and transliterations in quotations have been modified according to the latest SBL standards.

In order to keep the bibliography within reasonable limits, only books and a few articles frequently quoted are included in the bibliography. All other articles, essays, and books are fully referenced in each chapter when first mentioned and in shorter form thereafter.

May this book help pastors to preach the psalms and to preach Christ from the psalms so that the church may not only *pray* the psalms with Israel and *praise* God with their songs but also *hear* the psalms as God's Word proclaiming good news for hurting people living in a broken world.

Grand Rapids, Michigan   SIDNEY GREIDANUS

---

5. The different numbering of the Psalms in the Hebrew Bible and the Septuagint:

Hebrew (MT)	Greek (LXX) followed by Latin
1–8	(1–8)
9–10	(9)
11–113	(10–112)
114–115	(113)
116:1–9	(114)
116:10–19	(115)
117–146	(116–145)
147:1–11	(146)
147:12–20	(147)
148–150	(148–150)

Acknowledgments

I would like to thank the John Stek family for giving me some forty of his books on the psalms after he went to glory. John Stek, my former professor and later colleague, was an expert on the psalms and wrote the introduction and notes to the psalms for the *NIV Study Bible* (1985). At first, the many books added to my own and the ones from the Calvin library almost swamped me. But in the end it was handy to have these books readily available in my study. I shall seek to pass them on to good homes.

I am also very grateful for the work of my readers and proofreaders. I began with three: my former seminary student, the Rev. Ryan Faber of Pella, Iowa; my brother, the Rev. Morris N. Greidanus of Grand Rapids, Michigan; and my colleague at Calvin Seminary, Dr. John Witvliet, Professor of Worship. Unfortunately, because of illness, my brother Morris soon had to withdraw. Then two of my seminary colleagues offered to help out: Dr. Howard Vanderwell, Adjunct Professor of Worship, read and commented on all the chapters, while the Rev. Carl Bosma, Professor of Old Testament, read and commented on several of the psalms. I am grateful to all for their questions, suggestions, corrections, and encouragement. Special thanks to Ryan Faber for sticking with me as a proofreader for my last four books, for doing such an excellent job, for preaching on these psalms during Advent and Lent, and for allowing me to publish his Advent sermons on Psalms 78 and 80 in Appendix 4.

I also express my appreciation to the many authors quoted in this book and to the staff of the library of Calvin College and Calvin Theological Seminary for their courteous, helpful service, especially Paul Fields, Theological Librarian. I thank the staff of Eerdmans Publishing Company for their competent work, especially the copy editor, Dr. Andrew Knapp. In this connection, I particularly wish to express my gratitude to Mr. Jon Pott, Vice President, Editor-in-Chief, who suggested after publishing my book *Preaching Christ from the Old Testament* that I write my next book on an individual Old Testament book. This suggestion led to publications on Genesis (narrative), Ecclesiastes (wisdom), Daniel (prophecy / apocalypse), and now I finish the series with the genre of psalms. Writing these books has made for a most joyful, fulfilling "retirement."

Again I am grateful to my wife, Marie, for taking care of most of the household chores so that I could concentrate on the research and writing of this book. Last but not least, I am immensely thankful to the Lord for providing me with health, strength, and insights for writing this book and for having used me to help thousands of preachers and student preachers to preach Christ from the Old Testament. To God be the praise and glory.

Abbreviations

ANET	*Ancient Near Eastern Texts Relating to the Old Testament*
ATJ	*Asbury Theological Journal*
Bib	*Biblica*
BR	*Bible Review*
BSac	*Bibliotheca Sacra*
CBQ	*Catholic Biblical Quarterly*
cf.	compare
CML	*Canaanite Myths and Legends*
CTJ	*Calvin Theological Journal*
ed.	edited by
ESV	English Standard Version
ExpTim	*Expository Times*
GTJ	*Grace Theological Journal*
HCSB	Holman Christian Standard Bible
Heb.	Hebrew
HKAT	Handkommentar zum Alten Testament
HorBT	*Horizons in Biblical Theology*
HTR	*Harvard Theological Review*
IDB	*Interpreter's Dictionary of the Bible*
Int	*Interpretation*
JATS	*Journal of the Adventist Theological Studies*
JBL	*Journal of Biblical Literature*
JBQ	*Jewish Biblical Quarterly*
JETS	*Journal of the Evangelical Theological Society*
JEvHS	*Journal of the Evangelical Homiletics Society*
JPr	*Journal for Preachers*

JPS	Jewish Publication Society
JRT	*Journal of Religious Thought*
JSOT	*Journal for the Study of the Old Testament*
KJV	King James Version
LXX	Septuagint
MT	Masoretic Text of the Hebrew OT
n(n).	footnote(s)
NAB	New American Bible
NASB	New American Standard Bible
NEB	New English Bible
NIV	New International Version (2011)
NJB	New Jerusalem Bible
NKJV	New King James Version
NLT	New Living Translation
NovT	*Novum Testamentum*
NRSV	New Revised Standard Version
NT	New Testament
OT	Old Testament
p(p).	Page(s)
par(s).	Parallel(s)
PRSt	*Perspectives in Religious Studies*
REB	Revised English Bible
RevExp	*Review and Expositor*
RSV	Revised Standard Version
SBLDS	Society of Biblical Literature Dissertation Series
SJOT	*Scandinavian Journal of the Old Testament*
SWJT	*Southwestern Journal of Theology*
TDOT	*Theological Dictionary of the Old Testament*
trans.	translated by
TrinJ	*Trinity Journal*
TWOT	*Theological Wordbook of the Old Testament*
TynBul	*Tyndale Bulletin*
v(v)	verse(s)
Vol.	Volume
VT	*Vetus Testamentum*
W & W	*Word and World*
WTJ	*Westminster Theological Journal*
ZAW	*Zeitschrift für die alttestamentliche Wisssenschaft*

CHAPTER 1

Issues in Preaching Christ from Psalms

The Hebrew title for the Psalter is *Təhillîm,* "Praises,"[1] which the Septuagint translated as *Psalmoi,* "referring to songs sung to the accompaniment of stringed instruments."[2] Via the Latin Vulgate's *psalmus,* the English words *psalms* (Luke 24:44) and *book of Psalms* (Luke 20:42; Acts 1:20) originated.[3] The book of Psalms is the largest book in the Old Testament (2,527 verses in the Masoretic Text) and is quoted or alluded to in the New Testament more than any other book (some 560 times).[4] James Mays observes that "the psalms are especially crucial in Christology. They are the primary scriptural context for the titles by which Jesus is identified."[5]

For detailed introductions to the psalms, I refer the reader to the Introductions found in most psalm commentaries.[6] In this Introduction I wish to

---

1. Cf. the verb form, *hallēl,* "to praise," as in *hallelujah (haləlû-yāh),* "praise the LORD."

2. Bernhard Anderson, *Out of the Depths,* 3.

3. The Septuagint A used *psalter* or *psalterion* which led to the Latin *psalterium* and our English Psalter.

4. See the appendix in the Nestle-Aland, *Novum Testamentum Graece,* 1993. Henry Shires, *Finding the Old Testament in the New* (Philadelphia: Westminster, 1974), 126–27, breaks the quotations and allusions down into 70 quotations introduced by formulas such as, "As it is written," 60 quotations without an introductory formula, and another 220 citations and references. Bruce Waltke and James Houston, *The Psalms as Christian Worship,* 110, state, "Of the 283 direct quotes from the Old Testament in the New Testament, 116 (41 percent) are from the Psalter."

5. Mays, *Psalms,* 2.

6. Brief but good introductions can also be found in Study Bibles, e.g., John H. Stek's in *The NIV Study Bible* (1985, 2011) and C. John Collins's in *The ESV Study Bible.* See also N. H. Ridderbos and P. C. Craigie, "Psalms," in the *International Standard Bible Encyclopedia,* III (Grand Rapids: Eerdmans, 1986), 1030–40, and J. D. S. S. Thomson and F. D. Kidner, "Psalms, Book of," in the *New Bible Dictionary,* 2nd ed., ed. J. D. Douglas (Leicester: InterVarsity, 1982), 992–96.

concentrate on the essentials for interpreting and preaching the psalms. But first we need to respond to two objections that are frequently raised about preaching Christ from Psalms.

Objections to Preaching Psalms

The first objection is to *preaching* Psalms in general: since most of the psalms are prayers and praises offered in Israel's worship services, they ought to be prayed and sung but not preached. The second objection focuses on preaching *Christ* from Psalms: since Jesus was born centuries after the psalms were composed, one cannot preach Christ from Psalms. We shall discuss each objection in turn.

Is It Proper to Preach Biblical Prayers?

Claus Westermann, an expert on Psalms, held that it is improper to preach Psalms: they can be prayed, they can be sung — but most of them should not be preached.[7] In his book *Reclaiming the Old Testament for the Christian Pulpit,* Donald Gowan follows Westermann and omits reclaiming the psalms for the Christian pulpit. His justification for this omission is that "most of the psalms were used in worship; they are human language addressed to God. . . . That suggests that the integrity of the psalmists' words addressed to God in praise and lamentation ought to be preserved and that ordinarily they ought not to be considered as texts to be expounded to a congregation. We ought to use them, certainly, but in their appropriate place; we ought to pray them and sing them rather than preach them."[8]

Gowan also realizes, however, that "not all of the psalms are addressed exclusively to God, and when they contain testimony addressed to fellow worshipers such language ought to be fully appropriate material for preaching. . . . Indeed, some of the psalms are didactic in purpose and are addressed to human beings throughout (e.g., Pss 1, 37, 49). . . . [In addition] *hymns* contain recitals of God's

---

7. Westermann, *Verkündigung des Kommenden: Predigten alttestamentlicher Texte* (Munich: Kaiser Verlag, 1978), 135, mentioned by Donald E. Gowan, *Reclaiming the Old Testament for the Christian Pulpit* (Atlanta: Knox, 1976), 146, 159 n. 2. Clinton McCann, "Hearing the Psalter," in *Hearing the Old Testament : Listening for God's Address,* ed. Craig G. Bartholomew and David J.H. Beldman (Grand Rapids: Eerdmans, 2012; pp. 277–301), 277–78, reports, "Many pastors over the years have told me that it never occurred to them to preach on the Psalms, and that even if it had occurred to them, they would not have known how to proceed."

8. Gowan, *Reclaiming the Old Testament,* 145–46.

saving acts in history (e.g., Pss 103, 135) and descriptions of his work as creator and sustainer of the world (e.g., Pss 8, 29), *thanksgivings* sometimes recount God's acts of deliverance at length (e.g., Ps 107), while the psalms of *trust* . . . contain humanity's finest expressions of certainty in God's help (Pss 4, 11, 16, 23, 27:1–6, 62, 131)."[9]

But preachers need not pick and choose which psalms can be preached and which cannot because they are "exclusively addressed to God." Though it may not be easy, every psalm can be preached! There are several reasons for this claim. First, the editors of the Psalter have placed Psalm 1, a *torah* (wisdom) psalm, at the head of this collection in order to signal that every following psalm is to be read as part of God's *torah,* teaching, instruction, for Israel[10] (see pp. 25–28 below).

Second, though many psalms originated as a human word to God, every psalm is now part of the Psalter and was accepted in the canon as God's word for Israel.[11] James Mays observes that "the function of psalms shifted from a focus on performance in ritual proceedings toward instruction. The intention to propagate and preserve the piety of the righteous became increasingly important."[12] As

9. Ibid., 146.

10. "The placement of Psalm 1 as introduction decisively explodes this view of the Psalter [as a collection of hymns to be sung in public worship]. The psalms are no longer to be sung as human response to God but are to be meditated upon day and night as the source of the divine word of life to us." Gerald H. Wilson, "The Shape of the Book of Psalms," *Int* 46, no. 2 (1992; pp. 129–42): 137. In my opinion Wilson overstates the case: I think the church can still sing the psalms as Israel did "as human response to God" but preachers can also preach them as God's word to his people.

11. Cf. Brevard Childs, *Introduction to the Old Testament as Scripture,* 513, "Because Israel continues to hear God's word through the voice of the Psalmist's response, these prayers now function as the divine word itself. The original cultic role of the Psalms has been subordinated under a larger category of the canon." Cf. McCann, "Hearing the Psalter," 278, "The material in the Psalter that originated from, and is a record of, human response to God was ultimately received and transmitted as God's address to humankind — that is, as Scripture." Ellen Davis, *Wondrous Depth,* 26, offers another reason for preaching the psalms: "The main reason to preach the psalms is not the bare fact that they contain great lines or great metaphors. Rather, it is because the poets who composed them thought differently about God than we ordinarily do, and more deeply." Thomas G. Long, *Preaching and the Literary Forms of the Bible* (Philadelphia: Fortress, 1989), 43, offers still another reason for preaching the Psalms: "In the same way that the Apostles' Creed, normally a liturgical confessional statement, at times becomes the focus of a series of doctrinal sermons, the rich theological texture of the Psalms justifies their liturgical use as sermon texts as well as musical texts."

12. Mays, *Psalms,* 11, with references to Pss 15; 33; 34; 90; 135. Cf. McCann, "The Psalms as Instruction," *Int* 46, no. 2 (1992; pp. 117–28): 117–18, "Although [the psalms] may have originated primarily within the liturgical life of ancient Israel and Judah, [they] were finally appropriated, preserved, and transmitted as instruction to the faithful." Cf. Walter Brueggemann, *The Message of the Psalms,* 15, "The psalms are not only addressed to God. They are a voice of the gospel, God's good word addressed to God's faithful people. In this literature the community of faith has heard

God's word for Israel, modern preachers can preach the messages of the psalms, in the context of the canon, to God's people today.

Third, the New Testament authors accepted the Psalter not just as Israel's word to God but as God's word to his people. For example, Hebrews 1 introduces quotations from three psalms with God "says,"[13] and Paul certainly did not exclude the psalms when he wrote, "*all* scripture is inspired by God and is useful for teaching, for reproof, for correction, and for training in righteousness" (2 Tim 3:16). We can preach the psalms because they are part of the canon, God's inspired word.

Fourth, Jesus not only prayed the psalms but used them, more than any other Old Testament book, for his preaching and teaching. As we can preach sermons on the Lord's Prayer, so we can preach sermons on every psalm.

Is It Proper to Preach Christ from Psalms?

Objections are also raised about preaching Christ from Psalms. A major problem in the discussion about preaching Christ is that it is not at all clear what it means to preach Christ. Some hold to a very narrow definition — preaching Christ is "preaching Christ crucified" — which frequently leads to forced interpretations in order to land at Calvary. Others broaden the definition to "preaching Christ's death and resurrection." Still others broaden the definition to "preaching the eternal logos, active in Old Testament times as the Angel of Yahweh and the Wisdom of God." Others broaden the definition even more to "preaching Jehovah" because "'Jehovah' of the Old Testament [is] the Christ of the New." And still others equate preaching Christ-centered sermons with preaching God-centered sermons, since Christ, as the second person of the Trinity, is fully God.[14]

In view of this confusion, it would be well to begin with a clear definition of what we mean by "preaching Christ." For the New Testament church preaching Christ meant preaching the incarnate Christ: Jesus' birth, ministry, death,

---

and continues to hear the sovereign speech of God, who meets the community in its depths of need and in its heights of celebration."

13. See the quotations on p. 7 below. In fact, John H. Eaton, "The Psalms and Israelite Worship" in *Tradition and Interpretation* (Oxford: Clarendon, 1979; pp. 238–73), 260, notes that Mowinckel designated "as oracular psalms: 2, 12, 14, 20, 21, 45, 50, 60, 72, 75, 81, 82, 87, 89, 91, 95, 108, 110, 132. Further, he agreed with Gunkel that many of the laments will have been answered by an encouraging oracle, not preserved in the text of the Psalm, but giving rise to a concluding statement of relief by the Psalmist (e.g., 13, 22). . . . Whatever might be said or done from the human side was outweighed by the action and words of the divine party to the meeting." On the priestly and prophetic contributions to the Psalms and the authority of wisdom teaching, see Leslie Allen, *Psalms*, 118–20.

14. For references, see my *Preaching Christ from the Old Testament*, 3.

resurrection, ascension, rule at God's right hand, his presence with us today in the Spirit, and his imminent return.[15] Therefore I define preaching Christ as "preaching sermons which authentically integrate the message of the text with the climax of God's revelation in the person, work, and/or teaching of Jesus Christ as revealed in the New Testament."[16]

The main objection to preaching Christ from Psalms is that Christ came in the flesh long after the psalms were composed, and reading the incarnate Christ back into the psalms is eisegesis.[17] I agree that we should not read Christ back into the psalms, but from the message of a psalm we can certainly move forward to Jesus in the New Testament. A psalm may mean one thing in its own historical context, say the time of the monarchy. But it may acquire a fuller meaning in a later historical and literary context. For example, the Babylonian exile brought an end to the Davidic monarchy. At that later stage in redemptive history, the prayers for the Davidic king no longer applied to a specific Davidic king but began to be heard as a prayer for a coming Davidic king.[18]

Beyond the Babylonian exile, redemptive history moved on to the actual coming of Christ. This means that the psalm is now heard in the literary context not only of the Old Testament but also of the New Testament. In preaching psalms, therefore, one can do justice to the psalm in its own historical context and yet preach Christ from it because the psalm is now heard in the broader horizons of redemptive history and the whole canon of Scripture.

Another objection to preaching Christ from Psalms is that this confuses the

---

15. See ibid., 4–10.

16. Ibid., 10.

17. See, e.g., the Presidential Address George Dahl delivered at the meeting of the Society of Biblical Literature and Exegesis in 1937: "The . . . serious spiritual flaw in recent psalm literature . . . is the . . . trend toward minimizing both the extent and religious importance of the Messianic element in the Psalter. This has resulted in the wrong of giving a purely secular interpretation to many Psalms, especially the so-called Royal Psalms. . . . Whenever in the psalms the word 'Messiah' appears, every nerve is strained, and every device of a forced exegesis utilized, in order to make it refer merely to the secular king and his mundane affairs." "The Messianic Expectation in the Psalter," *JBL* 57, no. 1 (1938; pp. 1–12): 2. Cf. Brevard Childs, *Introduction to the Old Testament as Scripture*, 515, "The majority of modern scholars are fully in accord with Gunkel and Mowinckel in rejecting the traditional interpretation of messianic psalms." Childs is not part of that majority (see n. 20 below).

18. "The disappearance of kingship, then, is the new cultural context that effects a semantic shift in Israel's royal texts: they refer to the King who is to come." Stanley D. Walters, "Finding Christ in the Psalms," in *Go Figure!: Figuration in Biblical Interpretation* (Eugene, OR: Pickwick, 2008; pp. 31–47), 36. For both secular and biblical examples "that second meanings arise through a semantic shift when a text comes to stand in a different context," see ibid., 32–33. Cf. Mays, *Psalms*, 11, "When there were no longer reigning kings in Israel, the psalms written for use in royal ceremonies were re-read as divine promises and prophecies of a future messiah."

genre of psalms with that of prophecy: the psalms do not contain predictions of a coming Messiah.[19] God's promises of a coming Messiah King, of course, are not limited to the genre of prophecy: we find God's promises also in Hebrew narrative, apocalyptic literature, and in Psalms. For example, in Psalm 2 God says, "Ask of me, and I will make the nations your heritage, and the ends of the earth your possession" (Ps 2:8). Since no king in Israel ever saw the fulfillment of this promise, it is clear that it points to a future fulfillment. Mays observes, "It is . . . generally agreed that by the time the Psalter was being completed, the psalms dealing with the kingship of the Lord were understood eschatologically. They no longer refer only to what was enacted in cult, but as well to what was promised in prophecy. . . . The end of the wicked and the vindication of the righteous can be understood in terms of the coming kingdom of God."[20] Since Psalm 2 functions as the second psalm to introduce the Psalter (see pp. 25-28 below), the editors thereby signaled that the psalms should be read "in the light of promises of a future Davidic messiah."[21]

Still another objection is that in this modern age we cannot adopt the New Testament way of preaching Christ from Psalms.[22] But this objection assumes that we can only preach Christ from the psalms by adopting the "method" used by the writers of the New Testament. In fact, the authors of the New Testament never intended to teach a normative method for interpreting the psalms. They did not begin by interpreting a psalm in its historical setting and then moving to Christ

19. See, e.g., Christoph F. Barth, *Introduction to the Psalms* (Oxford: Blackwell, 1966), 69, to the effect that we cannot say "that the Psalms *predicted* or *foretold* His [Jesus'] life. . . . Actually, they speak of the history and reality of *Israel*." Barth's italics.

20. Mays, "The Place of the Torah-Psalms in the Psalter," *JBL* 106, no. 1 (1987; pp. 3-12): 10. Cf. Mays, "Isaiah's Royal Theology and the Messiah," in *Reading and Preaching the Book of Isaiah*, ed. Christopher R. Seitz (Philadelphia: Fortress, 1988), 39-51, esp. p. 48. Cf. Childs, *Introduction to the Old Testament as Scripture*, 517: the royal psalms "were treasured in the Psalter . . . as a witness to the messianic hope which looked for the consummation of God's kingship through his Anointed One." Cf. John Stek, "Introduction: Psalms," *NIV Study Bible* (1985), 786, "When the Psalms speak of the king on David's throne, they speak of the king who is being crowned (as in Pss 2; 72; 110 . . .) or is reigning (as in Ps 45) at the time. They proclaim his status as God's anointed and declare what God will accomplish through him and his dynasty. Thus they speak of the sons of David to come — and in the exile and the postexilic era, when there was no reigning king, they spoke to Israel only of the great Son of David whom the prophets had announced as the one in whom God's covenant with David would yet be fulfilled." Cf. Elizabeth Achtemeier, *Preaching from the Old Testament*, 145.

21. Mays, "The David of the Psalms," *Int* 40, no. 2 (1986; pp. 143-55): 154. Mays continues, "The role of Psalm 2 as introduction to the canonical book is only one piece of evidence that prophecy has become a rubric in terms of which all the psalms may be read."

22. E.g., Christoph Barth, *Introduction to the Psalms*, 67, "This [NT] way of handling the psalms can not in fact be reconciled with the principles of scientific Biblical exegesis."

as we would do; rather, they moved in the opposite direction. They "began with Jesus and the messianic events associated with him and then used the psalm verse to explain or illuminate those events."[23] They knew their psalms well, and after Jesus' resurrection and his claim "that everything written about me in the law of Moses, the prophets, and *the psalms* must be fulfilled" (Luke 24:44), the psalms lit up with "a thousand points of light." Thus, in seeking to preach Christ, the New Testament writers were able to use many psalms. For example, Hebrews reads,

> For to which of the angels did God ever say,
>   "You are my Son,
>   today I have begotten you"? (1:5; cf. 5:5; Ps 2:7)

> But of the Son he says,
>   "Your throne, O God, is forever and ever,
>   and the righteous scepter is the scepter of your kingdom.
>   You have loved righteousness and hated wickedness;
>   therefore God, your God, has anointed you
>   with the oil of gladness beyond your companions." (1:8–9; Ps 45:6–7)

> But to which of the angels has he ever said,
>   "Sit at my right hand
>   until I make your enemies a footstool for your feet"? (1:13; Ps 110:1)

Hebrews 5:6 reads,

> As he [God] says also in another place,
>   "You are a priest forever,
>   according to the order of Melchizedek." (Ps 110:4)

In using the psalms this way, the New Testament writers followed the example of Jesus who frequently used the psalms in his teaching (e.g., Matt 5:35; 7:23; 13:35; 21:16, 42; 23:37) and saw his life portrayed in some psalms (see, e.g., Matt 27:46; Luke 23:46). The Gospel writers' intent was to preach the good news of Jesus, persuading people that Jesus was indeed the promised Messiah. To ac-

---

23. William L. Holladay, *The Psalms Through Three Thousand Years: Prayer Book of a Cloud of Witnesses* (Minneapolis: Fortress, 1993), 128–29. Cf. Fredrick C. Holmgren, *The Old Testament and the Significance of Jesus* (Grand Rapids: Eerdmans, 1999), 47, "The New Testament authors, looking back from their experience of Christ's ministry, death, and resurrection, have selected certain passages from the Old Testament which remind them of him." See also my *Preaching Christ from the Old Testament,* 182–85.

complish this goal they frequently quoted the Old Testament or alluded to it, especially the psalms.[24] They did not set out to interpret the psalms in their Old Testament setting but "used" them to accomplish their purpose of preaching Christ.[25] Even though, like the Gospel writers, we should continue to preach Christ from the psalms, today preachers cannot simply copy their way of doing so but will have to use a responsible, modern hermeneutical method.[26]

Still another objection is that preaching Christ from Psalms leads to the allegorical interpretation promoted by the Church Fathers.[27] Allegorical interpretation, of course, is subjective and arbitrary; it is not convincing in this day and age. But one can preach Christ from Psalms without resorting to allegorical interpretation (see below, pp. 34–37, "Seven Ways of Preaching Christ from Psalms").

The question remains, can we legitimately preach Christ from every psalm, also non-messianic psalms? I think we can and that for two reasons. First, in addition to Psalm 1 the editors of the Psalter also introduced the Psalter with the messianic Psalm 2, thereby signaling that the following psalms ought to be read not only as part of God's *torah*, teaching for Israel (Ps 1), but also with a view to the Messiah and his coming worldwide kingdom (see pp. 25–28 below). Second, as explained above, we can preach Christ from every psalm because every psalm must be understood not only in its own historical context but also in the context

---

24. "The apostles established Jesus' suffering (Pss 22; 35; 41; 55; 69; 109), messianic claims (Pss 2; 72; 89; 110; 132), priestly ministry (Ps 95), his being the Son of Man (Pss 8; 16; 40), and the coming judgment and redemption (Pss 18; 50; 68; 96–98; 102) by appealing to the psalms." VanGemeren, *Psalms,* 26-27,

25. On the New Testament use of the Old Testament, see the many references in my *Preaching Christ from the Old Testament,* 185–91. To these references should be added concerning the Psalms: William Holladay, "Texts for the First Christians," in his *The Psalms Through Three Thousand Years,* 113–33; Hans-Joachim Kraus, "The Psalms in the New Testament," in his *Theology of the Psalms,* 177–203; J. Clinton McCann, "The Psalms and Jesus Christ," in his *A Theological Introduction to the Book of Psalms,* 163–75; and Fredrick C. Holmgren, *The Old Testament and the Significance of Jesus : Embracing Change — Maintaining Christian Identity.* On p. 42 Holmgren argues "that the Greek word translated 'fulfill' has the meaning of 'correspond to,' 'is similar / analogous to,' or even 'reminds one of.'" When we think of "fulfill" as "filling up," the word can apply to either the way of promise-fulfillment or typology.

26. For the method I propose, see "Christocentric Interpretation," pp. 33–37 below.

27. According to Bruce Waltke, "Augustine, who dominated all subsequent interpretations of the Psalter in the Western church, was never surpassed in seeing Christ everywhere. According to Augustine, our method of interpretation should be 'Him first, Him last, Him midst and without end.'" Waltke, "A Canonical Process Approach to the Psalms," in *Tradition and Testament,* ed. John S. and Paul D. Feinberg (Chicago: Moody, 1981; pp. 3–18), 4, quoting J. M. Neale and R. F. Littledale, *A Commentary on the Psalms: From Primitive and Mediaeval Writers* (London: John Masters, 1884), 77.

of the progression in redemptive history and its coinciding expanding literary contexts of the Psalter, the Old Testament, and the New Testament.

Literary Interpretation of Psalms

Proper interpretation seeks to understand each psalm in four dimensions: literary, historical, theocentric, and christocentric. Literary interpretation (broadly conceived as inclusive of grammatical concerns) is the first and foundational entrance into understanding a psalm. Literary interpretation investigates each psalm concerning its grammar, form (type), its poetic devices, its rhetorical structures, and its literary contexts in the Psalter, the Old Testament, and the New Testament. We shall begin with the rather recent scholarly concern for the form of each psalm.

Literary Forms (Types) of Psalms

It was not until the 1920s that scholars began to analyze the psalms according to their literary forms. Hermann Gunkel was the first to distinguish five different major forms and some minor ones. He named the five major forms: hymns, community laments, thanksgiving songs of the individual, spiritual laments of the individual, and mixed types.[28] He called them *Gattungen,* which is frequently translated as "types" or "genres," but we shall use the word "forms" for these sub-genres in order to avoid confusion with the "type" that is standard terminology in typology. Although Gunkel's categories have been refined somewhat, they have basically stood the test of time.[29] For the purpose of this book we shall simply accept the designations provided by Bernhard Anderson in 2000.[30]

Before we look at the typical characteristics of the major forms of psalms, we should be aware that, although the psalmists were able to use standard literary forms to shape their prayers and songs, they were free to mix forms and "refash-

---

28. Hermann Gunkel, *The Psalms: A Form-Critical Introduction,* trans. Thomas M. Horner (Philadelphia: Fortress, 1967), 30-39.

29. "Gunkel's classification continues to be accepted with only minor modifications by many commentators and writers on the Psalms." D. J. Clines, "Psalm Research since 1955: II. The Literary Genres," *TynBul* 20 (1969; pp. 105-25): 106. In 1995 Brueggemann, *The Psalms and the Life of Faith* (Minneapolis: Fortress, 1995), 4, agreed: "We have not moved very far from Gunkel's fivefold classification." Kraus, *Psalms 1–59,* 39, has a different opinion: "In the last decades it has become more and more clear that the investigation of types as Gunkel and Begrich presented it is in need of considerable correction — and, in part, of basic reorganization."

30. B. Anderson, *Out of the Depths,* 219-24.

ion" these forms.[31] Therefore, after identifying a particular form of a psalm, we should not rigidly impose its standard features on the psalm but allow the psalm to reveal its alterations of these features since these alterations may well be keys to its interpretation.

Still, identifying a psalm's basic literary form offers preachers several advantages. It enables us to follow the thought sequences of the psalm more easily, the intensification that frequently takes place, and the turning point or hinge in the psalm. It will also aid in preparing an outline of the psalm (its structure). And it will help in understanding the mood and emotion the psalmist sought to convey as well as his goal, that is, the response sought from Israel.

The most used forms in order of frequency are laments, hymns, and thanksgivings[32] — they give voice to the emotions of distress, joy, and gratitude.

Individual and Community Laments

Laments are cries, even angry cries, to God for help from an individual or the community in deep distress. They are the most common forms in the Psalter, numbering more than sixty.[33] "For the individual, sickness and unjust accusation, even ostracism, are frequent complaints, and for the community, famine, military defeat, and exile."[34] The structure of lament psalms present some or all of these elements:[35]

---

31. Robert Alter, "Psalms," in *The Literary Guide to the Bible*, ed. Robert Alter and Frank Kermode (Cambridge, MA: Harvard, 1987, pp. 244-61), 247, cautions, "The most pervasive form-critical misconception about psalmodic genre is the notion that genre, apart from the occasional mixed type, is a fixed entity. . . . We are likely to perceive the poetic richness of psalms more finely if we realize that there is a good deal of . . . refashioning of genre in the collection, even when the recurrence of certain formulas tells us that a particular generic background is being invoked." Cf. Brueggemann, *The Message of the Psalms*, 54, "It will be understood that no single psalm follows exactly the ideal form." We must also keep Mays's caution in mind, "Form criticism looks for the typical. It is important to ask also what constitutes a psalm's individuality." *Psalms*, 20-21.

32. Brueggemann, *The Message of the Psalms*, 25-167, calls hymns and a few other forms "psalms of orientation," laments "psalms of disorientation," and thanksgivings "psalms of new orientation."

33. All numbers given are according to Bernhard Anderson's categories in *Out of the Depths*, 173-77. Anderson himself reminds us, "There are too many uncertainties to permit an exact and rigid classification according to type" (p. 173).

34. Norman K. Gottwald, "Poetry, Hebrew," *IDB*, 837. For differences between the individual and community laments, see Westermann, *Praise and Lament in the Psalms*, 52-71.

35. Stek, *NIV Study Bible*, 783, goes into much more detail listing fourteen elements: 1) address to God, 2) initial appeal, 3) description of distress, 4) complaint against God, 5) petition, 6) motivation for God to hear, 7) accusation against the adversary, 8) call for redress, 9) claims of

1) Introductory petition for God's help   E.g., Ps 80 vv 1–3
2) Description of the trouble or complaint   vv 4–6, 12–13, 16a
3) Petitions for God's help   vv 7, 14–15, 17, 19
4) Reasons why God should hear
5) Examples of God's saving acts in history   vv 8–11
6) A vow to praise   v 18

Some have objected to the name "lament" since lament is but a small part of these psalms and most end in praise. However, "lament" is what distinguishes this form from the others. Laments can include anger, confrontation with God, and accusations against God (see, e.g., Ps 80:4–6, 12).

All laments, except Psalm 88, move from lament to praise. They can do this because God's positive response is expected or because of an oracle from God which is either explicitly stated (see Ps 35:3) or assumed to have been given by a priest at the temple.[36] The goal of lament is to cry out to God for help when in distress and to rest in him.

Hymns

Hymns are the next largest category in the Psalter (some twenty-five).[37] They are songs of praise to God for his great works in creating this world, for creating and choosing Israel, and for being the Lord of history. The typical pattern of a hymn consists of most of the following elements:

1) A call to praise the LORD   E.g., Ps 117 v 1
2) Transition (*kî*, for, because)   v 2a
3) Reasons why the LORD is to be praised   v 2b–c
4) Conclusion: Praise the LORD!   v 2d

The goal of a hymn is for Israel, all nations and peoples, and all the earth to praise the LORD: "Let everything that breathes praise the LORD! Praise the LORD!" (Ps 150:6). "Praising God is the goal of human life, the goal of every living thing, the goal of all creation!"[38]

---

innocence, 10) confessions of sin, 11) professions of trust, 12) vows to praise for deliverance, 13), calls to praise, and 14) motivations for praise.

36. See, e.g., Bellinger, *Psalms*, 56.

37. Mays, *Psalms*, 27, counts "some thirty-five" but includes "hymns with specialized topics."

38. McCann, "The Psalms as Instruction," *Int* 46, no. 2 (1992): 124.

Individual and Community Thanksgivings

Thanksgiving psalms express gratitude to God for some special blessing, deliverance, or an answer to prayer. They usually exhibit most of these elements:[39]

1) An invitation to or statement of giving thanks
   Sometimes a beatitude instead   E.g., Ps 32 vv 1–2
2) Account of the trouble   vv 3–4
3) Report that God heard and delivered   v 5
4) Generalized teaching   vv 6–10
5) Praise or a vow to give thanks   v 11

There are sixteen thanksgiving psalms: ten individual and six community. Their goal is to help individuals and communities to express their thanks to God for deliverance.

Other Forms

Some of the other forms are the *psalms of Ascents* (fifteen: Pss 120–134), which the Israelites sang as they made their way up to Jerusalem to celebrate the festivals; *songs of trust* (about ten), which express the psalmist's trust in the Lord; the *royal psalms* (about ten),[40] which are psalms concerning, for, or by the king; *songs of Zion* (five to eight) about the city of God; *salvation history psalms* (five), which celebrate God's acts of redemption; the *torah (wisdom) psalms* (only three, but at strategic places in the psalter): Psalm 1 introducing the whole Psalter, Psalm 19 (the center of Pss 15–24),[41] and Psalm 119 (the longest psalm) — all three highlighting God's teachings for living happily before God's face.[42]

Poetic Devices Used in the Psalms

With the analysis of poetic devices we dig deeper into the details of the psalm. As Hebrew poetry, the psalms are more dense, intense, and emotional than prose

---

39. Adapted from Allen, *Psalms*, 20.

40. A. Anderson, *Psalms 1–72*, 39, does not regard these psalms as an "independent literary type; rather they comprise psalms of various categories."

41. Cf. Ps 15:1, "Who may dwell on your holy hill?" and Ps 24:3, "Who shall ascend the hill of the LORD?"

42. See Mays, *Psalms*, 27–29, on the "psalms of instruction," and Kraus, *Psalms 1–59*, 58–60, on "didactic poetry."

and can best express the acute desire to lament or praise. Poetry is also easier to memorize and recite communally in worship. Hebrew poetry is marked especially by terseness, imagery, and parallelism,

Terseness

The first marker of Hebrew poetry is terseness. Tremper Longman observes, "Psalms are noted for their brief poetic phrases, usually containing three words in the Hebrew, rarely more than four. The effect of this technique is achieved in part by the repression of conjunctions ('like,' 'but,' 'or,' 'and,' 'therefore'). . . . A second type of omission that leads to terseness is ellipsis" — the second colon of the verse omits one of the parts (e.g., the verb) of the first colon."[43] Usually units consist of two lines (bicola), but occasionally of three lines (tricola). The terseness of Hebrew poetry is also enhanced by the frequent use of imagery.[44]

Imagery

A second marker of Hebrew poetry is the frequency of imagery. "By using figurative language, the poet not only makes his work more striking and colorful but also invites the reader to observe and meditate more closely on what he is saying. At the same time, the compressed language of figures makes for a conciseness of expression that is more easily remembered."[45] We shall look in turn at some examples of simile, metaphor, anthropomorphism, and zoomorphism.

43. Longman, "Psalms," 249–50. Cf. Patrick D. Miller, "The Theological Significance of Biblical Poetry," in *Language, Theology and the Bible: Essays in Honour of James Barr,* ed. Samuel E. Balentine and John Barton (Oxford: Clarendon, 1994; pp. 213–30), 215, "Clearly *terseness* is one of the most obvious features of biblical poetry." His emphasis. Cf. J. P. Fokkelman, *Reading Biblical Poetry: An Introductory Guide* (Louisville: Westminster John Knox, 2001), 15, "Poetry is the most compact and concentrated form of speech possible. By making the most of his or her linguistic tools, the poet created an immense richness of meaning, and this richness becomes available if we as readers know how to handle the density: how we can cautiously tackle complexity, probe the various layers one by one and unfold them."

44. "Imagery is a concise way of writing, because an image conveys not only information but also evokes an emotional response." Longman, "Psalms," 251.

45. Andreas Köstenberger and Richard Patterson, *Invitation to Biblical Interpretation: Exploring the Hermeneutical Triad of History, Literature, and Theology* (Grand Rapids: Kregel, 2011), 272. Cf. Raymond Dillard and Tremper Longman, *Introduction to the Old Testament,* 28, "Imagery contributes to the compactness of poetry, because it allows the authors to communicate their message using fewer words." For many of the metaphors used in the Psalter, see William Brown's *Seeing the Psalms: A Theology of Metaphor.*

Simile Simile is easily recognized because it signals a comparison with "like," or "as." But for the modern preacher the point of comparison is not always easy to detect.[46] For example, Psalm 133:1–2 offers a clear analogy:

> How very good and pleasant it is when kindred live together in unity!
> It is *like* the precious oil on the head, running down upon the beard,
>   on the beard of Aaron, running down over the collar of his robes.

What is the point of this comparison? G. B. Caird humorously shows up the difficulty: "When the psalmist tells us that a united family is like oil dripping down Aaron's beard on to the skirts of his robe, he is not trying to persuade us that family unity is messy, greasy, or volatile; he is thinking of the all-pervasive fragrance which so deeply impressed itself on his memory at the anointing of the high priest."[47]

Other similes are easier to understand because the psalmist gives the point of comparison in a following line. For example, Psalm 1:2–3,

> [Those whose] delight is in the law of the LORD. . . .
>   are *like* trees planted by streams of water,
>   which yield their fruit in its season,
>   and their leaves do not wither.
>   In all that they do, they prosper.

Metaphor Metaphor is defined by Webster as "a figure of speech in which a term or phrase is applied to something to which it is not literally applicable in order to suggest a resemblance."[48] Longman offers an interesting definition: "A metaphor is an image based on similarity within difference."[49] Again, the point of resemblance or similarity is not always easy to detect, partly because we live in a different time and place. For example, Psalm 84:11 calls God "a sun." Frequently the sun is a symbol of evil from which we need protection: "The sun shall not

---

46. "Metaphor and simile place immense demands on a reader. They require far more activity than a direct propositional statement. Metaphor and simile first demand that we take the time to let the literal situation sink in. Then we must make a transfer of meaning(s) to the topic or experience the poem is talking about." Leland Ryken, *How to Read the Bible as Literature* (Grand Rapids: Baker, 1984), 95.

47. G. B. Caird, *The Language and Imagery of the Bible* (Philadelphia: Westminster, 1980), 145.

48. *Webster's Unabridged Dictionary.*

49. Longman, *Literary Approaches to Biblical Interpretation,* 130. He continues on p. 131, "The similarity is unstated or hidden, and the reader must meditate on the metaphor to arrive at its interpretation. The result is a lack of precision."

strike you by day" (Ps 121:6). But in Psalm 84 *God* is compared to a sun — the only time in the Bible.[50] Is God at all like the capricious pagan sun-gods? Is God like the physical sun ready to strike us with heat-stroke? The context offers us the right interpretation:

> For the Lord God is a sun and shield;
>   he bestows favor and honor.
> No good thing does the Lord withhold
>   from those who walk uprightly. (Ps 84:11)

God resembles the sun by spreading light and warmth, thus producing life and food.

Another example: more than thirty times the psalmists speak of God as their "rock." In Psalm 42:9 the psalmist cries out, "I say to God, my rock, 'Why have you forgotten me?'" How does God resemble a rock? Does God, like a rock, have no memory? Is God as hard as a rock? As heavy as a rock? As lethal as a rock hurled from a sling? As precious as a "rock" (a diamond)? Or is he like a fortress, for example, the rock Masada in Israel or the rock Gibraltar in Spain? Frequently the context of the Psalm or the synonyms used will help us decide. In Psalm 18:1-2 the psalmist leaves no doubt what he means by calling God "my rock":

> I love you, O Lord, my strength.
> The Lord is my rock, my fortress, and my deliverer,
>   my God, my rock in whom I take refuge,
>   my shield, and the horn of my salvation, my stronghold.

Three psalms refer to God as shepherd (23:1; 28:9; 80:1). Even city-dwellers who have never seen a shepherd, let alone a Middle Eastern shepherd, will understand the basic resemblance of God to a shepherd. Psalm 23:1-4 spells it out. These four verses consist of extended metaphor:

> The Lord is my shepherd, I shall not want.
>   He makes me lie down in green pastures;
> he leads me beside still waters;
>   he restores my soul.
> He leads me in right paths for his name's sake.
> Even though I walk through the darkest valley, I fear no evil;

---

50. J. Bardarah McCandles, "Enfleshing the Psalms," *Religious Education* 81, no. 3 (1986; pp. 372–90): 376, "The term 'sun,' an ancient symbol for divine power, is used only once in the Bible, possibly because of its pagan connotations."

for you are with me;
>   your rod and your staff — they comfort me.

Anthropomorphism Anthropomorphism ascribes human form, attributes, or actions to God. For example,

When I look at your heavens, the work of *your fingers* . . . (Ps 8:3).

He bowed the heavens, and *came down;*
>   thick darkness was under *his feet* (Ps 18:9).

Truly *the eye* of the LORD is on those who fear him . . . (Ps 33:18).

Incline your ear to me and save me (Ps 71:2).

His right hand and his holy *arm* have gotten him victory (Ps 98:1).

Zoomorphism Zoomorphism ascribes animal form or attributes to God. "Wings" is a favorite in the psalms. For example,

Hide me in the shadow of your wings . . . (Ps 17:8).

He will cover you with his pinions,
>   and under his wings you will find refuge (Ps 91:4).[51]

Summing up, all these poetic devices make the psalms more dense, intense, and emotional than prose and fascinating to explore in depth.

Parallelism

A third important marker of Hebrew poetry is parallelism. Adele Berlin states, "The predominance of parallelism combined with terseness . . . marks the poetic expression of the Bible." "Parallelism sets up relationships of equivalence or opposition between two propositions."[52] Scholars usually distinguish three major kinds of parallelism: synonymous or affirming parallelism, synthetic or advancing parallelism, and antithetic or opposing parallelism.[53] Another rather

---

51. See also Pss 36:7; 57:1; 61:4; and 63:7.

52. Adele Berlin, *The Dynamics of Biblical Parallelism* (Bloomington: Indiana University Press, 1985), 5 and 135.

53. Douglas K. Stuart, "Preaching from Old Testament Poetry," in *The Newell Lectureships,*

common form is climactic parallelism, which is basically advancing parallelism over three or more lines.

But Hebrew parallelism is too versatile to be caught in three or four airtight compartments. Especially the difference between synonymous and advancing parallelism is not always clear cut. Wherever I sense that one or more elements in the second line move beyond the first line I will mark it as advancing parallelism.

In the following chapters I will identify for every selected psalm its parallelisms as a first step of entering into understanding the movements in the psalm. To do this efficiently we need a shorthand way of marking these different forms of parallelism. Since the common way of marking the two parallel lines A and B is not very helpful, I am taking my cue from the standard way of marking inclusios and chiasms: A A' for inclusios, ABCB'A' for chiasms. Hence I will mark the various forms of parallelism as follows:

Synonymous parallelism	A
	A'
Advancing parallelism	A
	+ A'
Antithetic parallelism	A
	− A'
Climactic parallelism	A
	+ A'
	+ A''
Different topic in stanza	B
Different topic in stanza	C

I will use the "stanzas" as they are designated in the NRSV.[54] Noting the parallelisms in each stanza will give us a quick snapshot of the movements in the

---

Vol. I, ed. Timothy Dwyer (Anderson, IN: Warner, 1992; pp. 133–206), 143–44, estimates that synonymous parallelism "accounts for somewhere around thirty-five percent of all Old Testament poetry. Antithetical parallelism is not more than ten percent. . . . Synthetic parallelism accounts for about fifty-five percent."

54. I may not always agree with the way the NRSV lays out the stanzas (see the differences between versions), but using the NRSV's layout will give us a common starting point. I am using the word *stanza* in a loose sense to indicate a division or paragraph in a psalm. Concerning the NIV's divisions, John H. Stek writes: "Since the judgment that regular stanza formation was not an 'essential element' (however occasionally present) in Hebrew poetic form . . . , the NIV translators . . . opted for the less controversial general policy of marking off verse paragraphs by spacing." In addition, they would "set off by spaces" even a single line if it represented "a particular function" of a prayer psalm. "When the Spirit Was Poetic," in *The NIV: The Making of a Contemporary Translation,* ed. Kenneth L. Barker (Grand Rapids: Zondervan, 1986; pp. 72–87, 158–61), 78.

psalm as well as the subjects that are repeated or picked up again after a small break. This snapshot may also help us in determining the psalm's structure, which tends to be the most controversial.

Before proceeding, it may be helpful to note some examples of each kind of parallelism as well as the variety produced by inversion and ellipsis.

Synonymous Parallelism Synonymous parallelism repeats in the second line the thought of the first line but in different words.[55] For example, Psalm 19:1 reads,

| The heavens are telling the glory of God; | A | a | b | c |
| and the firmament proclaims his handiwork. | A' | a' | b' | c'[56] |

Synonymous with ellipses. For example, Psalm 24:1 reads,

| The earth is the Lord's and all that is in it, | A | a | b | c[57] |
| the world, and those who live in it. | A' | a' | | c' |

Inverted synonymous. For example, Psalm 103:1,

| Bless the Lord, O my soul, | A | a | b | c |
| and all that is within me, bless his holy name. | A' | c' | a' | b'[58] |

---

55. Scholars have discovered both in Ugaritic and Hebrew some seven hundred word pairs "that appear in a fixed parallel relationship to each other. These conventionally linked pairs of words are balanced off against each other in such a way that the 'A' word appears in the 'A' line and the parallel 'B' word appears in the 'B' line." Walter C. Kaiser, Jr., *Toward an Exegetical Theology: Biblical Exegesis for Preaching and Teaching* (Grand Rapids: Baker, 1981), 213. George L. Klein, "Preaching Poetry," in *Reclaiming the Prophetic Mantle: Preaching the Old Testament Faithfully*, ed. George L. Klein (Nashville: Broadman, 1992; 71–92), 78, offers some specifics: "Examples of common Old Testament word pairs are: 'heaven/earth,' 'day/night,' 'sun/moon,' 'sin/transgression' and the like. From this vast collection of word pairs the poet could shape his text in a marvelously creative way, all the while utilizing familiar themes for his hearers." For other examples from the psalms, see John H. Stek, "The Stylistics of Hebrew Poetry: A (Re) New (ed) Focus of Study," *CTJ* 9, no. 1 (1974; pp. 15–30): 22–23.

56. In these examples I will follow the word order of the NRSV translation. The word order in Hebrew reveals inverse synonymous parallelism:
    A a b c
    A' c' b' a'

57. The Hebrew omits the verb "is" in the first line. The word order in Hebrew is
    A a (YHWH) b c
    A' b' c'

58. The Hebrew omits "bless" in the second line. The Hebrew is not inverted:
    A a b c
    A' b' c'

Advancing Parallelism Advancing or synthetic parallelism advances or completes in the second line the thought of the first line.

Regular advancing. For example, Psalm 1:2,

but their delight is in the law of the LORD,	A	a	b	c[59]	
and on his law they meditate day and night.	+A′	$c′$		d	e

Inverted advancing. For example, Psalm 130:1,

Out of the depths I cry to you, O Lord.	A	a	b	c	
Lord, hear my voice!	+A′			$c′$	d e

Advancing with ellipses. For example, Psalm 95:3,

For the Lord is a great God,	A	a	b	c[60]
and a great King above all gods.	+A′	$c′$		d

Antithetic Parallelism Antithetic parallelism states in the second line the opposite of the thought in the first line.

Regular antithetic. For example, Psalm 90:6,

In the morning it flourishes and is renewed;	A	a	b	c
in the evening it fades and withers.	$- A′$	$- a′$	$- b′$	$- c′$

Antithetic with ellipsis. For example, Psalm 7:9,

O let the evil of the wicked come to an end,	A	a	b	c
but establish the righteous.	$- A′$		$- c′$	$- b′$[61]

---

59. The Hebrew has ellipsis in the first line. The Hebrew word order is,
    "but in the law of the LORD is their delight,   A a c
    and on his law they meditate day and night." $+ A′$ $a′$ d e
60. The Hebrew omits the verb also in the first line. The word order in Hebrew is
    A a c
    $+A′$ $c′$ d
61. The second line omits the opposite of "evil," which would be "the good" of the righteous.

Inverted antithetic with ellipsis. For example, Psalm 1:6,

For the Lord watches over the way of the righteous,	A	a b c	
but the way of the wicked will perish.	$-A'$	$-c' - b'^{62}$	

Climactic Parallelism   Climactic parallelism repeats words of the first line in the second line, adding words to complete the sentence, repeating the words again in a third line bringing the whole to a climax. Classic examples are Psalms 93:3 and 96:7–8:

The floods have lifted up, O Lord,	A a b c	
the floods have lifted up their voice;	$+A'$ a' b'	d
the floods lift up their roaring.	$+A''$ a'' b''	e

Ascribe to the Lord, O families of the peoples,	A a b c	
ascribe to the Lord glory and strength.	$+A'$ a' b'	d
Ascribe to the Lord the glory due his name.	$+A''$ a'' b''	d' e

Some scholars take the analysis of parallelism down to the details of the word order within lines (a b c). This is very time-consuming because, as can be seen in the footnotes above, the Hebrew word order is often different from the English word order. Moreover, the "payoff" in terms of understanding the meaning of the psalm is minimal.[63] In the following chapters, therefore, I will only indicate the parallelism between lines and based on the NRSV translation and stanzas.

The value for preachers of observing the parallelisms in the psalms is that they will avoid the mistake of trying to discover a separate exegetical or homiletical point in each poetic line. "Each line is attached to its parallel and considered along with it. There is only one thought and we need to consider it as a whole."[64] Moreover, we will begin to see a depth dimension in the psalms that is not evident

---

62. The second line omits the "for the Lord" of the first line. The Hebrew word order is

   A a b c
  $-A' - c'$ $-a'$

63. In discussing synonymous parallelism, A. Anderson, *Psalms 1–72,* 41, notes that "the order of the parallel terms need not be the same in both lines." The Hebrew word order is important primarily for identifying the first word in a line because this is often the word the author wishes to emphasize. For example, the NRSV translates Psalm 1:4 "The wicked are not so." The Hebrew indicates a stronger contrast with the word order, "Not so the wicked!" Also the Hebrew makes one aware of ellipses, which are filled in in English translations (e.g., in Ps 1:4a, b, the translators have added the verb "are").

64. W. H. Bellinger, "Let the Words of My Mouth: Proclaiming the Psalms," *SWJT* 27, no. 1 (1984; pp. 17–24): 18.

from a cursory reading; we will see the psalms in 3-D so to speak. In addition, we will be more aware of the movement in each psalm. Robert Alter observes, "The dominant pattern is a focusing, heightening, or specification of ideas, images, actions, themes from one verset to the next."[65]

Rhetorical Structures

Aside from parallelism, we need to review a few other common rhetorical structures. We shall look at repetition, inclusio, and chiasm.

Repetition of Keywords

Repetition of keywords or their synonyms will frequently reveal the point of a whole psalm or section.[66] Martin Buber writes, "The recurrence of the key-words is a basic law of composition in the Psalms. This law has a poetic significance — rhythmical correspondence of sound values — as well as a hermeneutical one: the Psalm provides its own interpretation, by repetition of what is essential to its understanding."[67] For example, in Psalm 119 the psalmist uses the keyword *torah* (law, teaching, instruction) twenty-five times and its synonyms ("decrees," "precepts," "statutes," "commandments," "ordinances," "word," etc.) many times more. In this way he reveals the topic that drives his long poem. Thus we are not surprised when he states his overriding theme in verse 1:

> Happy are those whose way is blameless,
> who walk in the *law of the* Lord.

In Psalm 98 the psalmist repeats the word "victory" ("salvation") three times in the first three verses and then no longer uses the word:

65. Robert Alter, "The Characteristics of Ancient Hebrew Poetry," in *The Literary Guide to the Bible,* ed. Robert Alter and Frank Kermode (Cambridge, MA: Harvard, 1987; pp. 611–24), 615. Cf. p. 620, "The poetry of the Bible is concerned above all with dynamic process moving toward some culmination. The two most common structures . . . of biblical poetry are a movement of intensification of images, concepts, themes through a sequence of lines, and a narrative movement — which most often pertains to the development of metaphorical acts but can also refer to literal events. . . ."

66. Unfortunately, these repetitions in Hebrew are often lost in translation. Repetition can also serve "passion, as in the *'Elî, 'elî* (My God, my God) of Ps 22:1 [and] the fourfold *'ad–'ānâ* (How long?) of Ps 13:1f." Stek, "The Stylistics of Hebrew Poetry," *CTJ* 9, no. 1 (1974; pp. 15–30): 17.

67. Martin Buber, *Good and Evil* (New York, 1953), 52, as cited by Stek, "The Stylistics of Hebrew Poetry," 18–19.

> O sing to the LORD a new song,
>> for he has done marvelous things.
> His right hand and his holy arm have gotten him *victory*.
> The LORD has made known his *victory*;
>> he has revealed his vindication in the sight of the nations.
> He has remembered his steadfast love and faithfulness to the house of Israel.
>> All the ends of the earth have seen the *victory* of our God.

This limited repetition marks the first stanza in this psalm and indicates why we have to sing a new song to the LORD: he has gained victory, salvation; he has made known his victory, and everyone has seen this victory.

Repetition can consist not only of words (concepts) but also of verbal forms, especially imperatives. For example, the repetition of imperatives shows that Psalm 98 has three stanzas. The first stanza begins with an imperative call to praise: "O sing to the LORD!" The second stanza (vv 4-6) begins with another imperative call to praise: "Make a joyful noise to the LORD all the earth." And the final stanza begins with a triple jussive call to praise: "Let the sea roar. . . . Let the floods clap their hands; let the hills sing together for joy" (vv 7-8).

Psalmists can also use repetition to arrive at meaningful numbers. For example, in Psalm 29 "the name Yahweh is repeated precisely *four* times in both introduction and conclusion [forming an inclusio]. But even more significantly, within the body of the Psalm 'the voice of Yahweh' (allusion to thunder) is sounded a perfect *seven* times and 'Yahweh' is named a full *ten* times. In Psalm 30 . . . 'Yahweh' is named *seven* times, twice he is called 'Yahweh my God' (vss 2a, 12b — inclusio), and once 'Adonay' — for a total of ten references. In Psalm 19 . . . 'Yahweh' occurs also precisely seven times."[68]

Inclusio

Inclusio — also called "ballast lines," "ring structure," "envelope structure," and "bookends" — marks a unit of thought by repeating the beginning at the end. Inclusio helps preachers determine the parameters of a sub-unit (stanza) or the whole preaching text. For example, Psalm 8 begins and ends with, "O LORD, our Sovereign, how majestic is your name in all the earth!" (vv 1, 8 [9]). Psalms 103 and 104 both begin and end with "Bless the LORD, O my soul" (vv 1, 22; 1, 35). Psalms 146–150 all begin and end with the imperative, "Praise the LORD!"

---

68. Stek, "The Stylistics of Hebrew Poetry," 20.

Chiasm

Chiasm — also called "concentric structure" and "introversion" — forms parallel lines around one or two central lines. The outer parallel lines indicate the unit (A-A', like an inclusio) while the central line(s) usually disclose the key point of the psalm. For example,[69] Psalm 102:1–2 with its repetition of A, A' reveals a sub-unit in the psalm while its center, C, discloses its major concern: "Do not hide your face from me."

> A Hear my prayer, O LORD;
>   B let my cry come to you.
>   C Do not hide your face from me in the day of my distress.
>   B' Incline your ear to me;
> A' answer me speedily in the day when I call.

The Literary Contexts of the Psalm

We must also understand each psalm in its literary contexts: in expanding order, the neighboring psalms, the Psalter, the Old Testament, and the New Testament. We will begin with the neighboring psalms and the Psalter, and deal further with the contexts of the Psalter and the Old Testament under "Theocentric Interpretation" (pp. 31–33) and the context of the New Testament under "Christocentric Interpretation" (pp. 33–37).

The Context of Neighboring Psalms

Interpreting a psalm in the context of its neighboring psalms is a controversial topic. Dillard and Longman maintain, "Most psalms do not have a normal literary context. Except under rare circumstances, it is inappropriate to exegete a psalm in the literary context of the psalms that precede and follow it."[70] It is well to note that the psalms are not connected to each other as, say, the gospel stories in John. At the same time we must be aware of the fact that some psalms have

---

69. For more details and examples, see the following chapters. See also John V. Tornfelt, "Preaching the Psalms: Understanding Chiastic Structures for Greater Clarity," *JEvHS* 2, no. 2 (2002): 4–31.

70. Dillard and Longman, *Introduction to the Old Testament*, 227. Cf. Petersen and Richards, *Interpreting Hebrew Poetry*, 90, "The surrounding psalms provide little specific information for the interpretation of a given psalm. . . . Hence the interpreter regularly focuses almost exclusively on an individual psalm, and not the psalm within its literary surroundings."

deliberately been set next to each other so as to color their interpretation. For example, "Psalm 135 picks up the emphases on praise and ministry in the house of the Lord expressed in Psalm 134 (cf. Ps 134:1 with 135:1–2). In turn, Psalm 135 prepares the reader for Psalm 136 with its emphasis on God's goodness (cf. Ps 135:3 with Ps 136:1)."[71] Also, Psalms 103 and 104 are clearly connected by their shared inclusios: each begins and ends with, "Bless the Lord, O my soul" — a phrase that occurs only here in the Psalter. "The topic of the first [Ps 103] is God as savior, who forgives sinners, and of the second [Ps 104] is God as creator, who sustains all life. Together they provide a meditation on the two typical works of the Lord."[72] Granted that neighboring psalms do not offer a literary context for the interpretation of many psalms, but when there is evidence that the editor has deliberately placed a psalm next to another because of its contents, that context should be considered.

One can also compare a psalm with other psalms that have the same form: compare a lament psalm with other lament psalms, a hymn with other hymns, etc. The objective of this comparison is not to generalize the psalm to be preached but to discover what is distinctive about this particular psalm and preach its specific message.

The Context of the Psalter

In the past the psalms were interpreted individually, isolated from their context in the Psalter. The Psalter was "treated as an anthology, a collection that contains the psalms."[73] Recently, however, more attention has been paid to the Psalter as an edited collection in which the editor(s) in various ways indicate(s) how a psalm is to be understood. Just as the stories about Jesus have to be understood in their original historical setting of Jesus *and* in their setting in a particular Gospel, so the psalms have to be understood both in their original setting (if possible) *and* in their setting in the Psalter. Unfortunately, there is still much uncertainty as to how and how much the context of the Psalter changes the interpretation of a

---

71. Andreas J. Köstenberger and Richard D. Patterson, *Invitation to Biblical Interpretation: Exploring the Hermeneutical Triad of History, Literature, and Theology* (Grand Rapids: Kregel, 2011), 282.

72. Mays, *The Lord Reigns,* 121. In "The Place of the Torah-Psalms," *JBL* 106, no. 1 (1987; pp. 3–12): 10–11, Mays identifies Psalms 111 and 112, 105 and 106, 9 and 10, 18 and 19, and 118 and 119 as arranged "in pairs to bring topics together to create a more comprehensive theological statement." Psalms 42 and 43, of course, are often identified as a single psalm and Psalms 32 and 33 as "a conjoined set." Miller, *The Way of the Lord,* 169. See also Leslie Allen, *Psalms,* 16, with other examples on pp. 15–17.

73. Mays, *The Lord Reigns,* 119,

psalm.[74] But there is general agreement that the editor(s) intended to mark off five books of psalms to duplicate the five books of Moses, to have Psalms 1 and 2 function as an introduction to the Psalter in whose light the following psalms ought to be understood, and to conclude the Psalter with a burst of praise. We shall discuss each claim in turn.

Five Books of Psalms As many English translations indicate, the editors have divided the Psalter into five books — 1–41; 42–72; 73–89; 90–106, and 107–150 — each book concluding with a doxology (Pss 41, 72, 89, 106, and 150). The five books are clearly intended to remind the reader of the five books of Moses. Midrash Tehillim on Psalm 1 says, "Moses gave Israel the five books, and David gave Israel the five books of Psalms."[75] This allusion to the five books of Moses is confirmed by the introductory *torah* psalm, Psalm 1, which encourages meditation on God's teaching. It is also confirmed by the inclusion of other *torah* psalms, Psalm 19 and especially Psalm 119, the longest psalm.[76] "Like the Pentateuch, the Psalter is to be read and heard as God's instruction to the faithful."[77]

Psalms 1 and 2 as Introduction to the Psalter There are several reasons for understanding Psalms 1 and 2 as an intentional introduction to the Psalter.[78] First, in contrast to most if not all the psalms in book I (Pss 1–41) which have superscriptions,[79] these two psalms have no headings that would seek to ground them in some historical setting. Since they "are not identified with an author or speaker, they have a purely literary role in the framework of the book."[80]

Second, Psalms 1 and 2 are linked together in various ways. The first line of Psalm 1 begins with the word "happy" ("blessed") and the last line of Psalm 2 begins with the word "happy." If this is an intended inclusio, it suggests that these

---

74. See, e.g., Tremper Longman's critique of Gerald Wilson's *The Editing of the Psalter* in Longman's "The Messiah: Explorations in the Law and Writings," in Stanley E. Porter, *The Messiah in the Old and New Testaments* (Grand Rapids: Eerdmans, 2007: pp. 13–34), 21–24.

75. Quoted by Mays, *Psalms*, 15.

76. Westermann, *Praise and Lament in the Psalms*, 253, claims that "there was once a Psalter which began with Ps 1 and ended with Ps 119," thus seeking to determine a point in tradition history when a Psalter framed by Psalms 1 and 119 turned the corner from prayers and songs to *torah*, God's instruction. Cf. Westermann, *Living Psalms*, 294.

77. McCann, "The Psalms as Instruction," *Int* 46, no. 2 (1992): 119.

78. "The notion that Psalm 1 constitutes an introduction to the Psalter is an ancient one that goes back at least as far as Jerome." R. N. Whybray, *Reading the Psalms as a Book* (Sheffield: Sheffield Academic, 1996), 38.

79. The exceptions are Psalms 10 and 33. Mark Futato, *Transformed by Praise*, 55, suggests that originally Psalms 9 and 10 were one psalm, as were Psalms 32 and 33.

80. Mays, *The Lord Reigns*, 123.

two psalms belong together. Further, the last verse of Psalm 1 and the last verse of Psalm 2 both use the words "way" and "perish":

but *the way* of the wicked *will perish* (Ps 1:6).

kiss his feet, or he will be angry,
    and you *will perish* in *the way* (Ps 2:12).

Both psalms also use the word "meditate," but in different senses:

and on his law they meditate [*yehge(h)*] day and night (Ps 1:2).

and the people plot [*yehgû*] in vain? (Ps 2:1).

In Psalm 1 people meditate on God's law in order to learn from it; in Psalm 2 they meditate on how to rebel against God. "The repetition of ['happy'] 'blessed,' 'way/perish,' and 'meditate' serves to bind Psalms 1 and 2 together as a literary unit."[81]

Third, each Psalm "contains a distinctive topic and set of themes that recur throughout the book."[82] Mays explains, "Psalm 1 introduces the psalms as *torah*, as Scripture to be studied, heeded, and absorbed. . . . In the psalms, says this directive, you may find instruction about what God is like and how God deals with people and the world. You can learn about the human predicament and human possibilities in a world populated by the powerful and the lowly, the wicked and the righteous. . . . You will be taught trust and the language of trust, prayer and praise."[83] Gerald Wilson adds, "Psalm 1 seems . . . to encourage an attitude of constant delight in, and meditation on, the Torah as the guide to life rather than to death."[84] In addition, Psalm 1 raises the topic of "the opposition between the righteous and the wicked."[85]

81. Futato, *Transformed by Praise*, 54. Peter Craigie, *Psalms 1-50*, 59, notes that "there is some evidence, in both the early Jewish and Christian traditions, to suggest that . . . the two psalms together were considered to be the first psalm of the Psalter." For example, the oldest Greek text of Acts 13:33 quotes Psalm 2:7 "but introduces it as coming from the first psalm." The NEB (1961 and 1971) footnote to "second psalm" in Acts 13:33 reads, "*Some witnesses read* first." It is also possible that Psalm 1 was unnumbered as preface to the Psalter so that our Psalm 2 was Psalm 1. See Wilson, *Psalms*, I, 92 n. 8.

82. Mays, *The Lord Reigns*, 120.

83. Mays, *Psalms*, 15-16. Cf. Bellinger, *Psalms*, 130, "Placing this wisdom psalm as the introduction to the Psalter helps readers view the Psalms as having significance for the life of faith beyond the texts' original cultic setting."

84. Wilson, "The Shape of the Book of Psalms," *Int* 46, no. 2 (1992): 137.

85. Mays, *The Lord Reigns*, 122.

Psalm 2 also introduces the opposition between the righteous and the wicked, this time between "the LORD and his anointed" and "the peoples" and their "kings."[86] But, as Bernhard Anderson points out, its main theme is "the theme of the kingdom or dominion of God, which is manifest through the Davidic king (God's anointed one) and which will come fully 'on earth as it is in heaven.' . . . The psalms invite us into a God-centered world, the dominion of God, which was, which is, and is to come. The theme of God's kingship is rooted primarily in royal covenant theology. . . . God made 'an everlasting covenant' with the Davidic dynasty, assuring David and his successors that God would not go back on the 'promises of grace' made to David."[87] Psalm 2 as introduction to the Psalter suggests that in meditating on the following psalms we should be listening for the coming kingdom of God and for the coming king.[88]

Summing up, Psalms 1 and 2 together as introduction to the Psalter introduce two major themes of the Old Testament: "law and kingship, conditional covenant

86. "Psalm 2 escalates the wicked of Psalm 1 to whole nations and narrows the righteous individual to the Davidic king." Waltke and Houston, *The Psalms as Christian Worship*, 103. Cf. McCann, "Hearing the Psalter," 290, Psalms 1–2 introduce us to the "'the wicked' (1:1, 4–6), who have no intention of listening to or obeying God's *torah*, along with 'the nations,' 'the peoples,' 'the kings,' and 'the rulers,' who collaborate 'against the LORD and his anointed' (2:1–2)." Cf. Brown, *Psalms*, 115, "Psalm 2 plunges the reader into the savage world of international conflict. . . . This 'loud' and vivid picture of military conflict against Zion sets up what will prove to be a type-scene in the Psalter."

87. B. Anderson, *Out of the Depths*, 206–7. See also p. 205 on "the basic themes of Judaism: the revelation of God's will in the Torah (Ps. 1), the dominion of God manifest in a Davidic king (Ps. 2)." Cf. McCann, "The Psalms as Instruction," *Int* 46, no. 2 (1992): 123, "The central theological affirmation of the Psalter is that the Lord reigns! Given the crucial placement of the enthronement psalms at the editorial 'center' of the Psalter [book 4], it seems very likely that the placement of Psalm 2 at the beginning of the Psalter was intended primarily as an affirmation of God's reign and not simply as a statement about the Davidic monarchy (see esp. Ps 2:11, 'Serve the LORD with fear'). After Psalm 1 orients the reader to receive what follows as instruction, Psalm 2 introduces the essential content which the Psalter intends to teach — that the LORD reigns! . . . As a proclamation of God's reign, the Psalter calls people to a decision."

88. "Psalm 2 was apparently destined to confer an eschatological significance on the whole Psalter and to present King David, its symbolic author, as the prophet par excellence of the Messiah to come." Terrien, *The Psalms*, 21. Cf. McCann, "Hearing the Psalter," 281, "Psalm 2 seems to be performing its introductory function by anticipating the Psalter's theological heart and the message that the enthronement collection will make explicit: God reigns." Cf. Calvin Seerveld, "Reading and Hearing the Psalms: The Gut of the Bible," *Pro Rege* (June 1999; pp. 20–31): 23, "The first two untitled psalms . . . have been set there like a preface or foreword to give you a prospectus of what follows in the book. . . . Psalm 1 centers around *torah*, and Psalm 2 introduces Messiah. Those are the orienting horizons, I think, to the book of the psalms: God's will which when followed satisfies, and the LORD's anointed one here and coming."

and unconditional promise, Sinai and Zion."[89] In addition, the thrust of Psalm 1, "*Happy* are those . . . [whose] delight is in the law of the LORD," is expanded by Psalm 2, "*Happy* are all who take refuge in him." "The entire psalter will be about the 'happy' / 'blessed' life, and it will affirm throughout that this life derives fundamentally from the conviction that God rules the world."[90]

Psalms 146–150 as a Climax of Praise The last five psalms are meant to conclude the Psalter with doxologies. Wilson argues that "this final *hallel* is set in motion by the personal and universal calls to praise that are expressed at the end of Psalm 145:21 ('My mouth will speak the praise of Yahweh, and let all flesh bless his holy name for ever and ever')." "This is not to deny," he writes, "that Psalm 150 has a concluding force and function of its own."[91] Mays adds, "All five praise the LORD for his mighty deeds as sovereign of the world and God of his people. The themes of this praise summarize and repeat the characterizations of the LORD throughout the Psalter."[92] Mays further observes that the "massive concentration of psalms of praise in the last third of the Psalter creates the movement from the dominant tone of prayer in the first two-thirds to praise as climax and consummation."[93]

Historical Interpretation of Psalms

Historical interpretation raises the questions, Who wrote this text? When? Where? Why? and to Whom?

The Psalm's Original Historical Setting

The individual psalms were originally addressed to God or to fellow believers. Unfortunately, questions about the original author and the occasion for writing are difficult to answer because most psalms originated as individual cries to God for help or songs of praise that were later taken over by the community.[94] The

---

89. Steven Shawn Tuell. "Psalm 1," *Int* 63, no. 3 (2009; pp. 278–80): 279. See also VanGemeren, *Psalms*, 38.

90. McCann, "Psalms," 688–89. Cf. Brown, *Psalms*, 116–17, "Psalms 1 and 2 . . . serve as programmatic pieces designed to influence how one reads the Psalter selectively yet discerningly."

91. Wilson, "The Shape of the Book of Psalms," *Int* 46, no. 2 (1992): 133 and n. 15.

92. Mays, *The Lord Reigns*, 120.

93. Mays, *Psalms*, 17.

94. Robert Alter, *Book of Psalms*, xv, calls the dating of individual psalms "a region of treach-

closest we can come to answering these questions are the superscriptions that were added to 116 psalms.[95] But here, too, we must acknowledge that the Hebrew particle *lə* (of) is ambiguous, so that "of David" can mean "belonging to David," "for David," "concerning David," "dedicated to David," etc.[96]

In fact, most scholars agree that these superscriptions are not original but were added by later editors when the psalms were collected and shaped into the Psalter. Craigie notes, "While a few of these titles may have been composed at the same time as the psalm, the majority of them reflect later tradition concerning the use of the psalm in Israel's worship. The psalm titles are, nevertheless, a part of the canonical text of the Hebrew Bible, not merely the notations of a post-biblical editor."[97] When these superscriptions do identify the author and the occasion for writing (e.g., Ps 51, "To the leader. A Psalm of David, when the prophet Nathan came to him, after he had gone in to Bathsheba."),[98] they offer the editor's invitation for reading the psalm from that historical perspective.[99]

When the psalm has no historical superscription, we can "examine the internal evidence for clues. . . . For instance Psalm 2 arose out of international turmoil, though the specific situation is not clear; yet the anonymous historical crisis lends

---

erous scholarly quicksand. The one safe conclusion is that the writing of psalms was a persistent activity over many centuries."

95. "The contents of the superscriptions vary but fall into a few broad categories: (1) author, (2) name of collection, (3) type of psalm, (4) musical notations, (5) liturgical notations and (6) brief indications of occasion for composition." Stek, *NIV Study Bible* (1985), 782.

96. Ibid. Cf. Alter, *Book of Psalms*, xv.

97. Craigie, *The Old Testament*, 212. Cf. Bellinger, *Psalms*, 8–9.

98. See also Psalms 3, 7, 18, 30, 34, 52, 54, 56, 57, 59, 60, 63, 142.

99. "While they [the superscriptions] may not be read to identify the precise situation in which the prayer was first composed, they indicate how the community of faith and those responsible for the transmission of these prayers associated them with varying human predicaments, primarily in the life of David." Miller, *They Cried to the Lord*, 83. Cf. Tate, *Psalms 51–100*, 13, "The historical note is a way of saying that the understanding of the psalm is helped when it is read in a particular context." Cf. Mays, "The David of the Psalms," *Int* 40, no. 2 (1986): 152, "The psalm titles do not grow out of or function in behalf of a historical interest of any kind. They are rather hermeneutical ways of relating the psalms to the lives of those who lived in the face of threats from enemies within and without and from their own sin, and who sought to conduct their lives according to the way of David." Cf. Brueggemann, "Psalms in Narrative Performance," in *Performing the Psalms*, ed. David Fleer and Dave Bland (St. Louis: Chalice, 2005), 20, "The value of the superscription and the narrative connection is that we read the Psalm with specificity. . . . The superscriptions are a scribal strategy whereby the now-lost particularity of the Psalms can be recovered in a second wave of narrative concreteness." See also Paul Wilson, "Reading the Psalms for Preaching: Fictive Plot," in *Performing the Psalms*, ed. David Fleer and Dave Bland (St. Louis: Clalice, 2005; pp. 105–20), 116–17.

a definite orientation to the psalm."[100] We can also "explore the general historical / cultural backdrop of the psalm."[101] But Allen Ross rightly states, "In the final analysis, the message of the psalm will come from the exegesis of the psalm itself, without the need for a reference to a specific event."[102]

The Psalm's Later Historical Settings

In addition to seeking to determine the psalm's original historical setting, we can seek to understand it in its later historical horizons as it was incorporated into the Psalter. But here, too, we face some difficult issues. Gordon Wenham raises the questions, "Should we see the Psalter as compiled during the exile, after the exile, or even later? It could make a difference to the way we read it."[103] Unfortunately, we do not know the exact history of the formation of the Psalter.

Peter Craigie, however, suggests a possible way out of this dilemma. He writes, "The psalms, in most cases, need to be examined in *functional* terms. . . . If we are to understand the psalms, then, we must try to envision each one in its appropriate social setting."[104] Sometimes the psalm itself provides that setting, such as meeting God in his holy temple. For example:

> But I, through the abundance of your steadfast love, will enter your house,
>   I will bow down toward your holy temple in awe of you (Ps 5:7).

> I was glad when they said to me,
>   "Let us go to the house of the Lord!"
> Our feet are standing within your gates, O Jerusalem (Ps 122:1–2).

In the following chapters I will combine historical interpretation with determining the author's / editor's goal in order to avoid needless duplication.

---

100. Greg W. Parsons, "Guidelines for Understanding and Proclaiming the Psalms," *BSac* 147 (1990; pp. 169–87): 172.

101. Ibid.

102. *Commentary on the Psalms*, I, 47.

103. Wenham, *The Psalter Reclaimed*, 78.

104. Craigie, *The Old Testament*, 213. Cf. Dillard and Longman, *Introduction to the Old Testament*, 217, "It is futile to reconstruct the elusive historical background of individual psalms. In place of it, the psalm interpreter must rather ask, How did this psalm function in the worship of Old Testament Israel?" Cf. Tate, *Psalms 51–100*, 370.

Theocentric Interpretation of Psalms

So far we have discussed literary and historical interpretation. A third dimension of biblical interpretation is theocentric interpretation. Theocentric interpretation is necessary as a corrective to a general inclination to use an anthropocentric approach for understanding the psalms. Preachers sometimes use psychology to focus on the psalmist's emotions and link it to our emotions or they use sociology to analyze Israel's religious culture.[105] But that is to miss the point of the psalms, as the Psalter itself makes clear.

The Theocentric Focus of the Psalter

We have seen that the strategic position of Psalm 1 encourages delight in meditating on God's teaching (*torah*) while Psalm 2 highlights the sovereign reign of God and his anointed — themes that recur throughout the Psalter. Moreover, each of the five books of the Psalter ends with a doxology: "Blessed be the LORD, the God of Israel, from everlasting to everlasting. Amen and Amen" (Ps 41:13).[106] The doxologies reach a climax in the final book of the Psalter with six hymns of praise to God the King (145–150), the last one culminating in, "Let everything that breathes praise the LORD! Praise the LORD!" Paul Wilson rightly contends that "the key player . . . is not David or any other named or unnamed psalmist. The key player is God. When the church reads the Bible as scripture, it reads for a Word that is from, about, and embodying God in one instance, and about humanity's relationship to God in another."[107]

The theocentric focus of the Psalter also becomes evident when we inquire about its central, underlying theme. Mays argues persuasively that this central theme is "Yahweh reigns": "The declaration '*YHWH mālak*' involves a vision of reality that is the theological centre of the Psalter. . . . The psalmic understanding of the people of God, the city of God, the king of God, and the law of God depends on its validity and implications." Mays calls "the LORD reigns" "a

---

105. For example, in the nineteenth century, a major approach to the psalms was the biographical-psychological approach that centered on the author of the psalm. Another popular approach was psychologizing which focused primarily on human emotions. See Carl J. Bosma, "Discerning the Voices in the Psalms: A Discussion of Two Problems in Psalmic Interpretation," *CTJ* 43, no. 2 (2008; pp. 183–212) and *CTJ* 44, no. 1 (2009; pp. 127–70).

106. See also Pss 72:18–19; 89:52; 106:48; and 150:1–6.

107. Paul Wilson, "Reading the Psalms for Preaching," 118–19. Cf. Brueggemann, "Psalms in Narrative Performance," 10, "The *little narratives* and the sustaining *meta-narrative* [of the Psalter] share together the attestation that *YHWH is the central and decisive character* in the plot."

metaphor that transcends and lies behind the variety [of metaphors]. It is what every reader and user of the psalms may know as the code for understanding all of them."[108] As he writes elsewhere, "The psalms are the poetry of the reign of the LORD."[109]

The theocentric focus of the Psalter also comes to expression in the many different metaphors the Psalter uses to reveal God. The basic metaphor is that God is a covenant God, a God who has established a relationship with his people. "This relationship is described by means of a variety of images of God: shepherd, warrior, father, mother, king, husband, to name a few. Each emphasizes a particular aspect of God's relationship with his people."[110] Elizabeth Achtemeier adds, "The Psalter is not a humanistic book. Every experience and condition of humankind is set in relation to the God of Israel; therein lies the Psalter's greatness. . . . Therefore no psalm can properly be understood outside of God's relation with his elected people."[111]

In view of the theocentric focus of the Psalter, each psalm requires not only literary and historical interpretation but also theocentric interpretation. In other words, a key question that must be raised in interpreting a psalm is, What does this psalm say about God and God's relationship with his creation and his people? The necessity of theocentric interpretation is also underscored by the broader context of the Old Testament.

The Theocentric Context of the Old Testament

The Old Testament story consists of four major episodes: 1) God created the world and its people good (Genesis 1–2); 2) our ancestors fell into sin, bringing

---

108. Mays, "The Centre of the Psalms," in *Language, Theology and the Bible: Essays in Honour of James Barr*, ed. Samuel E. Balentine and John Barton (Oxford: Clarendon, 1994; pp. 231–46), 245–46. Cf. Mays, *The Lord Reigns*, 122, "A topic is identified that is central and recurrent in the book as a whole: the kingship of the LORD. . . . His reign in the work is represented by a place and a person. The place is Zion. The person is his chosen king. Zion as city of God and king as the LORD's anointed will themselves be the subject of many particular psalms. What happens to and through them involves the reign of the LORD. And it is this theme of the reign of God that is the integrating center of the theology of the entire book."

109. Mays, *Psalms*, 30. Cf. Anderson, *Out of the Depths*, 207, "The psalms invite us into a God-centered world, the dominion of God, which was, which is, and is to come."

110. Dillard and Longman, *Introduction to the Old Testament*, 228. Some of the other metaphors for God are: the Most High, our Sovereign, my rock, God of hosts, judge, shield, fortress, deliverer, redeemer, my light, my salvation, my strength, helper, upholder, refuge, hope, trust, maker, and keeper. See the lengthy list in John Witvliet's *The Biblical Psalms in Christian Worship*, 18–20.

111. Achtemeier, *Preaching from the Old Testament*, 140.

about the pain and brokenness we experience in this world (Genesis 3); 3) God redeems his people, and 4) God promises to renew his creation (the remainder of the Old Testament). Since God is the main character in the Old Testament, the whole Old Testament requires theocentric interpretation, including the psalms.

The context of the Old Testament also enables us to better understand the psalm in the light of similar literature in the Old Testament. For example, the context of a creation psalm like Psalm 8 can be compared with Genesis 1–2 and other creation passages. A *torah* psalm like Psalm 119 can be compared with God's teachings in Exodus, Leviticus, Numbers, and Deuteronomy. Even a superscription about king David may be a reason to compare the psalm with Samuel and Chronicles. A wisdom psalm like Psalm 49 can be compared with other wisdom literature such as Proverbs, Ecclesiastes, and Job. Again, the objective of comparing the psalm to be preached with other passages of the Old Testament is not to generalize the message of the psalm but to understand it better in the context of the Old Testament and discern its distinctive message.

Christocentric Interpretation of Psalms

The contexts for interpreting psalms are not only neighboring psalms, the whole Psalter, and the Old Testament, but now also the New Testament.

The Context of the New Testament

According to the Bible, God's work progresses from his good creation, which was spoiled by the human fall into sin, to God's redemption (eventually in Christ's First Coming), to his promised new creation (at Christ's Second Coming). Because of this progression in redemptive history, we find in the psalms promises God made at a certain stage of that history which come to fulfillment in Christ later in that history; we find types (especially King David) at a certain stage of redemptive history that come to fulfillment in Christ, the antitype, later in that history; and we can discover more general analogies or contrasts between the teaching of the psalms and the teaching of Jesus Christ. Since the Bible reflects this progression in redemptive history, we can also trace through the Bible longitudinal themes[112] from the psalms to Jesus Christ in the New Testament.

---

112. For an explanation of "longitudinal themes" see p. 36 below, "Longitudinal themes."

Seven Ways of Preaching Christ from Psalms

In my book *Preaching Christ from the Old Testament* I identify seven (sometimes overlapping)[113] ways that preachers can use to move legitimately from an Old Testament passage to Jesus Christ in the New Testament. These seven ways are: redemptive-historical progression, promise-fulfillment, typology, analogy, longitudinal themes, New Testament references, and contrast. I will briefly explain each of these seven ways.[114]

1. Redemptive-historical progression

Redemptive-historical progression considers how the message of the passage changes as redemptive history progresses from the text's historical setting to Jesus' First and/or Second Coming. For example, the theme of the shortest hymn, Psalm 117, is, "Praise the LORD, all you nations, for great is his steadfast love toward us." If the psalmist in Old Testament times encouraged the nations to praise the LORD because of his steadfast love, how much more should the nations in New Testament times praise the LORD since we have experienced God's love in the sending of his only Son to redeem his creation and his people. This move can be supported by John 3:16, "For God so loved the world that he gave his only Son. . . ."[115]

2. Promise-fulfillment

Promise-fulfillment moves from God's promise of a coming Messiah to its fulfillment with Jesus' First or Second Coming. For example, in the royal Psalm 2 the LORD promises that his anointed king will possess "the ends of the earth." This promise will be fulfilled on the last day when Jesus establishes his universal kingdom on earth.[116] This move can be supported by Philippians 2:9-11, "Therefore

---

113. The issue, of course, is not so much to identify the precise classification as it is to find a legitimate way forward from the Old Testament text to Christ in the New Testament.

114. For an extended explanation, see my *Preaching Christ from the Old Testament,* 203–77. When I began writing *Preaching Christ from the Old Testament,* my first inclination was to place the way of New Testament references first. But considering that the New Testament does not intend to teach a hermeneutical method, I placed New Testament references last in the six positive ways to move from the Old Testament to Christ so that it performs more of a supporting role to the first five ways as well as to the way of contrast.

115. Redemptive historical progression is a natural move when psalms speak about the coming kingdom of God and the coming king who ushers in this kingdom, as in the royal psalms, Pss 2, 18, 20, 21, 45, 72, 89, 101, 110, 132, 144:1–11.

116. The ways of promise-fulfillment or typology also work well with the royal psalms (listed above in n. 115).

God also highly exalted him and gave him the name that is above every name, so that at the name of Jesus every knee should bend, in heaven and on earth and under the earth, and every tongue should confess that Jesus Christ is Lord, to the glory of God the Father." It can also be supported by Revelation 11:15, "The Kingdom of the world has become the kingdom of our Lord and of his Messiah, and he will reign forever and ever."

3. Typology

Typology moves from an Old Testament type prefiguring Jesus to the antitype, Jesus himself. For example, when the speaker in a psalm is the Davidic king or speaks about a Davidic king, one can move forward in redemptive history from that type to the greater antitype, "Jesus the Messiah, the son of David" (Matt 1:1), "the Lord of lords and King of kings" (Rev 17:14). One can use typology not only with the royal psalms but also with laments that speak of intense suffering (Pss 22, 35, 41, 55, 69, 109) to move to the suffering Jesus in the New Testament.[117]

4. Analogy

Analogy notes the similarity between the teaching or goal of the psalmist and the teaching or goal of Jesus. Analogies exist because through Christ Christians are grafted into Israel (e.g., Rom 11:17–24; Eph 2:11–22). Since the church is the new Israel, one can find analogies between what God did for Israel and what God through Christ does for the church and analogies between what God required of Israel and what God through Christ requires of the church. For example, in preaching Psalm 1, "Happy are those . . . [whose] delight is in the law of the LORD," one can use analogy to move to Jesus' teaching: "Blessed [happy] are those" whose delight is in the law of Christ (the ninefold "blessed," "happy," followed by the law of Christ in Matt 5–7). The possibility of using analogy for preaching Christ from Psalms is underscored by McCann's judgment that "the 'theological heart' of the Psalter is essentially the same as Jesus' fundamental proclamation — the Lord reigns!"[118]

---

117. "Christ is the summing up of all the psalmists' laments and suffering — he bears it all on the cross. He is the bearer to us of all the forgiveness the psalmists knew, all the gladness they voiced, all their joy in God's abundant life." Elizabeth Achtemeyer, *Preaching as Theology and Art* (Nashville: Abingdon, 1984), 449.

118. McCann, *A Theological Introduction to the Book of Psalms*, 163.

5. Longitudinal themes

"Longitudinal themes" is a technical term in biblical theology for uncovering themes that run through several Bible books and even through both the Old and the New Testaments.[119] The way of longitudinal themes traces the theme (or sub-theme) of the text through the Old Testament to Jesus Christ in the New Testament. For example, the royal Psalm 72 is a prayer that the king may judge God's people "with righteousness," defending "the cause of the poor." One can trace this theme through the Psalter, the prophets, and into the New Testament where Jesus not only teaches this theme but lives it . This bridge can be supported by New Testament references such as Luke 4:18 where Jesus says, "The Spirit of the Lord is upon me, because he has anointed me to bring good news to the poor."

6. New Testament references

New Testament references usually support the other six ways to Christ by quoting New Testament verses that cite or allude to the preaching text and link it to Christ (see the examples above). But sometimes one can also move directly from a psalm to the New Testament reference. For example, when preaching Psalm 22, the lament, "My God, my God, why have you forsaken me," is repeated by Jesus on the cross, which allows one to move directly from Psalm 22 to Mark 15:34.[120] As mentioned above, the New Testament quotes or alludes to the psalms more than 560 times.[121]

7. Contrast

The way of contrast moves to Christ by noting the contrast between the message of the text and that of the New Testament — a contrast that exists because Christ has come or because Christ teaches the opposite. For example, in Psalm 137:8–9 the psalmist exclaims, "O daughter Babylon, you devastator! Happy shall they

---

119. See my *Modern Preacher,* 67–70, and *Preaching Christ from the Old Testament,* 222–24.

120. With Psalm 22 one can also use typology: Jesus sees the suffering psalmist as a type of himself; one can then support this move with Mark 15:34.

121. See p. 1 above. "Several Psalms such as Psalms 118, 110, 41, 31, and 22 are central to the Passion narratives in all the gospels. At least three of the reported 'seven words' spoken by Jesus from the cross are words of the Psalter (Matt 27:46 par.; Luke 23:46; John 19:28). References in the book of Acts to the foundational message of the apostles as well as references in the epistle to the Hebrews to the basic christological argumentation of the second generation make prolific use of texts from the Psalter and their new Christian interpretation." Karlfried Froehlich, "Discerning the Voices: Praise and Lament in the Tradition of the Christian Psalter," *CTJ* 36, no. 1 (2001; pp. 75–90): 77.

be who take your little ones and dash them against the rocks!" Jesus, by contrast, teaches, "Love your enemies and pray for those who persecute you" (Matt 5:44). This contrast can be further supported by Jesus' prayer on the cross, "Father, forgive them; for they do not know what they are doing" (Luke 23:34).

Preaching Psalms

Ellen Davis suggests that "the best way to prepare to preach a psalm is to read it over and over aloud, until you can see how and why one line yields to the next, until its images are haunting your imagination, until its phraseology and its particular pattern of repetition-with-variation . . . becomes distinctive in your mind."[122] This is good advice, but more can be said.

Preaching Poetry

The psalms as Hebrew poetry, we have seen, are marked by terseness, vivid imagery, and parallelism. It would be good if these characteristics would also guide to some extent our crafting of sermons on the psalms.[123]

Terseness

Although the hearers at times may wish for more terseness (shorter sermons), for the sake of understanding the psalm, preachers cannot give in to that desire. Sermons are not poetry; sermons *explain* the message of the psalm's poetry. As such they require many more words than the psalmist used. But preachers can mimic terseness by using oral style, which includes short sentences and vivid images.

Vivid Images

The vivid images of the psalms will play the most important role in preaching psalms. Jeffrey Arthurs explains: "Poetry uses concrete nouns and verbs to create a *picture* of abstract ideas. The word *anger* does little to conjure up an image in our

---

122. Davis, *Wondrous Depth*, 24.

123. "The Psalms are both models and permits. We stand under their discipline, and we are authorized by their freedom." Clinton J. McCann and James C. Howell, *Preaching the Psalms* (Nashville: Abingdon, 2001), 51. Cf. Kenneth Smith, "Preaching the Psalms with Respect for Their Inspired Design," *JEvHS* 3, no. 2 (2003; pp. 4–31): 6, "Just as each psalm is designed in specific ways to maximize its impact on readers and listeners, our sermons can be similarly crafted."

minds, but in the psalms *wrath* 'kindles' and 'burns.' *Confusion* makes us 'stagger'; *trouble* is an 'arrow that flies by day'; *security* is a 'shelter' from the sun or a 'wing' to hide under; and *jubilation* causes 'trees to clap their hands' and 'seas to lift their voices.'"[124] For preaching purposes, he writes, "concretizing the abstract produces three rhetorical effects. First, it sparks the imagination. . . . Hear the roaring sea and the roaring lions. Feel the cold shadows and the hot sun. . . . The second effect of concretizing is to foster identification. Although David's headache is not my headache, when he describes his headache with concrete nouns and verbs, I identify. . . . The third effect is to aid memory."[125]

Parallelism

Awareness of parallelism is important for interpreting psalms and in expository preaching we can certainly expose the parallelisms in the psalm. But it is not likely that parallelism will be as dominant a feature in the sermon as it is in the psalm.[126] Arthurs proposes, "Not only can we use parallelism for small units, but we can also use it to organize the entire sermon. State your point and develop it, then restate the point and develop it with more intensity, then restate it again."[127]

Appeal to the Emotions

Related to the vivid images, the psalms, more than any other biblical genre, appeal to the emotions. Fee and Stuart contend that psalms are "intended to appeal to the emotions, to evoke feelings rather than propositional thinking, and to stimulate a response on the part of the individual that goes beyond a mere cognitive understanding of certain facts."[128] Preachers need to take this appeal to emotions into account when preaching psalms. Arthurs asserts, "The goal is not

---

124. Arthurs, *Preaching with Variety,* 46 (my emphasis on picture).

125. Ibid., 46–47.

126. "The preacher must pay attention in interpreting the psalm to the ways in which the psalmist, through parallelism, unfolds and nuances the central ideas and images around which the psalm is built. The effect on the reader is that those ideas and images begin to take on life in her or his imagination. The sermon should seek to create a similar effect for hearers, even if the rhetorical strategies employed are quite different." Thomas Long, *Preaching and the Literary Forms of the Bible,* 49–50.

127. Arthurs, *Preaching with Variety,* 47. Cf. David Bartlett, "Texts Shaping Sermons," in *Listening to the Word,* ed. Gail R. O'Day and Thomas G. Long (Nashville: Abingdon, 1993; pp. 147–63), 150, "All of us can find ways to reinforce a theme or an image by repetition that both underlines and expands what has gone before."

128. Gordon D. Fee and Douglas K. Stuart, *How to Read the Bible for All It's Worth* (Grand Rapids: Zondervan, 1982), 171.

to mimic the *exact form* of the text but to reproduce the *impact* of the text. . . . If the text prompts emotion, we should too."[129] Although this is true, we should be careful not to target the hearers' emotions exclusively. The psalms' appeal to the emotions is always balanced by the editor's introduction to the Psalter with the *torah* Psalm 1, which appeals primarily to the intellect and the will. According to Ellen Davis, "Calvin is the great master at comprehending the reasoning of both heart and mind that generated these poem-prayers, and his core insight is that the psalmists are not responding solely or directly to immediate circumstance. Certainly they register the pressure of the present situation; after all, a large proportion of the psalms are laments. Yet their response to trouble is based on something more fundamental than trouble itself, namely, on what they know to be true about God. A lamenting psalmist is 'emotional,' of course, but the emotions are those of second nature, of nature instructed by both faith and close observation of how God characteristically acts."[130]

Selecting the Preaching Text

Text selection with psalms is fairly simple because over three-quarters of the psalms have a superscription indicating the beginning of a new psalm. Since preaching texts should be literary units, not just a verse or two, the divisions into individual psalms in our English Bibles accurately reflect the literary units.[131] Whenever feasible, we should select as preaching text the whole psalm so that we can do justice in the sermon to the movement in the psalm: for example, the movement from lament to trust or praise. With a lengthy psalm like Psalm 119 we can select a smaller unit as long as it is a literary unit, e.g., one or more of the twenty-two Hebrew alphabet sections, and understood in the context of the whole psalm.

Generating Questions about the Psalm

Fred Craddock taught preachers to raise questions about the selected text. In my sermons I often used these questions in the introduction of the sermon both to

---

129. Arthurs, *Preaching with Variety*, 49.

130. Davis, *Wondrous Depth*, 22.

131. "In psalms . . . there are very often clear markers of beginnings and endings in the formulaic devices . . . , and in almost all instances chapter divisions dependably indicate individual poems." Alter, "Psalms," 255. Cf. Davis, *Wondrous Depth*, 24, "One of the peculiar pleasures and even sources of confidence for the preacher is that when you choose a psalm as your text, you get to work with a complete literary unit. . . ."

gain the attention of the congregation and to create a desire to *hear* the sermon. Our present pastor, a former educator, uses these questions effectively to keep the hearers listening throughout the sermon. "If I have these questions about the text," he says, "many in the congregation will have the same questions and want to hear the answers."[132] So he uses these questions to set and reset tension throughout the sermon to keep the congregation listening for the answers.

Determining the Psalm's Theme and Goal

Before writing their sermon, preachers need to determine the theme of the psalm: what is the point the psalmist seeks to make? what is his message for Israel? In order to keep the sermon focused, this theme should be formulated as a short sentence: subject, verb, object.

Next preachers need to determine the psalmist's goal with the psalm for Israel. Identifying the form of the psalm will pay off here, for the form of the psalm usually discloses its goal: a *hymn,* to urge Israel to praise God; a *song of thanksgiving,* to encourage Israel to thank God for blessings received; a *lament,* to embolden Israel to bring their complaints before God and to praise God for his response; a *torah (wisdom) psalm,* to persuade Israel to walk in God's ways.[133] The psalmist's specific goal can be determined by historical interpretation: hearing the message (theme) of the psalm as it spoke to Israel at a certain time in its history and inquiring about the response sought from God's people.

Formulating the Sermon's Theme, Goal, and Need Addressed

Ideally the sermon theme will be the same as the theme of the psalm. If progression in redemptive history and revelation calls for a different theme for the Christian church, one should try to stay as close as possible to the theme of the psalm. If one changes the theme too much, the psalm will no longer support the sermon theme and one is really preaching on a different text (from the New Testament) rather than the psalm. The theme sentence should be inserted in the

132. Randy Buursma, a former professor in the Communication Arts and Sciences Department at Calvin College, in one of his presentations at the 2013 Calvin Symposium on Worship held at Calvin College and Calvin Theological Seminary.

133. "Catching the mood and thrust of such psalm-types is the key to discovering their use in Israel's life. That discovery, in turn, gives us clues for their use in contemporary preaching, liturgy, and music." Robertson McQuilkin, "Understanding and Applying the Text," in *Leadership Handbooks of Practical Theology,* vol. 1, ed. James D. Berkley (Grand Rapids: Baker, 1992), 25.

sermon in various key places. "This strategic repetition helps to ensure that both the psalm and the sermon arrive at the intended theological outcome."[134]

The preacher's goal for the sermon must be in harmony with the psalmist's goal for the psalm.[135] Elizabeth Achtemeier articulates the general goal for all sermons on psalms: "The purpose of preaching from the Psalter [is] to so instruct a congregation in the life of faith, set forth in these songs, that such a life becomes the congregation's life; to let the words of the psalms so inspire and work among the gathered people that Israel's stance before God becomes the congregation's stance, Israel's depth of devotion becomes their devotion, Israel's heartfelt response to God's deeds becomes their response."[136] The more specific sermon goal will need to be determined by carefully examining how the psalmist's goal for Israel applies to the church today.

The sermon's goal, in turn, reveals the need addressed. The need addressed is the congregation's *lack of* faith, trust, thanksgiving, praise, etc. which the goal seeks to fill. The need addressed is like the negative pole on a battery while the goal is the positive pole — when the two are connected the current flows. I recommend using the sermon introduction to explore briefly the need addressed.[137] The body of the sermon responds to that need by expositing the psalm and driving home its theme: the current begins to flow; there is "a word from the Lord" for this situation. The sermon conclusion clinches the goal and the congregation can respond with a song of thanksgiving, trust, or praise.[138]

---

134. Paul Wilson, "Reading the Psalms for Preaching," 119.

135. "When the preacher is preaching from a hymn text, the sermon should duplicate the function [goal] of the hymn: namely, to call forth praise of God because of who he is and what he has done." Achtemeier, *Preaching from the Old Testament,* 50.

136. Achtemeier, ibid., 138. Ellen Davis, *Wondrous Depth,* 24, adds, "The gifted poet uses words to yield a changed perception of what we cavalierly call 'reality,' as though that were a fixed quantity. But more than that, the poet's words change us. The best poems persuade us to think and act differently."

137. Preachers can also present the need addressed before the sermon introduction. The "prayer for illumination" often focuses on the preacher with the beautiful words of Psalm 19:14, "Let the words of my mouth and the meditation of my heart be acceptable to you, O LORD, my rock and my redeemer." More effective, I think, would be a prayer for illumination for the *hearers,* such as, "Gracious God, We ask now that you would meet us here. We ask that you would meet us in the midst of our questions, in the midst of our anxiety, in the midst of our depression, and in the midst of our fog. Meet us in the midst of our poverty and affluence, joy and pain. . . ." This prayer before the sermon was recently prayed by Fred Harrell, Senior Pastor of City Church San Francisco, as reported by Keith Adams, *Calvin Theological Seminary Forum* 20, no. 2 (2013): 7.

138. Whenever I have difficulties applying a biblical text or find my prepared sermon not particularly relevant, I have found it helpful to go back and check again the author's specific goal; this move usually clarifies the direction for applying that text today.

Producing the Sermon Outline

Expository sermon outlines usually expose the structure of the text in order to transmit its message. The structure of a psalm may indicate its major divisions into stanzas, which may become the major points in a sermon outline. The structure of the psalm may also reveal repetition of words, phrases, or sentences and parallelisms that may find their place in a sermon outline. But Duane Garrett rightly cautions that "using the structure of the psalm as the outline of the sermon may be impossible. . . . What works well in a poem may not work well in a speech." Also, "the psalm may have a structure that is simply too long or complex to work well as a sermon."[139] Because the psalms appeal to the emotions, Arthurs suggests the possibility of an "emotional outline": In contrast to a logical outline, an emotional outline will follow the valleys and peaks of the psalm. "There need to be moments of effective intensity and then backing off and moments of relief for the congregation. . . . We can achieve a similar effect [as the psalm] by carefully choosing and arranging materials not only for their ideational content (remember that we *are* teachers of the Word) but also for their emotional content."[140]

Applying the Psalm

David Bartlett observes, "Preaching on the Psalms will usually not . . . end with imperatives. . . . Preaching on the psalms will end with praise or with repentance. Praise or repentance will well up among the people in the presence of God. We will not need to enjoin what the psalm will induce."[141] Although this is a good general principle for applying the psalms, there will be exceptions, as Bartlett also indicates ("usually"). For example, the salvation history Psalm 105 states its goal in its conclusion (v 45), "that they might keep his statutes and observe his laws." And, as we noted earlier, Psalms 146–150 all begin and end with the imperative, "Praise the Lord!" In concluding the Psalter, Psalm 150 enjoins, "Let everything that breathes praise the Lord!" Only the goal of each individual psalm can determine the form the application will take.

For applying laments, Elizabeth Achtemeier argues that we should have the congregation identify with the psalmist: "We do not want to tell *about* the Psalm,

---

139. Duane A. Garrett, "Preaching from the Psalms and Proverbs," in *Preaching the Old Testament,* ed. Scott M. Gibson (Grand Rapids: Baker, 2006; pp. 101–14), 103.

140. Arthurs, *Preaching with Variety,* 53.

141. Bartlett, "Texts Shaping Sermons," 157.

to stand back and describe the psalmist's experience: 'The psalmist says . . . the psalmist feels . . . the psalmist experiences. . . .' No! By means of the sermon, we want the congregation so to live into the text that they recognize themselves in its words and expressions; so to identify with the text that these songs are understood as their songs."[142]

Insofar as the original recipients, Israel, identified with the psalmist, preachers can have the congregation identify with the psalmist.[143] But we can also have the congregation identify directly with Israel. The psalms, after all, are mostly addressed to Israel.[144] As part of the canon, the psalms are the word of the LORD for Israel then and now also for the church. We ask therefore, What need in Israel did this psalm seek to address? And how is Israel's need in the past like our need today? Now the message of the psalm can fill this need and the current begins to flow between the negative and the positive pole.

Some of the lament psalms, such as Psalm 22, are difficult to apply to a prospering congregation in North America. Many of us have a hard time relating to "I am poured out like water, and all my bones are out of joint" (22:14). People who prosper cannot identify with such intense suffering. Yet even these psalms are relevant for a flourishing congregation if we remember two things. First, as Mays reminds us, in the "I-psalms" "the first-person pronoun had a different content and structure then. The Jews received identity and significance from identity with the group. To say 'I' meant to speak of one's group as well as one's person. . . . In Israel, there was a real corporate identity which could say 'I' authentically."[145] Second, as Ellen Davis observes, "We are articulating that word of God, not just for ourselves individually, but for the whole body of Christ. The psalm is connecting us with the hope, the need, the spiritual insight of people whose experience, in some respects at least, differs vastly from our own. Putting time-tested words of prayer in our mouths, then, the psalm is offering us a place from which to move forward faithfully in the company of saints (big S and little s) who are journeying to God."[146]

In preaching these psalms, then, we should not limit the need addressed

---

142. Achtemeier, "Preaching the Praises and Laments," *CTJ* 36 (2001; pp. 103–14): 105.

143. On the use of identification, see my *Modern Preacher and the Ancient Text,* 179–81.

144. Cf. Mays, *Psalms,* 23, "There is an individual *in* each psalm, known through the first person voice and its self-descriptions and self-designations. But the individual *in* the psalm is not the same as the individual for whom the prayer was composed."

145. Mays, "A Question of Identity: The Threefold Hermeneutic of Psalmody," *ATJ* 46, no. 1 (1991; pp. 87–94): 92.

146. Davis, *Wondrous Depth,* 19. Mays asks, "Could the use of these prayers remind us and bind us to all those in the worldwide Church who are suffering in faith and for their faith?" "A Question of Identity," *ATJ* 46, no. 1 (1991): 92.

solely to the needs of individual hearers before us, though these needs will surely be present. But we can open the umbrella to cover the needs of all Christians suffering in this world: because of the unity of the church their needs are our needs, their suffering is our suffering. As Paul puts it, "If one member suffers, all suffer together with it; if one member is honored, all rejoice together with it" (1 Cor 12:26).

Reading the Psalm in the Worship Service

Usually, before preaching the sermon, the psalm is read. It should be read well, that is, as John Witvliet puts it, the reader should be "alert to a Psalm's pace, form, script, and any poetic devices that contribute to its meaning."[147] There are many options for reading the psalm. The preacher him- or herself could read the psalm or have a good reader from the congregation read it. Such a reading could be supported by mime or drama. The congregation could also read the psalm in unison, or the congregation and pastor could read it responsively, or the congregation and choir could read it antiphonally.[148] Another option is to have two readers read the psalm verse by verse, the first using the pew Bible (NRSV, NIV, etc.), the second reading each verse from a paraphrase such as *The Message*.[149] William Hull suggests that after the psalm is read, it be "sung as an anthem or solo," then preached "in expository fashion, thereby combining these three modes of expression in the unity of proclamation."[150]

Witvliet advises that worship leaders should "imagine scripting the Psalm for a choral reading group of four or forty people. Who should say what line — and why?" When possible, they should "assign roles in the assembly that call attention to dramatic shifts in voice."[151] The advantages of a choral reading, he writes, "are many: multiple readers convey the communal nature of many Psalm texts; a rehearsed reading promises to capture more of the poetic nuance than unrehearsed congregational reading; and the interplay among readers is useful for capturing the dialogic nature of many Psalm texts."[152]

---

147. Witvliet, *The Biblical Psalms in Christian Worship*, 86.

148. *Psalms for All Seasons: A Complete Psalter for Worship* provides all 150 psalms, most in multiple formats for singing, responsive reading, or chanting.

149. Suggested by Laura and Robert J. Keeley at the 2013 Calvin Symposium on Worship held at Calvin College and Calvin Theological Seminary in Grand Rapids, Michigan.

150. Hull, "Preaching on the Psalms," *RevExp* 81, no. 3 (1984; pp. 451–56): 454.

151. Witvliet, *The Biblical Psalms in Christian Worship*, 80.

152. Ibid., 87. See also Witvliet's suggestions for responsive readings on pp. 91–92.

Using Verses of the Psalm in the Liturgy

We can further unify the worship service and its focus on the message of a particular psalm by using some of its verses for the call to worship, the confession of sin, the assurance of pardon, the offertory sentence, or for introductions to prayer or praise. "When verses drawn from the psalm being treated that day are forged into liturgical links connecting various elements in the order of service," it reinforces the sermon.[153] Another suggestion is to structure a service "entirely around a Psalm, taking time to expand on each section of a given Psalm."[154]

Preaching Series of Sermons on Psalms

In this book I will present the foundations for several series of sermons on the psalms. A sermon series should never be so rigid, of course, that it would ignore the needs of the congregation. If a disaster strikes the congregation, community, or nation, preachers should suspend the series or substitute a lament for a hymn of praise. But in planning a series of sermons, preachers can use this book for a series of sermons on the psalms for Advent, or Lent, or the Christian feast days, or all of them. In addition, preachers can use this book to preach one or more series of four to eleven sermons on the vital biblical story-line Creation–Fall–Redemption–New Creation or a series of two or three sermons on a lengthy psalm (for more possible series, see Appendix 6, pp. 581–84 below).[155]

---

153. Hull, "Preaching on the Psalms," *RevExp* 81, no. 3 (1984): 453.

154. Witvliet, *The Biblical Psalms in Christian Worship,* 68. See there also for other suggestions for using the psalms in worship.

155. These sermon series can be reinforced with congregational singing of each preached psalm as suggested in *Psalms for All Seasons: A Complete Psalter for Worship* and *Lift Up Your Hearts: Psalms, Hymns, and Spiritual Songs.* The first part of *Lift Up Your Hearts* traces in its selected songs "The Story of Creation and Redemption: Old Testament Life and Witness, Advent Expectation, Christ's Life, Christ's Passion and Exaltation, Joining in the Spirit's Work, Trusting the Triune God, and Hope for Things to Come" (p. v, Contents).

CHAPTER 2

"Happy Are Those Whose Delight Is in the Law of the LORD"

Psalm 1

Psalm 1, along with Psalm 2, is intended to introduce the Psalter and guide the understanding of the following psalms (see above, pp. 25–28). As such, this psalm, as well as Psalm 2, can be used to start almost any series of sermons on the psalms.[1] We shall use it here to introduce the following series of psalms *The Revised Common Lectionary (Year A)* assigns for reading for Advent, Lent, and Christian feast days.

There is general agreement that Psalm 1 is a *torah* (wisdom) psalm.[2] Although *torah* is often translated as "law," its meaning is much broader than what we usually understand by law. The five books of Moses are called *Torah* and they reveal not only God's laws but also God's works of creation and redemption. *Torah* basically means God's teaching or instruction.

Text and Context

Although some think that at one time Psalm 1 may have been united with Psalm 2 (see above, p. 26 n. 81), Psalm 1 is a literary unit in its own right as can be seen by its subject matter (meditating on the *torah*), which is different from that of Psalm 2 (the battle between "the LORD and his anointed" and "the kings of the earth"). Also, Psalm 1 is marked off by its own inclusios: "*Happy are those* who do not . . . take the path (*derek*) that sinners tread" (v 1) and "*the LORD watches*

---

1. *The Revised Common Lectionary* lists Psalm 1 for the seventh Sunday of Easter, Year B, the eighteenth Sunday after Pentecost, Year B, and the sixth Sunday after the Epiphany, Year C. Psalm 2 is assigned for reading on Transfiguration Sunday (see Chapter 10 below).

2. See Bernhard Anderson, *Out of the Depths,* 219.

over the way (*derek*) of the righteous, but the way (*derek*) of the wicked will perish" (v 6).[3]

Psalm 1 also offers more subtle clues to its being a literary unit. It begins with the word "happy" and ends with its antithetical "perish" (cf. Ps 112).[4] Moreover, "the first word in this psalm began with *alef*, the first letter of the Hebrew alphabet. The last word in this psalm begins with *tav*, the last letter of the alphabet. This first psalm offers the '*alef* to *tav*,' the 'A to Z' of living the life of the godly."[5]

As to its context, the introductory Psalm 1 has connections with many of the following psalms. We have already seen its links with Psalm 2 (above pp. 25–28). The opening "Happy" ("Blessed," NIV) is found in many other psalms (e.g., 32:1, 2; 41:1; 112:1; 119:1, 2; 128:1, 2)[6] as well as Proverbs (e.g., 3:13; 8:32, 34). The assurance that "the LORD watches over the way of the righteous" (1:6) is echoed in many of the following psalms,[7] as is the final line "but the way of the wicked will perish.[8]

As a *torah* psalm it links up with the *torah* Psalms 19 and 119. For example, the "*delight . . . in the law of the LORD*" (Ps 1:2) becomes in Psalm 19:7–8,

> *The law of the LORD is perfect,*
> *reviving the soul. . . .*
> the precepts of the LORD are right,
> *rejoicing the heart. . . .*

And the *meditating* on God's law "*day and night*" (Ps 1:2) is echoed in Psalm 119:97,

> Oh, how I love your law!
> It is my *meditation all day long.*[9]

As a *torah* psalm, Psalm 1 also reaches back to the *Torah,* the five books of Moses. Psalm 1 pictures two ways, one leading to life, the other to death. In Deuteronomy 30:19–20 Moses also speaks of two contrasting ways: "I have set

---

3. See also Petersen and Richards, *Interpreting Hebrew Poetry,* 91, "We would contend that the poetic analysis, genre issues, dominant motifs, and a series of other arguments sustain the conclusion that Ps 1:1–6 may be understood as an interpretive unit or poem separable from Ps 2:1–11." Cf. Willem VanGemeren, *Psalms,* 78.

4. Mark Futato, *Transformed by Praise,* 56.

5. James Limburg, *Psalms,* 3.

6. Kidner, *Psalm 1–72,* 47 n. 1, lists 26 instances in the Psalter.

7. See, e.g., Psalms 5:12; 14:5; 34:15; 37:17, 29; 112:6; 145:20; 146:9.

8. See, e.g., Psalms 2:12; 9:5, 6, 16–17; 34:21; 37:20; 68:2; 73:27; 92:9; 146:9; 147:6.

9. For "meditation" see also Ps 119:15, 23, 48, 99, and 148.

before you life and death, *blessings and curses.* Choose life so that you and your descendants may live, loving the LORD your God, obeying him, and holding fast to him; for that means life to you and length of days. . . ."

Several ideas in Psalm 1 are also reflected in Joshua 1:8 (note the italicized words), "This book of the *law* shall not depart out of your mouth; you shall *meditate on it day and night,* so that you may be careful to act in accordance with all that is written in it. For then you shall make your way *prosperous,* and then you shall be successful."

As a wisdom psalm, Psalm 1 also has connections with other wisdom psalms (Pss 36, 37, 49, 73, 78, 112) and Old Testament wisdom literature, especially the Book of Proverbs which equally emphasizes the two ways (cf. Prov 2:12–15, 20–22) and the importance of not associating with the wicked (e.g., Prov 1:10–19; 14:14–19).

The picture of the fruitful tree "planted by streams of water" (Ps 1:3) is similar to Jeremiah 17:7–8,[10]

> Blessed are those who trust in the LORD,
>   whose trust is the LORD.
> They shall be *like a tree planted by water,*
>   sending out its roots by the stream.
> It shall not fear when heat comes,
>   and *its leaves shall stay green;*
> in the year of drought it is not anxious,
>   and it does not cease to *bear fruit.*

Literary Interpretation

As noted above, there is general agreement that Psalm 1 is a *torah* (wisdom) psalm, that is, it exhibits characteristics of both *torah,* God's teaching or instruction, and wisdom literature. Since detecting a psalm's structure is often the most contentious issue among scholars (witness nine different proposals for the structure of Psalm 1; see p. 52 below), we shall begin each of the following chapters with a snapshot of its parallelisms, which provides a rather objective entry into and quick scan of the psalm. Next we shall investigate the psalm's imagery and repetition of keywords. With this information in hand, we will finally seek to determine the psalm's structure.

---

10. See also Ezek 17:5–6; 47:12; and Rev 22:1–2. We shall explore the context of the New Testament below under "Ways to Preach Christ," pp. 56–58.

Parallelisms[11]

Here then is a quick overview of the parallelisms in Psalm 1:

₁Happy are those who do not follow the advice of the wicked,	A
or take the path that sinners tread,	+ A′
or sit in the seat of scoffers;	+ A″
₂but their delight is in the law of the LORD,[12]	– B
and on his law they meditate day and night.	+– B′[13]
₃They are like trees planted by streams of water,	C
which yield their fruit in its season,	+ C′
and their leaves do not wither.	+ C″
In all that they do, they prosper.	+ C‴
₄The wicked are not so,	– A
but are like chaff that the wind drives away.	+– A′[14]
₅Therefore the wicked will not stand in the judgment,	B
nor sinners in the congregation of the righteous;[15]	+ B′
₆for the LORD watches over the way of the righteous,	C
but the way of the wicked will perish.[16]	– C′

The psalm begins with three lines of advancing parallelism, therefore, climactic parallelism. Some scholars claim that verse 1 offers synonymous parallelism.[17] "The wicked," "sinners," and "scoffers," are indeed synonymous, but the important verbs, "walk," "stand," and "sit," are a form of advancing (synthetic) parallelism of what happy people do not do. As Tremper Longman explains, "Look at the verbs: *walk, stand,* and *sit*. In the development of the metaphor of the righteous man, his connection with evil is more and more strongly denied. As we move from walk to

11. To simplify this presentation I will use in this and the following chapters the NRSV translation rather than the Hebrew, which often has inversions as well as ellipses (see pp. 18–20 above). I will also use the NRSV stanzas as a common starting point even though I may see the structure differently, as in the case of Psalm 1 (see pp. 52–54 below).

12. The strong "but" indicates a contrast with verse 1, therefore, antithetic parallelism (–).

13. This is as complicated as our short-hand for parallelisms will get: + is advancing, – is antithetic, B′ is the same topic as the first B line.

14. Advancing (+) antithetic (–) A′ (same subject as A, the wicked). See also n. 12 above.

15. This is a close call. It looks like synonymous parallelism, but because "the congregation of the righteous" is more specific than "the judgment," I call it advancing parallelism (+).

16. Clearly antithetic parallelism (–).

17. E.g., A. Anderson, *Psalms 1–72,* 58, and Leland Ryken, *The Literature of the Bible* (Grand Rapids: Zondervan, 1977), 127.

sit, we are progressing from a casual acquaintance with evil to a settled one."[18] In contrast, verse 2 follows up with antithetic parallelism: "*but* their delight is in the law of the LORD." The psalmist next likens these happy people to "trees planted by streams of water," which results in a second climactic parallelism concluding with the climax, "In all that they do, they prosper" (v 3d).

The second stanza switches back to the wicked with strong antithetic parallelism (the Hebrew *lo'*, "not," being the first word), "Not so the wicked!" (NIV), and advancing antithetic parallelism about the wicked (v 4). Verse 5 turns to the final outcome of the way of the wicked with advancing parallelism in 5b. Finally verse 6 presents the reasons for the different outcomes of the two ways with antithetic parallelism.

Imagery

Psalm 1 contains metaphors as well as similes. Verse 1 has the metaphors of walking, standing, and sitting: "Happy are those[19] who do not follow [*walk*] the advice of the wicked, or take [*stand*] the path that sinners tread, or *sit* in the seat of scoffers." "The *path* [or way] that sinners tread" is also a metaphor. "In its figurative sense 'way' evokes three notions: 1) 'course of life' (i.e., the character and context of life); 2) 'conduct of life' (i.e., the specific choices and behavior); and 3) 'consequences of that conduct' (i.e., the inevitable destiny of such a lifestyle)."[20]

Verse 2b says about the happy person that he meditates on the law *"day and night."* The Qumran community took this literally and "established a rotation of interpreters to study and expound *torah* twenty-four hours a day."[21] But the expression "day and night" could be hyperbole for continuously meditating on God's teaching or a merism, "in which the two extremes are mentioned to include all in between as well."[22] In either case, it would be a figure of speech not to be interpreted literally.

Verses 3 and 4 consist of contrasting similes of "the happy / righteous one" being like a tree[23] and the wicked like chaff. In detail these two similes contrast

18. Tremper Longman III, *Reading the Bible with Heart and Mind* (Colorado Springs: Nav-Press, 1997), 133.

19. The Hebrew reads, "Happy is the man" (*hā'îš*) and has the singular through verse 3, "He is like a tree." The NRSV turns the singular into the plural to avoid gender specificity.

20. Waltke, *Psalms as Christian Worship*, 134–35.

21. Wilson, *Psalms*, I, 103.

22. Ibid., 96.

23. "In the ancient world, the tree was a symbol of divine blessing. It was a symbol of the temple where God dwelled (cf. Ezek 41:18), it was a symbol of paradise (cf. Genesis 2), it was

being a planted, stable tree and being directionless chaff blown by the wind, being well-watered and being dried out, bearing fruit and being worthless, being prosperous and being a failure; in short, being alive and being dead.

Verse 5 contains the metaphor that "the wicked will not *stand* in the judgment, while verse 6 uses the contrasting metaphors of "*the way* of the righteous" and "*the way* of the wicked."

Repetition of Keywords

Repetition may alert us to the presence of parallelism and other rhetorical structures such as inclusios and chiasms. Repetition of *keywords* frequently shows what the author wishes to emphasize and thus may help us in formulating the textual theme.

The negative particle "not" (*lo'*) is repeated 6 times: 3 times in verse 1, once at the end of verse 3, once in verse 4a, and once in verse 5a. This frequent use of "not" indicates that a major concern of the psalmist is contrast.

Repetition also indicates between whom the contrast is drawn. "The wicked" and its synonyms "sinners" and "scoffers" are mentioned 7 times: verses 1 (3×), 4, 5 (2×), 6. "The righteous" (those who are right with God) are mentioned only once, but this is at the climax of the psalm (v 6). Looking back over the psalm we discover several descriptions of "the righteous": "Happy are those" (v 1), "their delight is in the law of the LORD and on his law they meditate day and night" (v 2), and "they are like trees" bearing fruit; "in all that they do, they prosper" (v 3). The major contrast, therefore, is being drawn between "the wicked" and "the righteous."

"The way" (*derek*) is mentioned 3 times: verses 1 and 6 (2×). This narrows the contrast down to "the way of sinners / the wicked" and "the way of the righteous." It "suggests that this Psalm and the entire Psalter will offer a choice between two fundamentally different ways of life or lifestyles. The outcomes of one's choice of ways are described by the first and last words of the psalm ['happy' and 'perish']. . . . In short, the way one chooses is a matter of life and death."[24] The key to that choice is whether one delights "in the *torah* of the LORD" (v 2).

---

a symbol of God's kingly reign and of the Davidic kings who reigned as God's representatives (cf. Isa 11:1; Zech 6:12). . . ." Jacobson in deClaissé-Walford, Jacobson, and Tanner, *The Book of Psalms,* 64.

24. McCann, "Psalms," 684. Cf. McCann, *Theological Introduction to the Book of Psalms,* 33, "The structure, movement, vocabulary, and imagery of the psalm combine to emphasize that there should be absolutely no confusion about the two ways and their results."

Structure

Psalm 1 is a perfect example of the difficulty of getting scholarly consensus on the structure of a psalm, its stanzas or strophes. Experts have proposed at least nine different structures for the six verses of Psalm 1.[25]

Verse Divisions	Advocates
1 – 3 / 4 – 5 / 6	NIV; REB; NKJV; HCSB; Goerling; Broyles; Kraus; Craigie*; Gerstenberger*; Williams*; Ross*
1 – 3 / 4 – 6	NRSV; RSV; NASB; NAB; JPS; Bratcher-Reyburn; Anderson; Delitzsch
1 – 2 / 3 – 4 / 5 – 6	ESV; Hakham; Webster and Beach*;[26] Waltke,*[27] Collins*[28]
1 – 2 / 3 – 4a / 4b – 6	NJB
1 – 2 / 3 / 4 – 6	Terrien; Fokkelman*[29]
1 / 2 – 3 / 4 – 6	Hosch
1 / 2 – 3 / 4 – 5 / 6	Beaucamp
1 / 2 – 3 / 4 / 5 – 6	Auffret
1 / 2 / 3 / 4 – 6	Jacobson*[30]

For preachers it is important to know the structure of a psalm because it informs to a large extent the outline of an expository sermon. So how do we make a responsible choice when the experts are so divided?

As we have seen in the parallelisms and imagery, the core of Psalm 1 consists of the contrast between "the righteous" (those who are right with God) and "the

---

25. See C. John Collins, "Psalm 1: Structure and Rhetoric," *Presbyterion* 31, no. 1 (2005; pp. 37–48): 37. I have added to his list the names marked by stars.

26. "Verses 1–2 contrast the influence one chooses, the counsel of the wicked or the Law of God. Verses 3–4 contrast a well-watered tree with chaff as an image of the enduring strength that comes from the choice in verses 1–2. Verses 5–6 directly contrast the fate of the wicked and the righteous." Webster and Beach, *Essential Bible Companion to the Psalms,* 37.

27. Waltke, *Psalms as Christian Worship,* 132

28. Collins himself, "Psalm 1: Structure and Rhetoric," *Presbyterion* 31, no. 1 (2005): 40, makes a case for the following structure:
vv 1–2   Contrasting sources of guidance and values
vv 3–4   Contrasting similes of the effects of their lives
vv 5–6   Contrasting outcomes of their ways

29. J. P. Fokkelman, *Major Poems of the Hebrew Bible,* II, 53–55, argues from "the exact 9 as the average number of syllables per colon. This has been realized here by arranging 144 syllables in 16 cola" and thus he arrives at three strophes: vv 1–2/3/4–6.

30. Jacobson in deClaissé-Walford, Jacobson, and Tanner, *The Book of Psalms,* 59–60.

wicked" (those who are not right with God). A key question concerns verse 1: Does this verse speak about "the righteous" or "the wicked"? It is true that it speaks of the way of the wicked: the advice of the wicked, the path that sinners tread, the seat of scoffers. But actually verse 1 is about "the righteous":

> Happy are those
>> who do *not* follow the advice of the wicked,
>>> or take the path that sinners tread,
>>>> or sit in the seat of scoffers. . . .

This means that verse 1 speaks about "the righteous" in terms of what they do *not* do; verse 2 follows up with what they do: "their delight is in the law of the LORD"; and verse 3 likens what they are to a fruitful tree by streams of water. That is the first stanza.

Verse 4 switches abruptly to "the wicked" with "Not so the wicked" (Hebrew word order). Verse 4b follows with the contrasting, antithetic, simile, "but are like chaff that the wind drives away." Verse 5 continues with the outcome for the wicked:

> Therefore the wicked will not stand in the judgment,
>> nor sinners in the congregation of the righteous.

Verse 6 switches back to "the righteous," then "the wicked," in that order:

> for the LORD watches over the way of the righteous,
>> but the way of the wicked will perish.

In terms of the contents of Psalm 1, we can conclude, therefore, that it has a three-part structure consisting of verses 1–3, 4–5, and verse 6:[31]

---

31. Cf. Craigie, *Psalms 1–50*, 59, "(1) the solid foundation of the righteous (1:1–3); (2) the impermanence of the wicked (1:4–5); (3) a contrast of the righteous and the wicked (1:6)." Cf. Gerstenberger, *Psalms,* I, 40,

I.	Encouragement: profile of a just man		1–3
	A.	Negative description	1
	B.	Positive description	2
	C.	Promise	3
II.	Discouragement: the fate of the wicked		4–5
III.	Motivation for promise and determent		6

I. A description of what the righteous do not do, what they do, illustrated with the agricultural simile of a fruitful tree by streams of water (vv 1–3)
II. A negative statement that the wicked are not at all like that, illustrated with a contrasting agricultural simile of chaff being blown away by the wind (vv 4–5)[32]
III. The reasons for the contrasting outcomes: "for the LORD watches over the way of the righteous," not "the way of the wicked" (v 6).

A major advantage of recognizing this particular structure is that it clearly shows where the psalmist places the relative weight of "the righteous" and "the wicked." "The righteous" receive the first 3 verses for a total of 9 lines. "The wicked," by contrast, receive only 2 short verses (vv 4–5) for a total of 4 lines. Finally in verse 6 each receives 1 line concerning the reason for the outcome: "the LORD watches over (intimately knows) the way of the righteous," and the contrast, "but the way of the wicked will perish." The psalmist seeks to focus more on "the righteous" than on "the wicked"[33] — a point we need to take into account in formulating the theme of Psalm 1.

Theocentric Interpretation

Although God is the explicit subject only in the final verse (v 6), "the LORD watches over the way of the righteous," he is present from the beginning. Verse 1's "Happy are those" raises the question, Who or what makes them "happy"? Verse 2 responds, "their delight is in the law of the LORD." With his teaching God makes them happy. Happiness "is a gift of God."[34]

Verse 3 reads, "They are like trees *planted* by streams of water." Who planted this tree by streams of water? God did (divine passive participle). In fact, the Hebrew means "transplanted."[35] God transplanted a wild shoot from an arid re-

---

32. "The wicked are not even accorded the dignity of being a proper grammatical subject of an active verb: windblown like chaff, whatever way they go on is trackless, directionless, doomed." Robert Alter, *The Art of Biblical Poetry*, 116–17.

33. Petersen and Richards, *Interpreting Hebrew Poetry*, 96, overstate the case: "There are twice as many words regarding the righteous as there are about the wicked. The poem is not about the wicked, nor is it an elaboration on the two ways. Rather, it uses the negative way to illumine the way of the happy individual."

34. "Blessedness is not deserved; it is a gift of God." VanGemeren, *Psalms*, 78.

35. "The tree is actually said to have been *transplanted* (*šātûl*; cf. Ps 92:12–13; Ezek 17:7–10, 22–23; 19:10–13)." Brent Strawn, "Psalm 1," in Van Harn and Strawn, eds., *Psalms for Preaching*, 52. Cf. C. Broyles, *Psalms*, 43, "It is planted (lit. 'transplanted') by streams (lit. '[irrigation] channels') of water. This word choice implies that the tree is able to transcend natural circumstances, but

54

gion to a well-watered area where it could flourish, bear "fruit in its season," "not wither" in the dry season, but "prosper."

Verse 5 states that "the wicked will not stand in the judgment," which ultimately refers to God's judgment at the end time. And then comes the climax in verse 6, "for the LORD *yôdēaʿ* [intimately knows, embraces,[36] cares for, watches over] the way of the righteous." From the beginning of Psalm 1 to its end the LORD is central.

Textual Theme and Goal

Having looked at Psalm 1 from these several angles, we should be ready to formulate its theme. We have seen that the psalmist contrasts the righteous and the wicked. The question is whether he presents them in a balanced way so that the theme should encompass the righteous and the wicked equally or whether one is dominant. It is clear from the first word "happy" (for the righteous) to the last word "perish" (for the wicked) and from the space given to describe the righteous (3½ long verses) to the space to describe the wicked (2½ short verses) that the psalmist's message focuses on the righteous.[37]

Webster and Beach propose as theme, "A righteous individual is established and prospers by attending to God's Word."[38] Unfortunately, this is not only a dual theme (is the focus on "established" or "prospers"?) but it ignores the wicked entirely. The theme formulation should indeed keep the righteous dominant while not ignoring the wicked. We can accomplish this by formulating the theme of Psalm 1 as follows: *In contrast to the wicked who will perish, happy are the righteous who delight in the teaching of the LORD, for the LORD watches over them.*[39]

---

not because of its natural or inherent abilities." Cf. Brown, *Seeing the Psalms,* 76–78, and 231 n. 8; A. Anderson, *Psalms 1–72,* 60; and Rogerson and McKay, *Psalms 1–50,* 17. Delitzsch, *Biblical Commentary on the Psalms,* I, 85, argues for the meaning of "firmly planted."

36. Alter, *Book of Psalms,* 4 n. 6.

37. The psalmist presents "the righteous as central and preeminent, both literarily and theologically. In vv 5–6, the wicked perish on the periphery (note 'judgment' in v 5a and 'perish' in v 6b), while the righteous are at the center of God's attention [v 6a]." McCann, "Psalms," 686. Cf. Brown, *Seeing the Psalms,* 56, "The wicked are purely passive, driven away, while the image of the righteous commands the position of subject. Whereas the chaff is blown away by the winds of judgment, the tree not only has standing: it bears fruit."

38. Webster and Beach, *Essential Bible Companion,* 37. Cf. Limburg, *Psalms for Sojourners,* 20, "The central theme of the first psalm is meditation on Torah or Scripture as the pathway to a happy and blessed life." Cf. Mays, *Psalms,* 40, The central statement of Psalm 1 is, "Blessed the one whose delight is in the law of the LORD."

39. Cf. Kraus, *Psalms 1–59,* 121, "The dreadful lot of the wicked, that is, of those who have

For the goal of the psalmist we usually want to consider its historical setting. That setting is not given with this psalm nor even suggested by way of a (later) superscription. Scholars generally consider Psalm 1 to be postexilic "when the book was put into final form."[40] Since Psalm 1 is intended to introduce the Psalter, its specific historical setting does not play a major role in determining its goal. We could possibly formulate the goal as to urge Israel to walk in the way of the righteous, but "to urge" is too strong, since the psalmist does not use any imperatives. Instead he presents two pictures, the righteous and the wicked, the one happy, stable, fruitful, prospering, and intimately known by the LORD; the other directionless, dead, and perishing. His goal, therefore, is *to persuade Israel to walk in the way of the righteous by delighting in the teaching of the LORD.*[41]

Ways to Preach Christ

There is no promise of the coming Messiah in Psalm 1, but traditionally typology has been used to preach Christ. A better way to Christ, however, is the way of analogy supported by New Testament references. We shall discuss these two options in turn.

Typology

Those who use typology to preach Christ from Psalm 1 take "the happy person" to be a type of Christ. For example, Patrick Reardon argues that "the man" (*hā'îš*) of verse 1 is "emphatically masculine — that is gender specific. . . . The 'man' of reference here is a particular man. According to the Fathers of the Church, he is

---

separated themselves from the 'direction' of God, is only the somber contrast to a life that alone is worth recommending and truly happy. For that reason the psalm as a whole can be understood correctly only from this viewpoint."

40. Walter Brueggemann, "Bounded by Obedience and Praise: The Psalms as Canon," *JSOT* 50 (1991; pp. 63–92): 64. Cf. A. Anderson, *Psalms 1–72*, 57–58; Petersen and Richards, *Interpreting Hebrew Poetry*, 91; and Vos, *Theopoetry of the Psalms*, 57. The similarities with Jeremiah 17:7–8 and Ezekiel 17:5–6; 47:12 (see p. 48 above) would also argue for this late dating.

41. "The reason for using nondirective discourse in Psalm 1 is plainly that the psalmist considers objective description a strong enough appeal to invoke God-fearing behavior. The statements about the just and the wicked bear in themselves the thrust of moral and religious *instruction*." Gerstenberger, *Psalms,* I, 42. Cf. Mays, *Psalms,* 41, "That is the central purpose of the psalm, to commend joyous and continuous concern with the law of the LORD." Cf. Vos, *Theopoetry of the Psalms*, 58, "By contrasting the way of the righteous and that of the wicked and describing the way of the righteous in a positive manner, the psalm attempts to persuade us to make the right choice."

the one Mediator between God and man, the Man Jesus Christ."[42] However, to base this argument on the masculine nature of *hā'îš* is decidedly weak because the word can also be gender neutral, simply meaning "someone" or "one."[43]

Others argue that "everything that is stated in Psalm 1 about 'the righteous' basically entails a character that transcends any one individual. . . . The picture of the fortunate 'righteous' definitely bears the features of the super individual, the paradigmatic person. . . . The NT declares that Jesus Christ, 'whom God made our . . . righteousness' (1 Cor 1:30), is the fulfillment of this original picture that the OT had in mind."[44] The weakness of this approach is that identifying the happy person with a "super individual" removes the message of Psalm 1 from ordinary folk: the goal can no longer be "to persuade Israel to walk in the way of the righteous by delighting in the teaching of the LORD."

Analogy Supported by New Testament References

A much stronger way to Jesus Christ in the New Testament is the way of analogy with Jesus' teachings supported by New Testament references. With the images of Psalm 1 in mind I read through Jesus' Sermon on the Mount and was amazed at the similarity in words and images. Jesus' Sermon is saturated with Psalm 1. It's almost as if Jesus (Matthew) had Psalm 1 in mind when he composed the Sermon on the Mount.

Psalm 1 begins with "Happy." Jesus begins his sermon with a ninefold "Happy" / "Blessed" — the same Greek word *makarioi* used in the Greek translation (LXX) of Psalm 1 (*makarios*). Like Psalm 1, Jesus highlights "the law": "Do not think that I have come to abolish the law or the prophets; I have come not to abolish but to fulfill. For truly I tell you, until heaven and earth pass away, not one letter, not one stroke of a letter, will pass from the law until all is accomplished" (Matt 5:17-18; see Matt 5:21–7:27).

---

42. Reardon, *Christ in the Psalms*, 2. Using allegorical interpretation, the Fathers of the Church could then go on to Psalm 1:3 and identify the tree with the cross of Christ. See my *Preaching Christ from the Old Testament*, 69–109, esp. p. 89.

43. See *TDOT*, I, 224, with references to Gen 13:16 for "someone, one" and to Gen 40:5 for "each." Samuel Terrien, *The Psalms*, 72, observes, "To choose the right way, in a nomadic society, is the responsibility of 'the man,' the husband and head of the family, but the use of the male gender in such a metaphor does not exclude the woman."

44. Kraus, *Psalms 1–59*, 121. Cf. Graeme Goldsworthy, *Preaching the Whole Bible as Christian Scripture: The Application of Biblical Theology to Expository Preaching* (Grand Rapids: Eerdmans, 2000), 203, "In the final analysis the righteous, *Torah*-oriented person who is the object of God's care and preservation is a foreshadowing of the righteous Man for us, Jesus Christ." Cf. J. H. Eaton, *Psalms* (1967), 31, and *The Psalms* (2003), 64, and Williams, *Psalms 1–72*, 32–33.

Psalm 1:2 seems to call for perfection: "their delight is in the law of the LORD, and on his law they meditate day and night." Jesus also demands perfection: "I tell you, unless your righteousness exceeds that of the scribes and Pharisees, you will never enter the kingdom of heaven." "Be perfect, therefore, as your heavenly Father is perfect" (Matt 5:20, 48).

Psalm 1 presents two ways (v 6), the way of "the one" (*hā'îš*, sing. v 1) and the way of "the wicked" (plural). Jesus also presents two ways, the way of the few and the way of the many: "Enter through the narrow gate; for the gate is wide and *the road* is easy that leads to destruction, and there are *many* who take it. For the gate is narrow and *the road* is hard that leads to life, and there are *few* who find it" (Matt 7:13–14). Psalm 1:3 pictures the happy person as a tree bearing fruit. Jesus also speaks about a "good tree" bearing "good fruit" (Matt 7:17). Psalm 1 concludes with the comforting message, "the LORD watches over the way of the righteous" (Ps 1:6). In the Sermon on the Mount Jesus similarly assures us, "Strive first for the kingdom of God and his righteousness, and all these things [food, drink, or clothing] will be given to you as well" (Matt 6:33).

As a wisdom psalm, the goal of Psalm 1 is to persuade Israel to be wise, to walk in the way of the righteous by delighting in the teaching of the LORD. Jesus' goal in the Sermon on the Mount is also to persuade people not to be foolish but wise (see Matt 7:24–27). One can also use other New Testament references, such as Matt 3:12, John 4:9–10, 14; 7:37–39; 15:1–2, 5, Eph 2:8–10, and 1 John 5:11–12, to move from Psalm 1 to Jesus in the New Testament (see "Sermon Exposition" below).

Sermon Theme, Goal, and Need

Since the New Testament agrees with the theme and goal of Psalm 1, we can use the textual theme and goal for the sermon theme and goal. The sermon theme, then, will be, *In contrast to the wicked who will perish, happy are the righteous who delight in the teaching of the LORD, for the LORD watches over them.* For the sermon goal we only need to change "Israel" to "people." The sermon goal, then, is *to persuade people to walk in the way of the righteous by delighting in the teaching of the LORD.*

The need addressed in this sermon is the negative side of the goal. In the words of Psalm 1:1 this need is that we are tempted to "follow the advice of the wicked," "take the path that sinners tread," and even "sit in the seat of scoffers." Clinton McCann writes perceptively, "What is so unsettling about all of this is that what Psalm 1 and the rest of the Psalter call 'wickedness' is perhaps what

North American culture promotes as the highest virtue — autonomy,"[45] being a law unto oneself, self-made people, sovereign, subject to none. The introduction to the sermon can illustrate this need in order to focus attention on hearing this specific word of the Lord.

Liturgy, Scripture Reading, Sermon Outline, and PowerPoint

Before writing the sermon, we need to give some thought to the context in which the sermon will be preached and how we can enhance it with PowerPoint. We shall briefly suggest some options for the liturgy, scripture reading, sermon outline, and PowerPoint.

The Liturgy

To reinforce the message of Psalm 1 and the sermon, one can utilize parts of Psalm 1 in the worship service. For example, one can make Psalm 1:1-2 the call to worship and close the service by singing a version of Psalm 1:1-3,[46] forming a neat liturgical inclusio.

One can also utilize the other *torah* psalms (19 and 119) in the worship service. For example, one can read Psalm 19:7-9 before or after the reading of God's law. Or one can read Psalm 119:1-8 or verses 9-16, or 97-104, or 105-12 after the reading of God's law or sing them after the sermon or to conclude the worship service.[47]

Scripture Reading

To highlight for the congregation the contrasts in Psalm 1, one can select two good readers — one to introduce the righteous and the other the wicked. For Psalm 1:1-3 I suggest a female reader who emphasizes the three "not"s / "or"s of verse 1. Next a male reads verses 4-5, stressing the three "not"s / "nor" in both verses. In conclusion the female reads verse 6a and the male verse 6b.

45. McCann, "Psalms," 687.
46. See, e.g., *Psalms for All Seasons,* 4-10 (1A, 1B, 1C, 1E, 1F).
47. See the many options offered in *Psalms for All Seasons,* 95-106, 761-87.

Sermon Outline

The sermon outline can follow the structure of the psalm, adding here and there moves to Jesus in the New Testament with a major move in the conclusion. This leads to the following sermon outline:

I. The righteous: what they do not do; what they do; they are like a fruitful tree (vv 1–3)
II. The wicked: not fruitful; they are like blowing chaff (vv 4–5)
III. Their outcomes: "the LORD watches over the righteous"; "the wicked will perish" (v 6)
IV. Analogous teachings of Jesus Christ (NT)

PowerPoint

The contrasting structure of Psalm 1 can be illuminated by PowerPoint. For example, one can start the first slide with I. A, then add B, then C:

I. The righteous (those who are right with God) — verses 1–3
  A What they do *not* do: Walk, stand, sit with the wicked — verse 1
  B What they do — verse 2
    delight in the law of the LORD and
    meditate on it day and night
  C They are like trees by water — verse 3
    (Show a picture of a fruitful palm tree by water)
II. New slide: the contrasting outcome of the wicked
  A "Not so the wicked; they are like chaff driven by wind" — verse 4
  B Show a picture of a threshing floor with winnowing fork: explain
  C Show a split screen with a tree on one side and chaff on the other
    Move through the contrasts:
    1 stable vs wind-blown
    2 well-watered vs dry as dust
    3 fruit-bearing vs worthless
    4 alive vs dead
  D Show the outcome:
    "The wicked will not stand in the judgment" — v 5a
    "nor in the congregation of the righteous" — v 5b
III. New slide: The reasons for the contrasting outcomes:
  A The LORD watches over the way of the righteous — v 6a
  B The way of the wicked will perish — v 6b

Sermon Exposition

We all want to be happy, don't we? Unfortunately, we are tempted to follow the crowd in looking for happiness. In North America we want to live the American dream. We think we will be happy when we are rich — then we can buy whatever our heart desires. Or we think we will be happy when we own the company — then no one can tell us what to do. Or we seek immediate gratification in living for our own pleasure. We all want to be happy. The United States Declaration of Independence enshrines the right of "the pursuit of happiness." Yet the United States, one of the wealthiest nations on earth, has many citizens who are decidedly unhappy. Happiness is not found in "the pursuit of happiness"; in the pursuit of riches; in the pursuit of pleasure. Happiness is found in a different direction. Psalm 1 will tell us where to find happiness.

Psalm 1 is a beatitude, just like Jesus' beatitudes at the beginning of the Sermon on the Mount. Psalm 1 begins with, "Happy (or blessed) are those."[48] Jesus uses the very same word from the Greek translation of Psalm 1,[49] "Blessed (or happy) are the poor in spirit, for theirs is the kingdom of heaven" (Matt 5:3). Nine times Jesus uses that word "blessed," "happy."

The word translated as "happy" or "blessed" means something like "fortunate are those," or better, "privileged are those."[50] It denotes "the contented state of being that comes from the directed life." It is marked by a sense of well-being, "contentment and satisfaction."[51] As a beatitude, Psalm 1 does not use commands to tell us what to do. But with its descriptions and pictures, it surely tells us which is the wise choice and which is foolish.

"Happy are those." Who does Psalm 1 say are happy, contented persons? Verse 1 says, "Happy are those who do *not* follow the advice of the wicked, or take the path that sinners tread, or sit in the seat of scoffers."[52] Three times this

---

48. The Hebrew reads, "Happy is the man" and has the singular through verse 3, "He is like a tree." The NRSV turns the singular into the plural to avoid gender specificity. Unfortunately, this translation loses the contrast between the one and the many ("the wicked" is plural throughout) and the link to Jesus' teaching about the many who travel the road to destruction and the few who find the road to life (Matt 7:13–14).

49. The Hebrew word *'ašrê* (a plural construct noun) is translated in the LXX as the singular *makarios*. Jesus uses the plural *makarioi*.

50. Davis, *Wondrous Depth,* 146.

51. Raymond Apple, "The Happy Man of Psalm 1," *JBQ* 40, no. 3 (2012; pp. 179–82): 180 and 181. Cf. Wilson, *Psalms,* I, 93–94, "The word 'blessed' conveys the idea of happiness that flows from a sense of well-being and rightness." Cf. Waltke, *Psalms as Christian Worship,* 133, "The popular, modern rendering of *'ašrê* as 'happy' conceals both that suffering saints are fortunate and that the focus is on life that outlasts clinical death."

52. The Hebrew verbs are all perfect, indicating completed action.

verse states that those people are happy who do *not* associate with the wicked. The psalm contrasts truly happy people with the wicked, sinners, and scoffers. Interestingly, the Hebrew literally reads that those people are happy who do not *walk* by the advice of the wicked, do not *stand* on the path of sinners, and do not *sit* in the company of scoffers. Notice the progression from walking[53] according to the advice of the wicked, then taking a stand[54] with sinners (who miss the mark in life), then sitting or dwelling[55] with scoffers.[56] "The three complete phrases show . . . three degrees of departure from God by portraying conformity to this world at three different levels":[57] accepting the world's advice instead of God's teaching, being party to the world's ways, and dwelling with scoffers of God and his Word[58] (cf. Mal 3:13–18).

This raises the question, Who are the wicked in this psalm? The wicked are clearly portrayed in contrast to the happy / righteous person. For the psalmist it is an either / or. A person is either righteous or wicked, either right with God or not right with God. There is "no partly righteous, no a-little-bit-wicked."[59] The wicked are "those who are self-ruled, self-grounded, self-centered, self-seeking. The essence of wickedness in the psalms is autonomy. . . . To be wicked is finally to praise the self instead of God, . . . to trust the self instead of God."[60]

53. "Walking on a way is a traditional metaphor for pursuing a set of moral choices in life. In this verse that idea is turned into an elegant narrative sequence in the triadic line — first walking, then standing, then sitting, with the attachment to the company of evildoers becoming increasingly more habitual from one verset to the next." Alter, *Book of Psalms*, 3.

54. "The verb *ʿāmad* has more the sense of 'take a stand' than simply 'stand still.' There is volition (and therefore responsibility) assumed in this action." Wilson, *Psalms*, I, 94 n. 15. Cf. A. Anderson, *Psalms 1–72*, 59, "'To stand in the way of sinners' is to share their way of life (cf. Prov 1:10–19)."

55. "The verb *yāšab* can mean 'sit down' or often 'dwell, take up permanent residence' in a place." Wilson, *Psalms*, I, 94 n. 16. Ellen Davis, *Wondrous Depth*, 149, suggests, "In our culture, in Christian homes . . . , the functional equivalent of 'the sitting-place of the scornful' is often the easy chair in front of the television set. . . . [This distracts] us from giving our best attention to God . . . [and hurts] us by filling our thoughts and imagination with things that have no substance."

56. "A progression seems to be intended: first an occasional compliance, then a lingering, and finally a settled identification." Eaton, *The Psalms*, 62. Cf. Marlin Thomas, "Psalms 1 and 112," *JETS* 29, no. 1 (1986; pp. 15–24): 20, "The progression from the 'counsel' to the 'way' to the 'assembly' (of the wicked) parallels the realms of thinking, behaving, and belonging." Cf. Waltke, *Psalms as Christian Worship*, 135, The poet "accelerates patterns of sinful behavior from *ʿēṣâ* ('counsel'), a pattern of thinking, to *derek* ('way'), a pattern of behavior, to *môšāb* ('sitting' / 'seat'), a pattern of identification."

57. Kidner, *Psalms 1–72*, 48.

58. "'To sit in the seat of the scoffers' amounts to making light of God's law which ought to be one's delight." A. Anderson, *Psalms 1–72*, 59. Cf. Waltke, *Psalms as Christian Worship*, 134.

59. Mays, *Psalms*, 42.

60. McCann, "The Psalms as Instruction," *Int* 46, no. 2 (1992; pp. 117–28): 127.

Today, we are immersed in a culture that is thoroughly selfish. People live for themselves, buy for themselves, seek to please themselves. Hedonism, they call it. People tend not to reckon with God and his law. Modern scientists even seek to explain the universe by deliberately leaving God out of the equation. Donald Williams observes, "We have been so indoctrinated by the modern scientific worldview with its anti-supernatural bias that we are practically closed to the presence and power of God in our day-by-day existence."[61]

Three times verse 1 reiterates that those people are happy who do *not* associate with the wicked. Does this mean, then, that we should not have contact with unbelievers? That we should isolate ourselves?[62] Some Christians have thought so and separated themselves from the world by entering monasteries. But the New Testament reports that Jesus "ate with sinners" and interacted with Gentiles. So the message is not to avoid contact with unbelievers but not to choose their way of life, to avoid a lifestyle that centers on oneself instead of God.

After the three negatives, verse 2 adds two positive characteristics of the happy person: "but their *delight*[63] is in the law of the LORD, and on his law they meditate[64] day and night." How can people delight in *the law?* The law seems to hem us in. We cannot do whatever we want. We may not drive over the speed limit. We may not let our lawn go to seed. We may not take what is not ours. How can we delight in the law?

The answer is that the word "law" (*torah*) does not mean a law that restricts us. Rather, it means the LORD's *instruction,* the LORD's *teaching.* The LORD who created us presents us with a manual of teachings on how to live our life to its fullest potential. *Torah* shows us the direction our life ought to take so that we can indeed be happy and content. "*Torah* is the LORD God's graciously extended hand to steady us on our feet like a child learning to walk."[65] Thus we can "*delight* . . . in the law of the LORD." As Psalm 19:8, 10 states,

---

61. Williams, *Psalms 1–72,* 27.

62. Cf. John Calvin, *Commentary on the Book of Psalms,* I, 4, "If in the time of the Psalmist it was necessary for the devout worshipers of God to withdraw themselves from the company of the ungodly, in order to frame their life aright, how much more in the present day, when the world has become so much more corrupt, ought we carefully to avoid all dangerous society, that we may be kept unstained by its impurities."

63. The wicked do not delight in God's law: "A fool takes no pleasure in understanding, but only in expressing personal opinion" (Prov 18:2).

64. This verb and the following ones are all imperfect, meaning incompleted action. "According to Lambdin, paragraph 91, imperfect verbs can refer to simple future action, to habitual action, iterative action or modal (=subjunctive or optative) actions. Here it expresses habitual action." Comment of my colleague Carl Bosma.

65. Calvin Seerveld, "Reading and Hearing the Psalms: The Gut of the Bible," *Pro Rege* (June 1999; pp. 20–31): 24.

The precepts of the LORD are right,
    rejoicing the heart; . . .
More to be desired are they than gold,
    even much fine gold;
sweeter also than honey,
    and drippings of the honeycomb.

Psalm 119:103, 105 echoes,

How *sweet* are your words to my taste,
    sweeter than honey to my mouth! . . .
Your word is a *lamp* to my feet
    and a *light* to my path.

The psalmist even declares,

Oh, how I *love* your law!
    It is my *meditation* all day long (Ps 119:97; cf. 119:131)

"Psalm 119 gives the impression that obedience to God's law was not a slavish servant-to-master duty but more like a response to a magnet pulling one toward the source of life's true fulfillment."[66]

Psalm 1 gives the same impression. Verse 2 says, "their *delight* is in the law of the LORD," and then adds, "and on his law they *meditate* day and night." The experience of delight will lead to action.[67] If we delight in friends, we will want to be with them. If we delight in children, we will want to look after them. If we delight in a song, we will want to sing it. "If we delight in God's law, we will want to meditate upon it."[68]

The question now is, Where do we find God's *torah*? At its broadest level we find God's law in all of creation (see Psalm 19).[69] But verse 2 goes on to say "and on his law they *meditate* day and night." This seems to narrow the intended law down to a written word.

66. J. Bardarah McCandles, "Enfleshing the Psalms," *Religious Education* 81, no. 3 (1986; pp. 372–90): 385–86, referring to Ps 119:16, 20, 35, 47–48, 54, 97, 103, 105, 127, 131, and 165.
67. Psalm 1:2 has advancing (synthetic) parallelism.
68. Williams, *Psalms 1–72*, 27.
69. See Calvin Seerveld, *Take Hold of God and Pull* (Palos Heights, IL: Trinity Pennyasheet Press, 1966), 22, his "Reading and Hearing the Psalms," *Pro Rege* (June 1999; pp. 20–32): 24, and his *Voicing God's Psalms* (Grand Rapids: Eerdmans, 2005) 3. See also my article "The Universal Dimension of Law in the Hebrew Scriptures," *Studies in Religion / Sciences Religieuses* 14, no. 1 (1985): 39–51.

Verse 2 reminds us of God's words to Joshua as he was leading Israel into the Promised Land. The LORD said, "This *book of the law* shall not depart out of your mouth; you shall *meditate* on it *day and night,* so that you may be careful to act in accordance with all that is written in it. For then you shall make your way *prosperous,* and then you shall be successful" (Josh 1:8).[70] So when Psalm 1 says that those people are happy and content who meditate on God's *torah,* it refers first of all to the "book of the law," "the Deuteronomic code of laws," then to the five books of Moses, Genesis to Deuteronomy,[71] and ultimately to all the collected teachings of the LORD, the holy Bible.[72]

What is it to "meditate" on God's word? Does it mean to set aside time for personal devotions? Or does it mean to withdraw to a retreat and to turn inward? Webster's Dictionary gives as one of the meanings, "to engage in transcendental meditation, devout religious contemplation." But that is not what it means here. The word translated as "meditate" is literally to "recite aloud," to "murmur."[73] In those days people did not read silently as we do today. They read aloud. Think of Jews reading Scripture at the Wailing Wall or in their synagogues, murmuring the words while bowing whenever they come across the name of the LORD.

So to meditate on God's law means to read God's word and reflect and act on its meaning. As we read, we should ask ourselves, What is God saying here about himself and what he has done for us? And what is God saying about us and what he requires of us? Are we living in accordance with God's teachings? Are we living for ourselves or for God? In contrast to the wicked, writes John Stott, the truly happy people look for guidance for their daily conduct "not to public opinion, the unreliable fashions of the godless world, but to the revealed Word of God, in which they delight and meditate."[74]

---

70. For the similarities in Hebrew vocabulary between Ps 1:2–3 and Josh 1:7–8, see R. N. Whybray, *Reading the Psalms as a Book,* 39.

71. See ibid. Cf. B. Anderson, *Out of the Depths,* 190.

72. "Here [Ps 1:2] the psalmist seems to refer primarily to the heart of the *Torah,* the Pentateuch, but this does not preclude meditation on God's *torah* that is given in other places, including the book of Psalms itself." B. Anderson, *Out of the Depths,* 206. Cf. Craigie, *Psalms 1–50,* 60, "*Torah* . . . may include that which is technically law, but it also includes other more general parts of God's revelation." Cf. Kraus, *Psalms 1–59,* 116, "The *Torah* in this sense is the authoritatively valid 'Sacred Scripture.'" Cf. Wilson, *Psalms,* I, 95–96; VanGemeren, *Psalms,* 79; and Mays, *Psalms,* 41–42.

73. "The common English translation of 'meditate' (so NRSV and NIV) draws from the Vulgate *meditabitur.* The Hebrew, however, carries a wider range of meaning, from moan and growl to speak and consider. . . ." Brown, *Psalms,* 82.

74. John Stott, *Favorite Psalms,* 7. Cf. McCann, "The Psalms as Instruction," *Int* 46, no. 2 (1992): 128. "In a real sense, 'a teachable spirit' [Calvin's phrase] is what Psalm 1 means by being 'happy' and 'righteous': an openness to God's instruction and a commitment to live under God's reign."

Verse 2 says, "on his [God's] law they meditate *day and night*." That means that they meditate on it continuously.[75] But there may be a deeper meaning to "day and night" than simply "continuously." The LORD instructed Israel, "Hear, O Israel: The LORD is our God, the LORD alone. You shall love the LORD your God with all your heart, and with all your soul, and with all your might. Keep these words that I am commanding you today in your heart. Recite them to your children and talk about them when you are *at home* and when you are *away*, when you *lie down* and when you *rise*" (Deut 6:4–7). Jesus also said to those who believed in him, "If you *continue in my word*, you are truly my disciples; and you will know the truth, and the truth will make you free" (John 8:31–32).

Verse 3 pictures the happy person (who does not stand on the path of sinners but who delights in the teaching of the LORD) as a fruitful tree: "They are like trees planted by streams of water, which yield their fruit in its season, and their leaves do not wither. In all that they do, they prosper."

"They are like trees *planted* by streams of water." The Hebrew actually says that they are "*transplanted*"[76] by streams of water. Imagine yourself in parched Palestine. Wild palm shoots are growing in the wet wadis (river beds). But in the dry season these wadis dry up and the shoots die. Gardeners would transplant some of these shoots to areas where there were "streams of water," that is, irrigation ditches. Here these small palm trees could flourish, bear "their fruit in its season," "their leaves do not wither" in the dry season, and "in all that they do, they prosper."

The Gardener who transplanted these happy people by streams of water can only be God. God transplants his people by streams of water where they will be nourished and bear fruit. "The lesson of the metaphor is that spiritual happiness is God-given, not naturally attained."[77]

What are these streams of water that nourish these people so that they can be happy and fruitful? The streams of water are the *torah* of the LORD, the LORD's teaching.[78] Since we find the LORD's teachings in the whole Bible, we

75. "'Day and night,' in the sense of 'continuously,' is another common phrase (Pss 1:2; 32:4; 42:3; 55:10)." John Stek, "The Stylistics of Hebrew Poetry," *CTJ* 9, no. 1 (1974; pp. 15–30): 23. Cf. A. Anderson, *Psalms 1–72*, 60, "The righteous man's dependence upon the revealed will of God must be *unbroken*."

76. "The word used here for planting (*šātûl*) denotes 'transplanting' and, according to rabbinic tradition, means a firm planting to withstand tempest." Eaton, *The Psalms*, 62. See also p. 54 n. 35 above.

77. Rogerson and McKay, *Psalms 1–50*, 17.

78. "As the righteous individual delights *in* and reflects *on* YHWH's *tôrâ* (v 2), the tree is planted *by* ever-flowing streams (v 3). The juxtaposition is deliberate. . . . The image of flowing channels signifies *tôrâ*, on which the individual reflects. . . . Without *tôrâ*, the individual would wither, as it were, and dry up like chaff (v 4)." Brown, *Seeing the Psalms*, 131. See p. 232 n. 21, "In later Jewish Hellenistic literature, the Torah is given the epithet 'the tree of life' (Michael V. Fox, *Proverbs 1–9* [New York: Doubleday, 2000], 159)."

can say that the nourishing streams of water are the Old and New Testaments. As we read the Bible with longing hearts to hear more about God and his will for our lives, the Holy Spirit nourishes us, teaches us, comforts us, and instructs us in how to live.[79]

Jesus also spoke of these nourishing streams of water. He called them "living water." One day as Jesus traveled through Samaria he rested beside a well. When a Samaritan woman came to the well to draw water, Jesus asked her for a drink. She said to him, "How is it that you, a Jew, ask a drink of me, a woman of Samaria?" Jesus answered, "If you knew the *gift of God,* and who it is that is saying to you, 'Give me a drink,' you would have asked him, and he would have given you *living water.* . . . Those who drink of the water that I will give them will never be thirsty. The water that I will give will become in them a spring of water gushing up to *eternal life*" (John 4:9–10, 14). Ultimately, Jesus is the source of this living water. He is the one who can give us this living water.

Jesus spoke of the living water again at the Feast of Tabernacles. At this feast people remembered God's care of Israel as they wandered forty years through the desert. On the last day of this feast, Jesus cried out, "Let anyone who is thirsty *come to me,* and let the one who believes in me *drink.* As the scripture has said, 'Out of the believer's heart shall flow *rivers of living water.*'" The Gospel writer John adds, "Now he said this about the *Spirit,* which believers in him were to receive" (John 7:37–39).

The Gardener, God, by grace has transplanted us by streams of water. The streams of water are God's teachings on who he is, what he has done for us, and what he expects of us. We find these teachings in the Bible. By reading and meditating on God's teachings, the Holy Spirit gives us faith in Jesus. Faith in Jesus, in turn, gives us eternal life. John writes, "This is the testimony: God gave us eternal life, and this life is in his Son. Whoever has the Son has life; whoever does not have the Son of God does not have life" (1 John 5:11–12).

Verse 3 lists three benefits of being "transplanted by streams of water." First, these trees "yield their fruit in its season."[80] Notice that these trees do not bear fruit all the time but in its season, when it is time to bear fruit. As God's people we may suffer through hard times when we cannot bear fruit. This is okay; we don't have to feel guilty about this. We don't have to bear fruit all the time.[81] But

---

79. "As the tree draws constant nourishment from the water through its roots, so through daily meditation in the law of the Lord the righteous refresh and replenish their soul in God." Stott, *Favorite Psalms,* 8.

80. The verbs "yield," "not wither," and "prosper," are the imperfect tense, expressing repeated action.

81. "The phrase, 'which yields its fruit in season' (lit. 'in its time'), is a simple image illustrating a profound truth: while believers may be able to sustain spiritual life through times of adversity,

we *will* bear fruit "in its season."[82] Jesus said, "I am the true vine, and my Father is the vinegrower. He removes every branch in me that bears no fruit. Every branch that bears fruit he prunes to make it bear more fruit. . . . I am the vine, you are the branches. Those who abide in me and I in them bear much fruit, because apart from me you can do nothing" (John 15:1-2, 5).

Do we receive eternal life, then, by bearing fruit? Clearly not. "Apart from me you can do nothing," Jesus said. We can only bear fruit when we abide in Jesus and he in us. So our fruit-bearing is a gift of Jesus. We bear fruit only by God's grace. Remember also that the divine Gardener transplanted us by nourishing streams of water where we can grow and bear fruit. Again, bearing fruit is not our accomplishment; we bear fruit only by God's grace. Paul writes, "By grace you have been saved through faith, and this is not your own doing; it is the gift of God — not the result of works, so that no one may boast. For we are what he has made us, created in Christ Jesus for good works, which God prepared beforehand to be our way of life" (Eph 2:8-10).

So the first benefit of having been "transplanted by streams of water" is that we can yield "fruit in its season." The second benefit for these trees is that "their leaves do not wither." During the dry season in Palestine, the leaves of trees wither — unless they are close to a source of water. These trees have been transplanted by streams of water, so their leaves do not wither. This means that even in the dry season, the integrity of God's people remains constant.[83] Even in times of suffering, God's people keep their faith. In fact, God's people often grow in their faith in times of suffering. They experience that *in* their suffering they are "more than conquerors" (Rom 8:37).

The third benefit of having been transplanted by streams of water is, "In all that they do, they prosper." This sounds like "the health and wealth gospel" one hears so often on TV: "Just obey the Lord, send us some seed money, and the Lord will give you great health and abundant wealth." Does God here promise his people good health and great wealth?

This interpretation misses the point of this introductory Psalm as well as the following psalms. Several psalms struggle with the fact that it is the wicked who seem to prosper. The wicked are often the ones who have health and wealth while God's people experience trouble and pain. Take, for example, Psalm 73 where the psalmist confesses,

---

they may be productive only at certain times, whose determination is beyond their control." Broyles, *Psalms,* 43.

82. "As the tree bears fruit 'in due season,' so the individual knows the right time in which to act and speak, as well as to find success." Brown, *Seeing the Psalms,* 58, with references to Prov 15:23; 25:11; and Eccl 3:1-8 (see p. 232 n. 20).

83. Brown, *Seeing the Psalms,* 58.

But as for me, my feet had almost stumbled;
　　my steps had nearly slipped.
For I was envious of the arrogant;
　　I saw the *prosperity of the wicked.*
For they have no pain;
　　their bodies are sound and sleek.
They are *not in trouble* as others are;
　　they are not plagued like other people. . . . [84]

Also today we know of wicked people who are filthy rich and sincere Christians who are dirt poor. We know of wicked people who are in excellent health and Christians who suffer from various diseases. The health and wealth gospel not only misses the point of this Psalm, it also contradicts our experience of life on earth.

Those who interpret the final line in verse 3 as a promise of health and wealth separate this line from the rest of verse 3. Remember, verse 3 is a simile: "They are *like* trees planted by streams of water, which yield their fruit in its season, and their leaves do not wither. In all that they [the trees] do, they prosper." This last line is still talking about these trees.[85] It says, "*In all that they do,* they prosper." What do these trees do? They bear fruit! John Collins astutely observes that bearing fruit is "to bring refreshment to others. (Trees do not yield fruit for themselves!) Hence we see that the 'prosperity' is not materialistic or self-centered, but for the sake of others."[86] As these trees prosper / succeed[87] in bearing fruit, so God's people prosper / succeed in bearing fruit for the benefit of others.[88]

84. Ps 73:2–5. Cf. Pss 10:1–18; 37:7; 44:23–25.

85. "The Hebrew grammar permits one to read the subject of prospering as either tree — thus a continuation of the simile — or the happy individual. In our judgment, the poet created intentional ambiguity, since the tree clearly is prospering, and by analogy so also will the happy individual, the one who focuses on the torah." Petersen and Richards, *Interpreting Hebrew Poetry,* 95. I see no valid reason, however, for separating this final line from the simile and applying it directly to the happy person. I think it is more appropriate to interpret this line as part of the simile (it speaks of the tree) and then apply this part of the simile to the happy person (cf. the contrasting simile in v 4).

86. Collins, "Psalm 1," *Presbyterion* 31, no. 1 (2005; pp. 37–48): 47. Cf. McCann, "Psalms," 685, "The final line of v. 3, . . . has often been interpreted to mean that obedience is materially rewarded. Instead, to 'prosper' in 'all that they do' should be understood as an affirmation that persons who trust God have a resource for sustaining their lives under any circumstance." Cf. VanGemeren, *Psalms,* 82, "The prosperity of the righteous does not necessarily extend to the assurance of great wealth but primarily to God's blessing on their words and works (cf. 90:14–17)."

87. "The term translated 'prospers' here has more the sense of 'be successful, bring to a successful conclusion.'" Wilson, I, *Psalms,* 98.

88. "For Psalm 1 (and the rest of the Psalter), happiness involves not enjoying oneself but

Again, our success is not our doing. We succeed only by God's grace. As Peter Craigie put it, "Just as a tree with a constant water supply *naturally* flourishes, so too the person who avoids evil [v 1] and delights in Torah [v 2] *naturally* prospers, for such a person is living within the guidelines set down by the Creator. Thus the prosperity of the righteous reflects the wisdom of a life lived according to the plan of the Giver of life."[89]

Having spent considerable time describing the happy person, Psalm 1 dismisses the wicked in two short verses. Verse 4, "The wicked are not so, but are like chaff that the wind drives away."[90] The Hebrew has a stronger contrast: "*Not so* the wicked!"[91] Not like a tree planted by streams of water, bearing fruit, always green, prospering. "Not so the wicked!" They "are like chaff that the wind drives away." It's another agricultural image but antithetical to that of the fruitful tree. The wicked are like worthless chaff.

At harvest time, farmers would gather the sheaves of grain, lay them on a threshing floor, crush them with a threshing sledge, and then with a winnowing fork toss the grain into the air. The heavier grain would fall back on the threshing floor but the dry chaff would be blown away by the wind. "Without root below, without fruit above, devoid of all the vigour and freshness of life, . . . a prey of the slightest breeze — thus utterly worthless and unstable."[92]

In contrast to the stable tree standing by the water, chaff is extremely dry and unstable[93] — blown away by the wind. Note the contrasts between the tree and the chaff:

stable	vs	wind-blown
well-watered	vs	dry as dust
fruit-bearing	vs	worthless
alive	vs	dead

---

delight in the teaching of God. The goal of life is to be found not in self-fulfillment but in praising God. . . . Prosperity does not involve getting what one wants; rather, it comes from being connected to the source of life — God." McCann, "Psalms," 687.

89. Craigie, *Psalms 1–50,* 61. I knew Peter Craigie from meetings at the Canadian Society of Biblical Literature. He indeed flourished in Calgary, Alberta. But a few years after writing these words, this gracious, promising scholar lost his life in a tragic car accident in the Rocky Mountains. The health and wealth gospel is far too simplistic.

90. The verb "drives away" is imperfect, expressing repeated action.

91. "Verse 3 is introduced by an emphatic form of the negative particle, which has already occurred three times in v 1 and once in v 3 and will occur again in v 5. This sixfold repetition sharpens the contrast between the righteous and the wicked." McCann, "Psalms," 685.

92. Delitzsch, *Biblical Commentary on the Psalms,* I, 87.

93. The wicked "are not the subject but rather the object of a verb, and one that denotes unstable motion, a scattering action." Alter, *The Art of Biblical Poetry,* 116.

The wicked are compared to chaff because they are unstable and worthless. They are not grounded in God's teachings. They do not bear fruit. They are dead. "The life of the wicked, a life lived apart from God, is just as empty, just as meaningless and worthless as the chaff."[94] "The wicked life has no weight of worth, no root against the tempest, no abiding in God's world."[95]

Verse 5 continues, "Therefore the wicked will not stand in the judgment, nor sinners in the congregation of the righteous." "The wicked will *not stand* in the judgment."[96] As the happy person does "not stand" in the way of sinners (v 1), so the wicked will "not stand"[97] in the judgment.

As the parallel line "nor sinners in the congregation of the righteous" suggests, initially this judgment refers to the judgment made by the righteous.[98] The righteous would meet at the city gate and adjudicate cases. The wicked will not stand in that judgment. They are too light when weighed in the scales.[99]

But "the judgment" also has the fuller sense[100] of God's final judgment.[101] The Old Testament frequently uses the image of chaff to portray those falling under God's judgment.[102] In the New Testament John the Baptist also uses this image to predict what Jesus will do: "His winnowing fork is in his hand, and he will clear his threshing floor and will gather his wheat into the granary; but the chaff he will burn with unquenchable fire" (Matt 3:12). John is speaking of the final judgment.

The righteous and the wicked are headed in opposite directions. Of the righteous the psalm says, "In all that they do, they prosper." Of the wicked it says, "the wicked will not stand in the judgment." Verse 6 gives the reasons for these

---

94. Weiser, *The Psalms*, 106. Cf. Ross, *Commentary on the Psalms*, I, 191, "The figure shows that the ungodly are not only of no value, but also will eventually be removed."

95. Eaton, *The Psalms*, 63,

96. "The YQTL [= imperfect] verb in v 5 can be either habitual or iterative." Comment of my colleague Carl Bosma.

97. A different Hebrew word for to stand: v 1 *'āmad*, v 5 *qûm*.

98. "We are best advised to begin with the clue offered by the psalm's own parallel line: 'nor sinners in the assembly of the righteous.' The judgment relates to the righteous assembly, that is, the worshiping congregation (cf. 74:2; 111:1)." Broyles, *Psalms*, 43. Cf. Goldingay, *Psalms*, I, 87, "It is the assembly of the faithful that makes the judicial decision to which the psalm refers." Cf. Waltke, *Psalms as Christian Worship*, 142.

99. Cf. Daniel 5:27, "TEKEL, you have been weighed on the scales and found wanting."

100. For a discussion of the fuller sense, *sensus plenior,* see my *Modern Preacher and Ancient Text*, 71–72, 111–13.

101. "Almost certainly verse 5 came to be understood in the light of apocalyptic eschatology like that of Daniel (see Daniel 7; 12) as a reference to a vindicating judgment beyond this life." Mays, *Psalms*, 44.

102. See Ps 35:5; Isa 29:5; Hos 13:3; and Zeph 2:2.

opposite destinies: "For the LORD *watches over* the way of the righteous,[103] but the way of the wicked[104] will *perish.*"

"The LORD watches over the way of the righteous." This is the first time we hear about the LORD in this psalm. But the LORD was there all along: with his teaching making his people happy (vv 1–2); the divine Gardener transplanting the wild shoot by streams of water where it can bear fruit (v 3); and judging the wicked in the final judgment (v 5).

"The LORD *watches over* the way of the righteous" is literally, the LORD *intimately knows* the way of the righteous. He embraces, cares for, "watches over the way of the righteous." The LORD protects their life so that they do not perish.[105] "The psalmist uses a verb form that indicates that the LORD 'keeps on knowing' the way of the righteous. His eye is upon them, His ear is open to them, and in Christ His Spirit abides in them forever (John 14:17)."[106] "The righteous can be assured of Yahweh's loving protection. He will secure their future. However, the wicked have no future and are destined to perish."[107]

Psalm 1 ends with the words, "but the way of the wicked will perish."[108] "No divine action is explicitly predicated for the way of the wicked; it simply 'will perish.' The implication is that without divine intervention life will degenerate into death; it is only with divine aid that it is possible to sustain life."[109]

---

103. "The term righteous does not signify sinless persons. Rather, it points to persons who have experienced mercy and forgiveness and who as a consequence have sought to lead a moral life." N. H. Ridderbos and P. C. Craigie, "Psalms," in the *International Standard Bible Encyclopedia*, III (Grand Rapids: Eerdmans, 1986; pp. 1030–40), 1037. Cf. VanGemeren, *Psalms*, 83, "The ṣaddîqîm, righteous, are those who love God and do his will. They have close fellowship (cf. Ps 15) as they practice the will of the Most High in all areas of life."

104. "The way of the righteous" and "the way of the wicked" is "idiomatic for the course of action that people follow (how they live, their motives, what they produce)." Ross, *Commentary on the Psalms*, I, 194.

105. Antithetic parallelism with "the way of the wicked will perish." Cf. Ross, *Commentary on the Psalms*, I, 193.

106. Williams, *Psalms 1–72*, 30. Cf. Ross, *Commentary on the Psalms*, I, 192–93, "The LORD knows them. This verb is a participle . . . , emphasizing the knowing as continuous or durative in nature."

107. The verb "perish" is imperfect and thus signals incompleted or future action.

108. "To *perish* is used in many senses: here . . . of a road or course that comes to nothing or to ruin." Kidner, *Psalms 1–72*, 49. Cf. Alter, *The Art of Biblical Poetry*, 116, "The very 'way' of evildoers on which at the beginning of the poem the fortunate man did not stand is here at the end seen to lead nowhere, or to perdition." Cf. Goldingay, *Psalms*, I, 89. "The psalm notes God's personal involvement specifically in the positive, while picturing the negative simply working itself out."

109. Broyles, *Psalms*, 43. Cf. Goldingay, *Psalms*, I, 90, "The psalm began with the misapprehension that the path of the faithless could lead to a good place. It closes by affirming that this path leads over a cliff and takes with it those who walk it (cf. Prov 4:18–19; 14:12; Ps 37 expounds this conviction at length)."

That the way of the wicked will perish is also the conclusion reached by Psalm 73. Its author started off with his bewilderment at seeing "the prosperity of the wicked." He writes,

> I was envious of the arrogant;
>> I saw the *prosperity of the wicked*. . . .
> Such are the wicked;
>> always at ease, they *increase in riches*. . . .
> But when I thought how to understand this,
>> it seemed to me a wearisome task,
> until I went into the sanctuary of God;
>> then I perceived *their end*. . . .
> Indeed, those who are far from you will *perish*;
>> you put an end to those who are false to you (Ps 73:3, 12, 16–17, 27).

The message of Psalm 1 is simple: There are two ways: the way of the wicked and the way of the righteous. In contrast to the wicked who will perish, the LORD watches over the righteous who delight in the teaching of the LORD. Which way will we choose? Will we walk with the wicked or stand with those who are right with God? If we are wise, we will choose to order our life according to God's teaching. That is the way to life.

In the New Testament we also read of the two ways. For example, John 3:16, "God so loved the world that he gave his only Son, so that everyone who believes in him may *not perish* but may *have eternal life*." There are the two ways again: the way that leads to perishing and the way that leads to eternal life. John 3:36 says, "Whoever believes in the Son has *eternal life*; whoever disobeys the Son *will not see life, but must endure God's wrath*."

Jesus himself speaks about these two ways in his Sermon on the Mount. Like Psalm 1, which begins with the word "Happy" or "Blessed," the Sermon on the Mount begins with a ninefold "Blessed." How can we be happy? Jesus encourages us to choose wisely, "Enter through the narrow gate; for the gate is wide and *the road* is easy that leads to *destruction,* and there are many who take it. For the gate is narrow and *the road* is hard that leads to *life,* and there are few who find it" (Matt 7:13–14).

A little later in his Sermon on the Mount Jesus likens the two ways to two builders, one wise, one foolish. Jesus said, "Everyone then who hears these words of mine and *acts on them*[110] will be like a *wise* man who built his house on rock.

---

110. Cf. Jesus' words, "Blessed rather are those who hear the word of God and *obey it!*" (Luke 11:28).

The rain fell, the floods came, and the winds blew and beat on that house, but it did not fall, because it had been founded on rock [it was stable]. And everyone who hears these words of mine and *does not act on them* will be like a *foolish* man who built his house on sand. The rain fell, and the floods came, and the winds blew and beat against that house, and it fell — and great was its fall!" (Matt 7:24–27).[111] Will we be wise by delighting in God's teaching and living accordingly? Or will we be foolish by ignoring God's teaching? In contrast to the wicked who will perish, the LORD watches over the righteous who delight in his teaching. Psalm 1 and Jesus himself encourage us to choose wisely.

Prayer[112]

O God, we chafe under your commands when we should be reveling in them. Make us teachable people, glad to learn your blessed recipe for life. Make us humble enough to think we actually have something to learn from your Word. Then let us delight in your sound instruction and mull it over. In other words, O God, we pray to you for basic wisdom, the knack of living effectively within your world. We pray in Jesus' name. Amen.

Song[113]

I sought the Lord, and afterward I knew
    he moved my soul to seek him, seeking me;
it was not I that found, O Savior true;
    no, I was found, was found of thee.
It was not I that found, O Savior true;
    no, I was found, was found of thee.

Thou didst reach forth thy hand and mine enfold;
    I walked and sank not on the storm-vexed sea;
'twas not so much that I on thee took hold,
    as thou, dear Lord, took hold on me.
'Twas not so much that I on thee took hold,
    as thou, dear Lord, took hold on me.

---

111. Jesus further encourages us in the Sermon on the Mount, "Ask, and it will be given you; search, and you will find; knock, and the door will be opened for you. For everyone who asks receives, and everyone who searches finds, and for everyone who knocks, the door will be opened (Matt 7:7–8).

112. Cornelius Plantinga, Jr., Christian Classics Ethereal Library, Calvin Institute of Christian Worship, Calvin College.

113. Anonymous, 1878. Public Domain. *Psalter Hymnal* (1987) #498; *Lift Up Your Hearts*, #685.

I find, I walk, I love; but, oh, the whole
    of love is but my answer, Lord, to thee!
For thou wert long beforehand with my soul;
    always, always, thou lovedst me.
For thou wert long beforehand with my soul;
    always, always, thou lovedst me.

CHAPTER 3

"Pray for the Peace of Jerusalem"

Psalm 122 (121)

The next five chapters (3–7) will help pastors preach an Advent series of four sermons on the psalms plus one for Christmas. The psalms selected are those *The Revised Common Lectionary* assigns for Advent Year A. Since the Lectionary selected these psalms not for preaching but as responses to the Old Testament lessons, preaching them as a series has advantages and disadvantages. The advantages are that pastors from various denominations using the Lectionary can study the assigned psalms together while members of their congregations who wish to study these psalms can also do so interdenominationally. One disadvantage is that the *occasion* for preaching sometimes tends to trump the meaning of the text. We will have to be vigilant, therefore, to clearly establish the theme of each psalm and preach it in the light of later revelation. Another disadvantage is that, though all these psalms point to Christ's First or Second Coming, they do not follow one another in an orderly manner reaching a climax at Christmas. Pastors not strictly following the Lectionary can change the order into a more climactic sequence. It seemed to me particularly awkward to preach on Psalm 80, a community lament, on the Sunday before Christmas. My proofreader Ryan Faber, who preached this series for Advent, solved this problem brilliantly. He preached this lament as part of a "blue Christmas" or "Longest Night" service[1] (see his sermon in Appendix 4). As an alternative, one could move Psalm 80 to the first Sunday of Advent where the Lectionary, Year B, places it. The series would then be,

1. Chapter 6, Psalm 80, the community lament, "Restore Us, O LORD God of Hosts"
2. Chapter 3, Psalm 122, the song of Zion, "Pray for the Peace of Jerusalem"

---

1. This service remembers especially people who have lost loved ones in the past year.

3. Chapter 4, Psalm 72, the royal Psalm, " Give the King Your Justice, O God"
4. Chapter 5, Psalm 146, the hymn, "Happy Are Those Whose Help Is the God of Jacob."
5. Chapter 7, Christmas, Psalm 96, the hymn, "Sing to the LORD a New Song"

The Lectionary, Year A, designates Psalm 122 for the First Sunday of Advent as a response to Isaiah 2:1–5, "In days to come the mountain of the LORD's house shall be established as the highest of the mountains. . . ." But Psalm 122 in its own right can be preached as a text for Advent. It is a Song of Ascents celebrating the pilgrimage to Jerusalem. A pilgrimage to Jerusalem entails "the movement from the periphery to the center, from the ordinary to the holy, from the mundane to the meaningful, . . . from the famine of the ordinary to the festivities and feasting of the special."[2] In this respect a pilgrimage to Jerusalem in the Old Testament is similar to our celebration of Advent. Irene Nowell observes, "We begin the Church year singing the pilgrimage song which expresses our desire to be home at last."[3]

The psalmist encourages us to pray for the peace (*šālôm* 3×) of Jeru*salem*, the city of peace. In today's context of strife between Israel and Palestinian and other states, our prayer for peace for the city of peace is still urgent. But with the forward movement of redemptive history, the earthly city of Jerusalem has been superseded by the true city of peace, the heavenly Jerusalem (Revelation 21). Although we still need to pray for peace for the city of Jerusalem, today we need to pray especially for the peace of the church (Eph 2:19–22) and the coming (Advent) new Jerusalem when Jesus comes again.

Text and Context

Psalm 122 is one of fifteen "Songs of Ascents" and has been classified more specifically as a "Song of Zion."[4] As an individual psalm it is a literary unit and therefore a good preaching text. The author has confirmed the literary unit by the inclusio of the first and last verses: "Let us go to the house of the LORD!" (v 1) and "For the sake of the house of the LORD our God, I will seek your good" (v 9).[5]

The editor(s) of the Psalter have placed Psalm 122 immediately after Psalms 120 and 121, which describe a world of dangers, violence, and war. Although Psalm

2. John Hayes, *Preaching the New Common Lectionary, Year A, Advent . . .* , 15.
3. Irene Nowell, *Sing a New Song*, 282.
4. Bernhard Anderson, *Out of the Depths*, 223.
5. For a more detailed analysis of the inclusio, see J. P. Fokkelman, *Major Poems of the Hebrew Bible*, II, 295.

121, amid the dangers, offers the assurance, "My help comes from the LORD, who made heaven and earth" (v 2), Psalm 122 takes the assurance a step further: it "sets the solidly built city of Jerusalem as a place of shelter and community over against the warlike and dangerous 'world' described in Psalms 120 and 121."[6]

Psalm 122 can also be compared with the other Songs of Ascents (Pss 120–134) and the other Songs of Zion, especially Psalms 46, 48, 76, 84, 87, and 121, in order to home in on its specific focus. Verses 1–2 about being "glad" and "Our feet are standing within your gates, O Jerusalem" remind us of Psalm 1:1 where "the happy person" does "not stand [same Hebrew word] on the path of sinners." The city of the LORD is where the righteous should take their stand.

A broader context for the pilgrimage to Jerusalem takes us back to Deuteronomy 16:16, "Three times a year all your males shall appear before the LORD your God at the place that he will choose. . . ."[7] The opening of Psalm 122 is similar to Isaiah 2:3a, part of the Lectionary reading,

> Many peoples shall come and say,
> "Come, let us go up to the mountain of the LORD,
>   to the house of the God of Jacob. . . ."[8]

And, of course, for preaching Psalm 122 it must be understood not only in the context of the Old Testament but now also of the New Testament.

Literary Interpretation[9]

We shall work our way into understanding Psalm 122 by examining in turn its parallelisms, imagery, repetition of keywords, and its structure.

---

6. Zenger, *Psalms 3*, 330. Cf. p. 342, "If one reads the sequence of Psalms 120–122 as a single context (cf. the keyword links 'peace': Pss 120:6–7; 122:6–8; 'foot/feet': Pss 121:3; 122:2, and the arcs of events 'going out and coming in, going and coming in Jerusalem': Pss 121:8; 122:1–2), one perceives a movement from the margins of the world to Jerusalem as the world's center, where, or because, there is the protecting and hospitable 'house of YHWH.'"

7. Cf. Deut 12:5 "The place that the LORD your God will choose . . . as his habitation."

8. "Based on this psalm are the pilgrimage songs found in Isa 2:3 and Micah 4:2; Jer 31:6; Isa 30:29; it recurs in Gen 35:3; Ps 132:7." Westermann, *The Psalms*, 105.

9. Historical interpretation will be combined with the search for the textual goal in order to avoid needless repetition.

Parallelisms

Psalm 122 is stitched together with stairlike or steplike parallelism, which repeats a word or phrase of one verse in the next verse or line.[10] It links verses 2–3, 4–5, 6–7, and 8–9 (see the italicized words below). The psalm exhibits mostly advancing (synthetic) parallelism, blossoming twice into climactic parallelism (vv 4c–5 and 6–9), the last one being interrupted by advancing parallelism (vv 8a, 9a). Here is our snapshot picture of the psalm's parallelisms.

A Song of Ascents. Of David.	
₁I was glad when they said to me,	A
"Let us go to the house of the LORD!"	B
₂Our feet are standing within your gates, O *Jerusalem.*[11]	+ B′
₃*Jerusalem*—built as a city	A
that is bound firmly together.	+ A′
₄To it *(šām)* the tribes go up,	B
the tribes of the LORD,	+ B′
as was decreed for Israel,	C
to give thanks to the name of the LORD.	+ C′
₅For there *(šāmmâ)* the thrones for judgment were set up,	+ C″
the thrones of the house of David.	+ C‴
₆Pray for the *peace* of Jerusalem:	A
"May they prosper who love you.	+ A′
₇*Peace* be within your walls,	+ A″
and security within your towers."[12]	+ A‴
₈*For the sake* of my relatives and friends	B
I will say, "Peace be within you."[13]	+ A″″
₉*For the sake* of the house of the LORD our God,	+ B′
I will seek your good.	+ A″″′

10. "Stairlike or steplike repetition . . . is especially appropriate for a psalm about a journey, which in ancient times would literally have proceeded step by step." McCann, "Psalms," 1180. See deClaissé-Walford in deClaissé-Walford, Jacobson, and Tanner, *The Book of Psalms*, 887–90.

11. The line advances from the invitation to go to Jerusalem (v 1b) to standing in Jerusalem (v 2).

12. Whether this is synonymous or advancing parallelism is a tough call. "Within your walls" and "within your towers" are synonymous. I take it that "security" adds to "peace," hence advancing parallelism (+), all the more since it is part of (broken) climactic parallelism.

13. This line as well as 9b pick up the topic of vv 6–7 and therefore continue the (broken) climactic parallelism.

Verses 1b–2 show advancing parallelism from the invitation to go to Jerusalem to arriving there. Verses 3 and 4a-b each also show advancing parallelism. Verses 4c-d and 5 exhibit advancing parallelism over four lines, that is, climactic parallelism. Verses 6–9 present another series of climactic parallelism, interrupted by advancing parallelism of the motivation to pray for the peace of Jerusalem in verses 8a and 9a.

Imagery

Psalm 122 portrays Jerusalem very concretely with its gates (v 1), walls and towers (v 7), a city "bound firmly together" (v 3). But the name "Jerusalem" has several levels of meaning: as the capital city of Israel it is the city of David. Since God's house is located in Jerusalem, it is also the city of God. Moreover, *yərûšālāim*, meaning foundation or city of *shalom*,[14] is also the city of peace. "Jerusalem represents in the psalms not just a place but [is] a symbol of God's presence in space and time."[15] Ultimately Jerusalem and the house of David are symbols of the kingdom of God.[16]

Verse 5 employs two metaphors: "For there *the thrones for judgment* were set up, the thrones of the *house of David*." "The thrones[17] for judgment" allude to the king's obligation to maintain justice while "the house of David" refers to the dynasty of David.

Repetition of Keywords

The word "Lord" occurs four times (vv 1, 4 [2×], 9). The psalm mentions Jerusalem three times (vv 2, 3, 6). It also repeats peace (*shalom*) three times (vv 6, 7, 8) and the word "house," twice in the inclusio "house of the Lord" (vv 1, 9) and once in the center, "house of David" (v 5). Repetition of syllables leads to a neat alliteration in verse 6, *ša'ălû šəlôm yərûšālāim*, "Pray for the peace of Jerusalem."

Repetitions also alert us to a possible chiastic structure. Clinton McCann proposes the following chiasm:

---

14. "What people of that time heard in the two elements *yərûšālāim*, namely *'îr šālôm*, 'city of peace.'" Zenger, *Psalms 3*, 334.
15. McCann, "Psalms," 1185.
16. Rogerson and McKay, *Psalms 101–150*, 118.
17. "'Thrones' is metonymy for the people who sat on thrones." Goldingay, *Psalms*, III, 466.

A vv 1–2   the psalmist and his companions ("I" / "us")
              and "house of the LORD"
 B vv 3–4   Jerusalem
   C v 5   "house of David"
 B' vv 6–7   Jerusalem
A' vv 8–9   the psalmist, companions ["I" / "friends"]
              and "house of the LORD"

"While 'the house of David' is central," writes McCann, "its position in the psalm and thus its authority are encompassed by 'the house of the Lord.' David's power is derivative. . . . David's reign is to manifest God's reign."[18]

Structure

Most versions (e.g., NRSV, NIV, ESV) and commentators agree that Psalm 122 has three stanzas: verses 1–2, 3–5, and 6–9.[19] The contents as well as repetitions mark these three stanzas. Eric Zenger notes the contents: "From the perspective of time the three sections, taken in terms of their discourse situation, evoke the present (vv 1–2), the past (vv 3–5), and the future (vv 6–9)."[20] Michael Wilcock highlights the repetitions: "The house of verse 1 and the city of verse 2 provide an inclusio for each of the main sections of the psalm (vv 3–5, 6–9). Both begin with the city (vv 3 and 6) and end with the house, though in two different senses (vv 5 and 9): Jerusalem / the house of David, Jerusalem / the house of the LORD our God."[21] "The thrones of the house of David" (v 5) represent justice in Jerusalem (see Ps 72, pp. 100–101 below) while "the house of the LORD our God" represents God's presence in his chosen city.

We can outline the structure of the psalm as follows:

I. Departure for Jerusalem and arrival (vv 1–2)
II. Jerusalem itself (vv 3–5)
III. Pray for the peace of Jerusalem (vv 6–9)[22]

18. McCann, *Theological Introduction*, 153; and McCann, "Psalms," 1183.
19. See Zenger, *Psalms 3*, 335. Eaton, *The Psalms*, 427, argues for two stanzas, "The psalm may be divided into two parts: praise of the Lord's city (vv 1–5), and prayer for her (vv 6–9)," while Fokkelman, *Major Poems of the Hebrew Bible*, II, 295, argues for five strophes of four cola each.
20. Zenger, *Psalms 3*, 335. Zenger, ibid., 335–36, also states that this threefold structure is strengthened "by the threefold naming of Jerusalem" in each of the three sections: vv 2b, 3a, 6a.
21. Wilcock, *Message of Psalms 73–150*, 225.
22. Verses 6–9 are held together by climactic parallelism (see p. 79 above).

Theocentric Interpretation

While it seems that Psalm 122 focuses on the city of Jerusalem, the name Jerusalem occurring in each stanza, the psalm is really God-centered. For what makes Jerusalem important is that it is the place the LORD selected for a dwelling place on earth, emphasized in the inclusio, "the ballast lines": "the house of the LORD" (v 1), expanded to "the house of the LORD our God" (v 9). God stipulated that the tribes of Israel — here called by the unique name "the tribes of the LORD" (v 4) — make pilgrimages to Jerusalem at the Feast of Unleavened Bread (Passover), the Feast of Weeks (Harvest), and the Feast of Tabernacles (Booths). Israel is to remember God's redemption from Egypt, God's provision of the harvest, and God's care in the desert. They go up to Jerusalem specifically "to give thanks to the LORD" (v 4). Even the psalmist's urging people to "pray for the peace of Jerusalem" (v 6) and seeking the good for Jerusalem (v 9) is "for the sake of the house of the LORD our God" (v 9).

Textual Theme and Goal

Webster and Beach suggest a double theme, "It is a joy to go to Jerusalem to worship at the LORD's house; may the city be blessed with peace."[23] Actually, each of the three stanzas has its own theme so that the psalm has three themes. First, "I was *glad* when they said to me, 'Let us go to the house of the LORD!'" These words, being glad, are laid on the lips of the Israelites. Second, the psalmist and Israel come to Jerusalem *"to give thanks to the name of the LORD"* (vv 3–5). And third, the psalmist urges the Israelites to *"Pray for the peace of Jerusalem"* (vv 6–9). For a unified sermon, however, we need to discover a single theme. It is difficult to come up with an overarching theme that encompasses all three themes. The question then is, Which is the dominant theme under which the other two can be subsumed? Clearly the dominant theme is "Pray for the peace of Jerusalem" because it is the only imperative and it comes at the climax of the psalm. Therefore we can formulate the textual theme as, *While Israel should be glad to go on pilgrimage to the house of the LORD to give thanks to him, they ought to pray especially for the peace of Jerusalem.*

The goal of this psalm would be more precise if we knew its historical setting. The superscription "of David" does not help because the house of the LORD was built by Solomon after David's death. "The psalm has been dated anywhere from the time of David (about 1000 B.C.) and the time of Nehemiah (fifth cen-

---

23. Webster and Beach, *Essential Bible Companion,* 157.

tury B.C.)."[24] Fortunately, knowing the historical setting is less important for the psalms than for other biblical genres. What is clear from the psalm itself ("Pray for the peace of Jerusalem") is that it was a time when there was no peace in Jerusalem. McCann suggests that "especially in the post-exilic era, during which it is likely that the Songs of Ascents were collected, Jerusalem existed in anything but 'security' (v 7b; see 'prosper' in Lam 1:5; see also Neh 1:3; Jer 15:5)."[25] The psalm, then, has a threefold goal, the main goal being to pray for the peace of Jerusalem (v 6, imperative). We can formulate this threefold goal as follows: *to encourage Israel not only to be glad to go to the house of the LORD to give thanks to him but to urge the pilgrims especially to pray for the peace of Jerusalem.*

Ways to Preach Christ

Psalm 122 contains no promise of the coming Messiah, and longitudinal themes is an elaborate, lengthy way to move to Christ in the New Testament. The way of contrast,[26] by definition not very positive, can be incorporated to some extent in redemptive-historical progression. The best way to preach Christ from Psalm 122, I think, is redemptive-historical progression supported by New Testament references. But typology supported by New Testament references offers another option. We shall first consider typology and next redemptive-historical progression.

Typology and New Testament References

The final admonition of Psalm 122 is to pray for the *shalom* (3× in the last stanza) of Jerusalem, the city of peace. The psalmist wants Israel to pray for the peace of Jerusalem because that is where God had chosen to dwell in "the house of the LORD" (vv 1 and 9, inclusio). When Solomon completed the temple, the LORD made his presence known by filling the temple with a cloud, "the glory of the LORD."[27] The temple was a symbol of the LORD dwelling in the midst of his people.

This symbol of the Old Testament temple is a type of Jesus Christ entering

24. Rogerson and McKay, *Psalms 101–150*, 117.

25. McCann, "Psalms," 1184.

26. The psalmist was *glad* when he was invited to go on pilgrimage to Jerusalem. Jesus, by contrast, was *sad* on his final pilgrimage to Jerusalem: Jesus "wept over" Jerusalem (Luke 19:41).

27. "And when the priests came out of the holy place, a cloud filled the house of the LORD, so that the priests could not stand to minister because of the cloud; for the glory of the LORD filled the house of the LORD" (1 Kings 8:10–11; cf. Exod 40:34–35).

our world, God incarnate, Immanuel, "God with us" (Matt 1:23). John writes, "And the Word became flesh and lived [tabernacled] among us, and we have seen his glory, the glory as of a father's only son, full of grace and truth" (John 1:14).

Jesus also saw himself as the new temple where God dwells. When he cleansed the temple, the Jews asked, "What sign can you show us for doing this?" Jesus answered, "Destroy this temple, and in three days I will raise it up. . . . He was speaking of the temple of his body" (John 2:18–21). But even as Jesus in his life fulfilled the Old Testament type of the temple, further fulfillment of this type is yet to come. In Revelation 21:3 John reports, "And I heard a loud voice from the throne saying,

> See, the home of God is among mortals.
> He will dwell with them as their God;
> they will be his peoples,
> and God himself will be with them.

Redemptive-Historical Progression and New Testament References

Although typology can be used to move to Christ, I think a clearer way is redemptive-historical progression supported by New Testament references.

In Old Testament times the command "Pray for the peace of Jerusalem" meant "Pray for the peace of the city of Jerusalem, the political and religious capital of Israel." With the house of David ruling Israel / Judah from Jerusalem and the house of God being in Jerusalem, this city was both the city of David and the city of God. God required of Israel regular pilgrimages to Jerusalem (Deut 16:16–17). They were to "seek the place that the LORD your God will choose out of all your tribes as his habitation to put his name there. You shall go there, bringing there your burnt offerings and your sacrifices. . . . And you shall eat there in the presence of the LORD your God, you and your households together, *rejoicing* in all the undertakings in which the LORD your God has blessed you" (Deut 12:5–7).

In the New Testament, on his final pilgrimage to Jerusalem, Jesus "wept over it, saying, 'If you, even you, had only recognized on this day the things that make for *peace!*'" (Luke 19:41–42). Jesus is quoting Psalm 122:8 from the Septuagint. Then Jesus predicts the fall of Jerusalem (Luke 19:41–44), which was fulfilled in A.D. 70 when Roman soldiers led by Titus razed the city and temple.

With the death and resurrection of Jesus and the outpouring of the Holy Spirit, the Old Testament temple as God's house was replaced by God's people, the church (1 Cor 6:19; Eph 2:19–22), and ultimately by the New Jerusalem (Rev 21:1–3) (see further the "Sermon Exposition" below).

Psalm 122 (121)

Sermon Theme, Goal, and Need

We formulated the textual theme as, "While Israel should be glad to go on pilgrimage to the house of the Lord to give thanks to him, they ought to pray especially for the peace of Jerusalem." In considering the New Testament context (see above, "Ways to Preach Christ"), we noticed that redemptive history has moved on from the temple in Jerusalem being the house of the Lord to God's people, the church of Christ, being the temple where the Holy Spirit dwells. The church now looks forward to the new Jerusalem which Jesus will bring on earth at his Second Coming. We will need to change the sermon theme accordingly: *While God's people should be glad to go to the house of the Lord (church) to give thanks to him, they ought to pray especially for the peace of the church and the new Jerusalem.*

The goal of the psalm was "to encourage Israel not only to be glad to go to the house of the Lord to give thanks to him but to urge the pilgrims especially to pray for the peace of Jerusalem." In line with the sermon theme, the goal of this sermon is *to encourage God's people not only to be glad to go to the house of the Lord to give thanks to him but to urge them especially to pray for the peace of the church and the new Jerusalem.* The main goal shows that the need addressed in this sermon is that the church is not at peace: there is division within the church — strife within, persecution from without — while the promised peace of the new Jerusalem seems very distant.

Liturgy, Scripture Reading, and Sermon Outline

Verse 1, "I was glad when they said to me, 'Let us go to the house of the Lord!'" can be used as the call to worship.

Scripture reading can be done by two good readers: the first reading the first stanza (vv 1–2, the "I"); the second reading the second stanza (vv 3–5, about Jerusalem); and the first reading the third stanza (vv 6–9, the "I" again).

The structure of this psalm can be used for the sermon outline, adding moves to Christ at appropriate places and especially at the end.

    I. Departure for Jerusalem and arrival (vv 1–2)
    II. Jerusalem itself (vv 3–5)
    III. Pray for the peace of Jerusalem (vv 6–9)[28]
    IV. Pray for the church and the new Jerusalem (NT)

28. VanGemeren, *Psalms,* 897, suggests "the following expository structure."
    A The Pilgrim's Joy (vv 1–2)
      B The Pilgrim's Praise (vv 3–5)
        C The Pilgrim's Prayer (vv 6–9)

Sermon Exposition

Since the need addressed is that the church today is not at peace, one can use the sermon introduction to demonstrate this need. One can remind the congregation of divisions within the church or relate specific instances of persecution of the church today.[29] Next, transition to Old Testament Jerusalem, which was seldom at peace. Yet it was called the city of God because God's house, God's temple, was there. God had chosen Jerusalem as his dwelling place on earth. Moreover, God had instructed Israel to make pilgrimages to Jerusalem at the three great feasts: the Feast of Unleavened Bread or Passover, the Feast of Weeks or Harvest, and the Feast of Tabernacles or Booths.

Psalm 122 was associated with these pilgrimages to Jerusalem. That is why its heading reads "A Song of Ascents." The pilgrims would sing this psalm and others as they ascended Mount Zion where the temple was located. The Psalm has three stanzas: verses 1–2, 3–5, and 6–9.

The psalmist begins the first stanza in the past. Verse 1, "I was glad when they said to me, 'Let us go to the house of the LORD!'" The invitation to go to the house of the LORD may have come from family or friends.[30] They would travel together and have a good time together. At night they would probably sit around campfires sharing news, telling stories, and singing songs.

The best-known pilgrimage is that of Mary and Joseph with the twelve-year-old Jesus going "to Jerusalem for the festival of the Passover"[31] (Luke 2:41). Luke relates that at the end of the festival, Mary and Joseph journeyed home without Jesus. They simply assumed that Jesus was with a group of travelers ahead of them. They walked the whole day and then at night began to look for him among relatives and friends. They could not find him anywhere. The next morning, almost in a panic, they walked back all the way to Jerusalem, perhaps some twelve miles. They could not find him that second day. Finally,

---

29. See, e.g., Paul Marshall, with Lela Gilbert, *Their Blood Cries Out: The Worldwide Tragedy of Modern Christians Who Are Dying for Their Faith* (Dallas: Word Books, 1997) and Paul Marshall, Lela Gilbert, and Nina Shea, *Persecuted: The Global Assault on Christians* (Nashville: Thomas Nelson, 2013). For up-to-date examples, googling "Persecution of Christians" provides an abundance of examples.

30. Cf. Isa 2:3, "Many peoples shall come and say, 'Come, let us go up to the mountain of the LORD, to the house of the God of Jacob . . .'" and Jer 31:6, "For there shall be a day when sentinels will call in the hill country of Ephraim: 'Come, let us go up to Zion, to the LORD our God.'"

31. Although God had commanded the Israelites in Deuteronomy 16:16, "Three times a year all your males shall appear before the LORD your God at the place that he will choose," those who could make the pilgrimage only once a year tended to come to Jerusalem for the Passover Feast.

on the third day, they found Jesus in the temple "sitting among the teachers," the wisest rabbis in Israel.

Understandably, Mary said to Jesus, "Child, why have you treated us like this? Look, your father and I have been searching for you in great anxiety." Amazingly, twelve-year-old Jesus said to them, "Why were you searching for me? Did you not know that I must be in my Father's house?" (Luke 2:48–49). Jesus had to be in his Father's house. That was the goal of all Israelites on pilgrimage: they had to be in God's house.

The psalmist says, "I was glad when they said to me, 'Let us go to the house of the Lord!'" He is glad not merely because they will have a good time on the journey together. He is glad especially because of *where* he is going. The destination of this journey is "the house of the Lord."[32] That fills him with tremendous joy. Psalm 84 (vv 2, 4) puts it this way:

> My soul longs, indeed it faints for the courts of the Lord;
>   my heart and my flesh sing for *joy* to the living God. . . .
> *Happy* are those who live in your house, ever singing your praise.

Interestingly, the psalmist does not spend any time on the journey. That is not important for him. Crucial is the destination: "the house of the Lord."

Verse 2 describes the psalmist's arrival in Jerusalem: "Our feet are standing[33] within your gates, O Jerusalem." Jerusalem is so important because that is where "the house of the Lord" is located. Jerusalem is the city of God. Psalm 132:13 says,

> For the Lord has *chosen* Zion [Jerusalem];
>   he has desired it for his [earthly] habitation.

Another psalm declares that "the Lord *loves the gates of Zion* more than all the dwellings of Jacob" (Ps 87:2). This first stanza of Psalm 122 is filled with gladness at being invited to "go to the house of the Lord" and arriving in Jerusalem, the city of God.

---

32. The Hebrew word order is "to the house of the Lord let us go," thus emphasizing "the house of the Lord."

33. Goldingay, *Psalms*, III, 463, argues that v 2 "suggests that it specifically looks back on coming to the city and thus belongs to the moment of leaving to go back home." On p. 264 he allows that "the verbal expression in v 2 could signify 'our feet have become standing,' and therefore are standing now (so NRSV, NIV) rather than 'our feet have been standing,' but a noun clause would be the more natural way to say 'our feet are standing.'" Eaton, *The Psalms*, 427, states, "The construction can be understood: 'our feet have become standing, have come to stand,' rather than 'were standing' as Dahood."

The second stanza (vv 3–5) deals with the reasons why the pilgrims go to Jerusalem. It offers four reasons: first, they go up to Jerusalem because *it is a beautiful city offering safety to its inhabitants.* Verse 3, "Jerusalem — built as a city that is bound firmly together." We can see the pilgrims viewing the city from a distance as a compact, beautiful communal group of houses and buildings surrounded by enormous city walls.[34] This city is secure; its inhabitants are safe.[35] Psalm 48 encourages pilgrims, "Walk about Zion, go all around it, count its towers, consider well its ramparts; go through its citadels, that you may tell the next generation that this is God, our God forever and ever. He will be our guide forever" (Ps 48:12–14). The security Jerusalem offers its inhabitants and pilgrims is practically equated with the security God offers.

The second reason for traveling to Jerusalem is to express *the unity of the different tribes.* Verse 4 reads, "To it the tribes go up, the tribes of the LORD as was decreed for Israel, to give thanks to the name of the LORD." This verse says that "the *tribes* go up." There were twelve tribes in Israel: the tribe of Judah, Benjamin, Levi, Dan and eight others. The tribes were distinguished by their differences in their forebears and their location in the Promised Land: north or south, west of the Jordan river or east. But here, and only here in the Bible, they are called not tribe of Judah or the tribes of Israel but "the tribes *of the LORD.*" In spite of their differences in heritage and geography, they are all united in being "the tribes of the LORD." The different tribes are one in "their common loyalty to the LORD."[36] The second reason, then, for traveling to Jerusalem together is to express the unity of God's people.

The third and main reason for going up to Jerusalem is *to give thanks to the LORD.* As verse 4 puts it, "To it the tribes go up, the tribes of the LORD as was decreed for Israel, *to give thanks to the name of the LORD.*" In Deuteronomy 16:16 we read that the LORD decreed: "Three times a year all your males shall appear before the LORD your God at the place that he will choose: at the festival of unleavened bread [Passover],[37] at the festival of weeks [Harvest], and at the

---

34. McCann, "Psalms," 1184, remarks, "It is possible that it is not so much Jerusalem's architecture that is being praised but Jerusalem's ability to bring people together." Indeed, the NEB translates, "where people come together in unity." But I think the psalmist has in mind the architecture of Jerusalem, which the pilgrims would see from a distance: Jerusalem with its gates (v 1), walls and towers (v 7), and here a city "bound firmly together" (v 3). Cf. Alter, *Book of Psalms,* 439, "'Joined fast together.' The most probable reference is to the fortifications of Jerusalem or, specifically, to the protective wall that encloses it."

35. "In times of dangers from wars, the city offered protection not only for its inhabitants but also for peasant families living in the neighborhood (cf. Lev 26:25; Josh 10:20; Jer 4:5; 8:14; 35:11)." Zenger, *Psalms 3,* 339.

36. Davidson, *Vitality of Worship,* 410.

37. The LORD had decreed, "You shall offer the passover sacrifice to the LORD your God,

festival of booths [Tabernacles]." At the Passover Feast the pilgrims would especially thank the LORD for freeing Israel from the slavery in Egypt. At the Harvest
Festival the pilgrims would thank the LORD especially for providing their daily
bread. And at the Feast of Booths the pilgrims would thank the LORD especially
for providing for their daily needs in hard times, such as when their fathers and
mothers wandered in the desert for forty years.

The pilgrims are to express their thanks to the LORD not just in words but
also in deeds. The LORD stipulated, "They shall not appear before the LORD
empty-handed; all shall give as they are able, according to the blessing of the
LORD your God that he has given you" (Deut 16:16–17).

The fourth reason for the pilgrims to go up to Jerusalem is *to celebrate and
receive justice.* Verse 5 reads, "For there [in Jerusalem] the thrones for judgment
were set up, the thrones of the house of David." "The thrones for judgment" are
the seats where judges dispense justice. This verse equates "the thrones for judgment" with "the thrones[38] of the house of David." In Israel the supreme judge
was the king.[39]

"Pilgrimage season was likely a time when conflicts and disputes unsettled in
the country courts were brought to the royal officials."[40] In Psalm 72 Israel prays,

> Give the king your justice, O God,
>   and your righteousness to a king's son.
> May he judge your people with righteousness,
>   and your poor with justice. . . .
> May he defend the cause of the poor of the people,
>   give deliverance to the needy,
>   and crush the oppressor (Ps 72:1–2, 4).

This second stanza of Psalm 122, then, gives four reasons for the pilgrimage
to Jerusalem. First, they travel to Jerusalem because it is a beautiful city that

---

from the flock and the herd, at the place that the LORD will choose as a dwelling for his name"
(Deut 16:2).

38. "'Thrones' is metonymy for the people who sat on thrones. . . . The plurality of thrones
reflects the king's associating his son(s) and potential successor(s) ('David's household') with him
in such aspects of government; further, the demands of dispute resolution could be overwhelming
and would not be undertaken by the king alone but by a judiciary appointed by him (cf. 2 Sam
15:2–6; also Exod 18:13–26)." Goldingay, *Psalms,* III, 466.

39. See, e.g., 2 Samuel 8:15, "So David reigned over all Israel; and David administered justice
and equity to all his people." 1 Kings 7:7 tells us that Solomon "made the Hall of the Throne where
he was to pronounce judgment, the Hall of Justice."

40. Mays, *Psalms,* 393.

offers God's safety and security. Second, people from all twelve tribes journey to Jerusalem to express the unity of "the tribes of the LORD." Third, and this is the main reason, they go up to Jerusalem to give thanks to the LORD for his deliverance from slavery and for his provisions for them. And finally, they journey to Jerusalem to celebrate and receive justice.

And now comes the third and final stanza, the climax of this psalm. Verse 6a, "Pray for the peace of Jerusalem!"[41] The verb "pray" is the only imperative in this psalm. It is a command. The pilgrims must "pray for the peace of Jerusalem!"

The psalm gives three reasons why the pilgrims should pray for Jerusalem. The first reason, "Jerusalem must be prayed for because it is the religious and political capital of the nation."[42] The pilgrims must pray for the peace, the *shalom*, of the city. They are to pray for a "calm undisturbed by social conflict within and dread of enemies without. . . . It is the well-being that is composed of both well-doing and doing well (see 'good' in v 9)."[43]

Verses 6b–7 are set off in quotation marks because they express the prayer of the pilgrims: "May they prosper who love you. Peace be within your walls, and security within your towers." When the pilgrims say, "May they prosper who love you," they mean "prosper" in the broadest sense: "May all that is needful be granted to such as love the Lord's holy city."[44]

The pilgrims go on to say, "Peace be within your walls, and security within your towers." The "walls" and "towers" are signs of the city's secure defenses against the enemy without. But notice that this "is more than a prayer against external foes . . . ; it asks above all for concord: peace 'within . . . within . . . within.'"[45] "Peace be *within* your walls, and security *within* your towers."

Verse 8 offers a second reason why the pilgrims should pray for the peace of Jerusalem. Not only should they pray for Jerusalem because it is "the religious and political capital of the nation." Verse 8 adds, "*For the sake of* my relatives and friends I will say, 'Peace be within you.'" Apparently the psalmist has relatives and friends living in this embattled city. Thinking of them he will naturally pray, "Peace be *within* you."

But even more important than relatives and friends is the third reason. The

---

41. "The opening line of verse 6 reads in Hebrew *ša'ălû šəlôm yərûšālāim* and such assonance suggests that it may be a proverbial expression — 'ask about [pray for] the peace of Jerusalem.'" Hayes, *Preaching the New Common Lectionary, Year A, Advent . . .* , 16–17.

42. Leopold Sabourin, *The Psalms*, 214.

43. Mays, *Psalms*, 393.

44. Leupold, *Exposition of the Psalms*, 876. Cf. A. Anderson, *Psalms 73–150*, 857. The verb translated as "prosper" "usually means 'to be quiet, secure.'"

45. Kidner, *Psalms 73–150*, 434.

house of the LORD is in Jerusalem. Therefore verse 9 concludes with the climax, *"For the sake of the house of the LORD our God,* I will seek your good."[46]

The main point of this psalm is that Israelites should *pray for the peace of Jerusalem.* Is this also its message for Christians today? Should we Christians pray for the peace of Jerusalem? Of course, we should — even as we should pray for the peace of Damascus, Gaza City, Boston, and Paris. But the Jerusalem for which Psalm 122 urges us to pray has evolved.

When Jesus made his final pilgrimage to Jerusalem to celebrate the Passover Feast, he was not glad but sad. Jesus wept over Jerusalem, saying, "If you, even you, had only recognized on this day the things that make for *peace!*[47] But now they are hidden from your eyes. Indeed, the days will come upon you, when your enemies will set up ramparts around you and surround you, and hem you in on every side. They will crush you to the ground, you and your children within you, and they will not leave within you one stone upon another; because you did not recognize the time of your visitation from God" (Luke 19:41–44). Jesus' prediction of the destruction of Jerusalem and the temple was fulfilled in A.D. 70 when Roman soldiers led by Titus destroyed the city and God's temple.

With the death and resurrection of Jesus and the outpouring of the Holy Spirit, the New Testament church now replaces the Old Testament temple as "a dwelling place for God." Paul writes in Ephesians 2:19–22 that the church, "the household of God," is "built upon the foundation of the apostles and prophets, with Christ Jesus himself as the cornerstone. In him the whole structure is joined together and grows into a holy temple in the Lord; in whom you also are built together spiritually into a dwelling place for God."

The Christian church worldwide has replaced the Old Testament temple as the "dwelling place for God." Think of it: our local church is "a dwelling place for God"! If the Old Testament pilgrims were glad to "go to the house of the LORD," how much more should we be *glad* to go to church, the dwelling place for God. If the Old Testament pilgrims traveled to Jerusalem to express the *unity* of "the tribes of the LORD," how much more should we be eager to go to church to exhibit the unity of the body of Christ. And if the Old Testament pilgrims went up to Jerusalem to give thanks to the LORD, how much more should we yearn to go to church to *thank* the Lord for giving us his only Son, Jesus; for forgiveness of sins; for making us members of the body of Christ; for his daily provisions.

46. "The final wish for peace is accompanied by reasons: friends and relatives live there (v 8), and the temple is there (v 9). Because of all this, the psalmist promises the city, 'I will seek your good.'" Limburg, *Psalms,* 428. Cf. Leupold, *Exposition of the Psalms,* 877, "Concern for God's sanctuary should motivate the prayer for the city that houses that sanctuary."

47. Jesus is quoting Psalm 122:8 from the LXX.

The psalmist urged Israel, "Pray for the peace of Jerusalem." Today we should pray for the peace of the church of Jesus! Pray that the enmity between groups within the church may be overcome; that the wounds we have caused each other will be healed; that we may be eager to forgive even as we ourselves have been forgiven; that Christians of all denominations may truly love each other as brothers and sisters in the Lord Jesus.

Pray for the peace of the church of Jesus! Pray that the violence aimed at the church from without may cease. Pray that the persecuted church of Jesus around the world may experience peace so that it can perform its mission in the world without hindrance. Pray that the church of Jesus may be a safe haven for all peoples and nations.

But the church as the "dwelling place for God" is not the final goal of redemptive history. In the book of Revelation John writes that he saw "a new heaven and a *new earth*. . . . And I saw the *holy city, the new Jerusalem,* coming down out of heaven from God, prepared as a bride adorned for her husband. And I heard a loud voice from the throne saying, 'See the home [tabernacle] of God is among mortals. He will dwell [tabernacle] with them as their God'" (Rev 21:1-3).[48] Soon Jesus will come again (Advent) to bring this new Jerusalem, his church in heaven, to this earth and establish God's perfect kingdom on earth.

While we pray for the peace of the church on earth, we await the *new* Jerusalem. We live in the time of Advent. We look forward to Jesus' coming again to establish his perfect kingdom on earth. As we pray for the church today, we should also pray for the coming of this new Jerusalem. We will be ever so glad when it comes. It will be far more beautiful than the old Jerusalem.[49] It will demonstrate the perfect *unity* of God's people. It will manifest the *justice* of God's kingdom, which the old Jerusalem could not attain. It will truly be a city of *peace.* It will offer God's people the perfect opportunity to thank and praise the LORD.

Prayer[50]

O Lord, we long for the day when our feet will stand
    within the gates of the new Jerusalem.
Until then, as we journey toward home, guide and protect your church:
    be our unity, clothe us in truth, and keep us in your peace.
We pray in the name of Jesus the Christ. Amen.

---

48. Cf. Hebrews 12:22-24, "But you have come to Mount Zion and to the city of the living God, the heavenly Jerusalem . . . , and to Jesus, the mediator of a new covenant, and to the sprinkled blood that speaks a better word than the blood of Abel."

49. See Rev 21:10-27 on the beauty of the new Jerusalem.

50. From *Psalms for All Seasons,* 806.

Psalm 122 (121)

Song[51]

Jerusalem the golden, descending from above,
    the city of God's presence, the vision of God's love –
I know not, oh, I know not what joys await us there,
    what radiancy of glory, what bliss beyond compare!

They stand, those halls of Zion, all jubilant with song,
    so bright with many an angel and all the martyr throng.
The Prince is ever in them, the daylight is serene;
    the tree of life and healing has leaves of richest green.

There is the throne of David, and there, from pain released,
    the shout of those who triumph, the song of those who feast.
And all who with their leader have conquered in the fight,
    forever and forever are robed in purest white.

How lovely is that city, the home of God's elect!
    How beautiful the country that eager hearts expect!
O Christ, in mercy bring us to that eternal shore
    where Father, Son, and Spirit are worshiped evermore.

51. Bernard of Cluny, 12th cent.; trans. John M. Neale, 1858, alt. Public Domain. *Psalter Hymnal* (1987), # 618; *Lift Up Your Hearts,* # 488; and 16 other hymnals (see *Lift Up Your Hearts*).

CHAPTER 4

"Give the King Your Justice, O God"

Psalm 72 (71)

The Revised Common Lectionary assigns Psalm 72:1–7, 10–14 for reading for Epiphany during all three years (see Chapter 8 below), while it assigns Psalm 72:1–7, 18–19 for the second Sunday of Advent in Year A as a response to the reading of Isaiah 11:1–10, "The Peaceful Kingdom." The whole psalm makes a wonderful preaching text for Advent. But preachers should not be too eager to move to Christ in their sermons, for this familiar psalm is first of all a prayer for the king of Israel.

Text and Context

Selection of the preaching text is not as easy with Psalm 72 as it is with most psalms. The problem arises because Psalm 72 concludes Book II of the psalms, and the editor, as he does to conclude every one of the five books, has added a doxology (vv 18–19). He has also added in verse 20, "The prayers of David son of Jesse are ended." The question is, therefore, shall we select as preaching text the verses 1–17[1] or extend it to verse 19 or even to verse 20?

Although the verses 1–17 are a literary unit and probably the original psalm,[2] there are good reasons for extending the text to verse 19 and even to verse 20. In its final canonical form verses 18–20 are now part of Psalm 72. Moreover, literarily

---

1. Cf. Robert Alter, *Art of Biblical Poetry,* 130, "In what follows, I omit the last three verses of Psalm 72, which clearly belong to the editorial formula of conclusion of Book Two of Psalms, and not to the poem itself." For arguments pro and con adding verses 18–19, see Erich Zenger, *Psalms 2,* 209–10.

2. John Kselman, "Psalm 72: Some Observations on Structure," *Bulletin of the American Schools of Oriental Research* 220 (1975; pp. 77–81): 78, argues for an inclusio of vv 1 and 15–17.

this doxology provides an inclusio for the psalm. The verses 1–17 mention the name of God only once: "O God, give the king your justice" (v 1, with the name of God in the prominent first position in Hebrew). The doxology suitably doubles back to that beginning: "Blessed be the LORD, the God of Israel" (v 18). We can also include verse 20 in the reading since it will help us determine whether the editor ascribes this psalm to Solomon (superscription, "Of Solomon") or to David ("The prayers of David son of Jesse are ended").

As to its context, since Psalm 72 is a royal psalm, we can compare it with other royal psalms, especially Psalm 2 which the editor has placed in the prominent position of introducing all the following psalms (see pp. 25–28 above). As "the LORD and his anointed" work in tandem in Psalm 2:2, so Psalm 72:1 asks, "Give the king *your* justice, O God, and *your* righteousness to a king's son." Moreover, Psalm 2:8 promises the king universal dominion: "Ask of me, and I will make the nations your heritage, and the ends of the earth your possession." Psalm 72:8 expresses the same desire: "May he have dominion from sea to sea, and from the River to the ends of the earth." Psalm 2:11 urges the rulers of the earth, "Serve (*'ābad*) the LORD with fear," while Psalm 72:11 voices the wish, "May all kings fall down before him, all nations give him service (*'ābad*)."

The superscription "Of Solomon," or "For Solomon," signals the editor's hint to read this psalm against the background of Solomon's reign (1 Kings 1–10). The links between 1 Kings 1–10 and Psalm 72 are indeed remarkable. When Solomon was anointed king, "All the people said, 'Long live King Solomon!'" (1 Kings 1:39). Psalm 72:15 prays for the king, "Long may he live!" Solomon asked the LORD for "an understanding mind to govern your people, able to discern between good and evil" and the LORD gave him "a wise and discerning mind; no one like you has been before you and no one like you shall arise after you" (1 Kings 3:9, 12). Psalm 72:1–2 similarly asks God, "Give . . . your righteousness to a king's son. May he judge your people with righteousness, and your poor with justice."

Under Solomon's kingship, "Judah and Israel were as numerous as the sand by the sea; they ate and drank and were happy" (1 Kings 4:20). Psalm 72:16 requests, "May there be abundance of grain in the land . . . ; and may people blossom in the cities." During Solomon's rule "people came from all nations to hear the wisdom of Solomon" (1 Kings 4:34), also the queen of Sheba (1 Kings 10:1–10), and brought him gifts (1 Kings 10:10, 24–25). Psalm 72:10, 15 asks: "May the kings of Tarshish and of the isles render him tribute, may the kings of Sheba and Seba bring gifts. . . . May gold of Sheba be given to him." The queen of Sheba concludes her speech to Solomon with a doxology: "Blessed be the LORD your God, who has delighted in you and set you on the throne of Israel!" (1 Kings 10:9). Psalm 72 concludes with a similar doxology, "Blessed be the LORD, the God of Israel, who alone does wondrous things" (72:18).

We should also note the context of prophets who express similar thoughts to those in Psalm 72. For example, Psalm 72:8 says, "May he have dominion from sea to sea, and from the River to the ends of the earth." Zechariah 9:10 uses identical words to describe the coming king of Israel, "He shall command peace to the nations; his dominion shall be from sea to sea, and from the River to the ends of the earth." The lectionary itself assigns Psalm 72 as a response to Isaiah 11:1–10. Note the similar ideas expressed in the two passages. Isaiah 11:1–5 predicts, "A shoot shall come out from the stump of Jesse [Ps 72:1, "a king's son"]. . . . The spirit of the LORD shall rest on him [Ps 72:1, "Give the king *your* justice, O God"]. . . . With righteousness he shall judge the poor, and decide with equity for the meek of the earth [Ps 72:2, "May he judge your people with righteousness, and your poor with justice"]; he shall strike the earth with the rod of his mouth, and with the breath of his lips he shall kill the wicked [Ps 72:4, 9, "May he . . . crush the oppressor. . . . May his foes bow down before him, and his enemies lick the dust"]. Righteousness shall be the belt around his waist [Ps 72:7, "In his days may righteousness flourish"]."

Literary Interpretation

Psalm 72 is classified as a royal psalm because it deals with the person or office of the king. "More specifically, Psalm 72 is probably also an accession or coronation psalm, a prayer for the king at the beginning of his reign."[3] Before we look at the psalm's parallelisms, imagery, repetition, and structure, we need to discuss the difficulty of translating the Hebrew imperfect tenses.

Ambiguous Verb Tenses

A key interpretive issue is whether Psalm 72 is a prophecy about a coming king or a prayer for the king of Israel, or both. The issue turns on the ambiguity of the Hebrew imperfect verb tense. Verse 1 begins with the imperative, "Give the king your justice, O God. . . ." All the following verbs are imperfects, which can be translated into English either as future tenses (predictions, "he will") or as jussives (prayers, "may he"). The Authorized Version (as well as the Septuagint) translated all thirty-one Hebrew imperfects in verses 2–17 as future tenses; e.g., vv 5, 7–8: "They *shall* fear thee as long as the sun and moon endure throughout all generations. . . . In his days *shall* the righteous flourish; and abundance of

---

3. Tate, *Psalms 51–100*, 222.

peace so long as the moon endureth. He *shall* have dominion also from sea to sea, and from the river unto the ends of the earth." Small wonder Isaac Watts, in *The Psalms of David, Imitated in the Language of the New Testament,*[4] began Psalm 72 with,

> Jesus shall reign where'er the sun
>   does his successive journeys run,
> his kingdom stretch from shore to shore,
>   till moons shall wax and wane no more.

Modern translations are not so quick to translate the Hebrew imperfects as future tenses. For example, the NRSV (similarly the NIV) translate the verses 5, 7–8 as,

> *May* he live while the sun endures,
>   as long as the moon, throughout all generations. . . .
> In his days *may* righteousness flourish
>   and peace abound, until the moon is no more.
> *May* he have dominion from sea to sea,
>   and from the River to the ends of the earth.

The context will have to decide whether a Hebrew imperfect should be translated as a future (prediction) or a wish (prayer).[5] It is clear that Psalm 72 is first of all a prayer for the king of Israel, for it opens with, "O God, give the king your justice" (v 1) and the editor closes it with, "Amen and Amen" (v 19). Therefore, the modern translations are correct in translating the Hebrew imperfects as wishes ("may he").

But this conclusion still leaves a few questions. Since this canonical psalm is God's Word for his people, could God have embedded in this prayer for Israel's current king predictions about a coming king? Or, to put it another way, Could the progression in redemptive history later change the meaning of this psalm from a prayer for Israel's current king to a prayer for Israel's coming King?

Another question concerns the ambiguity of the Hebrew imperfect verbs. Is it possible that the continuous use of this ambiguous verb form in this psalm is intentional? Purposeful ambiguity is at home in poetry. Metaphors reveal surprising shifts in meaning; synonymous parallelism does not intend an ei-

---

4. Michael Wilcock, *Message of Psalms 1–72*, 249.

5. See ibid., 250; Gerald Wilson, *Psalms*, I, 986–87, 992–93; and Gordon Wenham, *The Psalter Reclaimed*, 179.

ther–or but a both–and. Could the use of this ambiguous verb tense in this psalm indicate not an either–or but a both–and? Not just a wish but also a prediction?[6] We will have to leave these questions open-ended for now (see "Promise-Fulfilment" below). But we shall first seek to enter further into the meaning of Psalm 72 by analyzing its parallelisms, imagery, repetition of key-words, and its structure.

Parallelisms

The psalm was composed with intricate parallelisms, one synonymous (v 1), one antithetic (v 4c), five climactic (vv 2 and 4a,b, 8–11, 12–14, 16, 18a–19), and the remainder some form of advancing parallelism. Here is the snapshot of the parallelisms of Psalm 72.

1Give the king your justice, O God,	A
and your righteousness to a king's son.[7]	A'
2May he judge your people with righteousness,	B
and your poor with justice.[8]	+ B'
3May the mountains yield prosperity (šālôm) for the people,	C
and the hills, in righteousness.	+ C'
4May he defend the cause of the poor of the people,[9]	+ B''
give deliverance to the needy,	+ B'''
and crush the oppressor.[10]	− D

6. Cf. Alter, *Art of Biblical Poetry*, 131, "Taking advantage of the ambiguity of Hebrew verb tenses, the poem manages at once to be prayer, prophecy, portrait, and benediction. Strictly speaking, there are only two tenses in biblical Hebrew, the perfect and the imperfect. The latter, which is employed throughout Psalm 72, can be used for future actions, or habitual repeated actions, or as a jussive or optative, for actions the speaker wishes would happen, and the force of the verbs in our poem seems to overlap all these possibilities."

7. This would be advancing parallelism if "the king" and "a king's son" were two different people, such as the king and the crown prince. But it can be argued that they refer to the same person; hence synonymous parallelism. Cf. Williams, *Psalms 1–72*, 520, "The reason that the King is also identified as the King's Son is to assert that He is legitimate, standing in the royal line."

8. "Your poor" is more specific than "your people"; therefore advancing parallelism (+).

9. Picks up on the people and the poor in verse 2; therefore +B''. We can call this "broken climactic parallelism." For other examples of this, see vv 15a, 17a, b and 18a, 19a, b below. See also p. 79 n. 13 above.

10. A new topic, "the oppressor," and "crush" is antithetic parallelism vs "deliverance" in v 4b.

₅May he live while the sun endures,	A
and as long as the moon, throughout all generations.	+ A′
₆May he be like rain that falls on the mown grass,	B
like showers that water the earth.	+ B′
₇In his days may righteousness flourish	C
and peace (*šālôm*)¹¹ abound, until the moon is no more.	+ C′

₈May he have dominion from sea to sea,	A
and from the River to the ends of the earth.	+ A′
₉May his foes bow down before him,	+ A″
and his enemies lick the dust.	+ A‴
₁₀May the kings of Tarshish and of the isles render him tribute,	+ A⁗
may the kings of Sheba and Seba bring gifts.	+ A⁗′
₁₁May all kings fall down before him,	+ A⁗″
all nations give him service.	+ A⁗‴

₁₂For he delivers the needy when they call,	A
the poor and those who have no helper.	+ A′
₁₃He has pity on the weak and the needy,	+ A″
and saves the lives of the needy.	+ A‴
₁₄From oppression and violence he redeems their life;	+ A⁗
and precious is their blood in his sight.	+ A⁗′

₁₅Long may he live!	A
May gold of Sheba be given to him.	B
May prayer be made for him continually,	C
and blessings invoked for him all day long.	+ C′
₁₆May there be abundance of grain in the land;	D
may it wave on the tops of the mountains;	+ D′
may its fruit be like Lebanon;	+ D″
and may people blossom in the cities like the grass of the field.	E

₁₇May his name endure forever,¹²	+ A′
his fame continue as long as the sun.	+ A″
May all nations be blessed in him;¹³	+ B′
may they pronounce him happy.	+ B″

11. Picks up the *šālôm* of verse 3.
12. Picks up on v 15a but advances with "forever"; therefore +A′.
13. Advances from "Sheba" (v 15b) to "all nations"; therefore +B′.

18Blessed be the LORD, the God[14] of Israel,	A
who alone does wondrous things.	B
19Blessed be his glorious name forever;	+ A'
may his glory fill the whole earth.	+ A''

Amen and Amen.

20The prayers of David son of Jesse are ended.

Imagery

Psalm 72 uses similes and metaphors associated primarily with nature: "May he be *like rain* that falls on *the mown grass, like showers* that water the earth" (v 6). "The similes signify that his reign should be beneficial to the lives of the people as well as refreshing."[15] "May he have dominion . . . to *the ends of the earth*" (v 8). "May . . . his enemies *lick the dust*"(v 9).[16] "Precious is their *blood* [life] in his sight" (v 14). "May people *blossom* [flourish] in the cities *like the grass of the field*" (v 16). "May his *name* [person] endure forever" (v 17).

Repetition of Keywords

A major concern in Psalm 72 is "righteousness" and its synonyms, as can be seen in its frequent repetitions:

1Give the king your *justice*, O God,
and your *righteousness* to a king's son.
2May he *judge* your people with *righteousness*,
and your poor with *justice*.
3May the mountains yield prosperity (*šālôm*) for the people,
and the hills, in *righteousness*.
4May he defend (*šāpaṭ*[17]) the cause of the poor of the people,
give deliverance to the needy. . . .
7In his days may *righteousness* flourish
and peace (*šālôm*) abound, until the moon is no more.

14. Inclusio with "God" in verse 1.

15. Ross, *Commentary on the Psalms*, II, 538.

16. "'Lick the dust' is figurative (a metonymy of adjunct) for either subjugation or self-humiliation (Isa 49:23; Mic 7:17)." Ross, ibid., 539.

17. *Šāpaṭ* is a synonym of *dîn* ("judge") in verse 2. See A. Anderson, *Psalms 1–72*, 519–20. Alter, *Book of Psalms*, 248, translates v 4a, "May he bring justice to the lowly of the people."

In fact, verses 1 and 2 stress this concern for righteousness / justice with inverted parallelism (ABBA): justice, righteousness, righteousness, justice.

Related to this concern for righteousness / justice is the concern for those who are frequently denied justice: "the poor" (3×, vv 2, 4, 12) and "the needy" (4×, vv 4, 12, 13 [2×]). In addition we find the name "God" (*'ĕlohîm*) twice (vv 1, 18), "prosperity / peace" (*šālôm*) twice (vv 3, 7), "sun" twice (vv 5, 17), "moon" twice (vv 5, 7), and "earth" three times (vv 6, 8, 19).

David Dorsey uses some of these repetitions to propose a three-part chiastic structure for verses 1–17:[18]

    A prayer for justice, prosperity, and the king's long life (72:1–7)
- "may he defend the *afflicted* (*'ānî*)"; "may he save the *needy* (*'ebyôn*)"
- "may the *mountains* yield prosperity"
- "as long as the *sun* endures"

      B   CENTER: prayer for ascendency over all nations (72:8–11)

    A' prayer for justice, prosperity, and the king's long life (72:12–17)
- "may he defend the *needy* (*'ebyôn*). . . .and the *afflicted* (*'ānî*); "may he pity . . . the *needy* (*'ebyôn*); and may he save the lives of the *needy* (*'ebyôn*)"
- "may there be abundance of grain . . . on the *mountains*"
- "may his name endure as long as the *sun*"

Structure

Bible translators and commentators are not agreed on the structure of Psalm 72. At least nine proposals are current:

Verse Divisions										Advocates
1	–	4 / 5–7 / 8	–	11 / 12–14 / 15	–	17	/	18–19 / 20		NRSV, ESV, Tanner[19]
1	–	4 / 5–7 / 8	–	11 / 12–14 / 15 / 16 / 17			/	18–19 / 20		NKJV
1	–	4 / 5–7 / 8	–	11 / 12	–	15 / 16 –17	/	18–19 / 20		NASB
1–2 / 3	–	7 / 8	–	11 / 12–14 / 15	–	17b / 17c, d / 18–19 / 20				NIV
1 / 2	–	4 / 5–7 / 8	–	11 / 12–14 / 15	–	17	/	18	– 20	Kselman, Zenger[20]

---

18. David A. Dorsey, *The Literary Structure of the Old Testament: A Commentary on Genesis-Malachi* (Grand Rapids: Baker, 1999), 175.

19. Tanner in deClaissé-Walford, Jacobson, and Tanner, *The Book of Psalms*, 574, has the five stanzas from vv 1–17 and combines vv 18–20 under "Editorial addition to close Book Two."

20. Kselman, "Psalm 72," *Bulletin of the American Schools of Oriental Research* 220 (1975) 77; Zenger, *Psalms 2*, 206–7.

Verse Divisions							*Advocates*
1	– 4 / 5 – 8 / 9–11 / 12	–	15 / 16 – 17 / 18	–	20		Tate, Tournay[21]
1	– 7 / 8	–	14 / 15	–	17 / 18–19 /	20	Goldingay[22]
1	– 7 / 8	–	14 / 15	–	17 / 18	– 20	Miller, Kaiser[23]
1	– 3 / 4	–	11 / 12	–	17 / 18	– 20	Broyles[24]

Gunkel already noted that "the thought process of the poem is not altogether strict and moves by repetition."[25]

As one reads through Psalm 72 several times, one indeed begins to notice repetition of words and ideas in different sections. We have already noticed the repetition of "God" in verses 1 and 18–19, forming an inclusio providing the parameters of the literary unit. Further, we have seen the repetition of "righteousness" and its synonyms in verses 1–4 and 7 and of the "poor" and "needy" in verses 2–4 and 12–13. In addition we notice the repetition of "May he live while the sun endures" (v 5) and "Long may he live!" "May his name endure forever" (vv 15, 17). Further, "May he have dominion from sea to sea" (v 8) and "May all nations be blessed in him" (v 17). Is there a way to organize these repetitions into a coherent structure for the psalm?

Willem VanGemeren proposes six sections in an ABCB'C'A' pattern:[26]

A   Prayer for Davidic Kingship (v 1)
  B   Hope for Righteousness and Justice (vv 2–4)
    C   Prayer for Longevity and Universal Rule (vv 5–11)
  B'   Hope for Righteousness and Justice (vv 12–14)
    C'   Prayer for Longevity and Universal Rule (vv 15–17)
A'   Praise of God's Kingship (vv 18–20)

---

21. Tate, *Psalms 51–100*, 223; Raymond J. Tournay, *Seeing and Hearing God with the Psalms*, trans. J. Edward Crowley (Sheffield: JSOT Press, 1991), 225.

22. Goldingay, *Psalms*, II, 381.

23. Patrick D. Miller, "Power, Justice, and Peace: an Exegesis of Psalm 72," *Faith and Mission* 4, no. 1 (1986; pp. 65–70): 66. Walter C. Kaiser, *Preaching and Teaching the Last Things* (Grand Rapids: Baker, 2011), 68, also has vv 1–7 and 15–17 but divides vv 8–14 into 8–11 and 12–14.

24. Broyles, *Psalms*, 295.

25. Hermann Gunkel, *Die Psalmen übersetzt und erklärt* (HKAT II/2. 4th ed. Göttingen: Vandenhoeck & Ruprecht, 1926), 302, cited by Zenger, *Psalms 2*, 205–6.

26. VanGemeren, *Psalms*, 548. Wilson, *Psalms*, I, 985, proposes a similar structure: "Opening entreaty (72:1), hope for just rule (72:2–4), desire for enduring reign (72:5–7), plea for worldwide dominion (72:8–11), hope for compassionate justice (72:12–14), desire for prosperous kingdom (72:15–17), doxology concluding Book 2 (72:18–19), and postscript concluding the 'prayers of David' (72:20)."

More helpful for expository preachers is to identify the stanzas of the psalm. We can do so by checking for inclusios, climactic parallelisms (see pp. 98–100 above), and, of course, the contents. Thus we arrive at six stanzas:

I. Prayer that God give his justice to the new king (vv 1–4)
    A. Request (imperative): "O God, give the king your justice" (v 1)
    B. Three petitions (imperfect) for the king's righteous actions (vv 2–4)
       "May he judge your people with righteousness. . . ."
II. Three petitions for the king's long life and flourishing justice (vv 5–7):[27]
    "May he live while the sun endures. . . ."
III. Five petitions for the king's worldwide dominion (vv 8–11):[28]
    "May he have dominion from sea to sea. . . ."
IV. Six reasons for answering the prayer (vv 12–14):[29]
    "For (*ki*) he delivers the needy when they call. . . ."
V. Ten petitions for the king, the land, the people, and the nations (vv 15–17):[30]
    "Long may he live! . . ."
VI. Doxology (vv 18–19):[31]
    "Blessed be the LORD. . . . May his glory fill the whole earth"

Theocentric Interpretation

Most of Psalm 72 seems to deal with the king — seventeen out of nineteen verses. But the psalm begins, significantly, with "O God" (*'ĕlohîm*) and the first seventeen verses are petitions addressed to that God of the universe. Moreover, the first petition is, "Give the king *your* justice, O God, and *your* righteousness to a king's son" (v 1). Israel prays that its king will administer *God's* justice. Clinton McCann comments, "Justice and righteousness are first and foremost characteristics of God's reign (see Pss 96:13; 97:2, 6; 98:9; 99:4; 146:7); they describe God's royal policy. . . . In short, the role of the king is to enact God's rule."[32]

In addition, we have noted that the editor has added a doxology to this psalm: "Blessed be the LORD, the God (*'ĕlohîm*) of Israel, who alone does wondrous things. Blessed be his glorious name forever; may his glory fill the whole earth"

---

27. Inclusio vv 5 and 7, "the moon."
28. Inclusio of vv 8 and 11, worldwide dominion, as well as climactic parallelism.
29. Climactic parallelism.
30. Inclusio vv 15–17, long life and blessings.
31. Inclusio of vv 18 and 19, "blessed be," as well as climactic parallelism.
32. McCann, "Psalms," 963.

(vv 18–19). This doxology concludes not only Book II of the psalms but is a fitting conclusion to Psalm 72 because it encloses all these petitions in an inclusio framed by "God." This doxology also reveals that the kingdom of the Davidic king for which Israel prayed is really the kingdom of God: "May he [the Davidic king] have dominion from sea to sea, and from the River to *the ends of the earth*" (v 8); "may his ['the LORD, the God of Israel'] glory fill *the whole earth*" (v 19).

Finally, as McCann states, "It is significant that royal psalms (Psalms 2, 72, 89) appear at the seams of the psalter; they focus attention on God's reign at crucial points, and they lead up to the climactic proclamation of God's reign (Psalm 93; 95–99) that forms the theological heart of the Psalter."[33]

Textual Theme and Goal

In seeking to discern the textual theme, we note that verse 1 is key: "Give [imperative] the king *your* justice, O God." The following petitions (all imperfects) for a just rule, prosperity / peace, dominion from sea to sea, an endless reign, basically ask God to spread this peaceable kingdom to the ends of the earth. The final petition in the doxology confirms the implication of verse 1 that this is really God's kingdom: "May his [the LORD's] glory fill the whole earth" (v 19). We can, therefore, formulate the textual theme as follows, *Pray*[34] *that through God's righteous king, God's peaceable kingdom may spread to the ends of the earth.*

For determining the author's goal, knowing the historical background will be helpful. The editor has given us a clue by providing the superscription, "Of Solomon." "Of Solomon" can mean "to," "for," "concerning," as well as "by Solomon."[35] Since the editor concludes the psalm with, "The prayers of David son of Jesse are ended" (v 20), we can deduce that the editor wishes us to hear Psalm 72 as a prayer of David for his son Solomon.[36] The psalm could have been used at the coronation of King Solomon and of later Davidic kings. In any event, the

---

33. Ibid.

34. Although the psalm itself is a prayer and does not command Israel to pray, as part of the canon it is now God's word to Israel encouraging them to pray this prayer. See pp. 3–4 above.

35. See p. 29 above.

36. See p. 95 above for the connections of this psalm with Solomon's reign. "LXX and many subsequent interpreters regard the *li šalomô* heading as meaning *for Solomon* rather than *by Solomon.* The Syriac heading is, 'A Psalm of David, when he had made Solomon king.'" David C. Mitchell, *The Message of the Psalter: An Eschatological Program in the Book of Psalms* (Sheffield: Sheffield Academic, 1997), 250. Cf. Eaton, *The Psalms,* 262, "The heading 'Of Solomon' . . . might suggest the psalm originated at Solomon's coronation, or it could be a deduction from the phrase 'son of the king' in verse 1."

author's / editor's goal with this psalm is *to encourage Israel to pray that through God's righteous king, God's peaceable kingdom may spread to the ends of the earth.*

Ways to Preach Christ

Is Psalm 72 a prayer for Solomon / the reigning Davidic king or is it a prayer for the coming Messiah? Or is it both a prayer for the reigning king and the coming Messiah? Commentators spend much time debating these questions (see "Ambiguous Verb Tenses" above, pp. 96–98). If it is a prayer for Solomon or a later reigning Davidic king, one could preach Christ by way of typology: the Davidic king prefigures King Jesus (see p. 180 below). But a more direct way would be either promise-fulfillment or redemptive-historical progression supported with New Testament references.

Promise-Fulfillment

If the ambiguity of the Hebrew imperfect verbs is intentional, one can understand these verbs both as wishes and predictions.[37] Then one can preach Christ by way of *promise-fulfillment:* in this prayer for the reigning king, God has embedded promises of a great coming King — promises that are fulfilled in Jesus' First and Second Coming.[38] But the clearest, least "ambiguous," bridge to Christ in the New Testament is the way of redemptive-historical progression supported by New Testament references.

Redemptive-Historical Progression and New Testament References

In its original historical setting Psalm 72 is a prayer for Solomon or a later Davidic king. But Solomon "in all his glory" never attained the just rule, peace, domin-

---

37. The LXX translates the verbs in vv 4–16 as future tenses. Cf. Alter, *Art of Biblical Poetry,* 131, "Taking advantage of the ambiguity of Hebrew verb tenses, the poem manages at once to be prayer, prophecy, portrait, and benediction."

38. Matthew seems to have read Psalm 72 this way when he reports that wise men from the East came to Jerusalem to pay homage to the child Jesus. When they found him in Bethlehem, they opened their treasure chests and "offered him gifts of gold, frankincense, and myrrh" (Matt 2:11), possibly in fulfillment of Isa 60:6 and Ps 72:10, "May the kings of Tarshish and of the isles render him tribute, may the kings of Sheba and Seba bring gifts." By using the prophets (Isa 11:4–5 and Zech 9:10) as partial bridge to the New Testament we still use an element of promise-fulfillment (see "Sermon Exposition" below).

ion from sea to sea, and endless reign for which Israel prayed in this psalm. In fact, after Solomon's death, ten tribes rebelled against his son and seceded. The following Davidic kings did not even come close to the glory of Solomon, and in 586 B.C. the last Davidic king went into Babylonian exile.[39]

How did Israel pray Psalm 72 for the king later in redemptive history when there was no Davidic king? Israel focused on a future King, a king like David and Solomon but much greater — a King who would indeed rule justly, whose kingdom would be marked by righteousness, peace, and prosperity, whose kingdom would spread to the ends of the earth and "endure *forever.*"[40]

The prophets lent support to this way of understanding Psalm 72 by casting their predictions of a future Messiah in words similar to Psalm 72. Isaiah 11:4–5[41] announced the coming of another Davidic king: "With righteousness he shall judge the poor, and decide with equity for the meek of the earth [cf. Ps 72:2], he shall strike the earth with the rod of his mouth, and with the breath of his lips he shall kill the wicked [cf. Ps 72:4, 9]. Righteousness shall be the belt around his waist [cf. Ps 72:7]." Zechariah 9:10 used the very words of Psalm 72:8 to describe the dominion of the coming king, "His dominion shall be from sea to sea, and from the River to the ends of the earth."

Moreover, the editor of the Psalter, having introduced the Psalter with the royal Psalm 2, has deliberately placed the royal Psalm 72 at the end of Book II.[42] The LORD's opening decree in Psalm 2:7–8, "You are my son; today I have begotten you. Ask of me, and I will make the nations your heritage, and the ends of the earth your possession" is now echoed in Psalm 72:8–11, "May he have dominion . . . from the River to the ends of the earth. . . . May his foes bow down before him. . . . May all kings fall down before him, all nations give him

---

39. "The language of the Psalm and the actual reigns of the successive Davidic kings are such as to suggest that the Psalm must have looked not only to the present but also to the future . . . , when the ideals and hopes expressed by this poem would be realized." A. Anderson, *Psalms 1–72*, 518–19.

40. "When there were no longer reigning kings in Israel, the psalms written for use in royal ceremonies were reread as divine promises and prophecies of a future messiah." Mays, *Psalms*, 11. Cf. Stanley D. Walters, "Finding Christ in the Psalms," in *Go Figure!: Figuration in Biblical Interpretation* (Eugene, OR: Pickwick, 2008; pp. 31–47), 36, "The disappearance of kingship . . . is the new cultural context that effects a semantic shift in Israel's royal texts: they refer to the King who is to come — and that reference constrains what those texts can mean."

41. The Lectionary assigns Isaiah 11:1–10 as the "First Lesson."

42. "The drastic change of historical context in 586 is matched by the changed literary context as the book of Psalms grows and takes its present shape. In response to seismic changes in Israel's life, the royal psalms have all 'moved over,' as earthly kingship becomes a figure for the rule of God through the King who is to come." Walters, "Finding Christ," 42.

service." Small wonder that early Jewish interpreters already understood Psalm 72 as a messianic psalm.[43]

Although the New Testament does not explicitly quote Psalm 72,[44] it contains many allusions to Jesus' fulfilling the expectations of this psalm. To support our move to Christ in the New Testament, we can refer to texts such as Matthew 5:3, 6; 11:3–5; perhaps 25:31–46; Mark 1:14–15; Luke 1:31–33; 4:18–21; Acts 1:8; Philippians 2:9–11; and Revelation 21:23–26 (see "Sermon Exposition" below).

Sermon Theme, Goal, and Need

We formulated the textual theme as, "Pray that through God's righteous king, God's peaceable kingdom may spread to the ends of the earth." This prayer was answered in part with Jesus' First Coming when his life, death, resurrection, missionary mandate, and ascension advanced God's kingdom on earth. But we still await Jesus' Second Coming when he will bring God's kingdom in perfection to the ends of the earth. Since "God's righteous king" can refer to the Davidic kings as well as to Jesus, the textual theme can serve as sermon theme: *Pray that through God's righteous king, God's peaceable kingdom may spread to the ends of the earth.*

The textual goal was "to encourage Israel to pray that through God's righteous king, God's peaceable kingdom may spread to the ends of the earth." For the sermon goal we need only change "Israel" to "God's people," so that the sermon goal becomes, *to encourage God's people to pray that through God's righteous king, God's peaceable kingdom may spread to the ends of the earth.*

This goal points to the need addressed by this sermon: God's people do not pray ardently enough for Jesus to come again to establish God's perfect kingdom on earth. The sermon introduction can focus on this need by raising the question whether we earnestly long and pray for Jesus' Second Coming or whether we would rather not have Jesus come today.

---

43. "Ben Sira refers to verse 8 in the context of Israel's eschatological hope, saying that Abraham's seed will inherit from sea to sea and from the River to the ends of the earth (44:21): The Targum renders verse 1 as 'God, give King Messiah the precepts of your judgments.' PRE 14a and Num. R. 13.14 interpret the psalm of Messiah ben David. Midr. Pss. 72.6 regards it as referring to Solomon and to the Messiah. Ibn Ezra adopts the same dual interpretation, as does Kimhi, who notes that the messianic interpretation was widespread among his predecessors." Mitchell, *The Message of the Psalter*, 251. For other references, see Tournay, *Seeing and Hearing God*, 226–27.

44. But see Craig C. Broyles, "The Redeeming King: Psalm 72's Contribution to the Messianic Ideal," in *Eschatology, Messianism, and the Dead Sea Scrolls* (Grand Rapids: Eerdmans, 1997; pp. 23–40), 28–29, who notes "literary echoes" in the Greek of Matthew 2:11 and Psalm 72 (LXX): 9, 11, and 10; and Luke 1:68 and Psalm 72:18.

Scripture Reading and Sermon Outline

We have seen that the psalm in different parts repeats certain topics such as justice for the poor and needy, a long life for the king, and dominion to the ends of the earth. This shows up clearly in the above-mentioned ABCB'C'A' structure:[45]

A Prayer for Davidic kingship (v 1)
   B Hope for righteousness and justice (vv 2–4)
      C Prayer for longevity and universal rule (vv 5–11)
   B' Hope for righteousness and justice (vv 12–14)
      C' Prayer for longevity and universal rule (vv 15–17)
A' Praise of God's Kingship (vv 18–20)

To emphasize these topics in the scripture reading, we could have three persons read the following verses:

Reader 1.   Prayer for righteousness and justice (vv 1–4)
Reader 2.   Prayer for longevity and universal rule (vv 5–11)
Reader 1.   Prayer for righteousness and justice (vv 12–14)
Reader 2.   Prayer for longevity and universal rule (vv 15–17)
Reader 3.   Praise of God's Kingship (vv 18–20)

This division could also be used for a four-point sermon outline.

  I. Prayer for Righteousness and Justice (vv 1–4, 12–14)
 II. Prayer for Longevity and Universal Rule (vv 5–11, 15–17)
III. Praise of God's Kingship (vv 18–20)
IV. Move to Christ's First and Second Coming (NT)

The downside is that this outline requires the hearers to skip ahead from verses 1–4 to 12–14, then back to verses 5–11, and ahead again to verses 15–20. Although it will have more points than is ideal, for an expository sermon outline it is better to follow the stanzas we found in analyzing the psalm's structure above.

  I. Prayer that God give his justice to the new king (vv 1–4)
    A. Request: "O God, give the king your justice" (v 1)
    B. Three petitions for the king's righteous actions (vv 2–4)
 II. Three petitions for the king's long life and flourishing justice (vv 5–7)

45. See p. 102 and n. 26 above.

III. Five petitions for the king's worldwide dominion (vv 8–11)
IV. Six reasons for answering the prayer (vv 12–14)
V. Ten petitions for the king, land, people, and nations (vv 15–17)
VI. Doxology (vv 18–19)
VII. Move to Christ's First and Second Coming (NT)

Sermon Exposition

How urgently do we pray that Jesus will come again to establish God's perfect kingdom on earth? Do we ask for this kingdom to come today or can it wait a few days or years? Would we first like to have that long-planned vacation or see our grandchildren? There could be many reasons why we don't want Jesus to come back today. But when we focus on the injustices in this world, the mindless killings, the senseless beheadings, the starving refugees, we may be more inclined to pray that Jesus will come back today. Psalm 72 seeks to encourage us to pray urgently that God's peaceable kingdom may spread to the ends of the earth.

Notice that the heading of this psalm is "Of Solomon," which can mean, "For Solomon." Notice also that the last verse says, "The prayers of David son of Jesse are ended." These are clues that this psalm may originally have been a prayer of David for his son Solomon when he became king of Israel.[46] In any case, this psalm is a prayer for the king of Israel. It was probably used when a new king was crowned.

Psalm 72 encouraged Israel to pray that through God's righteous king, God's peaceable kingdom might spread to the ends of the earth. The prayer focuses on justice. There often was much injustice in ancient Israel. Frequently the rights of the poor and needy were trampled by the powerful.[47] God had given Israel specific instructions to care for the poor and needy. For example, we read in Deuteronomy 15:11, "Since there will never cease to be some in need on the earth, I therefore command you, 'Open your hand to the poor and needy neighbor in your land.'"

---

46. "The translation of the superscription in the Greek and Syriac versions interprets it as a prayer for Solomon, or a prayer where Solomon is the object." Ross, *Commentary on the Psalms,* II, 532.

47. See, e.g., Jeremiah 22:3, 13–15, "Thus says the LORD: Act with justice and righteousness, and deliver from the hand of the oppressor anyone who has been robbed. And do no wrong or violence to the alien, the orphan, and the widow, or shed innocent blood in this place. . . . Woe to him who builds his house by unrighteousness, and his upper rooms by injustice; who makes his neighbors work for nothing, and does not give them their wages. . . . Did not your father eat and drink and do justice and righteousness? Then it was well with him."

The first stanza begins, "Give the king your justice,[48] O God, and your righteousness to a king's son."[49] Did you notice that the prayer asks God not merely that the king may be just? That would have been good. But the prayer asks for much more: "Give the king *your* justice, O God." It asks God to give *God's* justice to the king. This is confirmed in the second line, "Give *your* righteousness to a king's son." God is perfectly just and perfectly righteous. Now in this prayer Israel asks God to share his justice and righteousness with the new king. The king's actions are to be an extension of God's actions. He is to rule not by human conventions but by God's norms for justice.

God is the ultimate King. The king of Israel is king under God.[50] The king rules Israel on behalf of God. If God will give his justice and righteousness to the king, the king will be able to rule according to the will of God. The kingdom of Israel will then be a manifestation of the kingdom of God on earth. So verse 1 is the foundation of this prayer, "Give the king your justice, O God, and your righteousness to a king's son." The following petitions depend on God giving his justice to the king.[51]

Verse 2, "May he judge your people with righteousness, and your poor with justice."[52] Again justice and righteousness are mentioned, now in reverse order.

---

48. The Hebrew has the plural *mišpāṭêkā* (your justices, statutes, ordinances). The plural "ordinances" "has in view above all the laws for social order that, both in the 'book of the covenant' (cf. Exodus 21–23 ['These are the *ordinances* that you shall set before them. . . .' Exod 21:1]) and in the Deuteronomic law (cf. esp. Deuteronomy 15, 23–24) aim at the rescue of the poor, the weak, and the stranger." Zenger, *Psalms 2*, 213. At his coronation the king received a copy of God's law (see Deut 17:18–20; 1 Sam 10:25). The LXX translates the plural as a singular.

49. If verse 1 is synonymous parallelism, "the king" in line 1 is the same person as "a king's son" in line 2. "The reason that the King is also identified as the King's Son is to assert that He is legitimate, standing in the royal line." Williams, *Psalms 1–72*, 520.

50. "The underlying view is that perfect kingship belongs to God alone; the vocation of the Davidic king is to be the instrument of God's rule on earth (2:7)." Eaton, *Psalms*, 181. Cf. Weiser, *The Psalms*, 503, "In direct contrast to the autocracy of oriental despotism the Old Testament kingship is *subject* to the statutes of God for the execution of which the king is responsible to his divine Lord."

51. "Justice and righteousness became the first and organizing responsibility of the king upon which all else depended. They are not one item in a list but the foundation on which the other possibilities rest." Mays, *Psalms*, 237.

52. Some versions (e.g., NIV [84], NKJV) as well as commentators (e.g., Eaton, *The Psalms*, 262) translate the verses 2 and following as future tenses: "He will judge your people in righteousness, your afflicted ones with justice." I would not make a major issue of this but just follow the pew Bible. In the final analysis there is little difference between verse 2 speaking of a future result or being a prayer that God will answer in the future. Cf. Isa 11:4–5, "With righteousness he shall judge the poor, and decide with equity for the meek of the earth. . . . Righteousness shall be the belt around his waist, and faithfulness the belt around his loins."

God, the King over all, is deeply concerned about social justice in Israel. Notice, "May he judge *your* people with righteousness, and *your* poor with justice." The people are *God's* people; the poor are *God's* poor. And God wants justice for them all. God wants his people to be treated justly or fairly. In Isaiah 1:17 God says, "Learn to do good; seek *justice,* rescue the oppressed, defend the orphan, plead for the widow." And in Amos 5:15, 24 God commands, "Hate evil and love good, and establish *justice* in the gate. . . . Let *justice* roll down like waters, and *righteousness* like an everflowing stream." Ultimately the king of Israel is responsible for establishing justice in the land. He is king under the God who demands justice.

Verse 3, "May the mountains yield prosperity for the people, and the hills, in righteousness." There is that word "righteousness" again, but now in the context of "the mountains" and "the hills." Mountains and hills describe the landscape of Israel. The hills were fertile but the mountains were barren. Now with verse 3 Israel asks God that even the mountains may "yield prosperity for the people." The word translated as "prosperity" is *šālôm.*[53] It means well-being: everyone has what is needed. The prosperity refers not to riches or wealth but to sufficient food. This prayer is echoed in verse 16, "May there be abundance of grain in the land; may it wave on the tops of the mountains."[54] The psalmist paints a beautiful picture of the barren mountains waving with an abundance of grain. When not only the hills but even the mountains wave with grain there will be plenty of food for all. There will no longer be hungry people in the land, no needy people. Righteousness will be found in the land.[55]

How will this prosperity come about? The God of all creation will bring it about. He promised Israel, "If you follow my statutes and keep my commandments and observe them faithfully, I will give you your rains in their season, and the land shall yield its produce, and the trees of the field shall yield their fruit. . . . You shall eat your bread to the full, and live securely in your land. And I will grant peace (*šālôm*) in the land . . ." (Lev 26:3–6).[56]

---

53. "*Shalom* is much more than just the absence of war ['peace'], and likewise, 'prosperity' in modern cultural usage indicates monetary success instead of a completeness of life." Tanner in deClaissé-Walford, Jacobson, and Tanner, *The Book of Psalms,* 575 n. 6.

54. "Though there was terraced farming on the hillsides in the ancient period, this phrase ['on the tops of the mountains'] may be hyperbolic: grain will flourish not only in the flat fields but on the very mountaintops." Alter, *Book of Psalms,* 250 n. 16.

55. Delitzsch, *Psalms,* II, 301, suggests, "The wish of the poet is this: By righteousness may there in due season be such peaceful fruit adorning all the heights of the land."

56. Alter, *Art of Biblical Poetry,* 131, writes, "Once there is justice, the natural world, as though sympathetically influenced, confers its blessing of 'peace' or 'well-being' (*šālôm*) on man. . . ." Rogerson and McKay, *Psalms 51–100,* 114, correctly caution, "It is, however, possible to exaggerate the Hebrew view of the 'sympathy' between the created order and social justice. A more straight-forward interpretation is to regard the verse in the light of Lev 26:3–6." Cf. Tanner in

Verse 4, "May he defend the cause of the poor of the people, give deliverance to the needy, and crush the oppressor." In ancient Egypt, Assyria, and Babylonia, and even in nations today, kings and presidents are judged successful when they do well in military campaigns and building projects. Not so in Israel. According to this psalm, Israelite kings were to be judged by how well they looked after the poor and needy, the marginalized and the defenseless.[57]

Again we see the close connection between the king of Israel and God. "The king does what is ordinarily attributed to God: He 'delivers' when people cry out (see Exod 2:23); he 'saves' (see Exod 15:2); he redeems (see Exod 15:13). He values the lives of those entrusted to his care (v 14b; see Ps 116:15)."[58]

So the first stanza is a prayer that God give *his* justice to the new king. The second stanza contains three petitions for the king to live forever and for flourishing righteousness and peace. Verse 5, "May he live while the sun endures, and as long as the moon, throughout all generations." In Britain and other countries, people still sing, "Long live our gracious queen / king." But this prayer asks for much more: "May he live while the *sun endures,* and *as long as the moon,* throughout *all generations.*" In short, this prayer asks God that the king may live forever.[59]

Verse 6 echoes verse 3, the grain growing on the hills and even waving on the mountains. "May he be like rain that falls on the mown grass, like showers that water the earth." Compare this prayer to Proverbs 28:3, "A ruler who oppresses the poor is a beating rain that leaves no food." For this king who defends the poor, Israel prays, "May he be like rain that falls on the mown grass." As I recall from my childhood, farmers do not like rain on mown grass. They cannot harvest wet grass as hay — it will heat up and set the barn on fire. But "it is likely that *gēz* [mown grass] denotes young growth on a freshly mown field (cf. Amos 7:1)."[60] That would be a blessing, a guarantee of another good crop in the future.

Verse 7 summarizes the prayer for righteousness of the first three verses: "In his days may righteousness flourish and peace abound, until the moon is no

---

deClaissé-Walford, Jacobson, and Tanner, *The Book of Psalms,* 577–78, "Instead of the good rule of the king causing a good response by nature, the structure of the poem apparently is stressing that the king and the creation work in tandem for the good of the world."

57. "According to the theology of this psalm, power is to be achieved not by grasping for the most but by caring for the least." Broyles, "The Redeeming King," 38.

58. McCann, "Psalms," 964.

59. Some interpreters understand verse 5 as referring to the dynasty of David while others think that it refers to a specific king but is typical hyperbole of the ancient court style. I think verse 5 refers to a specific king (cf. v 15, "Long may he live!" and v 17, "May his name endure forever, his fame continue as long as the sun"). It may well be hyperbole but open to literal fulfillment in Jesus.

60. VanGemeren, *Psalms,* 551. Cf. A. Anderson, *Psalms 1–72,* 521.

more." This kingdom will be marked by righteousness and peace (*šālôm*) "until the moon is no more," that is, forever.

So far we have heard in the first stanza the request that God give his justice and righteousness to the king, and that the king may judge God's people with righteousness and the poor with justice. In the second stanza we heard Israel pray in verse 5 that the king might live forever and in verse 7 that his kingdom of righteousness and peace might last forever.

The third stanza has five petitions for the king's worldwide dominion. Verse 8, "May he have dominion from sea to sea, and from the River to the ends of the earth." These words probably referred to God's promise to Israel in Exodus 23 to set its borders from the Red Sea to the Mediterranean Sea[61] and from the Euphrates to the ends of the earth. King Solomon indeed had dominion "from sea to sea."[62]

The next verses go on to specify details of this worldwide rule of Israel's king. Verses 9–11, "May his foes bow down before him, and his enemies lick the dust. May the kings of Tarshish [an ancient Mediterranean seaport in Spain][63] and of the isles [in the Mediterranean] render him tribute, may the kings of Sheba [today's Yemen] and Seba [in Africa][64] bring gifts. May *all kings* fall down before him, *all nations* give him service."[65] Israel prays that former enemies will bow down before Israel's king, that kings from the far west and the east and south will bring him gifts, and that *all* kings and nations will serve him. Dominion from sea to sea!

Yet this dominion is not gained by a powerful army or a superior navy. Rather, it is gained by worldwide recognition of this king's concern for justice and righteousness. We can see this in the fourth stanza, which begins with "For."[66]

---

61. Cf. Exodus 23:31: "I will set your borders from the Red Sea to the sea of the Philistines [the Mediterranean], and from the wilderness to the Euphrates."

62. Cf. 1 Kings 4:21, "Solomon was sovereign over all the kingdoms from the Euphrates to the land of the Philistines, even to the border of Egypt. . . ."

63. "Far off to the westernmost limits of the then-known world lies the famous old city of Tartessus in Spain, commonly known as Tarshish." Leupold, *Exposition of the Psalms*, 519–20.

64. Seba "may refer to a region in present-day Sudan, south of Egypt." Stek, *NIV Study Bible*, Psalm 72:10 n.

65. "The final verb is especially important, for it is always a keyword for Israel. Hebrew *'ābad* means both to 'serve' and 'worship'. It is the keyword in the Exodus narrative. Israel goes from being 'slaves' of the bad reign of Pharaoh to being 'servants / worshippers' in God's kingdom. In the poem here, all the world, through Israel and its king, will become servants in the kingdom of God." Tanner in deClaissé-Walford, Jacobson, and Tanner, *The Book of Psalms*, 578.

66. "For" (*kî*) makes verses 8–11 (dominion from sea to sea) dependent on vv 12–14 (justice for the needy). "It will not be by force of arms, but by the recognition of his justice, that the king will get universal homage. Cp. Ps 82:3f." Rogerson and McKay, *Psalms 51–100*, 116.

Verses 12–13, Dominion from sea to sea — "For [because][67] he delivers the needy when they call, the poor and those who have no helper. He has pity on the weak and the needy, and saves the lives of the needy." Three times these two verses mention the needy. To have "pity" on the weak and needy is to "be troubled about, look compassionately on" them. This compassion "mirrors the compassion of God" for the weak and needy.[68]

Verse 14, "From oppression and violence he redeems their life; and precious is their blood in his sight." "Oppression and violence" are two evils that threaten the poor and needy. "Oppression" "emphasizes the exploitation of the powerless by the powerful." The powerless have "no helper" (v 12). "Violence" refers to "the ruthless disregard for life that characterizes such exploitation."[69]

Oppression and violence are still rampant in this world, as we can see all around us. But the expectation in this prayer is that this king of Israel *redeems* the life of the weak and needy from oppression and violence. To redeem is "to buy back." In Leviticus 25:25 God stipulated, "If anyone of your kin falls into difficulty and sells a piece of property, then the next of kin shall come and redeem what the relative has sold." The next of kin is to buy it back for his relative. But this psalm prays not for the next of kin but for the *king* to redeem his people. "Precious is their blood [their life] in his sight."

The original psalm ends in the fifth stanza with ten petitions for the king, the land, the people, and the nations. Verses 15–17, "Long may *he* live! May gold of Sheba be given to him. May prayer be made for him continually, and blessings invoked for him all day long. May there be abundance of grain in *the land;* may it wave on the tops of the mountains;[70] may its fruit be like Lebanon;[71] and may *people* blossom in the cities like the grass of the field. May his name endure forever, his fame continue as long as the sun. May *all nations* be blessed in him; may they pronounce him happy."[72]

"May all nations be blessed in him" recalls God's ancient promise to Abraham, "I will make of you a great nation, and I will bless you, and make your name

67. "The Hebrew *kî* ('for') may imply that the King's universal rule is based upon his just government (so Kirkpatrick). It is possible, however, that *kî* in this verse serves as an emphatic particle (cf. Dahood, *UHP,* p 22), hence 'He will certainly deliver.'" A. Anderson, *Psalms 1–72,* 523–24.

68. Wilson, *Psalms,* I, 989.

69. Ibid.

70. "When the tops of the mountains are brought into the picture, fertile cornfields are thought of as extending to the very peak, that is to say, no sterile areas will be left." Leupold, *Exposition of the Psalms,* 521.

71. "Either Lebanon is thought to symbolize the best fertile land, or the wish is that the crops will grow as tall and strong as do cedars in Lebanon." Rogerson and McKay, *Psalms 51–100,* 116.

72. Cf. Psalm 1:1, "Happy are those" forming a giant inclusio around Psalms 1–72, books I and II of the Psalter.

great, so that you will be a blessing. . . . *In you all the families of the earth shall be blessed*" (Gen 12:2–3).[73] Through this great king of Israel, God's ancient promise will come to fulfillment. Psalm 72, then, encouraged Israel to pray that through God's righteous king, God's peaceable kingdom might spread to the ends of the earth.

The editor of the Psalter has added a fitting doxology to the psalm. The psalm names God only once but in an important place, right at the beginning: "O God, give the king your justice." After that request the prayer concentrates on the king of Israel. In concluding this psalm, the editor doubles back to God. Verse 18, "Blessed be the LORD, the *God* of Israel, who alone does wondrous things." The God of Israel alone is sovereign. No other gods can do such wondrous things. He alone can endow the king with God's justice and righteousness. He alone can make not only the hills but even the mountains wave with gorgeous grain. He alone can give the king dominion "to the ends of the earth." He alone can provide a king who will live "while the sun endures," that is, forever.

Verse 19 concludes, "Blessed be his glorious name forever; may his glory fill the whole earth. Amen and Amen." Verse 17 prayed for the king, "May his *name* endure *forever*." Verse 19 prays, "Blessed be his glorious *name forever*." In this case it is the LORD God's glorious name that is blessed forever. We see again how closely linked are the king of Israel and the sovereign God of the universe.

The final petition is, "May his [the LORD's] glory fill the whole earth."[74] In verse 8 Israel prayed that their king might have dominion to "the *ends of the earth*." Here they pray that God's glory may "fill *the whole earth*." Clearly, the psalm is speaking about the kingdom of *God*.

In its original historical setting Psalm 72 is a prayer for Solomon or a later Davidic king. But Solomon "in all his glory" (Matt 6:29) never attained the just rule, peace, dominion to the ends of the earth, and the endless reign for which Israel prayed in this psalm. In fact, after Solomon's death, "all the assembly of Israel came and said to Rehoboam [Solomon's son], 'Your father made our yoke heavy. Now therefore lighten the hard service of your father and his heavy yoke that he placed on us, and we will serve you'" (1 Kings 12:3–4). When Rehoboam failed to comply, ten tribes rebelled against him and seceded. Ruling in Judah, the following Davidic kings did not even come close to the glory of Solomon. And in 586 B.C. the last Davidic king went into Babylonian exile. No more kings from the house of David.

---

73. Cf. Gen 22:18, "By your offspring shall all the nations of the earth gain blessing for themselves, because you have obeyed my voice."

74. "The king's reign and its blessings are the reflection of the sovereign rule of God and of his salvation, and his fame is overshadowed by the 'glory' (*kābôd*) of God who alone does wondrous things." Weiser, *The Psalms*, 505.

How did Israel pray Psalm 72 later in its history when there was no Davidic king? God had promised King David, "Your house and your kingdom shall be made sure *forever* before me; your throne shall be established *forever*" (2 Sam 7:16). Praying Psalm 72, Israel naturally focused on a future King, a king like David and Solomon but much greater — a King who would indeed rule justly, whose kingdom would be marked by righteousness, peace, and prosperity, whose kingdom would spread to the ends of the earth and "endure *forever.*" In fact, Zechariah 9:10 used the words of Psalm 72:8 to describe the dominion of the coming Messiah: "His dominion shall be from sea to sea, and from the River to the ends of the earth."

In the New Testament we read that the angel Gabriel came to Mary and told her that she would conceive and bear a son. He said, "You will name him Jesus. He will be great, and will be called the Son of the Most High, and the Lord God will give to him *the throne of his ancestor David.* He will reign over the house of Jacob *forever,* and *of his kingdom there will be no end*" (Luke 1:31–33).

Jesus began his ministry by "proclaiming the good news of God, and saying, 'The time is fulfilled, and *the kingdom of God* has come near; repent, and believe in the good news'" (Mark 1:14–15).[75] In the synagogue in Nazareth Jesus read the words of Isaiah that echo Psalm 72, "The Spirit of the Lord is upon me, because he has anointed me to bring good news to *the poor.* He has sent me to proclaim release to the captives . . . , to let *the oppressed* go free, to proclaim the year of the Lord's favor. . . ." Then Jesus said, "Today this scripture has been fulfilled in your hearing" (Luke 4:18–21).

In his ministry Jesus indeed brought "good news to the poor." In his Sermon on the Mount Jesus preached, "Blessed are *the poor* in spirit, for theirs is the kingdom of heaven. . . . Blessed are those who hunger and thirst for *righteousness,* for they will be filled" (Matt 5:3, 6).

Jesus brought good news to the poor not only in words but also in deeds. When John the Baptist heard in prison what Jesus was doing, he sent his disciples to ask, "Are you the one who is to come, or are we to wait for another?" Jesus answered them, "Go and tell John what you hear and see: the *blind* receive their sight, the *lame* walk, the *lepers* are cleansed, the *deaf* hear, the *dead* are raised, and the *poor* have good news brought to them" (Matt 11:3–5). That's quite a list of poor and needy people Jesus helped: the blind, the lame, the lepers, the deaf, the dead, and the poor. Jesus fulfilled the prayer of Psalm 72:12–13, "He delivers the

---

75. "Christians have always known that they can pray this psalm in its fullness only for the heir of David who was Jesus of Nazareth. Through him the God of the universe has already bestowed righteousness, peace, and victory upon those who find in him the nearness of the reign of God. For them, the prayer is a form of petition for the consummation of the kingdom of God." Mays, *Psalms,* 238.

needy when they call, the poor and those who have no helper. He has pity on the weak and the needy, and saves the lives of the needy."

But where is Jesus' dominion "to the ends of the earth"? With Psalm 72 we still have to pray that through God's righteous king, Jesus, God's peaceable kingdom may spread to the ends of the earth. Along with John the Baptist we have to be patient. When Jesus came to earth he brought God's kingdom of justice — but not yet in perfection nor worldwide. Jesus healed some sick people, but not all. He preached good news to the poor, but not all. After Jesus died and rose again he sent his disciples as his witnesses "*to the ends of the earth*" (Acts 1:8). Having given his church the mandate to spread his kingdom "to the ends of the earth," Jesus ascended into heaven. There he is seated at the right hand of God the Father. Jesus rules as King of the universe. Paul quotes an ancient Christian hymn about Jesus: "Therefore God also highly exalted him and gave him the name that is above every name, so that at the name of Jesus *every knee should bend* . . . , and every tongue should confess that Jesus Christ is Lord, to the *glory* of God the Father" (Phil 2:9–11).

When Jesus comes again he will establish God's kingdom in perfection "to the ends of the earth." In Revelation 21 John describes the New Jerusalem: "The city has no need of sun or moon to shine on it, for *the glory of God* is its light, and its lamp is the Lamb. *The nations* will walk by its light, and *the kings of the earth* will bring their glory into it. . . . People will bring into it the glory and the honor of *the nations*" (Rev 21:23–26).

During Advent we focus on Jesus' coming again to establish God's kingdom in perfection. With Psalm 72 we pray that through Jesus, God's righteous king, God's peaceable kingdom may spread to the ends of the earth. Jesus himself taught us to pray for this coming kingdom. He said, "Pray then in this way: Our Father in heaven, hallowed be your name. *Your kingdom come. Your will* be done, on earth as it is in heaven" (Matt 6:9–10). Let us continue to pray that Jesus will soon come again to establish God's peaceable kingdom to the ends of the earth. The ascended Lord promised (Rev 22:20), "Surely I am coming soon." And God's people responded with, "Amen. Come, Lord Jesus!"[76]

---

76. Preaching a twenty-five-minute sermon on such a lengthy text as this will be a challenge. But it can be done: see the fine Advent sermon by Ryan Faber in Appendix 4 below. Alternatively, since the psalm's structure divides into two sections with similar contents (see p. 102 above), one could preach a series of two sermons on this psalm, vv 1–11 and 12–20 (see pp. 581–82 below).

Prayer[77]

O God, eternal King, who caused the hope for the Messiah to arise,
and answered it in your Son Jesus,
we bless you for his care of the needy,
and for the peace and salvation which he brings to those who love him;
and we ask that his work be completed,
and all the earth be filled with your glory;
Amen and Amen.

Song[78]

1Jesus shall reign where'er the sun
    does its successive journeys run,
his kingdom stretch from shore to shore,
    till moons shall wax and wane no more.

4Blessings abound where'er he reigns:
    the prisoners leap to lose their chains,
the weary find eternal rest,
    and all who suffer want are blest.

5Let every creature rise and bring
    the highest honors to our King,
angels descend with songs again,
    and earth repeat the loud amen.

---

77. Eaton, *The Psalms,* 264.
78. Isaac Watts, 1719. Public Domain. *Psalter Hymnal* (1987) # 412:1, 4, 5; *Psalms for All Seasons,* # 72B; *Lift Up Your Hearts,* # 219.

CHAPTER 5

"Happy Are Those Whose Help Is the God of Jacob"

Psalm 146 (145)

For the third Sunday of Advent, *The Revised Common Lectionary, Year A,* assigns Psalm 146:5–10 as a response to Isaiah 35:1–10, "The Return of the Redeemed to Zion." Unfortunately, by selecting only the second half of the psalm,[1] the hearers miss out on the inclusio, "Praise the LORD!" (vv 1, 10), and, more importantly, they miss out on the contrast, "Do not put your trust in princes . . ." (vv 3–4), and the message of this psalm, Put your trust in the God of Jacob. As a preaching text we need to select the whole of Psalm 146.

Text and Context

The entire Psalm 146 is a literary unit as indicated by the inclusio *halǝlû yāh* ("Praise the LORD!") in verses 1a and 10c.[2] This inclusio is repeated in each of the following psalms: 147, 148, 149, and 150.

Limburg, for one, has pointed out that in these last psalms in the Psalter there is roughly step-by-step progression in those invited to praise the LORD.[3] Psalm 146 begins with the psalmist calling *himself* to praise the LORD: "Praise the LORD, O *my soul! I* will praise the LORD as long as I live" (vv 1b, 2a). Psalm 147:12

---

1. The Lectionary does select the whole psalm for Year B (the twenty-fourth Sunday after Pentecost) and for Year C (the third Sunday after Pentecost).

2. The inclusio is more extensive when we compare vv 1–2 with v 10. "O my soul" (v 1) and "O Zion (v 10), "my God" (v 2) and "your God" (v 10), "as long as I live" with its parallel "all my life long" (v 2) and "forever" with its parallel "for all generations" (v 10). See Kselman, "Psalm 146 in Its Context," *CBQ* 50, no. 4 (1988; pp. 587–99): 592.

3. Limburg, *Psalms,* 494. See Zenger, *Psalms 3,* 616, for detailed connections between Psalms 145–150.

extends the invitation to the people of Jerusalem: "Praise the LORD, O Jerusalem! Praise your God, O Zion!" Psalm 148 expands the invitation to the whole cosmos: "Praise the LORD from the heavens; praise him in the heights! Praise him, all his angels; praise him, all his host! Praise him, sun and moon; praise him, all you shining stars! . . . Praise the LORD from the earth, you sea monsters and all deeps . . . ! Mountains and all hills . . . ! Wild animals and all cattle . . . ! Kings of the earth and all peoples, princes and all rulers of the earth! Young men and women alike, old and young together!" (148:1–3, 7–12). Psalm 149:2 focuses on Israel again, "Let Israel be glad in its Maker; let the children of Zion rejoice in their King,"[4] while Psalm 150:6 concludes with, "Let everything that breathes praise the LORD!" The relevance of this overview for preaching Psalm 146 is that this psalm is unique in this final series of praise psalms because of its personal invitation and commitment: "Praise the LORD, O my soul! I will praise the LORD as long as I live; I will sing praises to my God all my life long."

In the context of the whole psalter, the introductory Psalms 1 and 2 have many connections with Psalm 146. The opening words of Psalm 1, "Happy are those . . . [whose] delight is in the law of the LORD" (cf. Ps 2:12) are reflected in Psalm 146:5, "Happy are those whose help is the God of Jacob, whose hope is in the LORD their God." The same opening words in Psalm 1 introduce us to "the law [the instruction, the teaching] of the LORD." This instruction materializes in Psalm 146:3–5 in the teaching, "Do not put your trust in princes. . . ." The contrast between the righteous and the wicked of Psalm 1:6, "the LORD watches over the way of the righteous, but the way of the wicked will perish" (cf. Ps 2:2),[5] is echoed in Psalm 146:8–9, "The LORD loves the righteous . . . but the way of the wicked he brings to ruin." Further, as McCann points out, "One of the effects of placing Psalms 1 and 2 at the beginning of the Psalter is to present the whole book as a call to decision, and this call to decision is explicit in Ps 146:3–4 [–5] and implicit in vv 8c–9."[6]

Psalm 146 has many other connections with the Old Testament.[7] Verse 6, the

---

4. "In this alternating sequence, Psalm 149, with its focus on Israel, is interposed between Psalms 148 and 150, with their universal and inclusive scope. Thus positioned, it may seem to interrupt an escalating line. . . . However, the present ordering makes another point. . . . Pss 148:14 and 149 put Israel's praise of God in the center of the chorus of praise from heaven and earth (Ps 148:1–13) and from all that have breath (Psalm 150)." Kselman, "Psalm 146 in Its Context," *CBQ* 50, no. 4 (1988): 598.

5. The word *'ābad* ("perish") is repeated in Psalm 2:12 and also in Psalm 146:4, "their plans perish."

6. McCann, "Preaching on Psalms for Advent," *JPr* 16 (1992; pp. 11–16): 14.

7. For a detailed list of parallel Hebrew quotations from the Old Testament, see Kselman, "Psalm 146 in Its Context," *CBQ* 50, no. 4 (1988): 589–90. See also Zenger, *Psalms 3*, 610–11.

LORD "who made heaven and earth, the sea, and all that is in them," obviously recalls the creation story of Genesis 1. The words *'ādām* and *'ădāmâ* (earth, ground) in verses 3–4 recall Genesis 3:17–19, "And to the man (*'ādām*) he said, . . . By the sweat of your face you shall eat bread until you return to the ground (*'ădāmâ*) for out of it you were taken. . . ." "The God of Jacob" in verse 5 reminds us of Genesis 28:13–18 when God appeared to Jacob at Bethel and made wonderful promises to him which God subsequently fulfilled. The acts of God described in verses 7–9 about God's help for the oppressed resonate with the assigned lectionary reading of Isaiah 35:1–10.

Literary Interpretation

With its inclusio of *halǝlû yāh* ("Praise the LORD!") Psalm 146 is clearly composed as a hymn. But within this hymnic structure we can see several other literary forms. The "Do not put your trust in princes . . ." (vv 3–4) is an instruction, while the "Happy are those whose help is the God of Jacob . . ." (v 5) is a beatitude.

We will seek to gain entry into understanding the psalm by analyzing in turn its parallelisms, imagery, repetition of keywords, and its structure.

Parallelisms

Psalm 146 is artfully crafted with a series of three lengthy climactic advancing parallelisms (vv 1–2; 5–7b; 7c–9) and strategically placed antithetic parallelisms (vv 3 and 9c).

₁Praise the LORD!	A
Praise the LORD, O my soul!	+ A'
₂I will praise the LORD as long as I live;	+ A''
I will sing praises to my God all my life long.	+ A'''
₃Do not put your trust in princes,	– A
in mortals, in whom there is no help.[8]	+– A'
₄When their breath departs, they return to the earth;	B
on that very day their plans perish.	+ B'

---

8. The "mortals, in whom there is no help" advances on the "princes" in the first line; therefore +–A' or advancing antithetic parallelism.

₅Happy are those whose help is the God of Jacob,	A
whose hope is in the LORD their God,	+ A'
₆who made heaven and earth,	+ A''
the sea, and all that is in them;	+ A'''
who keeps faith forever;	+ A''''
₇who executes justice for the oppressed;	+ A'''''
who gives food to the hungry.	+ A''''''
The LORD sets the prisoners free;	A
₈the LORD opens the eyes of the blind.	+ A'
The LORD lifts up those who are bowed down;	+ A''
the LORD loves the righteous.	+ A'''
₉The LORD watches over the strangers;	+ A''''
he upholds the orphan and the widow,	+ A'''''
but the way of the wicked he brings to ruin.	− A
₁₀The LORD will reign forever,	A
your God, O Zion, for all generations.	+ A'
Praise the LORD!	B

Verses 1 and 2 show advancing (synthetic) parallelisms over four lines, resulting in climactic parallelism. Verse 3 starts with antithetic parallelism ("do not") and continues with ellipsis and advancing parallelism (giving another reason for not putting your trust in princes). Verse 4 adds the reasons for there being no help in mortals (new topic, B), with advancing parallelism (+B').

Verse 5 starts a string of advancing parallelisms that run to verse 7b, resulting in climactic parallelism. Verses 7c–9 also exhibit climactic advancing parallelism in expanding on the acts of the LORD for the needy, concluding with antithetic parallelism, "but the way of the wicked he brings to ruin" (v 9c). Verse 10 shows advancing parallelism, concluding with "Praise the LORD!" (v 10c) — a different topic; hence B.

Imagery

The imagery in this psalm raises an interesting question for interpretation: Are the prisoners, the blind, those bowed down, etc. to be understood literally or figuratively? Mays suggests that "the terms are used for both physical and spiritual need (for instance, the use of hunger and blindness for the condition of the exiles in Isaiah 40–55)."[9] A. Anderson comments that "The LORD opens the eyes of the blind" "is probably to be taken figuratively: Yahweh is able to help even the most helpless."[10] Although we should be open to a metaphorical understanding of these needy people, this does not rule out a literal interpretation: God did indeed set free his people imprisoned in Egypt and Babylonia and Jesus did indeed open the eyes of the literally blind.

The psalmist also personifies Zion in verse 10: "The LORD will reign forever, your God, O *Zion*, for all generations." By Zion he means not the hill in Jerusalem but the people of God (cf. Isa 52:7).

Repetition of Keywords

The keyword that stands out in Psalm 146 is the name of Yahweh: twice the abbreviated *Yah* in the inclusio of verses 1a and 10c and nine times the full name of *Yahweh* (vv 1b, 2a, 5c, 7c–9a [5×], and 10a). In addition the psalmist uses the name "God" (*'ēl, 'ĕlohîm*) four times (vv 2, 5 [2×], and 10). The word "praise" also stands out. Twice the psalmist encourages Zion to praise *Yah* (vv 1a, 10c) and three times he expresses his own intention to praise God (vv 1, 2a, 2b).

In addition, the psalmist links the repetition of the name of Yahweh to the various acts of Yahweh: the LORD their God "who made heaven and earth, the sea, and all that is in them; who keeps faith forever; who executes justice for the oppressed; who gives food to the hungry" (vv 6–7b). The list of the LORD's acts continues in verses 7c–9 with what the LORD does for the prisoners, the blind, those who are bowed down, the righteous, the strangers, the orphan and the widow, and, yes, the wicked.

Structure

Some commentators have suggested that Psalm 146 has a chiastic structure. For example, John Kselman proposes a chiasm focusing on "God Creator and Redeemer":[11]

---

9. Mays, *Psalms*, 441. Cf. Gerstenberger, *Psalms*, II, 439, "The book of Isaiah sometimes names 'blind' ('deaf,' 'mute') ones and 'bound,' 'imprisoned,' or 'poor,' 'miserable' ones together (cf., e.g., Isa 29:18–19; 42:7, 18–22). We may surmise that physical deficiencies have acquired metaphorical value in such theological discourse."

10. A. Anderson, *Psalms 73–150*, 942.

11. Kselman, "Psalm 146 in Its Context," *CBQ* 50, no. 4 (1988): 591.

A   Opening (vv 1–2)
   B   Wisdom (vv 3–4)
      C   God Creator and Redeemer (vv 5–8b)
   B'   Wisdom (vv 8c–9)
A'   Conclusion (v 10)

Of the Bible versions proposing different stanzas,[12] the most convincing are the NRSV and ESV, who have a structure of five stanzas: verses 1–2, 3–4, 5–7b, 7c–9, and 10.[13] Adding specific literary forms, the structure looks as follows:

    I. The liturgist's call, "Praise the Lord!" (vv 1–2)
   II. Instruction to congregation: "Do not put your trust in princes" (vv 3–4)[14]
  III. Benediction: "Happy are those who trust the God of Jacob . . . ," followed by five participial clauses (vv 5–7b)
      A. "who made heaven and earth,"
      B. "the sea, and all that is in them";
      C. "who keeps faith forever";
      D. "who executes justice for the oppressed";
      E. "who gives food to the hungry."[15]
  IV. The Lord's acts for various classes of needy people (vv 7c–9): five statements with *Yahweh* as subject of the participles plus two with imperfect tenses (F, G) for a total of seven:
      A. "The Lord sets the prisoners free;
      B. the Lord opens the eyes of the blind.
      C. The Lord lifts up those who are bowed down;
      D. the Lord loves the righteous.
      E. The Lord watches over the strangers;
      F. he upholds the orphan and the widow,
      G. but the way of the wicked he brings to ruin."
   V. Confession: "The Lord will reign forever. . . ." followed by the closing call "Praise the Lord" (v 10)

---

12. The NIV suggests six sections: vv 1a, 1b, 2–5, 6–9, 10a,b, 10c; the NASB (95) has two stanzas, vv 1–7, 8–10.

13. See the climactic parallelisms above (uniting the verses 1–2, 5–7b, and 7c–9) and the comments below.

14. "Your" in verse 3 is plural. Cf. verse 10, "O Zion."

15. "According to its nature this work would seem to belong among those in the next class, but according to the grammatical construction it is listed in the first group." Leupold, *Exposition of the Psalms*, 985.

Theocentric Interpretation

There is no question that Psalm 146 centers on God. As we saw, the name *Yahweh* is mentioned eleven times and God four times; that is fifteen references to God in ten verses. Terrien notes the progression from "my God" in verse 2, to "his God" in verse 5, to "your God, O Zion" in verse 10. He writes, "The theological outlook embraces the passion of the individual, extends itself to the holy people, and crowns this ascension with the hope of universal worship in the presence of the eternal King."[16]

The God-centered nature of this psalm is also underscored by the fact that God is the object of praise in verses 1–2 and 5; God is the subject who acts as Creator and Redeemer in verses 6–9; and God is again the object of praise in verse 10.

Textual Theme and Goal

In formulating the textual theme, we are faced with an interesting problem. On the one hand, the inclusio "Praise the LORD!" (vv 1, 10) as well as the "I will praise the LORD as long as I live" (v 2) suggest a theme about praising the LORD. On the other hand, the "Do not put your trust in princes" (v 3) and its contrast, "Happy are those whose help is the God of Jacob, whose hope is in the LORD their God" (v 5), suggest a theme about trusting the LORD.[17] We cannot eliminate the one or the other. Yet for the sake of a unified sermon, we need a single theme. Since it is practically impossible to formulate an overarching theme that covers these two themes equally, we have to ask which theme is dominant and subsume the other theme under the dominant one.

I think that the theme of trusting the LORD is the dominant one.[18] Although the theme of praising the LORD is mentioned at the beginning (vv 1–2) and the end (v 10c), the following psalms (147–150) have the same inclusio, which might lead to similar themes. What is unique about Psalm 146 in these praise psalms — apart from its personal commitment to "praise the LORD, O my soul!" — is its message about trusting the LORD. The psalmist uses more than seven of the

16. Terrien, *The Psalms*, 911.

17. Leupold, *Exposition of the Psalms*, 982, formulates the problem as follows, "We have, therefore, a psalm of praise which has the didactic purpose to urge men to put their trust in the Lord."

18. Cf. Broyles, *Psalms*, 509, "Here surfaces the chief issue of the psalm: whom will you trust, mortal men (vv 3–4) or the God of Jacob (vv 5–9)?" Cf. also Hermann Gunkel, cited by Zenger, *Psalms 3*, 610, "The beatitude 5 ['Happy are those whose help is the God of Jacob, whose hope is in the LORD their God'] is the real center of the psalm: what precedes it states the contrary, and what follows gives the reason."

ten verses to convey this message (vv 3–10b). Moreover, this theme begins as an "instruction" which is introduced with the imperative, "Do not put your trust in princes, in mortals, in whom there is no help" (v 3). The psalmist next declares that person "happy" "whose help is the God of Jacob" (v 5) and follows this up with a long list of what this God has done in the past (v 6a, b), does in the present (vv 6c–9), and will do in the future (v 10a, b). This God is indeed worthy of our trust as well as our praise. In fact, people who do not trust God will hardly praise him. Only they can sincerely praise God who trust God.[19] This makes trusting God the dominant theme, both textually and logically. We can therefore formulate the theme of this psalm as, *Put your trust in the only being worthy of our trust, the God of Jacob, praising him as long as you live.*[20]

The goal of this psalm can be determined by its historical setting and/or its theme. The Septuagint added the title, "Of Haggai and Zechariah," suggesting that this psalm was composed when Israel returned from the Babylonian exile. The "Do not put your trust in princes" (v 3) would fit that setting: "Do not trust foreign overlords."[21] But since this historical setting is conjecture, the best way to determine the goal is to consider how the psalm's themes would play out in Israel. This leads to a dual goal: *to urge Israel not to put their trust in princes but in the God of Jacob and to praise their faithful* LORD *their whole life long.*

Ways to Preach Christ

Psalm 146 contains neither a promise of the coming Messiah nor a type of Christ. To move to Christ in the New Testament one can use either analogy or redemptive-historical progression, both supported by New Testament references.

Analogy Supported by New Testament References

One can use analogy in at least two ways. One can draw an analogy between the works of the LORD mentioned in Psalm 146:6–9 and Jesus' works mentioned in the New Testament (e.g., Matt 11:3–5).

19. "To praise God is even the very fulfillment of human existence. But only he can praise God who trusts in God." Kraus, *Psalms 60–150,* 553.

20. Cf. Webster and Beach, *Essential Bible Companion,* 181, "Theme: Trust in the Lord, who is faithful, just, and compassionate, rather than in human leaders."

21. "They may be foreign overlords . . . in the postexilic period when national independence was but a dream. Equally they could be anyone holding positions of power and influence in the community." Davidson, *Vitality of Worship,* 469–70.

A stronger analogy would focus on the theme of Psalm 146: as the psalmist instructed Israel to trust the Lord, so Jesus instructed his followers to trust his Father in heaven (e.g., Matt 6:31–33; see "Sermon Exposition" below).

Redemptive-Historical Progression Supported by New Testament References

Redemptive-historical progression offers a more comprehensive way to move to Christ in the New Testament because it can include the above analogies but move beyond them to Jesus' Second Coming.

The psalmist urges Israel to put its trust only in the God of Jacob. He shows that this God alone is worthy of our trust, for this is the great Creator God, the Lord, "who keeps faith forever" (v 6). How did the Lord keep faith forever? The psalmist lists in detail what God did for Israel. Indeed, the Lord "keeps faith forever."

In the fullness of time God kept faith by sending his only Son to this earth to die for our sins and reconcile us to God. Jesus also taught us to trust God for our every need: food, drink, clothing, etc. He said, "your heavenly Father knows that you need all these things. But strive first for the kingdom of God and his righteousness, and all these things will be given to you as well" (Matt 6:31–33).

In fact, Jesus began his ministry by proclaiming that "the kingdom of God has come near" (Mark 1:15). Jesus then demonstrated the reality of the kingdom of God by preaching the good news of the kingdom and healing the sick (e.g., Matt 9:35; 15:30–31). Jesus died, rose again, and ascended into heaven. But he gave his church the mission to be his witnesses, to represent him in this world until he comes again. At his Second Coming Jesus will complete his work of redeeming God's whole creation (Rev 21:3–5; see further "Sermon Exposition" below).

Sermon Theme, Goal, and Need

Since the New Testament affirms the message of Psalm 146, the textual theme can become the sermon theme: *Put your trust in the only being worthy of our trust, the God of Jacob, praising him as long as you live.*

By changing "Israel" to "God's people" the textual goal can also become the sermon goal: *to urge God's people not to put their trust in princes but in the God of Jacob and to praise their faithful Lord their whole life long.* The need addressed by this psalm is therefore that we do not sufficiently trust God nor praise our faithful Lord our whole life long.

Liturgy, Scripture Reading, and Sermon Outline

A fitting call to worship would be for the liturgist, in the name of the Lord, to instruct the congregation, "Praise the LORD!" (Ps 146:1a) and the congregation responding in unison, "Praise the LORD, O my soul! I will praise the LORD as long as I live; I will sing praises to my God all my life long" (vv 1b–2). In concluding the worship service the liturgist could assure the congregation, "The LORD will reign forever, your God, O Zion, for all generations. Praise the LORD!" (v 10).

For Scripture reading before the sermon, the liturgist could again cry out the opening "Praise the LORD!" (v 1a), followed by a second voice reading the admonition to him- or herself to praise the LORD (vv 1b–2). The liturgist could read the admonition to the congregation not to put their trust in princes (vv 3–4), while the second reader lists the reasons for trusting the LORD (vv 5–10b). Finally the liturgist could conclude with a strong "Praise the LORD!" (v 10c).[22]

The sermon outline can follow the structure of the text with a final move to Jesus Christ in the New Testament:

    I. The call to "Praise the LORD!" (vv 1–2)
    II. The admonition to the congregation: "Do not put your trust in princes" (vv 3–4)
    III. Four reasons why people are happy when they trust the LORD (vv 5–7b)
    IV. Seven acts of the LORD for specific groups of people (vv 7c–9)
    V. Assurance that "The LORD will reign forever"; therefore, "Praise the LORD" (v 10)
    VI. Jesus teaches us to trust the LORD and will complete his redemption when he comes again (NT)

Sermon Exposition

Because of the dual goal, the introduction to the sermon could illustrate either our lack of trust in God or our lackluster praise of God. Since Psalm 146 is the first of five hymns of praise concluding the Psalter, I will here illustrate briefly our lack of praise.

How often would you say that we really praise our God from the heart? In

22. Verses 1a and 10c are both "a proper frame for the hymn either in a mere literary or a truly liturgical way. In the latter case someone would introduce and end the song by crying aloud: *hallelu-yah!*" Gerstenberger, *Psalms*, II, 440.

church we sing praise to God but frequently we don't even reflect on the words we sing. During the week we are consumed by worries about our health, our kids, where the next meal is coming from — and again we fail to praise God.

Psalm 146 has a timely reminder for us. It is the first of five hymns of praise that conclude the psalter with a burst of praise for the Lord. Each of these hymns begins and ends with the command, "Praise the Lord!" Five Psalms beginning and ending with "Praise the Lord!" — that is ten times "Praise the Lord!" The number ten is the number of fullness. We are called to praise the Lord with our whole being and in our whole life. And that is how Psalm 146 begins and ends, "Praise the Lord!"

Verse 1 begins with the command, "Praise the Lord!" In Hebrew it is the familiar phrase *halǝlû yāh! Halǝlû*, "praise"; *yāh*, a shortened form for Yahweh, Israel's covenant God, the God who revealed himself to Moses as "I am what I am" (Exod 3:14).[23] In our English Bibles this special name for God is always printed with four capitals, Lord.

"Praise the Lord!" The command is in the plural. This command is addressed to all Israelites, to all God's people. To praise the Lord sounds quite simple, but what does it mean exactly? How does one praise the Lord? Parallel verbs in the Old Testament give us some clues: "sing," "sing praises, make melody," "tell," "thank," "glorify," "magnify," "extol," "bless," "invoke," "rejoice."[24] To praise the Lord is to admire the Lord, to thank the Lord, to honor the Lord, to glorify the Lord.

The command to "praise the Lord!" has several implications. It means first of all that we acknowledge the Lord as our sovereign King upon whom we are completely dependent. It also means that our whole life ought to be a thank and praise offering to God.[25] And it means that we should be eager to offer up songs of praise to the Lord.

After this general call to praise the Lord, the psalmist exhorts himself, "Praise the Lord, O my soul!"[26] We may wonder, Does this mean that the psalmist wants to praise the Lord only with his soul? Sometimes we think of the soul as our inner, spiritual self as distinct from our outer, physical body. But for the

---

23. God also said to Moses, "Thus you shall say to the Israelites, 'The Lord, the God of your ancestors, the God of Abraham, the God of Isaac, and the God of Jacob [cf. Ps 146:5], has sent me to you': 'This is my name forever, and this my title for all generations'" (Exod 3:15).

24. For biblical references, see Ringgrenn, *TDOT,* III, 406. Webster defines praise as "1. the act of expressing approval or admiration; commendation; laudation. 2. the offering of grateful homage in words or song, as an act of worship: a hymn of praise to God."

25. "Praise — the offering of the whole self to God in worship and work — is the lifelong vocation of the human creature in response to God's cosmic sovereignty." McCann, "Psalms," 1263.

26. Similar expressions are found in Pss 103:1, 22 and 104:1, 35.

Hebrew writer the soul is "his very self as a living, conscious, personal being."[27] The soul is the whole person.

This becomes clear in verse 2 where the psalmist continues, "I will praise the Lord as long as I live; I will sing praises to my God all my life long." Not just some inner soul but *"I will praise the* Lord *as long as I live."*[28] The psalmist wants to praise the Lord as long as he lives; he wants to sing praises to his God his whole life long. Not just the little time he spends in the temple but his whole life long. "We are to praise God, not just for an hour a week in song, but with the whole of our being at all times and in all places."[29] Our whole life, then, is to be a song of praise. The worship service on Sunday should set the tone for the rest of the week and the whole of our lives.[30]

Our praise of God should spring from our awareness of who God is and what he has done for us. God is the almighty King of creation. He made us; we are his. God is our Father in heaven. He provides for us; we are his. Every step we make, every breath we take is under God's sovereign control. When we become aware of our utter dependence on God, our whole life will become a song of praise to the Lord for his many gifts to us. Not that we will literally sing all the time but, recognizing our dependence on God, our whole life will glorify our Maker. In looking to God for our every need, we acknowledge God as our King and Provider. In trusting God as our provider, we praise him.[31] If we do not trust God, we cannot praise him.

Consequently, the psalmist admonishes people in verse 3, "Do not put your trust in princes [leaders], in mortals, in whom there is no help [literally, 'no salvation']." This advice may well reflect Israel's experience with its leaders.[32] These

27. Stek, *NIV Study Bible*, 791, Psalm 6:3 n. Soul and body and soul and bones "did not for the Hebrew writer involve reference to two distinct entities but constituted for him two ways of referring to himself."

28. "The psalmist puts his mind and his will to the matter: His hallelujahs are not empty-headed repetitions, triggered by certain kinds of atmosphere or music. Nor are they songs for the good days only, when he is in the mood. He has learned to look for the facts behind the appearances, and to see the Lord at work in everything." Wilcock, *Message of Psalms 73–150*, 275.

29. Knight, *Psalms*, II, 348. Cf. Brueggemann, *The Psalms and the Life of Faith*, 126, "There will be, for this singer, no 'postpraise' existence; praise and life are coterminal."

30. "The psalmist's most precious possession resulting from his faith is an immense, selfless and wholehearted devotion to God." Weiser, *The Psalms*, 830.

31. "The movement from vv 1–2 to vv 3–4 to vv 5–10 suggests that praise is not only a liturgical act (see 'sing praises' in v 2), but also a way of living characterized by the disavowal of human autonomy (vv 3–4) in favor of living constantly in fundamental dependence upon God (v 5). As such, praise is the source of what makes human beings genuinely 'happy.'" McCann, "Preaching on Psalms: Psalm 146:5–10, Third Sunday in Advent," *JPr* 31, no. 1 (2007; pp. 37–41): 39.

32. "Do not put your trust in princes may reflect the exilic disillusionment with the Davidic monarchy and the postexilic hopes of its revival." Broyles, *Psalms*, 509.

princes could not save them from the Babylonian armies. The whole nation went into exile. Today many people still look to their leaders to save them. Some look for security to their president or government. Others put their trust for their welfare in the CEO of their company. Still others put their trust for their financial well-being in their broker. Others put their trust for their health in their medical doctors.

But princes cannot offer salvation. That is because, as verse 3 says, princes are "mortals," literally "*ben-'ādām*, son of Adam," a person made from the earth, *'ădāmâ* (cf. Gen 2:7). Verse 4 continues, "When their breath departs, they return to the earth; on that very day their plans perish." When their breath departs, the children of the earth, *'ādām*, return to the earth, *'ădāmâ*. Earthlings return to the earth (cf. Gen 3:19). Ecclesiastes 12:7 describes the end of mortals as follows: "The dust returns to the earth as it was, and the breath returns to God who gave it."

Human beings are transitory; they are here today and gone tomorrow. "When the wind [breath] leaves the powerful, they die. They become powerless, futile, helpless, unable to deliver, and unable to keep promises."[33] Verse 4 says, "On that very day [when they die] their plans perish." Why would anyone trust such fleeting persons who "have the mark of death on them"?[34] Why would anyone trust such temporary, short-lived people, or their plans, especially when there is a much superior option?

Verse 5 turns to that superior option: "Happy are those whose help is the God of Jacob, whose hope is in the LORD their God." What does it mean to be "happy" or "blessed"? An expert on the psalms writes, "As the whole sweep of the psalter makes clear, happiness is not the absence of pain and trouble but the presence of a God who cares about human hurt and who acts on behalf of the afflicted and the oppressed."[35]

The psalmist says, "Happy are those whose help is the God of Jacob." The mention of "the God of Jacob" brings to mind how God helped Jacob.[36] When Jacob had to flee from his brother Esau, God met him at night in a dream. God had said to Jacob, "I am the LORD, the God of Abraham your father and the God

---

33. Brueggemann, *The Psalms and the Life of Faith*, 126. Brueggemann continues, "In an affluent society like ours, besot with self-sufficiency, the question of basic trust is a profound public issue."

34. Kraus, *Psalms 60–150*, 552.

35. McCann, "Psalms," 1264. Cf. Hayes, "Psalm 146" in *Preaching the New Common Lectionary: Year A, After Pentecost* (Nashville: Abingdon, 1987), 235, "The term 'happy' denotes a state of well-being and contentment but not necessarily a state of extravagance and luxury."

36. "The divine name chosen in verse 5 [the God of Jacob] may aim to awaken the memory of how Yahweh proved to be the God of Jacob, the patriarch who similarly experienced 'famine' or 'hunger' (Heb. *rā'āb*, Gen 42:5; 43:1) and whose son Joseph was a 'prisoner' (39:20; 40:3, 5). When Jacob blessed Joseph, he called Yahweh 'your father's God, who helps you' (49:25)." Broyles, *Psalms*, 510.

of Isaac; the land on which you lie I will give to you and to your offspring; and your offspring shall be like the dust of the earth . . . ; and all the families of the earth shall be blessed in you and in your offspring. Know that I am with you and will keep you wherever you go, and will bring you back to this land; for I will not leave you until I have done what I have promised you" (Gen 28:13-15). And the LORD came through for Jacob. The LORD blessed Jacob as he worked for his uncle Laban. The fugitive became rich and returned to Palestine with twelve sons who became the twelve tribes of Israel. In due time the tribe of Judah brought forth a young woman named Mary who would give birth to Jesus. God had promised Jacob, "All the families of the earth shall be blessed in you and in your offspring." They were blessed in Jesus' coming to earth.

"Happy are those whose help is the God of Jacob." The God of Jacob can help us the way he helped Jacob. The word "help" "is not only about comprehensive and enduring protection and support in situations of distress but also about powerful support in undertakings and throughout life itself."[37] In Psalm 121:1 a pilgrim traveling to (or from) Jerusalem calls out, "I lift up my eyes to the hills — from where will my help come?" And he answers, "My help comes from the LORD, who made heaven and earth" (v 2). In spite of the dangers facing the pilgrim, he feels secure because his "help comes from the LORD, who made heaven and earth." In contrast to mortal princes, the LORD does not "have the mark of death on him." The LORD will not die. His plans never perish. The LORD is always there to help. And he is *able* to help. After all, he is the one "who made heaven and earth." Therefore, "Happy are those whose help is the God of Jacob, whose hope[38] is [not in princes who will die but] in the LORD their God."

Verses 6-7b give four reasons why we are happy, blessed, when our hope and trust is in the LORD our God. First, this LORD "made[39] heaven and earth, the sea, and all that is in them." He is the great Creator God. Almighty! Able to help, no matter what. Not subject to death. Eternal! Always there for us. As someone said, "Rather than aspiring for a great faith, one should aspire for a little faith in a great God."[40]

---

37. Zenger, *Psalms 3*, 613. Cf. Davidson, *Vitality of Worship*, 470, "Help" connotes "strength and security."

38. "The word translated 'hope' occurs only here and in 119:116, but elsewhere the verb is translated by the NRSV as 'look to you' (104:27; 145:15). It points in this context to people who refuse to be dazzled by human power but keep their eye firmly and expectantly fixed on the LORD." Davidson, *Vitality of Worship*, 470.

39. "The formula is expressed in a participial statement and thus shows that this is a matter not only of the *creatio prima* but especially of the *creatio continuata* or *gubernatio mundi*, that is, of YHWH's ongoing work that gives life to the world and creates it ever anew." Zenger, *Psalms 3*, 614.

40. Broyles, *Psalms*, 510. Cf. Calvin, *Commentary on the Book of Psalms*, V, 288, "The power

The second reason why we are happy when our hope and trust is in the LORD is that he "keeps faith forever." "Unlike humans whose plans and programs die with them, God and his help endure forever."[41] God is always faithful to his people. He will never forsake us. When Israel, coming from enslavement in Egypt, was about to enter the Promised Land with its well-fortified cities and its many giants, Moses encouraged them, "Be strong and bold; have no fear or dread of them, because it is the LORD your God who goes with you; he will not fail you or forsake you" (Deut 31:6). This is also true for us. No matter what challenges and dangers we face, "It is the LORD your God who goes with you; he will not fail you or forsake you." Put your trust in the LORD your God.

The third reason for being happy when our hope is in the LORD is that the LORD, as verse 7 says, "executes justice for the oppressed." The LORD is deeply concerned about justice in his world. We saw this (last Sunday) in Psalm 72: "Give the king your justice, O God." God desires justice in the land. Unfortunately, we see much injustice in this world. Many people in this world are oppressed. You may be among them. But don't give up hope; take heart: the LORD is on your side. He "executes [guarantees] justice for the oppressed."

Fourth, he "gives food to the hungry." All of us will grow hungry when there is no food. Where does food come from? The farm? The grocery store? Ultimately, the psalm confesses, all food is a gift from "the LORD, who made heaven and earth." The God who created us gives us the food we need to survive.

So we can put our trust in the God of Jacob. First, he is the almighty Creator God. Second, he "keeps faith forever." Third, he "executes justice for the oppressed." And finally, he is the one who "gives food to the hungry."

Beginning with the last line of verse 7 the psalm lists seven acts the LORD carries out for specific groups of people. First, "The LORD sets the prisoners free." The LORD liberates those who are enslaved or unjustly imprisoned.[42] Think of Joseph in Egypt. Falsely accused by Potiphar's wife, he was imprisoned. We read in Genesis, "But the LORD was with Joseph and showed him steadfast love; he gave him favor in the sight of the chief jailer" (Gen 39:21). And eventually the LORD set him free. Later the God of Jacob freed the Israelites enslaved by Pharaoh in Egypt. "The LORD sets the prisoners free."

Second (verse 8), "the LORD opens the eyes of the blind." Blindness affected

---

of God bears most pertinently upon his helping us whenever danger is near. We know how easily Satan tempts to distrust, and we are thrown into a state of trembling agitation by the slightest causes. Now, if we reflect that God is the Maker of heaven and earth, we will reasonably give him the honour of having the government of the world which he created in his hands and power."

41. Hayes, *Preaching the New Common Lectionary, Year A, Advent, Christmas, Epiphany,* 35.

42. "The prisoners will be people in confinement for political reasons, the usual reason for imprisonment in the ancient world." Goldingay, *Psalms,* III, 712.

a lot of people in the ancient world. "Blindness was not only a very common affliction in Palestine, but it was also a most distressing condition in which the unfortunate man was entirely at the mercy of his fellow-men."[43] But even for these helpless people, this psalm holds out hope: "the LORD opens the eyes of the blind."

Third, "the LORD lifts up those who are bowed down." In those days, many people were literally bowed down from hard labor; others were in debt, burdened, and discouraged. The good news for these discouraged people is that "the LORD lifts up those who are bowed down."

Fourth, "the LORD loves the righteous." "While it may seem that 'the righteous' (v 8c) do not belong in this series, we must remember that it is precisely 'the righteous' in the Psalter who are constantly besieged, assaulted, and oppressed."[44] Psalm 34 says, "Many are the afflictions of the righteous, but the LORD rescues them from them all" (Ps 34:19). People who are right with God, who know they are completely dependent on God and trust him, should know that "the LORD loves the righteous." They can trust him for their every need.

Fifth (v 9), "the LORD watches over the strangers." "The strangers" in those days were the sojourners, the resident aliens in Israel. Again, a class of people that was easily exploited and required special protection. We read in Deuteronomy 10, The LORD "executes justice for the orphan and the widow, and . . . loves the strangers, providing them food and clothing. You shall also love the stranger, for you were strangers in the land of Egypt" (Deut 10:18–19).

Sixth, the LORD "upholds the orphan and the widow." Orphans and widows were among the most helpless people in Israel. They had no father or husband to defend them. People often took unfair advantage of orphans and widows. Well, the LORD "upholds orphans and widows."

Now notice the contrast in verse 9 for the LORD's seventh act, "the LORD *upholds* orphans and widows, but the way of the wicked he brings to *ruin*."[45] "The way of the wicked he brings to ruin."[46] God's people need not fear the assaults of the wicked, for God will bring their way to ruin. God demonstrated in the history of his people that he "keeps faith forever." We can trust God completely.

The psalm ends with a final reason why we can trust God completely. Verse 10, "The LORD will reign forever, your God, O Zion,[47] for all generations." The psalm here turns to the future. "The LORD will reign *forever*." He will not die like

---

43. A. Anderson, *Psalms 73–150*, 942.

44. McCann, "Psalms," 1264.

45. "Over against this open outreach to those in need, the section ends, as does 145:20, with the door being firmly closed against the wicked." Davidson, *Vitality of Worship*, 471.

46. "The verb '-w-t means 'to be bent, crooked'; hence Yahweh bends the path of the wicked, i.e. he frustrates their crookedness so that they miss the goal." A. Anderson, *Psalms 73–150*, 943.

47. "Zion" here means not the hill in Jerusalem but the people of God (cf. Isa 52:7).

human kings but "will reign forever," "for all generations." The LORD is King of kings, King of the universe. As the Great King he will surely bring into this unjust world his perfect kingdom of justice and peace.[48]

"The words ring out like triumphant shouts":[49] "The LORD sets the prisoners free; the LORD opens the eyes of the blind. The LORD lifts up those who are bowed down; the LORD loves the righteous. The LORD watches over the strangers; he upholds the orphan and the widow." Salvation is on the way! The LORD will do it!

But still we see many in this world who are wrongfully imprisoned (think of the sex-trade), people who are blind (think of Africa), people who are bowed down (think of the depressed people in our society), righteous people who are persecuted (think of Syria, Egypt, Iran, Iraq), people who are strangers (think of refugees and aliens), helpless orphans and widows. Can we really trust the LORD to bring healing to the many people who are hurting in this world?

We can. God "kept faith" by sending his only Son to this earth to die for our sins and reconcile us to God. Jesus also taught us to trust God for our every need. Jesus said, "Therefore do not worry, saying, 'What will we eat?' or 'What will we drink?' or 'What will we wear?' For it is the Gentiles who strive for all these things; and indeed your heavenly Father knows that you need all these things. But strive first for *the kingdom of God and his righteousness,* and all these things will be given to you as well" (Matt 6:31–33). Striving for "the kingdom of God and his righteousness" has to be the goal of our life. Then we will experience that God will provide for all our needs.

We noted (last Sunday) with Psalm 72 that John the Baptist in prison questioned if Jesus was really the Messiah. He sent his disciples to Jesus to ask, "Are you the one who is to come, or are we to wait for another?" Jesus answered them, "Go and tell John what you hear and see: the *blind* receive their sight, the *lame* walk, the *lepers* are cleansed, the *deaf* hear, the *dead* are raised, and the *poor* have good news brought to them" (Matt 11:3–5). Jesus performed the saving acts described in Psalms 72 and 146.[50] His miracles were signs that Jesus was bringing God's kingdom into this world. Jesus was indeed the promised Messiah. But he

---

48. "Verse 10 adds an eschatological note to the text and points to the future as the time when the intervention of God on behalf of society's rejects and subjects will occur. In this forward-looking thrust, the psalm participates in and contributes to the expectations of Advent." Hayes, *Preaching the New Common Lectionary, Year A, Advent, Christmas, Epiphany,* 36. Cf. McCann, "Psalms," 1264, "Psalm 146 conveys the eschatological perspective of the psalter: God's reign is proclaimed amid circumstances that seem to deny it (see Psalms 2; 93; 95–99)."

49. Gerstenberger, *Psalms,* II, 439.

50. See Matt 9:35, "Jesus went about all the cities and villages, teaching in their synagogues, and proclaiming the good news of the kingdom, and curing every disease and every sickness." See also Matt 15:30–31.

did not set *all* prisoners free — John the Baptist was beheaded in prison. He did not all at once establish God's good kingdom on earth. God is patient, desiring that many be saved.[51] With his first coming Jesus inaugurated God's kingdom on earth. But he was not finished yet. He promised to come again.[52]

Meanwhile Jesus sent his church on a mission. He said, "You will be my witnesses in Jerusalem, in all Judea and Samaria, and to the ends of the earth" (Acts 1:8). He charged his followers to represent him in the world, to be his body, his hands and feet to help the needy. We read in Luke that Jesus sent his disciples "out to proclaim the kingdom of God and to heal. . . . They departed and went through the villages, bringing the good news and curing diseases everywhere" (Luke 9:2, 6). Later Jesus told one of his hosts, "When you give a banquet, invite the poor, the crippled, the lame, and the blind. And you will be blessed, because they cannot repay you, for you will be repaid at the resurrection of the righteous" (Luke 14:13–14). How will they be repaid at the resurrection of the righteous?

Jesus told them, when he comes again he will be the Judge and will judge people according to their deeds. He will say to the righteous, "Come, you that are blessed by my Father, inherit the kingdom prepared for you from the foundation of the world; for I was hungry and you gave me food, I was thirsty and you gave me something to drink, I was a stranger and you welcomed me, I was naked and you gave me clothing, I was sick and you took care of me, I was in prison and you visited me." When the righteous wonder when they did this for Jesus, he will say, "Truly I tell you, just as you did it to one of the least of these who are members of my family, you did it to me" (Matt 25:34–36, 40).

When Jesus comes again, he will complete his work of redeeming God's creation. There will be no more prisoners, blind people, those who are bowed down, strangers, orphans, and widows. John received a glimpse of this wonderful future. He heard a loud voice from the throne saying, "'God himself will be with [his people] . . . ; he will wipe every tear from their eyes. Death will be no more; mourning and crying and pain will be no more, for the first things have passed away.' And the one who was seated on the throne said, 'See, I am making all things new.' Also he said, 'Write this, for these words are *trustworthy* and true'" (Rev 21:3–5).

God has promised us this wonderful future. We can trust him. In spite of the

---

51. 2 Pet 3:9. Cf. the Parable of Weeds among the Wheat (Matt 13:24–30). Cf. James 5:7–8, "Be patient, therefore, beloved, until the coming of the Lord. The farmer waits for the precious crop from the earth, being patient with it until it receives the early and the late rains. You also must be patient. Strengthen your hearts, for the coming of the Lord is near."

52. See Luke 21:25–28; John 14:1–3; Acts 1:11. Jesus' First and Second Coming have been likened to D-Day, June 6, 1944, the day when the Allied forces invaded western Europe, and V-Day, when the victory was won in 1945.

dangers and troubles we face in this world, we can trust our faithful God. "Do not put your trust in princes. . . . Happy are those whose help is the God of Jacob, whose hope is in the LORD their God." If we fully trust the LORD, our whole life will be a song of praise to the LORD.

Prayer[53]

Lord God, Creator and King, help us in every need
to put our trust and hope in you,
that we may know the happiness of your salvation,
and all our life long make music to your name. Amen.

Song[54]

O God, our help in ages past,
    our hope for years to come,
our shelter from the stormy blast,
    and our eternal home:

Under the shadow of your throne
    your saints have dwelt secure;
sufficient is your arm alone,
    and our defense is sure.

Before the hills in order stood
    or earth received its frame
from everlasting you are God,
    to endless years the same.

O God, our help in ages past,
    our hope for years to come,
still be our guard while troubles last,
    and our eternal home!

---

53. Eaton, *The Psalms*, 476.
54. Isaac Watts, 1719. Public Domain. *Psalter Hymnal* (1987), # 170:1, 2, 3, 6; *Psalms for All Seasons*, # 90B; *Lift Up Your Hearts*, # 405.

CHAPTER 6

"Restore Us, O LORD God of Hosts"

Psalm 80 (79)[1]

For the fourth Sunday of Advent, *The Revised Common Lectionary, Year A,* assigns the reading of Psalm 80:1–7, 17–19 as a response to the first lesson, Isaiah 7:10–16. This reading of Psalm 80 thus omits the wonderful allegory of God bringing a vine out of Egypt and planting it in Canaan where it flourished and subsequently was ravaged by a boar from the forest. Since this allegory lends special force to the appeal, "Restore us, O LORD" (see vv 14–16), we should choose the whole psalm as our preaching text.

Since Psalm 80 "does not appear to be a favorite preaching text among pastors,"[2] it is good that the Lectionary places this psalm on our agenda. But preachers should realize that Psalm 80 may not be a good fit for preaching on the Sunday before Christmas. A major catastrophe has befallen Israel (probably attacks by the Assyrians between 732–722 B.C.) and Israel pleads with God to restore them. Thus a better occasion for preaching this psalm would be earlier in the Advent season or for a "blue Christmas" service (see the fitting, pastoral sermon of Ryan Faber in Appendix 4), or when the church is suffering through a major calamity.

---

1. Psalm 80 is number 79 in the Septuagint and Vulgate, the numbering used in Orthodox churches. Instead of the 19 verses of our English Bibles, the Hebrew (Masoretic) text counts the superscription as verse 1 and thus has 20 verses.

2. Leonora Tubbs Tisdale, "Psalm 80:1–7," *Int* 47, no. 4 (1993; pp. 396–99): 396, cites as evidence, "A survey of the extensive sermonic holdings of one theological seminary library revealed that only four sermons in the entire collection were based upon Psalm 80. (By way of contrast, the collection included ninety sermons based on Psalm 23 and eighty sermons on Psalm 90.)."

Text and Context

Psalm 80 is a literary unit not only because it is a complete psalm (see the new superscription for Psalm 81) but also because its refrain, "Restore us, O God; let your face shine, that we may be saved" (v 3), is repeated in verse 7 with "O God of hosts," and comes to a climax at the end of the psalm with "O Lᴏʀᴅ God of hosts" (v 19; inclusio).

As to its literary context, Psalm 80 is part of the collection of psalms of Asaph (76–83). It has a particularly close connection with Psalm 79 which concludes, "Then we your people, the flock of your pasture, will give thanks to you forever; from generation to generation we will recount your praise" (v 13). Psalm 80 continues this Shepherd / flock imagery with, "Give ear, O Shepherd of Israel, you who lead Joseph like a flock!" (v 1). In both psalms we hear the appeal for help (79:11; 80:3, 7, 14–15, 19), meet mocking neighbors (79:4, 12; 80:6), hear the call for vengeance on the enemies (79:6; 80:16), hear the questions "How long?" (79:5; 80:4) and "Why?" (79:10; 80:12) as well as references to God's "face" (79:11, *pānêkā* translated as "before you"; 80:3, 7, 19).[3] "Psalm 79 almost certainly bewails the catastrophe in 586 BCE. So the collectors that placed Psalm 80 after Psalm 79 conceived and used the psalm as an appropriate reaction to the destruction of Jerusalem and the Exile."[4]

Although the name "Shepherd of Israel" is found only in Psalm 80:1, the images of God as a Shepherd and Israel as a flock / sheep are common in the Asaph psalms (74:1; 77:20; 78:52–53; 79:13) as well as other psalms (23:1; 28:9; 119:176). The image of Israel as a vine / vineyard is also found in the prophets (see, e.g., Isa 5:1–7; 27:2–6; and Ezek 15:1–8; 17:6–8; 19:10–14).

Literary Interpretation

Psalm 80 is a community lament.[5] To enter into the meaning of the psalm, we shall first analyze its parallelisms, next its imagery, repetition of keywords, and finally its structure.

---

3. See Thomas Hieke, "Psalm 80 and Its Neighbors," *Biblische Notizen* 86 (1997; pp. 36–43): 38.
4. Ibid., 39. Cf. Erich Zenger, *Psalms 2*, 317.
5. Note that it has most of the elements of lament psalms (see pp. 10–11 above):

1) Introductory petition for God's help	Psalm 80:1–3
2) Description of the trouble or complaint	4–6, 12–13, 16a
3) Petitions for God's help	7, 14–15, 17, 19
4) Reasons why God should hear	
5) Examples of God's saving acts in history	8–11
6) A vow to praise	18

Parallelisms

Here is a snapshot of the parallelisms in Psalm 80:

> To the leader: on Lilies, a Covenant. Of Asaph. A Psalm.

₁Give ear, O Shepherd of Israel,	A
you who lead Joseph like a flock!	+ A′
You who are enthroned upon the cherubim,	B
shine forth (2) before Ephraim and Benjamin and Manasseh.	+ B′
Stir up your might,	+ B″
and come to save us!⁶	+ B‴
₃Restore us, O God;	A
let your face shine, that we may be saved.⁷	+ A′
₄O LORD God of hosts,	A
how long will you be angry with your people's prayers?	B
₅You have fed them with the bread of tears,	+ B′
and given them tears to drink in full measure.	+ B″
₆You make us the scorn of our neighbors;	+ B‴
our enemies laugh among themselves.	+ B⁗
₇Restore us, O God of hosts;	A
let your face shine, that we may be saved.	+ A′
₈You brought a vine out of Egypt;	A
you drove out the nations and planted it.	+ A′
₉You cleared the ground for it;	+ A″
it took deep root and filled the land.	+ A‴
₁₀The mountains were covered with its shade,	+ A⁗
the mighty cedars with its branches;	+ A″″′
₁₁it sent out its branches to the sea,	+ A″″″
and its shoots to the River.	+ A″″″′
₁₂Why then have you broken down its walls,	B
so that all who pass along the way pluck its fruit?	+ B′
₁₃The boar from the forest ravages it,	+ B″
and all that move in the field feed on it.	+ B‴

6. Three advancing imperatives reaching a climax in "come to save us!"
7. Advancing parallelism which will be repeated as a refrain in vv 7 and 19.

₁₄Turn again, O God of hosts;	A
look down from heaven, and see;	+ A'
have regard for this vine,	+ A''
₁₅the stock that your right hand planted.	+ A'''
₁₆They have burned it with fire, they have cut it down;	B
may they perish at the rebuke of your countenance.	+ B'
₁₇But let your hand be upon the one at your right hand,⁸	– C
the one whom you made strong for yourself.	+– C'
₁₈Then we will never turn back from you;	D
give us life, and we will call on your name.	+ D'
₁₉Restore us, O LORD God of hosts;	A
let your face shine, that we may be saved.	+ A'

The opening advancing parallelism (v 1a, b) describes the "Shepherd of Israel." This is followed by a four-line climactic parallelism with three imperatives: the urgent request, "Shine forth. . . . Stir up your might," climaxing with "come to save us!" This leads to the psalm's refrain of advancing parallelism, "Restore us, O God; let your face shine, that we may be saved" (two more imperatives; v 3).

The lament of verses 4b–6 in the form of climactic parallelism calls attention to God's anger and Israel's increasing suffering, reaching a climax in verse 6. The refrain sounds again, "Restore us, O God of hosts; let your face shine, that we may be saved" (v 7).

The longest climactic parallelism (vv 8–11) deals with the past, tracing the progression in God's loving care over the vine he brought out of Egypt with the climax being its tremendous growth (v 11). This is followed by another climactic parallelism (vv 12–13), a lament that belabors Israel's present anguish. With four imperatives the next climactic parallelism (vv 14–15) urges God to "turn again," to "look down from heaven," to "see," and to "have regard for this vine."

Verse 16 shows advancing parallelism from the enemy burning the vine to the request "may they perish." By contrast, "let your hand be upon the one at your right hand," verse 17a, is antithetic parallelism which advances in verse 17b. This request is followed by the promise that Israel will never turn back from God and will call on his name (advancing parallelism). The psalm ends by repeating for the third time its refrain, "Restore us, O LORD God of hosts; let your face shine, that we may be saved." Tracing the parallelisms gives us a good clue to the theme and goal of this psalm.

---

8. In contrast to the "perish" in v 16b, antithetic parallelism in 17a (–), advancing in 17b (+–).

Imagery

Psalm 80 contains many metaphors and anthropomorphisms. God is called the "*Shepherd* (metaphor) of Israel" who "leads Joseph *like a flock*" (simile). God is said to be "*enthroned* upon the cherubim." Israel calls upon God to "*give ear*," and to "*let your face shine*." The "let your face shine" echoes the Aaronic blessing, "the LORD make his face to shine upon you" (Num 6:24–25). They call God the "God *of hosts*," of heavenly armies. They ask, "how long will you *be angry?*" and complain that God has "fed them with *the bread of tears* and given them *tears to drink*" (their food and drink consist of tears). Turning to the past, the psalm pictures God as a *Gardener* who transplanted *a vine* (Israel) from Egypt to Canaan where it flourished because God "*cleared the ground* for it." The extended metaphor turns this section (vv 8–12) into an allegory. God not only cared for the vine but he broke down the walls of the vineyard so that *passers-by* (enemies) could pluck its fruit and an unclean (Deut 14:8) *boar* (gentile nation) could ravage the vineyard (Israel).

Finally, the psalm pleads with God to "*turn again*," to "*look down* from heaven, and *see*" (v 14). The psalm asks that the enemies "may perish at the rebuke of your *countenance* [face], but let your *hand* be upon the one *at your right hand*" — a picture of God prospering his appointed king.

Repetition of Keywords

The keyword "save" appears four times (vv 2, 3, 7, 19). It is part of the threefold refrain of this psalm, "Restore us, O God; let your face shine, that we may be saved." "The effect of the repetition is to express the urgency of the plea that pervades the psalm."[9] This urgency is underscored by the repetition of six imperatives: "Give ear!" "Shine forth!" "Stir up your might, and come to save us! Restore us, O God; let your face shine!" (vv 1–3; cf. v 14 with four imperatives). In the refrain the "O God" of verse 3 is expanded to "O God of hosts" (v 7) and "O LORD God of hosts" (v 19). "The title is probably deliberately expanded throughout the psalm for the sake of emphasis."[10] A variation of this refrain occurs in verse 14, "Turn again, O God of hosts."

Structure

The threefold refrain marks the conclusion of three major stanzas: verses 1–3, 4–7, and 8–19. Goldingay makes a good case for splitting the final stanza into

9. McCann, "Psalms," 1000.
10. Davidson, *Vitality of Worship*, 264.

two: verses 8–13 and 14–19. He notes that verses 1, 4, and 14 "all begin with appel-latives. I thus take the psalm to divide into two sections of four lines and two of six, each with some coherence. Verses 1–3 focus on appeal, on describing God. Verses 4–7 focus on protest at the calamity that has overcome the community. Verses 8–13 retell the story of the exodus and occupation of the land and ask how the calamity fits into that. . . . Verses 14–19 focus on a petition that takes up the recollection in verses 8–13."[11] We can, therefore, view the structure of Psalm 80 as follows:

    I. Petition for God's help: Shepherd of Israel, hear and save! (vv 1–3)
   II. Complaint: O God of hosts, how long will you be angry? (vv 4–7)
  III. Allegory of the transplanted vine flourishing, now ravaged. (vv 8–13)
  IV. Petition: "Turn again, O God of hosts" and restore us. (vv 14–19).

Theocentric Interpretation

This entire psalm is focused on God as can be seen in the repeated refrain, "Re-store us, O God; let your face shine, that we may be saved" (vv 3, 7, 19) and the petition "Turn again, O God of hosts" (v 14).[12] It can also be seen in the two metaphors for God. God is the "Shepherd of Israel" who guides his people like a flock of sheep. God is also the Gardener who brought a vine out of Egypt and planted it in the ground he had cleared in Canaan. Israel is completely dependent on its Shepherd and Gardener. The theocentric nature of this psalm is particularly evident where the psalmist blames God for Israel's misfortunes: "You [God] have fed them with the bread of tears. . . . You make us the scorn of our neighbors. . . . Why then have you broken down its walls, so that all who pass along the way pluck its fruit?" (vv 5–6, 12). Israel's God is the sovereign God. The hardships that befall Israel are not outside God's will. Only God can turn from his anger, let his face shine, and restore them.

---

11. Goldingay, *Psalms*, II, 533. The NASB has the same structure, as do the NRSV and ESV which, however, separate the three refrains from the stanzas. Ross, *Commentary on the Psalms*, II, 687–89, suggests four stanzas but includes verse 14 in the third stanza. Gerstenberger, *Psalms II*, 103, 105, also has four stanzas but includes verses 14 and 15 in the third stanza. Stek, *NIV Study Bible*, Psalm 80 n., suggests "five stanzas of four (Hebrew) lines each."

12. "The prayer concentrates with a single focus on one thing and one thing alone — the divine Thou." Mays, *Psalms*, 264. Cf. Broyles, *Psalms*, 332, "In the clear majority of cases Yahweh is the subject of the verbs. Even where he is not the grammatical subject, the action follows as a result of divine initiative."

Textual Theme and Goal

Psalm 80, we have seen, addresses God directly. But now the psalm is part of the psalter and the word of God for his people. What is its message for Israel? That message comes out clearly in the refrain, "Restore us, O LORD God of hosts; let your face shine, that we may be saved" (v 19; cf. vv 3, 7). This refrain encouraged Israel to pray that the LORD God of hosts would restore his people. In fact, some think that in the temple liturgy a priest would read the psalm with the people sounding out the refrain three times.[13] If this was the case, the people were actually doing what the psalm encouraged them to do. In any case, we can formulate the theme as follows, *Pray that the LORD God of hosts will restore his people.*[14]

The textual goal comes into clearer view when we know the historical background. From the psalm it is evident that Israel was suffering through a major disaster that allowed its neighbors to scorn them, its enemies to "laugh among themselves" (v 6), passers-by to "pluck its fruit," gentile nations to ravage them (vv 12–13), and burn their possessions with fire (v 16). Because of the names of Joseph, Ephraim, Benjamin,[15] and Manasseh in verses 1–2, it is likely that the reference is to the northern tribes of Israel as they were being attacked by the Assyrian armies after 732 B.C.[16] The Assyrians destroyed Israel's homes and farms, plundered whole towns and set them on fire, and in 722 B.C. destroyed the capital Samaria. This historical background is supported by the Septuagint's superscription of the psalm, "concerning the Assyrian."

But, as we saw above, the editor(s) of the Psalter have placed Psalm 80 after 79, which bewails the fall of Jerusalem in 586 B.C. Thus the editor(s) saw Psalm 80 "as an appropriate reaction to the destruction of Jerusalem and the Exile."[17]

---

13. See Hayes, *Preaching Through the Christian Year, Year A,* 25, quoted on p. 147 below.

14. If one considers "God of hosts" to be unclear for the theme, one could substitute the NIV translation, "God Almighty": "Pray that the LORD God Almighty will restore his people." This way one gains some clarity but at the cost of the vivid image "God of hosts," "God of heavenly armies." Webster & Beach, *Essential Bible Companion,* 115, propose the theme, "Our only hope in this disaster is that the Lord will look on us favorably and restore us."

15. "Benjamin belonged to the northern kingdom [see 1 Kings 11:13, 32, 36]. However, part of Benjamin must always have remained with the southern kingdom since its territory actually bordered on Jerusalem itself, and the southern kingdom continued to control Jerusalem's environs (see 1 Ki 12:21). This suggests that the disaster suffered was the Assyrian campaign that swept the northern kingdom away (see 2 Ki 17:1–6)." Stek, *NIV Study Bible,* Ps 80 n.

16. "The mention of the tribes of Ephraim, Benjamin and Manasseh . . . may indicate that the psalm originated among these tribes in the north, or that the psalm was composed in Jerusalem [it is a psalm of Asaph] after these northern tribes were overrun by the Assyrians, say, 732–722 B.C., and constituted a prayer for their restoration." Rogerson and McKay, *Psalms 51–100,* 156.

17. Hieke, "Psalm 80 and Its Neighbors," 39.

In other words, Psalm 80 could function as an appropriate reaction to the Assyrian attack on the northern tribes (732–722 B.C.), the Babylonian attack on the southern tribes and subsequent exile (586 B.C.), and later national disasters. Thus this psalm has relevance whenever God's people suffer on a great scale. As Mays writes, "Whatever the original historical setting, the psalm in its continued use belongs to the repertoire of the afflicted people of God on their way through the troubles of history."[18] The goal of Psalm 80, then, is *to encourage God's suffering people to pray that the* LORD *God of hosts will restore them.*

Ways to Preach Christ

How can we best link the message of Psalm 80 to Jesus Christ in the New Testament? The most straightforward way is redemptive-historical progression supported with New Testament references. But we should also consider the ways of promise-fulfillment and analogy.

Redemptive-Historical Progression with New Testament References

The theme of Psalm 80 is, "Pray that the LORD God of hosts will restore his people." In the fullness of time God answered this prayer by sending his Son Jesus Christ. The angel told Joseph in a dream, "Joseph, son of David, do not be afraid to take Mary as your wife, for the child conceived in her is from the Holy Spirit. She will bear a son, and you are to name him Jesus, for *he will save his people* from their sins" (Matt 1:20–21). Jesus will restore God's people by saving them from their sins. Later the angels told the shepherds, "Do not be afraid; for see — I am bringing you good news of great joy for *all the people:* to you is born this day in the city of David *a Savior, who is the Messiah,* the Lord" (Luke 2:10–11). In Jesus, God let his face shine and saved his people. As Paul put it, "Just as one man's trespass led to condemnation for all, so one man's act of righteousness leads to justification and *life* for all" (Rom 5:18). When Jesus comes again he will completely restore God's people.

Promise-Fulfillment with New Testament References

A more complicated way to Christ is the road of promise-fulfillment. With the introductory Psalm 2 setting the stage for a messianic understanding of the fol-

18. Mays, *Psalms,* 264.

lowing psalms, we can also see in the prayer of Psalm 80 the expectation of a coming Messiah King. In Psalm 80 Israel prayed that the Lord would restore his people. In verse 17 they linked this restoration to a person at God's right hand: "But let your hand be upon the one *at your right hand,* the one [*ben-'ādām,* son of man] whom you made strong for yourself." Psalm 110:1 also speaks about a person seated at God's right hand: "The LORD says to my LORD, 'Sit at my *right hand* until I make your enemies your footstool.'" In the New Testament Jesus says that this person is the Messiah (see Matt 22:42–45). In Psalm 80:17 the "son of man" at God's right hand also refers to the Messiah King.[19] This claim is supported by the Aramaic translation (Targum) which speaks of "the King Messiah."[20] The New Testament and Jesus himself claimed that Jesus was the Son of Man, the Messiah.

Psalm 80:18 continues, "Then we will never turn back from you; give us *life,* and we will call on your name." God answered this prayer for life by giving his Son Jesus. Jesus said, "I came that they may have life, and have it abundantly" (John 10:10; cf. 14:6; see further "Sermon Exposition" below).[21]

Analogy with New Testament References

Another option is to use the way of analogy supported by New Testament references. Psalm 80 vividly describes Israel with the allegory of a vine. God brought a vine out of Egypt and planted it in Canaan where it flourished until it was ravaged by a boar from the forest. The vine was being punished for having become unfaithful to God. Israel pleads with God, "Restore us, O LORD."

In the New Testament Jesus calls himself "the *true vine*": "I am the true vine, and my Father is the vinegrower. . . . Abide in me as I abide in you. Just as the branch cannot bear fruit by itself unless it abides in the vine, neither can you unless you abide in me" (John 15:1, 4). "In Jesus, God answered Israel's plea in ways

19. "The identity of 'the man at your right hand, the son of man,'" is discussed by A. Gelston ("A Sidelight on the 'Son of Man,'" *SJT* 22 [1969; pp. 189–96]) and David Hill ("'Son of Man' in Psalm 80 v 17," *NovT* 15 [1973; pp. 261–69]). Both conclude that the term refers not to Israel as a nation but to the king, and that this may denote an early messianic reference." VanGemeren, *Psalms,* 617. See also nn. 52 and 53 below.

20. The Aramaic targum reproduced verse 16b [15b] as, "and the King Messiah . . . whom you have made strong for yourself." "Analogously, then, in v 18 [17] the designation 'son of man / human one' [*ben-'ādām*] . . . was probably read messianically, in the horizon of Daniel 7 and other texts." Zenger, *Psalm 2,* 318.

21. "The church in her turn sees Christ as the bearer of life and salvation; through him may be known already the blessing of the face of God (cf. Num 6:25); the light of the knowledge of the glory of God is given in the face of Jesus Christ (2 Cor 4:6), and in him shall be made perfect the restoration of the suffering world." Eaton, *The Psalms,* 292.

beyond their wildest imaginings. And through Jesus God has smiled on us. He's no longer smouldering in anger against us. We're saved; we're restored — through Jesus who behaved as the perfect Son on our behalf."[22]

Sermon Theme, Goal, and Need

Since the New Testament does not change the message of Psalm 80, the textual theme can become the sermon theme: *Pray that the LORD God of hosts will restore his people.* The goal of Psalm 80 can also become the sermon goal: *to encourage God's suffering people to pray that the LORD God of hosts will restore them.* This goal indicates that the need addressed in this sermon is that God's people today are suffering. The worldwide church is being attacked by enemies and persecuted.

Liturgy, Scripture Reading, and PowerPoint

Psalm 80:19 would make a good call to worship. As to Scripture reading, John Hayes states, "Perhaps in the service of communal lamentation, these refrains [vv 3, 7, 19] represent the part of the liturgy spoken by the entire congregation while the rest of the psalm was voiced by the priest or person in charge."[23] Whether or not this was done in Israel's worship, it certainly makes sense to do this today since it highlights the theme of this preaching text. Therefore the liturgist can read the verses 1–2, 4–6, and 8–18, and the congregation responds with the refrain, vv 3, 7, and 19. A fitting benediction would be Hebrews 13:20–21.

PowerPoint can show slides of the verses being explained. This could be enhanced with a slide of "the cherubim" (v 1), a branching vine (v 11), supplemented by a slide of the land God gave Israel, from the Sinai mountain range in the south to the cedars of Lebanon in the north and from the Mediterranean Sea in the west to the Euphrates River in the east (vv 10–11).

Sermon Exposition

One could get the goal of this sermon into focus by relating a recent incident of the pain and persecution the Christian church suffers in this world. As I write this, Coptic churches in Egypt are being torched and Christians in Syria are being

---

22. Peter H. W. Lau, "Proper 15: Psalm 80," *ExpTim* 121, no. 10 (2010; pp. 509–12): 511.
23. Hayes, *Preaching Through the Christian Year, Year A,* 25.

kidnapped and fleeing the country in droves.[24] That may seem far away from us and not touch us. But Paul writes, "If one member suffers, all suffer together with it" (1 Cor 12:26). So as members of the church, the body of Christ, we suffer along with all members who suffer.

Psalm 80 is a lament of the people of Israel. It is an anguished cry to God. Israel is in deep despair. Enemies are mocking them, attacking their homes and farms. Their towns are being burned. Relatives and friends are dying. Why is all this happening? And how long will it last?

Three tribes of northern Israel are mentioned in verse 2: Ephraim, Benjamin, and Manasseh. Therefore it is likely that this psalm originally responded to Israel's persecution by the mighty armies of Assyria. The raids started in 732 B.C. and lasted a whole decade. Slowly but surely the nation of Israel was being swallowed up by this pagan nation. The desperate situation leads Israel to scream at God with four commands: "Give ear, O Shepherd of Israel . . . ! Shine forth! . . . Stir up your might, and come to save us!"

Verse 1,[25] "Give ear, O Shepherd of Israel, you who lead Joseph like a flock!" "Give ear!" Give us your ear! Grant us a hearing! Listen! This demand is followed by several titles for God. The first is, "O Shepherd of Israel."[26] "Shepherd is the title for God as king who leads, protects, and provides for his people."[27] The image of God as shepherd is expanded in the next phrase, "you who lead Joseph like a flock." Joseph probably refers to the ten northern tribes who were under attack by Assyria.[28]

The next title for God follows at the end of verse 1, "You who are enthroned upon the cherubim." Cherubim were angel-like, winged figures. God instructed Moses to make the ark of the covenant with two cherubim on top of the mercy seat (see Exod 25:20–22). The ark represented God's throne on earth; it was an earthly symbol of God's heavenly throne. The title of God "enthroned upon the cherubim," then, refers to God as the king of heaven who has heavenly armies

24. The number of Christian martyrs in the twentieth century has been estimated at 45 million. See David Barrett and Todd M. Johnson, *World Christian Encyclopedia* (2nd ed.; New York: Oxford University Press, 2001), I, 11. A web search "Persecution of Christians" will provide countless recent examples.

25. Since the superscription does not contribute much to the meaning of the Psalm, I would skip over it.

26. "The psalm begins with an epithet for God that appears only here." Tanner in de-Claissé-Walford, Jacobson, and Tanner, *The Book of Psalms*, 631. "'Israel' may denote either the northern tribes or, more likely, the people of God in their totality." A. Anderson, *Psalms 73–150*, 582.

27. Mays, *Psalms*, 262.

28. The tribes descended from Joseph, Ephraim, and Manasseh (see v 2) were the major tribes of the northern kingdom. "The tribe of Benjamin will be included since he, with Joseph, was the other son of Rachel." Eaton, *The Psalms*, 290.

("hosts") at his disposal.[29] In Psalm 99:1 Israel confesses, "The LORD is king; let the peoples tremble! He sits enthroned upon the cherubim; let the earth quake!"

But even as Israel confesses that God is King of the universe, in its severe suffering it makes bold to tell God what to do with four imperatives. *"Give ear!* ... You who are enthroned upon the cherubim, *shine forth* before Ephraim and Benjamin and Manasseh (three of the northern tribes directly related to Joseph).[30] *Stir up* your might, and *come* to save us!" Israel is desperate. It begs God to "leave his heavenly throne and 'shine forth in (specifically divine) splendor.'"[31]

Verse 3 adds another two imperatives, "*Restore* us, O God; *let* your face *shine*, that we may be saved." This is the first of three refrains in this psalm. "Restore us, O God." Restore us to our former prosperity; return us to the land from which we have been displaced; return us to our tribes, homes, and farms.[32]

Their prayer continues, "Let your face shine, that we may be saved." The fact that the Assyrians are conquering Israel indicates that God's face is frowning upon them. God's face is clouded with anger.[33] That's why Israel suffers such agony. So they plead: "Let your face *shine* that we may be saved." The "let your face shine" echoes the Aaronic blessing, "The LORD bless you and keep you; the LORD make his face to *shine* upon you" (Num 6:24–25). If the LORD will let his face shine on them, they will be saved; if the LORD will smile down on them, they will be saved from the ferocious Assyrians.

In the second stanza Israel complains bitterly to God. Verse 4, "O LORD God

---

29. "The title of God as the one 'enthroned on / over the kerubs' reflects the idea of God as king in heaven on a throne supported and borne by celestial creatures, a conception represented by kerub-figures in the sanctuary." Ibid.

30. "Possibly all the ten northern tribes are meant, or merely the rump of the hill country of Ephraim, which was all that remained of the northern kingdom in the second half of the eighth century (2 Kings 15:29)." Rogerson and McKay, *Psalms 50–100*, 157.

31. Zenger, *Psalms 2*, 313. Zenger adds in n. 7, "'Shine forth' is a term for a theophany in which God leaves his 'divine seat' and comes to a particular place in order to act or speak there; cf. Deut 33:2; Pss 50:2; 94:1."

32. "Restore us" can mean both return us to our former prosperity and return us to God. Many commentators argue for a deliberate ambiguity in Psalm 80. E.g., McCann, "Psalms," 999, writes, "'Restore us' (*hăšîbēnû*; more lit., 'cause us to return') has several dimensions that are appropriate to Psalm 80. The word is used elsewhere to describe God's bringing the people back from exile (see 1 Kgs 8:34; Jer 27:22; cf. Dan 9:25). The word may also denote repentance, literally 'causing people to return' to God (see Neh 9:26; Lam 5:21). . . ." However, Goldingay, *Psalms, II*, 536, correctly observes, "The parallelism [with 'that we may be saved'] supports Calvin's view that the prayer refers to the restoration of the nation's fortunes, not its spiritual or inner renewal." See Calvin, *Commentary on the Book of Psalms*, III, 298. To be saved from the Assyrians was the immediate need.

33. See Psalm 74:1, "O God, why do you cast us off forever? Why does your anger smoke against the sheep of your pasture?" Cf. Deut 29:20 and Lam 3:43–44.

of hosts, how long will you be angry with your people's prayers?" When people suffer terribly, they often raise the question of "how long"? How long will this suffering go on? But here the "how long" concerns God's anger at Israel's prayers. They have been praying for years, "Restore us, O God; let your face shine, that we may be saved." But God did not save them. After years of prayer, Israel is still suffering from the attacks of its enemies. Why is that? It's not that God cannot save them. They call God the "LORD God of hosts," that is, the God of the heavenly armies. This God can call on the heavenly armies to do his will. This God is God Almighty. Nothing is too hard for this God. But why, then, has God not come through for them? Does God not like their prayers? "O LORD God of hosts, how long will you be angry with your people's prayers?"

Literally, verse 4 reads, "How long will you smoke against the prayers of your people?" In the temple the fragrant smoke of rising incense was a sign that God accepted the prayers of his people.[34] But now they think that God is smoking against the prayers of his people. They think that their prayers are not rising to God in heaven.

In verses 5–6 Israel goes on to complain that the LORD is the one who brought about all this suffering.[35] Notice the "you's." Verse 5, "*You* have fed them with the bread of tears, and given them tears to drink in full measure." Can you imagine, the Shepherd of Israel has not led his flock into "green pastures"; he has not led them "beside still waters" (Ps 23:2). He has not protected his flock as a good shepherd should. Instead he has abandoned them. More than abandonment, he has personally "fed them with the bread of tears, and given them tears to drink in full measure."[36] Their food and drink is severe suffering, "Suffering and sorrow [have] become a regular part of their daily routine."[37] Another psalmist complains, "My tears have been my food day and night, while people say to me continually, 'Where is your God?'" (Ps 42:3). Where is God when his people suffer day and night?

Verse 6 follows up with another accusation. "*You* make us the scorn of our neighbors; our enemies laugh among themselves." Israel's neighbors scorn de-

---

34. Davidson, *Vitality of Worship*, 265.

35. "Every lament [in the Old Testament] somewhere strikes at the one who as Creator and Lord of creation permits the trouble. The laments . . . search for the cause of suffering not in some power hostile to God but in God alone." Westermann, *The Psalms*, 34.

36. The Hebrew word for "in full measure" is literally "by the third" — a third of some large measure. Because the English "by the third" denotes something small, the NRSV translates "in full measure." Kidner, *Psalms 73–150*, 290, suggests the rough equivalent "by the quart." Tate, *Psalms 51–100*, 306, suggests "by the keg." Cf. Tanner in deClaissé-Walford, Jacobson, and Tanner, *The Book of Psalms*, 631, "you have caused them to drink tears in triple."

37. Ross, *Commentary on the Psalms*, II, 693–94.

fenseless Israel and fight over the spoils.[38] Their enemies laugh among themselves and mock them. What has happened to the good Shepherd who "prepares a table before me in the presence of my enemies" (Ps 23:5)? The Shepherd has given them over to their enemies. Soon Israel will be no more.

In the depths of their despair they sound the refrain again. Verse 7, "Restore us, O God of hosts; let your face shine, that we may be saved." The refrain is the same as in verse 3, except that here they address God as "O God *of hosts*." God of heavenly armies. God Almighty. Israel has fallen so far that only an almighty God can save them.

With the third stanza Israel begins to recount the good things God did for them in the past. God is now pictured as a Gardener and Israel as a precious vine.[39] Verse 8, "You brought a vine out of Egypt; you drove out the nations and planted it." We see God bringing Israel out of Egypt to the Promised Land. God drove out the pagan nations and planted Israel in the fertile soil.[40]

God took good care of this tender plant.[41] Verses 9–11, "You cleared the ground for it; it took deep root and filled the land. The mountains [the Sinai mountain range in the south] were covered with its shade, the mighty cedars[42] with its branches; ['Even the mighty cedars (of Lebanon in the north) were overshadowed by the vine: Israel was the absolute master of the land.'];[43] it [the vine] sent out its branches to the sea [the Mediterranean Sea in the west], and its shoots to the River [the Euphrates in the east]."[44] Thus the vine filled the whole land from south to north and west to east. God had richly blessed Israel; under King David Israel began to fill the whole land.[45] Israel was the vineyard of the Lord.

38. "The Hebrew reads 'strife,' which might mean that the community had become a 'bone of contention' in the eyes of neighbors quarreling over the spoils." Davidson, *Vitality of Worship*, 265.

39. In blessing Joseph, Jacob promised that he would be "a fruitful vine" (Gen 49:22). It is most efficient to communicate the allegory of the vine as a running commentary as I will do in verses 8–11.

40. "By 'transplanting' the nation from Egypt to Palestine God assumed responsibilities like those of a gardener." Broyles, *Psalms*, 331.

41. "The metaphor of the vine indicates careful planning, preparation, and patient nurturing, which makes possible growth and fruitfulness. Thus the metaphor appropriately represents the commitment that God shows to God's people (see Isa 5:1–7; Jer 2:21; 6:9; Ezek 17:1–10; 19:10–14; Hos 10:1; 14:7; John 15:1)." McCann, "Psalms," 1000.

42. Literally "cedars of *'ēl*." "The word 'God' (*'ēl*) may be used to express the superlative degree (cf. *VT* 3 (1953), pp. 210 ff.; *VT* 18 (1968), pp. 121f.)." A. Anderson, *Psalms 73–150*, 584.

43. Ibid.

44. Cf. God's promise in Deut 11:24, "Your territory shall extend from the wilderness to the Lebanon and from the River, the river Euphrates, to the Western Sea." Broyles, *Psalms*, 331, comments, "As a recitation of God's saving history and the splendor that he bestowed on the vine . . . , these verses remind God of the historical precedent he himself set in saving his people."

45. "This recollection of God's 'primeval' powerful and loving action for Israel . . . , and the contrasting depiction of the horrible present are meant to move this very God, for the sake of his

But then Israel goes back to the bold accusations of verses 5–6: "*You* have fed them with the bread of tears. . . . *You* make us the scorn of our neighbors." Verse 12, "Why then have *you* broken down its walls, so that all who pass along the way pluck its fruit?" Vineyards had stone fences around them to keep out destructive animals. After reminding God that he first carefully built up his vineyard, now they accuse God of breaking down this protective wall. We can hardly believe what they are saying. Would God himself break down the protective wall of his vineyard?

But God is the God of hosts, the sovereign God. No foreign god could have broken down the wall. Only the God of hosts is in control. He must have broken down the protective wall, allowing passers-by easy access to the fruit. Verse 13 speaks of even more damage to the vineyard: "The boar from the forest ravages it and all that move in the field feed on it." The boar, hog, would savagely root up the plants. For Israel the boar was an unclean animal and thus refers to gentile nations such as Assyria ravaging God's vineyard. "And all that move in the field feed on it."[46] This refers to field animals or insects moving into the vineyard and devouring its foliage.[47] An early Jewish commentary (the Midrash) explains, "Once a vineyard has been breached, everyone goes up into it and plunders it; so also everyone who rises up — Babylon, Media, Greece, Edom — plunders Israel. Come a ruler he plunders it, come a general he plunders it."[48] Israel is about to be annihilated.

At this low point for Israel, stanza 4 begins with a variation on the refrain "Restore us, O God of hosts." God has turned away from Israel in anger; now he needs to turn again. Again Israel makes bold to tell God what to do with four imperatives. Verse 14, "*Turn again,*[49] O God of hosts; *look down* from heaven, and *see; have regard* for this vine, the stock that your right hand planted." The "have regard for this vine" is literally "visit this vine."[50] In its distress Israel feels not only

---

own divine identity, to eliminate this divine contradiction and fulfill his obligation of care and protection. The whole lament section of vv 5–14 is thus a passionate struggle with God himself — for the sake of his very being as God." Zenger, *Psalms 2,* 315.

46. "*The swarm.* The Hebrew *zîz* suggests 'moving thing,' in all likelihood a reference to insects and other crawling things. In the quasi-allegorical vehicle of the violated vine, the Assyrian army is imagined as other than human — a wild boar, a ravenous swarm of pestilential crawling creatures." Alter, *Book of Psalms,* 286 n. 14.

47. "Unprotected, Israel lies open to the casual (12b) and piecemeal (13b) plundering, as well as to more formidable foes (13a), the one kind completing what the other has begun." Kidner, *Psalms 73–150,* 291.

48. Quoted by Davidson, *Vitality of Worship,* 265.

49. "The fact that 'turn' is the qal of *sub,* while 'restore' is the hiphil of the same verb, heightens the impression that v 14a is a variant on the refrain. But 'turn' is what a psalm needs Yhwh to do before 'restoring' (cf. 90:13). At the moment Yhwh has turned away; the community needs Yhwh to turn back." Goldingay, *Psalms,* II, 541.

50. A. Anderson, *Psalms 73–150,* 585.

that God has turned his back on them but that God has abandoned them. They think God is far away in heaven, does not see what is going on, and does not care. Hence, "Turn again!" "Look down!" "See!" "Visit this vine!" Israel calls God to action. It wants God the Gardener to look after his vine again: "have regard for this vine, the stock that your right hand planted."[51]

Israel has accused God of being responsible for their terrible suffering. But in verse 16 they also point at their hostile neighbors: "They have burned it [the vine] with fire, they have cut it down." This shows the brutality of Israel's neighbors. They probably practiced the scorched earth policy. Israel has only one wish for these cruel neighbors who sought to annihilate them: "May they perish at the rebuke of your countenance" (v 16b).

In contrast to the destruction they wish on their enemies, Israel wants God to bless their king. Verse 17, "But let your hand be upon *the one* at your right hand, the one whom you made strong for yourself." From the communal "restore *us*," the psalm now focuses on "the one." Restoration of *us* will come about through "the one." When God's hand is on someone, amazing things happen (see Ezra 7:6, 9, 28; 8:18, 31; Neh 2:8). For Israel to be restored, amazing things will need to happen. So they pray, "But let your hand be upon the one at your right hand."

Who is that person at God's right hand? In the psalms God's right hand is associated with Israel's king (see Pss 18:35; 20:6). In this psalm, too, the prayer for the one at God's right hand refers to Israel's king.[52] But more can be said. Psalm 110:1 says of Israel's king, "The LORD says to my LORD, 'Sit at my right hand until I make your enemies your footstool.'" In the New Testament Jesus says that this person is the Messiah (see Matt 22:42–45). So the prayer for the one at God's right hand refers more specifically to the Messiah King.[53]

---

51. The Hebrew adds in verse 15b, "and for the son (*bēn*) whom you made strong for yourself." The NRSV judges that this line erroneously came from verse 17b and therefore omits it (see NRSV footnote). The NIV keeps both lines: "the root your right hand has planted, the son you have raised up for yourself." Kidner, *Psalms 73–150*, 292, calls the omission arbitrary and suggests that "the word 'son,' used here for the vine-shoot, will be upgraded in 17b, a line which carries the whole thought a stage further. Here it simply continues the metaphor and emphasizes the growth of what was planted, as in 9b–11."

52. "The reference is to the King, who can be described as sitting at the right hand of God (cf. Ps 110:1)." A. Anderson, *Psalms 73–150*, 586. Zenger, *Psalms 2*, 316, makes the point that "the one at your right hand" is identified in verse 17 with "the one whom you made strong for yourself." "The verb 'make strong' (*'āmaṣ*), also in 89:22 [21], describes YHWH's strengthening of the Davidic king for his royal office." Cf. Ps 2:8–9.

53. "Analogous texts and expressions (cf. Ps 110:1; Ezek 8:2, 8; Dan 7:13–14) suggest that we are dealing with messianic terminology. Thus our communal complaint in fact culminates with an eschatological petition, asking God to protect a royal figure considered a divine savior (cf. Isa 9:5–6 [NRSV 6–7]; 11:1–5; Hag 2:23; Zech 4:6–10)." Gerstenberger, *Psalms II*, 105. Cf. Terrien, *The*

"The one at your right hand" is literally "the son of man (*ben-'ādām*) at your right hand." Daniel also speaks of a "son of man": "I saw one like a son of man coming with the clouds of heaven. . . . To him was given dominion and glory and kingship, that all peoples, nations, and languages should serve him" (Dan 7:13–14). In the New Testament Jesus often used the title "Son of Man" to refer to himself. He claimed to be the "son of man" of Daniel. At Jesus' trial the high priest said to Jesus, "I put you under oath before the living God, tell us if you are the Messiah, the Son of God." Jesus responded, "You have said so. But I tell you, 'From now on you will see the Son of Man seated at *the right hand* of Power and coming on the clouds of heaven'" (Matt 26:63–64).

Israel's prayer, "Let your hand be upon the one at your right hand," was fulfilled in Jesus. God's hand was upon him and Jesus did amazing things. With his death on the cross he paid the price for our sins and restored us to fellowship with God. With his resurrection he conquered death for us and gave us eternal life. Jesus is the person at God's right hand — even today. Paul writes, "God put this power to work in Christ when he raised him from the dead and seated him at his right hand in the heavenly places (Eph 1:20).[54]

Israel's prayer in Psalm 80 continues with a vow of renewed commitment. Verse 18, "Then we will never turn back from you; give us life, and we will call on your name." Here Israel finally acknowledges that they had turned their back on God before God turned his back on them. But now they promise that they will never turn back from God. "*Give us life,* and we will call on your name." Jesus came and gave us life. Jesus said, "I came that they may have *life,* and have it abundantly. I am the good shepherd. The good shepherd lays down his life for the sheep" (John 10:10–11).

The psalm ends with the refrain, "Restore us, O Lord God of hosts; let your face shine, that we may be saved." This is the strongest of the three appeals. The first, in verse 3, was addressed to, "O God." The second, in verse 7, was addressed to, "O God of hosts." Now this final appeal is addressed to, "O Lord God of hosts." The added, "Lord," "Yahweh," is a reminder that this prayer is addressed to Israel's faithful covenant God. Yahweh will come through for them. "Restore us, O Lord God of hosts; let your face shine, that we may be saved." And the Lord did come through for them. He sent his son Jesus to save his people. At the birth of Jesus the angel told Joseph to name this baby, "Jesus, for *he will save his people* from their sins" (Matt 1:20–21). Jesus restored God's people by saving them from their sins.

Psalms, 580, and VanGemeren, *Psalms,* 616. Ross, *Commentary on the Psalms,* II, 697, notes that "the Targum sees this clearly as prophetic of 'King Messiah.'" See also p. 146 nn. 19 and 20 above.

54. Cf. Hebrews 1:13, "To which of the angels has he ever said [as he did to the Son], 'Sit at my right hand until I make your enemies a footstool for your feet'?"

But still the church of Jesus suffers in this world. Churches in Egypt are torched. Priests in Syria are kidnapped and never seen again. Christians in African countries are persecuted. Personally we may not be persecuted today. But, to quote Paul again, "If one member suffers, all suffer together with it" (1 Cor 12:26). So we suffer together with persecuted sisters and brothers around the world. In this Advent season, we ought to earnestly pray, "Restore us, O LORD God of hosts; let your face shine, that we may be saved."[55] Pray that Jesus will come again soon to restore all of God's people.[56]

Prayer[57]

Lord God, you reveal to us that the vine of your church is
one with the vine of all your creation,
one in the sap of life, in health and in suffering;
we pray you to care for this your vine,
that is so plundered and harmed;
stir up your mighty strength
and come and save us by the light of your face,
through the Son whom you raised in power to your right hand. Amen.

Song[58]

1O Shepherd, hear and lead your flock,
   as lambs we crave your care;
what strength on earth approaches yours,
   what mercies can compare?
Restore, O God, your favor,
   the radiance of your face
to lighten and reveal the gift
   of your redeeming grace.

---

55. Israel originally prayed for restoration probably when the Assyrian armies attacked them from 732 B.C. to 722 B.C. Israel prayed this prayer again when the Babylonian armies attacked the remaining two tribes and took them into exile (see pp. 144–45 above). Psalm 80 is a prayer for God's people whenever they face calamities.

56. "Just as Israel gave thought and expression in this psalm to its need for God's help and saw its situation as desperate without divine aid, so we in the Advent Season think of the misery of human existence and look forward to the shining of God's face in the coming of the Redeemer. Advent, like Israel's lamentation services, should be a time to ponder the conditions of life under the wrath of the Divine and life's futility without the presence of God's shining face." Hayes, *Preaching Through the Christian Year, Year A*, 26.

57. Eaton, *The Psalms*, 292.

58. *Lift Up Your Hearts*, #64. Words: Michael Morgan. Copyright © 1999, 2011 Michael Morgan, admin. Faith Alive Christian Resources. Used with permission.

2Our selfish prayers deserve God's wrath,
    our pride, a sudden burst;
we have but stones to serve as bread,
    and tears to quell our thirst.
Restore, O God Almighty,
    the radiance of your face
to lighten and reveal the gift
    of your redeeming grace.

3God's lineage, like a vine, once spread
    and flourished in the land;
but now the vineyard fails, the fruit
    lies withered in the sand.
Restore, LORD God Almighty,
    the radiance of your face
to lighten and reveal the gift
    of your redeeming grace.

CHAPTER 7

"Sing to the LORD a New Song"

Psalm 96 (95)

The Revised Common Lectionary assigns Psalm 96 as a responsive reading to Isaiah 9:2–7 ("The Righteous Reign of the Coming King") for Christmas Day in all three years, A, B, and C.[1] Reading this psalm on Christmas Day is one thing; preaching it is quite another. But preaching Psalm 96 on Christmas Day will provide the congregation with a wonderfully new perspective on Jesus' birth, a surprising historical panorama of the impact of Jesus' birth on Israel, the nations, and all of creation. "Joy to the *World! The* Lord Is Come."[2]

Text and Context

Psalm 96 is a literary unit because it is a complete psalm. It may also be marked by an inclusio in its first and last verse: "Sing to the LORD, all *the earth*" (*hā'āreṣ,* v 1) and "the LORD . . . is coming to judge *the earth*" (*hā'āreṣ,* v 13).

As to its context, Psalm 96 is in the middle of a series of psalms (93–99) that celebrate the kingship of the LORD. It has a similar structure and phrases as Psalm 95.[3] Psalm 96 has the same opening as Psalm 98, "O sing to the LORD a new song" (so also Isa 42:10 and Rev 5:9; 14:3) as well as similar images in closing (cf.

1. The connection with Isaiah 9:2–7 is that Isaiah here pictures God's salvation as a military victory while Psalm 96 commands Israel to sing to the LORD a new song, which was sung in response to God's military victory. But including Isaiah in a sermon on Psalm 96 would detract from the theme of the psalm. I would rather make use of the assigned New Testament lesson, Luke 2:1–14.

2. Isaac Watts, 1719, based on Psalm 98.

3. For details, see Hossfeld, *Psalms 2,* 466–67. See also Tanner in deClaissé-Walford, Jacobson, and Tanner, *The Book of Psalms,* 719.

96:11–13; 98:7–9). Psalm 96:7–8 is also similar to Psalm 29:1–2 with its climactic parallelism. There are also many echoes of Isaiah 40–55 (see esp. Isa 44:23 and 55:12).[4] Psalm 96 has been called a "mosaic," "a weaving together of phrases and whole lines that appear elsewhere."[5] The whole psalm, in a somewhat abbreviated form, appears in 1 Chronicles 16:23–33 when David "first appointed the singing of praises to the LORD by Asaph and his kindred."

Literary Interpretation

Psalm 96 is a hymn. Some scholars, following Mowinckel, call it an enthronement psalm, but the background of an annual enthronement festival in Israel is speculation[6] and therefore not helpful for interpreting this psalm. An *annual* enthronement festival would hardly call forth the *new* song for the *new* thing the LORD has done (see Ps 144:9–11; Isa 42:6–10; 43:19; 48:6). It is better, with A. Anderson, to call this psalm "a hymn celebrating the kingship of the LORD."[7]

We shall again begin our entree into understanding the psalm by examining its parallelisms, imagery, repetition of keywords, and structure.

Parallelisms

Psalm 96 contains the classic examples of climactic (staircase) parallelism in verses 7–8a and 13:

4. Isa 44:23, "Sing, O heavens, for the LORD has done it; shout, O depths of the earth; break forth into singing, O mountains, O forest, and every tree in it! For the LORD has redeemed Jacob, and will be glorified in Israel."

Isa 55:12, "For you shall go out in joy, and be led back in peace; the mountains and the hills before you shall burst into song, and all the trees of the field shall clap their hands."

Cf. Williams, *Psalms 73–150*, 186, "Several themes, such as the new song, the denunciation of the idols, and the exaltation of God's reign connect this psalm to sections of Isaiah 40–66, making it missionary and eschatological."

5. Robert Alter, *Book of Psalms*, 338, who continues, "Yair Hoffman actually characterizes it as a 'mosaic' of lines drawn from familiar psalms." Knight, *Psalms*, II, 111, claims "that this whole psalm is made up of twenty-five quotations of the OT."

6. "The nature and occasion of the enthronement to which they refer remain hypothetical." Rogerson and McKay, *Psalms 51–100*, 220. See also Tate, *Psalms 51–100*, 504–5.

7. A. Anderson, *Psalms 73–150*, calls this "a more non-committal description." Other scholars, e.g., Grogan, *Psalms*, 165, identify this psalm as "a descriptive praise psalm."

Ascribe to the Lord, O families of the peoples,	A	*a*	*b*	*c*	
ascribe to the Lord glory and strength.	A′	*a′*	*b′*		*d*
Ascribe to the Lord the glory due his name.	A″	*a″*	*b″*		*d′* *e*

for he is coming,	A	*a*	*b*			
for he is coming to judge the earth.	A′	*a′*	*b′*	*c*	*d*	
He will judge the world with righteousness,	A″			*c′*	*d′* *e*	
and the peoples with his truth.	A‴				*d″*	*f*

But recognizing advancing parallelism over three or more lines reveals more subtle forms of climactic parallelism. Except for verse 4, which I have marked as advancing parallelism,[8] the whole psalm is composed of strings of climactic parallelism.

1O sing to the LORD a new song;	A
sing to the LORD, all the earth.	+ A′
2Sing to the LORD, bless his name;	+ A″
tell of his salvation from day to day.	+ A‴
3Declare his glory among the nations,	+ A⁗
his marvelous works among all the peoples.	+ A⁗′
4For great is the LORD, and greatly to be praised;	B
he is to be revered above all gods.	+ B′
5For all the gods of the peoples are idols,	C
but the LORD made the heavens.[9]	− C′
6Honor and majesty are before him;[10]	+− C″
strength and beauty are in his sanctuary.	+− C‴

7Ascribe to the LORD, O families of the peoples,	A
ascribe to the LORD glory and strength.	+ A′
8Ascribe to the LORD the glory due his name;	+ A″
bring an offering, and come into his courts.	B
9Worship the LORD in holy splendor;	+ B′
tremble before him, all the earth.	+ B″

8. One could argue that verses 5 and 6 continue the advancing parallelism of verse 4, resulting in a six-line climactic parallelism (B) interrupted by antithetic parallelism in v 5b. But the *kî* in v 5a and the switch in subject to idols persuaded me to mark 5a with a C. The precise designation is not as important, of course, as getting a feeling for the movement in the various sections of the psalm.

9. In contrast to the idols, "the LORD made the heavens"; therefore, antithetic parallelism (−).

10. Verse 6 offers two more reasons why the LORD is not an idol; therefore +−C″ or advancing antithetic parallelism.

10Say among the nations, "The LORD is king!	A
The world is firmly established; it shall never be moved.	+ A'
He will judge the peoples with equity."	+ A''
11Let the heavens be glad, and let the earth rejoice;	B
let the sea roar, and all that fills it;	+ B'
12let the field exult, and everything in it.	+ B''
Then shall all the trees of the forest sing for joy	+ B'''
13before the LORD; for he is coming,	C
for he is coming to judge the earth.	+ C'
He will judge the world with righteousness,	+ C''
and the peoples with his truth.	+ C'''

Imagery

This psalm, as many others, personifies nature. For example, "Let the *heavens* be glad, and let the *earth* rejoice; let the *sea* roar . . . ; let the *field* exult. . . . Then shall all the *trees* of the forest sing for joy" (Ps 96:11-12).[11] Verse 6 may also offer personification: "*Honor* and *majesty* are before him; *strength* and *beauty* are in his sanctuary." Williams suggests that "honor," "majesty," "strength," and "beauty" "become God's kingly attendants, standing 'before him' (literally, 'before his face'). . . . All are in Yahweh's 'sanctuary,' either the earthly tabernacle, or temple, or heaven itself where He reigns (see 1 Kings 8:27)."[12]

Repetition of Keywords

The psalm begins with three plural imperatives, "Sing!" followed three times by "to the LORD," which is followed by three more imperatives: "bless! . . . tell! . . . declare!" Verse 7 similarly begins with three imperatives, "Ascribe!" followed three times by "to the LORD," which is followed by five more imperatives: "bring! . . . come! . . . worship! . . . tremble! . . . say! . . ." Clearly Psalm 96 wants people to do something, to be active in worship. And it includes "all" — *kol* repeated seven times (vv 1, 3, 4, 5, 9, 12 [2×]).

11. Brueggemann, *Message of the Psalms*, 145, calls this "poetic hyperbole, the delight of Israel writ as large as possible."

12. Williams, *Psalms 73-150*, 188. Cf. Stek, *NIV Study Bible*, Ps 96:6 n., "Two pairs of divine attributes personified as throne attendants whose presence before the Lord heralds the exalted nature of the one, universal King. For similar personifications see 23:6." So also Wilcock, *Message of Psalms 73-150*, 97.

We also notice that the psalm is filled with indescribable joy. It accomplishes this with the introductory repetitions of "sing" (3× in vv 1–2), and the concluding synonyms for joy: "be glad," "rejoice," "roar," "exult," climaxing with "sing for joy" (vv 11–12).[13] Finally, the psalm gives the reason for all this activity and all this joy in verse 13: "for he [the LORD] is coming, for he is coming to judge the earth. He will judge the world with righteousness" (twice "for he is coming" and twice "judge"). The fact that the LORD "will judge the world *with righteousness*" is the reason for all the joy.

Structure

Bible translators and commentators are not agreed on the structure of Psalm 96.[14] It would be well to start with the typical structure of a hymn. As we saw in Chapter 1, p. 11, the typical pattern of a hymn consists of most of the following elements:

1) A call to praise the LORD
2) Transition (*kî*, for, because)
3) Reasons why the LORD is to be praised
4) Conclusion: Praise the LORD!

In Psalm 96 we see these elements doubled or tripled:

1) A threefold call for Israel to praise the LORD — vv 1–3
2) Transition (*kî*, for, 2×) — vv 4–5
3) Reasons why the LORD is to be praised — v 6
4) A second threefold call for all peoples to praise the LORD — vv 7–9
5) "Say among the nations, 'The LORD is king!'" — v 10
6) All nature invited to praise the LORD — vv 11–12
7) Transition (*kî*, for, 2×) — v 13a, b
8) Reasons why the LORD is to be praised — v 13c, d

---

13. "A sermon on Psalm 96 must, if it is to be faithful to its text, under all circumstances bear some witness to the great joy that pervades it and, by means of a correct definition of its nature, aid the congregation in achieving this expression of faith that has become foreign to the church to a large extent." Von Rad, *Biblical Interpretations*, 80.

14. "There is no consensus among scholars as to the poetic structure of the psalm. Some propose two strophes (vv 1–6 / vv 7–13), and others subdivide these two strophes and add a third either starting with v 10 or with v 11." Hossfeld, *Psalms 2*, 464.

In analyzing the psalm's structure the main issue is the function of verse 10. The NRSV divides the psalm into three stanzas: verses 1–6, 7–9, and 10–13.[15] This division sees the "Say among the nations" of verse 10 as a new imperative starting the last stanza. The NIV, on the other hand, proposes four stanzas: verses 1–3, 4–6, 7–10, and 11–13. This division sees verse 10 as providing the reason why the nations are to ascribe to the LORD glory (v 7): "Say among the nations, 'The LORD is king!'"[16] While the NRSV's stanzas do more justice to the grammar (imperatives starting each stanza), the NIV's configuration does more justice to the usual structure of hymns: the call to praise the Lord, and reasons for praising the LORD.[17]

If it be objected that verse 10 does not have the tell-tale *kî* for the reasons, the answer is that it is superfluous at this point. Note the progression in the psalm: *Israel*[18] is to sing to the LORD a new song (vv 1–3). This requires the *kî* clause that Israel's God is the greatest (vv 4–6). Next *the nations* ("families of the peoples") are commanded to ascribe to the LORD glory and strength (vv 7–9). But they do not know Israel's God the LORD. Therefore Israel is to tell them: "Say among the nations, 'The LORD *is king!* . . . He will judge *the peoples* with equity'" (v 10). This is the reason why the nations are to ascribe glory to the LORD. Finally the psalm calls on *all nature* to praise the LORD.[19] This invitation is followed by another double *kî* clause with reasons: "for he is coming, for he is coming to judge the earth . . . in righteousness" (v 13).

Thus we arrive at a three-part symmetrical structure:

---

15. The ESV has four stanzas: 1–6/ 7–9/ 10/ 11–13. The NASB adds verse 10 to the second stanza: 1–6/7–10/11–13. The issue is the function of verse 10.

16. Besides the NIV, I found support for this analysis in only a few commentaries: Goldingay, *Psalms*, III, 101; Fokkelman, *Major Poems of the Hebrew Bible*, III, 188–89; McCann, "Psalms," 1064; and, with more details, Hossfeld, *Psalms 2*, 464.

17. In addition, Fokkelman, *Major Poems of the Hebrew Bible*, III, 190, notes, "The careful construction of the song is also demonstrated by the fact that its fourteen verses score an exact average on two levels, that of words and that of syllables. As there are 112 words and 252 syllables, the average per poetic line is exactly 8 words and 18 syllables."

18. "The call to praise in the first strophe suggests Israel as subject of the praise, both because of the verbs of speaking (praise, proclaim, tell) and because of the content of the message (YHWH's name, salvation, glory, wonders)." Hossfeld, *Psalms 2*, 465. See also the reference to "his sanctuary" in verse 6. Verse 1b, of course, does say, "Sing to the LORD, all the *earth.*" This could be explained as an inclusio between verses 1 and 13 and an anticipation of the third stanza (vv 11–13).

19. "The shift from imperative to jussive in vv 11–12 is conditioned by the content. Extrahuman creation, nature, is not addressed directly, but is metaphorically drawn into the act of praise." Hossfeld, *Psalms 2*, 464.

A   A threefold call for Israel to praise the LORD (vv 1–3)
B   Reasons for Israel to praise the LORD (vv 4–6)
A'   A threefold call for the nations to praise the LORD (vv 7–9)
B'   Reason for the nations to praise the LORD: He is King (v 10)
A'' All of nature invited to praise the LORD (vv 11–12)
B'' Reasons for nature (and peoples) to praise the LORD (v 13)

We can consolidate these six points into three stanzas:

Stanza 1, Israel, sing to the LORD a new song, for he is great (vv 1–6)
Stanza 2, Nations, ascribe to the LORD glory, for the LORD is king (vv 7–10)
Stanza 3, Let all nature rejoice, for the LORD is coming to judge (vv 11–13)

Theocentric Interpretation

The theocentric nature of Psalm 96 is obvious. Israel, the nations, and all of nature are called to praise the LORD. As Elizabeth Achtemeier puts it, "It is precisely the hymn-form . . . that is primarily concerned with God. Indeed, the hymns in the Bible have one purpose — to glorify and honor God — and they call on individuals, the covenant people, and even all nature and nations to join in that glorification."[20]

In addition, the psalm gives reasons for singing a new song to the LORD. These reasons describe the LORD and his mighty acts: The LORD is great "and greatly to be praised" (v 4); "the LORD made the heavens" (v 5); "honor and majesty are before him" (v 6); "the LORD is king! . . . He will judge the peoples with equity" (v 10); the LORD "is coming to judge the earth. He will judge the world with righteousness, and the peoples with his truth" (v 13).

Textual Theme and Goal

We are now ready to formulate the theme of this psalm. It is clear that the three-fold imperative, "Sing to the LORD a new song" (vv 1–2), echoed in verses 7–8, has to be part of the theme — but not by itself. Why sing to the LORD a new song? The psalm gives many reasons for praising the LORD. One reason that stands out, however, because it comes at the climax of the psalm and is repeated twice,

20. Achtemeier, "The Use of Hymnic Elements in Preaching," *Int* 39, no. 1 (1985; pp. 46–59): 46–47.

is in verse 13: "for he is coming, for he is coming to judge the earth." Therefore the overall theme could be formulated as "Sing to the LORD a new song, for he is coming to judge the earth." But the word "judge" is not clear; it often has negative connotations for us; it does not give us a good reason to sing a new song. Verse 13, however, goes on to explain the LORD's judgment: "He will judge the world with righteousness, and the peoples with his truth." This allows us to phrase the textual theme as follows: *Sing to the LORD a new song, for he is coming to restore justice on the earth.*

For determining the specific goal of this psalm, it would be good to know the occasion for which it was composed. Unfortunately, the historical background of this psalm is not clear.[21] On the one hand, the fact that 1 Chronicles 16 incorporates Psalm 96 into its narrative of the entry of the ark of the covenant into Jerusalem suggests a preexilic date. On the other hand, the LXX adds the superscription, "When the house was built after the exile. A song of David." But VanGemeren points out that "these traditions . . . have little bearing on the original life situation."[22] Verses 6 and 8 do indeed speak of God's "sanctuary" and bringing an offering "into his courts," but this could be either preexilic or postexilic. In any event, since Israel used this psalm in its temple worship on many occasions we need not look for one specific occasion to determine the goal. We can just examine the psalm itself: the threefold imperative "sing!" and the threefold imperative "ascribe!" indicate that the goal of this psalm is *to urge Israel and the nations to praise the* LORD *with a new song.*[23]

Ways to Preach Christ

Psalm 96 presents neither a promise of Christ nor a type. It does present, however, several topics that link directly to Christ in the New Testament: the new song, the kingdom of God, the nations, and the judge. One could develop one or more of these strands to Christ by way of longitudinal themes. The best way, however, is to carry all of them forward together by way of redemptive-historical progression supported by New Testament references.

---

21. "As is usually the case, the psalm is cast into so general a form as to have lost almost all specific references to the occasion that gave rise to its composition." Leupold, *Exposition of the Psalms,* 681.

22. VanGemeren, *Psalms,* 722.

23. Cf. Ps 150:6, "Let everything that breathes praise the LORD! Praise the LORD!" Cf. McCann, "The Psalms as Instruction," *Int* 46, no. 2 (1992; pp. 117–28): 124, "Praising God is the goal of human life, the goal of every living thing, the goal of all creation!"

Redemptive-Historical Progression Supported by New Testament References

The theme of Psalm 96 is "Sing to the LORD a new song, for he is coming to restore justice on the earth." In Isaiah, too, the LORD tells Israel to sing a new song in response to God's new acts of salvation: "See, the former things have come to pass, and *new* things I now declare; before they spring forth, I tell you of them. Sing to the LORD a *new* song, his praise from the end of the earth!" (Isa 42:9–10). At that time the "new things" Isaiah would declare was God's saving Israel from exile in Babylonia (Isa 43:19–21). In Psalm 96 God's new act of salvation is God's coming to restore justice on the earth, to set things straight, to bring in the perfect kingdom of God.

The coming of God's kingdom came close when God sent his son Jesus to earth. At his birth in Bethlehem, angels as well as people sang a new song. Jesus began his ministry by proclaiming the nearness of the kingdom of God (Mark 1:14–15). Jesus showed how near the kingdom of God had come when he preached the good news, healed the sick, gave sight to the blind, restored the lame, fed the hungry, raised people from death. Jesus began to set things right.

After his resurrection, Jesus sent his disciples out to make disciples of all nations. Then he ascended into heaven to reign at God's right hand. But he promised to come again to judge the earth and restore God's perfect kingdom on earth. Then the whole church will sing a new song (for more New Testament references, see "Sermon Exposition" below).

Sermon Theme, Goal, and Need

Since the New Testament does not change the message of Psalm 96, the textual theme can become the sermon theme: *Sing to the LORD a new song, for he is coming to restore justice on the earth.*

We formulated the goal of this psalm as, "to urge Israel and the nations to praise the LORD with a new song." By changing "Israel" to "God's people" the textual goal can become the sermon goal: *to urge God's people and the nations to praise the LORD with a new song.* This goal indicates that the need addressed in this sermon is insufficient praise of the LORD by God's people and the nations. When God's people focus on the pain in this world, the injustice, the violence, the persecution, it is indeed difficult to praise the LORD.

Liturgy, Scripture Reading, and Sermon Outline

For the call to worship one could use Psalm 96:1–3 or 7–9. Verse 8 could function as the offertory sentence. Since the psalm has three stanzas, this is best communicated by having a different reader for each stanza. Alternatively, one could highlight the call to praise and the reasons for it by having two readers:

> Reader 1. A threefold call for Israel to praise the LORD   vv 1–3
> Reader 2. Reasons why the LORD is to be praised: He is great   vv 4–6
> Reader 1. A threefold call for all nations to praise the LORD   vv 7–9
> Reader 2. Reason: "The LORD is king!"   v 10
> Reader 1. All nature called to "sing for joy"   vv 11–12
> Reader 2, Reason: the LORD is coming to restore justice   v 13

The three stanzas also provide a clear, expository sermon outline followed by a solid move to Christ in the New Testament:

> I. Israel, sing to the LORD a new song, for he is great (vv 1–6)
> II. All nations, ascribe glory to the LORD, for the LORD is king (vv 7–10)
> III. All nature, rejoice, for the LORD is coming to restore justice on earth (vv 11–13)
> IV. Christ came and will come to restore justice on earth (NT)

Sermon Exposition

Since the need addressed is that God's people and the nations do not sufficiently praise the LORD, one can use the sermon introduction to illustrate this need. This lack of praise may be due to the pain we experience in this world: cancer, depression, violence, persecution, terrorism. . . . If this sermon is preached on Christmas day, one can read Luke 2:1–14, as the Lectionary suggests, and contrast our lack of praise with the exuberant praise that rang out in the fields of Bethlehem when Jesus was born.

Psalm 96 anticipates this vigorous praise. The Psalm consists of three stanzas, with each stanza calling on more and more people and creatures to praise the LORD. The first stanza, verses 1–6, is addressed to Israel.[24] It begins with a threefold command to "sing to the LORD." Verse 1, "O sing to the LORD a new song; sing to the LORD, all the earth." "Sing!" is a command (imperative) and it is repeated for emphasis. Singing is not optional. Israel is commanded to "sing to the LORD!" They are commanded to sing not to just any god. They are to "sing to the LORD" — all capitals L O R D. The Hebrew word behind this translation is *Yahweh,* that is, Israel's faithful covenant God, the God who revealed himself to Moses as the great "I AM WHO I AM" (Exod 3:14).

24. See n. 18 above.

Israel is commanded to "sing to the LORD a *new song.*" Usually they would sing a *new* song when the LORD gained a military victory for his people.[25] But the psalm sets suspense. It does not tell us what this victory is till the very last verse. So Israel and we have to wait patiently to find out why we have to sing a *new* song. In the meantime the Psalm commands Israel to sing a new song to its LORD.

And not just Israel. Verse 1 continues, "sing to the LORD, *all the earth.*" The whole earth now receives the command to sing to Israel's God. Why is that? They don't even know the LORD. Again we are kept in suspense and have to wait till later.

Verse 2 repeats for the third time, "Sing to the LORD" and adds, "bless his name." "His name" stands for the LORD himself.[26] To "*bless* his name" is to "praise his name" (NIV).

But then verse 2 adds a new command, "Tell of his salvation from day to day." The word for "tell" (*biśśar*) is literally, "proclaim the good news."[27] And the good news is God's salvation. Proclaim the good news of God's salvation not just once but "from day to day," that is, daily, continually. Israel is to praise the LORD by singing songs about the LORD's saving acts and proclaiming this good news daily.[28]

Verse 3, "Declare his glory among the nations, his marvelous works among all the peoples." Now the nations come into view. They do not know Israel's LORD. So Israel is to declare the LORD's "glory among the nations." The LORD's glory (*kābôd*) is the LORD's standing in the world, his weight, his magnitude, his significance, what makes him majestic, impressive. It "is his presence, power, and action in the world."[29] Verse 3 adds, declare "his marvelous works among all the peoples." The LORD's marvelous works began with his creating the heavens and the earth (cf. vv 5, 10). But then came the human fall into sin. Since then

25. See Tremper Longman III, "The Divine Warrior: The New Testament Use of an Old Testament Motif," *WTJ* 44 (1982): 290–307.

26. Note the *a b / a' b'* parallelism: "Sing to the LORD, bless his name." The "name" refers more specifically to the LORD's character and reputation. See "Name" in Leland Ryken et al., *Dictionary of Biblical Imagery* (Downers Grove, IL: InterVarsity, 1998), 582–86.

27. "The Hebrew word is the verb for the duty of the herald who precedes a victor to bring a report to those who wait for good news from the battle." Mays, *Psalms,* 308. Cf. Isaiah 52:7, "How beautiful upon the mountains are the feet of the messenger (*məbaśśēr*) who announces peace, who brings good news (*məbaśśēr ṭôb*), who announces salvation, who says to Zion, 'Your God reigns.'" Cf. Isa 40:9. The LXX translates *biśśar* in Ps 96:2 as *euangelizesthe.*

28. "At first only the elect community knows of this cosmic turning point that has come about; this knowledge is both its blessing and its commission (Isa 40:9–10; 60:1ff.). Thus it has a twofold obligation: (1) that of praise, and (2) that of proclamation to the world." Von Rad, *Biblical Interpretations,* 79.

29. Tate, *Psalms 51–100,* 512. See the many biblical references there. See also von Rad, *Old Testament Theology,* I, 239–40.

the Lord's marvelous works are his marvelous works of salvation. The Lord is working to save his people and to restore his broken creation.

Why does Israel have to sing to the Lord, praise his name, proclaim the good news of his salvation daily, and declare his marvelous works among the nations? Verses 4–6 give the reasons for these commands.

The first reason is given in verse 4. Note the "for": "For great is the Lord, and greatly to be praised; he is to be revered above all gods." All the nations have their own gods which they worship and praise. But only Israel's God, the Lord, is great "and greatly to be praised." Therefore, "he is to be revered above all gods."

The second reason, given in verse 5, builds on the first with another "for": "For all the gods of the peoples are idols, but the Lord made the heavens." This is a devastating description of the gods of the nations: they are mere idols. The Hebrew word for idols is *'ĕlîlîm* while the word for God is *'ĕlohîm.* Obviously this is a pun. In English we might say that "all the gods of the peoples are ungods."[30] The word "designates something as ineffective, worthless, and futile."[31] These worthless idols were made by human hands. But Israel's God, the Lord, "made the heavens." What a contrast! No human hands could have made the heavens. No idols either could have made the heavens. "But the Lord made the heavens." "The creation of the heavens is viewed as a particularly mighty work of power of the God of Israel, one that stretches over the whole earth."[32] Therefore Israel should praise its Lord and declare his marvelous works among the nations.[33]

The third reason for Israel to praise the Lord is given in verse 6, "Honor and majesty are before him; strength and beauty are in his sanctuary." In contrast to the idols, the no-gods, "honor and majesty" are before the Lord.[34] This is the real

30. "'Ungods,' *'ĕlîlîm,* is a polemic coinage that appears frequently elsewhere, punningly formed on *'al* ('no,' 'not') and *'ēl* ('god'), to which a diminutive or pejorative suffix is appended." Alter, *Book of Psalms,* 339 n. 5. Cf. Brueggemann, *The Psalms and the Life of Faith,* 118, "Doxology to Yahweh attacks the claim of every other god and every other loyalty. Israel freely confesses that the other gods have no gifts to give, no benefits to bestow, no summons to make, no allegiance to claim. They are massively and forcefully dismissed."

31. Goldingay, *Psalms,* III, 104, with references to Job 13:4; Zech 11:17.

32. Kraus, *Psalms 60–150,* 253. Also, the pagan nations thought of the heavens as the abode of their gods (cf. Deut 4:19; 17:3). The conviction that the Lord made the heavens established the Lord as far superior to their ungods.

33. "It is relatively easy for us to imagine the dismissal of ancient godly rivals. It is a more difficult contemporary matter to recognize that the alternatives to Yahweh in our time and idiom are not nameable gods but 'isms' of all kinds that want our loyalty and chase after our life commitment. In our social context, some of the more seductive of these idolatries are consumerism, militarism, ageism, racism, sexism, and capitalism. Praise [of the Lord] is a dismissal of every such claim. . . ." Brueggemann, *The Psalms and the Life of Faith,* 119.

34. "Many exegetes suggest that these two attributes of God are personified and are regarded as his personal attendants, just as earthly kings are waited upon by their servants. Whether this is

God, the real King. The second part of verse 6 reminds Israel of God's temple: "strength and beauty are in his sanctuary." The sanctuary can be both the temple in Jerusalem and heaven.[35] According to the letter to the Hebrews, the earthly sanctuary "is a sketch and shadow of the heavenly one" (Heb 8:5). "Strength and beauty are in his sanctuary." "Both words have royal associations."[36] In the sanctuary Israel meets the LORD as its powerful, radiant King. "Honor and majesty," "strength and beauty," characterize Israel's God. This is another reason why Israel should sing to the LORD, praise his name, proclaim the good news of his salvation daily, and declare his marvelous works among the nations.

Stanza two, like stanza one, begins with a threefold command, this one to "ascribe to the LORD glory." Verses 7–8a, "Ascribe to the LORD, O families of the peoples, ascribe to the LORD glory and strength. Ascribe to the LORD the glory due his name." These commands are addressed not to Israel but to the "families[37] of peoples" or families of nations. They are to ascribe glory and strength to the LORD. "To ascribe" is "to give."[38] When the nations did not know the LORD, they ascribed glory and strength to their pagan gods. But Israel has just been instructed in verse 3 to declare the LORD's glory "among the nations." Now that the nations know the LORD's glory, "his presence, power, and action in the world," they are to ascribe, to give, to the LORD "glory and strength." They are to give not to their idols but "to the LORD the glory due his name."

Verse 8b follows up with an astonishing command: "Bring an offering, and come into his courts." The *nations* are commanded to "bring an offering, and come into his courts" by the holy temple. The nations were Gentiles. Gentiles were considered unclean. They could not come near the temple. The Herodian temple had a Court of Priests, a Court of Israel (men), a Court of Women, and a Court of Gentiles — as far away from the Holy of Holies as possible. There were even warning inscriptions to Gentiles not to enter the other courts and come closer to the Holy of Holies. But in bringing an offering to the temple, the Gentile nations

---

so or not, the phrase means that true honour and majesty belong to God." A. Anderson, *Psalms 73–150*, 683. See p. 160 above. Although personification can make the image more concrete and support that the LORD is king (v 10), it does not change the meaning of the words. Note that Psalm 104:1 expresses the same thought with a different image, "You are *clothed* with honor and majesty."

35. Cf. Solomon's prayer at the dedication of the temple, "But will God indeed dwell on the earth? Even heaven and the highest heaven cannot contain you, much less this house that I have built!" (1 Kings 8:27).

36. Davidson, *Vitality of Worship*, 318.

37. "The 'families of nations' probably relates to the characteristic OT designations, 'children of Edom,' 'children of Ammon,' and so on." Grogan, *Psalms*, 166. Cf. Gen 12:3.

38. "As in Ps 29, the verb (*yāhab*) does not mean merely ascribe or recognize, but give (cf. 60:11 [13]; 108:12 [13])." Goldingay, *Psalms*, III, 105. See also Tanner in deClaissé-Walford, Jacobson, and Tanner, *The Book of Psalms*, 721.

would bring a tribute to the LORD. By way of this tribute they would acknowledge that Israel's LORD was also their sovereign King.[39] "Bring an offering, and come into his courts." The Gentile nations are urged to come into the courts of the temple. They are invited "to take their place alongside the Israelites."[40]

Verse 9, "Worship the LORD in holy splendor; tremble before him, all the earth." To *worship* the LORD is to bow down before him, to submit to God. The nations are commanded to bow down before the LORD, to submit to him, to acknowledge that he is the sovereign King. The nations are to worship the LORD in holy splendor, that is, in "garments that are ritually clean."[41] They are to be holy because God is holy. And they are to "tremble before him" because God is awesome.[42]

Why should the nations "ascribe to the LORD the glory due his name; bring an offering, and come into his courts, worship the LORD in holy splendor [and] tremble before him"? The reasons are given in verse 10, "Say among the nations, 'The LORD is king! The world is firmly established; it shall never be moved. He will judge the peoples with equity.'"

The first reason is that "the LORD is king!" Or, as the NIV translates, "The LORD reigns!" No other god is king. No other god reigns. Only the LORD reigns. "This confession challenges all other gods, all other rulers and authorities. There is only one King."[43] That is why the nations must ascribe to him the glory due his name, bring tribute to him, come into his courts, bow down and tremble before him.

The second reason why the nations are commanded to ascribe glory to the

39. The LORD "is like an imperial ruler whom other peoples come to recognize as sovereign, abandoning the lords they previously recognized. They come to this emperor's courts with an 'offering' (*minḥâ*), a word that usefully doubles as both a term for a gift to Yhwh (141:2) and for tribute offered to a sovereign (72:10)." Goldingay, *Psalms*, III, 105.

40. A. Anderson, *Psalms 73–150*, 684, "It is possible that the Psalmist now invites the Gentiles to take their place alongside the Israelites." Cf. Robert L. Foster, "A Plea for New Songs: A Missional / Theological Reflection on Psalm 96," *Currents in Theology and Mission* 33, no. 4 (2006; pp. 285–290): 288, "The psalmist's message is quite prophetic, perhaps even eschatological, mirroring the promises recorded in several prophets that the nations will one day stream into Zion, the courts of YHWH (Isa 56:1–8; 66:18; Zech 14:16–19)."

41. A. Anderson, *Psalms 73–150*, 684. See also p. 194 nn. 17–18 below. It might be tempting at this point to follow Williams, *Psalm 73–150*, 200, with a move to Christ in the New Testament: "While holiness here implies ritual purity, there is more involved. For us this holiness is now ours in Christ. As Paul says, Jesus cleanses the church 'so as to present the church to himself in splendor, without a spot or wrinkle or anything of the kind — yes, so that she may be holy and without blemish' (Eph 5:27)." But it is more powerful to make the move to Christ not on an element in the psalm but on its theme.

42. "'Quake' (*ḥâlâ*) is a powerful word to describe this diffidence: it suggests shuddering, or classically the agonized twisting of a woman giving birth (cf. 90:2)." Goldingay, *Psalms*, III, 105–6.

43. Williams, *Psalms 73–150*, 189.

LORD is also given in verse 10, "The world is firmly established; it shall never be moved." The LORD is King because he is the one who created the world. In verse 5 we already heard that "the LORD made the heavens." In verse 10 the reference is to God making this world. And because the LORD made it, "the world is firmly established; it shall never be moved."[44] "The world is reliable, the earth is stable, the human home is dependable. Life does not need to be lived in anxiety."[45] The dependable Creator King is in control; that's why the nations are ordered to give glory to the LORD.

The last line of verse 10 offers the third reason why the nations are to give glory to God: "He [the LORD] will judge the peoples with equity."[46] "The affairs of people will be ordered according to equity. History and society are not left to the capriciousness of fickle gods or the arbitrary decisions of human rulers. Instead the LORD will rule with righteousness and faithfulness. There is a power that sets things right, a might that can be trusted."[47] That power is the LORD.

The psalmist, then, has offered three reasons why the nations should give to the LORD the glory due his name and worship the LORD. First, the LORD is King of the universe. Second, as Creator King he firmly established the world so that the nations have a safe home. And third, as Judge he will set things right by judging the nations fairly.

Thus far we have seen that stanza 1 commands *Israel* "to sing to the LORD a new song." In stanza 2 the commands are broadened to *all nations* to give to the LORD the glory due his name. The third stanza, finally, invites *all nature* to rejoice before the LORD.

Verse 11, "Let the heavens be glad,[48] and let the earth rejoice; let the sea roar, and all that fills it." The heavens, the earth, and the sea. These are the three domains God created in the beginning.[49] The psalm invites the heavens to be glad, the earth to rejoice, and even the sea to roar. It is surprising that the sea is part of this choir praising the LORD. In the Bible the sea is usually a symbol of evil,

---

44. "It is the sturdy Old Testament immanent will of God that is attested here: God will not liquidate his creation." Von Rad, *Biblical Interpretations*, 81.

45. Mays, *Psalms*, 309. Cf. Hayes, *Preaching the New Common Lectionary, Year A, Advent . . .*, 53, "The belief that Yahweh was in control meant for the ancient Hebrew that life could make sense, that life could be lived in some consistency and hope, and that even consolation could be found in calamity."

46. Equity. "The Hebrew *mêšārîm* . . . is an abstract noun derived from *yāšar*, 'straight' or 'upright,' and has the sense of fairly, even generously, administered justice." Alter, *Book of Psalms*, 339 n. 10.

47. Mays, *Psalms*, 309.

48. Note that Rev 12:12 quotes Psalm 96:11, "Let the heavens be glad."

49. "'Heavens . . . earth . . . sea' constitute the universe of the peoples of antiquity." A. Anderson, *Psalms 73–150*, 685.

chaos. When John received a vision of the new heaven and new earth, he noted, "and the sea was no more" (Rev 21:1). But here even the sea will roar to the glory of God.[50] All evil is overcome and praises its creator God.

But the joy spreads even farther. Verse 12, "Let the field exult, and everything in it. Then shall all the trees of the forest sing for joy before the LORD." "The contents of the fields are their wheat and grass, waving in exultation like a congregation in worship."[51] "Then shall all the trees of the forest sing for joy before the LORD." In the ancient world, trees were often associated with the worship of pagan gods.[52] But just as the chaotic sea is invited to roar praise to the LORD, so all the trees shall "sing for joy before the LORD."

This final stanza, then, addresses the heavens, the earth, the sea "and all that fills it," the field "and everything in it" and all the trees. The *whole* of creation is invited to "sing for joy before the LORD."[53] Again we ask, why?

Verse 13 offers the reasons why. "For he [the LORD] is coming, for he is coming to judge the earth." "For he is coming" is repeated for emphasis.[54] We should not miss this point: The LORD "is coming to judge the earth." Here finally we learn why we and all creation have to sing a *new* song. The LORD is coming to judge the earth.

Is that a reason for joyful singing? When we hear that the LORD is coming to *judge* the earth, we are not joyful. We tend to equate judgment with punishment. Instead of joy we may feel fear. But read on in verse 13, "For he [the LORD] is coming, for he is coming to judge the earth. He will judge the world with *righteousness,* and the peoples with his *truth.*"

"In the context of the Psalms, Yahweh's 'judging the world in righteousness' means 'putting things right' and restoring order and harmony."[55] The LORD will

---

50. "Given its associations with chaos elsewhere, the image of the roiling sea is the perfect choice as the metonym of universal praise. . . . Stripped of all associations of hostility and conflict, the sea's discourse of praise parallels God's solitary, uncontested reign." Brown, *Seeing the Psalms,* 129.

51. Goldingay, *Psalms,* III, 107.

52. For example, when Abram claimed the land of Canaan for the LORD, he built an altar to the LORD at Shechem by the *oak* of Moreh (a Canaanite shrine), another altar east of Bethel, and another by the *oaks* of Mamre at Hebron (Gen 12:6–7, 8; 13:18).

53. "The creator of the world and the judge of the world has to be praised by the entire range of his lordship and his possessions." Kraus, *Psalms 60–150,* 252.

54. "The psalm is coming to its point, so the action is slowed up." Goldingay, *Psalms,* III, 107.

55. Broyles, *Psalms,* 377. Cf. von Rad, *Biblical Interpretations,* 81, to whom "to judge" (*šāpaṭ*) means "a 'settling,' a 'helping one to gain one's rights.' The positive predicates in verses 10b and 13b show how this judging is something of a helping and saving kind: 'equity,' 'righteousness' (meaning loyalty), and 'truth.' Injustice and oppression will disappear from the world of nations." Cf. Leupold, *Exposition of the Psalms,* 685, "In the days of the Old Testament this judgment was

also judge "the peoples with his truth," that is, "with self-consistency and without arbitrariness."[56] The LORD's coming to judge means that the King is coming to restore his created order. The LORD is coming to restore justice on the earth, to set things straight, to bring in the perfect kingdom of God. This is all good news that calls for Israel to "sing to the LORD a new song," for the nations to "worship the LORD in holy splendor,"[57] and for the heavens to be glad, the earth to rejoice, the sea to roar, the field to exult, and all the trees of the forest to sing for joy. It's a picture of a worldwide celebration praising the LORD.

We, too, are part of that celebration. We can rejoice because the LORD is coming to set things right. When Jesus first came to this earth, his birth in Bethlehem was greeted with singing. An angel told the shepherds, "'I am bringing you good news of *great joy* for *all the people:* to you is born this day in the city of David a Savior, who is the Messiah, the Lord.' . . . Suddenly there was with the angel a multitude of the heavenly host, praising God and saying, 'Glory to God in the highest heaven, and on earth peace among those whom he favors!'" (Luke 2:10–14). A new song. Then Simeon praised God with a new song (Luke 2:28–32), then the old prophetess Anna (Luke 2:38).

The nations were next bringing tribute to this "king of the Jews." Wise men came from the East following a star. "When they saw that the star had stopped, they were overwhelmed with *joy.* On entering the house, they saw the child with Mary his mother; and they knelt down and paid him homage. Then, opening their treasure chests, they offered him gifts of gold, frankincense, and myrrh" (Matt 2:10–11). These Gentiles gave tribute to Jesus, acknowledging him as their King.[58]

Jesus began his ministry by "proclaiming the good news of God, and saying, 'The time is fulfilled, and the kingdom of God has come near; repent, and believe in the good news'" (Mark 1:14–15). "The kingdom of God has come near!" Jesus showed how near the kingdom of God had come when he preached the good news, healed the sick, gave sight to the blind, restored the lame, fed the hungry, raised people from death. The world was beginning to look a little more like God intended it in the beginning. Jesus began to restore justice on earth.

---

also thought of with most joyful anticipation, for judgment involved the fact that all things now in disarray and disharmony, suffering from injustice and violence, shall be set right and adjusted." Cf. Brueggemann, *Message of the Psalms*, 145.

56. A. Anderson, *Psalms 73–150.* 686.

57. Cf. Rev 15:3–4, "And they sing the song of Moses, the servant of God, and the song of the Lamb: 'Great and amazing are your deeds, Lord God the Almighty! Just and true are your ways, King of the nations! Lord, who will not fear and glorify your name? For you alone are holy. All nations will come and worship before you, for your judgments have been revealed.'"

58. A little foretaste of the new Jerusalem: "The kings of the earth will bring their glory into it" (Rev 21:24).

With his death on the cross Jesus atoned for our sins. John writes that Jesus "is the atoning sacrifice for our sins, and not for ours only but also for the sins of the *whole world*" (1 John 2:2). Jesus' death on the cross atoned for the sins of Gentiles as well. Paul writes to the Gentiles in Ephesus, "Remember that you were at that time without Christ, being aliens from the commonwealth of Israel, and strangers to the covenants of promise, having no hope and without God in the world. But now *in Christ Jesus* you who once were far off have been brought near by the blood of Christ. For he is our peace; in his flesh he has made both groups into one and has broken down the dividing wall, that is, the hostility between us" (Eph 2:12–14). Gentile nations can now "bring an offering, and come into his courts [and] worship the LORD in holy splendor" (Ps 96:8–9).[59]

After his resurrection, Jesus sent his disciples out to the nations. Jesus said, "Go therefore and make disciples of all nations" (Matt 28:19). Then he ascended into heaven to reign at God's right hand. With Jesus' coronation, God's people in heaven begin to sing a new song. We read in Revelation 5, "They sing *a new song*." What are the words of that new song? "They sing *a new song*: 'You are worthy to take the scroll and to open its seals, for you were slaughtered and by your blood you ransomed for God saints from *every tribe and language and people and nation*; you have made them to be a kingdom and priests serving our God, and they will reign on earth" (Rev 5:9–10).[60]

They will reign on earth when Jesus comes again. For Jesus promised that he would come again. In fact, Jesus claimed to be the judge who is coming. Jesus said, "When the Son of Man [Jesus] comes in his glory, and all the angels with him, then he will sit on the throne of his glory. All the nations will be gathered before him, and he will separate people one from another as a shepherd separates the sheep from the goats. . . . Then the king will say to those at his right hand, 'Come, you that are blessed by my Father, inherit the *kingdom* prepared for you from the foundation of the world'" (Matt 25:31–34).[61] Jesus is the king who is coming

59. "We cannot doubt that the Psalmist refers here to that great change which was to take place in the Church upon the advent of Christ. An opposition or distinction is intended between God's ancient people and the Gentile tribes, which were to be afterwards adopted into the same fellowship." Calvin, *Commentary on the Book of Psalms*, IV, 53.

60. Cf. Revelation 7:9–10, "After this I looked, and there was a great multitude that no one could count, from every nation, from all tribes and peoples and languages, standing before the throne and before the Lamb, robed in white, with palm branches in their hands. They cried out in a loud voice, saying, 'Salvation belongs to our God who is seated on the throne, and to the Lamb!'"

61. Jesus explained his Parable of the Weeds as follows: "Just as the weeds are collected and burned up with fire, so will it be at the end of the age. The Son of Man will send his angels, and they will collect out of his kingdom all causes of sin and all evildoers, and they will throw them into the furnace of fire, where there will be weeping and gnashing of teeth. Then the righteous

to "judge the peoples with equity," to "judge the world with righteousness, and the peoples with his truth" (Ps 96:10, 13).[62] When Jesus comes again and restores God's kingdom on earth, the whole church will sing a new song.[63]

What do we do in the meantime? When we reflect on the increasing persecution of Christians in the world, we hardly feel like singing. When we see the pain people suffer in this world, we hardly feel like singing. When we think of all the injustice in this world, we hardly feel like singing. However, Clinton McCann points out that "in both Psalm 96 and Isaiah 40–55, the proclamation of God's reign occurs in a context (literary, historical, or both) in which it appears that God does *not* reign." He asks, "Can we, shall we say 'the Lord reigns' when the forces of evil seem overpowering? Can we, shall we say 'the world is firmly established' when things around us seem to be falling apart?"[64] But strangely, persecution, pain, and injustice are all the more reason for singing. For we sing in anticipation of what is coming.[65]

For he is coming. Jesus is coming. Jesus is coming to set things right, to make straight what is crooked, to restore justice. So we can sing a *new song* even in our pain and suffering.[66] Paul, who was harshly persecuted, wrote, "I consider that the sufferings of this present time are not worth comparing with the glory about to be revealed to us" (Rom 8:18).

At Christmas we celebrate that Jesus has come to establish God's kingdom on earth. God's kingdom is here now, but not yet fully. We look forward to the day when Jesus will come again to bring it in perfection. In anticipation of that great day of Jesus' victory, let us daily sing to the Lord a *new* song.

---

will shine like the sun in the kingdom of their Father" (Matt 13:40–43). Cf. 2 Cor 5:10, "All of us must appear before the judgment seat of Christ."

62. Cf. Rev 19:11, "Then I saw heaven opened, and there was a white horse! Its rider is called Faithful and True, and in righteousness he judges and makes war."

63. Cf. Rev 14:1–3, "I looked, and there was the Lamb, standing on Mount Zion! And with him were one hundred forty-four thousand who had his name and his Father's name written on their foreheads. . . . And they sing a *new* song before the throne and before the four living creatures and before the elders."

64. McCann, *Theological Introduction*, 46. McCann answers his questions with, "We can, we shall, we must. The only possible source of happiness is to proclaim God's reign and to 'take refuge in' God (Ps 2:12)."

65. "All true praise lives out of the certainty of the eschatological kingdom; it does not stop at what is subjected to our human calculation, but it knows that already even now the kingdom belongs to God." Von Rad, *Biblical Interpretations*, 79.

66. "The 'new song' is to express a new realization and acknowledgement that the future belongs to Yahweh. . . . The new song is the song which breaks through the restraints of the present circumstances and voices expectation and confidence in the future works of God." Tate, *Psalms 51–100*, 719.

Prayer[67]

Great and wondrous God,
your love and your mercy are new every morning.
Do not let your people be content with the repetition of threadbare praise.
Inspire us to join with all of your creation in fresh songs of hope and blessing
offered to you each new day,
through Jesus Christ our Lord. Amen.

Song[68]

Joy to the world! the Lord is come;
    let earth receive her King.
Let every heart prepare him room,
    and heaven and nature sing.

Joy to the earth! the Savior reigns:
    let all their songs employ,
while fields and floods, rocks, hills, and plains
    repeat the sounding joy.

No more let sin and sorrow grow
    nor thorns infest the ground;
he comes to make his blessings flow
    far as the curse is found.

He rules the world with truth and grace,
    and makes the nations prove
the glories of his righteousness
    and wonders of his love.

---

67. *Psalms for All Seasons*, 596.

68. Isaac Watts, 1719 (based on Psalm 98). Public Domain. *Psalter Hymnal* (1987), # 337; *Psalms for All Seasons*, # 98D; *Lift Up Your Hearts*, # 92.

CHAPTER 8

"May the Kings of Seba and Sheba Bring Gifts"

Psalm 72:8–11 (71:8–11)

The Revised Common Lectionary assigns Psalm 72:1–7, 10–14 for reading for Epiphany during all three years in response to the reading of Isaiah 60:1–6. Since we have used the whole psalm as preaching text for Advent (Chapter 4 above), we need not repeat here explanations on the whole psalm. Instead we shall concentrate on the verses 8–11, the literary unit that is really the reason why the *Lectionary* chose verses 10–14 for reading at Epiphany.[1]

Text and Context

Psalm 72:8–11 is a literary unit marked by the inclusio of worldwide dominion (v 8) and all nations giving him service (v 11). This literary (sub)unit may not be understood and preached in isolation, of course, but must be interpreted in the context of the whole psalm.

A broader context for our text is Psalm 2, the royal psalm which, along with Psalm 1, serves as an introduction to the Psalter. Psalm 2:8 promises the king universal dominion: "Ask of me, and I will make the nations your heritage, and the ends of the earth your possession." Psalm 72:8 similarly prays, "May he have dominion from sea to sea, and from the River to the ends of the earth." Psalm 2:11 urges the rulers of the earth, "Serve (*'ābad*) the LORD with fear." Psalm 72:11 similarly wishes, "May all kings fall down before him, all nations give him service (*'ābad*)."

The superscription, "Of Solomon," signals the editor's clue to read this psalm

---

1. We cannot select the verses 10–14 as a preaching text because they are not a literary unit. For literary units we have the option of choosing either the verses 8–11 or 8–14.

against the background of Solomon's reign (1 Kings 1–10). There are many links between 1 Kings 1–10 and Psalm 72 (see p. 95 above). Specifically related to the verses 8–11, during Solomon's rule "people came from all nations to hear the wisdom of Solomon" (1 Kings 4:34), among them the queen of Sheba who brought him gifts (1 Kings 10:1–10, 24–25). Psalm 72:10, 15 asks, "May the kings of Tarshish and of the isles render him tribute, may the kings of Sheba and Seba bring gifts. . . . May gold of Sheba be given to him."

In addition, the Old Testament prophets expressed ideas similar to those in Psalm 72:8–11. Psalm 72:8 says, "May he have dominion from sea to sea, and from the River to the ends of the earth." Zechariah 9:10 uses identical words to describe the coming king of Israel, "He shall command peace to the nations; his dominion shall be from sea to sea, and from the River to the ends of the earth." The lectionary itself assigns Psalm 72 as a response to Isaiah 60:1–6. In Psalm 72:11 the author prays, "May all kings fall down before him, all nations give him service." Isaiah 60:3 predicts, "Nations shall come to your light, and kings to the brightness of your dawn." As mentioned, the psalmist prays, "May the kings of Tarshish and of the isles render him tribute, may the kings of Sheba and Seba bring gifts" (Ps 72:10). Isaiah 60:5–6 promises, "The wealth of the nations shall come to you. A multitude of camels shall cover you . . . ; all those from Sheba shall come. They shall bring gold and frankincense, and shall proclaim the praise of the LORD."

Literary Interpretation

We noted in Chapter 4 that Psalm 72 is classified as a royal psalm because it deals with the person or office of the king. "More specifically, Psalm 72 is probably also an accession or coronation psalm, a prayer for the king at the beginning of his reign."[2] We shall briefly analyze parallelisms, imagery, and repetition of keywords in our text.

Parallelisms

The verses 8–11 are crafted with climactic advancing parallelism and framed with an inclusio of the king's worldwide dominion (vv 8 and 11):

2. Tate, *Psalms 51–100*, 222.

8May he have dominion from sea to sea,	A
and from the River to the ends of the earth.	+ A'
9May his foes bow down before him,	+ A''
and his enemies lick the dust.	+ A'''
10May the kings of Tarshish and of the isles render him tribute,	+ A''''
may the kings of Sheba and Seba bring gifts.	+ A'''''
11May all kings fall down before him,	+ A''''''
all nations give him service.	+ A'''''''

Imagery

Our preaching text uses imagery in verse 8, "May he have dominion . . . to *the ends of the earth.*" Verse 9 offers two images, "May his foes *bow down* before him, and his enemies *lick the dust*" — a picture of defeat, the enemies groveling like a snake[3] before the Davidic king.[4]

Repetition of Keywords

Three times our short text mentions foreign kings. The kings of Tarshish and of the isles rendering tribute; the kings of Sheba and Seba bringing gifts; and finally *all kings* falling down before the Davidic king (vv 10–11). The focus in this text is on all foreign kings submitting to the king of David's House.

Textual Theme and Goal

We formulated the textual theme of the whole psalm as, "Pray that through God's righteous king God's peaceable kingdom may spread to the ends of the earth." The sub-unit of verses 8–11 will have a theme different from that of the whole psalm: a sub-theme. The inclusio or "ballast lines" of this unit give us a solid clue to its theme: "May he have dominion from sea to sea, and from the River to the ends of the earth" (v 8), and "May all kings fall down before him, all nations give him service" (v 11). Therefore the theme of this sub-unit is, *Pray that God's righteous king may have dominion to the ends of the earth, all nations serving him.* The au-

---

3. Cf. Micah 7:16–17, "The nations . . . shall lick the dust like a snake, like the crawling things of the earth."

4. "Hyperbole of self-humiliation." A. Anderson, *Psalms 1–72,* 523.

thor's goal with this text was *to encourage Israel to pray that God's righteous king may have dominion to the ends of the earth, all nations serving him.*

Ways to Preach Christ

One could preach Christ from this text by way of redemptive-historical progression supported by New Testament references (see Chapter 4 above). But because the focus in verses 8–11 is specifically on the Davidic king and his worldwide dominion, the best way to preach Christ is typology supported by New Testament references.

Typology and New Testament References

It is clear that in its original historical setting Psalm 72 is a prayer for King Solomon or a later Davidic king. This king of the house of David is a type of king Jesus:[5] he prefigures Jesus Christ who will indeed bring in the anticipated worldwide kingdom of justice. One can perhaps use the prophecies of Isaiah 60:2–6 and Zechariah 9:10, which are similar to our text, as a bridge to the New Testament (this would add the bridge of promise-fulfillment). For Epiphany the major New Testament reference will be the story of the visit of the wise men to Bethlehem, Matthew 2:1–12, expanded perhaps with references to Matthew 28:18–20 and other passages about all nations becoming part of God's kingdom (see "Sermon Exposition" below).

Sermon Theme, Goal, and Need

Since "God's righteous king" can refer to both the Old Testament Davidic king and King Jesus, the textual theme can function as the sermon theme: *Pray that God's righteous king may have dominion to the ends of the earth, all nations serving him.*

By changing "Israel" to "God's people," the textual goal can become the sermon goal: *to encourage God's people to pray that God's righteous king may have dominion to the ends of the earth, all nations serving him.* This goal points to the

---

5. See, e.g., Belcher, *The Messiah and the Psalms*, 137, "Although some take this psalm as a direct prophecy of the reign of Christ, it is better to take the reign of the king in Psalm 72 as a type of the reign of Christ because the psalm clearly reflects the historical reality of Solomon's reign."

need addressed by this sermon: God's people do not pray ardently enough that Jesus will be acknowledged as King of kings by all nations. The sermon introduction can focus on this need by raising the question how urgently we pray for all nations to acknowledge Jesus as King of kings and Lord of lords.

Scripture Reading and Sermon Outline

Although our preaching text is Psalm 72:8–11, it would be well for the congregation to hear its immediate context. Therefore one should first read the verses 1–14, followed by the reading of this short text, verses 8–11. As suggested in Chapter 4 above, p. 108, we can best use two readers and the preacher:

Reader 1: Prayer for righteousness and justice (vv 1–4)
Reader 2: Prayer for longevity and universal rule (vv 5–11)
Reader 1: Prayer for righteousness and justice (vv 12–14)
Preacher: Prayer for the king's universal rule (vv 8–11)

The sermon outline can follow the text verse by verse and conclude with the New Testament:

    I. Prayer for the Davidic king's dominion to the ends of the earth (v 8)
   II. Prayer for the submission of the king's enemies (v 9)
  III. Prayer for gentile kings to bring tribute to the Davidic king (v 10)
  IV. Prayer for all nations to serve the Davidic king (v 11)
   V. Move to Epiphany: Matthew 2:1–12 and other passages (NT)

Sermon Exposition

At Christmas time we frequently hear the refrain of Handel's *Messiah*, "King of kings and Lord of lords; King of kings and Lord of lords." It's a wonderful line from Revelation 19:16. It's the name of the conquering rider on the white horse. Jesus is the "King of kings and Lord of lords." But not all nations acknowledge this. Many rulers today still believe that they are all-powerful. Many lords would not have anyone "lord it" over them. Many people serve other gods. How earnestly do we pray that all nations might acknowledge Jesus as "King of kings and Lord of lords"? Our text for this Epiphany Sunday encourages us to pray sincerely that all nations would submit to King Jesus, serve him, and declare him to be "King of kings and Lord of lords."

According to verse 20, Psalm 72 was a prayer of King David. And according to the heading above this psalm, "Of Solomon" or "For Solomon," it is a prayer for Solomon. So originally this psalm was probably a prayer of David for his son Solomon when he became king of Israel. It may also have been used later at the coronation of other kings from the house of David. We shall simply call this Davidic king, Solomon.

The psalm begins with many petitions for Solomon: verses 1–2, "Give the king your justice, O God, and your righteousness to a king's son. May he judge your people with righteousness, and your poor with justice." The psalm is all about the Davidic king promoting justice for the poor and needy. Verse 7 concludes this first section of the psalm: "In his days may righteousness flourish and peace (*šālôm*) abound, until the moon is no more." David prays that this righteous kingdom may last forever.

In verse 8 David turns to the geographical dimensions of this kingdom. He implores God: "May he have *dominion* from sea to sea, and from the River to the ends of the earth." When God created human beings, "God blessed them, and God said to them, 'Be fruitful and multiply, and fill the earth and subdue it; and have dominion . . .'" (Gen 1:28). But humans misused their dominion, resulting in many injustices on earth. But this king will head a righteous kingdom. So David prays, "May he have dominion from sea to sea, and from the River to the ends of the earth."

"From sea to sea" probably refers to the realm God promised Israel in Exodus 23:31: "I will set your borders from the Red Sea to the sea of the Philistines [the Mediterranean], and from the wilderness to the Euphrates."[6] The words "from the River to the ends of the earth" mean from the river Euphrates "to the ends of the earth," that is, to "its farthest borders."[7]

Solomon was indeed king over a large empire. The book of First Kings tells us that "Solomon was sovereign over all the kingdoms from the Euphrates to the land of the Philistines, even to the border of Egypt; they brought *tribute* [a sign of allegiance] and served Solomon all the days of his life. . . . People came from all the nations to hear the wisdom of Solomon; they came from all the kings of

---

6. Kidner, *Psalms 1–72*, 256. By contrast, Rogerson and McKay, *Psalms 51–100*, 115, think it probably refers to "the Mediterranean sea in the west to the Persian Gulf in the east"; while A. Anderson, *Psalms 1–72*, 522, thinks it more likely that this is "an allusion to the cosmic sea."

7. A. Anderson, *Psalms 1–72*, 523. Cf. Psalm 2:8, "Ask of me, and I will make the nations your heritage, and the ends of the earth your possession." "'The ends of the earth' reprises a significant theme that binds together the group of psalms beginning with Ps 56 and here culminating at the end of Book 2 of the Psalter. This segment presents the growing expectation of the divine rule of God in which all kings and nations will acknowledge his rule and will join in his praise." Wilson, *Psalms*, I, 988 n. 11.

the earth who had heard of his wisdom" (1 Kings 4:21, 34). Solomon indeed had "dominion from sea to sea."

"Dominion from sea to sea." Some nations later adopted this slogan for their nation. Canada's coat of arms has the Latin words *a mari usque ad mare,* "from sea to sea" — meaning, from the Atlantic to the Pacific. In the United States, people sing "America the Beautiful" with the lines, "America! America! God shed his grace on thee. And crown thy good with brotherhood from sea to shining sea!" Again, from the Atlantic to the Pacific.

But the prayer in this psalm asks for much more than dominion from one sea to another or from one ocean to another. It asks for dominion "to *the ends of the earth*" — which is the entire earth. A. Anderson rightly comments, "If this request were thought of merely in political terms, the wish might be absurd." But, he points out, "the writer links the rule of the earthly king with the universal rule of God. It is only as Yahweh's representative that the king has a claim to dominion over the world; in a way the king sits upon Yahweh's throne (1 Chron 28:5, 29:23; 2 Chron 9:8)."[8] And Yahweh's rule, of course, covers the entire world. The kingdom of God has no borders.

The next verses provide more details for this prayer for the worldwide rule of Israel's king. Verse 9 begins with the king's enemies: "May his foes bow down before him, and his enemies lick the dust."[9] The prayer for his foes to bow down before Solomon is a prayer for their submission to Solomon. It is a petition that they no longer fight Solomon but acknowledge Solomon as their sovereign. May "his enemies lick the dust" takes the bowing down one step further. This line asks that his enemies will be completely defeated, that they will grovel like a snake before the king of the house of David.

Verse 10 moves to the kings of other nations: "May the kings of Tarshish and of the isles render him tribute, may the kings of Sheba and Seba bring gifts." Tarshish is a Mediterranean seaport far west of Israel, close to Gibraltar, Spain, at the edge of the then-known world.[10] "The isles" are the islands in the Mediterranean. The prayer is that these kings in western nations may render

---

8. A. Anderson, *Psalms 1–72,* 522. For example, in 1 Chronicles 28:5 David says, "And of all my sons, for the LORD has given me many, he has chosen my son Solomon to sit upon the throne of the kingdom of the LORD over Israel." Cf. Weiser, *The Psalms,* 503–4, "The wishes expressed for the expansion of the power of the king's dominion . . . come . . . from this linking of the earthly kingship to the idea of the Kingdom of God as embodied in the dominion of the king and aiming at the subjection of all the nations to God."

9. Cf. Psalm 2:10–12, "Now therefore, O kings, be wise; be warned, O rulers of the earth. Serve the LORD with fear, with trembling kiss his feet. . . ."

10. "Far off to the westernmost limits of the then-known world lies the famous old city of Tartessus in Spain, commonly known as Tarshish." Leupold, *Exposition of the Psalms,* 519–20.

tribute to Solomon. By bringing tribute, these gentile kings express allegiance to Israel's king.

From the west verse 10 turns to the east and south: "may the kings of Sheba and Seba bring gifts." Sheba[11] is today's Yemen, southeast of Israel. Seba is south of Israel in Africa.[12] We read in 1 Kings 10:10 that the queen of Sheba gave King Solomon "one hundred twenty talents of gold" — an astonishing amount of gold, about four and a half tons.[13] Other kings also came to Solomon bearing gifts: "objects of silver and gold, garments, weaponry, spices, horses, and mules" (1 Kings 10:25). By bringing gifts, these kings to the east and south also acknowledge Solomon as their sovereign king.

Verse 11 broadens the range to *all* kings, and *all* nations: "May all kings fall down before him, all nations give him service."[14] If *all* kings of the earth will fall down before Solomon, they will publicly demonstrate that Israel's king is King of kings, also their King. If *all* nations will give him service,[15] they will show by their actions that the Davidic king is Lord of lords, also their Lord.

But this worldwide dominion is not gained by a powerful army or a superior navy. Instead, it is gained by worldwide recognition of this king's concern with justice and righteousness, as the following verses explain. Verse 12 begins with the important word "for." Why should all nations serve this king of the house of David? "*For* [because] he delivers the needy when they call, the poor and those who have no helper. He has pity on the weak and the needy, and saves the lives of the needy." Three times verses 12–13 mention the needy. It is because of "the recognition of his justice, that the king will get universal homage."[16]

Although Solomon's kingdom was extensive, he was never hailed as King of kings. Solomon prefigured a coming King of kings. The extent of Solomon's

---

11. "The Greek version interpreted this word Sheba; it has Ἀράβων, 'Arabs.'" Ross, *Commentary on the Psalms*, II, 531 n. 14.

12. Seba "may refer to a region in present-day Sudan, south of Egypt." Stek, *NIV Study Bible*, Ps 72:10 n. A. Anderson, *Psalms 1–72*, 523, notes that "the various geographical locations mentioned are representative of all the world, near and far."

13. NIV, 1 Kings 10:10 n. f. If a talent is 75 pounds, 120 talents adds up to 9,000 pounds.

14. "The final verb [serve him] is especially important, for it is always a key word for Israel. Hebrew *'ābad* means both to 'serve' and 'worship.' It is a key word in the Exodus narrative. Israel goes from being 'slaves' of the bad reign of Pharaoh to being 'servants / worshippers' in God's kingdom." Tanner in deClaissé-Walford, Jacobson, and Tanner, *The Book of Psalms*, 578.

15. "May . . . all nations give him service (*'ābad*)." Cf. Psalm 2:11 which urges the kings of the earth, "Serve (*'ābad*) the LORD with fear."

16. "For" (*kî*) makes verses 8–11 (dominion from sea to sea) dependent on verses 12–14 (justice for the needy). "It will not be by force of arms, but by the recognition of his justice, that the king will get universal homage. Cp. Ps 82:3f." Rogerson and McKay, *Psalms 51–100*, 116.

kingdom and the justice and peace he promoted were small but promising signs of this worldwide kingdom that would come in the future.

Zechariah prophesied about this coming king and kingdom with the words of Psalm 72: "Rejoice greatly, O daughter Zion! . . . Lo, your king comes to you; triumphant and victorious is he, humble and riding on a donkey. . . . He shall command peace (*šālôm*) to the nations; his dominion shall be *from sea to sea, and from the River to the ends of the earth*" (Zech 9:9–10).[17]

The prophet Isaiah also spoke of this glorious future. He predicted, "The LORD will arise upon you, and his glory will appear over you. Nations shall come to your light, and kings to the brightness of your dawn. . . . A multitude of camels shall cover you, the young camels of Midian and Ephah; all those from *Sheba* shall come. They shall bring *gold and frankincense,* and shall proclaim the praise of the LORD" (Isa 60:2–6). In Jesus Christ these Old Testament promises were fulfilled. The nations did indeed come to Jesus' light when he was born.

Today is Epiphany Sunday. Epiphany is a Greek word meaning appearance or manifestation. On Epiphany Sunday the Christian church remembers the manifestation of Christ to the gentiles in the persons of the wise men. We read the story in Matthew 2:1–12:

> In the time of King Herod, after Jesus was born in Bethlehem of Judea, wise men from the East came to Jerusalem, asking, "Where is the child who has been born *king of the Jews?* For we observed his star at its rising, and have come *to pay him homage.*" When King Herod heard this, he was frightened, and all Jerusalem with him; and calling together all the chief priests and scribes of the people, he inquired of them where the Messiah was to be born. They told him, "In Bethlehem of Judea; for so it has been written by the prophet:
>
> > 'And you, Bethlehem, in the land of Judah, are by no means least among the rulers of Judah; for from you shall come *a ruler who is to shepherd my people Israel.*'"
>
> Then Herod secretly called for the wise men and learned from them the exact time when the star had appeared. Then he sent them to Bethlehem, saying, "Go and search diligently for the child; and when you have found

17. Cf. Micah 7:11–12, "In that day the boundary shall be far extended. In that day they will come to you from Assyria to Egypt, and from Egypt to the River, from sea to sea and from mountain to mountain." "The basis for such cosmic claims on behalf of the Judean monarch was the belief in God as creator. As creator of the world, God could make his earthly representative ruler of the world." Hays, *Preaching Through the Christian Year,* 74.

him, bring me word so that I may also go and pay him homage." When they had heard the king, they set out; and there, ahead of them, went the star that they had seen at its rising, until it stopped over the place where the child was. When they saw that the star had stopped, they were overwhelmed with joy. On entering the house, they saw the child with Mary his mother; and *they knelt down and paid him homage.* Then, opening their treasure chests, *they offered him gifts of gold, frankincense, and myrrh.* And having been warned in a dream not to return to Herod, they left for their own country by another road.

Matthew is the only gospel writer who records this story of the wise men. He does not mention, as does Luke, the angel telling Mary in Nazareth that she will become the mother of God's Son, the birth of John the Baptist, Mary and Joseph's journey from Nazareth to Bethlehem, the birth of Jesus, and the angels and shepherds glorifying God at Jesus' birth. Matthew zeroes in on the wise men offering their gifts to Jesus. Why? Why did Matthew want to record just this story? What was his message?

In contrast to Luke who wrote his gospel for gentiles, Matthew wrote his gospel for Jews. His goal was to convince the Jews that Jesus was the long-expected Messiah. So he begins his gospel with a genealogy of Jesus: "An account of the genealogy of Jesus the Messiah, the *son of David,* the son of Abraham" (Matt 1:1). To convince the Jews that Jesus was indeed the Messiah, Matthew emphasizes that Jesus was "the son of David," from the royal house of David. So he does not spend time in Nazareth but goes directly to Bethlehem, the city of David. Matthew 2:1, "In the time of King Herod, after Jesus was born in *Bethlehem of Judea,* wise men from the East came to Jerusalem." He calls the town "Bethlehem *of Judea*" "to emphasize that Jesus came from the tribe and territory that produced the line of Davidic kings."[18]

Matthew knew Psalm 72. He knew Israel's prayer for the Davidic king: "May the kings of Tarshish and of the isles render him tribute, may the kings of Sheba and Seba bring gifts. May all kings fall down before him, all nations give him service" (vv 10–11). And here come the wise men from the East. Matthew mentions no country. They could be gentiles from any country. They were astrologers. They had studied the stars and had seen a new star rising. They interpreted this as a sign of the birth of a king of the Jews. So they loaded up their camels with gifts

---

18. "Matthew says nothing of the events in Nazareth (cf. Luke 1:26–56). Possibly wanting to emphasize Jesus' Davidic background, he begins with the events that happened in David's city. It is called 'Bethlehem of Judea,' not to distinguish it from the town of the same name about seven miles northwest of Nazareth, but to emphasize that Jesus came from the tribe and territory that produced the line of Davidic kings." *NIV Study Bible,* Matt 2:1 n.

and headed for the capital city of Judea, Jerusalem. Naturally, that's where the king of the Jews would have been born. When they arrived there, they asked, "Where is the child who has been born king of the Jews? For we observed his star at its rising, and have come to pay him homage."

But the Jews could not answer the question about the child "born king of the Jews." Neither could King Herod. He was frightened. Was there a pretender who would usurp his throne? He asked the chief priests and scribes who knew their Bible well. And they immediately had the answer. Micah had prophesied, "But you, O Bethlehem of Ephrathah, who are one of the little clans of Judah, from you shall come forth for me one who is to rule in Israel, whose origin is from of old, from ancient days" (Micah 5:2). The great Messiah King would be born not in the capital city Jerusalem but in the little town of Bethlehem.

The wise men immediately set out for Bethlehem, about six miles southwest of Jerusalem. There they found the child. Matthew writes, "They knelt down and paid him homage." Here are the first gentiles from the East paying homage to the child Jesus. These gentiles publicly submitted to Jesus as their king. "Then, opening their treasure chests, they offered him gifts of gold, frankincense, and myrrh." As the queen of Sheba gave gold to king Solomon, these gentiles gave their royal gifts, their tribute, to King Jesus. They confirmed that Jesus is the King of kings, also their king.

In relating this story, Matthew's message is that Jesus is indeed the great Messiah King, the King of kings. Even gentiles recognize this. They kneel down before the child, pay him homage, and offer him royal gifts. But this is only the beginning of Jesus' story. Matthew continues to tell the story of Jesus' teachings and miracles, of his death and resurrection. After his resurrection Jesus declared, "*All authority* in heaven and on earth has been given to me." Jesus is indeed the King of kings and King of all nations. Jesus commanded his disciples, "Go therefore and make disciples of *all* nations." Then Jesus ascended to his heavenly throne — the King of kings, the ruler of all nations. But he did not leave us alone. He promised, "I am with you always, to the end of the age" (Matt 28:18–20).

Meanwhile we are mandated to "make disciples of *all nations.*" The apostle John was privileged to see the fantastic future that awaits God's people. He records in the book of Revelation that he saw "a great multitude that no one could count, *from every nation,* from all tribes and peoples and languages, standing before the throne and before the Lamb, robed in white, with palm branches in their hands" (Rev 7:9). Later he saw the New Jerusalem. He writes, "The city has no need of sun or moon to shine on it, for the glory of God is its light, and its lamp is the Lamb. *The nations* will walk by its light, and *the kings of the earth* will bring their glory into it" (Rev 21:23–24).

Jesus Christ is indeed King of kings and Lord of lords. Pray that more and more people and earthly powers may submit to King Jesus. Pray that all nations may declare that Jesus Christ is King of kings and Lord of lords and serve only King Jesus.

Prayer[19]

Everlasting God,
> you brought the nations to your light
>> and kings to the brightness of your rising.
> Fill the world with your glory,
>> and show yourself to all the nations,
> through him who is the true light
>> and the bright morning star,
> Jesus Christ, your Son, our Lord,
>> who lives and reigns with you and the Holy Spirit,
> one God, now and forever. Amen.

Song[20]

1 Hail to the Lord's Anointed,
> great David's greater Son!
Hail in the time appointed,
> his reign on earth begun!
He comes to break oppression,
> to set the captive free;
to take away transgression,
> and rule in equity.

2 He comes with succor speedy
> to those who suffer wrong;
to help the poor and needy,
> and bid the weak be strong;
to give them songs for sighing,
> their darkness turn to light,
whose souls, condemned and dying,
> are precious in his sight.

---

19. *Worship Sourcebook,* Edition Two, quoted in *Lift Up Your Hearts,* # 109.

20. James Montgomery (1822). Public Domain. *The United Methodist Hymnal; Psalms for All Seasons,* # 72A; *Lift Up Your Hearts,* # 109.

₃He shall come down like showers
    upon the fruitful earth;
love, joy, and hope, like flowers,
    spring in his path to birth.
Before him on the mountains,
    shall peace, the herald, go,
and righteousness, in fountains,
    from hill to valley flow.

₄To him shall prayer unceasing
    and daily vows ascend;
his kingdom still increasing,
    a kingdom without end.
The tide of time shall never
    his covenant remove;
his name shall stand forever;
    that name to us is love.

CHAPTER 9

"The Voice of the LORD Is Powerful"

Psalm 29 (28)

Although Psalm 29 has been called one of the most beautiful psalms,[1] it is also one of the more difficult psalms to interpret.[2] Because of its sevenfold repetition of "the voice of the LORD," *The Revised Common Lectionary, Year A,* selected it for the Baptism of the Lord, the first Sunday after the Epiphany.[3] At the baptism of Jesus "a voice from heaven said, 'This is my Son, the Beloved, with whom I am well pleased'" (Matt 3:17). John Hayes rightly asserts, "The connection of the psalm with the baptism of Jesus is . . . very secondary and simply draws on some imagery in the psalm."[4] The baptism of Jesus is a detail in Jesus' life that no psalm anticipates. But the baptism of Jesus can be a stepping stone for a solid connection to the works the powerful voice of Jesus performed during his ministry on earth (see "Sermon Exposition" below).

---

1. Ross, *Commentary on the Psalms,* I, 652.

2. See some of the different interpretations in Lowell K. Handy, ed., *Psalm 29 through Time and Tradition* (Eugene, OR: Pickwick, 2009).

3. "The Eastern Church celebrates the baptism of Jesus on the Feast of the Epiphany. By contrast, the Western Church observes the coming of the Magi on Epiphany and celebrates the Baptism of the Lord on the Sunday after Epiphany." Bert Polman, "The Liturgical Use of Psalm 29," *Psalm 29 through Time and Tradition,* ed. Lowell K. Handy (Eugene, OR: Pickwick, 2009; pp. 90–98), 94.

4. Hayes, *Preaching the New Common Lectionary, Year B, Advent . . . ,* 102. But Mays, *Preaching and Teaching the Psalms,* 64, considers the choice "a profound interpretation of the occasion." See the full quotation in n. 75 below.

Text and Context

Some biblical scholars think that verse 11 was added later and that the original literary unit was verses 1–10. But the verses 1–11 are marked as a literary unit by the inclusio of verses 1–2 and 10–11: "Verses 1–2 contain sixteen words in the Hebrew text. Four of the sixteen are the divine name *Yahweh* ('the Lord'). Verses 10–11 also contain sixteen words in the Hebrew text. Again, four of the sixteen are the divine name *Yahweh* ('the Lord')."[5] In addition the word "strength" (*'oz*) appears in both verses 1 and 11.[6]

The context of neighboring psalms may help elucidate the message of Psalm 29. In Psalm 28:1 the psalmist cries out, "To you, O Lord, I call; my rock, do not refuse to hear me, for if you are silent to me, I shall be like those who go down to the Pit." Psalm 29 answers with a deafening roar as "the voice of the Lord" thunders over the waters a complete seven times.[7] Psalm 28:8–9 declares, "The Lord is the strength of his people; he is the saving refuge of his anointed. O save your people, and bless your heritage." Similarly Psalm 29:11 asks, "May the Lord give strength to his people! May the Lord bless his people with peace!"

More helpful for understanding the specific message of Psalm 29 are other hymns such as Psalm 96. Both psalms have the threefold climactic or staircase parallelism, "Ascribe to the Lord." But whereas Psalm 29:1 addresses the angels, "Ascribe to the Lord, O heavenly beings," Psalm 96:7 addresses the "families of the peoples." Mark Futato writes, "Although Psalm 29:1–2 summons the angelic hosts to worship the Lord, this summons is rightly extended to humans, since Psalm 96 does just this."[8]

Further, verse 10, "The Lord sits enthroned over the flood" (*mabbûl*) will be understood better in the context of Genesis 6–11, the Genesis flood, the only other place in the Bible that uses the term *mabbûl*.[9] The flood narrative, in turn, takes us back to the beginning when the Lord set bounds to the chaotic waters; the Lord was sovereign and in control (Genesis 1; see "Sermon Exposition" below).[10]

---

5. Futato, *Interpreting the Psalms*, 211. In the Hebrew Bible the superscription is not part of verses 1–2.

6. For more details on the inclusio, see John H. Stek, "Stylistics of Hebrew Poetry," *CTJ* 9, no. 1 (1974; pp. 15–30): 20; Fokkelman, *Major Poems of the Hebrew Bible*, III, 46; and Freedman and Hyland, "Psalm 29," *HTR* 66 (1973; pp. 237–56): 240.

7. See Futato, *Interpreting the Psalms*, 211–12, on the context of Pss 28, 30, and the "Kingship of Yahweh psalms."

8. Ibid., 212.

9. The Hebrew word for "flood" in Psalm 29:10, *mabbûl*, is used in the Old Testament only for Noah's flood (Gen 6:17; 7:6, 7, 10, 17; 9:11 [2×], 15, 28; 10:1, 32; 11:10).

10. See also Pss 77:16–19 and 89:8–10. For connections with the Song of the Sea (Exod 15:1–18), see Craigie, *Psalms 1–50*, 245.

Literary Interpretation

Although some scholars classify Psalm 29 as a "theophany psalm,"[11] it is generally identified as a hymn. In seeking to understand this hymn, we shall first examine it with respect to its parallelisms, imagery, repetition of keywords, and structure.

Parallelisms

Psalm 29 begins with a classic example of climactic (staircase) parallelism (similar to Ps 96:7–8a):

1Ascribe to the LORD, O heavenly beings,	A *a* *b* *c*
ascribe to the LORD glory and strength.	+ A′ *a′ b′* *d*
2Ascribe to the LORD the glory of his name;	+ A″ *a″ b″* *d′ e*

But awareness of advancing parallelism over three or more lines will disclose more subtle forms of climactic parallelism in verses 3, 5–6, and 7–8. Advancing parallelism over two lines is found in verses 4, 9, 10, and 11. Here is a snapshot of the psalm's parallelisms:

A Psalm of David.

1Ascribe to the LORD, O heavenly beings,	A
ascribe to the LORD glory and strength.	+ A′
2Ascribe to the LORD the glory of his name;	+ A″
worship the LORD in holy splendor.	B

3The voice of the LORD is over the waters;	A
the God of glory thunders,	+ A′
the LORD, over mighty waters.	+ A″
4The voice of the LORD is powerful;	B
the voice of the LORD is full of majesty.[12]	+ B′

---

11. Gerstenberger, *Psalms*, I, 132, names Weiser, Jeremias, and Stolz.

12. This could be synonymous parallelism (see n. 54 below). But since I understand "full of majesty" to be more than just powerful (it connotes royalty; see v 10b), I have marked it as advancing parallelism.

₅The voice of the LORD breaks the cedars;	A
the LORD breaks the cedars of Lebanon.¹³	+ A'
₆He makes Lebanon skip like a calf,	+ A''
and Sirion like a young wild ox.	+ A'''
₇The voice of the LORD flashes forth flames of fire.	A
₈The voice of the LORD shakes the wilderness;	+ A'
the LORD shakes the wilderness of Kadesh.	+ A''
₉The voice of the LORD causes the oaks to whirl,	A
and strips the forest bare;	+ A'
and in his temple all say, "Glory!"	B
₁₀The LORD sits enthroned over the flood;	A
the LORD sits enthroned as king forever.	+ A'
₁₁May the LORD give strength to his people!	B
May the LORD bless his people with peace!	+ B'

Imagery

The imagery in Psalm 29 offers real challenges to interpretation. Verse 1 presents the first image, "Ascribe to the LORD, O heavenly beings," Hebrew, *bǝnê 'ēlîm,* "sons of gods."¹⁴ The Canaanites believed that their lower gods were "sons of gods." Should this phrase be taken literally or figuratively or both?¹⁵ Most commentators opt for a figurative interpretation: "sons of gods" refers not to the Canaanite gods but to angels in God's heavenly council.¹⁶

---

13. Westermann, *The Living Psalms,* 230, classifies verses 5 and 8 as synonymous parallelism. I have classified these as advancing parallelisms because the second line specifies more precisely "the cedars *of Lebanon*" and "the wilderness *of Kadesh.*" "The Germans call this 'the parallelism of *Aufsprung*' (holding in reserve)." Leupold, *Exposition of the Psalms,* 248.

14. "The formally plural word *'ēlîm* always has a plural meaning, at least as it is used in the Bible." Brooks Schramm, "Adapting Psalm 29 through Translation," in *Psalm 29 through Time and Tradition,* ed. Lowell K. Handy (Eugene, OR: Pickwick, 2009; pp. 9–24), 13.

15. Ross, *Commentary on the Psalms,* I, 656–57, argues that the phrase can have a double reference. The Canaanites would hear it as a call for their gods to ascribe glory to Israel's LORD while the Israelites would hear it as a call for God's attendants, the angels, to give glory to the LORD. It is not very likely, however, that the Canaanites would have heard Psalm 29.

16. E.g., Broyles, *Psalms,* 152, "In the Old Testament, comparable expressions designate the angelic host in Yahweh's heavenly council," with references to 1 Kings 22:19; Isa 6:2–4; Pss 8:6; 82:1–7; 89:6–9; 97:7; 103:20; 148:1–2; Job 1:6; 2:1; 38:7.

Verse 2 contains a double metaphor: "Worship the LORD in holy splendor."
"Worship" is literally to bow low, to lie prostrate. "In holy splendor" is the second
metaphor. The Hebrew has *hadrat qodeš*, "splendid holy attire." Does this phrase
refer to the LORD or the worshipers? The various translations indicate that the
meaning is not entirely clear: the NRSV translates, "in holy splendor" (either
the LORD's or the worshipers'); the NIV translates, "the splendor of his holiness"
(the LORD's, but the footnote allows for the worshipers': "Worship the LORD with
the splendor of holiness"), which is how the ESV translates the phrase. "In holy
splendor" probably refers to the holy garments the priests had to wear[17] — a picture here transferred to angels who did not wear garments but were to worship
the LORD with the "appropriate attitude."[18]

Thunder as "the voice of the LORD" (v 3) is both an anthropomorphism and a
metaphor. God does not have a human voice nor is thunder actually the voice of
the LORD. "These are poetic illustrations or symbols (i.e., implicit comparisons)
helping us to gain a sense of what Yahweh's majesty is like."[19]

Verse 6 contains hyperbole as well as two similes: "He makes [the giant
mountains of] Lebanon skip like a calf, and Sirion [Mount Hermon] like a young
wild ox." Verse 10 offers another double metaphor, "The LORD sits enthroned
over the flood [chaos]," which is explained in the parallel line, "the LORD sits
enthroned as king forever." "The metaphor maps God's sovereignty as universally
cosmic"[20] and "forever."

Repetition of Keywords

The most obvious repetition is that of "the voice of the LORD." The phrase occurs
in verses 3, 4 (2×), 5, 7, 8, and 9 for a total of seven times — the perfect number
(cf. the seven days of Genesis 1–2 and "the seven thunders" of Revelation 10:3).[21]

---

17. "The expression 'in holy array' borrows the picture from the earthly ministrants, who
were, according to Old Testament regulations (cf. Exod 28:2; 2 Chron 20:21), to appear for service
in God's sanctuary only when properly vested." Leupold, *Exposition of the Psalms*, 246. Cf. Van-
Gemeren, *Psalms*, 293, "Only when arrayed in a manner fit for the worship of the Great King, and
when consecrated to him like the priests at the temple, are God's servants prepared to serve him."

18. "'Holy splendor'. . . . may refer to the appropriate attitude or even the proper attire of those
called upon to glorify Yahweh (see 1 Chron 16:29; 2 Chron 20:21; Ps 96:9)." McCann, "Psalms," 792.

19. Broyles, *Psalms*, 150. He adds, "It would not be consistent with the rest of the OT to
assume Hebrews actually identified Yahweh's voice with the thunder, any more than 84:10[11]
identifies Yahweh as 'a sun and shield.'"

20. Brown, *Seeing the Psalms*, 187.

21. "The Canaanite texts refer to the seven peals of thunder from Baal." Ross, *Commentary
on the Psalms*, I, 658.

In the central section of the psalm (vv 3–9) the name *Yahweh* (LORD) appears ten times — the number of fullness. In the whole psalm, the name *Yahweh* occurs eighteen times: verses 1–2 (4×), verses 3–9 (10×), and verses 10–11 (4×).

Another keyword is "glory" (*kābôd*—weightiness), which is repeated four times (vv 1, 2, 3, and 9). Other repetitions are the result of Hebrew parallelisms. In its climactic parallelism the psalm urges the angels three times to "ascribe to the LORD" (vv 1–2). Advancing parallelism leads to the twofold use of "breaks the cedars" (v 5), "shakes the wilderness" (v 8), and "the LORD sits enthroned" (v 10).

Structure

Biblical scholars are not agreed on the structure of Psalm 29. Some propose a chiastic structure such as: A (vv 1–2), B (vv 3–4), C (vv 5–9b), B' (vv 9c–10), A' (v 11).[22] Others suggest different chiastic structures.[23] The NRSV and ESV subdivide the psalm into six stanzas: vv 1–2, 3–4, 5–6, 7–8, 9, and 10–11. The NIV keeps the central section together and therefore has three stanzas: vv 1–2, 3–9, 10–11.[24] For preachers, it is most helpful to go back to the basic structure of a hymn.

As noted in Chapter 1, p. 11, the typical pattern of a hymn consists of most of the following elements:

1) A call to praise the Lord
2) Transition (*kî*, for, because)
3) Reasons why the Lord is to be praised
4) Conclusion: Praise the Lord!

Psalm 29 exhibits three of these elements (it lacks the transition *kî*):

---

22. Goldingay, *Psalms*, 1, 413. In opposing Goldingay's break between v 9b and c, Jacobson in deClaissé-Walford, Jacobson, and Tanner, *The Book of Psalms*, 283, states, "It would fall outside of the rhythm of the psalm to have the closing stanza begin with the *waw* or for that stanza to include five cola."

23. See, e.g., Robert L. Alden, "Chiastic Psalms: A Study in the Mechanics of Semitic Poetry in Psalms 1–50," *JETS* 17, no. 1 (1974; pp. 11–28): 21, who suggests the following structure: A (vv 1–2), B (v 3), B' (v 4), B'' (v 5), B''' (v 6), B (v 7), B' (v 8), B'' (v 9b), B''' (v 9a), A' (vv 10–11).

24. Cf. John H. Stek, "When the Spirit Was Poetic," in *The NIV: The Making of a Contemporary Translation*, ed. Kenneth L. Barker (Grand Rapids: Zondervan, 1986; pp. 72–87, 158–61), 80. In Psalm 29 "couplets (vv 1–2, 10–11) frame the whole. The body of the psalm is a seven-line hymn celebrating 'the voice of the LORD.'"

1) A call to praise the LORD (vv 1–2)
   Sixteen words in Hebrew[25] including four times *Yahweh*
2) Reasons why the LORD is to be praised (3–9)
   Seven times "the voice of the LORD"
   Marked as a unit by the inclusio "glory" in verses 3 and 9[26]
3) Conclusion: The LORD is praised as king forever (10–11)
   Sixteen words in Hebrew including four times *Yahweh*

Freedman and Hyland propose that, according to the movement of the thunder storm, we can subdivide the central section (vv 3–9) into three strophes, verses 3–4, 5–6, and 7–9. "Thus, in the first strophe the storm gathers force over the Mediterranean. In the second, it shatters the mighty cedars of Lebanon, while shaking the highlands of Syria. In the third, it thunders on into the plains, having left a trail of devastation in the forests. Each strophe begins, appropriately, with *qôl yhwh*. The expression occurs three times in the first strophe, and an equal number of times in the third strophe; the remaining occurrence is in the second strophe."[27]

We can, therefore, sketch the structure of Psalm 29 as follows:

I.   The call to ascribe to the LORD glory and strength (vv 1–2)
II. Reasons for ascribing to the LORD glory and strength (vv 3–9)
     A. The voice of the LORD thunders over the waters of the Mediterranean Sea (vv 3–4)
     B. The voice of the LORD causes destruction in Lebanon (vv 5–6)
     C. The voice of the LORD shakes the wilderness of Kadesh (vv 7–9)
III. Praise and prayer: The LORD sits enthroned as king forever (v 10)
                          May the LORD bless his people with peace (v 11)

25. Not counting the superscription.

26. A key question is whether "and in his temple all say, 'Glory!'" (v 9c) belongs with the verses 3–9 or 10–11. Some commentators divide the psalm as follows: verses 1–2; 3–9b; and 9c–11, while others insist that verse 9c belongs to the central section of verses 3–9. Because of the inclusio of verses 1–2 and 10–11 (see p. 191 above) and the inclusio "glory" surrounding verses 3–9, I side with the latter. See also n. 24 above.

27. Freedman and Hyland, "Psalm 29," *HTR* 66 (1973): 241. Terrien, *The Psalms*, 276, also opts for three strophes but selects vv 3–4, 5–7, and 8–9. Freedman and Hyland's selection is more convincing. They add (pp. 241–42) that "the word Yahweh by itself occurs once in each strophe. The distributional pattern is outlined in the following table:

	qôl yhwh	*yhwh*
Strophe I (vv 3–4)	3	1
Strophe II (vv 5–6)	1	1
Strophe III (vv 7–9)	3	1
	7 +	3 = 10

Theocentric Interpretation

There is no question that Psalm 29 centers on the LORD: it is his voice that is heard a perfect seven times in nature and his name, *Yahweh,* that is sounded a full ten times in the central section (vv 3–9). The LORD is the only sovereign God; he controls the mighty forces of nature. Therefore the "heavenly beings" are "to ascribe to the LORD glory and strength" and prostrate themselves before the LORD (vv 1–2).

Altogether the LORD's name is heard eighteen times in eleven verses. The psalm concludes with "The LORD sits enthroned over the flood [the destructive, chaotic waters; the LORD is sovereign!]; the LORD sits enthroned as *king forever.*" This confession is followed by the prayer,[28] "May the LORD give strength to his people! May the LORD bless his people with peace!" Glory to God is the psalm's beginning and peace on earth its conclusion.[29]

Textual Theme and Goal

Some scholars look for the theme in the sevenfold use of the powerful "voice of the LORD" (vv 3–9).[30] But it seems clear that this message is subordinate to the main theme introduced by the three opening imperatives: "Ascribe to the LORD, O heavenly beings, ascribe to the LORD glory and strength. Ascribe to the LORD the glory of his name" (vv 1–2a). The addressees, "O heavenly beings," presents us with a unique challenge for determining the textual theme. The theme seems to be, "Angels, ascribe glory to the LORD!" But this leaves Israel out of the picture. The textual theme should capture the psalm's message for Israel.

What, then, was the message for Israel? Earlier (p. 191 above) we heard Mark Futato's solution: "Although Psalm 29:1–2 summons the angelic hosts to worship the Lord, this summons is rightly extended to humans, since Psalm 96 does just this."[31] With the same threefold climactic parallelism as Psalm 29, Psalm 96 says, "Ascribe to the LORD, O *families of the peoples,* ascribe to the LORD glory and strength." But we cannot base the theme of Psalm 29 on Psalm 96. We should find the theme for Psalm 29 in the psalm itself.

Where is Israel in this psalm? We find Israel in verse 9c which reads, "and

---

28. See n. 72 below.

29. "*Gloria in excelsis* is its beginning, and *pax in terris* its conclusion." Delitzsch, *Biblical Commentary on the Psalms,* I, 373.

30. E.g., Williams, *Psalms 1–72,* 235, "The voice of Yahweh, the theme of this psalm, is 'over the waters,' even 'over many waters.'"

31. Futato, *Interpreting the Psalms,* 212.

in his temple all say, 'Glory!'" The "all" is Israel worshiping in God's temple in Jerusalem.[32] Mays writes, "The description [of the theophany] concludes in verse 9c with the effect the majesty of the Lord has on the temple congregation: They are saying (the Hebrew participle implies continuously): 'Glory!'"[33]

We can picture the use of this psalm in the Jerusalem temple as follows: A priest or God's people begin this psalm by calling upon the angels in heaven to "ascribe to the LORD glory."[34] Why should angels give glory to the LORD? The priest or God's people enumerate seven reasons that describe the awesome power of the voice of the LORD on this earth. At the end of this enumeration, God's people on earth join in with the heavenly choir: "and in his temple *all*[35] say, 'Glory!'" The two choirs singing glory to the LORD are like a giant liturgical inclusio joining heaven and earth.[36] Therefore the theme of Psalm 29 is, *Angels and Israel should join in giving glory to the LORD whose powerful voice in nature reveals his sovereignty over all.*

The goal of the psalm for Israel needs to be determined by the theme and the historical circumstances addressed. "Most modern scholars associate Psalm 29 with the Feast of Tabernacles, which may have included as one of its aspects the so-called New Year Festival."[37] The Feast of Tabernacles or "ingathering" was held on the fifteenth day of the seventh month (September-October) and lasted seven days (Exod 23:16; Lev 23:34). People lived in tents and brought fruit to the LORD. On the final day of this feast, according to the Septuagint, they would sing Psalm 29. A month or two later the thunderstorms would roll in, breaking the summer drought.

There is a general consensus that Psalm 29 is a polemic against the worship

32. Some commentators argue that "his temple" refers to God's heavenly temple implied in vv 1–2. But this whole central section, verses 3–9, marked as a unit by the inclusio "glory" (vv 3 and 9c), takes place on earth. It would be strange indeed if the psalmist in the last line of the theophany switched from earth to heaven. Moreover, the word "temple" is not even mentioned in verses 1–2.

33. Mays, "Psalm 29," *Int* 39, no. 1 (1985; pp. 60–64): 60. Freedman and Hyland, *HTR* 66 (1973) 244, argue for the Jerusalem temple on the basis of similarities with Psalm 96: "The cultic addition in Ps 96:8, "Bring an offering, and enter into his courts" fixes the setting in the temple area, and lends further support to the identification of the *qodeš* in v 9 [96:9] as the holy place."

34. "The opening call for the heavenly host to glorify the LORD is a liturgical way for the congregation to equate its own praise with what is right and required in the heavenly palace-temple. The congregation's doxologies correspond to the doxologies of heaven." Mays, *Psalms*, 136.

35. "The sense is that all those who serve God join in the cry." Bruce Chilton, *Pure Kingdom: Jesus' Vision of God* (Grand Rapids: Eerdmans, 1996), 153 n. 24.

36. "Hence the worship of earth becomes united with the song of the angels in the temple of heaven (vv 1–2). The psalmist may have in mind a picture of the temple crowded at festival time, which is perhaps the occasion when this psalm was originally used in ancient Israel." Rogerson and McKay, *Psalms 1–50*, 131–32. Cf. Eaton, *Psalms*, 89, "Jerusalem's worship is felt to be one with that of heaven."

37. A. Anderson, *Psalms 1–72*, 232. So also the LXX.

of Baal. The Canaanites (and the people of Lebanon [vv 5–6]) believed that their storm god Baal was responsible for the storms, the thunder, the lightning, and the rains that made the earth fertile. Some scholars think that the psalm was a Canaanite hymn in which the psalmist merely replaced the name of Baal with Yahweh. It is more likely, however, that the psalmist used phrases from Canaanite literature in order to show that not Baal but Yahweh is the sovereign God.[38] The goal of the psalm, then, was *to urge Israel to give glory not to Baal but to the* LORD *whose powerful voice in nature reveals his sovereignty over all.*

Ways to Preach Christ

"There are no explicit references to Psalm 29 in the New Testament"[39] nor does it have a promise of the coming Messiah nor a type. But we can still preach Christ in several ways: longitudinal themes and redemptive historical progression, both supported by New Testament references.

Longitudinal Themes

One can trace the sub-themes of God's powerful voice and that of glory from Psalm 29 to Jesus Christ in the New Testament. For example, one can trace "the voice of the LORD" back to the creation account where in six days God's powerful voice spoke the creation into being. In the New Testament John links this voice to Jesus: "In the beginning was the *Word,* and the Word was with God, and the Word was God. . . . All things came into being through him. . . . And the Word became flesh and lived among us, and we have seen his *glory, the glory* as of a father's only son, full of grace and truth" (John 1:1–3, 14).

One can also trace the theme of glory from Psalm 29 directly to the New Testament. James Mays writes, "In the New Testament the subject of doxology

38. "Many of the details of Psalm 29 remind us of a Canaanite poem. It shares many traits with the type of poetry discovered at Ugarit. . . . The psalm is unusually heavy with tricola, and its parallelism is very repetitive. These are characteristics of Ugarit poetry as contrasted with Hebrew. . . . Besides the details of the psalm, the imagery associated with Yahweh bears a striking resemblance to the descriptions of Baal in the Ugaritic texts." Dillard and Longman, *Introduction to the Old Testament,* 232. See also Westermann, *The Living Psalms,* 235–36, and Futato, *Interpreting the Psalms,* 219–20.

39. Craigie, *Psalms 1–50,* 249, "There are no explicit references to Ps 29 in the NT, though it has been suggested that the 'seven thunders' of Rev 10:3 have Ps 29 as their background; such a view is far from certain."

[glory] undergoes a surprising personal concentration. With few exceptions, the subject is Jesus, the Son of God. For John the deeds of Jesus were signs, a disclosure of his participation in the majesty of God (2:11; 11:4, 40), and to know Jesus by faith as Son of God was to behold his glory (1:14). For Paul the crucified Christ is the Lord in whom glory is manifest (1 Cor 2:8); the light of the knowledge of the glory of God is seen in the face of Jesus Christ (2 Cor 4:6)."[40]

Redemptive-Historical Progression and New Testament References

A more comprehensive and satisfying way to Christ in the New Testament is redemptive-historical progression supported by New Testament references. The theme of Psalm 29 is that Israel join the angels in giving glory to the LORD whose powerful voice in nature reveals his sovereignty over all. The psalm begins with glory to God in heaven (vv 1–2) and ends with peace on earth (v 11),[41] similar to the angel song at the birth of Jesus. Before he began his ministry Jesus was baptized and "the heaven was opened, and the Holy Spirit descended upon him in bodily form like a dove. And a *voice* came from heaven, 'You are my Son, the Beloved; with you I am well pleased'" (Luke 3:21–22; cf. Luke 9:35). John calls Jesus "the Word" that was in the beginning — the powerful Word through whom "all things came into being" (John 1:1–3). In his ministry on earth Jesus demonstrated that he was God's powerful Word (see other New Testament references in the "Sermon Exposition" below).

Sermon Theme, Goal, and Need

Since the New Testament does not change the message of Psalm 29, by changing "Israel" to "all God's people" the textual theme can become the sermon theme: *Angels and all God's people should join in giving glory to the LORD whose powerful voice in nature reveals his sovereignty over all.*

The textual goal was "to urge Israel to give glory not to Baal but to the LORD whose powerful voice in nature reveals his sovereignty over all." Today people are no longer tempted to ascribe glory to Baal, the storm god, when witnessing a thunderstorm or longing for rain. But people today are tempted to ascribe glory to meteorologists for forecasting how much rain will fall and where; to ascribe glory to scientists in general for protecting our buildings from lightning

40. Mays, *Preaching and Teaching the Psalms*, 63–64.
41. See n. 29 above.

strikes with lightning rods, for chasing and analyzing storms till all mystery has evaporated. The goal, then, should be updated to, *"to urge God's people to give glory not to human beings but to the* LORD *whose powerful voice in nature reveals his sovereignty over all."* The need addressed, then, is that God's people today are tempted to glorify human experts instead of the LORD.

Liturgy / Scripture Reading / Sermon Outline / PowerPoint

Psalm 29:1–2 can serve as the call to worship while verses 10–11 are a fitting parting blessing. For Scripture reading, the liturgist could read Psalm 29:1–2, another reader could read verses 3–9 (or split this central section among three readers: vv 3–4; 5–6; 7–9) and the liturgist concludes with verses 10–11.

The sermon outline can utilize the textual outline, with a final additional point:

>   Introduction: the historical setting of Baal worship
> I. The call to ascribe to the LORD glory and strength (vv 1–2)
> II. Reasons for ascribing to the LORD glory and strength (vv 3–9)
>   A. The voice of the LORD thunders over the waters of the Mediterranean Sea (vv 3–4)
>   B. The voice of the LORD causes destruction in Lebanon (vv 5–6)
>   C. The voice of the LORD shakes the wilderness of Kadesh (vv 7–9b) "and in his temple all say, 'Glory!'" (v 9c)
> III. "The LORD sits enthroned over the flood" and prayer (vv 10–11)
> IV. Jesus is the voice of the LORD (NT)

If PowerPoint is available, it would be well to show a map of Lebanon in order to follow the thunderstorm as it originates over the Mediterranean Sea, crashes into the coastal mountains of Lebanon, then Mount Hermon, and finally shakes the wilderness of Kadesh (II. A. B. C.). Projecting also the verses being explained enables the congregation to understand better the point being made.

Sermon Exposition

Psalm 29 gives us a graphic description of a powerful thunderstorm. When I was young and we heard thunder, my parents would huddle the kids together and start counting the time between seeing the lightning and hearing the thunder. When they could count to twenty we were relaxed because the lightning was still far away. When the count was seven or five we were more nervous because the lightning was closing in. One time they could not even count to one: we saw the lightning and immediately heard a deafening boom. We were all scared. The lightning had split a tree in our backyard.

Even today being caught in a thunderstorm is an awesome experience. It was that and more for ancient people. Thunder was the loudest noise they ever heard. It terrified them. Who could make such deafening sounds? It must be a god, they believed, a storm god. They had a name for this storm god: Baal-Hadad. When they heard the thunder, they believed they heard the voice of Baal. On the one hand, they were terrified by the destruction Baal could cause. On the other hand, they welcomed the arrival of Baal with the fall thunderstorms. For that is when Baal broke the summer drought and brought the welcome rain to their parched lands. Baal made the earth fertile.

When Israel entered the land of Canaan they were confronted by Baal worship. In Egypt they had irrigation when the Nile flooded the land (see Deut 11:10–16). Not so in Canaan. Just like the Canaanites, the Israelites were dependent on rain to make the land fertile. So they were tempted to worship Baal, the storm god.

Recall the story of Elijah and the priests of Baal. The LORD had punished Israel with a drought because they forsook "the commandments of the LORD and followed the Baals" (1 Kings 18:18). The drought was now in its third year. Elijah told King Ahab to meet him at Mount Carmel by the Mediterranean Sea. The king came with four hundred fifty prophets of Baal. Elijah proposed that they prepare an offering for Baal but put no fire to it. "So they took the bull that was given them, prepared it, and called on the name of Baal from morning until noon, crying, 'O Baal, answer us!' But there was *no voice,* and no answer. . . . Then they cried aloud and, as was their custom, they cut themselves with swords and lances until the blood gushed out over them. . . . But there was *no voice,* no answer, and no response." The storm god Baal failed to send lightning.

Next Elijah repaired the altar of the LORD, "put the wood in order, cut the bull in pieces, and laid it on the wood." He asked the people to drench the offering and the wood with water. Then he prayed, "O LORD, God of Abraham, Isaac, and Israel, let it be known this day that you are God in Israel, that I am your servant, and that I have done all these things at your bidding. Answer me, O LORD, answer me, so that this people may know that you, O LORD, are God, and that you have turned their hearts back." We read, "Then the fire of the LORD fell and consumed the burnt offering, the wood, the stones, and the dust, and even licked up the water that was in the trench. When all the people saw it, they fell on their faces and said, 'The LORD indeed is God; the LORD indeed is God'" (1 Kings 18:20–39). But it did not last long. Baal worship soon became popular again in Israel.

Psalm 29 is a protest against the worship of Baal. The psalmist has combined phrases that were used in Baal worship but substituted the name of the LORD (Israel's God Yahweh) for Baal. In eleven verses the psalm mentions the name of the LORD (Yahweh) eighteen times. It begins in verse 1: "Ascribe to the LORD, O heavenly beings, ascribe to the LORD glory and strength." "Ascribe" means to acknowledge, to give.[42] Give not to Baal but "give to the LORD, O heavenly beings, give to the LORD glory and strength."

Notice that with this psalm the priest or the people worshiping in the temple in Jerusalem tell the "heavenly beings" to "ascribe to the LORD glory and strength." Who are these "heavenly beings"? Literally the psalm says, "O sons of gods." The Canaanites believed that their lower gods were literally "sons of gods." So it is possible that the psalm tells the Canaanite gods to submit themselves to Israel's God and ascribe glory and strength to the LORD. But this psalm was not written for the Canaanites but for Israel. Moreover, Psalm 96, which is similar to Psalm 29, calls the Canaanite gods idols, ungods.[43] Idols cannot ascribe glory to the LORD. So it is more likely that the Jerusalem congregation is thinking of angels, more specifically "the angelic host in Yahweh's heavenly council."[44]

In Psalm 96 we also hear this threefold command to "ascribe," but there it is addressed to people: "Ascribe to the LORD, *O families of the peoples,* ascribe to the LORD glory and strength. Ascribe to the LORD the glory due his name" (Ps 96:7–8). In Psalm 29 the angels are ordered to "ascribe to the LORD glory and strength." How do they give glory and strength to the LORD?

Let's start with the word "glory." "Glory" is a keyword in this psalm. It occurs four times (vv 1, 2, 3, and 9). What does it mean to give "glory" to the LORD? In the Old Testament the word "glory" (*kābôd*) is literally "heavy," "weighty." For example, the cloud on Mount Sinai is described as "heavy" (*kābôd*) with rain (Exod 19:16). So to give glory to the LORD basically means to proclaim the LORD's weight, his worth, his importance, his majesty.[45] To give glory to the LORD is to give him the credit he deserves for his weight, his worth.

---

42. "The verb (*yāhab*) does not mean merely ascribe or recognize, but give (cf. 60:11 [13]; 108:12 [13])." Goldingay, *Psalms,* III, 105. See also Tanner in deClaissé-Walford, Jacobson, and Tanner, *The Book of Psalms,* 721.

43. The Hebrew word for idols is *'ĕlîlîm* while the word for God is *'ĕlohîm.* "'Ungods,' *'ĕlîlîm,* is a polemic coinage that appears frequently elsewhere, punningly formed on *'al,* ('no,' 'not') and *'ēl* ('god'), to which a diminutive or pejorative suffix is appended." Alter, *Book of Psalms,* 339 n. 5.

44. "In the Old Testament, comparable expressions designate the angelic host in Yahweh's heavenly council." Broyles, *Psalms,* 152, with references to "1 Kings 22:19; Isa 6:2–4; Pss 8:6; 82:1–7; 89:6–9; 97:7; 103:20; 148:1–2; Job 1:6; 2:1; 38:7."

45. "When used of the Lord, *kābôd* denotes splendor, majesty, magnificence." Limburg, *Psalms,* 93. Cf. Brown, *Psalms,* 154, "Elsewhere, 'glory' is described as a brilliant effulgence of overwhelming 'majesty' and 'splendor' (Pss 21:5; 45:3; cf. 104:1b–2a, 31), as well as 'power' and strength' (63:2; 96:7)."

The angels also are to ascribe "strength" to the LORD. "Strength" has to do with a king's military victories.[46] "Strength" refers to the LORD's royal power. Israel confessed, "By strength of hand the LORD brought us out of Egypt" (Exod 13:14, 16). "Strength," therefore, refers to God's power to gain the victory over his enemies and save his people. The LORD can display his strength in a destructive thunderstorm and can use that same strength to save his people.[47] "Ascribe to the LORD, O heavenly beings, ascribe to the LORD glory and strength." The heavenly beings are to give the LORD credit for his glory as well as his strength.

Verse 2 describes further *how* the angels are to "ascribe to the LORD glory": "Ascribe to the LORD the glory of his name; *worship* the LORD in holy splendor." They are to give glory to the LORD by worshiping the LORD. To "worship" is literally to bow low, to lie prostrate before the great King. To bow down before the LORD is to acknowledge that the LORD is glorious, almighty, sovereign. The LORD is King of the universe and even angels are to bow down before him.

Finally, the angels are told to "worship the LORD in holy splendor."[48] "In holy splendor" probably refers to the appropriate attitude of the angels.[49] Because worshiping the LORD is so weighty and the LORD is King of the universe, even angels are to worship the LORD with reverence and awe.

Why should the angels worship the LORD? The verses 3–9 give the reasons. These verses graphically describe the movement of a powerful thunderstorm. It begins far-out over the Mediterranean Sea (vv 3–4). Heading east it crashes into the coastal mountains of Lebanon (v 5), then Mount Hermon inland (v 6). Finally, heading farther east it shakes the wilderness of Kadesh (vv 7–9).

When the Canaanites heard thunder they thought they heard the voice of their storm god, Baal. Not so, says Psalm 29. It is the voice of the God of Israel, Yahweh, the LORD.

Verse 3, "The voice of the LORD [Yahweh] is over the waters; the God of glory thunders, the LORD, over mighty waters." "The voice of the LORD is over the waters." You can hear the voice of the LORD over the Mediterranean Sea. It is still distant, but you know that it is not the voice of Baal but "the voice of the

---

46. "The LORD's strength is to be praised in that it has been demonstrated in the victory following the battle." Craigie, *Psalms 1–50*, 246.

47. Cf. Psalm 74:12–13, "Yet God my King is from of old, working *salvation* in the earth. You divided the sea by your might [*strength*]; you broke the heads of the dragons in the waters."

48. "Holy splendor" could refer either to the LORD's holy splendor or to the worshipers' holy garments. The NRSV leaves the phrase ambiguous; the NIV translates, "the splendor of his holiness," that is the LORD's holiness; the ESV translates, "with the splendor of holiness," the worshipers' holiness. In the sermon I would just go with the pew Bible and not make an issue of this since it is a minor detail: "worship" is the primary image.

49. See p. 194 nn. 17 and 18 above.

LORD." "The God of glory thunders." The God of glory speaks in the thunder.[50] Again, it is not Baal, but "the God of glory" — the God of weight, the God who is much more weighty, much greater and more worthy than Baal.[51]

Verse 3 continues, "the LORD, over mighty waters." "'The waters' stand for tumultuous forces that threaten to overwhelm the regular order of life, in the way that a flood can overwhelm people, land, and even cities."[52] "Mighty waters" can cause indescribable chaos and grief, as we see in our days especially in destructive tsunamis. Who can forget the picture of a tsunami hitting Japan, flooding cities, and carrying off to sea houses, cars, and countless human bodies? But Psalm 93:4 proclaims, "More majestic than the thunders of *mighty waters,* more majestic than the waves of the sea, majestic on high is the LORD!"[53] Psalm 29 agrees, "The voice of the LORD is *over* the waters; . . . the LORD, *over* mighty waters."

Israel knew from experience that their LORD is mightier than mighty waters. When the LORD brought Israel out of slavery in Egypt, the Egyptian army chased after them. They caught up with Israel by the Red Sea and were about to slaughter them. Then "the LORD drove the sea back by a strong east wind all night, and turned the sea into dry land; and the waters were divided. The Israelites went into the sea on dry ground . . ." (Exod 14:21-22). The Israelites escaped while the Egyptians drowned. "The voice of the LORD is over the waters; . . . the LORD, over mighty waters."

Verse 4 wraps up the description of the LORD's voice: "The voice of the LORD is powerful; the voice of the LORD is full of majesty." "Powerful" and "full of majesty" describe the royal power of the voice.[54] Israel's God, the LORD, is

50. At Mount Sinai the LORD revealed himself in thunder and lightning (Exod 19:16; 20:18). "The voice of the LORD . . . means an articulate sound which communicates the awesome majesty and power of the LORD. . . . The voice of the LORD is not spoken of as identical with thunder and as only one feature of a storm along with wind and lightning." Mays, "Psalm 29," *Int* 39, no. 1 (1985): 61. Cf. Ross, *Commentary on the Psalms,* I, 659, "The psalmist probably means that the voice was commanding the elements of nature, causing the storm by his word to develop and then die out (metonymy of cause). . . . The LORD spoke the thunderstorm into existence."

51. The Canaanites considered the sea "to be the battle ground between Yam, the god of the sea and of chaos, and Baal, the god of fertility and thunderstorms. El, the chief of the Canaanite pantheon, was the benign father of the gods. The direct reference to Yahweh as the glorious El may contain a polemic allusion to the superiority of Yahweh over Baal." VanGemeren, *Psalms,* 294.

52. Goldingay, *Psalms,* I, 417. Goldingay continues, "They can also stand for such tumults as supernatural realities (e.g., 74:13; 93:4), the forces over which Yhwh asserted control at creation (e.g., 33:7; 74:13; Isa 51:10)."

53. "In Psalm 93:3-4 the 'mighty waters' are an image of the cosmic forces of chaos that the LORD vanquished at the time of creation." Futato, *Interpreting the Psalms,* 216. Cf. Westermann, *The Living Psalms,* 232.

54. "The use of these synonyms in verse 4 serves to tie the storm (vv 3-9) to the call to wor-

King of the universe. That's why even angels are to ascribe to the LORD glory and strength.

Verses 5–7 go on to recount the effects of the voice of the LORD on earth. The scene shifts to the mountains of Lebanon. This is where the Canaanites believed their gods lived.[55] The voice of the LORD wreaks utter destruction in the land of the pagan gods. Verse 5, "The voice of the LORD breaks the cedars; the LORD breaks the cedars of Lebanon."[56] The cedars of Lebanon were used in the construction of many pagan temples.[57] "The cedars of Lebanon, symbols of all that is lofty and proud . . . , tokens of all that is luxuriant and stable (Pss 92:12; 104:16), are shattered."[58] Isaiah 2:12–17 prophesied, "For the LORD of hosts has a day against all that is proud and lofty, against all that is lifted up and high; against *all the cedars of Lebanon,* lofty and lifted up; and against all the oaks of Bashan; against all the high mountains, and against all the lofty hills. . . . The haughtiness of people shall be humbled, and the pride of everyone shall be brought low; and the LORD alone will be exalted on that day." The destruction created by the thunderstorm of Psalm 29 is but a small foretaste, according to Isaiah, of the destruction that will take place on the day of judgment.

Verse 6, "He makes Lebanon skip like a calf, and Sirion like a young wild ox." Lebanon has two mountain ranges: the coastal mountains and those more inland with its southernmost peak Sirion, which we know as Mount Hermon. Mount Hermon, just north of Israel, reaches an altitude of 9,232 feet and is snow-capped in the winter. Even today it functions as a ski resort for Israelis. The mountains of Lebanon are massive and solid. Yet the voice of Israel's God "makes Lebanon skip like a calf, and Sirion like a young wild ox." The mountains of Lebanon skip not with joy, but in fear![59]

Verse 7 adds, "The voice of the LORD flashes forth flames of fire." In Canaanite

---

ship (vv 1–2). The 'splendor' [majesty] and 'power' witnessed in the storm are to be ascribed to the LORD and to no other deity." Futato, *Interpreting the Psalms,* 216–17.

55. VanGemeren, *Psalms,* 294.

56. "It is important to note the particular fashion in which the poet has utilized these northern references to make his point. He has taken two symbols of power and strength — 'cedars' (v 5) and the mountainous area of 'Lebanon / Sirion' — and illustrated in his poetry the weakness of those great symbols of strength in relationship to the LORD's strength (cf. 'strength,' v 1). The famous cedars of Lebanon are easily broken by the LORD's voice; the immobile mountains of Lebanon skip like calves frightened at the sound of the voice." Craigie, *Psalms 1–50,* 247.

57. "In the Mesopotamian tale of Gilgamesh and Enkidu, the forests of Lebanon were considered sacred to the gods, who used the cedars for the construction of their own dwellings." Wilson, *Psalms,* I, 505.

58. Kraus, *Psalms 1–59,* 349. Cf. Alter, *Book of Psalms,* "Throughout biblical poetry, these trees are the great emblem of proud loftiness."

59. See Psalms 77:16–19; 114:4–7.

art Baal "had a lightning bolt in his hand."[60] Psalm 29 once more reiterates that the awesome lightning does not come from Baal but from Israel's God, the LORD, the King of creation.

In verses 8–9 the mighty thunderstorm moves inland into the wilderness of Kadesh in Syria.[61] Here, too, it wreaks destruction: "The voice of the LORD shakes the wilderness; the LORD shakes the wilderness of Kadesh. [The booming explosions of thunder shake the wilderness.] The voice of the LORD causes the oaks[62] to whirl, and strips the forest bare." It sounds like a mighty tornado has reached the wilderness causing oaks to whirl and the forest to be stripped bare.

Seven times we hear "the voice of the LORD." In that culture seven was the number of perfection. Think of the seven days in which the LORD completed the creation of the heavens and the earth. Canaanite texts also speak of "the seven peals of thunder from Baal."[63] But again, Psalm 29 reiterates that Baal is not in the awesome thunderstorm. In the booming explosions of thunder we hear the voice of the LORD, Yahweh, the God of Israel.

The last line of verse 9 shifts back to the temple in Jerusalem. That is where God's people began to encourage the angels in heaven to ascribe glory to the LORD: "Ascribe to the LORD, O heavenly beings, ascribe to the LORD glory and strength" (Ps 29:1). Having heard the voice of the LORD breaking the cedars of Lebanon, causing Lebanon to skip like a calf, shaking the wilderness of Kadesh, causing the oaks to whirl and stripping the forest bare, God's people in the temple in Jerusalem now respond with the chorus: "Glory! Glory! Glory! . . ."[64] "They

60. Hilber, *Psalms*, 346.

61. An issue here is whether "the wilderness of Kadesh" is Kadesh in the south (the Sinai traditions, see Numbers 20:16) or Kadesh in the north (Syria) near the Orontes. The south is supported by, e.g., Alter, *Book of Psalms*, 99; Fokkelman, *Major Poems of the Hebrew Bible*, III, 48; and Nowell, *Sing a New Song*, 153. I favor the north primarily for three reasons: First, thunderstorms would usually not take a 90 degree turn south but continue east to the Syrian desert (see Futato, *Interpreting the Psalms*, 217). Second, Leupold, *Exposition of the Psalms*, 249, points out that "another such wilderness lying to the north by the side of the Lebanon range is meant because of the use of the same term in the Ras Shamra poem (so also Eaton, *The Psalms*, 140; and Hilber, *Psalms*, 346–47). And third, it is more likely that the shout "glory!" would sound from worshipers in the Jerusalem temple when the LORD's destructive power hammers the lands of Baal worshipers rather than the Promised Land.

62. "The NRSV translation, 'causes the oaks to whirl,' involves an alteration of the vowels of the traditional Hebrew text, its justification being that 'oaks' provides a neat parallel to forests. The text, however, may be referring not only to the forest, but to all animals who live in it." Davidson, *Vitality of Worship*, 103. E.g., the ESV translates, "The voice of the LORD makes the deer give birth." Ross, *Commentary on the Psalms*, I, 660, comments, If it does refer to "hinds to travail in birthpangs" it probably means "giving birth pre-maturely." Cf. Wilson, *Psalms*, I, 506.

63. Ross, *Commentary on the Psalms*, I, 658.

64. "The description concludes in verse 9c with the effect the majesty of the Lord has on

echo the heavenly anthem, picking up the one word which encapsulates the incomparable greatness of God, 'Glory.'"[65] They proclaim the LORD's worth, his splendor, his royal majesty.[66] They confess that the LORD is the great King of the universe.[67]

But after all the judgment and destruction caused by the voice of the LORD, we may wonder if the King of glory is favorably inclined to us. Verse 10 takes us back to the beginnings of human history: "The LORD sits enthroned over the flood; the LORD sits enthroned as king forever." The Hebrew word for flood here, *mabbûl*, is used elsewhere in the Bible only for Noah's flood (Genesis 6–11). So the words "The LORD sits enthroned over *the flood*" intend to remind us of the LORD's judgment early in human history. The flood narrative, in turn, takes us back to the waters of Genesis 1. In Genesis 1 we read: "When God created the heavens and the earth, the earth was a formless void and darkness covered the face of the deep, while a wind from God swept over the face of *the waters*. . . . And God *said* ["the voice of the LORD"], 'Let there be a dome in the midst of the waters, and let it separate the waters from the waters.' . . . And God *said,* 'Let the waters under the sky be gathered together into one place, and let the dry land appear.' And it was so" (Gen 1:1–9). In the beginning the LORD set bounds to the chaotic waters; the LORD was sovereign and in control. The LORD sat enthroned over the flood.[68] And eventually life flourished on earth.

Unfortunately, by Noah's time "the earth was corrupt in God's sight, and the earth was filled with violence. . . . And God said to Noah, 'I have determined to make an end of all flesh, for the earth is filled with violence because of them; now I am going to destroy them along with the earth'" (Gen 6:11, 13). God then withdrew his controlling hand and the chaotic waters returned. God's awful judgment destroyed all that was evil. But the story ends with the rainbow of hope: God made a new start with Noah and his family. God said, "I establish my covenant with you, that never again shall all flesh be cut off by the waters of a flood, and never again shall there be a flood to destroy the earth" (Gen 9:11). Never again! The LORD still sits enthroned above the flood; he controls the chaotic waters. He has

---

the temple congregation: They are saying (the Hebrew participle implies continuously): 'Glory!'" Mays, "Psalm 29," *Int* 39, no. 1 (1985): 60.

65. Davidson, *Vitality of Worship,* 103.

66. See n. 45 above.

67. Cf. Psalm 24:10, "Who is this King of glory? The LORD of hosts, he is the King of glory."

68. "Yahweh's power not only exceeds that of the 'many waters' (29:3); his kingship over the flood ascribes to Yahweh the highest possible sovereignty." Hilber, *Psalms,* 348. Cf. Mays, "Psalm 29," *Int* 39, no. 1 (1985): 62, "The assertion that the Lord reigns over the cosmic sea is tantamount to the claim that the entire cosmos is subject to his sovereignty."

the power to protect us from the flood.[69] And he promised to maintain control over the destructive waters: "Never again."[70]

Psalm 29:10 concludes, "the LORD sits enthroned as king forever."[71] Forever! That includes our time when our planet is threatened by floods caused by global warming, weapons of mass destruction that are out of control, and bacteria that are immune to antibiotics. But "the LORD sits enthroned as king forever." Our God is in control. That is our comfort in these trying times.

The psalm ends with a prayer.[72] Verse 11, "May the LORD give strength to his people!" The word "strength" is the same word used in verse 1 to describe the LORD's strength in the storm. It refers to the LORD's power to gain the victory. "The point is that the power of God manifested in the storm is the kind of power that the Lord is able and willing to give to his people."[73]

The final words are, "May the LORD bless his people with peace!" "May the LORD bless his people with *šālôm.*" After all the destruction caused by the voice of the LORD, the psalm concludes with a prayer for peace, for well-being, for security.

Psalm 29 urged Israel to ascribe glory not to Baal but to the LORD. Today, when we experience a thunderstorm, we are not tempted to ascribe glory to Baal. We are much too sophisticated for that. Our scientists know what causes lightning

---

69. "The Psalter also knows of other 'floods' [than Noah's], like the primordial chaotic waters subdued by God (Ps 74:12–17) or the celestial waters above the dome of the sky which God holds at bay, both of which are highly positive images in the sense that God is the controller or restrainer of the flood rather than the one who brings it." Schramm, "Adapting Psalm 29 through Translation," in Handy, *Psalm 29,* 13. Cf. Craigie, *Psalms 1–50,* 248–49.

70. The LORD's "enthronement over 'the flood' assures his children that in his great power he is sovereign. Even as in the days of the flood, when he destroyed creation with his power but saved his own, so it is at any time that God's glory is expressed in the severity of judgment." VanGemeren, *Psalms,* 296.

71. "Yahweh's lordship over the whole of nature means that he is indeed able to care effectively for his people, and that he *can* provide the seasonal rains that are so indispensable for the prosperity of the nation." A. Anderson, *Psalms 1–72,* 238–39.

72. "May the LORD bless" uses the Hebrew *yiqtol* (imperfect) form for incompleted action. Hence the NRSV translates it as a jussive, wish, the NIV as a present tense, "The LORD blesses," and Leupold, *Exposition of the Psalms,* 250, as a future: "The same Lord, whose control of the forces of nature is absolute, wields this control for the good of His people. He will grant them 'strength' whenever they need it; 'He will bless His people with peace.'" On the ambiguity of the Hebrew imperfect tense, see pp. 96–98 above.

73. Futato, *Interpreting the Psalms,* 219. Jacobson in deClaissé-Walford, Jacobson, and Tanner, *The Book of Psalms,* 286, adds, "The nature of God's strength . . . is qualified by the closing line: 'The LORD bless his people with peace!' The strength of God ['bestowed upon God's people in a free and gracious gift'] is given not for the purpose of warfare or conquering power, but paradoxically God's strength quells the warring madness of the children of Adam and Eve."

and what causes the following sound of thunder; they know the speed at which light travels and the speed of sound. They can predict where thunderstorms are likely to originate and where they will travel. They can protect our buildings with lightning rods and know how to seed clouds for fertile rain. When we see lightning and hear thunder in this day and age, we may be tempted to ascribe glory to the human experts. Or we just marvel at the forces of nature.[74]

The next time we experience a thunderstorm we should say to ourselves, "The voice of the LORD" and give God the glory. The next time we experience a thunderstorm we should tell our children, "The voice of the LORD," and give God the glory he deserves. In this secular age we need to hear again the voice of the LORD in nature. In this secular age we need to see again the revelation of the LORD in nature and give our sovereign God the glory he deserves.

In New Testament times the voice of the LORD came in Jesus. When Jesus was born in Bethlehem, an angel told the shepherds, "'I am bringing you good news of great joy for all the people: to you is born this day in the city of David a Savior, who is the Messiah, the Lord.' Suddenly there was with the angel a multitude of the heavenly host, praising God. . . .'" And just like Psalm 29, the song of the heavenly beings begins with "glory to God in the highest heaven" and ends with "on earth peace." The "multitude of the heavenly host" sang, "*Glory* to God in the highest heaven, and on earth *peace* among those whom he favors!" (Luke 2:10–14).

Jesus is the powerful voice of the LORD. John calls Jesus "the Word": "In the beginning was the *Word,* and the Word was with God, and the Word was God. He was in the beginning with God. *All things* came into being through him. . . . And the Word became flesh and lived among us, and we have seen his *glory,* the *glory* as of a father's only son, full of grace and truth" (John 1:1–3, 14).

Before he began his ministry, Jesus was baptized and "the heaven was opened, and the Holy Spirit descended upon him in bodily form like a dove. And a *voice* came from heaven,[75] 'You are my Son, the Beloved; with you I am well pleased'"

---

74. "Few if any of us are tempted to ascribe the power and glory seen in nature to Baal . . . but simply to the 'forces of nature.' In other words, we're not tempted to Baalism but to materialism or naturalism. . . . Psalm 29 instructs us to be theists as we go about our daily lives, to live with the awareness that what we witness in nature is a revelation of divine attributes such as power and glory, and to worship God whenever and wherever we perceive him." Futato, *Interpreting the Psalms,* 228.

75. Mays, *Preaching and Teaching the Psalms,* 64, considers the Lectionary choice of Psalm 29 for the baptism of Jesus "a profound interpretation of the occasion. The liturgical setting connects the psalm's mighty theophany with the quiet epiphany in the waters of the Jordan. The voice of the Lord in the thunderstorm is paired with the voice from heaven saying 'this is my Son.' The storm says, 'this is my cosmos'; the baptism, 'this is my Christ.' The two go inseparably together. The Christology is not adequate unless its setting in cosmology is maintained. The Old Testament doxology is necessary to the gospel."

(Luke 3:21–22). The LORD was well pleased with Jesus for his willingness to take on human flesh in order to advance God's kingdom on earth and spread God's peace to the ends of the world.

During his ministry Jesus demonstrated that he was indeed the powerful voice of the LORD. But instead of being a destructive voice, his was mostly[76] a healing voice. For example, one evening Jesus and his disciples were crossing Lake Galilee in a small boat. Suddenly a great storm arose, whipping up the waters. The mighty waves crashed into the boat and filled it with water. The disciples, who were experienced fishermen, were terrified. They woke Jesus who was asleep in the stern and shouted at him, "Teacher, do you not care that we are perishing?" Jesus "woke up and rebuked[77] the wind, and said to the sea, 'Peace! Be still!' Then the wind ceased, and there was a dead calm. He said to them, 'Why are you afraid? Have you still no faith?' And they were filled with great awe and said to one another, 'Who then is this, that even the wind and the sea obey him?'" (Mark 4:38–41). In the light of Psalm 29 the answer is clear, isn't it? Jesus is the powerful voice of the LORD. He "sits enthroned over the flood" (Ps 29:10); he can still a storm and mighty waves.

On another occasion, when Jesus entered Capernaum, a Roman centurion approached him. The centurion said, "Lord, my servant is lying at home paralyzed, in terrible distress." Jesus said, "I will come and cure him." The centurion answered, "Lord, I am not worthy to have you come under my roof; but only speak the *word,* and my servant will be healed." The centurion believed that Jesus' voice was so powerful that he could heal his servant at a distance. Matthew reports, "And to the centurion Jesus said, 'Go; let it be done for you according to your faith.' And the servant was healed in that hour" (Matt 8:5–8, 13). Jesus is the powerful voice of the LORD which can heal at a distance.

On still another occasion, a little girl, about twelve years old, was dying. We know her as the daughter of Jairus. Jairus begged Jesus to come to his house to heal her. But before they could get there, someone came from the house and said

---

76. Jesus' voice could also pronounce judgment. Jesus overturned the tables of the money changers in the temple and "told those who were selling the doves, 'Take these things out of here! Stop making my Father's house a marketplace!'" (John 2:16). Later Jesus' voice cried out in judgment, "Woe to you, scribes and Pharisees, hypocrites!" (Matt 23:13–36). At the final judgment, Jesus' voice "will say to those at his left hand, 'You that are accursed, depart from me into the eternal fire prepared for the devil and his angels'" (Matt 25:41).

77. "The Greek verb *epitimáō* in the Greek Old Testament is owned by Yahweh. Yahweh 'rebukes' the channels of the sea (Ps 18:15), the primordial Deep (Ps 104:5–9), the sea (Nah 1:3b–5), rivers (Isa 50:2), rider and horse (Ps 76:6), Assyrian armies (Isa 17:13), wicked nations (Ps 9:5), and Satan (Zech 3:1–2)." Foster R. McCurley, *Wrestling with the Word: Christian Preaching from the Hebrew Bible* (Valley Forge, PA: Trinity Press International, 1996), 21.

to Jairus, "Your daughter is dead; do not trouble the teacher any longer." "When Jesus heard this, he replied, 'Do not fear. Only believe, and she will be saved.' When he came to the house, . . . they were all weeping and wailing for her; but he said, 'Do not weep; for she is not dead but sleeping.' And they laughed at him, knowing that she was dead. But he took her by the hand and called out, 'Child, get up!' Her spirit returned, and she got up at once" (Luke 8:49–55). The powerful voice of the LORD can raise even the dead.

This voice of the LORD was so powerful, he could even raise himself from the dead. Jesus said to the Jews who asked for a sign, "Destroy this temple, and in three days I will raise it up" (John 2:19). Jesus was speaking of the temple of his body. People indeed destroyed Jesus' body by crucifying him. But three days later he rose from the dead, the powerful voice of the LORD which is sovereign over all.

Paul writes in Ephesians 1:20–21, "God put this *power* to work in Christ when he raised him from the dead and seated him at his right hand in the heavenly places, far above all rule and authority and power and dominion, and above every name that is named, not only in this age but also in the age to come." And just like Psalm 29, Paul assures us that this power or strength is also available for God's people: "Now to him who by *the power at work within us* is able to accomplish abundantly far more than all we can ask or imagine, to him be *glory* in the church and in Christ Jesus to all generations, forever and ever. Amen" (Eph 3:20–21).[78]

Prayer in unison[79]

Our Father in heaven, hallowed be Your name.
Your kingdom come.
Your will be done on earth as it is in heaven.
Give us this day our daily bread.
And forgive us our debts, as we forgive our debtors.
And do not lead us into temptation, but deliver us from the evil one.
For Yours is the kingdom
　　and the power
　　　　and the glory forever. Amen.

---

78. Cf. Rev 5:13, "Then I heard every creature in heaven and on earth and under the earth and in the sea, and all that is in them, singing, 'To the one seated on the throne and to the Lamb be blessing and honor and *glory and might* forever and ever!'"

79. Matthew 6:9–13, NKJV.

Song[80]

O Lord my God, when I in awesome wonder
 consider all the works thy hand hath made,
I see the stars, I hear the mighty thunder,
 thy power throughout the universe displayed.
Then sings my soul, my Savior God, to thee:
 how great thou art, how great thou art!
Then sings my soul, my Savior God, to thee:
 how great thou art, how great thou art!

But when I think that God, his Son not sparing,
 sent him to die, I scarce can take it in,
that on the cross my burden gladly bearing
 he bled and died to take away my sin.
(*Refrain*)

When Christ shall come, with shout of acclamation,
 and claim his own, what joy shall fill my heart!
Then I shall bow in humble adoration
 and there proclaim, "My God, how great thou art!"
(*Refrain*)

CHAPTER 10

"I Will Make the Nations Your Heritage"

Psalm 2

Handel's *Messiah* cites Psalm 2 extensively: "Why do the nations so furiously rage together, and why do the peoples imagine a vain thing? The kings of the earth rise up, and the rulers take counsel together against the LORD, and against His Anointed. 'Let us break their bonds asunder and cast away their yokes from us.' He that dwelleth in heaven shall laugh them to scorn: the LORD shall have them in derision. . . . Thou shalt break them with a rod of iron; Thou shalt dash them in pieces like a potter's vessel" (Ps 2:1–4, 9). With Handel's *Messiah* ringing in our ears, we might think that it will be easy to preach Christ from Psalm 2. But that is not the case. In its original setting the LORD's "anointed" was the Davidic king.[1]

The Revised Common Lectionary assigns Psalm 2 for reading on Transfiguration Sunday, immediately before Lent, because Matthew 17:5 alludes to Psalm 2: when Jesus was transfigured "a bright cloud overshadowed them, and from the cloud a voice said, '*This is my Son*, the Beloved; with him I am well pleased; listen to him!'" (cf. Ps 2:7, "He said to me, '*You are my son*; today I have begotten you'"). Preachers who do not follow the Lectionary can use Psalms 1 and 2 at the beginning of any series of sermons on the psalms since these two psalms introduce all the following psalms (see pp. 25–28 above).

---

1. Cf. Calvin's *Commentary on the Psalms*, I, 17, on Psalm 2:7, which was usually applied directly to Christ: "David, indeed, could with propriety be called the son of God on account of his royal dignity. . . . David was begotten by God when the choice of him to be king was clearly manifested." Cf. Balentine, "Royal Psalms and the New Testament: From 'messiah' to 'Messiah,'" *Theological Educator* 29 (1984; pp. 56–62): 58, "Thus in Ps 2, and throughout the royal psalms generally, Yahweh's 'anointed one' (*māšîaḥ*) should be understood in terms of the earthly Davidic king."

Text and Context

Psalm 2 is a literary unit as can be seen by its inclusio: the psalm begins with the rhetorical question, "Why do the nations conspire. . . . The kings of the earth set themselves . . . against the LORD and his anointed" and ends with an ultimatum for these kings, "Now therefore, O kings, be wise. . . ." Moreover, the concluding beatitude, "Happy are all who take refuge in him" (Ps 2:12) signals the end of the second introductory psalm to the Psalter even as the first introductory psalm opened with a beatitude, "Happy are those who do not follow the advice of the wicked . . ." (Ps 1:1).

As the second introductory psalm to the Psalter, Psalm 2 will have many connections with the following psalms. Gordon Wenham sees five themes in Psalm 2 that keep recurring in the Psalter:[2]

1. The divine choice of David as king (v 7)
2. The choice of Jerusalem or Zion as God's dwelling place (v 6)
3. The attack of the nations on the Davidic king in Jerusalem (vv 1–3)
4. The defeat of the nations (vv 8–9)
5. The invitation to the nations to serve the Lord (vv 11–12)

Psalm 2 can also be understood in the context of its twin introductory psalm, Psalm 1 (see pp. 25–28 above and n. 48 below) as well as the royal psalms: Psalms 18, 20, 21, 45, 72, 89, 101, 110, 132, and 144:1–11,[3] especially the coronation psalms, 72, 101, and 110. The historical narratives regarding God's covenant with King David also form part of its background, especially 2 Samuel 7:8–16[4] as well as the coronation rituals of 1 Kings 1:32–40 and 2 Kings 11:12. God's promise in verse 8, "I will make the nations your heritage," recalls God's original promise to Abram, "I will make of you a great nation, and I will bless you, and make your name great, so that you will be a blessing. . . . In you all the families of the earth shall be blessed" (Gen 12:2–3). And finally, we can take into account the vision of the prophets, such as Isaiah's picture of the Prince of Peace" (Isa 9:6–7; 11:1–16).

---

2. Wenham, *The Psalter Reclaimed*, 165.

3. "It is quite possible that other psalms should be added to this list, e.g., Pss 61, 63, 86, and 118." Craigie, *Psalms 1–50*, 456.

4. "Verse 7 is a poetic restatement of 2 Sam 7:14; vv 8 and 9 reflect vv 10, 11, 15, 16 of the same chapter." Leupold, *Exposition of the Psalms*, 50.

Literary Interpretation

Psalm 2 is usually identified as a royal psalm.[5] Yet, as Gerstenberger points out, it has "a puzzling variety and combination of forms and speech patterns. Lament, wisdom, and royal ceremonialism are fused into one."[6] Most helpful for understanding this psalm is to classify it by its content as a coronation psalm, as Craigie and others have done. "A coronation involved the setting of a crown upon the new king's head, the formal presentation of a document to the new king [the decree; v 7], and his proclamation and anointing (cf. 2 Kings 11:12)."[7] We shall in turn examine the psalm's parallelisms, imagery, repetition of keywords, and structure.

Parallelisms

Identifying the parallelisms requires some close calls between synonymous and advancing parallelisms (e.g., vv 3, 8, and 9) and between climactic and antithetic parallelism (vv 11–12). Again, sensing the forward movement in sections of the psalm is more important than getting the precise classification right.

1Why do the nations conspire,	A
and the peoples plot in vain?	+ A'
2The kings of the earth set themselves,	+ A''
and the rulers take counsel together,	+ A'''
against the LORD and his anointed, saying,	+ A''''
3"Let us burst their bonds asunder,	B
and cast their cords from us."	B'
4He who sits in the heavens laughs;	A
the LORD has them in derision.	+ A'
5Then he will speak to them in his wrath,	B
and terrify them in his fury, saying,	+ B'
6"I have set my king on Zion, my holy hill."	C

---

5. Bernhard Anderson, *Out of the Depths*, 171. Cf. von Rad, *Old Testament Theology*, I, 319 n. 1, "We designate as royal psalms those poems which had their functional place in ceremonies whose central figure was the king."

6. Gerstenberger, *Psalms*, I, 48. He could have added the beatitude in the last line of Psalm 2.

7. Craigie, *Psalms 1–50*, 64.

₇I will tell of the decree of the Lord:	A
He said to me, "You are my son;	+ A'
today I have begotten you.	+ A''
₈Ask of me, and I will make the nations your heritage,	B
and the ends of the earth your possession.	B'
₉You shall break them with a rod of iron,	C
and dash them in pieces like a potter's vessel."	C'
₁₀Now therefore, O kings, be wise;	A
be warned, O rulers of the earth.	+ A'
₁₁Serve the Lord with fear,	B
with trembling ₍₁₂₎kiss his feet,	+ B'
or he will be angry, and you will perish in the way;	– B''
for his wrath is quickly kindled.⁸	+– B'''
Happy are all who take refuge in him.⁹	– A

I see synonymous parallelism in verses 3, 8, and 9; advancing parallelism in verses vv 4, 5, 10; and climactic parallelism in verses vv 1–2, 7, 11–12c (including antithetic in v 12b, c). Having driven the poem relentlessly forward with advancing and climactic parallelisms, the final line surprises us with a single line of antithetic parallelism to perishing in the way (v 12b): "Happy are all who take refuge in him." The antithetic parallelism sets into bold relief the final words: "Happy," "all," "refuge" — Choose wisely where you look for refuge!

In addition, we see more intricate parallelism between verses 4–6 and 1–3. "We notice a threefold structuring that corresponds line by line to the preceding complaint: first, a description of heavenly reality (v 4) set against the rebellious uproar of v 1; second, divine counteraction (v 5) to defeat the plans of the enemy (v 2); and third, quotation of Yahweh's own words (v 6), which certainly will overrule enemy boastfulness (v 3). A certainty of victory thus pervades all the responses."[10]

Imagery

Psalm 2 is filled with imagery. The kings of the earth say about the Lord and his anointed, "Let us burst their bonds asunder, and cast their cords from us" (v 3).

8. The fact that the Lord's anger is quickly kindled offers a second reason to serve the Lord with fear; therefore +–B''' or advancing antithetic parallelism.

9. This final line clearly sets up a contrast with verse 12 from "perish" to "happy" and from "wrath" to "refuge." Therefore I have marked it –A, antithetic parallelism.

10. Gerstenberger, *Psalms*, I, 45–46. Cf. Terrien, *The Psalms*, 82–83.

The metaphors "bonds" and "cords" refer literally to the leather thongs that kept the yoke on oxen in place (cf. Jer 2:20; 5:5; 27:2; 30:8) or "the ropes and shackles conquering kings placed on their captives."[11] The kings of the earth are not literally tied in chains, of course, but they think that the LORD and his anointed keep them in bondage.

Verses 4 and 5 use anthropomorphic and anthropopathic language: "He who *sits* in the heavens *laughs;* the LORD has them in *derision.* Then he will *speak* to them in his *wrath,* and terrify them in his *fury.*"

Verse 7 contains two metaphors. The LORD's anointed recalls the decree of the LORD: "He said to me, 'You are *my son (bənî*); today *I have begotten* you." In Egypt the pharaoh was literally regarded as a son of god and therefore a god himself. The Old Testament makes clear, however, that the king of Israel was and remained human. But figuratively the king was a son of God. As the LORD promised David concerning Solomon, "I will be a father to him, and he shall be a son to me" (2 Sam 7:14). As son of God the Davidic king ruled God's people on God's behalf.

"Today I have begotten you" is also a figure of speech. It does not refer to a physical begetting of a baby. The "today" points to the day of coronation when the king was a grown man. The metaphor points to the close relationship between God and the Davidic king.[12] "The king certainly enjoys a privileged position with Yahweh . . . but he is not deified. The remarkable revelation of the New Testament, however, is that the fulfillment of 2:7 exceeds the original expectation. What was originally a figure of speech has become a literal historical reality."[13]

Verse 8 is frequently understood as hyperbole following the ancient "court style": "Ask of me, and I will make the nations your heritage, and the ends of

---

11. Bruce K. Waltke, "Ask of Me, My Son: Exposition of Psalm 2," *Crux* 43, no. 4 (2007; pp. 2–19): 6.

12. The question is whether "begotten" (*yālad*), in contrast to Near Eastern concepts of kingship, refers merely to "adoption" or to a genetic father-son relationship. Broyles, *Psalms,* 46, writes, "Within the horizon of the OT . . . this language points to legal adoption," not "a kind of genetic relationship between the Israelite king and God" as in the ancient Near East. So also von Rad, *Old Testament Theology,* I, 320. By contrast, Jacobson in deClaissé-Walford, Jacobson, and Tanner, *The Book of Psalms,* 69, states flatly, "In the texts as we have them, the verb always means to 'reproduce.' . . . The language emphasizes the special relationship that the king has with God." Peter Craigie, *Psalms 1–50,* 67, also writes, "'I have begotten you' is metaphorical language; it means more than simply adoption, which has legal overtones, and implies that a 'new birth' of a divine nature took place during the coronation." But this comment raises the question, What is this "'new birth' of a divine nature"? Craigie only answers, "It is important to stress, nevertheless, that the Davidic king, as son of God, was a *human being,* not a divine being, as was held in certain Near Eastern concepts of kingship." The NIV bypasses the issue by translating, "You are my Son; today I have become your Father."

13. Broyles, *Psalms,* 46.

the earth your possession." But Waltke argues cogently that these words are to be understood literally. He offers three reasons for taking them "at face value": "(1) The presence of rebellious nations would pose a constant threat to Israel's security (Micah 5:3 [4]). (2) The Old Testament ideal would not tolerate a notion of co-existence with pagan gods (cf. Jer 16:19). (3) Since *I Am* is the Creator and Lord of all his creation, his son's inheritance rightly consists of all lands (cf. Gen 48:4; Deut 20:16; Ps 72:8)."[14]

Verse 9 uses a metaphor and a simile: "You shall *break them with a rod of iron,* and dash them in pieces *like a potter's vessel.*" In ancient Egypt the pharaoh would literally smash potters' vessels that had the names of his enemies written on them.[15] The numerous potsherds could never be put together again as a complete vessel. This act, therefore, symbolized pharaoh's victory over his enemies. Psalm 2 refers to this practice but intends it only figuratively: the new king will crush the kings of the earth and be victorious.

Verses 11–12 warn the kings to "serve the LORD with fear, with trembling kiss his feet." Kissing the LORD's *feet* (NRSV) is anthropomorphic language for submission to the LORD. Even if the correct translation is "kiss his son" (NIV), the "kiss" is still a symbol of submission (cf. Isa 49:23). The image "is probably derived from the custom of kissing the feet of the king as an act of homage, a custom which is well known to us from Babylonian and Egyptian documents. We shall presumably have to understand this phrase in a figurative sense too — in the sense of submission and homage."[16]

The final line in Psalm 2 uses the metaphor "refuge": "Happy are all who take refuge in him." Mays writes, "To take refuge in the LORD is one of the most important expressions for the piety nurtured in the psalms. Literally, it means to seek shelter or protected space. Used as a metaphor, it belongs to the psalmic vocabulary of trust, the act of turning to and relying on the LORD's salvation."[17]

Repetition of Keywords

Psalm 2 repeats several keywords which help us discern the psalm's message. The word "LORD" occurs four times (vv 2, 4, 7, and 11), and the LORD's "wrath"

14. Waltke, "Ask of Me," *Crux* 43, no. 4 (2007): 10.
15. Terrien, *The Psalms,* 85.
16. Weiser, *The Psalms,* 115.
17. Mays, *Psalms,* 48. Cf. Brown, *Seeing the Psalms,* 19, "The first reference [in the Psalter] to 'refuge' is definitive, setting the tone for the rest of the Psalter. . . . Zion is the geographical embodiment of 'refuge.' To take refuge is to take shelter in Zion amid the swirling chaos and political clamor that threaten to engulf this rock of stability."

twice (vv 5 and 11). The LORD's "anointed" (v 2) is later referred to as the LORD's "king" (v 6), "my son" (Heb. *bēn;* v 7), and "his son" (Aramaic *bar;* v 12). The word "nations" (*gôyim*) occurs twice (vv 1 and 8). "The kings of the earth" and "the rulers" of verse 2 come back in verse 10 as "O kings" and "O rulers of the earth." These repetitions focus our attention on the major protagonists and antagonists in this psalm: the LORD and his son versus the kings and rulers of the nations of this earth.

Structure

Psalm 2 has been carefully designed as four stanzas of three verses each, with the stanzas arranged in a chiastic ABB'A' pattern. The scenes shift from stanza to stanza: from the earth (A), to heaven (B), to Mount Zion (B'), and back to the earth (A').[18] The first three stanzas each include a quotation from different speakers: the kings of the earth (v 3), the LORD in heaven (v 6), and the LORD's anointed quoting the LORD (vv 7–9). The psalmist concludes the final stanza with a beatitude (v 12). Thus we can sketch the structure of Psalm 2 as follows:

A. The kings (*malkê*) of the earth (*'ereṣ*) and rulers rebel against the LORD and his anointed:
"Let us burst their bonds asunder, and cast their cords from us."   (vv 1–3)

B. In heaven the LORD laughs derisively and says, "I have set my king on Zion, my holy hill."   (vv 4–6)

B'. The king says, "I will tell of the decree of the LORD, 'You are my son; today I have begotten you. Ask of me, and I will make the nations your heritage. . . .'" (vv 7–9)

A'. The kings (*məlākîm*), rulers of the earth (*'āreṣ*), are warned to serve the LORD:
"Happy are all who take refuge in him."   (vv 10–12)

Theocentric Interpretation

There is little danger that people will interpret Psalm 2 anthropocentrically. There is a question, however, whether the psalm centers on the LORD or on his anointed, the Davidic king. Although the two are closely related (father and son), the psalm

---

18. Waltke, "Ask of Me," *Crux* 43, no. 4 (2007): 3.

clearly centers on the LORD. As noted above, the word "LORD" occurs four times (vv 2, 4, 7, and 11) and "his wrath" twice (vv 5 and 11) for a total of six times in twelve verses. Moreover, when the kings of the earth plot against the LORD and the newly crowned king of Israel, it is the LORD in heaven who laughs derisively at their vain plotting (v 4). And it is the LORD who responds to their rebellion with a single statement: "I [the LORD] have set my king on Zion, my holy hill" (v 6). Next, the newly crowned king tells the decree of the LORD (v 7). Part of the LORD's decree is: "Ask of me [the LORD], and I [the LORD] will make the nations your heritage, and the ends of the earth your possession" (v 8). Next, the psalmist warns the kings of the earth to "serve the LORD with fear, with trembling kiss his [the LORD's] feet" (vv 11–12).[19] And he concludes with, "Happy are all who take refuge in him [the LORD]" (v 12). Thus, without taking anything away from the significance of the LORD's anointed, the psalm centers on the LORD.[20]

Textual Theme and Goal

McCann correctly states: "The real issue in Psalm 2 is this: Who rules the world? Is it the kings and rulers of the nations and peoples (vv 1–2)? Or is it the Lord (vv 10–12)?"[21] Mays agrees, "The issue that informs the psalm is the question of the ultimate power in the universe. The psalm is based on the faith that the Lord enthroned in heaven is the ultimate power."[22] Yet, to counter the rebellion of the kings of the earth, the sovereign LORD says, "I have set my king on Zion, my holy hill" (v 6). And he decrees, "Ask of me, and I will make the nations your heritage, and the ends of the earth your possession" (v 8).

In the textual theme, then, we will have to do justice both to the sovereignty of the LORD and to the role of his anointed. Therefore, we can formulate the textual theme as follows: *In his battle with the kings of the earth, the* LORD *will gain worldwide victory through his Davidic king.*[23]

19. The NIV translates verse 12, "Kiss his son." See n. 82 below.

20. For other arguments that Psalm 2, in the context of the Psalter, centers on the LORD's reign rather than the reign of the Davidic king, see, e.g., McCann, *Theological Introduction*, 43–45.

21. McCann, ibid., 43. Cf. Miller, *Interpreting the Psalms*, 88, "The fundamental and deepest question addressed by the psalm is whether the disorders of history are an indication that the forces of chaos still control, and whirl is king, or whether there is a power ruling in the cosmos that can bring order out of disorder and overcome the inevitably self-seeking and ultimately tyrannous character of all human powers."

22. Mays, *The Lord Reigns*, 47.

23. Cf. Leupold, *Exposition of the Psalms*, 41, "The theme of the psalm deals with victory so plainly that we have been moved to select the above caption: The Ultimate Victory of the Lord's Anointed." Cf. Belcher, *The Messiah and the Psalms*, 123: "The structure of Psalm 2 supports the

As to the goal of Psalm 2, Williams writes, "This psalm is evangelistic. It is addressed to the nations. . . . Psalm 2 directs the nations to the Son, warns them of the judgment to come, and promises them blessing if they will worship Him."[24] Kraus proposes, "The aim of the message of Psalm 2 could be summarized thus: The revolt of the nations and kings against the universal lordship of God and his anointed is a senseless undertaking."[25] The problem with these formulations of the goal is that they concentrate on the final stanza, which warns the kings of the earth to serve the LORD. But Psalm 2 is not written directly for the nations; they probably never even read it. The message of the psalm is aimed at Israel.[26]

For determining the goal of Psalm 2 for Israel it would be helpful to know the psalm's original historical setting. Unfortunately, since the psalm has no superscription providing some help from the editors of the Psalter, we have to determine a likely historical setting from the psalm itself.[27] Carl Armerding rightly notes that verse 6 "indicates the installation of a king on Zion, the holy hill of Jerusalem, while verses 7–8 speak of a decree by Yahweh specifically relating to the coronation of the king. The setting, then, is the coronation."[28] But

---

basic message of the psalm that God will establish his reign through his anointed king." Cf. Vos, *Theopoetry of the Psalms,* 62, "The theme of the psalm emerges here [vv 1–2], namely the futile rebellion of foreign nations and their kings against the Lord and his anointed, the Judean king." Cf. Mays, *Psalms,* 45–46, "Where does power to control the powers at work in world history ultimately reside? The thesis of the psalm is that the answer is given in the messiah, the son of God to whom the sovereign of heaven has given the right and power to rule the world. . . . The office, not the individual or the particular historical situation, was its theme."

24. Williams, *Psalms 1–72,* 38.

25. Kraus, *Psalms 1–59,* 133. Ross, *Commentary on the Psalms,* I, 178, also claims that "the expository idea" of Psalm 2 is: "It is wise to submit to the authority of the Messiah, because God has declared that he will rule the world."

26. See my *Modern Preacher and Ancient Text,* 259 n. 85: Sometimes "the group that the 'narrator' addressed directly . . . can be distinguished from the original audience and the original recipients of the book, particularly in the prophecies against the nations. For example, in Isa 14:28–32 Isaiah addresses an oracle directly to Philistia, but it is intended for the ears and later the eyes of Judah. Similarly, in Nahum the narrator addresses the Ninevites while his remarks are intended for the Judeans." Cf. Goldingay, *Psalms,* I, 96, "When prophets address the nations (e.g., Isa 13–23), generally the implicit real-life audience is Israel itself. When the psalm likewise addresses the nations, the audience overhears the psalmist indirectly encouraging it not to panic when nations threaten, and instead to join Yahweh in laughing." Cf. Mays, *Psalms,* 46, "Though it [Psalm 2] is at its conclusion rhetorically addressed to these other rulers, it was an interpretation of his [the Davidic king's] office for his own court and people."

27. For three different schools of interpretation on this issue, see James W. Watts, "Psalm 2 in the Context of Biblical Theology," *HorBT* 12, no. 1 (1990; pp. 73–87): 74–76.

28. Carl E. Armerding, *The Old Testament and Criticism* (Grand Rapids: Eerdmans, 1983), 60.

whose coronation? Some have suggested David's,[29] others Solomon's,[30] still others that "it is less likely that the writer had in mind a particular historical situation."[31] In any event, it is likely that this coronation psalm was used on more than one occasion. "Probably it became a kind of coronation liturgy, perhaps arising originally in the high hopes for Solomon that were generated by the Davidic covenant and later transferred to other kings who were less worthy."[32] The goal of Psalm 2, then, is *to encourage*[33] *embattled Israel with the good news that the* LORD, *in his battle with the kings of the earth, will gain worldwide victory through his Davidic king.*[34]

29. Tremper Longman, "The Messiah: Explorations in the Law and Writings," in Stanley E. Porter, *The Messiah in the Old and New Testaments* (Grand Rapids: Eerdmans, 2007; pp. 13–34), 18.

30. Armerding, *Old Testament and Criticism,* 60, "Vv 2 and 10 point to a time when there were vassal kings to revolt, and this situation would be truer to the occasion of Solomon's accession than to any time before or after." Cf. John L. McKenzie, "Royal Messianism," *CBQ* 19, no. 1 (1957; pp. 25–52): 33.

31. A. Anderson, *Psalms 1–72,* 65.

32. Armerding, *Old Testament and Criticism,* 60. Cf. Broyles, *Psalms,* 44, "Before Psalm 2 was placed near the beginning of the Psalms collection in postexilic times, it was probably used as a liturgy at the enthronement of the Davidic king in preexilic times (esp. vv 6–7)."

33. Cf. Waltke, "Ask of Me," 4, "In Israel's hymn book the psalm functions to encourage Israel with the assurance that their king will win the battle." Cf. Gerstenberger, *Psalms,* I, 49, "The writer insists that all the apparent strength of the nations and their gods is illusory. The real master of all the world is Yahweh, who one day will reveal the participation of his Anointed and his preferred people in the administration of the world. What a dream of greatness, and what a comfort and joy for the downtrodden, suffering Jewish communities!"

34. I will develop the application in line with this original textual goal, "*to encourage* embattled Israel." Others give more weight to the editor's placement of Psalm 2 next to Psalm 1. The goal of Psalm 1 is "to persuade Israel to walk in the way of the righteous"; it calls for a decision: "Happy are those who do not follow the advice of the wicked. . . ." Psalm 2 closes with, "Happy are all who take refuge in him." Therefore some commentators focus the application of Psalm 2 also on the decision the Israelites had to make then and we have to make today. See, e.g., McCann, *Theological Introduction,* 45, "The eschatological orientation of the final form of the Psalter — the affirmation that God's rule is effective *now* and will ultimately be fully manifest — means that the reader is called to a decision. Who is sovereign? In whom or in what will one trust? Will one trust the apparent power of the kings and rulers of the earth, the wicked? Or will one trust the Lord?" Cf. Davidson, *Vitality of Worship,* 19, "This psalm, like Psalm 1, speaks of a stark choice which has ultimate consequences. . . . It is the choice between believing that naked human power and military hardware decide the history of people and nations, or believing that true security and fulness of life can only be found in the fear of the LORD. The psalm invites us to ponder the consequences of the choices we make and challenges us to decide in what or in whom we are prepared to place our ultimate trust." Although the context of Psalm 1 informs the interpretation of Psalm 2 to some extent, I think that the theme and goal should reflect the theme and goal of the psalm itself and not its later literary context; otherwise one could come up with the same theme and goal for Psalm 1 as for Psalm 2. The theme and goal have to be textually specific.

Ways to Preach Christ

The New Testament quotes or alludes to Psalm 2 some eighteen times,[35] more than any other psalm. Psalm 2 is cited "especially in the Synoptic Gospels in connection with the baptism of Jesus and his transfiguration (Matt 3:17; 17:5; Mark 9:7; Luke 3:22; 9:35); 2 Peter 1:17 also cites it in reference to the transfiguration. Psalm 2 is also quoted in Acts (4:25f.; 13:33), in the letter to the Hebrews (1:5; 5:5; 7:28), and in Revelation (2:26f.; 6:15; 11:15, 18; 17:18; 19:19)."[36]

For preaching Christ from Psalm 2 there seem to be two main ways: typology and redemptive-historical progression, both supported by New Testament references.

Typology and New Testament References

The most direct way to Christ in the New Testament is the way of typology supported by New Testament references.[37] John Calvin, for example, saw the temporal kingdom of David as a type of the eternal kingdom of Christ. Calvin writes, "That David prophesied concerning Christ, is clearly manifest from this, that he knew his own kingdom to be a mere shadow. . . . David's temporal kingdom was a kind of earnest to God's ancient people of the eternal kingdom, which at length was truly established in the person of Christ. . . ."[38] And, of course, the Davidic king, described here as the LORD's "anointed" (v 2), "my king" (v 6), and "my son," "I have begotten you" (v 7), is a type of Jesus Christ. The relationship between an Old Testament type and its New Testament antitype is that of analogy and escalation.[39] There are clear analogies between the Davidic king and King Jesus: both anointed with the Holy Spirit (Matt 3:16, Acts 10:38), both kings of the Jews (Matt 2:2; Luke 23:2–3), both sons of God. But there are also clear escalations from the

35. Nestle Aland's *Novum Testamentum Graece* (1993), Appendix.

36. Kraus, *Theology of the Psalms*, 180. Cf. W. J. C. Weren, "Psalm 2 in LukeActs : An Intertextual Study," in *Intertextuality in Biblical Writings*, ed. Sipke Draisma (Kampen: Kok, 1989), 189–203.

37. An even more direct way is proposed by interpreters who "understand Psalm 2 as a direct prediction of Christ because David is presented as a prophet and the psalm is applied directly to Christ in the New Testament." Belcher, *Messiah and the Psalms*, 128, judges that this view is a possibility, but, he writes, it "makes it difficult to make sense of the psalm in its Old Testament context."

38. Calvin, *Commentary on the Book of Psalms*, I, 11. On Calvin's typological interpretation of Psalm 2, see Watts, "Psalm 2 in the Context of Biblical Theology," *HorBT* 12, no. 1 (1990): 83–84. Typological interpretation of Psalm 2 is further elucidated by, e.g., Patrick Fairbairn, *The Typology of Scripture* (Grand Rapids: Zondervan, *ca.* 1850), 122–25, and Leupold, *Exposition of the Psalms*, 42–43, 51, 53.

39. See my *Preaching Christ from the Old Testament*, 256–57.

Davidic king to King Jesus. Jesus is the literal Son of God, "begotten" by the Holy Spirit (Matt 1:18, 20; 3:17), the Word who was in the beginning with God (John 1:1), and not just "king of the Jews" but "King of kings" (Rev 19:16). Therefore typology would be a good way to preach Christ from Psalm 2.

Redemptive-Historical Progression and New Testament References

A more comprehensive way to Christ in the New Testament is the way of redemptive-historical progression supported by New Testament references. This way can take into account the progression in Old Testament times from a royal psalm that originally referred only to the Davidic king to a messianic understanding after the Babylonian exile.[40] In addition, redemptive-historical progression can do justice to the progression in the New Testament from Christ's First Coming to his Second Coming.

As to the progression in the Old Testament, Psalm 2 was originally used in Israel for the coronation of a new Davidic king. In this psalm Israel declared that the LORD, in his battle with the kings of the earth, would gain worldwide victory through his Davidic king. But that worldwide victory never materialized for any of Israel's kings: not David, not Solomon, and certainly not any Davidic kings after that. In fact, in 586 B.C. the Babylonian armies defeated Israel and took Israel (Judah) into exile. After that there were no more Davidic kings.

Yet Israel still preserved this royal psalm. When there were no Davidic kings, Israel began to understand this psalm differently. Psalm 2 began to speak to Israel of a future King from the line of David, a Messiah King, through whom the LORD would gain worldwide victory over the pagan nations. In fact, after the Babylonian exile, when Israel collected the various psalms and incorporated them into their Psalter, the editor(s) placed Psalm 2 at the beginning as an introduction to the following psalms. With this placement they signaled that the following psalms should be understood as looking forward to the coming Messiah King and the coming kingdom of God.[41]

---

40. "In the final form of the Psalter, the royal psalms and enthronement psalms function differently; they function eschatologically." McCann, *Theological Introduction,* 44. Cf. Waltke, "Ask of Me," *Crux* 43, no. 4 (2007): 16, "The psalm has a dual reference. During the existence of the first temple (960–586 BC) the psalm was used in the coronation of David's successors to his throne. In that context, the sobriquets 'king,' 'anointed one,' 'son' are written in lower case. But in the second temple period they referred to the Messiah, who in the New Testament is identified as the Son of God both by virgin birth in Matthean theology (Matt 1:18–25) and by his being the second person of the Trinity in Johanine theology (John 17)." Cf. Craigie, *Psalms 1–50,* 68–69, and Wilson, *Psalms,* I, 114.

41. "It is . . . generally agreed that by the time the Psalter was being completed, the psalms

Psalm 2 proclaims that in his battle with the kings of the earth, the LORD will gain worldwide victory through his Davidic king. This psalm, therefore, is a key link in the chain (theme) of the battle that began with God's words to Satan in Genesis 3:15, "I will put enmity between you and the woman, and between your offspring and hers; he will strike your head, and you will strike his heel." From there we could trace this theme of the LORD's ultimate victory through the Flood in Noah's time, the confusion of languages at Babel, the election and call of Abram to the Promised Land, the battles between Israel and the Gentile nations through the judges and Kings Saul, David, and Solomon until we arrive at Psalm 2. But for a sermon, this detailed approach would be too cumbersome. After a brief reference to Genesis 3:15, it will be better to move straight to Psalm 2 and trace its theme forward from preexilic Israel to postexilic Israel to Jesus' First Coming and then to his Second Coming (see "Sermon Exposition" below).

Sermon Theme, Goal, and Need

We formulated the textual theme as follows: "In his battle with the kings of the earth, the LORD will gain worldwide victory through his Davidic king." In the context of the whole Bible, this message does not change but the identity of the "Davidic king" is clarified: ultimately the "anointed" is the Messiah King, Jesus Christ, the son of David and the Son of God. To cover both the original message and its contemporary significance, we can therefore formulate the sermon theme as, *In his battle with the kings of the earth, the LORD will gain worldwide victory through his anointed king.*

The textual goal of Psalm 2 was "to encourage embattled Israel with the

---

dealing with the kingship of the Lord were understood eschatologically. They no longer refer only to what was enacted in cult, but as well to what was promised in prophecy.... The end of the wicked and the vindication of the righteous can be understood in terms of the coming kingdom of God." Mays, "The Place of the Torah-Psalms," *JBL* 106, no. 1 (1987; pp. 3–12): 10. Cf. Mays, "Isaiah's Royal Theology and the Messiah," in *Reading and Preaching the Book of Isaiah*, ed. Christopher R. Seitz (Philadelphia: Fortress, 1988), 39–51, esp. p. 48. Cf. Childs, *Introduction to the Old Testament as Scripture*, 517, The royal psalms "were treasured in the Psalter . . . as a witness to the messianic hope which looked for the consummation of God's kingship through his Anointed One." Cf. Stek, "Introduction: Psalms," *NIV Study Bible* (1985), 786, "When the Psalms speak of the king on David's throne, they speak of the king who is being crowned (as in Pss 2; 72; 110 . . .) or is reigning (as in Ps 45) at the time. They proclaim his status as God's anointed and declare what God will accomplish through him and his dynasty. Thus they speak of the sons of David to come — and in the exile and the postexilic era, when there was no reigning king, they spoke to Israel only of the great Son of David whom the prophets had announced as the one in whom God's covenant with David would yet be fulfilled."

good news that the LORD, in his battle with the kings of the earth, will gain worldwide victory through his Davidic king." In the light of the New Testament and the contemporary situation we can make the sermon goal: *to encourage God's embattled people today with the good news that the LORD, in his battle with the kings of the earth, will gain worldwide victory through his Messiah King, Jesus Christ.*

This goal points to the need addressed: God's embattled people tend to become discouraged in their lengthy struggle against evil powers in this world.

Scripture Reading and Sermon Outline

John Witvliet writes, "Any sermon on this text would benefit greatly from a reading that helped the congregation sense the interior drama, the shifts in voice, and the dramatic contrasts the text paints between the rulers and God's anointed."[42] To accomplish this we can choose from several options.

Broyles states that "the changing voices of the psalm indicate original liturgical performance: a narrator describes and quotes the subjected but conspiring nations (vv 1–3), a prophet or a priest quotes and describes 'the Lord . . . enthroned in heaven' (vv 4–6); the king quotes Yahweh's decree (vv 7–9); and the narrator then addresses the kings described in the opening verses with a warning and a promise (vv 10–12)."[43] Although we cannot be sure that such was the case in the temple liturgy,[44] we are certainly free to assign different readers for each stanza in order to make the congregation more cognizant of the structure (ABB′A′) and meaning of the psalm. This would call for three readers:

> *Preacher:* stanza 1 (vv 1–3), the kings of the earth conspire
> *Reader 2:* stanza 2 (vv 4–6), the LORD enthroned in heaven laughs
> *Reader 3:* stanza 3 (vv 7–9), the anointed king's speech
> *Preacher:* stanza 4 (vv 10–12), warning to the kings of the earth

One can also opt for a more complex choral reading. Calvin Seerveld suggests "the wise cantor" for verses 1–3, "another liturgete, perhaps a priest" for 4–6, "a princely ruler taking official part in the liturgy" for 7–9. Then the congregation

---

42. Witvliet, *The Biblical Psalms in Christian Worship*, 90.

43. Broyles, *Psalms*, 45.

44. Craigie, *Psalms 1–50*, 65, cautions that "the scant nature of the evidence makes any such analysis uncertain." Other commentators point out that "it is simpler to infer that the 'I' who speaks in vv 7–9, the king, is the speaker throughout." Goldingay, *Psalms*, I, 96. So also, e.g., A. Anderson, *Psalms 1–72*, 69; Kraus, *Psalms 1–69*, 125; and Weiser, *The Psalms*, 109.

stands as the cantor reads verses 10–12, and a "congregated chorus" repeats the final beatitude three times.[45]

Another meaningful option is to focus attention on the various voices quoted in Psalm 2. The first three stanzas quote three different people: the kings of the earth (v 3), the LORD (v 6), and the anointed king (vv 7–9). One can highlight these different voices as follows:

Preacher reads vv 1–2, the psalmist's voice
Choir reads v 3, the voices of the kings of the earth
Preacher reads vv 4–5, the psalmist's voice
Reader 3 reads v 6, the LORD's voice
Reader 4 reads vv 7–9, the anointed king's speech
Preacher reads vv 10–12d, the psalmist's voice,[46]
Preacher and/or congregation read v 12e, the beatitude

The sermon outline can follow the four stanzas, adding a fifth point to highlight the move to Christ in the New Testament:

    I. The kings of the earth rebel against the LORD and his anointed   (vv 1–3)
   II. In heaven the LORD laughs derisively, saying,
      "I have set my king on Zion, my holy hill."   (vv 4–6)
  III. The king relates the LORD's decree:
      "You are my son. . . . I will make the nations your heritage." (vv 7–9)
  IV. The kings of the earth are warned:
      "Serve the LORD with fear."
      "Happy are all who take refuge in him."   (vv 10–12)
   V. Jesus Christ is God's anointed King who will rule the nations.   (NT)

Sermon Exposition

In the sermon introduction one can focus on the need addressed by recalling a recent case of Christians being persecuted. God's people on earth have suffered persecution ever since the Fall into sin. In Genesis 3:15 God said to Satan, "I will put *enmity* between you and the woman, and between your offspring and hers; he will strike your head, and you will strike his heel." Although God promised

---

45. Calvin Seerveld, *Voicing God's Psalms* (Grand Rapids: Eerdmans, 2005), 19–20.
46. "Since the speaker of this stanza refers to *I AM* and his son in third person, presumably the speaker once again is" the psalmist. Waltke, "Ask of Me," *Crux* 43, no. 4 (2007): 11.

victory for the seed of the woman (strike Satan's head), Satan would be able to inflict severe damage on God's people ("strike his heel"). Genesis 4 follows up with Cain murdering the righteous Abel. Later, God's people Israel would be under constant attack by Gentile nations. King Saul was attacked by the Moabites, Ammonites, Edomites, Amalekites, Philistines, and other nations. King David had to defend Israel against the attacks of the same nations and others. In the words of Psalm 2:2, "The kings of the earth [did indeed] set themselves . . . against the Lord and his anointed."

In time, Israel became disheartened, discouraged. When would they ever find peace? But they took heart when a new Davidic king was crowned. For on that occasion they would hear the promise of Psalm 2 that the Lord and his anointed king would be victorious in their battle with the kings of the earth. This psalm encouraged them to continue serving the Lord their God. If ever we become discouraged by the attacks around the world on the Christian church, Psalm 2 will encourage us to continue to serve our Lord faithfully.

Psalm 2 consists of four stanzas of three verses each. Stanza 1 describes how the kings of the earth rebel against the Lord and his anointed. Verse 1, "Why do the nations conspire, and the peoples plot in vain?" The psalmist asks literally, "Why do the Gentiles (*gôyim*) conspire?"[47] The psalm deals with the enmity (Gen 3:15) between the Gentile nations who do not worship the Lord and the Lord and his anointed.[48]

When a new king was crowned in the ancient world, other nations thought this an opportune time to rebel against the untested king.[49] For example, when Rehoboam succeeded Solomon, the ten northern tribes rebelled and selected Jeroboam as their king (1 Kings 12).[50] Psalm 2 pictures the Gentile nations conspiring together and their peoples plotting rebellion against the Lord and his anointed. But why do they bother? They are plotting in vain. Why?[51]

---

47. "Not particular rebellious subject kingdoms, but all earth's pagan peoples who continually threaten the existence of Israel and challenge the universal rule of God." Rogerson and McKay, *Psalms 1–50*, 20.

48. "Psalm 2 escalates the wicked of Psalm 1 to whole nations and narrows the righteous individual to the Davidic king." Waltke, *The Psalms as Christian Worship*, 103. Cf. McCann, "Psalms," 689: "Psalm 2 portrays in corporate terms what Psalm 1 depicts in individual terms." Cf. VanGemeren, *Psalms*, 92.

49. "This psalm may reflect the fact that in the ancient Near East subjected territories often rebelled against their ruling empires when the king's inexperienced successor took over (cf. esp. vv 1–3)." Broyles, *Psalms*, 44. Cf. Weiser, *The Psalms*, 109.

50. For examples of other nations, see Hilber, *Psalms*, 320. Waltke, "Ask of Me," *Crux* 43, no. 4 (2007): 4, notes, "The El Amarna correspondence (fourteenth century BC) offers graphic descriptions of the petty kings of Syria-Palestine rebelling against the Egyptian suzerain."

51. "The interrogative *why* (*lāmmâ*) indicates puzzlement. This is not a literal question but

Verse 2 carries over the "Why?" of verse 1:[52] Why do "the kings of the earth set themselves, and the rulers take counsel together, against the LORD and his anointed"? "The kings of the earth set themselves" means that the kings of the earth prepare themselves for battle[53] "against the LORD and his anointed."[54] Why? It is a lost cause to rebel against the LORD of the universe and his anointed.

"His anointed" refers to the Davidic king. In the Old Testament kings were anointed to rule God's people on *God's* behalf.[55] "The king's anointing symbolized his consecration to and authorization for divine service, and a promise of divine empowerment for that service."[56] Now the kings of the earth prepare themselves for battle against the LORD and his anointed, the king of Israel. They think they have the advantage of numbers: many kings and rulers against two: the LORD and his anointed.[57] But it is a lost cause.

Being overconfident, however, the many kings and rulers cry out, verse 3, "Let us burst their bonds asunder, and cast their cords from us." "Bonds" and "cords" referred literally to the leather thongs that kept the yoke on oxen in place.[58] The kings of the earth are not actually tied with bonds and cords, of course, but they think that the LORD and his anointed keep them in bondage. "Bonds" and "cords" stand for being in submission, in subjection.[59] However, the kings of the earth refuse to be in subjection to the LORD and his anointed king. Instead they cry out, "Let us *burst* their bonds asunder, and *cast* their cords from us." "The yoke of God's kingship is not merely rejected; it is insolently thrown off (cf. Jer 2:20)."[60]

---

an exclamation of surprise." Jacobson in deClaissé-Walford, Jacobson, and Tanner, *The Book of Psalms*, 68.

52. "The word 'why' is used only once at the beginning of v 1a, but it dominates the whole introductory section (2:1–3) and is implied in the following lines." Craigie, *Psalms 1–50*, 63.

53. A. Anderson, *Psalms 1–72*, 66, "The underlying thought is that of preparing for a battle (cf. 1 Sam 17:16; Jer 46:4; 1QM viii:3, xvi:5, xvii:11)."

54. The Hebrew has "and his *məšîḥô*," from which we get our word "Messiah," meaning "anointed."

55. In 1 Samuel 16:13 we read that "Samuel took the horn of oil, and anointed him [David] . . . ; and the spirit of the LORD came mightily upon David from that day forward." Later Solomon was anointed king of Israel (1 Kings 1:45), then Rehoboam, and so on.

56. Waltke, "Ask of Me," *Crux* 43, no. 4 (2007): 5.

57. "The poetry of v 2 elegantly sets two pairs of antagonists against each other." *The kings of earth* and the *officials* (both plural nouns) stand *against the* LORD *and against his anointed* (both singular nouns). If this struggle were to be determined strictly by numbers, the kings and officials would obviously have the upper hand." Jacobson in deClaissé-Walford, Jacobson, and Tanner, *The Book of Psalms*, 68.

58. See pp. 217–18 above.

59. See e.g., Job 39:5; Jer 2:20; 5:5; 27:2; 30:8; and Nah 1:13.

60. VanGemeren, *Psalms*, 92.

The kings of the earth desire to be free, independent, autonomous. They do not want to be vassals, servants, of God.

How will God respond to this rebellion on earth? We're in for a surprise. In stanza 2 the scene shifts to heaven where God dwells. And God *laughs!* Verse 4, "He who sits in the heavens laughs." The Lord's laughter is a scoffing laughter. Verse 4 continues, "The Lord has them in derision." And small wonder. Note the contrast between "the kings *of the earth*" and "he who sits *in the heavens*." The Lord sits enthroned in the *heavens*.[61] Who do the kings of the earth think they are to even contemplate rebellion against the King of the universe? Such arrogance of puny humans!

Isaiah 40 puts matters into perspective: "Even the nations are like a drop from a bucket, and are accounted as dust on the scales. . . . All the nations are as nothing before him; they are accounted by him as less than nothing and emptiness. . . . It is he who sits above the circle of the earth, and its inhabitants are like grasshoppers . . . ; who brings princes to naught, and makes the rulers of the earth as nothing" (Isa 40:15–23). "He who sits in the heavens laughs;[62] the Lord has them in derision."

Patrick Miller observes perceptively about God's laughter, "In a strange way it is one of the most assuring sounds in the whole Psalter as it relativizes even the largest of human claims for ultimate control over the affairs of peoples and nations. The fiercest terror is made the object of laughter and derision and thus is rendered impotent to frighten those who hear the laughter of God in the background."[63]

God's derisive laughter next turns to anger. Verse 5, "Then he will speak to them in his wrath, and terrify them in his fury." We expect harsh words of rebuke and vengeance. Perhaps the Lord will call out the heavenly armies to snuff out the rebellion on earth. Perhaps the Lord himself will be the divine Warrior, incinerating all who oppose him. But here comes another surprise in verse 6: instead of a battle cry, the Lord declares simply, "I have set my king on Zion, my holy hill."

Will these simple words strike terror into the hearts of the kings of the earth? They should! Verse 6 begins with an emphatic "I," the Lord, or, "as for me."[64] I,

---

61. "The description of God as 'enthroned in heaven' is not an attempt to stress his distance and removal from the fray. It is a sign of his exaltation and power that is 'out of this world.' How can these puny, earthbound 'kings of the earth' (2:2) presume to reject and resist the rightful authority of the creator God who sits enthroned in heaven over all the earth?" Wilson, *Psalms*, I, 110.

62. Cf. Psalm 59:8, "But you laugh at them, O Lord; you hold all the nations in derision." Also Ps 37:13, "the Lord laughs at the wicked, for he sees that their day is coming."

63. Miller, *Interpreting the Psalms*, 90.

64. "What is 'terrifying' in these words is . . . [the] 'I ['*ănî*] have installed' him (the Heb. text makes this emphasis clear). The intimidation that Zion's king possesses stems not from an earthly

the LORD, "have set my king on Zion, my holy hill."[65] The LORD himself has installed the new Davidic king in Jerusalem. The King of the universe himself has given this king his authority and power.

In the third stanza the scene shifts back to earth, this time to Zion[66] where new Davidic kings were crowned. The new king begins to speak in verse 7, "I will tell of the decree of the LORD: He said to me, 'You are my son; today I[67] have begotten you.'" "The decree of the LORD" is a document the king received at his coronation. This document contained the words of the LORD appointing the new king, and probably his responsibilities.[68] The king recalls the words on this document. The LORD had said to him, "You are my son; *today* I have begotten you."[69] The "today" speaks of the day of coronation. On that occasion, the LORD begot the king as his son.[70] The Davidic king, therefore, rules on

---

military but from a heavenly King." Broyles, *Psalms,* 45–46. VanGemeren, *Psalms,* 94, suggests the "I" "could be translated 'as for me.'"

65. "God's agency is further underscored by the pronouns *my* king and *my* mountain. These dual pronouns reflect the Old Testament tradition of God's 'double election' of David and Jerusalem; in this tradition, God chose David and his descendants to be kings and Mount Zion in Jerusalem as the divine dwelling place." Jacobson in deClaissé-Walford, Jacobson, and Tanner, *The Book of Psalms,* 68.

66. "In the time of David the stronghold of Zion was identified with the city of David (2 Sam 5:7), but later the name 'Zion' was transferred to the Temple hill (cf. Ps 132:13; Mic 4:2) and to the whole city of Jerusalem (cf. Isa 10:24; Jer 3:14; Amos 6:1). In the present verse it is used of Jerusalem (cf. Ps 48:1f.)." A. Anderson, *Psalms 1–72,* 67.

67. "The initial 'I' is, as usual, emphatic. This is as much as to say: It is not you who inaugurated this very special relationship; I did it; take comfort from that fact." Leupold, *Exposition of the Psalms,* 50. Cf. McCann, "Psalms," 689, "The second 'I' in v 7, like the 'I' in v 6, is emphatic; God's initiative and activity are crucial."

68. "As part of the installation, the king has been given a document containing oracles of God; these appoint and acknowledge him, bestow blessings and probably make requirements. This document, called here the 'decree of the LORD,' is probably the 'testimony' given with the crown in the story of 2 Kings 11:12." Eaton, *The Psalms,* 66. Craigie, *Psalms 1–50,* 67, adds, "The 'decree' . . . is his [the king's] personal covenant document, renewing God's covenant commitment to the dynasty of David. The content of the decree establishes the nature and authority of the newly crowned king. . . . At the heart of the covenant is the concept of *sonship,* the human partner in the covenant is a *son* of the covenant God, who is *father.* This covenant principle of sonship is a part of the Sinai Covenant between God and Israel. . . . The Davidic covenant was eternal, but all covenants were renewed from time to time; the principal form of renewal in the royal covenant took place in the coronation, when a new descendant of the Davidic dynasty ascended to the throne. Thus, the divine words, 'you are my son' mark a renewal of the relationship between God and David's house in the person of the newly crowned king."

69. See n. 12 above. See also 2 Sam 7:14; 1 Chron 17:13; 22:10; 28:6; and Ps 89:26–27. On the theological problem of calling the king "The son of God," see Watts, "Psalm 2 in the Context of Biblical Theology," *HorBT* 12, no. 1 (1990): 76–80.

70. God promised David concerning the new king Solomon, "I will be a father to him, and

behalf of God himself. Thus his authority is not limited to Israel but extends to the ends of the earth.[71]

Consequently, the king quotes the LORD in verse 8 saying, "Ask of me, and I will make the nations your heritage, and the ends of the earth your possession." "Ask of *me*" — the King of the universe. When the Davidic king asks almighty God, then God promises, "I will make the nations[72] your heritage,[73] and the ends of the earth your possession." "The Davidic king's kingdom will not only endure the uprising, but will even be extended to the ends of the earth."[74] The kingdom of David will become coextensive with the LORD's kingdom which is worldwide.[75] Thus the LORD promises his anointed worldwide dominion (cf. Ps 72:8–11).

The LORD further says to his anointed, verse 9, "You shall break[76] them [the kings of the earth] with a rod of iron, and dash them in pieces like a potter's vessel." Note the contrast between the strong "rod of iron" and the fragility of "a potter's vessel."[77] There was no contest. In ancient Egypt the pharaoh would have the names of his enemies written on potters' vessels and then he would literally smash the vessels.[78] After it was broken into numerous potsherds, the vessel

---

he shall be a son to me. When he commits iniquity, I will punish him with a rod such as mortals use. . . . But I will not take my steadfast love from him, as I took it from Saul, whom I put away from before you. Your house and your kingdom shall be made sure forever before me; your throne shall be established forever" (2 Sam 7:14–16).

71. "Correspondence between the heavenly king and the anointed king is an important feature of the royal psalms. The human king is not equal to or identical with, but in certain respects corresponds to, the divine sovereign. So the inaugural of the anointed is a declaration that 'the Lord reigns' in the midst of a history whose powers deny it." Mays, *Psalms,* 47–48.

72. "The royal son's inheritance, nations (*gôyim*) . . . ends of the earth (*'apsê-'āreṣ*), matches the rebellious 'nations' (v 1) in corporate solidarity with 'the kings of the earth' (v 2)." Waltke, "Ask of Me," *Crux* 43, no. 4 (2007): 10.

73. "Most often the word [heritage / inheritance (*naḥălâ*)] describes the tribal allotments of the Promised Land or the whole land as the inheritance of the combined nation. Here, however, the vision of the Davidic monarchs expands to include as their divinely given inheritance the 'ends of the earth.'" Wilson, *Psalms,* I, 112.

74. Waltke, "Ask of Me," *Crux* 43, no. 4 (2007): 10.

75. "The dominion of the son must correspond to the sovereignty of the father." Mays, *Psalms,* 47.

76. As is clear from the parallelism, the MT's "break" (NRSV, NIV, 2011) is a better translation than the LXX's "rule" (NIV, 1984). For other reasons for preferring the MT, see Waltke, "Ask of Me," *Crux* 43, no. 4 (2007): 11.

77. "An 'iron rod' is something intrinsically strong, just as a potter's vessel is constitutionally fragile. This stark contrast between the power of the Davidic king and the fragility of earthly monarchs rested not in the human strength of the Hebrew king but in the strength of God, the speaker of these words." Craigie, *Psalms 1–50,* 67.

78. Terrien, *The Psalms,* 85. Cf. Kraus, *Psalms 1–59,* 132–33. For a similar custom in Assyria, see Vos, *Theopoetry of the Psalms,* 69.

could never be put together again.[79] Breaking the potter's vessels symbolized pharaoh's victory over his enemies. Psalm 2 alludes to this practice. It means to say that the Davidic king will smash the opposition and be victorious over the kings of the earth.

Stanza 4 speaks directly to these rebellious kings. The psalmist[80] now warns the kings of the earth to serve the LORD and his anointed king. Because the King of the universe himself had installed his king in Zion and commissioned him to rule to the ends of the earth, the psalmist begins with a "Now *therefore.*" Verses 10–11, "Now therefore, O kings, be wise; be warned, O rulers of the earth. Serve the LORD with fear, with trembling."

To "*serve* the LORD" means to *worship* the LORD and submit to his kingship. It "means to come under the King's rule and obey Him, as a slave surrenders to his master."[81] The psalmist urges the kings of the earth to "serve the LORD with fear, with trembling," that is, with reverence and awe.

Verse 12 continues, "kiss his feet,[82] or he will be angry, and you will perish

---

79. Cf. Isa 30:14, "Its breaking is like that of a potter's vessel that is smashed so ruthlessly that among its fragments not a sherd is found for taking fire from the hearth, or dipping water out of the cistern. Cf. Jer 19:11, "So will I break this people and this city, as one breaks a potter's vessel, so that it can never be mended."

80. "Since the speaker of this stanza refers to *I AM* and his son in third person, presumably the speaker once again is" the psalmist. Waltke, "Ask of Me," *Crux* 43, no. 4 (2007): 11.

81. Williams, *Psalms 1–72*, 37.

82. The NRSV adds the footnote, "12a is uncertain." If the pew Bible is the NRSV, I would go with its translation so as not to get side-tracked into technical details in the sermon. The main point is to submit. Moreover, this translation is consistent in that all the pronouns now refer to the LORD: "Kiss his [the LORD's] feet, or he [the LORD] will be angry . . . ; for his [the LORD's] wrath is quickly kindled."

The NIV (2011) translates, "Kiss his son." If the pew Bible is the NIV, I would go with this translation because there are good reasons for it (see, e.g., Craigie, *Psalms 1–50*, 64 n. on v 12a; Davidson, *Vitality of Worship*, 18; Terrien, *The Psalms*, 86; and VanGemeren, *Psalms*, 97–98 n. on v 12). Moreover, it establishes a solid inclusio in the psalm: the kings of the earth were rebelling "against the LORD *and his anointed*" (v 2c) and at the conclusion they are enjoined to submit not only to the LORD but also to his "*son*" (v 12a). Craigie, *Psalms 1–50*, 68, notes that "the word 'serve' has political overtones and implies that the foreign nations should submit as vassals to Israel's God. In order to submit to God, they would have to submit to his son, the king; thus, they are called upon to 'kiss the son,' for kissing was a sign of homage and submission (1 Sam 10:1; 1 Kings 19:18 [Ps 72:9; Isa 49:23])." Ross, *Commentary on the Psalms*, I, 211, observes, "For these pagan leaders, to serve him [the LORD] would mean changing loyalties from their gods to the one true God, but it would also mean accepting God's king and serving him." Ross adds, p. 212, "The imperative 'kiss [the] son' has the Aramaic word for 'son' probably because the psalmist was addressing pagan kings who would have likely spoken Aramaic."

Preachers using the NIV translation, however, will need to explain that the following pronouns in v 12 refer not to the son but to the LORD (see v 5 on the LORD's "wrath"). Cf. Waltke, "Ask

in the way; for his wrath is quickly kindled." In the ancient world, people would kiss the feet of a king as a sign of their homage and submission to the king.[83] So the psalmist here urges the kings of the earth, "Kiss his feet, or he will be angry, and you will perish in the way; for his wrath is quickly kindled." When the LORD is angry at the kings of the earth, they will surely perish. "His wrath is quickly kindled." The kings are pressed to submit to the LORD.

As a final encouragement to submit, the psalm ends with a beatitude, "Happy are all who take refuge in him." "Happy are *all*" — not just the kings of the earth but all who hear these words and take heed. "Happy are all who take refuge in him." When we hear the word "refuge," we should think of a shelter. When people are threatened by bombs, they take refuge in a bomb shelter. When there is a "tornado warning," we seek refuge in some kind of shelter. When we are threatened by the powers of this world, we also need a shelter.[84]

As I am writing this, we are threatened by the violence of ISIS: mass murders in Boston, Paris, Copenhagen, and who knows where next. We see on TV atrocious beheadings of people, one recent example being twenty-one Coptic Christians beheaded in Libya. When we are threatened by the powers of this world, we need a shelter. Psalm 2 encourages us to take refuge in God. "To 'take refuge' . . . in God means to depend on God, to trust God, to entrust one's life and future to God."[85] "Happy are all who take refuge" in the LORD, the King of the universe.

When Israel first heard this psalm they heard the message that the LORD in his battle with the kings of the earth would gain worldwide victory through his Davidic king. This message encouraged them not to give up, to keep serving the LORD. Even as pagan nations attacked them, they were assured that their LORD would gain worldwide victory through this new king. God promised the new king (verse 8), "I will make the nations your heritage, and the ends of the earth your possession." But even at its height the kingdom of David never reached to the ends of the earth. David's rule stretched from the River of Egypt to the Euphrates. And from that height it declined gradually. In the year 586 B.C. the

---

of Me," *Crux* 43, no. 4 (2007): 14: "The antecedent of the third masculine singular pronouns, 'he,' 'his,' 'him' is I AM, even though 'son,' according to the preferred interpretation of *bar*, is the nearest antecedent. In the other thirteen occurrences of the verb 'be angry' (*'ānap*), I AM is the subject. . . . This interpretation finds confirmation in 'seek refuge in him,' which always refers to trust in I AM."

83. See p. 219 above.

84. "The readers [of Psalm 2]. . . . are tempted to be afraid and discouraged, tempted to believe that the powers are the only reality, even in danger of submitting and trusting life to the purposes of the powers. The word to them is, 'Blessed are all who take refuge in him.'" Mays, *Psalms*, 48.

85. McCann, "Psalms," 690, with references to Pss 5:11; 7:1; 11:1; 16:1; and 25:20.

Babylonian forces conquered Israel (by that time just Judah) and carried the people into exile.

When there were no more Davidic kings, Israel began to understand this psalm as referring to a future anointed king.[86] They looked forward to an anointed King, a Messiah, who would rule the world. In fact, after the exile when the psalms were collected into the Psalter, the editor(s) placed this psalm immediately after Psalm 1 to introduce the following psalms. Their message with this placement of Psalm 2 was: Look in the following psalms for the coming Messiah King who will rule to the ends of the earth.

The New Testament quotes or alludes to Psalm 2 more than any other psalm, some eighteen times.[87] It does this to persuade people that Jesus is indeed the long-expected Messiah King of Psalm 2. When Jesus was born in Bethlehem, Matthew, for one, made sure that we would know that Jesus was born of David's line. Matthew begins, "An account of the genealogy of Jesus the *Messiah,* the son of *David,* the son of Abraham" (Matt 1:1). And Mark begins his narrative about Jesus as follows: "In those days Jesus came from Nazareth of Galilee and was baptized by John in the Jordan. And just as he was coming up out of the water, he saw the heavens torn apart and the Spirit descending like a dove on him. And a voice came from heaven, '*You are my Son,* the Beloved; with you I am well pleased'" (Mark 1:9–11; cf. Matt 3:17; Luke 3:22). The voice from heaven quotes the decree the LORD gave to the new king in Psalm 2:7, "He said to me, 'You are my son.'"

The *Lectionary* has assigned Psalm 2 for reading on Transfiguration Sunday. This is how Mark tells the story:

> Jesus took with him Peter and James and John, and led them up a high mountain apart, by themselves. And he was transfigured before them, and his clothes became dazzling white, such as no one on earth could bleach them. And there appeared to them Elijah with Moses, who were talking with Jesus. Then Peter said to Jesus, "Rabbi, it is good for us to be here; let us make three dwellings, one for you, one for Moses, and one for Elijah." . . . Then a cloud overshadowed them, and from the cloud there came a voice, "*This is my Son* [again a quotation from Psalm 2], the Beloved; listen to him!" Suddenly when they looked around, they saw no one with them any more, but only Jesus (Mark 9:2–8; cf. Matt 17:1–5; Luke 9:28–36).

---

86. "Finally a time came when there was no king, no Davidide, no anointed. The psalm could be read in the light of the prophets' foretelling of a descendant of David yet to come, that is, as eschatological promise, not as royal ritual. The genre of Psalm 2 and its companion royal psalms was revised by their inclusion in a book of Scripture." Mays, *Psalms,* 49.

87. Nestle Aland's *Novum Testamentum Graece* (1993), Appendix.

Moses represented the law and Elijah the prophets. Jesus superseded them all. The voice from heaven said, "This is my Son, the Beloved; listen to *him!*" Submit to him![88] Obey him! This is the Son Psalm 2 spoke about, the anointed King through whom the LORD would gain worldwide victory over the nations. But first Jesus would have to suffer and die and be raised on the third day.[89]

After his resurrection, Jesus told his disciples, "*All authority* in heaven and on earth has been given to me. Go therefore and make disciples of *all nations.* . . . And remember, I am with you always, to the end of the age" (Matt 28:18–20). Jesus now works through his followers to gain worldwide victory for the LORD. Then Jesus ascended into heaven where he is seated at the right hand of the Father ruling the nations. As Paul writes, "God put this power to work in Christ when he raised him from the dead and seated him at his right hand in the heavenly places, far above all rule and authority and power and dominion, and above every name that is named, not only in this age but also in the age to come" (Eph 1:20–21).

Two ages: this age and the age to come.[90] Already King Jesus rules the nations, but it is not yet visible to all. It will become obvious at the end of the age when Jesus comes again. In Revelation 19 John alludes to Psalm 2:9 and 11: "Then I saw heaven opened, and there was a white horse! Its rider is called Faithful and True, and in righteousness he judges and makes war. . . . He is clothed in a robe dipped in blood, and his name is called The Word of God. And the armies of heaven . . . were following him on white horses. From his mouth comes a sharp sword with which to strike down *the nations,* and *he will rule*[91] *them with a rod*

---

88. Cf. Ps 2:11–12 , "Serve the LORD with fear, with trembling kiss his feet."

89. Cf. Paul's sermon recorded in Acts 13, "But God raised him from the dead. . . . And we bring you the good news that what God promised to our ancestors he has fulfilled for us, their children, by raising Jesus; as also it is written in the second psalm, 'You are my Son; today I have begotten you'" (Acts 13:30–33). Balentine, "The Royal Psalms and the New Testament," *Theological Educator* 29 (1984): 60, comments, "The gospel writers do not intend to suggest that Jesus' sonship literally began with his baptism or transfiguration, hence they omit the word 'today' in their references to Ps 2:7. For Paul's argument, however, it was important to emphasize that it was especially through his resurrection from the dead that Jesus Christ was enthroned as God's Son. Thus Acts 13:33 does include the word 'today.'"

90. "With the advantage of retrospect and the knowledge that Jesus will have two advents, we can understand how Psalm 2 befits him. The Gospels' use of Psalm 2 is limited to verse 7. Verses 1–2 and 8–9, however, are frequently cited in Revelation (1:5; 2:26–27; 11:18; 12:5; 19:15, 19). Here he will appear not simply as God's Son but also as the warrior-king." Broyles, *Psalms,* 47. Cf. Kraus, *Psalms 1–59,* 133, "It is significant that Acts and Revelation cite Psalm 2 (Acts 4:25f.; 13:33; Rev 2:26–27; 19:15) in the contest between Christ the exalted king with the hostile Gentile nations."

91. Instead of the Hebrew for "break," Revelation follows the Septuagint and translates "rule." See also Rev 2:27 and 12:5.

of iron; he will tread the wine press of the fury of *the wrath* of God the Almighty. On his robe and on his thigh he has a name inscribed, 'King of kings and Lord of lords'"(Rev 19:11–16). It's a picture of Jesus coming on the final day to judge the nations. And then "he will reign forever and ever."[92]

"Thus it is that the kingship of Christ calls all other kingships into question and places them under the lordship of Christ. In every sphere of life Christ is the one who has ultimate rule over us. His kingship sets us free from the fear of all lesser lords whom we may serve obediently and even willingly, who may cause us trouble and suffering but who do not ultimately rule over us. The anointed of God alone claims and exercises that lordship."[93] Psalm 2, therefore, encourages us today to continue the battle for the kingdom of God against the evil powers in this world.

We should not be surprised that Christians around the world still suffer persecution. We should not be surprised that *we* may have to suffer persecution. Paul wrote to Timothy, "Indeed, all who want to live a godly life in Christ Jesus will be persecuted" (2 Tim 3:12). Jesus also predicted persecutions for his followers, but he still called them "blessed": "Blessed are those who are persecuted for righteousness' sake, for theirs is the kingdom of heaven" (Matt 5:10). They are "blessed" because "theirs is the kingdom of heaven." Jesus also said, "In the world you face persecution. But take courage; I have conquered the world!" (John 16:33). Take courage, for in the end the LORD, the King of the universe, will gain worldwide victory through his Messiah King, Jesus Christ.

Prayer[94]

Mighty God and Creator of all, we are made in your image,
    yet many deny you and despise the Messiah who is your Son.
By your Spirit, keep us humble and faithful
    so that our lives may proclaim our Savior's love
    and inspire others to find their refuge in you.
We pray in Jesus' name. Amen.

---

92. When the seventh angel blew his trumpet "there were loud voices in heaven, saying, 'The kingdom of the world has become the kingdom of our Lord and of his Messiah, and he will reign forever and ever'" (Rev 11:15).

93. Miller, *Interpreting the Psalms*, 93.

94. *Psalms for All Seasons*, 11. VanGemeren, *Psalms*, 91, suggests, "In the light of this psalm's message, our prayer should include (1) a petition for the full establishment of the messianic kingdom; (2) thanksgiving that Gentiles have been incorporated into God's kingdom; (3) an entreaty for the nations of the world that continue their rebellion against God; (4) a supplication for our brothers and sisters under governments hostile to Christianity; and (5) intercession for the Jewish people that they may soon be restored to Christ (Rom 11:25–32)."

Song[95]

Hallelujah!
For the Lord God Omnipotent reigneth.

The kingdom of this world is become the kingdom of our Lord,
    and of His Christ;
and He shall reign for ever and ever.

King of kings, and Lord of lords.
And He shall reign forever and ever.

King of kings! and Lord of lords!
Hallelujah!

95. Hallelujah Chorus of Handel's *Messiah*. Public Domain.

CHAPTER 11

"Create in Me a Clean Heart, O God"

Psalm 51 (50¹)

The *Revised Common Lectionary* assigns Psalm 51, *De Misere,* for Ash Wednesday to begin the Lenten season. Of the seven "penitential psalms" identified by the early church,² Psalm 51 is the most personal and vivid. As such it is a powerful introduction to the Lenten season.³ In Lent the church focuses on self-examination, penitence, and forgiveness through the blood of Christ. Thus the Lenten season reaches a climax with Jesus' death on Good Friday and his resurrection on Easter Sunday, forty weekdays after Ash Wednesday. "Psalm 51 with its movement beyond confession and forgiveness to renewal and praise can stand as a reminder that the season of Lent is one of repentance in preparation for God's new future in Resurrection, and it is not a time of breast-beating guilt."⁴ If no worship service is held on Ash Wednesday, Psalm 51 will be a fitting preaching text for any Sunday in Lent.

---

1. "Symbolically, as 'the fiftieth psalm' of the Vulgate, it was celebrant of the year of Jubilee, as described in Leviticus 25, when all debts were remitted, all slaves liberated, and all prisoners set free. And just as the ram's horn was uniquely blown on the great Day of Atonement, so we may describe this psalm as 'The Ram's Horn of the Church.' For it echoes the words of the apostle: 'where sin has abounded, grace has much more abounded' (Rom 5:20)." James M. Houston in Waltke, *Psalms as Christian Worship,* 446.

2. Psalms 6, 32, 38, 51, 102, 130, and 143.

3. Patrick Reardon, *Christ in the Psalms,* 99, notes "that Psalm 50 (Hebrew 51) is the only psalm prescribed to be recited in its entirety during every celebration of the Eastern Orthodox Divine Liturgy." Eaton, *The Psalms,* 206, relates that Psalm 51 was used for the Day of Atonement in later Jewish worship.

4. Bruce C. Birch, "Homiletical Resources: The Psalter as Preaching Text," *Quarterly Review* 1, no. 5 (1981; pp. 61–93): 88.

Text and Context

Many commentators consider the verses 18–19 a later addition to the original composition.[5] This observation, however, does not preclude using the whole psalm as preaching text. In preaching the psalms, our preaching text is the form of the psalm as it appears in the final Canon, not a possible earlier version. Psalm 51 is a literary unit as indicated by its inclusio of a two-verse prayer for David himself (vv 1–2) and a two-verse prayer for Zion (vv 18–19).[6] The literary unit is confirmed by the new superscription of Psalm 52. Our preaching text, therefore, is Psalm 51:1–19 [MT, vv 1–21].[7]

Psalm 51 needs to be understood in a broader biblical context. The immediate context is the neighboring psalm, Psalm 50. Both psalms warn against the mere bringing of sacrifices (50:9–13; 51:16). Instead, both encourage, "Offer to God a sacrifice of thanksgiving" (50:14; 51:19, "right sacrifices").[8] Psalm 50 concludes with, "Those who bring thanksgiving as their sacrifice honor me; to those who go the right way I will show the salvation of God" (50:23). Psalm 51 follows up with "a 'thank offering' of confession and an amended life made possible by a 'broken and contrite heart' (51:16–17), and it seeks the restoration of 'the joy of your [God's] salvation' (51:12)."[9]

Psalm 51 can also be compared with other individual laments, especially the other six penitential psalms identified by the early church, in order to determine the unique point of this particular psalm.[10] Gerstenberger observes that "Psalm 51 is unusual in its request for a 'clean heart' and a 'firm,' 'new,' 'holy,' and 'ready'

---

5. The reason most often cited is that verse 18 asks the Lord to "rebuild the walls of Jerusalem," which seems to indicate a time when the walls were destroyed, that is, during the Babylonian exile. E.g., Wilson, *Psalms*, I, 773, suggests that verses 18–19 "may well have been added to an essentially individual psalm in order to reflect the needs of the exilic community, who had lost Jerusalem and the temple and were struggling to understand what constituted 'righteous sacrifice' in their new circumstance scattered among nations, far from their ancestral home." For other reasons, such as a different rhythm and style, see Terrien, *The Psalms*, 403.

6. John Stek, *NIV Study Bible*, Ps 51 n.

7. The MT adds verse references 1–2 for the superscription and therefore has 21 verses. We will follow the verse references of most English versions, starting verse 1 *after* the superscription and ending with verse 19.

8. Psalm 50, therefore, confirms that our preaching text has to be the whole psalm, including the "right sacrifices" of v 19, unless we decide, because of the wealth of material, to preach two sermons on this psalm, vss 1–9 and 10–19 (see p. 582 below).

9. Wilson, *Psalms*, I, 772–73. Cf. Zenger, *Psalms 2*, 24. See also the two psalms as "mirror images of one another," in Frederick Gaiser, "The David of Psalm 51: Reading Psalm 51 in Light of Psalm 50," *W & W* 23, no. 4 (2003; pp. 382–94): 388.

10. Psalms 6, 32, 38, 51, 102, 130, and 143. Broyles, *Psalms*, 226, notes that actually "only Psalms 32, 51, and 130 give concerted attention to sin and forgiveness as their chief issue."

spirit (vv 12-14) [10-12]. . . . Complaint psalms usually ask for life, health, safety, strength, etc."[11]

The superscription — "A Psalm of David, when the prophet Nathan came to him, after he had gone in to Bathsheba" — encourages us to hear Psalm 51 in the context 2 Samuel 11-12. Note some of the similarities between 2 Samuel 11-12 and Psalm 51. Nathan says to David, "Why have you despised the word of the LORD, to do what is evil in his sight?" (2 Sam 12:9); the psalmist confesses, I have "done what is evil in your sight" (Ps 51:4). David said to Nathan, "I have sinned against the LORD" (2 Sam 12:13); the psalmist confesses, "Against you, you alone, have I sinned" (Ps 51:4). David "fasted and wept; for he said, 'Who knows? The Lord may be gracious to me (*yəḥānnanî*) and the child may live'" (2 Sam 12:22); the psalmist pleads, "Have mercy on me (*ḥānnēnî*), O God. . . . The sacrifice acceptable to God is a broken spirit" (Ps 51:1, 17). David's premeditated murder of Uriah (2 Sam 11:15) may be reflected in Psalm 51:14, "Deliver me from bloodshed, O God." The fact that "the spirit of the LORD departed from Saul" (1 Sam 16:14) may well be the background of Psalm 51:11, "Do not take your holy spirit from me."

A still broader context is the background of the ceremonial laws (e.g., Exod 12:22; Num 19:18) which elucidate the requests, "Blot out my transgressions. Wash me thoroughly from my iniquity, and cleanse me from my sin. . . . Purge me with hyssop, and I shall be clean" (51:1-2, 7).[12]

In addition we should be mindful of the testimony of the prophets. As Broyles points out, "The sequence of the petitions also matches the promises of a new covenant in Ezekiel 36:25-27. As they promise 'you will be clean' (Ezek 36:25), so verse 7 seeks the same claim, 'I will be clean.' As they promise 'a new heart' and 'a new spirit' (Ezek 36:26), so verse 10 seeks 'a clean heart' and 'a steadfast spirit.' As they promise God's 'Spirit' (Ezek 36:27), so verse 11 seeks to forestall the removal of 'your holy spirit.'"[13]

Literary Interpretation

Modern biblical scholars usually classify Psalm 51 as an individual lament,[14] though the early church identified it as one of seven penitential psalms. Willem

---

11. Gerstenberger, *Psalms*, I, 214.

12. See "Imagery" below, pp. 245-47.

13. Broyles, *Psalms*, 229. Broyles continues: "The new covenant passages in Jeremiah also promise a new 'heart' (24:7; 31:33) and add that Yahweh will forgive 'their iniquity' (NIV 'wickedness') and 'their sin' (31:34) — the same word pair used in Psalm 51:9."

14. For a detailed discussion of this classification, see Tate, *Psalms 51-100*, 8, and Zenger, *Psalms 2*, 15-16.

VanGemeren states that "the lament form of the psalm suitably fits the spirit of contrition and prayer for restoration."[15] But while most laments in the Psalter concern external causes (enemies, sickness), Psalm 51 laments an internal cause: the sinful self.[16] Originally this psalm was a cry to God for help by an individual whose sin brought him in deep distress: "Have mercy on *me*, O God" (51:1; cf. the fivefold *my* in vv 1–3). When the Psalter was compiled after the exile, the people of Judah whom God punished with exile from the Promised Land would have identified with this individual.

We shall seek to gradually understand the message of the psalm by exploring, in turn, its parallelisms, imagery, repetition of keywords, and structure.

Parallelisms

Psalm 51 uses some antithetic (–) parallelisms (vv 11, 16) but mostly advancing (synthetic, +) parallelisms that blossom into climactic parallelism when they cover three or more lines (vv 1–2, 14, 16–17, 19).

> To the leader. A Psalm of David, when the prophet Nathan came to him, after he had gone in to Bathsheba.

₁Have mercy on me, O God,	A
according to your steadfast love;	B
according to your abundant mercy	+ B'
blot out my transgressions.[17]	+ A'
₂Wash me thoroughly from my iniquity,[18]	+ A''
and cleanse me from my sin.[19]	+ A'''

---

15. VanGemeren, *Psalms*, 433.

16. In contrast to the lament form, "in the penitential psalm the crisis is spiritual. The affliction of the supplicant is not some external situation but a deep sense of one's own sin and unworthiness before God." Birch, "Homiletical Resources," *Quarterly Review* 1, no. 5 (1981): 84.

17. Completes the thought of v 1a, therefore +A': advancing parallelism.

18. A close call here with synonymous parallelism. Verse 2a continues the "transgressions" of verse 1d with "iniquity" but the image advances from "blot out" to "wash thoroughly," hence +A''.

19. Another close call with synonymous parallelism, but here the thought advances to being ritually clean (see p. 246 below and n. 32), hence +A'''.

₃For I know my transgressions,	A
and my sin is ever before me.²⁰	+ A′
₄Against you, you alone, have I sinned,	B
and done what is evil in your sight,	+ B′
so that you are justified in your sentence	C
and blameless when you pass judgment.²¹	+ C′
₅Indeed, I was born guilty,	D
a sinner when my mother conceived me.²²	+ D′
₆You desire truth in the inward being;	A
therefore teach me wisdom in my secret heart.²³	+ A′
₇Purge me with hyssop, and I shall be clean;	B
wash me, and I shall be whiter than snow.	+ B′
₈Let me hear joy and gladness;	C
let the bones that you have crushed rejoice.²⁴	+ C′
₉Hide your face from my sins,	D
and blot out all my iniquities.²⁵	+ D′
₁₀Create in me a clean heart, O God,	A
and put a new and right spirit within me.²⁶	+ A′
₁₁Do not cast me away from your presence,	− B
and do not take your holy spirit from me.²⁷	+− B′
₁₂Restore to me the joy of your salvation,	C
and sustain in me a willing spirit.	+ C′

20. The thought advances from knowing his transgressions to his sin being "ever before" him.

21. Advancing parallelism. "The intensification . . . that takes place between the two cola is that of a general statement ["justified in your sentence"] leading to a specific one [blameless judgments]." Longman, *Literary Approaches to Biblical Interpretation*, 143.

22. Advancing from birth to the earlier conception.

23. "The verbs 'desire' and 'teach', not being synonymous, suggest intensification of the second bicolon." VanGemeren, *Psalms*, 436.

24. Advancing from "me" to "the bones that you have crushed." Within the second line we find antithetic parallelism: from "the bones you have crushed" (*a*) to "let rejoice" (*−a*).

25. Advancing from "hide your face" to the more permanent "blot out."

26. According to Fokkelman, *Major Poems of the Hebrew Bible*, II, 165, this is the center of the psalm. "This poetic line contains nine words, arranged in a linear symmetry abcd//a'b'c'd' around the word 'God.'"

27. Verse 10b requested, "Put a new and right spirit within me." In contrast, verse 11a requests, "Do not cast me away," antithetic (−B). Verse 11b advances 11a by specifying "your holy spirit." This line, therefore, exhibits advancing parallelism supporting the antithetic −B; therefore +−B′.

₁₃Then I will teach transgressors your ways,²⁸	A
and sinners will return to you.	+ A′
₁₄Deliver me from bloodshed, O God,	B
O God of my salvation,	+ B′
and my tongue will sing aloud of your deliverance.	+ B″

₁₅O Lord, open my lips,	A
and my mouth will declare your praise.	+ A′
₁₆For you have no delight in sacrifice;	− B
if I were to give a burnt offering, you would not be pleased.	+− B′
₁₇The sacrifice acceptable to God is a broken spirit;	+ B″
a broken and contrite heart, O God, you will not despise.	+ B‴

₁₈Do good to Zion in your good pleasure;	A
rebuild the walls of Jerusalem,	+ A′
₁₉then you will delight in right sacrifices,	B
in burnt offerings and whole burnt offerings;	+ B′
then bulls will be offered on your altar.	+ B″

Imagery

"Of all the penitential psalms . . . only Psalm 51 employs the language of washing. . . . Psalm 51 views sin as an intractable stain, 'ever before' the psalmist's face, to be washed away or blotted out."²⁹ As such, much of the imagery in this psalm reflects the ceremonial laws that God instituted for the cleansing from sin. But these allusions to atonement rituals do not call for literal obedience; they are metaphors for a deeper meaning. No sacramental acts by sinners or priests can effect the cleansing called for; only God can do this. That's why the psalm begins with, "Have mercy on me, O God, according to your steadfast love; according to your abundant mercy blot out my transgressions."

"*Blot out (māḥâ)* my transgressions" (vv 1, 9) means wipe away my transgressions, as one wipes a dish clean (2 Kings 21:13). As Judge, God keeps a record of transgressions (Dan 7:10; Rev 20:12). The psalmist asks God to wipe his slate clean (cf. Exod 32:32–33).³⁰ "*Wash (kābas)* me thoroughly from my iniquity" (vv 2, 7)

---

28. Verses 13–15 in Hebrew use "three parallel lines, each including a first-person verb referring to the suppliant's speaking about God, about God's ways (v 13), God's faithfulness (v 14), and God's praise (v 15)." Goldingay, *Psalms,* II, 135.

29. Brown, *Seeing the Psalms,* 129.

30. "The traditional translation [blot out] has stayed with the psalm for centuries, but 'blot-

refers to washing clothes: "Literally it denotes 'treading,' as when one does laundry, a vigorous and thorough exercise presupposing serious dirt (cf. Jer 2:22)."[31] "*Cleanse (ṭāhar) me from my sin*" (v 2b) also refers to washing clothes but now with a view to making me "ritually clean" (Lev 13:6, 34, 58).[32]

"Purge me with hyssop, and I shall be clean; wash me, and I shall be whiter than snow" (v 7). Hyssop was a shrub with hairy leaves that could be used to sprinkle water (Numbers 19) or blood (Leviticus 14)[33] for becoming ritually clean. The psalmist uses this image as a metaphor for God's cleansing power.

The psalmist follows this up with another, "Wash me": "Wash me, and I shall be whiter than snow" (v 7). "Whiter than snow" is metaphor that contrasts the dirty stain of sin with pure white snow. It reminds us of the LORD's promise in Isaiah 1:18, "Though your sins are like scarlet, they shall be like snow."

In verse 8 the psalmist describes his distraught condition with another metaphor as "the bones that you have crushed."[34] In verse 9 he uses an anthropomorphic metaphor, pleading with God, "hide your face." The psalmist does not want God to look at his sins but to turn the other way.

Next he asks for "a clean heart" (v 10). In the Bible, the "heart" is an image for the center of our being,[35] while "clean," as a Levitical term, "describes someone as fit for the sanctuary and acceptable to God (see Ps 24:4)."[36] Then he pleads with God, "Do not cast me away from your presence" (v 11), that is, do not banish me from your covenant relationship. And he vows to teach transgressors God's

---

ting' as we know it only removes excess ink. The verb means 'to scrape off, remove.' The word is a figure of speech comparing divine forgiveness to God's scraping a slate clean (an implied comparison)." Ross, *Commentary on the Psalms*, II, 182.

31. Goldingay, *Psalms*, II, 127. Cf. Exod 19:10, 14.

32. Limburg, *Psalms*, 172. Cf. Goldingay, *Psalms*, II, 127, "The third verb . . . refers more intrinsically to a sacramental cleansing that makes something defiling into something pure."

33. At the exodus from Egypt, hyssop was also used to smear blood on the lintel and doorposts, so that the destroyer would pass over the Israelites (Exod 12:22–23). It was also used to clean people who had been healed of the dreaded disease of leprosy. God stipulated, the priest "shall sprinkle it [the blood] seven times upon the one who is to be cleansed of the leprous disease; then he shall pronounce him clean" (Lev 14:7). Although the comparison of sin and leprosy would be powerful in a sermon, Goldingay, *Psalms*, II, 131, rightly notes that "here the parallel with washing suggests sprinkling with water rather than with blood. . . . The supplicant asks God to act like a friend who sprinkles the people who live in that tent (and the tent itself and its furnishings) so that people and tent become pure again and able to live their ordinary lives."

34. "The bones refers to his spirit, and the verb 'crushed' is figurative (an implied comparison) for spiritual depression (as that described in Psalm 32)." Ross, *Commentary on the Psalms*, II, 190.

35. "'Heart' does not mean the organ, but the mind, the seat of the will within the human spirit (a metonymy of subject)." Ibid.

36. Ibid., 192.

"ways" (v 13) — literally roads; metaphorically, God's merciful ways of dealing with sinners and his requirements.[37]

He pleads again, "Deliver me from bloodshed, O God" (v 14). "The word used is 'bloods' (literally), the plural referring to shed blood ('bloods' is a metonymy of effect for murder); so it is translated 'bloodguiltiness.'"[38] And finally he speaks of "a broken spirit; a broken and contrite heart" (v 17), not literally a "broken" spirit and heart but as the parallelism shows, a "contrite heart," repentant, no longer self-sufficient, or, positively, "a willing spirit" (v 12).

Repetition of Keywords

Psalm 51 repeats many sets of three. The psalmist describes God's character with three different Hebrew words, translated as "mercy," "steadfast love," and "abundant mercy" (v 1). He recounts his problem with three different words for sin, translated as "my transgressions," "my iniquity," and "my sin" (vv 1–2). He portrays the solution to his problem with three different words for forgiveness, translated as "blot out," "wash me," and "cleanse me" (vv 1–2). He adds three requests for God to create something new in him, translated as "a clean heart," "a new and right spirit," and "a willing spirit" (vv 10–12). And finally he vows to do three things: "I will teach transgressors your ways," "my tongue will sing aloud of your deliverance," and "my mouth will declare your praise" (vv 13–15).

In addition, the psalm repeats many keywords with synonyms. The first word that stands out is the most general word for sin (*ḥaṭṭā'*), which, with its cognate, is used six times (vv 2, 3, 4, 5, 9, 13). It is supported by three synonyms: "transgressions" or rebellion (*pešaʿ*), which is used three times (vv 1, 3, 13); "iniquity" or guilt (*ʿāwon*), which is also used three times (vv 2, 5, 9); and "evil" (*rāʿ*), which is used once (v 4). All these repetitions reveal the problem addressed in this psalm: it is sin! sin! sin! — all kinds of sins.

The next keyword that stands out in the psalm is the word "wash" and its synonyms. "Wash" is used twice (vv 2, 7); "blot out" is also used twice (vv 1, 9); while "cleanse / clean" is used three times (vv 2, 7, 10) and "purge" once (v 7). Washing, cleansing, blotting out is the cure for the problem of sin.

The psalm probes even deeper for a cure to the problem of sin. Since the fountainhead of sinful acts is within human beings, the psalmist appeals to God:

37. "'Your ways' in v 15 may certainly include the ways God intends for the guidance of his people as expressed in commandments and teachings. In the context, however, the ways of God dealing with sinners must be included. Instruction in God's gracious, forgiving restoration of sinners would be an integral part of the teaching." Tate, *Psalms 51–100*, 26.

38. Ross, *Commentary on the Psalms*, II, 196.

"Create in me a clean heart, O God." The name "God / Lord" is repeated a perfect seven times (vv 1, 10, 14 [2×], 15, 17 [2×]). Notice that six of these references to God are in the second half of the psalm. In other words, the concentration on sin in the first half gives way to God in the second half.

In verses 10–12 the second line of each verse in Hebrew begins with *wərûaḥ* ("and a spirit") in the emphatic position: "Put a new and right spirit within me. . . . and do not take your Holy Spirit from me. . . . and sustain in me a willing spirit." Three times the psalm pleads with God for "a new spirit," the "Holy Spirit," and "a willing spirit" — an ABA' chiasm centering on the Holy Spirit.

Goldingay sums up well: "Words for sin come twelve times in vv 1–9 and twice in vv 10–19; God is named once in vv 1–9 and six times in vv 10–19. Sin gives way to God; with confession, sin gives way to God's presence."[39]

Structure

Three popular English versions are quite similar in the structure they propose for this psalm.

Verse Divisions	Versions
1–2 / 3–5 / 6 – 9 / 10–12 / 13–14 / 15–17 / 18–19	NRSV
1–2 / 3 – 6 / 7–9 / 10–12 / 13 – 17 / 18–19	NIV
1–2 / 3 – 6 / 7 – 12 / 13 – 17 / 18–19	ESV

The main question, as can be seen, is whether verse 6 belongs with verses 3–6 or 6–9. Technically the NIV may reflect a more precise literary structure. John Stek points out that the whole psalm is framed by a two-verse prayer for David himself (vv 1–2) and a two-verse prayer for Zion (vv 18–19). "The enclosed four stanzas in Hebrew consist of five lines, three lines, three lines and five lines respectively"[40] — an ABBA pattern. On the other hand, the NRSV's placement of verse 6 with "petitions for God's help" more closely follows the typical structure of laments (see below).

The repetition of keywords also enables us to discern the underlying structure of the psalm. Fokkelman rightly cautions, "The poet uses so many word repetitions that on this basis alone one can find (or impute) all sorts of structures."[41] Yet it is undeniable that the psalm reveals an underlying structure with two major

---

39. Goldingay, *Psalms*, II, 140.
40. Stek, *NIV Study Bible*, Ps 51 n.
41. Fokkelman, *Major Poems of the Hebrew Bible*, II, 165.

inclusios: "blot out" in verses 1 and 9 and the inversion of "clean heart" and "right spirit" of verse 10 into "broken spirit" and "contrite heart" in verse 17. The original psalm, then, consisted of two halves: verses 1–9 and verses 10–17.

Terrien further explores the artistry in the psalm's composition. He writes, "The psalm is clearly divided in two parts, each of which forms a mirror with two folding panels whose motifs reflect each other."[42] In other words, the original psalm consists of two chiasms:

PART I
A. "blot out" (v 1)
    B. "wash me" (v 2a)
        C. "cleanse me" (v 2b)
            D. "I know" (v 3a)
                E. "I have sinned" (v 4a)
                    F. "you are justified" (v 4b — core verse)
                E' "I was born a sinner" (v 5)
            D' "teach me" (v 6)
        C' "I shall be clean" (v 7a)
    B' "wash me" (v 7b)
A' "blot out" (v 9)

PART II
A. "a clean heart . . . right spirit" (v 10)
    B. "do not cast me . . . do not take" (v 11)
        C. "your salvation" (v 12)
            D. "I will teach your ways" (v 13 — core verse)
        C' "God of my salvation" (v 14)
    B' "you have no delight . . . would not be pleased" (v 16)
A' "a broken spirit . . . contrite heart" (v 17)

Aside from revealing its artistry, this rhetorical structure may be helpful in determining the specific emphases in this psalm.

For preaching purposes, it is more helpful to analyze the structure of Psalm 51 by comparing it with the typical structure of lament psalms. We have seen that laments usually have some or all of these elements:[43]

42. Terrien, *The Psalms*, 402–3. In the following diagram I have substituted my own design as well as the words and verse references of the NRSV. For a similar pattern, derived independently, see Gaiser, "The David of Psalm 51: Reading Psalm 51 in Light of Psalm 50," *W & W* 23, no. 4 (2003): 385–86.

43. See pp. 10–11 above.

1) Introductory petition for God's help
2) Description of the trouble or complaint
3) Petitions for God's help
4) Reasons why God should hear or confidence that God will save
5) Examples of God's saving acts in history
6) A vow to praise

Psalm 51 has four of these elements with a fifth point added in verses 18–19:

1) Introductory petition for God's help   (Ps 51:1–2)
2) Description of the trouble or complaint   (Ps 51:3–5)
3) Petitions for God's help   (Ps 51:6–12)
4) A vow to praise   (Ps 51:13–17)
5) Prayer for Zion, vow to bring "right sacrifices"   (Ps 51:18–19)

Theocentric Interpretation

Because of the temptation to use this psalm to focus exclusively on human sin, especially on Ash Wednesday, it is well to ask the question what Psalm 51 says about God. Right from the start God is the one who is addressed: "Have mercy on me, O God." The psalm names God's qualities that enable him to be gracious: "Have mercy . . . , according to your steadfast love; according to your abundant mercy [compassion, NIV]."[44] Throughout the psalm the psalmist keeps addressing God. In fact, "each of the repeated words for sin in verses 1–5 appears as the object of an imperative addressed to God in verses 1–2 — "blot out" . . . , "wash" . . . , "cleanse."[45] The psalmist also says to God, significantly at the center of the first chiasm, "You are justified in your sentence and blameless when you pass judgment" (v 4).

As we saw under "Repetition" above, the name "God / Lord" is repeated a perfect seven times: once in the first half of the psalm, six times in the second half (vv 1, 10, 14 [2×], 15, 17 [2×]). The second half begins with, "Create in me a clean heart, O God." The Hebrew Bible uses the verb "create" (*bāra'*) only for God.[46] No

---

44. "Before any mention of the vocabulary of sin, which dominates verses 1–5, the psalmist appeals to God's character, using three key words from God's self-revelation in Exodus 34:6: 'merciful' (*raḥûm*), 'gracious' (*ḥannûn*), and 'steadfast love' (*ḥesed*)." McCann, *Theological Introduction*, 102.

45. McCann, "Psalms," 886.

46. "This word (*bāra'*) in the Old Testament is absolutely strictly reserved for the creative work of God only . . . ; it is never used in reference to human undertaking. God alone is always the subject of this verb." Kraus, *Psalms 1–59*, 504.

one but God can create a clean heart. This request is followed by a threefold petition to God for "a new and right spirit": "Create in me a clean heart, O God, and put *a new and right spirit* within me. Do not cast me away from your presence, and do not take *your holy spirit* from me. Restore to me the joy of your salvation, and sustain in me *a willing spirit*" (vv 10–12).

The psalmist also calls God the "God of my salvation" (v 14). He asks God to open his lips so that he can declare God's praise (v 15). "Even the witness of thanksgiving (v 15) is exclusively left in the hands of powers furnished by Yahweh. Everything is God's act. The *sola gratia* shines forth from every verse."[47] The psalmist next tells God (and Israel and us), "a broken and contrite heart, O God, you will not despise" (v 17). He concludes with a prayer to God for Jerusalem: "Do good to Zion in your good pleasure; rebuild the walls of Jerusalem, then you will delight in right sacrifices" (vv 18–19).

Textual Theme and Goal

James Mays writes, "As a whole, the psalm is a prayer of unrelieved intensity and eloquence. Its theme is stated in the opening words, 'Be gracious to me, O God,' and the rest of the psalm unfolds that basic appeal."[48] Mays is right that the original psalm was a personal cry to God for mercy: "Have mercy on me, O God." But for preaching a text, the *theme* seeks to formulate the text's message for Israel. We ask, What is this psalm's message for Israel? Although the original psalm was addressed to God, it is now part of the Psalter which is addressed to God's people.

We can picture the switch in direction with a simple diagram:

The theme of the original psalm addressed God:

Forgive me, O God! ↑

The theme of the psalm as incorporated in the Psalter addresses Israel:

God forgives! →

Therefore we can formulate the theme of Psalm 51 as follows, *Because of his steadfast love and abundant mercy, God will forgive even the most heinous sins if people but ask with a contrite heart.*

47. Ibid., 507.
48. Mays, *Psalms*, 198.

The goal of the psalm depends on the historical situation it addressed. If the superscription is historically correct, David's goal was to cry out to God for forgiveness and to be forgiven because of God's steadfast love and abundant mercy. But most scholars agree that these superscriptions were added by later editors when the psalms were collected and shaped into the Psalter.[49] When these superscriptions identify the author and the occasion for writing, such as in Psalm 51, they offer the editor's invitation for reading the psalm from that historical perspective.[50] "The kingship characteristic of the psalm may be the result of the author consciously writing with David in mind; placing, as it were, the psalm in the mouth of David."[51] In other words, David would be the *implied* author of Psalm 51.

We know that the psalms were collected into the Psalter during or after the exile. That means that we should seek to determine the goal of Psalm 51 at some time in Israel's history during or after the exile when the walls of Jerusalem were still torn down (see 51:18).[52] This date comports well with similar ideas in Jeremiah and Ezekiel.[53] Israel is devastated by its punishment of exile. God has cast them off! God has removed them from the Promised Land. Why did this disaster come upon them? Their sins weigh heavily upon them. The goal of Psalm 51, then, is *to assure God's people that God, because of his steadfast love and abundant mercy, will forgive even the most heinous sins if people but ask with a contrite heart.*

49. "While a few of these titles may have been composed at the same time as the psalm, the majority of them reflect later tradition concerning the use of the psalm in Israel's worship. The psalm titles are, nevertheless, a part of the canonical text of the Hebrew Bible, not merely the notations of a post-biblical editor." Peter Craigie, *The Old Testament*, 212. Cf. Bellinger, *Psalms*, 8–9.

50. Eaton, *The Psalms*, 206, adds, "We may, however, consider whether the psalm could be the utterance of a king in his representative capacity; speaking in individual terms, he would be leading the penitence of the people incorporated in him, and so could naturally conclude with prayer for the well-being of Zion."

51. Tate, *Psalms 51–100*, 11.

52. A. Anderson, *Psalms 1–72*, 390, after evaluating suggestions for the date of composition, writes, "We may be on safer grounds, however, in placing its date of origin sometime between the period of Jeremiah and Ezekiel on the one hand, and that of Nehemiah on the other hand."

53. "In its present form, its language and thought are connected with that of Jeremiah, Ezekiel, and Isaiah 40–66. It reads like an anticipation of or response to the promises of a new heart and spirit in Jeremiah (Jer 24:7; 31:33; 32:39–40) and Ezekiel (Ezek 36:25ff.)." Mays, *Psalms*, 199. Cf. Broyles, *Psalms*, 227, "The main petition section of this psalm (vv 7–12) is, remarkably, unique in the Psalter but strongly paralleled by the promises of a new covenant found in exilic prophecies (Ezek 36:24–32; Jer 24:7; 31:31–34). Psalm 51 most likely originated within the same worshiping communities of the exilic period."

Ways to Preach Christ

There are at least two ways for preaching Christ from this psalm: analogy and redemptive-historical progression, both supported by New Testament references.

Analogy with New Testament References

One can use the way of analogy with the teaching of Jesus for preaching Christ from Psalm 51. Psalm 51 teaches that God will forgive even the most heinous sins if people but ask with a contrite heart. Jesus makes the same point in the parable of the prodigal son. After squandering his property in "dissolute living," the son returns to his father. Jesus has him quoting Psalm 51:4 (LXX, 50:6), "Father, I have sinned against heaven and before you" (Luke 15:21). The father not only forgives the son but throws a party, "for this son of mine was dead and is alive again; he was lost and is found!" (Luke 15:24, 32). "Luke 15 makes concrete, in paradigmatic fashion, the structure of events developed in that psalm: acknowledgment of guilt, confession before the merciful God, new creation, and festive meal."[54]

Redemptive-Historical Progression with New Testament References

Another way to preach Christ from Psalm 51 (perhaps combined with analogy and typology) is redemptive-historical progression supported by New Testament references. The message of Psalm 51 is that God will forgive even the most heinous sins if people but ask with a contrite heart. In Old Testament times God expressed his desire to forgive people by instituting an elaborate sacrificial system. "The sacrifices prescribed in Leviticus 1–7 addressed only sins committed 'unintentionally' or by omission of duty (Lev 4:2, 13, 22, 27; 5:1–4, 15; Num 15:22–29). Sins committed in a premeditated or defiant manner were not removed by these sacrifices (Num 15:30–36)."[55] David had committed premeditated sins: adultery with Bathsheba and the murder of her husband Uriah. No sacrifice he could offer would pay for these sins. He could only throw himself on God's mercy: "Have mercy on me, O God!" And God forgave him even these terrible sins. Psalm 51:17

---

54. Zenger, *Psalms 2*, 24–25.

55. Hilber, *Psalms,* 370. Appealing to the "all sins" in Lev 16:16, 21, 30, 34, Hilber, ibid., claims that "only on the Day of Atonement were all sins, even 'rebellion,' removed and God's wrath appeased. On this day, God expected an attitude of humble contrition (16:29–31)." But see n. 114 below.

declares confidently, "The sacrifice acceptable to God is a broken spirit; a broken and contrite heart, O God, you will not despise."

The Old Testament sacrifices, as types, prefigured the sacrifice of Jesus on the cross. When Jesus died "the curtain of the temple was torn in two, from top to bottom" (Matt 27:51). Jesus' sacrificial death opened the way to God. Jesus paid the penalty for sin once for all. People no longer had to slaughter animals to have their sins forgiven. In his mercy God provided a new way. His own Son would be the sin-sacrifice. Jesus was "the Lamb of God who takes away the sin of the world!" (John 1:29).

The psalmist asks God for a thorough cleansing from sin (vv 2, 7, 9), "a clean heart" and "a new and right spirit within" (v 10). Jesus' death, resurrection, and outpouring of the Holy Spirit can fulfill these requests in greater measure than the psalmist could have imagined. Jesus himself taught that we must be born again, born of the Spirit (John 3:3, 5, 8), and Paul writes that God, "even when we were dead through our trespasses, made us alive together with Christ . . . and raised us up with him and seated us with him in the heavenly places in Christ Jesus" (Eph 2:5–6). One can add more New Testament references such as 2 Cor 5:21; Col 2:13–14; 1 John 1:9; 2:1–2; 4:10 (see "Sermon Exposition" below).

Sermon Theme, Goal, and Need

Since the New Testament confirms God's willingness to forgive our sins, the textual theme and goal can function as the sermon theme and goal. Therefore the theme of the sermon is: *Because of his steadfast love and abundant mercy, God will forgive even the most heinous sins if people but ask with a contrite heart.* And the sermon goal is: *to assure God's people that God, because of his steadfast love and abundant mercy, will forgive even the most heinous sins if people but ask with a contrite heart.*

This goal points to the need being addressed in this sermon: people who have sinned grievously sometimes find it difficult to accept that God is eager to forgive their sins and fail to plead with God for forgiveness. The sermon introduction might illustrate this need.

Liturgy, PowerPoint, and Sermon Outline

Psalm 51:15 can serve as a call to worship: "O Lord, open my lips, and my mouth will declare your praise." Verses 1–5, or 10–12, or 10 by itself can be used as a prayer of confession: "Create in me a clean heart, O God, and put a new and right spirit within me." 2 Corinthians 5:17 offers a matching assurance of pardon: "If anyone is in Christ, there is a new creation: everything old has passed away; see, everything has become new!"[56]

PowerPoint can help the congregation understand better the artistry as well as the message of this psalm. Displaying on the screen the verses being explained will enable the congregation to read and reread the verses. The artistry can be communicated by highlighting the five sets of three, each time beginning with the first word, then adding to the slide the second, then the third word:

V 1, *God's character:* "mercy," "steadfast love," and "abundant mercy" [compassion].
Vv 1–2, *David's problem:* "my transgression," "my iniquity," and "my sin."
Vv 1–2, *The negative solution:* "blot out," "wash me," and "cleanse me."
Vv 10–12, *The positive solution:* create in me "a clean heart," "a new and right spirit," and a "willing spirit."
Vv 13–15, *David's vows:* "I will teach transgressors your ways," "my tongue will sing aloud of your deliverance," and "my mouth will declare your praise."

We may be able to use as sermon outline the lament structure we discovered earlier. Adding topical headings as well as the move to Christ results in the following sermon outline (the smaller font inserts the five sets of three with PowerPoint):

I. Prayer for God to blot out our sins (Ps 51:1–2)
   God's character: "mercy," "steadfast love," and "abundant mercy" [compassion].
   David's problem: "my transgression," "my iniquity," and "my sin."
   The negative solution: "blot out," "wash me," and "cleanse me."
II. Acknowledgment that we are born sinners (Ps 51:3–5)
III. Prayer for God to cleanse our "inward being" (Ps 51:6–9)[57]
IV. Prayer for God to create "a clean heart" in us (Ps 51:10–12)
   The positive solution: create in me "a clean heart," "a new and right spirit," and a "willing spirit."
V. Vow to spread the good news of God's "ways" (Ps 51:13–17)
   David's vows: "I will teach transgressors your ways," "my tongue will sing aloud of your deliverance," and "my mouth will declare your praise."

---

56. Or Ezekiel 36:26–27, "A new heart I will give you, and a new spirit I will put within you; and I will remove from your body the heart of stone and give you a heart of flesh. I will put my spirit within you, and make you follow my statutes and be careful to observe my ordinances."
57. Splitting verses 6–12 into two points acknowledges that verse 10 begins the second half of the psalm.

VI. Prayer for Zion and a vow of "right sacrifices"(Ps 51:18–19)

VII. Through Christ's sacrifice we are forgiven, a new creation (NT)[58]

As can be seen, this psalm has a lot of material for a single sermon. Preachers may wish to consider preaching two sermons on this psalm, one on each half (see Appendix 6, p. 582 below). In the sermon exposition below, I will not break the exposition into these seven points but seek to communicate the theme of this psalm by concentrating on the continuity between the verses and stanzas.

Sermon Exposition

The sermon introduction could focus the hearers on the need addressed with an illustration of contemporary people who sinned grievously and thought that God would never forgive them. Next move to David's sins. One can also follow the lead of the superscription and begin with David's sins.

The heading of this psalm reads, "To the leader. A Psalm of David, when the prophet Nathan came to him, after he had gone in to Bathsheba." This superscription invites us to read this psalm in the light of David's awful sins.[59] You know the story, don't you?

One late afternoon in the spring of the year, David was walking on the roof of his palace. Suddenly he saw a woman in a courtyard below the palace. She was bathing herself. He noticed right away that she was "very beautiful." This attracted him. He sent someone to check who this beautiful woman was. The report came back, "This is Bathsheba daughter of Eliam, the wife of Uriah the Hittite" (2 Sam 11:3). "The wife of Uriah" should have been enough for David: she was married to someone else. But that did not stop ancient Near Eastern kings. And it did not stop King David. He wanted this beautiful woman for himself. We read in 2 Samuel 11:4, "So David sent messengers to get her, and she came to him, and he lay with her. . . . Then she returned to her house." Premeditated adultery! A few months later Bathsheba sent David a three-word message: "I am pregnant!" (2 Sam 11:5).

What to do? David's adultery was about to become public. And the penalty for adultery according to God's law was death (Lev 20:10). What to do? David came up with a plan. He would try to hide his sin. We read in 2 Samuel, "So David

---

58. If the pew Bible is the NIV one may be able to use the six stanzas suggested by Stek (p. 248 above), although the contents of verse 6 fit better with verses 7–9.

59. King David is either the author of Psalm 51 or, if the psalmist wrote this psalm with King David in mind (see p. 252 above), the implied author. In either case we can use the name "David" in the sermon instead of "the author," or "the psalmist," or "the suppliant."

sent word to [his general] Joab, 'Send me Uriah the Hittite.' And Joab sent Uriah to David. . . . Then David said to Uriah, 'Go down to your house, and wash your feet'" (2 Sam 11:6–8). David wanted Uriah to sleep with Bathsheba so that he and everyone else would think that the baby was Uriah's. But it was a time of war, and the loyal soldier refused to go home, as he said, "to lie with my wife." He stayed that night at "the king's house with all the servants of his lord" (2 Sam 11:9–11). David tried again the next night to get Uriah to go home, "but he did not go down to his house" (2 Sam 11:13).

What to do now? How could he now hide his sin of adultery? He weighed his options overnight and came up with an appalling solution. "In the morning David wrote a letter to Joab, and sent it by the hand of Uriah. In the letter he wrote, 'Set Uriah in the forefront of the hardest fighting, and then draw back from him, so that he may be struck down and die'" (2 Sam 11:14–15). David made Uriah, of all people, carry his own death warrant. And Uriah died. Premeditated murder to hide the sin of premeditated adultery!

"If ever anyone deserved to be punished, it was David, whose afternoon stroll on the roof led him eventually to break fully half of the Ten Commandments (David killed, committed adultery, stole, bore false witness, and coveted). Remarkably, David is forgiven (2 Sam 12:13); he lives; he remains king."[60] Psalm 51 is in the Bible to assure us that God, because of his steadfast love and abundant mercy, will forgive even the most heinous sins if people but ask with a contrite heart.

David begins this psalm with, "Have mercy on me, O God, according to your steadfast love; according to your abundant mercy blot out my transgressions." Amazingly, he begins not with a list of his sins. He begins with God. He begins with an appeal to God's character with three keywords: "mercy," "steadfast love," and "abundant mercy." Verse 1, "Have *mercy* on me, O God, according to your *steadfast love;* according to your *abundant mercy.*" "Mercy" refers to God's grace or unmerited favor.[61] The second word is "steadfast love," which is God's covenant loyalty.[62] And the third word is "abundant mercy," which can also be translated

---

60. McCann, *Theological Introduction*, 102.

61. "The *ḥannēni*, 'be merciful to me' expresses the desire for favorable and beneficent action, usually involving the response of a superior to an inferior." Tate, *Psalms 51–100*, 13. Cf. Goldingay, *Songs from a Strange Land*, 160, "He refers first to God's *grace*, which means . . . the favorable attitude shown though not earned. . . . Grace or favor is the unearned, positive, friendly, giving attitude of someone."

62. Anderson, *Psalms 1–72*, 391, "*ḥesed* is essentially a Covenant word. . . . When it is used of God, it usually refers to his gracious and reliable Covenant promises." Cf. McCann, "Psalms," 885, "'Steadfast love' . . . is virtually a one-word summary of God's gracious, self-giving character." Cf. Psalm 63:3–4, "Because your steadfast love is better than life, my lips will praise you. So I will bless you as long as I live." Cf. Goldingay, *Songs from a Strange Land*, 160–61.

as "motherly compassion."[63] David begins this psalm by declaring that God is a God of grace, a God of covenant loyalty, a God of motherly compassion.

Jesus may have had this psalm in mind when he told the parable of the prodigal son. The son went to a far country and "squandered his wealth in wild living" (Luke 15:13, NIV). But when he came to his senses, he said, "I will get up and go to my father, and I will say to him, '*Father*, I have sinned against heaven and before you'" — an allusion to Psalm 51:4 — "Against you, you alone, have I sinned."[64] The son knew the character of his father; he knew that his father would forgive him.

So David here begins the psalm with the character of his heavenly Father. He begins with the reminder that God is a God of mercy, steadfast love, and motherly compassion. It is only on the basis of God's merciful character that he has any hope of forgiveness.

After he has described God's character with three profound words, he begins to list his offenses with three different words: "transgressions," "iniquity," and "sin." The end of verse 1, "Blot out my transgressions." "Transgressions" is a potent word. It does not mean merely to transgress, step over, the boundaries of God's law. "The picture behind 'transgressions' (vv 1, 3, 13) is rebellion, as when children rebel against their parents (Isa 1:2)" or people rebel against their king.[65] David has not merely broken God's law; he rebelled against his Lord.[66]

In verse 2 David adds two more words for his offenses: "Wash me thoroughly from my *iniquity*, and cleanse me from my *sin*." "Iniquity" is "a deliberate act" of going astray, deliberate "deviation from the right path."[67] The third word is "sin."

---

63. McCann, "Psalms," 885. Cf. Tate, *Psalms 51–100*, 14, "The form suggests the idea of the feelings of a mother toward her baby." Cf. A. Anderson, *Psalms 1–72*, 391, with a reference to Isa 49:15.

64. Luke 15:18 in part cites Psalm 51:4 (LXX, 50:6).

65. Limburg, *Psalms*, 172. Cf. A. Anderson, *Psalms 1–72*, 392. "The Hebrew *pešaʿ* primarily means a rebellion against an authority. . . . The cognate verb is often used to describe an act of revolt, e.g., when Israel rebelled against the house of David (1 Kings 12:19), or when Moab revolted against Israel (2 Kings 1:1). Consequently *pešaʿ* denotes sin as a deliberate defiance of God, and as a rebellion against his will." Cf. Goldingay, *Songs from a Strange Land*, 154, and Ross, *Commentary on the Psalms*, II, 180–81 n. 24.

66. I will go into some detail on the specific meanings of these words and others. Preachers will have to weigh whether such specificity will overload the sermon at the start so that instead of soaring it crashes. As an alternative to this detailed presentation, one can consider just giving the numbers, such as Walters, "I Talk of My Sin," *CTJ* 50 (2015; pp. 91–109): 91, "Its first part is overpopulated with words for sin and forgiveness: four different words for sin (if you're counting), used eleven times, and six different expressions for forgiveness, used nine times." Or one can summarize the specifics in general statements, such as Wilson, McCann, and Barentsen; see p. 259 and n. 70 below.

67. A. Anderson, *Psalms 1–72*, 393. As such it has the connotation of being guilty (cf. 51:5). Cf. McCann, "Psalms," 885, "'Iniquity' / 'guilty' ('*āwon*, vv 2, 5; see also v 9) involves the personal guilt or culpability of the sinner."

"Sin" evokes the picture of people aiming at a target and missing the mark (Judges 20:16); they fall short of the goal God has set for them; they fail to reach the goal.[68]

Three words to describe God's character and now three words to describe David's offenses: "transgressions," "iniquity," and "sin."[69] "The use of all three terms seems intended to be comprehensive, so that the psalmist's confession is far-reaching and complete."[70] David looks back at his life and sees various kinds of sin, sin! sin! He wants to be washed and cleansed from any and all kinds of sins.

In pleading for forgiveness, David again uses three different words: "blot out," "wash me," and "cleanse me."[71] These three words come from the rituals God had instituted for the forgiveness of sins. David requests in verse 1, "*Blot out my transgressions.*" To "blot out" means to wipe away as one wipes a dirty dish clean.[72] But there may be more involved in this image. As the final Judge, God keeps a record of sins. He writes them in a book, as it were.[73] So David here asks God to wipe the slate of his transgressions clean.[74]

In verse 2 David adds, "*Wash me* thoroughly." The "wash me" refers to the way people washed laundry in ancient times. You may have seen pictures of women gathered by the riverside placing dirty clothes on rocks in the running water. Then they tread on the laundry; they literally walk on it, rub it, and slap

---

68. "His sin has the character of failure. The word is the most frequent one here (2b, 3b, 4a, 5b, 9a, 13b) as elsewhere in the Old Testament. Perhaps 'failure' is then the dominant note in the Old Testament's understanding of sin." Goldingay, *Songs from a Strange Land*, 154.

69. The same six Hebrew words are found in Exod 34:6–7, "The LORD passed before him [Moses], and proclaimed, 'The LORD, the LORD, a God *merciful* and *gracious*, slow to anger, and abounding in *steadfast love* and faithfulness . . . , forgiving *iniquity* and *transgression* and *sin*. . . .'"

70. Wilson, *Psalms*, I, 774. Cf. McCann, *Theological Introduction*, 103, "The effect of the repetition is to drive home the point. Sin and its consequences are pervasive." Cf. Barentsen, "Restoration and Its Blessings," *GTJ* 5, no. 2 (1984; pp. 247–69): 261, "The three different words for sin . . . usually have different nuances, but here in parallel they indicate the totality of sin in which man is involved. Similarly, the three different words used for forgiveness indicate the complete forgiveness requested. Both observations show that sin is not a superficial characteristic of man but rather goes to the core."

71. "The words *blot out, wash,* and *cleanse* recur in reverse order in verses 7–9, forming a circle that speaks of forgiveness in terms of washing. . . . The two requests *blot out* frame this section (vv 1d and 9b), for in the Hebrew word order, no references to my sin stand outside these bookends. The two appeals, 'blot out' corral all references to sin, giving absolute closure." Walters, "I Talk of My Sin," *CTJ* 50 (2015): 93.

72. Cf. Isaiah 43:25, "I, I am He who blots out your transgressions for my own sake, and I will not remember your sins." Cf. 2 Kings 21:13; Isa 25:8; 44:22.

73. Cf. Exod 32:32–33; Pss 130:3; 139:16; Dan 7:10; Rev 20:12.

74. "The verb 'blot out' may have in its background the thought of a tablet or book in which the divine judge keeps a tally of all that people do. The psalmist is pleading that the debit account be erased." Davidson, *Vitality of Worship*, 167. Cf. Tate, *Psalms 51–100*, 14.

it against rocks above the water until it is clean. So David asks God to wash him *thoroughly.*

He adds a third word in verse 2, "*Cleanse me* from my sin." "Cleanse me" refers to washing that makes people ritually clean so they can appear in God's presence.[75] Sin is like leprosy; it renders people unclean. Then they can no longer appear before God in his temple. The "cleanse me from my sin" asks God for such cleansing that he can worship God again in his temple.[76]

David combines three different words for sin with three different words for forgiveness. He requests God to "blot out" his "transgressions," to "thoroughly wash" him from his "iniquity," and to "cleanse" him from his "sin." His problem of Sin-Sin-Sin can only be solved by Wash-Wash-Wash. Why is he repeating all these words?

He explains in verse 3, "For I know my transgressions, and my sin is ever before me." "For I *know* my transgressions," David says. I don't just acknowledge my sin; I don't just admit it; I *know* my transgressions personally. In fact, "my sin is ever before me."[77] My sin is always staring me in the face; I am always aware of it; my guilt is wearing me down. That's why I need cleansing so badly.

But there is a far more important reason. Verse 4, "Against *you, you alone,* have I sinned, and done what is evil[78] in your sight." He has sinned against his *God.* That is ultimately why he needs cleansing so badly.

Now we might raise a question here. Is it true that David sinned against God alone? Did he not also sin against Bathsheba by sleeping with her? And against Uriah by having sex with his wife and then murdering him?

Of course, he also sinned against Bathsheba and Uriah. Sin has social consequences. This becomes clear in the next (advancing) parallel line, "and done what is evil in your sight." When we hurt our neighbor, that is "evil in God's sight."[79]

---

75. "In the OT generally, uncleanness is essentially that which disqualifies from participation in ritual and excludes the worshiper from the presence of God." Tate, *Psalms 51–100,* 15.

76. Cf. Lev 13:6, 34, 58.

77. "My sin is 'before me', using the metaphor of space and place. I can see it, and I do not drag it off behind me or edge it to one side or the other. It is in the forefront of my awareness, within the range of my sight." Walters, "I Talk of My Sin," *CTJ* 50 (2015): 94.

78. "The comprehensive term 'what is evil' stands alone in verse 4b, at the center of verses 1–9, and echoes the identical expression in Nathan's rebuke, 'Why have you despised the word of the LORD, to do what is evil in his sight?' (2 Sam 12:9)." Ibid.

79. Evil in God's sight "includes offences against men and, indeed, elsewhere is always used with reference to such offences, for example Genesis 39:9. For in the Old Testament trespasses against men are viewed from the start as trespasses against God." Westermann, *The Living Psalms,* 96. Cf. Ross, *Commentary on the Psalms,* II, 186, "This word 'evil' . . . adds to the confession the clarification that the sin caused a great pain, for it describes any act that harms life in any way, including destroying life." Cf. Kraus, *Psalms 1–59,* "Already very early in the OT offenses against

When we do not love our neighbor as ourselves, that is "evil in God's sight." In verse 14 David will also confess to murder: "Deliver me from bloodshed, O God."

But the point David is making when he says, "Against *you, you alone,* have I sinned," is that ultimately sin is an affront to the holy God.[80] Sin is not only breaking God's law but rebelling against our King. So at its deepest level, when we sin, we sin against God.[81] For that reason David says, "Against you, you alone, have I sinned, and done what is evil in your sight" (cf. 2 Sam 12:13, "I have sinned against the LORD"). David concludes in verse 4, "so that[82] you are justified in your sentence and blameless when you pass judgment." God is the final Judge and he can rightly declare us guilty and sentence us to whatever sentence he deems appropriate. Even if God decides on the death penalty, God will be blameless.

In contrast to the blamelessness of God, David acknowledges in verse 5 that he is in the grip of sin: "Indeed,[83] I was born guilty, a sinner when my mother conceived me." David admits that his sinful acts spring from a deeper source. He was "*born* guilty"; born with iniquity.[84] And David moves back even further to the moment of his conception: "a sinner when my mother *conceived* me."

Being a sinner from the very beginning is no excuse for sinful acts, of course. David here points to the *origin* of his sinful acts. Sin is part of the human condition. We are born into it. We are infected with sin from birth, even from conception. We inherit this sinful human nature from our parents as they inherited it from their parents. Paul will later trace this sinful condition all the way back to the first man, Adam: "by the one man's disobedience the many were made sinners" (Rom 5:19).[85]

So David is aware that he not only needs to be cleansed from the stain of

---

other human beings are viewed as sin against God (Gen 39:9)." See also Nathan's accusations (2 Sam 12:9–10) and David's confession, "I have sinned against the LORD" (2 Sam 12:13; Ps 51:4). Cf. Prov 14:31 and 17:5.

80. "The confession must be understood within the context of this immediate encounter with the God of purity, truth, and holiness (vv 2, 6, 7, 11). As the rest of the verse makes plain, the point of this confession is to establish that the speaker has *done what is evil in your sight, so that you are . . . justified when you judge.*" Broyles, *Psalms,* 227. Broyles, p. 228, also points out that "elsewhere in the psalms, whenever the phrase 'you only' [Heb. *ləbaddəkā*] is used, its primary function is to denote Yahweh to the exclusion of other deities and powers. See, e.g., 83:18; [86:10]; 136:4."

81. "The problem is that sin violates God. This does not mean that others are not also hurt. But the righting of the wrong concerns the 'godness' of God, and none other. In the flat world of modernity, this psalm affirms a forgotten reality. Our skewed lives finally must deal with God." Brueggemann, *Message of the Psalms,* 99.

82. For arguments for the result clause ("so that") rather than the purpose clause ("in order that") see Tate, *Psalms 51–100,* 17–18.

83. "*Behold (hēn)* invites the audience to join the poet in observing the sonar graph of the unborn's spiritual state." Waltke, *Psalms in Christian Worship,* 472.

84. The same Hebrew word that is translated "iniquity" in verse 2. See p. 258 above.

85. Paul develops the doctrine of original sin in Rom 5:12–21.

particular sinful acts such as adultery and murder; he also needs to be delivered from the sinful nature with which he was born. Sin wells up within us. Sin's fountainhead is our depraved inward being.

That's why David continues in verse 6, "You desire truth in the inward being; therefore teach me wisdom in my secret heart."[86] God desires *truth* in our inward being. "'Truth' is the essential quality of reliability which is necessary for a proper relationship with God."[87] God desires truth, reliability, or, we could say, trustworthiness, faithfulness (Ps 26:3) on our part. David finds only corruption and deceit within. He is helpless. He cannot change his sinful condition. Only God can do that. Therefore he again appeals to God: "Teach me *wisdom* in my secret heart."

God has to teach him wisdom in his inward being. Wisdom is practical knowledge that enables us to navigate the difficulties and temptations of life successfully.[88] Wisdom begins with the fear of the LORD. So David asks God to teach him wisdom.

But there is more. David needs more than forgiveness for his sinful acts. He needs more than wisdom to chart his course through life. He realizes that he needs "deep cleaning" — cleaning that will go below the surface to his inner being. Therefore he requests in verse 7, "Purge me with hyssop, and I shall be clean; wash me, and I shall be whiter than snow." Hyssop was a shrub with hairy leaves that could soak up water. Hyssop was used to sprinkle water on people who had become unclean and could no longer appear in God's presence.[89] Once cleansed they could again worship God in his temple.

---

86. "As the parallelism shows by the repetition of two kindred phrases, the emphasis lies on the fact that God wants men to be upright down to the very core of their being." Leupold, *Exposition of the Psalms*, 403. Davidson, *Vitality of Worship*, 169, points out that "both the words translated 'inward being' and 'secret heart' (v 6) are unusual words, the first pointing to what is not visible on the surface, the second to what is there at the very core of someone's life." Cf. Waltke, *Psalms as Christian Worship*, 473, "The context of verse 6 and its parallel *ûbəsātūm* ('in the bottled up/shut up place) suggests these adjectival substantives are metonymies for the closed chamber of the womb."

87. Tate, *Psalms 51-100*, 20, with references to Gen 42:16; Deut 1:13; 1 Kings 2:4; Hos 4:1-2; Jer 4:2; Pss 15:2; 86:11; Isa 38:3; Zech 7:9; Ezek 18:8. Cf. Wilson, *Psalms*, I, 775, "The word *'emet* emphasizes reliability and trustworthiness over absolute accuracy."

88. "In general, it [wisdom] is the coping ability to deal with those skills, temptations, responsibilities, and sufferings which are common to human life in ways that enhance the performance of healthy and successful living." Tate, *Psalms 51-100*, 20.

89. For example, when someone died in a tent, the tent, its furnishings, and the people in it would be unclean. God stipulated, "A clean person shall take hyssop, dip it in the water, and sprinkle it on the tent, on all the furnishings, on the persons who were there, and on whoever touched the bone, the slain, the corpse, or the grave. The clean person shall sprinkle the unclean ones on the third day and on the seventh day, thus purifying them on the seventh day. Then they shall wash their clothes and bathe themselves in water, and at evening they shall be clean" (Num 19:18-19). Lev 14:49-52 calls for sprinkling with blood for cleansing.

"Purge me with hyssop." "Purge me" is a powerful word for the "deep clean-ing" David needs. "Purge me" can also be translated as "purify me from sin" or, more literally, "un-sin me," or "de-sin me."[90] Only God can "de-sin" a person. Only God can perform the deep cleansing we need. "Purge me with hyssop, and I shall be clean."

The next line vividly shows the result: "Wash me, and I shall be whiter than snow." What a transformation David is looking for. He knows how dark his inner self is. But if God will purge him, if God will "de-sin" him, he will be "whiter than snow" — completely clean; not one dark stain left on the outside or on the inside. God himself had promised, "though your sins are like scarlet, they shall be like snow" (Isa 1:18).

Having confessed his many sins and begged God for forgiveness, David next asks that he may move on to taste the joy of God's salvation again. Verse 8, "Let me hear joy and gladness; let the bones that you have crushed rejoice." The "joy and gladness" he wishes to hear probably refer to the joy and gladness that can be heard on feast-days at God's temple. Psalm 122:1 speaks of this gladness: "I was *glad* when they said to me, 'Let us go to the house of the LORD!'" David wishes to hear this joy and gladness of worshiping God again.

But right now he is far removed from "joy and gladness." He is a broken man, in agony, distraught. David prays, "Let the bones[91] that you have crushed *rejoice.*" If God will purge his sin and make him whiter than snow, he can again worship God at his temple with God's people. Then he will hear the joy and gladness of God's people again. Then he himself will rejoice. But his sin still stands in the way.

So in verse 9 he comes back one more time to his sins: "Hide your face from my sins, and blot out all my iniquities." David asks God to turn his face away from his sins, not to look at his sins. Instead of God looking at his sins, he asks God again to *"blot out"* all his iniquities. Notice that the word "blot out" is the same word with which he began this psalm in verse 1. "Blot out" frames the first half of the psalm.[92] It underscores his request for God to wipe away all his iniquities, to wipe his slate clean. If God blots out all his iniquities, they are gone. His sins will disappear as if they were never committed.

Verse 10 begins the second half of this psalm. In the first half David ac-knowledged that he was caught in the grip of sin, born in sin, in need of deep cleansing within. In this second half of the psalm he moves beyond his earlier requests. Even if God blots out all his iniquities, his sinful core will cause him to

---

90. Tate, *Psalms 51–100*, 21. Cf. McCann, "Psalms," 886.

91. "*Bones* ('*aṣāmôt*, see Ps 22:14) commonly refer to psyche (Pss 34:20 [21]; 35:10; Prov 3:8; 12:4; passim)." Waltke, *Psalms as Christian Worship*, 475.

92. "The parallel . . . brings closure to the petitions for forgiveness, heightened and reinforced by the closure technique of adding 'all.'" Ibid.

sin again. So he prays, "Create in me a clean heart, O God, and put a new and right spirit within me." The "heart" in the Bible is the center of a person, "the seat of all feeling, thinking, and willing."[93] Today we might call it the "mind."[94] We all know the song, "Create in me a clean heart, O God." Substituting "mind" for "heart" might clarify the image for us today: "Create in me a clean *mind,* O God."

"A *clean* heart" (mind) is what David needs above all so that he will not be dragged back into his cycle of sins. He knows that he himself cannot change his sinful core.[95] Therefore he asks, "Create in me a clean heart, O God." "Create" (*bāra'*) is the same word Genesis uses for God creating this world.[96] David pleads for a complete transformation of the core of his being. Only God can create such a clean heart, such a new creation. Centuries later, Paul will write, "If anyone is in Christ, there is a new creation: everything old has passed away; see, everything has become new!" (2 Cor 5:17; cf. Gal 6:15).

David continues in verse 10, "and put a new and right spirit within me." The "new and right spirit" refers to the action of God's "Holy Spirit" mentioned in the next verse.[97] "A new and right spirit" is "a steadfast spirit" (NIV).[98] "The 'right spirit' implies 'determination,' a 'disciplined' spirit."[99] A spirit that will not be so easily side-tracked by bad news (Ps 112:7–8) or temptation.

93. Kraus, *Psalms 1–59,* 505.

94. "The intellectual and rational function that we normally ascribe to the mind was located in the heart according to biblical language (Deut 29:4; Isa 6:10; Prov 15:14; Job 8:10; Ps 90:12)." Tate, *Psalms 51–100,* 22. Cf. Zenger, *Psalms 2,* 21, "The 'heart' is the seat of (practical) reason. It is the 'organ' with which the human being understands the order of the world and of life."

95. "As the seat of both the intellect and the power of decision, the heart cannot simply be improved. It requires a new creation." Terrien, *The Psalms,* 406. Cf. Kraus, *Psalms 1–59,* 507, "Only by God's creative, renewing power can the heart be cleansed and led to new obedience." For God creating "new things," see Isa 43:15–19; 48:6–7.

96. "While the prayer . . . is not for *creatio ex nihilo,* it is a bold one for a transformation which could be accomplished only by divine power and a work on the order of the first creation of the world." Tate, *Psalms 51–100,* 23.

97. "It is quite probable that the spirit in v 12 [10] is God's steadfast and firmly reliable spirit." Tate, *Psalms 51–100,* 22. Cf. Kraus, *Psalms 1–59,* 505, "*Rûaḥ* refers to the effective power emanating from Yahweh that pervades all feeling, thinking, and will." Cf. Ezek 36:25–27, "I will sprinkle clean water upon you, and you shall be clean from all your uncleannesses. . . . A new heart I will give you, and a new spirit I will put within you. . . . I will put my spirit within you, and make you follow my statutes and be careful to observe my ordinances."

98. The NIV and NASB translate, "and renew a steadfast spirit within me." Terrien, *The Psalms,* 406–7, comments, "The sinner, when forgiven, asks God for a spirit that is steadfast, well anchored, solidly grounded. Such a spirit will be firm in its fidelity to God and his covenant (Ps 78:37) because it will not deviate from complete trust in that God." Cf. Zenger, *Psalms 2,* 21.

99. Walters, "I Talk of My Sin," *CTJ* 50 (2015): 102. Cf. Waltke, *Psalms as Christian Worship,* 476, "*Steadfast (nākôn,* passive stem) spirit. *Kûn* means intransitively, 'to stand firm'; transitively, 'to establish, found, anchor'; passively, 'to be firm, true, certain.'"

In verse 11 David again speaks of God's spirit: "Do not cast me away from your presence [literally, 'from before your face'], and do not take your Holy Spirit from me." To be cast away from God's presence is to have the covenant relationship terminated. Saul had been king before David and God had rejected him because of his sin. In fact, we read in 1 Samuel 16:14 that "the spirit of the LORD *departed* from Saul, and an evil spirit from the LORD tormented him." In that same chapter we also read about David being anointed: "Then Samuel took the horn of oil, and anointed him in the presence of his brothers; and the Spirit of the LORD came mightily upon David from that day forward" (1 Sam 16:13). Now David pleads with God: "Do not cast me away from your presence, and do not take your Holy Spirit from me."[100] He does not want to be cast away like King Saul nor have God's Holy Spirit taken from him.

Instead he pleads in verse 12, "Restore to me the joy of your salvation, and sustain in me a willing spirit." He wishes to experience again the joy of God's salvation — the joy that comes with forgiveness, renewal, and the certainty of God's salvation. The joy of God's salvation is a powerful stimulus for continuing to walk in God's ways. But again, David cannot do this in his own strength. So he asks God, "and sustain in me a willing spirit."

This is the third time in three verses that David pleads with God for a new spirit: verse 10b, "put a new and right *spirit* within me"; verse 11b, "do not take your *Holy Spirit* from me"; and now verse 12b, "sustain in me a willing *spirit*."[101] It is clear that David is totally convinced of his own inability. He calls on God to create a clean heart in him and put a new, steadfast spirit within him, not to take his Holy Spirit from him, but instead sustain him with a willing spirit. Centuries later, Jesus would say to Nicodemus, "Very truly, I tell you, no one can see the kingdom of God without being born from above," "born of the Spirit" (John 3:3, 8).[102]

If God through his Holy Spirit will put a new, right, and willing spirit within him, David vows that he will do three things for God. First, he promises to teach other sinners about God's ways. Verse 13, "Then I will teach transgressors your ways, and sinners will return to you." Having been made new within, David will

---

100. "The appeal of Ps 51:11 seems to be for the continuing experience of the creative, life-giving, and empowering presence of God himself." Tate, *Psalms 51–100*, 23–24. For the progression of the work of the Spirit from the Old to the New Testament, see Goldingay, *Songs from a Strange Land*, 166.

101. Note that the Hebrew begins all three lines with *wərûaḥ* ("and a spirit"), the emphatic position. Note also the chiastic arrangement (ABA') in vv 10–12 centering on God's "Holy Spirit" (v 11b).

102. Cf. 1 Peter 1:23, "You have been born anew, not of perishable but of imperishable seed, through the living and enduring word of God."

teach other transgressors about God's ways.[103] He knows from experience that God is willing to forgive even the most heinous sins if people but ask him with a contrite heart (2 Sam 12:13). If he teaches transgressors about the merciful God and his gracious ways, he is certain that they will return to God.[104]

Second, David promises to praise God. Verse 14, "Deliver me from bloodshed,[105] O God, O God of my salvation, and my tongue will sing aloud of your deliverance." He begins with his most heinous sin, the premeditated murder of Uriah.[106] "Deliver me from bloodshed, O God, O God of my salvation." "Bloodshed" is murder and the guilt of murder. The NIV translates "Deliver me from the guilt of bloodshed." The penalty for premeditated murder was death.[107] Other sins could be forgiven by offering animal sacrifices.[108] But not premeditated murder. God had stipulated in Numbers 35:33, "Blood [murder] pollutes the land, and no expiation [atonement] can be made for the land, for the blood that is shed in it, except by the blood of the one who shed it."[109] God required the death penalty for premeditated murder (Num 35:16). David should die! But he throws himself on God's mercy. "Deliver me from bloodshed, O God, O God of my salvation."[110] And amazingly he does not die but is forgiven (2 Sam 12:5, 13). God proves to be the God of his salvation.

David continues in verse 14 with his promise, "Deliver me . . . O God, O God of my salvation, and my tongue will sing aloud of your deliverance." When God

103. "'Your ways' . . . may certainly include the ways God intends for the guidance of his people as expressed in commandments and teachings. In the context, however, the ways of God in dealing with sinners must be included. Instruction in God's gracious, forgiving restoration of sinners would be an integral part of the teaching." Tate, *Psalms 51–100*, 26.

104. "The psalmist who prayed 'restore to me' (v 12, *šwb*) also prays that he may be instrumental in restoring (*šwb*; NIV, 'turn back to you') sinners to the 'ways' of the Lord (v 13)." VanGemeren, *Psalms*, 439. Cf. Westermann, *The Living Psalms*, 99, "As one who has known forgiveness, he is able to help others find the path to repentance."

105. The RSV and ESV translate, "Deliver me from bloodguiltiness." The NIV 1984 translated, "Save me from bloodguilt," while the NIV 2011 clarifies, "Deliver me from the guilt of bloodshed."

106. "The use of 'bloods' [*dāmim*, intensive plural] could . . . be the result of the composition of the psalm with David in mind (. . . note the concern of David for the removal of blood-guilt in 2 Sam 3:28–29; 1 Kings 2:31–33; also 2 Sam 16:7, 8)." Tate, *Psalms 51–100*, 26.

107. "The word *damim* (RSV 'bloodguiltiness') probably means 'impending death' as the result of his previous misdeeds which may have included bloodshed and also bloodguiltiness. A parallel is found in [Ps] 30:9 (M.T. 10): 'What profit is there in my death (lit. 'my blood'). . . . Will the dust praise thee?'" A. Anderson, *Psalms 1–72*, 400. Cf. Zenger, *Psalms 2*, 13.

108. See n. 114 below.

109. Cf. Ezek 18:10–13, "If he has a son who is violent, a shedder of blood . . . he shall surely die; his blood shall be upon himself."

110. "David reinforces this final request for freedom by using the address, 'the God of my salvation,' as if he were reminding God of his grace." Williams, *Psalms 1–72*, 393.

delivers people from death, when he saves them, a natural response is to "sing aloud" of God's deliverance.[111] But even this natural response is beyond David's innate abilities. And so he prays in verse 15, "O Lord, open my lips, and my mouth will declare your praise." The Lord has to open his lips before his mouth can declare God's praise. Even singing aloud of God's deliverance is a gift of God's grace.[112] When the Lord opens his lips, his mouth will declare God's praise — not just once but continually. His life will be transformed to always praising God; transformed from self-centeredness to praising God; transformed from living for himself to living for God. Westermann observes, "The change brought about by forgiveness which we see here is to be understood as a change to a new and joyful life, in a new and right spirit, through a renewed fellowship with God."[113]

David promised to do three things. First, to teach other sinners about God's mercy and his ways. Second, to sing aloud of God's deliverance. And now third, he promises to sacrifice to God not animals but himself. Verse 16, "For you have no delight in sacrifice; if I were to give a burnt offering, you would not be pleased." David's sins are too great to be paid for by merely sacrificing an animal. Adultery and murder were considered "high-handed sins." Such sins could not be atoned for with animal sacrifice. The death penalty was required.[114] David deserves the death penalty on two counts: premeditated adultery and premeditated murder. Animal sacrifices cannot possibly pay the penalty for his sins.

But there is one sacrifice that can result in his sins being forgiven. Verse 17, "The sacrifice acceptable to God is a broken spirit; a broken and contrite heart, O God, you will not despise." God will accept the sacrifice of "a broken spirit."[115]

111. "Deliverance" here is a good translation for "righteousness" (ṣədāqâ). "Yahweh is 'a righteous God and saviour' (Isa 45:21) and his righteousness is most clearly manifested in his acts of deliverance." A. Anderson, *Psalms 1–72*, 400. Westermann, *The Living Psalms*, 99, notes, "From these words it is plain that, in the psalms, praising God is a completely human and natural reaction to the experience of being set free. . . ."

112. Cf. Psalm 40:3, "He put a new song in my mouth, a song of praise to our God."

113. Westermann, *The Living Psalms*, 100. Westermann adds (pp. 100–101), "It is not seen as consisting in a perpetual awareness of sin or an attitude of submissive penitence."

114. "Sins such as adultery and murder are not provided for in sacrificial instructions, and the execution of the adulterer or the murderer is required." Tate, *Psalms 51–100*, 28. Tate continues, "If Ps 51 was composed with David in mind (which is certainly possible), the writer may have had the nonsacrificial situation of David in view (note that in 2 Sam 12:13 forgiveness is given to David without mention of sacrifice, on the basis of his confession." So also Ross, *Commentary on the Psalms*, II, 183 (n. 28) and 188, and Waltke, *Psalms as Christian Worship*, 467, 469, 479. Cf. A. Anderson, *Psalms 1–72*, 401, "Sacrifice, as a God-given means [of forgiveness], functions only within the setting of the Covenant; if the Covenant relationship is broken by man, then also sacrifice and any other cultic means have lost their significance."

115. "This is the only damaged offering an Israelite was allowed to bring; every animal had to be perfect — but the heart of the sinner had to be broken . . . and contrite. . . . The words 'bro-

"A broken spirit" is like a horse that has been broken; it no longer does whatever *it* desires but obeys its master. For human sinners, "it is the hostile stance against the divine will which has to be broken. The sacrifice consists in abandoning that sacrilegious attitude which sets itself against God."[116] "A broken spirit" is one that begs God for "a new and right spirit," "a willing spirit," which can only be provided by God's "Holy Spirit."[117]

"A broken spirit" is similar to "a contrite heart." Note that the parallelism of verse 17 treats these two as synonyms. Verse 17 says, "The sacrifice acceptable to God is *a broken spirit; a broken and contrite heart,* O God, you will not despise."[118] "A broken and contrite heart" is one that gives up human self-will and surrenders itself completely to God.[119] It shows genuine humility and profound contrition.[120] In Isaiah God says, "This is the one to whom I will look, to *the humble and contrite in spirit,* who trembles at my word" (Isa 66:2; cf. 57:15). The sacrifice God will accept to forgive even the most heinous sins is a humble and contrite spirit.

Notice that towards the end of the psalm David does not dwell on his sin anymore. He began the psalm by pleading for God's mercy, listing his sins extensively, and pleading with God to blot them out. He also asked God to create a clean heart in him and a right spirit. And God forgave him his grievous sins. Nathan said to David, "The LORD has put away your sin; you shall not die" (2 Sam 12:13). Now David does not dwell on his sin any more. It is gone! Forgiven! The slate has been wiped clean! As a new creation he can now teach other sinners about this merciful God so that they too may return to God. He also intends to sing aloud of God's deliverance, praising God. And finally he promises to offer himself as a living sacrifice to God.[121] He does not dwell on his sin anymore. "The call to repentance

---

ken' and 'contrite/crushed' are figurative (implied comparisons); they refer to the penitence and submission of the sinner — he has to be humble and contrite, broken of self-will and arrogance." Ross, *Commentary on the Psalms,* II, 198.

116. Westermann, *The Living Psalms,* 100. Cf. McCann, "Psalms," 887, "Contemporary people tend to hear 'broken,' when used in regard to people, as something like 'dysfunctional.' . . . Rather, God desires humble, contrite persons who are willing to offer God their whole selves."

117. I have turned the chiasm of vv 10, 11, 12 into a climactic arrangement: vv 10, 12, 11.

118. "The word translated *broken* is from the Hebrew root *šābar* and includes the ideas of 'contrite, sorry, and humble.'" DeClaissé-Walford in deClaissé-Walford, Jacobson, and Tanner, *The Book of Psalms,* 457.

119. "The sacrifice that God demands is a sacrifice of human self-will and self-importance; . . . it is the surrender of a person's own self to God." A. Anderson, *Psalms 1–72,* 401.

120. "The 'broken spirit' (cf. Pss 34:19 [18]; 147:3; Prov 15:4, 13; Jer 23:9) and 'contrite heart' (lit. 'crushed' — used for bones in v 10 [8] . . .) describe the condition of profound contrition and awe experienced by a sinful person who becomes aware of the divine presence (cf. Isa 6; Job 42:1–6)." Tate, *Psalms 51–100,* 28.

121. Cf. Romans 12:1–2, "I appeal to you therefore, brothers and sisters, by the mercies of God,

is not a call to become mired in guilt. Guilt is oriented to the past and paralyzes persons in regret of things that cannot be changed. Repentance is oriented to the future as an alternative to the past, and it empowers a new response."[122] David's concern now is to live to the glory of God.

The psalm ends with a prayer for Zion. Verse 18–19, "Do good to Zion in your good pleasure; rebuild the walls of Jerusalem, then you will delight in right sacrifices, in burnt offerings and whole burnt offerings; then bulls will be offered on your altar." These two verses were probably added during Israel's exile to avoid misinterpretation of verse 16, "For you have *no delight in sacrifice;* if I were to give *a burnt offering,* you would *not be pleased.*"[123] God removed his people from the Promised Land precisely because their religion had become a mere formality. They thought they could continue to sin as long as they brought the right animal sacrifices. As punishment God sent the Babylonian armies to Judah. They tore down the walls of Jerusalem and burned the temple. Then animal sacrifices were no longer possible.

In reading this psalm, God's people in exile identified with David's pleading for mercy. They, too, had sinned and needed to appeal to God's mercy. They, too, needed God to forgive their sins and wipe the slate clean. They, too, needed God's deliverance from exile. They longed to be restored to the Promised Land. Therefore they pleaded with God, "Do good to Zion in your good pleasure; rebuild the walls of Jerusalem."[124]

"Then,"[125] they promise in verse 19, "then you will *delight in right sacrifices,* in *burnt offerings* and whole burnt offerings;[126] then bulls will be offered on your altar." Whereas verse 16 said, "you have *no delight in sacrifice,*" in verse 19 the psalm promises, "then you will *delight in right sacrifices.*" "Right sacrifices" are literally "righteous sacrifices." "Righteous sacrifices" are sacrifices that are offered to God

---

to present your bodies as *a living sacrifice,* holy and acceptable to God, which is your spiritual worship. Do not be conformed to this world, but *be transformed* by the *renewing of your minds....*"

122. Birch, "Homiletical Resources," *Quarterly Review* 1, no. 5 (1981): 88.

123. "The generations between the Captivity and the Rebuilding made David's penitence their own, adding these verses to make their prayer specific." Kidner, *Psalms 1–72,* 194. Cf. McCann, *Theological Introduction,* 108, "The effect of the final form of Psalm 51 is to give the intensely personal testimony of verses 1–17 a corporate dimension." Cf. VanGemeren, *Psalms,* 440, "The canonical significance of these verses lies in the community identification with David's sin, the need for grace, and the anticipation of divinely bestowed joy."

124. "'Rebuild' ... expresses the exilic Israelite hope for the restoration of Jerusalem (cf. Isa 26:1; 33:20; 62:6–7; Jer 31:38; Pss 102:13, 16; 147:2)." Tate, *Psalms 51–100,* 29.

125. "The adverb 'then' is repeated twice in v 21 [19], in emphatic positions, and has a temporal quality." Ibid.

126. "The root idea is that of wholeness and completeness ... and thus a sacrifice not eaten at all by the worshipers." Ibid.

in the right spirit and according to God's stipulations.[127] Psalm 4:5 admonishes Israel, "Offer right sacrifices, and put your trust in the LORD."

Thus Psalm 51 assured Israel that God, because of his steadfast love and abundant mercy, will forgive even the most heinous sins if people but ask with a contrite heart. By instituting an elaborate system of laws for animal sacrifices in Old Testament times, God gave expression to his desire to forgive people. People could pay for their sins by offering animals. These many animal sacrifices prefigured the later, one and only sacrifice of Jesus Christ.

For in the fullness of time God sent his Son to pay for our sins. Jesus died to pay the penalty for our sins. When he was dying on the cross, Jesus cried out, "My God, my God, why have you forsaken me?" (Matt 27:46). He was forsaken by God so that we would never be forsaken by him. When "he breathed his last . . . the curtain of the temple was torn in two, from top to bottom" (Matt 27:50–51). Jesus' sacrificial death opened the way to God for all of us. No more animal sacrifices. Jesus paid the penalty for our sins once for all. In his mercy God provided a new way. His own Son was the sin-sacrifice: Jesus, "the Lamb of God who takes away the sin of the world!" (John 1:29).

John writes, "In this is love, not that we loved God but that he loved us and sent his Son to be *the atoning sacrifice* for our sins" (1 John 4:10).[128] And again, "If we confess our sins, he who is faithful and just will forgive us our sins and cleanse us from all unrighteousness. . . . My little children, I am writing these things to you so that you may not sin. But if anyone does sin, we have an advocate with the Father, Jesus Christ the righteous; and he is *the atoning sacrifice* for our sins, and not for ours only but also for the sins of the whole world" (1 John 1:9; 2:1–2).

God reveals his abundant mercy and his steadfast love for us by sending his own Son to die for our sins. If God was willing to "blot out"[129] David's terrible sins; if God was willing to forgive Israel its grievous sins, how much more will

---

127. "'Righteous sacrifices' . . . may mean legitimate and proper sacrifices, i.e., according to the appropriate ritual prescriptions . . . , or sacrifices that are appropriate because they are offered in the right spirit and right relationship with God." Ibid. I don't think we have to choose one meaning or the other. In the context of verse 17, I think verse 19 means both. Cf. Ezek 36:26–28, "A new heart I will give you, and a new spirit I will put within you. . . . I will put my spirit within you, and make you follow my statutes and be careful to observe my ordinances. Then you shall live in the land that I gave to your ancestors; and you shall be my people, and I will be your God."

128. Cf. 2 Cor 5:21, "For our sake he [God] made him to be sin who knew no sin, so that in him we might become the righteousness of God."

129. David asked God, "according to your abundant mercy blot out my transgressions" (51:1b, LXX, 50:3). "Blot out," erase them, wipe the slate clean! Paul alludes to this request when he writes, "And when you were dead in trespasses and the uncircumcision of your flesh, God made you alive together with him, when he forgave us all our trespasses, *erasing* the record that stood against us with its legal demands. He set this aside, nailing it to the cross" (Col 2:13–14).

God be willing to forgive us our sins now that Christ has offered his life for "the sins of the world"? Because of Jesus' sacrifice, God will forgive even the most heinous sins if we but ask with a contrite heart. All praise and thanksgiving be to God!

Prayer[130]

God of mercy,
you know us better than we know ourselves,
and still you love us.
Wash us from all our sins,
create in us clean hearts,
and strengthen us by your Holy Spirit
that we may give you praise;
through Jesus Christ our Savior. Amen.

Song[131]

Create in me a clean heart, O God,
    and renew a right spirit within me.
Create in me a clean heart, O God,
    and renew a right spirit within me.
Cast me not away from your presence, O Lord,
    and take not your Holy Spirit from me.
Restore unto me the joy of your salvation,
    and renew a right spirit within me.

130. *Book of Common Worship*, 671.
131. Anonymous, Public Domain. *Psalms for All Seasons*, 332–33 (51F).

CHAPTER 12

"Happy Are Those Whose Transgression Is Forgiven"

Psalm 32 (31)

The *Revised Common Lectionary, Year A,* assigns Psalm 32 for reading on the first Sunday in Lent as a response to the "First Lesson: Genesis 2:15–17," God's prohibition not to eat from "the tree of the knowledge of good and evil."[1] This psalm celebrates God's readiness to forgive any and all sins upon sincere confession and moves beyond confession to God's instruction in the way we should go. As such, this preaching text provides a wonderful extension of the message of Psalm 51 and fits well in the Lenten season when the church focuses on sin, confession, forgiveness, and renewal through the death and resurrection of Christ.

Text and Context

The whole of Psalm 32 is a good preaching text. It is clearly marked as a literary unit by the inclusio of verses 1–2, two times "Happy are those. . . ." "Blessed is the one. . . ." (NIV) and verse 11: "Be glad in the LORD and rejoice, O righteous, and shout for joy, all you upright in heart." The inclusio is confirmed by the psalmist addressing his fellow worshipers at the beginning (vv 1–2) and doubling back to them at the end (vv 10–11).[2]

As to context, Psalm 32 is similar to Psalm 1 with its "Happy are those" (v 1), the contrast between "the wicked" and "the righteous" (1:4–6; 32:10–11), "the

---

1. Psalm 32 is also the assigned reading for the fourth Sunday in Lent, Year C, as a response to the "First Lesson: Joshua 5:9–12."

2. "For the first time the addressees are explicitly plural, in v 9a and again in v 11, and vv 10–11 refer to Yhwh in the third person. . . . The psalm thus closes as it began with the worshipper addressing the people who have listened to his testimony." Goldingay, *Psalms,* I, 459.

way" (1:1, 6; 32:8), and the LORD watching "over the way of the righteous" (1:6; 32:8).[3] But the particular emphasis in Psalm 32 is the happiness that results from being *forgiven* by the LORD.

The immediate context of Psalms 31 and 33 could also be taken into account.[4] One can also seek to determine the specific message (theme) of Psalm 32 by comparing it with the other thanksgiving psalms.[5] Further, the psalm needs to be understood in the context of the prophets since "Psalm 32 gives the impression of having learned from the prophets that the pardon of God is the first and principal basis of the life of the people of God (e.g., Isa 40:2; 55:6–7)."[6] And, of course, we need to consider the context of the New Testament.

Literary Interpretation

The editors of the Psalter have provided Psalm 32 with the superscription, "Of David. A Maskil." Since the editors attributed this psalm to David and the psalmist, if not David, may well have composed the psalm with David in mind, David would be the implied author. I will, therefore, use the name David instead of "psalmist" or "author" or "suppliant."

Bernhard Anderson identifies Psalm 32 as an "individual song of thanksgiving (penitential psalm with wisdom elements)."[7] Traditionally it was classified as one of seven penitential psalms — penitential because of its confession of sin (vv 3–5). Wisdom elements are found in its instruction in verses 8–9 as well as a proverb in verse 10. Peter Craigie suggests that the psalm should probably be understood "as a literary composition in which a basic thanksgiving psalm has been given literary adaptation according to the wisdom tradition."[8]

---

3. McCann, "Psalms," 805, calls attention to other similar words in the vocabulary, "sin" (1:1, 5; 32:1, 5), "day and night" (1:2; 32:4), and "teach" ("law," 1:2, the same Hebrew root as "teach," 32:8).

4. "Thematically Psalm 32 links back to Psalm 31 through the use of 'hiding place' terminology in 32:7 (cf. comments on 31:20) and links forward to Psalm 33. . . . Psalm 32 concludes with an exhortation to 'rejoice' and 'sing' directed to two groups: the 'righteous' (*ṣaddîqîm*) and the 'upright in heart' (*yišrê-lēb*). Psalm 33 opens with a similar exhortation to 'sing' directed to the same two groups." Wilson, *Psalms,* 544. Cf. VanGemeren, *Psalms,* 311.

5. Bernhard Anderson, *Out of the Depths,* 214, lists as "Individual Songs of Thanksgiving," Psalms 18, 30, 32, 34, 40:1–11, 66:13–20, 92, 116, 118, and 138.

6. Mays, *Psalms,* 146.

7. Anderson, *Out of the Depths,* 220.

8. Craigie, *Psalms 1–50,* 265. Cf. Goldingay, *Psalms,* I, 452, "The psalm is a thanksgiving or testimony, whose nature is thus to bring home in public worship the implications for other people of what Yhwh has done for the worshipper." Cf. VanGemeren, *Psalms,* 310, "The psalm shares the

We shall again begin our analysis of this psalm by providing a snapshot of its parallelisms, then its images, followed by repetition of keywords, and its structure.

Parallelisms

Although the difference between synonymous and advancing parallelism cannot always be scientifically precise, just the effort to identify the kind of parallelisms involved will provide insight into subtle moves within the psalm.

Of David. A Maskil.

1Happy are those whose transgression is forgiven,	A
whose sin is covered.	A'
2Happy are those to whom the LORD imputes no iniquity,	A''
and in whose spirit there is no deceit.[9]	B

3While I kept silence, my body wasted away[10]	– A
through my groaning all day long.	+– A'
4For day and night your hand was heavy upon me;	B
my strength was dried up as by the heat of summer. Selah	+ B'

5Then I acknowledged my sin to you,	A
and I did not hide my iniquity;	A'
I said, "I will confess my transgressions to the LORD,"	+ A''
and you forgave the guilt of my sin.[11] Selah	+ A'''

6Therefore let all who are faithful offer prayer to you;	A
at a time of distress, the rush of mighty waters shall not reach them.	B
7You are a hiding place for me;	+ B'

wisdom language and forms of expression ('blessed,' vv 1–2; 'instruct,' 'teach,' 'way,' 'counsel,' v 8; contrast between righteous and wicked, v 10; and advantages of godliness, vv 1–2, 7, 10)."

9. This could perhaps be marked as advancing parallelism (+A''') but because of the change in subject from forgiveness of "transgression," "sin," and "iniquity" to no deceit in one's spirit, I have marked it B.

10. In contrast to the "happy" person of vv 1–2, v 3 begins with the body wasting away, antithetic parallelism (–A), which advances in the second line to groaning all day long, therefore +–A'.

11. Since this line completes the thought of the prior line, I have marked it as advancing parallelism, now reaching a climax in climactic parallelism (+A''').

you preserve me from trouble;	+ B''
you surround me with glad cries of deliverance. Selah	+ B'''
₈I will instruct you and teach you the way you should go;	A
I will counsel you with my eye upon you.	+ A'
₉Do not be like a horse or a mule, without understanding,[12]	– B
whose temper must be curbed with bit and bridle,	+– B'
else it will not stay near you.	+– B''
₁₀Many are the torments of the wicked,	A
but steadfast love surrounds those who trust in the LORD.	– A'
₁₁Be glad[13] in the LORD	B
and rejoice, O righteous,	+ B'
and shout for joy, all you upright in heart.	+ B''

Psalm 32 starts with a beatitude ("Happy") with three synonymous lines resulting in climactic parallelism (vv 1–2a). Verse 3 begins with the contrast to that happy person, hence antithetic parallelism, which advances in verse 3b. Verse 4a gives the reason for his "groaning all day long": "your hand," a new topic, therefore B, followed by advancing parallelism in verse 4b (+B'). Verses 5 and 6–7 follow up with four-line climactic parallelisms. Verse 8 shows advancing parallelism, followed in verse 9 with antithetic climactic parallelism. Verse 10b exhibits antithetic parallelism followed in verse 11 by a new topic (B) and climactic parallelism.

Imagery

Psalm 32 bubbles over with pictures. Like Psalm 51, it uses the imagery of the ceremonial law: "transgression is forgiven . . . , sin is covered. . . . imputes no iniquity" (vv 1–2). "'Forgiven' is literally 'lifted up' (cf. 25:18; 85:2), as in the removal of a burden. The sins are also 'covered' [that is, concealed] and are 'not counted,' as in an accounting ledger (Lev 25:27, 52; 1 Kings 10:21; 2 Kings 12:15; 22:7)."[14] "In whose spirit there is no deceit" (v 2b). "'Spirit' here functions as a synecdoche

---

12. Clearly antithetic parallelism (–B) supported by two more reasons why we should not be like a mule (+–B'; +–B'').

13. "The closing line comprises three parallel two-stress cola, each beginning with a second-person plural imperative." Goldingay, *Psalms*, I, 460.

14. Broyles, *Psalms*, 161.

for the person's entire disposition . . . ; whole inner life . . . ; mind . . . ; will . . . ; and motives."[15]

Physical and/or mental ailments are pictured as "my body [bones] wasted away" (v 3).[16] "Your hand was heavy upon me" (v 4a) is not only an anthropomorphism but also a metaphor for God's punishment (cf. 1 Sam 5:6–7, 11; Ps 38:2). "My strength was dried up as by the heat of summer" (v 4b) is a simile in which David compares himself to a withering plant or the cracked earth in the summer heat.[17]

"At a time of distress, the rush of mighty waters shall not reach them" (v 6). The "mighty waters" are literally either the waters rushing down the wadis in the rainy season or the Noahic Flood (cf. Ps 29:3); as a metaphor the "mighty waters" portray the hardships of life. "You are a hiding place for me" (v 7a) means that God is a place of refuge for him. "You surround me with glad cries of deliverance" (v 7b) probably refers to the happy shouting and singing at the temple.[18]

"I will instruct you and teach you the way you should go" (v 8a). The "I" here is not David (as in vv 3–5) but the LORD whom he "is quoting . . . when he besought God during his time of affliction."[19] "I will counsel you with *my eye upon you*" (v 8b), then, is an anthropomorphism as well as a metaphor for God's watching over David ("you's" all singular). "The way" (v 8a) is a metaphor for a God-pleasing lifestyle. "Do not be like a horse or a mule" (v 9) are two similes advising God's people ("Do not be," second person, plural) not to be stubborn and "without understanding."

Repetition of Keywords

David begins Psalm 32 with a double note of joy in his opening beatitude (two times, "happy," vv 1–2). Then, just like Psalm 51's series of three, he explains his joy with three different Hebrew verbs for forgiving: "forgiven" (*nāśā'*, v 1), "having a

---

15. Waltke, *The Psalms as Christian Lament*, 112.

16. "Lit. 'My bones . . .' which seems to imply that the description is not to be taken literally. In a sense, the bones are the very last part of the body to disintegrate, and therefore the phrase may serve as a word-picture of a most serious and hopeless human situation." A. Anderson, *Psalms 1–72*, 257. Cf. Williams, *Psalms 1–72*, 256, "This could well be a metaphor for depression. . . . Moreover, this happened as he groaned 'all the day long.' The 'groaning' suggests continual emotional pain, perhaps repressed anger."

17. "In the heat of summer, one does not have to stay in the sun for long for one's body moisture to evaporate, and that is the psalm's image for the suppliant's inner and outward withering." Goldingay, *Psalms*, I, 456.

18. See n. 62 below.

19. A. Anderson, *Psalms 1–72*, 258. See p. 292 and n. 63 below.

burden lifted"; "covered" (*kāsâ*, v 1), "having a regretted action concealed"; and "not impute" (*ḥāšab*, v 2), "render a verdict of innocent (cf. Gen 15:6)."[20]

What has been forgiven? Sin! Every kind of sin! David uses three different Hebrew words for sin: "transgression" (*pešaʿ*) or "rebellion" against God's authority;[21] "sin" (*ḥāṭāʾâ*) or "missing the mark;[22] and "iniquity" or guilt (*ʿāwon*), deliberate "deviation from the right path" (vv 1–2a).[23]

He follows this up with three ways he suffered when he failed to confess his sins: "My body wasted away. . . . Your hand was heavy upon me; my strength was dried up" (vv 3–4).

God's punishment drives him to confess his sins. He uses the same three words for sin he used in verses 1–2a, but in verse 5 he personalizes them to "my sin," "my iniquity," and "my transgressions." In addition, he uses three synonyms for his confession: he "acknowledged" his sin; "did not hide" his iniquity; and decided to "confess" his transgressions to the LORD. He concludes verse 5 with the gospel in a nutshell: "You forgave the guilt of my sin."

In verse 7 he describes God's protection in three ways: "You are a hiding place for me; you preserve me from trouble; you surround me with glad cries of deliverance." In verse 8 he follows up with three synonyms for God's guidance: "I will *instruct* you and *teach* you the way you should go; I will *counsel* you with my eye upon you." And finally in the last verse he urges God's people three times to "Be glad in the LORD and rejoice . . . , and shout for joy" (v 11).

In addition to this threefold use of synonyms, David mentions the name of the LORD four times (vv 2, 5, 10, 11) and twice that the LORD "surrounds" him with "songs of deliverance" (v 7) and "surrounds" those who trust him with "steadfast love" (v 10).

Structure

Four popular English versions are in agreement about the structure of Psalm 32 except for the verses 8–11.

Verse Divisions   *Versions*
1–2 / 3–4 / 5 / 6–7 / 8–9 / 10 – 11   NRSV and ESV

---

20. Davidson, *Vitality of Worship*, 110.
21. See p. 258 above and n. 65.
22. See Judges 20:16. Falling short of the goal God has set for his people.
23. A. Anderson, *Psalms 1–72*, 393.

1–2 / 3–4 / 5 / 6–7 / 8 – 10 / 11   NIV
1–2 / 3–4 / 5 / 6–7 / 8   –   11   NASB

Like Psalm 51, Psalm 32 consists of two parts, verses 1–5 and 6–11. The unit of verses 1–5 is marked by an inclusio: verses 1–2a list three words for sin ("transgression," "sin," and "iniquity") which verse 5 repeats ("my sin," "my iniquity," "my transgressions"), an ABCB'C'A' order framed by "transgressions" (rebellions). After verse 5 sin is no longer mentioned.

Verse 6 begins with a strong logical particle, "Therefore" — indicating the beginning of a new section. The verses 6–11 are also marked off by an inclusio: the repetition of "faithful / steadfast love" (vv 6, 10), "mighty / many" (vv 6, 10), and "surround" (vv 7, 10),[24] as well as the exhortation of verse 6 ("let all") being balanced by the exhortation in verse 11 ("be glad").

In fact, like Psalm 51, the two sections may each be designed as a chiasm:

PART I

A Happy are those whose sin (*ḥăṭā'â*) is covered;   vv 1–2
     to whom the Lord imputes no iniquity (*'āwon*)
         double "happy"
     B David "kept silence . . . wasted away"   vv 3–4
         double *kî* ("while," "for")
A' David confessed his sin (*ḥaṭṭā'*) and iniquity (*'āwon*);   v 5
     the Lord forgave the guilt (*'āwon*) of his sin (*ḥaṭṭā'*)

PART II[25]

A Exhortation to faithful (*ḥāsîd*) to offer prayer   v 6
     "the mighty (*rabbîm*) waters shall not reach them"
     B Profession of faith: v 7
         "You are a hiding place for me . . . ;
         you surround (*sābab*) me"
         C Divine oracle: vv 8–9
            "I will instruct you and teach you the way. . . .
            Do not be like a horse or a mule."
     B' Profession of faith: v 10
         "Many (*rabbîm*) are the torments of the wicked,

---

24. Craigie, *Psalms 1–50*, 265.

25. McCann, "Psalms," 806, argues for a chiastic structure: "'invitation' (v 6), profession of faith (v 7), profession of faith (v 10), invitation (v 11)" but does not complete it with the divine oracle of vv 8–9 since he thinks "it more likely that the *psalmist* is speaking in vv 8–9 to offer instruction to others" (my emphasis). But see n. 35 below.

but steadfast love (*ḥesed*) surrounds (*sābab*). . . ."
A′ Exhortation to the "righteous" to be glad   v 11

This double chiasm first centers on the major problem, the sinner's silence (I. B) and contrasts it with the second center (II. C), God's gracious instruction in the way.[26] Interestingly, the psalm also adds a "Selah" (pause?) after the sinner's keeping silence (v 4), the LORD's forgiveness (v 5), and the sinner's profession of faith (v 7).

Awareness of the chiastic structure will help us in interpreting the psalm. Unfortunately, an ancient chiastic structure does not make for a good modern sermon outline. But we can still use its headings to indicate the moves we make in the sermon (see "Sermon Outline," p. 284 below).

Another possibility is to use the different speakers to structure the psalm:

David addressing his fellow-worshipers (vv 1–2)
David's personal testimony (vv 3–7)
God speaking to David (v 8)
David addressing his fellow-worshipers again (vv 9–11)[27]

Theocentric Interpretation

Because Psalm 32:5, at its turn, emphasizes human responsibility to "confess my transgressions to the LORD," the danger of anthropocentric interpretation is present, even in a semi-Pelagian sense. So it is well before preparing the sermon to highlight what the psalm says about God.

26. VanGemeren, *Psalms,* 311, suggests as expository structure:
    A Blessings of Forgiveness (vv 1–2)
    　　B Lesson from Experience (vv 3–5)
    　　　　C God's Protection (vv 6–7)
    　　　　　　D Promise of Wisdom (v 8)
    　　B′ Lesson from Experience (v 9)
    　　　　C′ God's Protection (v 10)
    A′ Rejoicing in Forgiveness (v 11)
"The advantage of this structure," he writes, "is that it sets apart the promise of God (v 8) as the center of the psalm."

27. The pronouns "you" in verse 8 are singular while the "Do not be like a horse" of verse 9 is the second-person plural, jussive. The best solution seems to be that verse 8 is the divine oracle delivered to the psalmist by a priest. "The plural in verse 9 suggests that the psalmist is using a traditional adage [wisdom] to connect individual experience to the experience of the listening community." Wilson, *Psalms,* I, 548.

The psalm starts out by declaring those "happy" (blessed) "whose transgression is forgiven, whose sin is covered" (v 1). Who did the forgiving? The divine passives[28] indicate that the LORD did the forgiving. This is confirmed by the parallel line in verse 2, "Happy are those to whom the LORD imputes no iniquity."

Human action (inaction) is emphasized in verse 3, "While I kept silence, my body wasted away," but the source of the punishment is immediately identified in verse 4, "For day and night your hand [the LORD's] was heavy upon me." Verse 5 follows up with, "Then I acknowledged my sin to you [the LORD] . . . ; I said, 'I will confess my transgressions to the LORD,' and you [the LORD] forgave the guilt of my sin."

Verse 6 follows up with exhorting the faithful to "offer prayer to you" [the LORD], while verse 7 professes with a triple "you": "You [LORD] are a hiding place for me; you [LORD] preserve me from trouble; you [LORD] surround me with glad cries of deliverance."

After this profession of faith, the LORD himself begins to speak in verse 8 (divine oracle): "I [the LORD] will instruct you and teach you the way you should go; I [the LORD] will counsel you with my [the LORD's] eye upon you." Verse 10 declares that the LORD's "steadfast love surrounds those who trust in the LORD" (cf. Exod 34:6–7). The psalm concludes with the exhortation: "Be glad in the LORD and rejoice, O righteous, and shout for joy, all you upright in heart" (v 11).

Textual Theme and Goal

Formulating the textual theme is no simple task because Psalm 32 makes several points. One theme is struck in the opening line, "Happy are those whose transgression is forgiven" (v 1a).[29] Although verse 11 doubles back to "be glad in the LORD," this opening theme cannot function as the theme of the whole psalm, for verses 3–5 add another message: Instead of keeping silence, hiding our sins, we should confess our sins to the LORD. So a good theme for the first half of the psalm would be, "Happy are those who, instead of keeping silence, honestly confess their sins to the LORD, for the LORD will surely forgive them."[30]

But the second half of the psalm leaves sin far behind: it's been forgiven! In this second half we hear the call to the faithful to "offer prayer" to the LORD (v 6), to "trust in the LORD" (v 10), to "be glad in the LORD" (v 11). And, most

28. On the "divine passive," see my *Modern Preacher*, 295.

29. Cf. Leupold, *Exposition of the Psalms*, 265, "The theme: the blessedness of forgiveness."

30. Ross, *Commentary on the Psalms*, I, 719, formulates the "expository idea" as follows: "Because forgiveness of sin brings joyful bliss with God and relief from guilty pain, it is wise to confess sin and not conceal it."

important, in the divine oracle we hear the LORD's promise, "I will instruct you and teach you the way you should go" (v 8).

As Lindsay Armstrong has pointed out, "though Psalm 32 is considered the second of the traditional penitential psalms, even this psalm does not stop with confession, but pushes past the temptation to dwell on one's crimes into the essential next steps taken by the righteous. . . . The happy acknowledge sin (v 5), accept forgiveness (v 7), attend God's instruction (vv 8–9), accentuate and trust God more than self (v 10), and act glad in God (v 11)."[31]

How shall we cover all these messages under a single theme? I think the opening and closing of the psalm (the "ballast lines") disclose the main message: "Happy are those whose transgression is forgiven" (v 1) and "Be glad in the LORD and rejoice, O righteous" (v 11). Further, we have seen above ("Structure," pp. 278–79) that the first chiasm centers on the sinner's silence while the second centers on God's gracious instruction in the way. We can, therefore, formulate the textual theme as follows: *Happy are those who honestly confess their sins to the LORD, for he will forgive their sins and guide them on the way they should go.*

For determining the original goal of this psalm we need to know how it functioned in Israel. A. Anderson suggests that "its *Sitz im Leben,* or life-situation, is to be found in the Temple worship (cf. 22:22 [M.T. 23]), during which the psalmist offered his song of thanks in the presence of his fellow-worshippers. This circumstance would also account for the didactic element in the Psalm."[32] Taking into account the jussive in verse 9 and the three imperatives in verse 11, we can formulate the goal of the author as, *to urge God's people to honestly confess their sins to the LORD, to rejoice in his forgiveness, and to walk in the LORD's way.*[33]

Ways to Preach Christ

In this psalm there is no promise of Christ nor a type of Christ. One could possibly trace from the Old Testament to Christ in the New Testament the longitudinal theme of confession followed by forgiveness. A more direct way is that of analogy: as Psalm 32 teaches us to confess our sins, so does Jesus when he teaches his followers to pray, "Forgive us our debts" (Matt 6:12). A more comprehensive way is redemptive-historical progression supported by New Testament refer-

31. Lindsay P. Armstrong, "Preaching the Lenten Texts," *JPr* 33, no. 2 (2010; pp. 3–13): 9.

32. A. Anderson, *Psalms 1–72,* 254.

33. Cf. Ross, *Commentary on the Psalms,* I, 707, "Having experienced divine chastening and then forgiveness for sin, the psalmist encourages others to seek the LORD who deals graciously with sinners, because the bliss of forgiveness is life changing."

ences. One can also consider just using New Testament references and sprinkling the sermon with appropriate New Testament quotations. We shall first explore the way of New Testament references and next that of redemptive-historical progression.

New Testament References

We have formulated the theme of Psalm 32 as, "Happy are those who honestly confess their sins to the LORD, for he will forgive their sins and guide them on the way they should go." 1 John 1 seems to allude to most parts of this theme, linking it directly to the sacrifice of Jesus Christ: "If we walk in the light as he himself is in the light, we have fellowship with one another, and the blood of Jesus his Son cleanses us from all sin. . . . If we confess our sins, he who is faithful and just will forgive us our sins and cleanse us from all unrighteousness" (1 John 1:7–9).

Another New Testament reference is much more complicated to communicate in a sermon. Paul quotes Psalm 32:1–2 in Romans 4:7–8 to make the point that we are not saved by works but by faith. Paul calls up two witnesses: Abraham and David. Paul writes, "For if Abraham was justified by works, he has something to boast about, but not before God. For what does the scripture say? 'Abraham believed God, and it was *reckoned* to him as righteousness.' Now to one who works, wages are not *reckoned* as a gift but as something due. But to one who without works trusts him who justifies the ungodly, such faith is *reckoned* as righteousness" (Rom 4:2–5). Notice that Paul uses the word *reckoned* three times: first quoting Genesis 15:6, then twice to make his point that we are saved not by works but by faith.

Next he uses *reckon* twice more to link Abraham to David, "So also David speaks of the blessedness of those to whom God *reckons* righteousness apart from works: 'Blessed are those whose iniquities are forgiven, and whose sins are covered; blessed is the one against whom the Lord will not *reckon* sin" (Rom 4:6–8). Paul concludes by basing his lengthy argument on the death and resurrection of Jesus: "Now the words, 'it was reckoned to him,' were written not for his sake alone, but for ours also. It will be reckoned to us who believe in him who raised Jesus our Lord from the dead, who was handed over to death for our trespasses and was raised for our justification" (Rom 4:23–25).

Redemptive-Historical Progression and New Testament References

Redemptive-historical progression supported by New Testament references can link the entire theme of Psalm 32 to Jesus Christ. Again, the theme of Psalm 32 is, "Happy are those who honestly confess their sins to the LORD, for he will forgive their sins and guide them on the way they should go." In Old Testament times God promised to forgive people their sins if they confessed their sins by bringing a guilt offering. For example, God said, "The priest shall make atonement for him with the ram of guilt offering before the LORD for his sin that he committed; and the sin he committed shall be forgiven him" (Lev 19:22). The act of the priest sacrificing an animal as a guilt offering would lead to God's forgiveness.

In the fullness of time, God sent his own Son to pay the penalty for sin. Jesus is both our eternal High Priest and the "once for all" sacrifice. Hebrews 7 says, "Unlike the other high priests, he has no need to offer sacrifices day after day, first for his own sins, and then for those of the people; this he did once for all when he offered himself. For the law appoints as high priests those who are subject to weakness, but the word of the oath, which came later than the law, appoints a Son who has been made perfect forever" (Heb 7:27–28).[34] Jesus is "the Lamb of God who takes away the sin of the world!" (John 1:29). Now we need no longer bring animal sacrifices nor do we need the intermediary of a priest. What remains is that we must still confess our sins in order to receive God's forgiveness. Jesus himself taught us to pray to our Father in heaven, "Forgive us our debts" (Matt 6:12; see further "Sermon Exposition" below).

Sermon Theme, Goal, and Need

Since the New Testament does not change the textual theme but focuses it on Christ, the textual theme can be used as the theme for the sermon: *Happy are those who honestly confess their sins to the LORD, for he will forgive their sins and guide them on the way they should go."*

The goal of this psalm can also remain as the goal of the sermon: *to urge God's people to honestly confess their sins to the LORD, to rejoice in his forgiveness, and to walk in the LORD's way.*

This goal exposes the possible needs addressed in this sermon: people do not confess their sins honestly or they cannot accept (let alone rejoice in) God's forgiveness, or they fail to walk in God's ways.

---

34. Cf. Heb 10:11–14, "And every priest stands day after day at his service, offering again and again the same sacrifices that can never take away sins. But when Christ had offered for all time a single sacrifice for sins, 'he sat down at the right hand of God.' . . . For by a single offering he has perfected for all time those who are sanctified."

Liturgy, Scripture Reading, Sermon Outline, and PowerPoint

Before Scripture reading, parts of Psalm 32 can be used in the liturgy. As the call to worship the liturgist could read verse 1, while the congregation responds with verse 2, and the liturgist reads verse 11, the triple imperative calls to be glad in the LORD. Verses 3–4 can be read prior to the prayer of confession, while verses 5 and 11 can serve as the assurance of pardon.

Since we hear different voices in Psalm 32, utilizing two or three voices in the public reading of the psalm will clarify its meaning.

> *The liturgist* reads the verses addressed to the fellow-worshipers (vv 1–2).
> *Another voice* reads David's personal testimony (vv 3–7).
> *A deep bass* reads the divine oracle (v 8).[35]
> *The liturgist* concludes by addressing the fellow-worshipers (vv 9–11)

The sermon outline can best follow the distinct sections:

I.	Happy are those whose sins are forgiven	vv 1–2
II.	The terrible results of keeping silent	vv 3–4
III.	Confession of sins to the LORD who forgave	v 5
IV.	Exhortation to all the faithful to pray	v 6
V.	Profession of faith: you are my hiding place	v 7
VI.	God's promise to teach the way to go	v 8
VII.	Exhortation not to be like a horse or mule	v 9
VIII.	Surrounded by steadfast love; be glad in the LORD	vv 10–11
IX.	Move to Christ — here and at earlier points	N.T.

I would not announce these points in the sermon (there are too many, anyway) but just highlight the flow of the psalm by moving from point to point with verse references.

PowerPoint can visually show the verse(s) being explained while it highlights the threefold repetitions in the psalm (as in Psalm 51):

Begin with a slide of verses 1–2: "Happy are those whose transgression is for-

---

35. "Without introduction, Yahweh himself speaks ('I will'). While the absence of a transition is awkward when the psalm is read as literature, it would not have been so when another voice, a prophet, stepped forward. Other psalms containing prophetic oracles proceed to them without giving notice of a change of speaker (50:7; 81:6, where the Heb. text lacks 'he says'; 75:2, where the Heb. text lacks 'you say')." Broyles, *Psalms*, 161. Verse 9 is probably a wisdom saying added by the psalmist to address Israel (see n. 27 above).

given, whose sin is covered. Happy are those to whom the Lord imputes no iniquity, and in whose spirit there is no deceit."

Highlight in turn the three different verbs for forgiving: "forgiven," "having a burden lifted"; "covered," "having a regretted action concealed"; and "not impute," "render a verdict of innocent."

Add what has been forgiven. In turn, the three different words for sin: "transgression," "rebellion against God's authority"; "sin," "missing the mark"; and "iniquity" or "guilt," "deliberate deviation from the right path."

New slide: Three ways David suffered when he tried to hide his sins: in turn, "My body wasted away." "Your hand was heavy upon me." "My strength was dried up" (vv 3–4).

New slide: David confesses his sins with the three words for sin in verses 1–2a but now the personal: "my sin," "my iniquity," and "my transgressions" (v 5).

Add in turn the three different verbs he uses to confess: he "acknowledged" his sin; "did not hide" his iniquity; and decided to "confess" his transgressions to the Lord.

Add the good news: "You forgave the guilt of my sin."

New slide: The exhortation to all the faithful to pray (v 6).

New slide: David describes God's protection in three ways: in turn, "You are a hiding place for me"; "you preserve me from trouble"; "you surround me with glad cries of deliverance" (v 7).

New slide: God's three promises to David: in turn, "I will instruct you"; "and teach you the way you should go"; "I will counsel you with my eye upon you" (v 8).

New slide: The proverb, "Do not be like a horse or a mule . . ." (v 9).

New slide: The assurance, "steadfast love surrounds those who trust in the Lord" (v 10).

New slide: David urges God's people three times: in turn, "Be glad in the Lord," "and rejoice," "and shout for joy" (v 11).

Sermon Exposition

The sermon introduction can focus attention on the need addressed by relating the story of an unnamed former parishioner who found little joy in the Christian faith and constantly focused on her sins. Her sins were such a burden that she felt she could not partake of the Lord's Supper. If you sometimes feel unworthy to partake of the Lord's Supper, Psalm 32 was written just for you.

The heading reads, "Of David. A Maskil." A Maskil is a psalm of instruction. This psalm instructs us in "the way" we should go.[36]

David begins with how happy, how blessed God's people are. Verses 1–2, "Happy are those whose transgression is forgiven, whose sin is covered. Happy are those[37] to whom the LORD imputes no iniquity, and in whose spirit there is no deceit." The double "happy" underscores how happy David is, how blessed. "The word describes the real joy and delight that comes from knowing that one is right with God." It's like the exclamation, "O the blessedness of . . ."[38]

Why is David so happy? Because each and every one of his sins are forgiven, covered, not counted against him. He uses three verbs for forgiving and three nouns for sins.[39] In the Hebrew "the three terms for sin are always preceded by a term for forgiveness (literally, 'is forgiven transgression,' 'is covered over sin,' and 'not held by the LORD his guilt,' vv 1–2). For the author of Psalm 32, the 'happy' one is someone whose sin cannot be spoken of before divine forgiveness is named."[40]

---

36. Basically the same Hebrew word is used in verse 8 where it is translated as *instruct:* "I will instruct you and teach you the way you should go." Cf. Craigie, *Psalms 1–50,* 264, "The term could mean 'didactic psalm.'" Cf. Stek, *NIV Study Bible,* Ps 32 title n., "The Hebrew word perhaps indicates that these psalms contain instruction in godliness."

37. The Hebrew has "Happy the man (*'ādām*)." Hence the NIV has the more personal "Blessed is the one."

38. Ross, *Commentary on the Psalms,* I, 710.

39. Craigie, *Psalms 1–50,* 266, cautions that because of the synonymous parallelism the three terms "transgressions," "sin," and "iniquity" as well as the three terms "forgiven," "covered," and "imputes" "should not be taken too precisely [in their potentially distinctive nuances], yet the three terms [for sin] as a whole specify the full dimensions of human evil. . . . Likewise, the three terms designating the manner of forgiveness are poetically parallel, but taken together, they indicate the completeness of the divine deliverance from evil which makes happiness possible." Although Craigie makes a valid point, preachers can still briefly indicate the specific meaning of each word for sin before making the point that the three terms together describe any and all sins, and the meaning of each word for forgive before making the point that the three words together "indicate the completeness of the divine deliverance." See also my caution from a homiletical perspective on p. 258 n. 66 above.

40. Melody D. Knowles, "Psalm 32," in Van Harn and Strawn, eds., *Psalms for Preaching and Worship,* 132. Cf. Carl Bosma, "Forgiveness — A Key to Happiness: A Meditation on Psalm 32:1–6," *Calvin Seminary Forum* (Spring 2014; pp. 10–12): 10, "This ordering of words emphasizes the fact that the forgiveness of sin is always the result of God's gracious initiative."

"Happy are those whose transgression is forgiven." "Transgression" is a terrible sin. It is not merely transgressing, stepping across a boundary, breaking a law or command. It is much more personal and deliberate. Transgression "denotes sin as a deliberate defiance of God, and as a rebellion against his will."[41] "Picture it as a raised fist against God."[42] But even this terrible sin is "forgiven," literally, "lifted up," "carried away."[43] The burden of carrying this sin is lifted up.

David adds a second set of forgiven sins: Happy are those "whose sin is covered." The word "sin" here denotes missing the mark; falling short of the goal God has set for us. Picture it as shooting at a target and falling short (Judges 20:6). This shortcoming, too, is forgiven; it is "covered," concealed, out of sight.

In verse 2 David adds a third set of forgiven sins: "Happy are those to whom the LORD imputes no iniquity." "Iniquity," also translated as "guilt," denotes "going astray," "deviation from the right path."[44] Picture it as deliberately taking the wrong road. Again a serious sin. Psalm 130:3–4 declares, "If you, O LORD, should mark iniquities, Lord, who could stand? But there is forgiveness with you, so that you may be revered." The LORD forgives also iniquity and guilt. He "imputes no iniquity." To "impute" is to reckon.[45] David says that the LORD "imputes [reckons] *no* iniquity." He does not count iniquity or guilt.[46] He has no record of it.

By using three different verbs for forgiving and three different words for sin, David is saying that the LORD can completely forgive any and all sins we commit, no matter how serious. God had provided Israel with a vivid picture of this forgiveness. We read in Leviticus 16 about the Day of Atonement:

> When he [Aaron, the high priest] has finished atoning for the holy place and the tent of meeting and the altar, he shall present the live goat. Then Aaron shall lay both his hands on the head of the live goat, and confess over it all the *iniquities* of the people of Israel, and all their *transgressions,* all their *sins,* putting them on the head of the goat, and sending it away into the wilderness

---

41. See p. 258 n. 65 above.

42. Waltke, *The Psalms as Christian Lament*, 111.

43. VanGemeren, *Psalms*, 312.

44. A. Anderson, *Psalms 1–72*, 255, 393.

45. "The verb means 'impute, reckon, credit'; it is the language of records, of accounting. . . . Here the psalm is using an implied comparison, as if there were record books in heaven that would record the sins. If the forgiven sins are not imputed, it means that there is no record of them — they are gone and forgotten." Ross, *Commentary on the Psalms*, I, 710–11.

46. "The sins are . . . 'not counted,' as in an accounting ledger (Lev 25:27, 52; 1 Kings 10:21; 2 Kings 12:15; 22:7)." Broyles, *Psalms*, 161. Cf. VanGemeren, *Psalms*, 312, It "expresses God's attitude toward those forgiven as 'justified.' (Cf. *TWOT* 1:330)."

by means of someone designated for the task. The goat shall bear on itself *all their iniquities* to a barren region. (Lev 16:20–22)

Perhaps with this picture in mind, David declares that God can forgive any and all sins, no matter how serious. That is the good news. Complete forgiveness of all our sins.

But there seems to be a catch. Verse 2 concludes, "and in whose spirit there is no deceit." Who among us can say that there is no deceit in our spirit? If there is deceit in us, then, do we risk not being forgiven? The question is, How should we understand "and in whose spirit there is no deceit"?

Basically "no deceit" means that we do not try to deceive God or ourselves about our sins.[47] Think of David trying to hide his sin after he committed adultery with Bathsheba, the wife of Uriah. First he called his soldier Uriah home from the front-lines and encouraged him to go home and sleep with his wife. Uriah and the people would then think that the expected baby was Uriah's. But the loyal soldier refused to go home and would eventually find out that the baby was not his. David's sin would become public. How could he now hide his sin? He ordered his general Joab, "Set Uriah in the forefront of the hardest fighting, and then draw back from him, so that he may be struck down and die" (2 Sam 11:14–15). In David's spirit was deceit, even to the point of having his loyal soldier killed. He tried to hide his sin (cf. v 5). "In whose spirit there is no deceit" means, then, that we are honest and open with God about our sins, that we don't try to hide them from God. It means that we confess our sins honestly and contritely.

In verse 3 David says, "While I kept silence, my body wasted away through my groaning all day long." Here he admits that his deceit was keeping silent. He was not open with God but tried to hide his sins. Do you know how long David "kept silence" after he committed adultery with Bathsheba and murdered her husband Uriah? For almost a year (cf. 2 Sam 11:5, 27; 12:1–23). For almost a year he lived with the guilt of these terrible sins. He kept silent.[48]

Meanwhile his body, he writes, "wasted away through my groaning all day long." He traces the cause of his distress not so much to his sin as to "his 'silence'"

47. "This phrase ['in whose spirit there is no deceit'] is exemplified by the confession that follows. This absence of 'deceit' is spelled out as acknowledging 'my sin to you' and by not covering up 'my iniquity.' . . . (Instead of 'spirit,' the LXX reads 'mouth,' and if correct provides further support for [this explanation])." Broyles, *Psalms*, 162. Cf. Ross, *Commentary on the Psalms*, I, 711, "The word refers to deceit or duplicity, here concerning one's sins; if the guilty sinner holds back or denies the sin, there is no genuine repentance and therefore no forgiveness."

48. "Where God is the other, silence is the performance of stubborn pride or of a spirit struck dumb for fear of being found out [cf. 2 Sam 12:12]. . . . The silence is the rejection of grace." Mays, *Psalms*, 147.

about his sin and to his 'covering it up.'"[49] His body (literally, "his bones") wasted away. He experienced such pain that he groaned all day long. Where did this horrific pain come from?

David knew the answer. Verse 4, "For day and night your hand was heavy upon me; my strength was dried up as by the heat of summer." God's hand was heavy on him. It was God's punishing hand[50] that caused the pain. And not just for a short time, but "day and night." Continuously. Without letup. "My strength was dried up as by the heat of summer," he writes. "His vitality for living, literally his life juices, dried up like the heat of summer."[51] He felt like a wilting plant drying up in the scorching summer sun. No energy left. He was dying under God's punishing hand.[52]

Here the psalm adds the word "Selah." We may not know its meaning precisely, but let's not just read over this word. In the Psalter the word "selah" is found seventy-one times. Some scholars suggest that "selah" signaled "an interlude of some kind in which something else was either sung or played." More recent studies suggest that the word may be derived from "to lift up," either one's voice or one's eyes, or "to turn, bend," for prayer.[53] In any case, the word "selah" seems to indicate some kind of pause.

So let's pause and reflect on the words we just heard. Do some of us keep silence, trying to hide our sins from God? Could it be that we are in pain of some kind because we fail to ask God for forgiveness? Of course, Jesus makes clear that not all sickness is the result of personal sin. When Jesus' disciples saw a blind man, they asked Jesus, "Rabbi, who sinned, this man or his parents, that he was born blind?" Jesus answered, "Neither this man nor his parents sinned; he was born blind so that God's works might be revealed in him" (John 9:2-3). In other words, there need not be a direct correlation between disability or sickness and personal sin. But there might be. David kept silence and experienced the punishing hand of God. "His mouth kept silence, so his body spoke. It wasted away." Lindsay Armstrong

---

49. Broyles, *Psalms*, 162. Broyles adds, "This cover-up is described as having its psychological and perhaps even physiological effects (cf. 31:9-10; 38:2-8; 102:3-5)."

50. "This is not simply the hand of God extended to help, protect, or deliver (cf. 2 Sam 24:14; 1 Kings 18:46; Ezra 7:6, 28; Ps 118:15-16; Isa 66:14). Rather, the characterization of the hand as heavy suggests a noticeable, if not decisively negative, presence (cf. Job 23:2; 1 Sam 5:6, 11; [Ruth 1:13; Ps 38:2])." Mignon R. Jacobs, "Sin, Silence, Suffering, and Confession in the Conceptual Landscape of Psalm 32," in *Text and Community*, II (Sheffield: Sheffield Phoenix, 2007; pp. 14-34), 29.

51. Ross, *Commentary on the Psalms*, I, 713.

52. "Neither the sin nor the form of suffering is identified, other than that the latter was physically and psychologically devastating. But it would be uncharacteristic of the Psalms to speak of mere emotional disturbance brought on by suppressed guilt. Some affliction, perhaps illness, was the instrument of God's chastisement (see Ps 38)." Stek, *NIV Study Bible*, Ps 32:3-5 n.

53. A. Anderson, *Psalms 1-72*, 48-49.

suggests, "Alternatively, we may exhibit extra pounds, knots in our back, higher blood pressure, shorter temper, or insomnia, but the result is the same: silence about sin makes us sick."[54] If we experience some kind of unexplained affliction, we should ask ourselves: Could this be God's punishing hand on me for trying to hide my sins? Is it time to be honest with God and sincerely confess my sins?

David continues in verse 5, "Then I acknowledged my sin to you, and I did not hide my iniquity; I said, 'I will confess my transgressions to the LORD,' and you forgave the guilt of my sin." God's punishment drives David to confess his sins. He uses the three different words for sin he mentioned in beginning the psalm but now he precedes each by "my," "my," "my": "my sin," "my iniquity," and "my transgressions." He seeks to include any and all of his sins. For *confessing* his sins he also uses three different words: "Then *I acknowledged* my sin to you, and *I did not hide* my iniquity; I said,[55] '*I will confess* my transgressions to the LORD.'" "Acknowledge," "not hide," "confess." He will be completely open and honest with God about all of his sins.

Did you notice something odd about the end of verse 5? "I said, 'I will confess my transgressions to the LORD,' and you forgave the guilt of my sin." The confession itself is missing. David just states his intent to confess his transgressions, "and you forgave the guilt of my sin."

We read David's confession in 2 Samuel 12. When the prophet Nathan confronted David with his sin, he confessed, "I have sinned against the LORD." Immediately Nathan said to David, "Now the LORD has *put away* your sin; you shall not die" (2 Sam 12:13). In verse 5 that confession itself is missing, as if to underscore God's rapid response: "I said, 'I will confess my transgressions to the LORD,' and you forgave the guilt of my sin."[56] Instant forgiveness! The burden lifted in a moment!

"Selah" — another pause for reflection. If God, before the coming of Christ, would immediately forgive David's sins, how much more will he instantaneously forgive us our sins after the coming of Christ. Christ already paid for our sins

---

54. Armstrong, "Preaching the Lenten Texts," *JPr* 33, no. 2 (2010): 9.

55. "Direct discourse . . . stresses the redemptive agency of spoken confession." Brown, *Psalms*, 63.

56. "The clause expressing an intent to confess is followed by the report of God's absolution: '*You* [emphatic] forgave . . .' (v 5). Curiously, the confession itself is lacking. . . . The absence of the confession poetically exhibits the rapidity of God's forgiveness." Knowles, "Psalm 32," in *Psalms for Preaching and Worship*, 132. Cf. Leupold, *Exposition of the Psalms*, 267, "The forgiveness followed hard on the heels of the confession. It might, in fact, almost be paraphrased: As soon as I said, I will confess, Thou forgavest. It was as simple as that. The writer is still filled with wonder." Cf. Tanner in deClaissé-Walford, Jacobson, and Tanner, *The Book of Psalms*, 308, "It has taken eight lines to describe the weight of the sin and the path of confession, and here it is reversed with four words describing God's act."

with his death and resurrection. Our sins *have been* paid for![57] All we have to do is confess our sins and be assured that they are forgiven. John writes, "If we confess our sins, he who is faithful and just will forgive us our sins and cleanse us from all unrighteousness" (1 John 1:9).

Is confession of sin, then, a good work we must do in order to be saved? The answer is that our confession of sin is not a good work[58] but an expression of our faith that God is a forgiving God — a God who has already paid for our sins in Christ. Confession of sin is our "Yes" to God's invitation to be forgiven. Confession is the open hand that receives forgiveness.

With the emphatic "therefore" of verse 6 we enter the second half of this psalm. David now leaves sins behind. He does not mention the word again, not even once. His sins have been forgiven; he need not dwell on them anymore; he can move on. It's almost as if David anticipates Paul's word in 2 Corinthians 5:17, "If anyone is in Christ, there is a new creation: everything old has passed away; see, everything has become new!"

Verse 6, "Therefore let all who are faithful offer prayer to you;[59] at a time of distress, the rush of mighty waters shall not reach them." "Therefore," because of the grief caused by not confessing our sins and God's eagerness to forgive, David urges God's people to offer prayer to God; to keep the lines of communication open.[60]

"At a time of distress, the rush of mighty waters shall not reach them." Times of distress will still come in the lives of God's people. But if they remain faithful in offering prayer to God, "the rush of mighty waters shall not reach them." "The rush of mighty waters" refers to imminent danger. With "mighty waters" we can think of the waters rushing down the wadis in the rainy season.[61] These flash floods sweep away everything in their path. But David assures God's people that these destructive waters shall not reach them. God will keep them safe.

57. "For our sake he made him to be sin who knew no sin, so that in him we might become the righteousness of God" (2 Cor 5:21).

58. Cf. Romans 4:6–8 where Paul quotes Psalm 32: "David speaks of the blessedness of those to whom God reckons righteousness *apart from works*: 'Blessed are those whose iniquities *are forgiven,* and whose sins *are covered;* blessed is the one against whom the Lord will *not reckon* sin.'"

59. David is addressing God, "you" (second person, masculine, singular), but clearly expects the reader to overhear and obey.

60. Cf. Isaiah 55:6–7, "Seek the LORD while he may be found, call upon him while he is near; let the wicked forsake their way, and the unrighteous their thoughts; let them return to the LORD, that he may have mercy on them, and to our God, for he will abundantly pardon."

61. "Mighty waters" could possibly refer to God's punishment of human sin with the Flood (cf. Ps 29:3). Goldingay, *Psalms,* I, 458, suggests that "mighty waters can be a figure for enemies, an imagery that may run through vv 6–7, and the surrounding shouts of rescue then contrast with the surrounding shouts of attack (109:3)."

In verse 7 he describes God's protection with three images, "You are a hiding place for me; you preserve me from trouble; you surround me with glad cries of deliverance." "You are a hiding place for me." You may have seen pictures of the caves of Qumran where the Dead Sea scrolls were found. Below the caves are the wadis where the rushing waters destroy everything in their path. But in the caves high up against the mountain the Dead Sea scrolls were kept safe for more than 2000 years. That is what God is for David and all the faithful: a hiding place, a place of refuge, a place of security, a place where even the most disastrous floods cannot reach us.

A second image: "you preserve me from trouble." "Trouble" can come from any direction. Psalm 138:7 declares, "Though I walk in the midst of trouble, you preserve me against the wrath of my enemies." Psalm 46:1 asserts confidently, "God is our refuge and strength, a very present help in trouble." "You preserve me from trouble."

A third image: "You surround me with glad cries of deliverance." Now we are at the temple surrounded by the glad cries of God's people.[62] God has delivered them; he has saved them. They shout and sing their praise to God.

"Selah" again. Another pause for reflection. What a loving, mighty God we serve! The rush of mighty waters shall not reach us. God is our hiding place, far above the mighty waters. God will preserve us from all kinds of trouble. In fact, he provides us with a community of believers who surround us "with glad cries of deliverance." When troubles come into our lives, we are not in this alone. God is there to preserve us and God's people are there to support us.

And there is even more good news. In verse 8 God himself begins to speak.[63] He promises to walk with David into the future. Specifically, God promises to do three things for David: "I will *instruct* you and *teach* you the way you should go; I will *counsel* you with my eye upon you." The repetition underscores God's "complete commitment to personal teaching."[64]

---

62. "The Hebrew reads 'enfold me with shouts of salvation,' suggesting that his embracing sense of security is enhanced by the presence of worshippers encompassing him and praising God for his salvation." Rogerson and McKay, *Psalms 1–50*, 146. Cf. Ross, *Commentary on the Psalms*, I, 716–17, "The reference may be to the congregation of people in the sanctuary who will sing and shout of God's great protection and salvation. A similar result is expressed in Psalm 51. . . ."

63. See nn. 27 and 35 above. Though not all scholars agree that this is a divine oracle, the "I will counsel you *with my eye upon you*" (v 8b) seems to settle that this could only be God speaking. Eaton, *Psalms*, 149 notes the connection between vv 7 and 8: "This promise of guidance is addressed first to a singular, and is best taken as words of the Lord in response to v 7." For detailed argumentation for "the words of a divine statement quoted in a song of thanksgiving," see Kraus, *Psalms 1–59*, 371.

64. Goldingay, *Psalms*, I, 459.

"I will instruct you," that is, give you insight, understanding. Second, "and teach you the *way you should go*," that is, a lifestyle that is pleasing to God and beneficial to David. Third, "I will counsel you with my eye upon you." God promises to be personally involved by guiding David with good advice. David does not have to face the future alone. God will be with him. God will be his personal counselor. Like a watchful Father, God will have his "eye" on him.

In verse 9 David addresses his fellow-worshipers.[65] "Do not be like a horse or a mule,[66] without understanding, whose temper must be curbed with bit and bridle, else it will not stay near you." Without a bit and bridle horses and mules would not stay near their masters. Stubborn as they are and without understanding,[67] they would strike out on their own. Especially in the rugged terrain of Israel they would soon be lost and probably die. David warns us not to be like that but to stay close to our Master, the LORD. He will teach us the way we should go.

Unfortunately, we cannot stay close to our Master in our own strength. So verse 10 provides even more good news: "Many are the torments of the wicked, but steadfast love surrounds those who trust in the LORD." In contrast to the wicked who suffer many torments, "steadfast love surrounds those who trust in the LORD." The key phrase is, "trust in the LORD." The wicked trust in themselves and suffer many torments. But "those who trust in the LORD" will be surrounded by "steadfast love." "Steadfast love" is another keyword. "Steadfast love" is the LORD's covenant loyalty.[68] The LORD surrounds those who trust in him with his enduring covenant love.

We have now seen through David's experience and eyes how good the LORD is for us, how gracious. Upon confession, he freely forgives us our sins (v 5). He protects us from the troubles in this violent, sinful world (vv 6–7). He instructs, teaches, and guides us in the way we should go (v 8). And his "steadfast covenant love" surrounds us on our journey through life (v 10). What will be our response to such good news? What will be our response when we come together to worship the LORD?

David concludes Psalm 32 with a triple call to exult in the LORD. Verse 11, "Be glad in the LORD and rejoice, O righteous, and shout for joy, all you upright in heart." Notice again, three synonyms: Be glad! Rejoice! Shout for joy!

---

65. See nn. 27 and 35 above.

66. "He explicitly compares a wrong response to that of a stubborn war *horse* (Prov 26:3; Jer 8:6) *or a mule*, a 'hybrid offspring of the stallion and she-ass,' a proverbial intractable animal." Waltke, *The Psalms as Christian Lament*, 118.

67. "'Understanding' (*byn*) is commonly used in wisdom literature to describe those who are perceptive, having clear understanding that informs right decision-making." Wilson, *Psalms*, I, 548–49.

68. See p. 257 n. 62 above.

These three commands are addressed to the "righteous," the "upright in heart." The "righteous" are not sinless people. The "righteous," according to Psalm 1, are those who walk on the right path. The "righteous," according to Psalm 32, are sinners whom God has forgiven and whom he now guides in the right path.[69] God's forgiven people are to "be glad in the LORD," not in themselves and their accomplishments. They live only by the LORD's forgiving grace. Therefore, "be glad in the LORD," "rejoice," and "shout for joy."[70]

If God's Old Testament people had so many reasons to rejoice in the LORD, how many more reasons do we have? Jesus has come and with his death paid for our sins. Jesus is "the Lamb of God who takes away the sin of the world!" (John 1:29). He died so that we might live. Now we can joyfully dedicate our lives to him and his service.

We will still face hardship in this world, perhaps even persecution. But that should not take away from our being glad in the Lord. Jesus teaches us that we can rejoice in any and all circumstances. Just like Psalm 32, Jesus begins the Sermon on the Mount with beatitudes. In one of these beatitudes Jesus says, "Blessed are you when people revile you and persecute you and utter all kinds of evil against you falsely on my account. Rejoice and be glad, for your reward is great in heaven" (Matt 5:11–12). "Rejoice and be glad!" even in difficult circumstances.

The apostle Paul similarly commands the church: "Rejoice in the Lord *always;* again I will say, Rejoice." And Paul continues, "Do not worry about anything, but in everything by prayer and supplication with thanksgiving let your requests be made known to God. And the peace of God, which surpasses all understanding, will guard your hearts and your minds in Christ Jesus" (Phil 4:4, 6–7).

Prayer[71]

Our Father in heaven, God of grace,
Thank you so much for your eagerness to forgive us our sins.
We sincerely confess that we have sinned against you in thought, word, and
    deed.
We pray that you will forgive us our sins through your Son Jesus Christ.

---

69. "To be righteous is to be forgiven (v 5). To be righteous is to be a witness to God's grace (vv 6–11)." McCann, "Psalms," 807.

70. This is not a call "for making a vain effort to be happy when one does not feel like it. The godly [righteous], who are mindful of all the benefits (forgiveness, protection, guidance) of the Lord, *will* rejoice!" VanGemeren, *Psalms,* 316. Cf. A. Anderson, *Psalms 1–72,* 259, with references to Deut 28:47 and Neh 8:10, "Joyful service of God is not an optional extra, but it is of the essence of all true service."

71. S.G.

Thank you for lifting the burden of guilt and making us new creations in
    Christ.
Thank you for sending your Holy Spirit to guide us in the way we should go.
May we truly be glad in the Lord and rejoice in the Lord always.
We pray this in Jesus' name. Amen.

Song[72]

To God be the glory, great things he has done;
so loved he the world that he gave us his Son,
who yielded his life an atonement for sin,
and opened the lifegate that we may go in.

Refrain:
Praise the Lord, praise the Lord; let the earth hear his voice!
Praise the Lord, praise the Lord; let the people rejoice!
O come to the Father through Jesus the Son,
and give him the glory; great things he has done.

O perfect redemption, the purchase of blood,
to every believer the promise of God;
the vilest offender who truly believes,
that moment from Jesus a pardon receives. *Refrain*

Great things he has taught us, great things he has done,
and great our rejoicing through Jesus the Son;
but purer and higher and greater will be
our wonder, our gladness, when Jesus we see. *Refrain*

72. Fanny J. Crosby, 1875. Public domain. *Psalter Hymnal* (1987), # 473; *Lift Up Your Hearts*, # 604.

CHAPTER 13

"The LORD Is Your Keeper"

Psalm 121 (120)

The Revised Common Lectionary, Year A, assigns Psalm 121 for the second Sunday in Lent as a response to the Old Testament reading of God calling Abram, "Go from your country and your kindred and your father's house to the land that I will show you . . ." (Gen 12:1–4a). This psalm is a fitting response to that reading because the psalm is filled with God's wonderful promises of safekeeping on a dangerous journey. As such it makes for a great preaching text for many journeys the church and its members may undertake. Traditionally, the church has used it for baptism and funeral services.[1] It is also a wonderful psalm for a New Year's service. Since the psalm is not particularly focused on the issues we consider during Lent, we must be careful not to allow the season of the church year to dictate the message of the psalm.

Text and Context

Psalm 121 makes for a good preaching text because it is a literary unit. This is indicated not only by its being a single psalm but also by a possible inclusio formed by verses 1 and 8: "From (*mē-*) where will my help come (*yābo'*)?" and "The LORD will keep your going out and your coming in from (*ûbô'ekā mē-*) this time on and forevermore." According to Robert Alter, "This concluding reference to the eternality of God's protection completes an arc begun with the reference

---

1. Zenger, *Psalms 3,* 331, who also notes that verse 8, "The Lord will keep your going out and your coming in from this time on and forevermore," "is still spoken in the Jewish tradition as one touches the mezuzah at the entry of a house or apartment, and . . . in Christian tradition (especially in the Byzantine context) is written on doorposts."

to creation at the beginning of the poem in the designation of God as 'maker of heaven and earth.'"[2]

The editor(s) of the Psalter have placed Psalm 121 immediately after Psalm 120, which describes a world of violence and war to which the psalmist is helplessly exposed. Psalm 121 also sees many dangers on life's journey but offers the assurance, "My help comes from the LORD, who made heaven and earth" (v 2). Psalm 122, in turn, "sets the solidly built city of Jerusalem as a place of shelter and community over against the warlike and dangerous 'world' described in Psalms 120 and 121."[3] Moreover, the superscription identifies Psalm 121 as "A Song of Ascents." Thus it can be compared with the other Songs of Ascents, Psalms 120–134, in order to capture its specific focus. In addition, other Old Testament passages can inform our understanding of this psalm, such as the Aaronic blessing (Num 6:22–27), and, of course, the New Testament.

Literary Interpretation

As noted, the superscription identifies Psalm 121 as "A Song of Ascents." Judging by its contents, Bernhard Anderson identifies the psalm as a "Song of trust."[4]

We shall again work our way into understanding the psalm first with a snapshot of its parallelisms, next its imagery, then repetition of keywords, and finally the psalm's structure.

Parallelisms

Psalm 121 is stitched together primarily with stairlike parallelisms (anadiplosis: to be doubled back). Stairlike or step parallelism repeats a word or phrase of one verse in the next verse or line.[5] It links verses 1–2, 3–4, 5–6, and 7–8 (see the italicized words below). Because of advancing parallelism all four stanzas of the psalm exhibit climactic parallelism.

---

2. Alter, *Book of Psalms*, 418 n. 8. Cf. Magonet, *A Rabbi Reads the Psalms*, 126.

3. Zenger, *Psalms 3*, 330.

4. Anderson, *Out of the Depths*, 223. So also, e.g., Zenger, *Psalms 3*, 320, who adds that it became a Song of Ascents "only when it was integrated into the Pilgrim Psalter."

5. "Stairlike or steplike repetition . . . is especially appropriate for a psalm about a journey, which in ancient times would literally have proceeded step by step." McCann, "Psalms," 1180. See also deClaissé-Walford in deClaissé-Walford, Jacobson, and Tanner, *The Book of Psalms*, 887–90.

₁I lift up my eyes to the hills —	A
from where will *my help* come?	+ A'
₂*My help* comes from the LORD,	+ A"
who made heaven and earth.	+ A'''
₃He will not let your foot be moved;	A
he who keeps you *will not slumber.*	+ A'
₄He who keeps Israel *will neither slumber* nor sleep.⁶	+ A"
₅The LORD is your keeper;	A
the LORD is your shade at *your right* hand.	+ A'
₆The sun shall not strike you by *day,*⁷	+ A"
nor the moon by night.	+ A'''
₇The LORD will keep you from all evil;	A
he will keep your life.	+ A'
₈*The* LORD *will keep* your going out and your coming in	+ A"
from this time on and forevermore.	+ A'''

Imagery

Five times this short psalm uses the Hebrew poetic device of merism, which we can call a form of imagery. It names a pair of opposites to include the whole: "heaven and earth" (v 2), "by day, by night," "sun and moon" (v 6), and "your going out and coming in," and "from this time on and forevermore" (v 8).

The underlying image of Psalm 121 is that of a person going on a dangerous journey.⁸ He raises the question, "I lift up my eyes to the hills — from where will my help come?" (v 1). Lifting up his eyes as well as hills can be understood liter-

---

6. The author uses three rhetorical devices to increase the intensity from verse 3 to 4. "First, by using intensifying negatives, he moves from a twofold usage of *'al* in verse 3 to a twofold usage of the stronger negative *lō'* in verse 4. Second, he intensified the names of God [from "your Watcher" to "the Watcher of Israel"]. Third, by the interjection 'Behold / Indeed' at the beginning of verse 4, he called attention to the unceasing vigil of the Keeper of Israel." David G. Barker, "'The LORD Watches over You': A Pilgrimage Reading of Psalm 121," *BSac* 152, no. 606 (1995; pp. 163–81): 175–76.

7. The Hebrew for "your right" (*yəmînekā*, v 5) and "day" (*yômām*, v 6) is paronomastic. Anthony R. Ceresko, "Psalm 121: A Prayer of a Warrior?" *Bib* 70, no. 4 (1989; pp. 496–510): 497.

8. "The psalm does evoke the sense of a journey. The idioms of the foot that does not slip (v 3) and departing and returning (v 8) form an interpretive inclusion around the main part of the psalm." Mays, *Psalms*, 390.

ally, but the question is, Which hills? Many scholars understand these hills to be the hills around Jerusalem. For example, McCann writes, "In the context of the Songs of Ascents, the hills in the distance might be intended to include Mount Zion, a symbol not of danger but of divine help."[9] However, the very question, "*From where* will my help come?" indicates that there is danger in these hills the pilgrim has to travel (see, e.g., 1 Kings 22:17; Jer 13:16; Lam 4:19; Luke 10:30).[10] So he is not lifting up his eyes to the comforting hills around Jerusalem but to dangerous hills he has to cross to get to his destination. Therefore he answers his own anxious question with, "My help comes from the LORD, who made heaven and earth." The Creator of heaven and earth can and will protect him on his dangerous journey.

Another issue is whether the pilgrim is heading *to* Jerusalem or *from* Jerusalem. Broyles writes, "The question must remain open as to whether the psalm was used originally on the departure to or from Jerusalem."[11] Unfortunately, preachers cannot leave this an open question because that will affect the design of the sermon. We cannot have the pilgrim both coming and going. So we have to decide which way our pilgrim is headed.

The superscription, "A Song of Ascents," does not decide the issue. First of all, scholars are not agreed on the meaning of this term.[12] Second, even if we agreed with "the most widely accepted explanation" that it indicates pilgrimage songs that would be "sung by the worshippers during the journey to Jerusalem,"[13] this does not mean that the song itself necessarily describes this ascent to Jerusalem. Of all the Songs of Ascents (Pss 120–134), only one *describes* going up to Jerusalem, and that very briefly: "I was glad when they said to me, 'Let us go to the house of the LORD!' Our feet are standing within your gates, O Jerusalem" (Ps 122:1–2). So the superscription of Psalm 121 cannot decide the issue.

How, then, can we decide whether the pilgrim is traveling to or from Jerusalem? Note that the verses 3–8 repeat the keyword "keep / keeper" six times (*šāmar*, vv 3, 4, 5, 7 [2×], 8). This is the same word that is used in the Aaronic blessing, "The LORD bless you and *keep* you" (Num 6:24). Therefore, the verses 3–8 can

9. McCann, "Psalms," 1180. Cf. Mays, *Psalms*, 389–90 , and Leupold, *Exposition of the Psalms*, 868.

10. "The adverb 'from where?' indicates a fateful interrogation, implying that the mountains shelter or constitute a deadly peril." Terrien, *The Psalms*, 811.

11. Broyles, *Psalms*, 448.

12. For different interpretations of "Song of Ascents," see A. Anderson, *Psalms 73–150*, 847–48; Vos, *Theopoetry of the Psalms*, 259–60; and deClaissé-Walford in deClaissé-Walford, Jacobson, and Tanner, *The Book of Psalms*, 887–88.

13. Vos, *Theopoetry of the Psalms*, 260.

probably be understood as an extended version of the Aaronic blessing. Certainly the verses 7–8 sound like a variation of the Aaronic blessing.[14]

Commentators who favor the pilgrim traveling *to* Jerusalem put the words of verses 3–8 in the mouths of the pilgrim's friends or relatives who are staying behind.[15] But pronouncing God's blessing belongs to the Aaronic priesthood (see Num 6:22–27) and these priests were in Jerusalem. Surely, a priest would not assure the pilgrim that the LORD would keep him safe on his journey *after* he had safely arrived in Jerusalem. Pilgrims needed that assurance *before* they set out on a dangerous journey.

For these two reasons ("from where my help" indicating danger and a priest assuring the pilgrim in verses 3–8) I side with those commentators who see the pilgrim not journeying towards Jerusalem but heading home after worshiping in Jerusalem.[16] With this picture in mind, all the images in this psalm fall into place.

The pilgrim has worshiped God in Jerusalem and is concerned about the dangers facing him on his way home. He asks, "From where does my help come?" He has just seen God's majesty in the temple and answers himself, "My help comes from the LORD, who made heaven and earth." Then the priest assures him: "He [the LORD] will not let your foot be moved; he who keeps you will not slumber" (v 3).

Kirsten Nielsen observes that the keyword "keeps" "is used in two different contexts: with regard to the shepherd who tends his flock (Jer 31:10) and with regard to guarding a city (Ps 127:1), a garden (Gen 2:15; 3:24), or a sacred object (1 Sam 7:1)."[17] The combination in verse 3 of "keeps" with "will not let your foot be moved" calls up the picture of a shepherd. Like a shepherd, the LORD will guide the pilgrim over dangerous mountains. Like a vigilant shepherd, "he who keeps you will not slumber."

In fact, "he who keeps Israel will neither slumber nor sleep" (v 4). The Canaanite god Baal was thought to sleep in the summer season when everything

---

14. "We get the impression that vv 7–8 are variations on Num 6:24." Gerstenberger, *Psalms,* II, 324.

15. E.g., Limburg, *Psalms,* 423.

16. "From vv 3–8 a different voice speaks: a priest utters a blessing as the departing pilgrim leaves the sanctuary." Westermann, *The Psalms,* 106. Cf. Kraus, *Psalms 60–150,* 428, "It would be better to think of a ceremonial of dismissal that has taken place at a farewell from the sanctuary." Cf. A. Anderson, *Psalms 73–150,* 852, "It is often suggested that the allusion [to the hills] is to the hills of Jerusalem . . . , but more probably the Psalmist was thinking apprehensively of the hills which he will have to cross on his homeward journey." So also Allen, *Psalms 101–150,* 207; Davidson, *Vitality of Worship,* 407–9; and Weiser, *The Psalms,* 746.

17. Nielsen, "Poetic Analysis: Psalm 121," in *Method Matters: Essays on the Interpretation of the Hebrew Bible* (Atlanta: SBL, 2009; pp. 293–309), 301.

withered.[18] But Israel's God never sleeps (anthropopathism), that is, he is always watchful. He will always watch over not only this individual pilgrim but he will always watch over his flock Israel.

The priest continues to assure the pilgrim in verse 5, "The LORD is your keeper; the LORD is your shade at your right hand." Here he uses a mixed metaphor that calls up the picture of God as a Guardian, a Protector. "Shade," think of a shade tree, guards from the dangerous rays of the sun (v 6) and refers therefore to protection. "At your right hand" is a military term. "The right side of the body is unprotected by a shield held in the left hand, so the person who stands to your right protects you from attack on that side."[19] The LORD being a "shade at your right hand" means therefore protection on one's vulnerable side.[20]

It follows, verse 6, that "the sun shall not strike you by day, nor the moon by night." By day the LORD's shade will protect you from sunstroke (cf. 2 Kings 4:19; Jonah 4:8). By night the LORD's shade will protect you from being moonstruck, suffering lunacy, becoming mentally deranged.[21] All-around protection!

Verses 7 and 8 reach the climax, "The LORD will keep you from all evil; he will keep your life [*nepeš*, soul = you]. The LORD will keep your going out and your coming in from this time on and forevermore." "Your going out and your coming in" "reflects typical city life in the ancient Near East, in which the worker left the protective confines of the walled city in the morning to carry out field and pasture work and returned in the evening to the shelter of the city walls."[22] This is another reason for seeing the pilgrim not coming to but leaving Jerusalem: he is leaving the safety of the strongly walled city of God to return across dangerous mountains to his village. But he goes with God's blessing, "The LORD will keep your going out [now] and your coming in" for the next festival.[23] The final phrase,

---

18. "The fertility gods of Canaan, who, when vegetation died off, were thought of as having gone off duty or as being asleep for a period." Leupold, *Exposition of the Psalms,* 869. See 1 Kings 18:27.

19. Magonet, *A Rabbi Reads the Psalms,* 123.

20. See, e.g., Psalm 16:8, "I keep the LORD always before me; because he is at my right hand, I shall not be moved."

21. "In all likelihood these words refer to the danger of being moonstruck, evidently thought to be a cause of madness in ancient Israel, as it is imagined in many cultures." Alter, *Book of Psalms,* 438 n. 6. Note that our English word "lunatic" for an insane or reckless person derives from the Latin "luna," moon.

22. DeClaissé-Walford in deClaissé-Walford, Jacobson, and Tanner, *The Book of Psalms,* 897, paraphrasing Loren D. Crow, *The Songs of Ascents (Psalms 120–134): Their Place in Israelite History and Religion* (SBLDS 148; Atlanta: Scholars, 1996), 39.

23. "The pair of verbs refers to daily work as primarily consisting of going out of the town to work in the fields and returning in the evening. . . . Here there is possibly also a nuance of going back from worship to daily life and in due course returning to the sanctuary at the time of the next festival." Allen, *Psalms 101–150,* 206.

"from this time on and forevermore," expands the literal journey from Jerusalem ("your going out") back home to our whole life's journey on earth and beyond.

Repetition of Keywords

The first prominent word in Psalm 121 is the word "help": "From where will my help come?" The answer repeats this keyword: "My help comes from the LORD" (vv 1–2). The remainder of the psalm expands on this answer.

Anthony Ceresko notes that the psalm uses different names for God a full ten times: "five times using the name *yhwh* [vv 2, 5 (2×), 7, 8] plus five further times employing three different titles ('*ōśê* 'Creator' v 2, *ṣēl* 'Shade' v 5, *šōmēr* 'Guardian' [Keeper] [3×; vv 3, 4, 5])."[24] As we have seen, the keyword "keep / keeper / watch / guardian / protector" (*šāmar*) is repeated six times (vv 3, 4, 5, 7 (2×), 8), three times in verses 7–8.[25] The "keeping" is connected to the second masculine singular "you," "your" (-*kā*, -*kâ*) a full ten times (vv 3 [2×], 5 [3×], 6, 7 [2×], 8 [2×]). The repetition of these keywords reveals that the basic message of this psalm is that the LORD is your personal keeper.[26]

Structure

The most obvious division of this psalm is between verses 1–2 and 3–8. Verses 1–2 use the first-person pronouns ("I," "my") while verses 3 and 5–8 use second-person pronouns ("you," "your"). This shift indicates a change of speaker and divides the psalm into two main parts: verses 1–2 and 3–8.

The second part can be divided further into two or three sections. Although some scholars argue for a total of three stanzas (vv 1–2, 3–5, 6–8),[27] most recognize four stanzas, verses 1–2, 3–4, 5–6, and 7–8 (see the NRSV, NIV, ESV). "The

---

24. Ceresko, "Psalm 121: A Prayer of a Warrior?" *Bib* 70, no. 4 (1989): 499 n. 13.

25. "The three instances of *šmr* 'to watch, guard' as a finite verb (vv 7 [2×], 8) in the latter part of the psalm balance its threefold participial usage as a divine title (vv 3, 4, 5) earlier in the poem." Ibid., 499. Cf. Alter, *Book of Psalms*, 438 n. 7, "In a climactic pattern of asserted trust, three of the six repetitions of 'guard' occur in the last two lines of the poem."

26. Cf. James K. Mead, "Psalm 121," in *Psalms for Preaching*, ed. Roger E. Van Harn and Brent A. Strawn (Grand Rapids: Eerdmans, 2009; pp. 312–16), 315. Verses 5–8 "contain six second masculine singular suffixes and four contrasting pairs (sun / moon, day / night, coming in / going out, now / and forever) so that the reader feels the personal nature and unlimited scope of divine protection."

27. See, e.g., Allen, *Psalms 101–150*, 207, arguing for "an introductory strophe of two lines and then two of three lines each."

four strophes are nicely linked by the keyword 'guard' [keep] and the tetragrammaton, and also by the attractive ploy of each unit mentioning one body part. Eye, foot and hand are followed by *nepeš*, a metonymy for 'person' and 'life' that nevertheless does not deny its semantic origin of 'throat.'"[28] Moreover, these four strophes are "of approximately equal length, with syllable counts of 29, 29, 32, and 32 syllables respectively (following the masoretic vocalization)."[29]

As noted above, the psalm may be framed by an inclusio: "*From* where will my help *come?*" (v 1) and "The LORD will keep your going out and your *coming in from* this time on and forevermore" (v 8). Counting syllables, the exact center of the psalm is verse 5a, "The LORD is your keeper": "58 syllables precede the phrase and 58 follow it."[30]

It should also be noted that the verses 7–8 form a climactic final unit. Here the keyword "keep / keeper," used three times as a participle (ongoing action) in verses 3–5, is used three times in the imperfect tense (incomplete action, future). David Barker observes, "This points to verses 7–8 as a final blessing for the pilgrim in the future ('he will keep you / your life / your goings and coming')."[31]

The basic structure of the psalm, then, is a dialogue between two persons, probably a pilgrim and a priest.[32] Verse 1 indicates that the pilgrim is about to go on a dangerous journey: "I lift up my eyes to the hills — from where will my help come?" Some commentators maintain that the rest of the psalm, from verse 2 onward, consists of the priest's answer. But because of the stairlike parallelism, especially the repetition of "*my* help" in verse 2, I understand the pilgrim to be answering his own question with a brief profession of faith: "My help comes from the LORD, who made heaven and earth."[33]

---

28. Fokkelman, *Major Poems of the Hebrew Bible*, III, 273. Ceresko, "Psalm 121: A Prayer of a Warrior?" *Bib* 70, no. 4 (1989): 500, observes, "This listing of the parts of the body contributes to the encompassing and totalizing nature of the psalm's rhetoric. In a kind of extended merismus, the poet explicitly includes even the singer's entire physical body under God's benevolent shelter within that secure microcosm created by the artistry of the psalm's language."

29. Ceresko, "Psalm 121: A Prayer of a Warrior?" *Bib* 70, no. 4 (1989): 496–97.

30. Ibid., 499.

31. Barker, "The LORD Watches over You," *BSac* 152, no. 606 (1995): 168. He also notes progression from one unit to the next by way of negative and positive statements: "Verses 3–4 include two negative statements, verses 5–6 have one positive and one negative statement, and verses 7–8 (the blessing) contain two positive statements."

32. "The solemn and formal administration of the blessing and the consolation of salvation in vv 3–8 gives precedence to the supposition that Psalm 121 contains a cultic dialogue between a pilgrim and a priest." Kraus, *Psalms 60–150*, 428.

33. "The NEB, which prefers 'Help' to 'My help,' implies that the psalmist's question is answered by another person, e.g., a priest. The Hebrew would imply that the psalmist answers his own question." Rogerson and McKay, *Psalms 101–150*, 116. Weiser, *The Psalms*, 747, incongruously

It is at that point (v 3) that the priest begins to speak: "He [the LORD] will not let your foot be moved; he who keeps you will not slumber. . . ."[34] Westermann points out the significance of understanding verse 2 as well as verse 1 as words from the pilgrim: "The fact that, as in Psalm 91, this avowal of trust precedes the bestowal of blessing, provides important evidence for how blessing is understood not only in the psalm but also throughout the entire Old Testament. The recipient shows that he does not just passively accept the blessing but receives it with a trusting heart."[35]

We can outline the four stanzas as follows:

I. A pilgrim's expression of trust:
   "My help comes from the LORD, who made heaven and earth" (vv 1–2)
II. A priest's assurance and blessing:
   A. "He [the LORD] keeps Israel" (vv 3–4)
   B. "The LORD is *your* keeper" (vv 5–6)
   C. "The LORD will keep your going out and your coming in from this time on and forevermore" (vv 7–8)

Theocentric Interpretation

We can be very brief here because Psalm 121's God-centeredness is so obvious. In eight verses the psalmist names God a full ten times (see p. 302 above). After the pilgrim's opening confession, "my help comes from the LORD" (v 2), the LORD is the subject of every verb but one, "The sun shall not strike you by day" (v 6). Even here it is understood that "the sun shall not strike you" because "the LORD is your shade" (v 5).

Textual Theme and Goal

With these literary considerations in mind we are ready to formulate the theme of the text. The original pilgrim expressed his trust in the LORD: "My help comes from the LORD" (v 2). On that basis he clearly heard the message at the very center of the psalm, "The LORD is your keeper" (v 5a). But in the context of the priest's

---

introduces a careless copyist: "The original text seems to have been altered merely as a result of the carelessness of a copyist who, as at the end of v 1, wrote 'my help' instead of 'help.'"

34. Cf. Westermann, *The Living Psalms,* 290, "Vv 1–2 have a first person subject, vv 3–8 are an address in the second person. The same applies to Psalm 91, where v 2 is in the first person, while 3–13 are an address in the second person, and these two psalms also correspond in content."

35. Ibid., 291.

response (vv 3–8), he heard the message, "On all your journeys, the LORD will constantly keep you."

As part of the Psalter, Psalm 121 is now addressed not to a single pilgrim but to Israel, many pilgrims (see also verse 4, "He who keeps *Israel* will neither slumber nor sleep"). As the single pilgrim expressed his trust in the LORD, the many pilgrims should also confess, "Our help comes from the LORD." The textual theme, then, can be formulated as follows: *On all your* (pl.) *journeys, the LORD will constantly keep you* (pl.) *if you* (pl.) *trust in him.*

Although it would be helpful to know the historical setting for determining the textual goal, unfortunately scholars are not agreed on that setting.[36] But under "Imagery" above we made the argument that the original pilgrim was not heading *for* Jerusalem but was leaving Jerusalem for home. From his question, "From where will my help come?" we can see that he is anxious. But the priest assures him with God's blessing that the LORD will keep him in all his going and coming. It is likely, therefore, that Psalm 121 was used in the temple liturgy especially when the pilgrims were leaving the temple for home.[37] The goal of Psalm 121, then, was *to assure the anxious pilgrims that the LORD will constantly keep them on all their journeys if they trust in him.*

Ways to Preach Christ

There is neither a promise nor a type of Christ in this psalm. One could possibly trace the longitudinal theme "God is our keeper" from the Old Testament to Christ in the New Testament, but I think the best way to Christ is redemptive-historical progression supported by New Testament references.

Redemptive-Historical Progression with New Testament References

The theme of Psalm 121 is, "On all your journeys, the LORD will constantly keep you if you trust in him." Abraham, Isaac, and Jacob experienced this safekeeping

36. John T. Willis, "An Attempt to Decipher Psalm 121:1b," *CBQ* 52, no. 2 (1990; pp. 241–51): 242 n. 1, writes, "Scholars have proposed no less than fifteen basic *Sitze im Leben* for this psalm. See J. T. Willis, 'Psalm 121 as a Wisdom Psalm,' *Hebrew Annual Review* 11 (1987), 435–51."

37. "Its *Sitz im Leben* is problematic; Schmidt links it with the Entrance Liturgies (cf. Pss 15 and 25), but it is more plausible that it should be associated with some ceremony in which the person departing (from the Temple for his own home?) is blessed by the one remaining behind. If so, the psalm might be described as a farewell liturgy, and the main speaker must be a priest." A. Anderson, *Psalms 73–150,* 851.

on all their journeys, as did David and other Israelites who trusted the LORD. God was for them a good Shepherd and Protector who constantly watched over them.

In the fullness of time, God sent his own Son to save his people. "God so loved the world that he gave his only Son, so that everyone who believes in him may not perish but may have eternal life" (John 3:16). Jesus called himself the good Shepherd. He said, "I am the good shepherd. The good shepherd lays down his life for the sheep" (John 10:11). We can use more passages from the New Testament, especially from John 10, but also Matthew 28:20, Romans 8:35–39, 1 Peter 2:25, Philippians 4:4–7, 2 Timothy 4:18, and perhaps Revelation 7:14–17 (see "Sermon Exposition" below).

Sermon Theme, Goal, and Need

We formulated the textual theme as "On all your journeys, the LORD will constantly keep you if you trust in him." Since the New Testament does not change this theme but focuses it on trusting Jesus, the sermon theme can become the textual theme with the understanding that "the LORD" applies both to God the Father and his Son Jesus. The sermon theme, then, is, *On all your* (pl.) *journeys, the LORD will constantly keep you* (pl.) *if you* (pl.) *trust in him.*

The goal of Psalm 121 was "to assure the anxious pilgrims that the LORD will constantly keep them on all their journeys if they trust in him." With a slight adjustment for the New Testament setting, the sermon goal can remain the same: *to assure God's anxious people that the LORD will constantly keep them on all their journeys if they trust in him.*

This goal points to the need addressed in this sermon: God's people are concerned about the harm that can befall them on their journey through life.

Liturgy, Scripture Reading, and Sermon Outline

When I was leading worship services as a young pastor, the congregation would begin the service by singing, "I lift up my eyes to the mountains, I look to Jehovah for aid; my help is the Lord God almighty; the earth and the heavens he made."[38] Then I would give God's greeting with Paul's words from Romans 1:7, "Grace to you and peace from God our Father and the Lord Jesus Christ." This was not inappropriate, but if I could do it over again after

---

38. Henry Zylstra, 1953, *Psalter Hymnal* (1987) # 448.

studying Psalm 121 in more depth, I would move the words of this psalm to the close of the service. Before heading home and another week of work, the congregation could sing or say in unison, "I lift up my eyes to the hills — from where will my help come? My help comes from the LORD, who made heaven and earth." Then the pastor, raising his hands in blessing, could recite verses 3–8, or at least the verses 7–8: "The LORD will keep you from all evil; he will keep your life. The LORD will keep your going out and your coming in from this time on and forevermore."

For scripture reading, it would be best to have two voices: for verses 1–2 a voice that starts out with some anxiety but becomes more confident reading verse 2, and a comforting voice reading verses 3–8.

The sermon outline can follow the four stanzas and add a final point for the move to Christ.

    I. A pilgrim's concern for the journey ahead and expression of trust (vv 1–2)
   II. The priest's assurance and blessing:
       A. The LORD like a shepherd keeps us (vv 3–4)
       B. The LORD like a guardian protects us (vv 5–6)
       C. The LORD will preserve us forevermore (vv 7–8)
  III. Jesus is the good Shepherd who keeps us, giving us eternal life (NT)

Sermon Exposition

The sermon introduction can begin with a personal illustration of being anxious before undertaking a dangerous journey. All people can relate to that anxiety. Then switch to the anxiety of the pilgrim in Psalm 121.

The psalm has the heading, "A Song of Ascents." This marks the psalm as a song of pilgrimage. It has to do with a journey. God had instructed Israel, "Three times in the year you shall hold a festival for me" (Exod 23:14).[39] These journeys to Jerusalem could be dangerous. The pilgrims had to contend with the heat of the scorching sun during the day and the cold at night. They had to walk narrow trails alongside steep cliffs. They might meet up with wild animals or robbers. In the parable of the Good Samaritan Jesus refers to robbers even close to Jerusalem: "A man was going down from Jerusalem to Jericho, and fell into the hands of robbers, who stripped him, beat him, and went away, leaving

---

39. The Israelites had to make pilgrimages to Jerusalem for the Feast of Unleavened Bread (Passover), the Feast of Weeks (Harvest), and the Feast of Tabernacles (Booths). See Exod 23:14–17.

him half dead" (Luke 10:30). A dangerous journey — both going to Jerusalem and returning home again.

Since a priest blesses the pilgrim, we can picture the pilgrim as having safely arrived in Jerusalem and now, after worshiping the LORD, being ready to head home again.[40] You can picture him on Mount Zion looking at the distant hills that impede his way home. In verse 1 we hear his anxious voice, "I lift up my eyes to the hills — from where will my help come?"[41] He needs help for the dangerous journey home, divine help. But the pilgrim has just seen God's majesty in the temple. So he knows where his help comes from.

He answers his own question in verse 2, "My help comes from the LORD, who made heaven and earth." LORD is the name of Israel's faithful covenant God. The LORD was the God who led Israel's father Abram out of Babylonia and brought him safely into the Promised Land. The LORD was the God who kept father Jacob safe on his many journeys. The LORD, the great I AM, was the God who brought Israel out of slavery in Egypt, who fed them manna in the wilderness, who provided water from the rock, who brought them safely back into the Promised Land. The pilgrim's faith has been strengthened by participating in the joyful worship in the temple. The pilgrims had been singing other Songs of Ascents, such as Psalm 125: "Those who trust in the LORD are like Mount Zion, which cannot be moved, but abides forever. As the mountains surround Jerusalem, so the LORD surrounds his people, from this time on and forevermore" (Ps 125:1-2). Of course, the pilgrim knows where his help comes from on his dangerous journey: "My help comes from the LORD!"

Then he adds to the name of the great I AM the phrase, "who made heaven and earth." In that ancient culture, this was a major statement of faith. For people believed that there were many gods who each controlled a different part of the journey. There was a god of the sea, a different god of the desert, a different god of the mountains, a different god of the rivers, etc. As the pilgrim traveled home crossing deserts, mountains, and rivers, which god would protect him? He answers his own question: "My help comes from the LORD, *who made heaven and earth.*" The LORD made[42] heaven and earth and everything in between. There

---

40. See pp. 299-300 above for reasons why the pilgrim is not going to but leaving Jerusalem.

41. "The adverb 'from where?' indicates a fateful interrogation, implying that the mountains shelter or constitute a deadly peril." Terrien, *The Psalms,* 811. That "deadly peril" could consist not only of deadly falls but also of angry foreign gods who lived on these mountains according to ancient Near Eastern beliefs.

42. "This invocation, which uses the word '*ōśe(h)* . . . , is in participial form; that is, it accents the idea of *creatio continuata:* YHWH is the creator God who is continually attentive to the world he has made and in a sense continues to 'create' it, that is, to keep it alive and protect it." Zenger, *Psalms 3,* 323.

is no greater God. The Creator of heaven and earth has the whole world in his hands.[43] The pilgrim trusts that the LORD can and will protect him on his dangerous journey.

In the following verses a priest assures the trusting pilgrim of God's safekeeping and blessing on his journey. Verses 3–4, "He will not let your foot be moved; he who *keeps* you will not slumber. He who *keeps* Israel will neither slumber nor sleep." This is the first time we hear the word *keeps*. This important word will be repeated six times in this psalm (*šāmar*, vv 3, 4, 5, 7 [2×], 8). This is the same word that is used in the Aaronic blessing, "The LORD bless you and *keep* you" (Num 6:24). The following verses, then, can probably be understood as an extended version of the priestly Aaronic blessing.[44]

"He will not let your foot be moved; he who *keeps* you will not slumber." The combination in verse 3 of "keeps" with "he will not let your foot be moved" pictures the LORD as a shepherd. Like a shepherd the LORD will guide the pilgrim up and down the steep trails. The LORD will keep the pilgrim's foot from stumbling over rocks. He will keep his foot from slipping and sliding down a cliff. Like a vigilant shepherd, "he who keeps you will not slumber."

In fact, verse 4, "he who keeps Israel[45] will neither slumber nor sleep." By repeating the "not slumber" and adding "nor sleep," the priest emphasizes that the LORD is ever watchful. Sometimes things happen in our lives that make us think that God may be sleeping. We are involved in an accident, we get sick, we lose a loved one — where is God? Is he aware of what is going on? Is he perhaps sleeping?

Israel had that same experience. In several psalms Israel complains that God seems to be asleep. For example, in Psalm 44 the psalmist cries out: "Because of you we are being killed all day long, and accounted as sheep for the slaughter. Rouse yourself! Why do you sleep, O Lord? Awake, do not cast us off forever!"[46]

But Psalm 121 assures us that the LORD never slumbers nor sleeps. The Ca-

43. "The festival is nearly over, and it is only here in this sacred mountain place of revelation and worship that he may find the key to coping with workaday life. Here in Zion, where traditionally Yahweh was acclaimed as 'maker of heaven and earth,' he has rediscovered that the whole world lies in his hands." Allen, *Psalms 101–150*, 208.

44. "The content of the confirmatory message is akin to the priestly blessing bestowed at the conclusion of worship (Num 6:24–26); but in form it is closer to a report of a divine oracle. It does not simply express powerful wishes evoking divine blessing, but carries the stronger tones of certain promise of such blessing." Ibid. Cf. Gerstenberger, *Psalms*, II, 324, "We get the impression that vv 7–8 are variations on Num 6:24."

45. "This 'guarding' of Israel by YHWH includes all YHWH's providential and saving care: protection from enemies, leading on the road, provision of food and water, provision of strength. . . ." Zenger, *Psalms 3*, 323–24.

46. Ps 44:22–23; cf. Pss 7:6; 10:12; 35:23; 59:4–5.

naanite god Baal was thought to sleep in the summer season when everything withered (see 1 Kings 18:27). But not the LORD, Israel's God. He never slumbers nor sleeps. He is always watchful.[47] We may not always know why bad things happen to us. But the LORD is not surprised or caught off guard by bad things. Of this we can be sure: the LORD, our good Shepherd, never slumbers nor sleeps!

The LORD does not only keep *Israel*. Verse 5 makes it very personal.[48] "The LORD is *your* keeper." Can you imagine that the God "who made heaven and earth" is your personal Keeper? That the God who controls the vast universe is your personal Guardian? You need not worry about anything. The Creator LORD is not far away; he is very close at hand.

In fact, verse 5 says, "the LORD is your shade at your right hand." Here the LORD is pictured as a Guardian, a Protector. The pilgrim would have to travel under the scorching rays of the sun. But shade guards against these dangerous rays. "The LORD is your shade at your right hand."

"At your right hand" seems odd. What does it mean? It goes back to ancient battles. Warriors would protect themselves with a shield in their left hand. But this meant that the right side of the body was unprotected. It was the person on their right side who had to protect that unprotected side.[49] For example, Psalm 16:8 says, "I keep the LORD always before me; because he is *at my right hand,* I shall not be moved." The LORD's being a "shade at your right hand" means therefore protection for your vulnerable side. So you have complete, all-around protection. Today we might say, "The LORD has your back." The LORD is your Shade,[50] your Guardian, your Protector.

It follows, verse 6, that "the sun shall not strike you by day, nor the moon by night."[51] The sun was a real danger for pilgrims. 2 Kings 4 tells the story

---

47. "YHWH does not leave creation to itself but remains actively engaged with it." Zenger, *Psalms 3*, 324. See also n. 42 above.

48. "The two remaining assurances (vv 5–6, 7–8) are construed in the personal-address mode throughout. . . . Every single line goes directly to the suppliant; note the grammatical singular: in three out of four lines Yahweh is the dominant substantive." Gerstenberger, *Psalms,* II, 323.

49. Magonet, *A Rabbi Reads the Psalms,* 123. Cf. Psalm 109:31, "For he stands at the right hand of the needy, to save them from those who would condemn them to death."

50. Cf. Psalm 91:1–2, "You who live in the shelter of the Most High, who abide in *the shadow* of the Almighty, will say to the LORD, 'My refuge and my fortress; my God, in whom I trust.'"

51. Barker, "The LORD Watches over You," *BSac* 152, no. 606 (1995): 177, points out that verse 6 "has been chiastically crafted to focus on the promise of protection":

> By day,
>> the sun
>>> shall not strike you,
>> or the moon,
> by night.

about a boy who went out one day to visit his father in the field. We read, "He complained to his father, 'Oh, my head, my head!' The father said to his servant, 'Carry him to his mother.' He carried him and brought him to his mother; the child sat on her lap until noon, and he died" (2 Kings 4:19–20). The sun could kill. But the priest promises the pilgrim, By day the LORD's shade will protect you from sunstroke. And by night the LORD's shade will protect you from being moonstruck.

In those days people thought that the moon's rays could also hurt a person.[52] Even today we still speak of lunacy and lunatic, which comes from the Latin *luna,* moon. The nights, of course, could also be very cold. But the LORD would guard the pilgrim also at night. Protection, therefore, both from the sun and from the moon.[53] Protection both by day and by night. All-around protection!

Verses 7 and 8 reach the climax. The tense here shifts from the present to the future[54] and the contents from a specific pilgrim's journey in Palestine to the journey of life: "The LORD will keep you from all evil; he will keep your life. The LORD will keep your going out and your coming in from this time on and forevermore."

"The LORD will keep you from *all* evil." "The LORD will keep you from *all* harm" (NIV).[55] "The 'all' (*kol*) points to the totality and comprehensiveness of God's protection. 'Life exposes people to a great variety of mishaps, but none are beyond God's sheltering care.'"[56] As Derek Kidner puts it, "In the light of other scriptures, to be kept from all evil does not imply a cushioned life, but a well-armed one." Psalm 23:4 says, "Even though I walk through the darkest valley, I fear no evil; for you are with me; your rod and your staff — they comfort me." The author "expects the dark valley but can face it."[57]

---

52. "The baleful effect of the moon was widely held in the ancient Near East: cf. Matt 4:24; 17:15 σεληνιάζεσθαι 'be moonstruck' [epileptic]." Allen, *Psalms 101–150,* 206 n. 6a. Kraus, *Psalms 60–150,* 430, adds another possibility: "In the Babylonian world disastrous effects are ascribed to the moon god. Fever and leprosy are caused by him."

53. "The juxtaposition of sun and moon may serve as a merism to indicate the total reach of God's protection." Brown, *Seeing the Psalms,* 201.

54. "These two final verses . . . stand apart from verses 3–6 as marked by a change from a substantival participial form of the key thematic term *šāmar* to an imperfect form. The description of Yahweh as 'Watcher / Keeper' now moves to an emphasis on the action of 'watching' or 'keeping.' This serves to identify a change from affirmation (vv 3–6) to benediction (vv 7–8)." Barker, "The LORD Watches over You," *BSac* 152, no. 606 (1995): 178.

55. "In light of the context of pilgrimage and concern for well-being on the journey, the amoral rendering 'calamity,' 'disaster,' or 'harm,' is the better way to render the term here." Ibid., 179.

56. Ibid., quoting A. Cohen, *The Psalms,* 421.

57. Kidner, *Psalms 73–150,* 432.

More than that, verse 7 states, "he will keep your life." Here the pilgrim's limited journey broadens to the journey of his whole life on earth. The LORD will guard your life!

Verse 8 explains further, "The LORD will keep your going out and your coming in from this time on and forevermore." "Your going out and your coming in" "reflects typical city life in the ancient Near East, in which the worker left the protective confines of the walled city in the morning to carry out field and pasture work and returned in the evening to the shelter of the city walls."[58] Our pilgrim is leaving the safety of Jerusalem, the strongly walled city of God, to return to his village on the other side of dangerous mountains. But he goes with God's blessing, "The LORD will keep your going out [now] and your coming in" for the next festival.

And not only for the festivals. "'Going out and coming in' . . . embraces and permeates the whole of life . . . : Every going out and every coming in, all coming and going, are under the protection of him who made heaven and earth."[59]

"From this time on and *forevermore*" expands the LORD's keeping even beyond our earthly journey. "God's care extends not just to all places and settings of life, but also to all time."[60] As Psalm 73:24 says, "You guide me with your counsel, and afterward you will receive me with honor" ["to glory," RSV, ESV; "into glory," NIV].[61] What a promise! "The LORD will keep your going out and your coming in from this time on and forevermore." On all our journeys, the LORD will constantly keep us.

The New Testament reveals even more clearly God's care for our lives and beyond. The familiar John 3:16 proclaims, "For God so loved the world that he gave his only Son, so that everyone who believes in him may not perish but may have *eternal life.*" Protection, even beyond death. God cared so deeply for us that he gave his only Son to protect us from death itself. God gave his Son so that we may have *eternal life.* Protection throughout our life's journey, even beyond death. Eternal life! Total protection!

But how does this protection come about? Jesus called himself the good

---

58. See p. 301 and nn. 22 and 23 above.

59. Kraus, *Psalms 60–150,* 430. Cf. Limburg, *Psalms,* 425. "The biblical expression 'going out and coming in' refers to all of one's activities, the 'comings and goings' that make up our day by day lives (see Deut 28:6; 31:2; Josh 14:11)."

60. Barker, "The LORD Watches over You," *BSac* 152, no. 606 (1995): 180. Barker adds, "Pious Jews today, as they leave or enter their house or a room in the house, touch the mezuzah, a small metal cylinder that is placed on the right hand door post and that contains a piece of parchment inscribed with Deuteronomy 6:4–9 and 11:13–21, and they recite Psalm 121:8."

61. Cf. Psalm 49:15, "But God will ransom my soul from the power of Sheol, for he will receive me."

Shepherd. He said, "*I am* the good shepherd. The good shepherd lays down his life for the sheep" (John 10:11). To keep his sheep safe, Jesus was willing to die for them. So he walked the road of suffering and died on a cross. "The good shepherd lays down his life for the sheep." But there is more. A dead shepherd cannot do anything for his sheep. Jesus continued: "For this reason the Father loves me, because I lay down my life *in order to take it up again.* No one takes it from me, but I lay it down of my own accord. I have power to lay it down, and *I have power to take it up again*" (John 10:17–18). And Jesus did. On Easter Sunday Jesus rose from the grave in order to continue keeping his sheep safe.[62] He said, "Remember, I am with you always, to the end of the age" (Matt 28:20). The good Shepherd is always with us.

Jesus' sheep are on a journey; they follow their good Shepherd. And he keeps them safe on all their journeys, even beyond death. Jesus said, "I give them *eternal life,* and they will never perish. No one will snatch them out of my hand" (John 10:27–28).[63] On all our journeys, Jesus will keep us safe; we can trust him.

The fact that Jesus our good Shepherd will keep us safe does not mean that our journey through life will be a bed of roses. Sometimes that journey will indeed go through deep, dark valleys. But Jesus will be with us in those dark valleys.

The apostle Paul experienced many dark valleys. He writes in one of his letters,[64] "Three times I was beaten with rods. Once I received a stoning. Three times I was shipwrecked . . . ; on frequent journeys, in danger from rivers, danger from bandits, danger from my own people, danger from Gentiles, danger in the city, danger in the wilderness, danger at sea. . . ." But those dark valleys did not discourage Paul. He writes in Romans 8, "Who will separate us from *the love of Christ?* Will hardship, or distress, or persecution, or famine, or nakedness, or peril, or sword? . . ." He answers his own questions, "No, *in* all these things [in these valleys] we are more than conquerors through him who loved us. For I am convinced that neither death, nor life, nor angels, nor rulers, nor things present, nor things to come, nor powers, nor height, nor depth, nor anything else in all creation, will be able to separate us from the love of God in Christ Jesus our Lord."[65]

The book of Revelation offers a marvelous picture of martyred Christians experiencing "the love of God in Christ Jesus our Lord." They find themselves in

---

62. Peter calls Jesus "the shepherd and guardian of your souls" (1 Pet 2:25).

63. Cf. Phil 4:7, "The peace of God, which surpasses all understanding, will *guard* your hearts and your minds in Christ Jesus."

64. 2 Cor 11:25–26.

65. Rom 8:35–39. Cf. 2 Tim 4:18, "The LORD will rescue me from every evil attack and save me for his heavenly kingdom. To him be the glory forever and ever. Amen."

heaven with God and the Lamb. We read in Revelation 7, "The one who is seated on the throne will shelter them. They will hunger no more, and thirst no more; *the sun will not strike them,* nor any scorching heat; for *the Lamb* at the center of the throne will be their *shepherd,* and *he will guide them to springs of the water of life,* and God will wipe away every tear from their eyes" (Rev 7:15–17).

But the journey of God's people does not end in heaven. Revelation 21 presents a picture of the final destination of our journey. John writes, "Then I saw *a new heaven and a new earth.* . . . And I heard a loud voice from the throne saying, 'See, the home of God is among mortals. He will dwell with them as their God; they will be his peoples, and *God himself will be with them;* he will wipe every tear from their eyes. *Death will be no more;* mourning and crying and pain will be no more, for the first things have passed away" (Rev 21:1–4). The new heaven and earth is the final destination of our journey through life. In Psalm 121 God promises, "The LORD will keep your going out and your coming in from this time on and forevermore." The New Testament affirms this. The LORD will keep and protect us throughout our earthly life "from this time on and forevermore."

Prayer[66]

Grant, Lord, that when we lift our eyes up to the hills in longing for your help,
we may hear and take to our hearts the promise of your unfailing care;
may we know that you are guarding us by day and night,
as we go out and come in,
and that whatever our share in the sufferings of the cross,
you are our shade and our Saviour,
now and forevermore. Amen.

Song[67]

1To the hills I lift my eyes;
    whence shall help for me arise?
From the Lord comes all my aid,
    who the heavens and earth has made.
He will guard through dangers all,
    will not let you slip or fall.
He who safe his people keeps
    never slumbers, never sleeps.

66. Eaton, *The Psalms,* 426.
67. Public Domain, *Psalter Hymnal* (1987), # 121; *Psalms for All Seasons,* # 121A; *Lift Up Your Hearts,* # 331.

2Your protector is the LORD;
    shade for you he will afford.
Neither sun nor moon shall smite;
    God shall guard by day and night.
He will ever keep your soul;
    what would harm he will control.
In the home and by the way
    God will keep you day by day.

CHAPTER 14

"Let Us Make a Joyful Noise to the Rock of Our Salvation"

Psalm 95 (94)

Psalm 95 in the Hebrew (MT), 94 in the Greek (LXX) and Latin (Vulgate), is known in the Christian tradition as the *Venite* (Latin for "come"), after the three Hebrew synonyms "come" [an invitation], "approach," and "enter" (95:1, 2, 6).[1] "From primitive times the Christian church has widely used this psalm . . . as a call and guide to worship."[2]

The *Revised Common Lectionary* assigns Psalm 95 for the third Sunday in Lent, Year A, as a response to the reading of Exodus 17:1–7. The latter passage records that Israel on its journey through the wilderness complained to Moses about the lack of water: "Why did you bring us out of Egypt, to kill us and our children and livestock with thirst?" Moses "called the place Massah [testing] and Meribah [contention], because the Israelites quarreled and tested the LORD, saying, 'Is the LORD among us or not?'" (Exod 17:3, 7). Psalm 95 refers to Massah and Meribah, warning later Israel not to put the LORD to the test (Ps 95:8–11). As such, the psalm is a fitting preaching text for Lent because it calls upon its readers to examine themselves whether they put God to the test.

Text and Context

Because Psalm 95 first calls God's people to worship the LORD (vv 1–7c) and next

---

1. Davidson, *Vitality of Worship,* 315.

2. Kidner, *Psalms 73–100,* 343. Cf. Leupold, *Exposition of the Psalms,* 675, "From days of old the church has always recognized that this psalm was an invitation to worship, witness its use in the Matins service, dating back even to the time of Athanasius and, for that matter, to the time of the ancient Jewish Church."

warns them not to test the LORD (vv 7d–11), some commentators believe that the psalm originally consisted of two separate psalms that were later brought together as one psalm.[3] Although it would be easier to formulate unified themes if we preached separate sermons on each section of the psalm (see Appendix 6, p. 582 below), the psalm as it is now found in the canon is a complete psalm, a literary unit,[4] and as such a proper preaching text.

To understand Psalm 95 in its canonical context, it can be compared to its neighboring psalms, especially psalms 96–100.[5] Limburg observes, "Psalm 95 is fitted carefully into its context. It is linked to Psalm 94 by the 'rock' picture in verse 1 (Ps 94:22; also 92:15). It is also tied to the 'kingship of the Lord' psalms with the king imagery (Pss 93:1; 96:10; 97:1; 98:6; 99:1)."[6] For preaching the specific message of this psalm, it is more important, of course, to note not what is similar but what is different in Psalm 95 from its neighboring psalms. That difference clearly is the sudden shift from the joy of worshiping God to the warning of the prophetic oracle in verses 7d–11.

We can also compare Psalm 95 to psalms that have a similar literary movement from call to worship to the exhortation to listen to God. Two other psalms have a similar movement: Psalms 50 and 81.[7] Again we ask, What is distinctive about Psalm 95? Both Psalms 50 and 81 end on positive notes[8] but Psalm 95 stops abruptly with God's judgment, "Therefore in my anger I swore, 'They shall not enter my rest.'" "This psalm leaves the people to ponder for themselves the dire consequences of disobedience."[9]

---

3. For an overview of commentators arguing for two psalms and those arguing for the original unity of this psalm, see Willem S. Prinsloo, "Psalm 95: If only you will listen to my voice!" in *The Bible in Human Society* (Sheffield: Sheffield Academic, 1995; pp. 393–410), 393–94.

4. Also, the verses 6 and 11 are linked by the use of the verb *bô'*: "O enter, let us worship," and, "They shall not enter my rest."

5. "It is possible that Psalms 95 and 100 are intended to serve as a frame around Psalms 96–99, the core of the enthronement collection (cf. 95:1–2, 6 with 100:1–2, 4; 95:7ab with 100:3)." McCann, "Psalms," 1061. Cf. Hossfeld, *Psalms 2*, 462, noting three functions of Psalm 95 in the context of Psalms 93–100.

6. Limburg, *Psalms*, 323.

7. See Hossfeld, *Psalms 2*, 459–60 on the "comparison of the three 'Festal Psalms' 50, 81, 95." For example, Psalm 81 also begins with a strong call to worship, followed by, "But my people did not listen to my voice; Israel would not submit to me" (Ps 81:11; cf. 81:8, 13, and compare with 95:7d).

8. Psalm 50:23 ends with, "to those who go the right way I will show the salvation of God." Psalm 81:16 concludes with, "with honey from the rock I would satisfy you."

9. Davidson, *Vitality of Worship*, 316. Cf. Prinsloo, "Psalm 95," 405, "Psalm 95 ends so abruptly that we can talk of an open ending where the readers / listeners must decide for themselves what else is going to happen."

Since the psalm mentions Massah and Meribah, Exodus 17:1–7 must obviously be taken into account.[10] Other psalms and the prophets may also shed light on certain concepts in Psalm 95.[11] And for Christian preaching the New Testament is part of the context.

Literary Interpretation

Bernhard Anderson identifies the form of Psalm 95 as a hymn.[12] This is a good classification for the verses 1–7c, but the hymn is unique in that it is followed by a prophetic oracle (vv 7d–11).

To enter into the meaning of the psalm, we shall again investigate in turn the psalm's parallelisms, its imagery, repetition of keywords, and its structure.

Parallelisms[13]

The hymn begins with impressive climactic parallelism (vv 1–2), followed by advancing parallelism in verse 3 and another climactic parallelism in verses 4–5. Verse 6 has advancing parallelism while verse 7a–c returns to climactic. Verse 7d begins climactic parallelism which turns into climactic antithetic parallelism in verses 8–9. Verse 10 exhibits climactic parallelism and verse 11 advancing.

₁O come, let us sing to the LORD;	A
let us make a joyful noise to the rock of our salvation!	+ A'
₂Let us come into his presence with thanksgiving;	+ A''
let us make a joyful noise to him with songs of praise!	+ A'''
₃For the LORD is a great God,	B
and a great King above all gods.	+ B'
₄In his hand are the depths of the earth;	C
the heights of the mountains are his also.	+ C'
₅The sea is his, for he made it,	+ C''
and the dry land, which his hands have formed.	+ C'''

10. Cf. McCann, *Theological Introduction,* 47, who argues for a background of Exodus 14–17.

11. For example, "the God of Israel is both creator and shepherd (the strongest parallels to this dual role for Yahweh are found in Second-Isaiah, e.g., 43:1, 15; see also Deut 32:6 and Ps 100:3). For v 7abc, note the similarity with Jer 31:33 [the new covenant]. For the shepherd concept, see Pss 23:1; 80:2; 100:3; Isa 40:11; John 10:11–14." Tate, *Psalms 51–100,* 501.

12. B. Anderson, *Out of the Depths,* 222.

13. For the internal parallelism of each line (*a b b' a'*, etc.) see Prinsloo, "Psalm 95," 397–406.

₆O come, let us worship and bow down,	A
let us kneel before the LORD, our Maker!	+ A'
₇For he is our God,	B
and we are the people of his pasture,	+ B'
and the sheep of his hand.¹⁴	+ B''
O that today you would listen to his voice!	A
₈Do not harden your hearts, as at Meribah,¹⁵	– A'
as on the day at Massah in the wilderness,	+– A''
₉when your ancestors tested me,	+– A'''
and put me to the proof, though they had seen my work.	+– A''''
₁₀For forty years I loathed that generation and said,	B
"They are a people whose hearts go astray,	+ B'
and they do not regard my ways."	+ B''
₁₁Therefore in my anger I swore,	C
"They shall not enter my rest."	+ C'

Imagery

As in Psalm 121 (p. 298 above), this psalm uses the poetic device of merism, naming a pair of opposites to include the whole: "the depths of the earth" and "the heights of the mountains," "the sea" and "the dry land" (vv 4–5). These four opposites are framed by the inclusio "in his hand" and "his hands" (anthropomorphisms, vv 4a and 5b). The combination of the inclusio and the merisms declares that the LORD made everything, vertically from low to high, and horizontally from the sea to the dry land and everything in between.

The three words translated "O come!" (v 1, imperative), "Let us come" (v 2, jussive), and "O come!" (v 6, imperative) are actually three different Hebrew verbs. Verse 1 uses the verb *hālak* "to come," verse 2 *qiddēm* "let us come / approach," and verse 6 uses the verb *bô'*, "to enter." The latter, *bô'*, is also used in verse 11: "They shall not enter my rest." "This suggests that both halves [vv 1–7c, 7d–11] are using the theme of travel and journey."¹⁶

---

14. This is a close call with synonymous parallelism, but I decided on advancing parallelism resulting here in climactic parallelism because "the sheep *of his hand*" is much more personal than the foregoing line "the people of his pasture." The LORD holds us in his hand as he does the universe (vv 4–5).

15. Antithetic parallelism supported in the following three lines by advancing antithetic parallelisms.

16. Massouh, "Psalm 95," *TrinJ* 4 (1983; pp. 84–88): 87. See also Tate, *Psalms 51–100*, 501; Kraus, *Psalms 60–150*, 246; and Mays, *Psalms*, 305.

Psalm 95 retraces the major stations on a pilgrimage to the temple.[17] As the procession is moving toward the temple complex, the pilgrims encourage each other, "O come, let us sing to the LORD; let us make a joyful noise to the rock of our salvation!" (v 1). As they enter the Court of the Gentiles, they spur each other on, "Let us come into his presence with thanksgiving; let us make a joyful noise to him with songs of praise!" (v 2). Finally they arrive at the gate that will bring them as close to the Holy Place as they are allowed, the Court of the Women and the Court of Israel. They encourage each other to enter with reverence: "O come [enter!], let us worship and bow down, let us kneel before the LORD, our Maker!" (v 6).

As the pilgrims lie prostrate they hear the voice of a priest or cultic prophet saying: "O that today you would listen to his [the LORD's] voice!" (v 7d). Then comes the LORD's message, "Do not harden your hearts, as at Meribah. . . . In my anger I swore, 'They shall not enter my rest'" (vv 8–11).

In addition to this underlying picture of a processional to the temple, the psalm uses several metaphors. God is called "the rock of our salvation" (v 1). Nineteen times the psalms speak of God as a "rock." In the context of this psalm with its reference to Meribah and Massah in the wilderness, the rock probably refers to the rock at Horeb through which God provided water for thirsty Israel (Exod 17:6).[18] When God is called a rock it "denotes God's reliability and stability,"[19] the safety and security he provides.[20]

"Let us come into his presence with singing" (v 2) is literally "come before his face" — an anthropomorphic metaphor meaning to come into God's presence. The verses 4–5 use another anthropomorphic metaphor: "In his *hand* are the depths of the earth. . . . the dry land, which his *hands* have formed." This metaphor stresses the greatness of God (see v 3) and his creative power. Verse 7 again uses the anthropomorphic metaphor "hand," this time in combination with another metaphor, "we are the people of his *pasture*, and the sheep of his *hand*." Actually, this verse contains two mixed metaphors since regular metaphors would have been, "we are his people, and the sheep of his pasture"

17. It is not likely that they would have sung parts of this psalm at the different stations. Rather, as they sang the whole psalm, they would have been reminded of their pilgrimage as the procession moved through these different stations.

18. G. Henton Davies, "Psalm 95," *ZAW* 85, no. 2 (1973; pp. 183–95): 189–90, argues, however, that "it is not too much to claim that 'Rock' has a reference to Jerusalem, and to that great Rock, formerly beneath either the Holy of Holies or the altar of burnt offering, and still to be seen under the great shrine in Jerusalem."

19. Hayes, *Preaching the New Common Lectionary, Year A: Lent . . .* , 45. Cf. A. Anderson, *Psalms 73–150*, 677.

20. Prinsloo, "Psalm 95," 397.

(Ps 100:3). In any case, the mixed metaphor "we are the people of his pasture, and the sheep of his hand" refers to "God's guidance and sustaining care of Israel."[21] It links right up with the earlier metaphor of the LORD being "a great King" (v 3).[22]

Finally, the prophetic oracle employs two major metaphors. The first is, "Do not *harden* your *hearts*" (v 8). "Heart" is a metaphor for the core of our being. The "heart" motivates our actions.[23] To "harden your hearts" is to decide not to obey God. "The 'hardened' heart is one without living relationship to the Lord, no longer hearing, attentive, trusting, centred on his will, but rather awake only to immediate desires and impulses."[24]

The second metaphor is "rest": "They shall not enter my *rest*" (v 11). With the psalm's reference to Israel's wilderness journey, the "rest" originally referred to entry into the Promised Land.[25] But in connection with the pilgrimage to Jerusalem, the rest in Psalm 95 can now also refer to the rest experienced in God's presence at the temple, for in verse 6 the pilgrims were invited to "enter" (*bô'*) into the LORD's presence while in verse 11 they are warned that if they harden their hearts, like their forefathers, "they shall not enter (*bô'*) my rest."[26] In either case, "rest" in God's Promised Land or "rest" in God's presence in his temple, "rest" is a state of not being threatened by enemies and being secure, safe, at peace in God's presence.[27] The author of Hebrews, after quoting Psalm 95, will later move from rest on earth to eternal rest: "So then, a sabbath rest still remains for the people of God" (Heb 4:9).

---

21. Brown, *Seeing the Psalms*, 151.

22. As Mays, *Psalms*, 306, points out, "The shepherd image used to interpret the relation of God to people is far more than a lovely pastoral metaphor. It is a royal image of the relation of a king to those he rules and portrays his role as leader, provider, and protector." Cf. Tanner in deClaissé-Walford, Jacobson, and Tanner, *The Book of Psalms*, 717, "The notion of shepherd here is more than a metaphor. In the ancient Near Eastern context, it is a title that means the same as king."

23. "Let your heart hold fast my words; keep my commandments, and live. . . . Keep your heart with all vigilance, for from it flow the springs of life." Proverbs 4:4, 23.

24. Eaton, *The Psalms*, 338.

25. "Not one of you shall come into the land in which I swore to settle you, except Caleb son of Jephunneh and Joshua son of Nun" (Num 14:30). Cf. Deut 12:9, "For you have not yet come into the rest and the possession that the LORD your God is giving you."

26. Cf. Psalm 132:13–14, "For the LORD has chosen Zion; he has desired it for his habitation: 'This is my resting place forever.'"

27. Cf. Deut 12:10, "When he [the LORD] gives you rest from your enemies all around so that you live in safety." Cf. Deut 25:19.

Repetition of Keywords

Although Psalm 95 repeats the name *Yahweh* only three times, together with its synonyms and pronouns *Yahweh* is referred to twenty-six times (see "Theocentric Interpretation," pp. 323–24 below).

Four times the hymn calls God's people to use their voices and instruments to praise the LORD: "let us sing," "make a joyful noise," "come into his presence with thanksgiving," and "make a joyful noise" (vv 1–2). This is followed in verse 6 with three more calls to display submission to the great King with bodily postures: "let us worship," "bow down," and "kneel." Thus the hymn has a perfect seven calls for worshiping the LORD with our whole being.

The hymn also mentions God's "hand(s)" twice to underscore that God's hands made all that exists (vv 4–5) and repeats "his hand" in verse 7 to indicate that the same great Creator God elected his people Israel from among the nations, made a covenant with them, and has them in "his hand."

Structure

Scholars are not agreed on the structure of Psalm 95. Some say it "consists of 2 or 3 or even 4 or 5 parts,"[28] though most would opt for two or three stanzas. For example, the NASB and ESV have two stanzas, verses 1–5 and 6–11, while the NRSV and NIV have three stanzas, verses 1–5, 6–7c, and 7d–11. It may be helpful again to begin with the typical pattern of a hymn. As we noted in Chapter 1, p. 11, a hymn usually consists of most of the following elements:

1) A call to praise the Lord
2) Transition (*kî,* for, because)
3) Reasons why the Lord is to be praised
4) Conclusion: Praise the Lord!

Psalm 95 has three of these elements twice in succession:

1) A call to praise the Lord	Ps 95:1–2
2) Transition (*kî,* for, because)	Ps 95:3a
3) Reason why the Lord is to be praised "For the LORD is a great God"	Ps 95:3–5

---

28. Davies, "Psalm 95," *ZAW* 85, no. 2 (1973): 187. See pp. 183–87 for a review of many commentators.

1) A call to praise the Lord   Ps 95:6
2) Transition (*kî*, for, because)   Ps 95:7a
3) Reason why the Lord is to be praised   Ps 95:7a-c
   "For the LORD is our God"

This double hymn is followed by a different form, a prophetic oracle (vv 7d–11). "Whereas the psalm began by urging people to make a noise, v 7d tells them to listen. Whereas vv 1–7c were an exhortation in which the speaker identified with the addressees ('Let us . . .'), in v 7d the speaker stands over against the addressees."[29] The psalm, therefore, has either two (vv 1–7c and 7d–11)[30] or three stanzas.

If we consider the double hymn as two stanzas, verses 1–5 and 6–7c,[31] the oracle (verses 7d–11) forms a final stanza, for a total of three stanzas. This division finds support in the number of lines in each stanza: the first stanza has a full ten lines, the second five lines, and the third again a full ten lines. "Setting out its twenty-five lines as 10 + 5 + 10 displays clearly both its symmetry and its keywords: sing, bow, hear."[32]

We can therefore outline the structure of Psalm 95, along with the NRSV and NIV, as three stanzas:

I. Make a joyful noise to the rock of our salvation, the great Creator God (vv 1–5)
II. Bow (submit) to the LORD, our Maker and Shepherd (vv 6–7c)
III. Listen today to his voice or you shall not enter his rest (vv 7d–11)

Theocentric Interpretation

From beginning to end Psalm 95 is centered on God. This short psalm uses the name LORD (3×), God (2×), as well as rock, King, and Maker. The first stanza begins with "O come, let us sing to the LORD; . . . the *rock* of our salvation! Let us come into his [the LORD's] presence . . . ; let us make a joyful noise to him [the LORD]. . . . For the LORD is a great *God,* and a great *King* above all gods. In his

29. Goldingay, *Psalms,* III, 89.

30. Stek, *NIV Study Bible,* Ps 95 n. has an interesting variation, similar to the NASB and the ESV: "The psalm is composed of two parts: (1) a call to praise the Lord of all the earth (vv 1–5); (2) a call to acknowledge by submissive attitude and obedient heart the Lord's kingship over his people (vv 6–11)."

31. See Prinsloo's arguments that vv 1–5 are "a complete stanza" and that "v 6 introduces a new stanza." "Psalm 95," 399.

32. Wilcock, *Message of Psalms 73–150,* 93.

[the Lord's] hand are the depths of the earth; the heights of the mountains are his [the Lord's] also. The sea is his [the Lord's], for he [the Lord] made it, and the dry land, which his [the Lord's] hands have formed. . . ."

Stanza 2 continues, "O come, . . . let us kneel before the Lord, our *Maker!* For he [the Lord] is our *God*, and we are the people of his [the Lord's] pasture, and the sheep of his [the Lord's] hand."

Stanza 3 begins with, "O that today you would listen to his [the Lord's] voice!" And then the Lord begins to speak through a priest. The Lord reminds Israel that their "ancestors tested me [the Lord], and put me [the Lord] to the proof, though they had seen my [the Lord's] work. For forty years I [the Lord] loathed that generation and said, . . . 'they do not regard my [the Lord's] ways.' Therefore in my [the Lord's] anger I [the Lord] swore, 'They shall not enter my [the Lord's] rest.'"

Textual Theme and Goal

As indicated earlier, the formulation of a single textual theme is complicated by the fact that Psalm 95 sends one message in the hymn and a different message in the prophetic oracle.[33] How do we merge two different themes into a single textual theme? It may be best to formulate the theme of each of the three stanzas and then see how we can unite them into a single theme. Stanza 1 (vv 1–5) presents the theme, "Make a joyful noise to the rock of our salvation, the great Creator God." Stanza 2 (vv 6–7c) expands on that theme with the message, "Bow down (submit) to the Lord, our Maker." Finally, stanza 3 (vv 7d–11) presents the theme, "If you do not listen to (obey) the Lord's voice, you shall not enter his rest." Can we find an overarching theme that covers all three? Or is one of the three themes dominant? It appears that the theme of stanza 1 is indeed dominant,[34] so that we can subordinate to it the themes of stanzas 2 and 3. The theme of the whole psalm, therefore, is, *Make a joyful noise to the rock of our salvation, submitting to him not only in worship but in your whole life.*[35]

---

33. One could, of course, avoid this difficulty by preaching two sermons on this psalm, respectively the verses 1–7c and 7d–11 (see Appendix 6, p. 582 below), but we have chosen to demonstrate preaching a single sermon on the whole psalm.

34. Cf. A. Anderson, *Psalms 73–150*, 677, "The main themes of the Psalm are the kingship of Yahweh, his ownership of the world because he had created it, his care for the Covenant people, and the responsibilities of those who are in a Covenant relationship with him."

35. "Psalm 95 is set up such that the entrance into the temple (and into God's rest) requires a proper relationship between word (vv 1–2) and deed (v 6). This relationship is contrasted to the 'improper' worship of their ancestors whose words at Meribah (Exod 17:2) and *mis*deeds (Exod

As to its goal, "the *Sitz im Leben* of the Psalm seems to be the entry of the worshippers into the Temple courts (cf. verses 2 and 6) during the [Feast of Tabernacles or New Year] festival."[36] With its imperatives and jussives this psalm seeks *to urge Israel to make a joyful noise to the rock of their salvation, submitting to him not only in worship but in their whole life.*[37]

Ways to Preach Christ

There is neither a promise nor an obvious type of Christ in Psalm 95. One way to move from this psalm to Christ in the New Testament is to use Hebrews 3:7–11, which quotes the whole third stanza (vv 7c–11) and links the warning to Christ: "But exhort one another every day, as long as it is called 'today,' so that none of you may be hardened by the deceitfulness of sin. For we have become partners of *Christ,* if only we hold our first confidence firm to the end" (Heb 3:13–14). However, this move is probably too complicated for a sermon on Psalm 95 since it would involve explaining the complex argumentation in Hebrews 3–4 which would shift the focus away from the psalm.[38] A better way for preaching Christ from this psalm is redemptive-historical progression supported by New Testament references.

17:7) evoked the word/deed response of God: "Therefore in my anger I *swore,* 'They shall not enter my rest'" (v 11)." Renz, "Come, Let Us Listen to the Voice of the Lord!" *Worship* 70, no. 2 (1996; pp. 140–53): 147. Cf. Goldingay, *Psalms,* III, 94, "The enthusiasm [in worship] concerns Yhwh's being king, and such liturgical submission to Yahweh as king presupposes that it is a liturgical expression of a submission in everyday life." Cf. Alter, *Book of Psalms,* 337 n. 8, "Perhaps the implicit connection with the acclaiming of God's kingship in the first part of the poem is that Israel can authentically recognize God as king only by obedience to His commands."

36. A. Anderson, *Psalms 73–150,* 677. Anderson continues, "Whether the different parts of the Psalm were sung by different choirs, groups, or solo singer(s) is a matter of conjecture, although some such procedure seems likely (cf. Sir. 50:16ff.)." On the divergent opinions about dating the psalm, see Prinsloo, "Psalm 95," 396.

37. Cf. Prinsloo, "Psalm 95," 406, "In opposition to all the praiseworthy things that Yahweh has done (stanza 1 and 2) we have the contemptible behaviour of Yahweh's people. The rhetorical function of this contrast and consequently of the whole psalm is to warn the readers/listeners and convince them that their association with Yahweh should not be taken for granted."

38. Cf. Ronald Cox, "The New Testament Preaches the Psalms," in *Performing the Psalms,* ed. Dave Bland and David Fleer (St. Louis: Chalice, 2005; pp. 83–104), 91, "The author focuses on three concepts: the consequences of an unbelieving (or 'hardened') heart; a reworking of the meaning of 'rest'; and an encouragement to enter that rest 'today' by means of faithfulness. His argumentation is complex, as it does not progress point by point but moves about in something of a circular fashion." See Simon Kistemaker, *The Psalm Citations in the Epistle to the Hebrews* (Amsterdam: Wed. G. van Soest, 1961), 108–16.

Redemptive-Historical Progression with New Testament References

Since Psalm 95 has two distinct forms (a double hymn and a prophetic oracle) and three distinct messages, it seems best to move to Christ in the New Testament first from each of the hymns and later in the sermon from the prophetic oracle. Beginning with the first stanza, the psalm urges God's people to "make a joyful noise to the rock of our salvation" (v 1). In Old Testament times "the rock of our salvation" probably referred to the rock at Horeb through which God provided water for thirsty Israel and thus saved them (Exod 17:6). In New Testament times Jesus Christ becomes "the rock of our salvation" to whom we ought to make a joyful noise. We can support this claim with a reference to John 4:10–14[39] (see "Sermon Exposition" below).

The second stanza urges us to submit to God the Shepherd (v 7). In New Testament times we ought to submit not only to God the Father but also to his Son, who called himself "the good Shepherd." We can support this claim with references to John 10:11, 27–30; Ephesians 5:18–20, and perhaps Revelation 5:11–12 (see "Sermon Exposition" below).

The last stanza of Psalm 95 encourages us to *listen* to God's voice, that is, to *obey* God's voice. God warns us not to harden our hearts as Israel did in the desert. Because they tested God, they failed to enter God's rest in the Promised Land. In the New Testament Jesus also warns us that we will not enter the kingdom of heaven if we fail to respond obediently to his Word (Matt 7:21). But the good news is that Jesus came for sinners and paid for our sins. He promised to give us "rest" if we will come to him. Moreover, he said, "Anyone who hears my word and believes him who sent me has eternal life, and does not come under judgment" (John 5:24). We can support these moves with references to Matthew 7:21–27; Mark 2:17; Matthew 11:28–29; John 5:24; and perhaps Hebrews 4:9, 11 (see "Sermon Exposition" below).

Sermon Theme, Goal, and Need

We formulated the textual theme of Psalm 95 as, "Make a joyful noise to the rock of our salvation, submitting to him not only in worship but in your whole life." Since the New Testament does not contradict this theme but expands "the

---

39. We could perhaps also support this move with typology, but this gets rather complicated for a sermon. "The rock of our salvation" may be understood as a type of Christ. See 1 Cor 10:4, Our ancestors "all drank the same spiritual drink. For they drank from the spiritual rock that followed them, and the rock was Christ."

rock of our salvation" to include Jesus Christ, the textual theme can become the sermon theme (changing "your" to the more inclusive "our"): *Make a joyful noise to the rock of our salvation, submitting to him not only in worship but in our whole life.*

We formulated the textual goal as, "to urge Israel to make a joyful noise to the rock of their salvation, submitting to him not only in worship but in their whole life." With slight modifications ("Israel" to "God's people," "their" to "our") the original goal of Psalm 95 can also become the sermon goal: *to urge God's people to make a joyful noise to the rock of our salvation, submitting to him not only in worship but in our whole life.* This goal points to the need addressed in this psalm and the sermon: we tend to fail to worship God enthusiastically and/or to submit to him in our whole life.

Liturgy, Scripture Reading, PowerPoint, and Sermon Outline

Psalm 95 verses 1–2 or 6–7 can be used as a call to worship. For Scripture reading, making use of different voices will enhance the understanding of the psalm:

> *Congregation:* "O come, let us sing to the LORD . . ." (vv 1–2).[40]
> *The liturgist:* "For the LORD is a great God . . ." (vv 3–5).
> *Congregation:* "O come, let us worship and bow down . . ." (v 6).
> *The liturgist:* "For he is our God . . ." (v 7a-c). *Pause:* "O that today . . . (v 7d).
> *A deep bass voice:* "Do not harden your hearts . . ." (vv 8–11).

PowerPoint can show the verses being explained. It will also be very helpful for the congregation to see a diagram of the temple complex, especially the Court of the Gentiles, the Court of the Women, and the Court of Israel (men), so that they can better understand the procession reflected in Psalm 95 (see p. 331 below). The sermon outline can follow the three stanzas with links to Christ at the end of each stanza.

    I. Make a joyful noise to the rock of our salvation, the great Creator God (vv 1–5)
    II. Bow down (submit) to the LORD, our Maker and Shepherd (vv 6–7c)
    III. Today listen to (obey) his voice, or you shall not enter his rest (vv 7d–11)

---

40. "In terms of liturgical functioning, we may say, the first person plural ['let us'] probably indicates the whole community speaking, or else a functionary in the name of the congregation." Gerstenberger, *Psalms*, II, 183.

Sermon Exposition

The sermon introduction can focus attention on the need addressed in this sermon by illustrating how our worship of God is often routine and/or how we may appear to submit to God in worship on Sunday but fail to obey God in our daily life. Psalm 95 would spark new, God-honoring zest into our worship as well as into our daily living.

This psalm with its three stanzas is all about worship. Pilgrims from far and wide would travel to Jerusalem on major feast days to worship God at his temple. This psalm reminds them of the major stations on their pilgrimage. Verse 1 reminds them of coming near to the temple complex. The pilgrims encouraged each other, "O come, let us sing to the LORD; let us make a joyful noise to the rock of our salvation!"

The Hebrew has, "O come, let us sing to Yahweh." Yahweh is the great I AM who led Israel out of slavery in Egypt. He led them through the Sea and at Mount Sinai made a covenant with them. "Let us sing to Yahweh," our faithful covenant God.

"Let us make a joyful noise to the rock of our salvation!" "A joyful noise" is the exuberant, noisy shouting that is heard when a king or president visits a city.[41] In this case the pilgrims have come to visit their heavenly King at the temple, God's palace on earth. And they encourage each other: "Let us make a joyful noise[42] to the rock of our salvation!" They call their King "the rock of our salvation." In the Bible God is often called a "rock." When you hear the word "rock," think of the rock of Gibraltar, or the rock of Masada. A rock is a fortress — solid, stable, a place of refuge and safety. Here God is called "the rock of our *salvation.*" The LORD is the rock who saves us.

In the context of this psalm "the rock" probably refers to the rock at Mount Horeb. Long ago, as Israel was traveling from Egypt through the wilderness to the Promised Land, they camped at a place called Rephidim. But they could not find any water there. Without water they would all die. So they began to quarrel with Moses. They said to him, "Why did you bring us out of Egypt, to kill us and our children and livestock with thirst?" (Exod 17:3). Then the LORD said to

---

41. Kraus, *Psalms 60–150*, 246. Cf. Eaton, *The Psalms*, 338, "The verb in vv 1b and 2b (corresponding to the noun tərû'â, 33:3; 47:5; 89:15) refers to the acclamations with voice and instruments for the God manifest in triumphant glory."

42. "Before making ourselves small before Him (as we must, v 6f.) we greet Him here with unashamed enthusiasm as our refuge and rescuer (v 1). The full-throated cries urged in the verbs of verses 1 and 2 suggest an acclamation fit for a king who is saviour of his people. . . . We address one another to make sure that we rise to the occasion, not drifting into His courts preoccupied and apathetic." Kidner, *Psalms 73–150*, 344.

Moses, "Go on ahead of the people . . . ; take in your hand the staff with which you struck the Nile, and go. I will be standing there in front of you on the rock at Horeb. Strike the rock, and water will come out of it, so that the people may drink" (Exod 17:5–6). Moses did so and life-giving water came out of the rock. By providing water from the rock, the LORD saved Israel from certain death. "Let us make a joyful noise to the rock of our salvation!" The rock who saved us from certain death.

Today the rock of our salvation is Jesus Christ.[43] Jesus gives us "living water." When Jesus met a Samaritan woman at a well, he said to her, "Everyone who drinks of this water will be thirsty again, but those who drink of the water that I will give them will never be thirsty. The water that I will give will become in them a spring of water gushing up to *eternal life*" (John 4:10–14). The rock of our salvation is Jesus Christ. He provides us with eternal life. So yes, "Let us make a joyful noise to the rock of our salvation!"

As the pilgrims come closer to the temple, they first enter the outer court called the Court of the Gentiles. Gentiles as well as Jews were allowed in this Court. This is the place where Jesus would later overthrow the tables of the money changers (Matt 21:12). Again the pilgrims encourage each other, verse 2, "Let us come into his presence with thanksgiving; let us make a joyful noise to him with songs of praise!"

"Let us come into his presence with thanksgiving." The Hebrew reads literally, "Let us come before *his face* with thanksgiving." "The reference to the LORD's 'face' underlines the reality of the meeting; it is as if we actually see the LORD, look into the LORD's eyes, catch sight of the LORD's smile."[44] The pilgrims are actually going to meet the LORD. So they spur each other on, "Let us come into his presence with thanksgiving."[45] We have so much for which to thank the LORD: the LORD made us; the LORD sustains us; the LORD provides for us; the LORD saves us. You fill in the blanks why we should come into the LORD's presence "with thanksgiving." And then the psalm repeats, "let us make a *joyful noise* to him with songs of praise!" Let's begin our worship with a joyful noise.

Why? Verse 3 begins to answer that question, "For the LORD is a great God, and a great King above all gods."[46] "The ancient pagan world had different gods for

---

43. See e.g., 1 Cor 10:4, "All drank the same spiritual drink. For they drank from the spiritual rock that followed them, and the rock was Christ," and 1 Peter 2:4, "Come to him, a living stone, though rejected by mortals yet chosen and precious in God's sight."

44. Goldingay, *Psalms*, III, 91 (I have changed four references from *Yhwh* to "the LORD").

45. Alter, *Book of Psalms*, 335, notes that "some interpreters think it refers here to the thanksgiving sacrifice" but argues against this notion because of "the strong poetic parallelism with 'songs.'"

46. "This way of speaking about a god belonged to the polytheistic culture in which Israel

---

different peoples, different geographical areas, different cosmic regions (heaven, earth, netherworld) and different aspects of life (e.g., war, fertility, crafts)."[47] But Yahweh, "the LORD is a great God,[48] and a great King above all gods."

Verses 4–5 go on to describe how great Yahweh really is. Verse 4, "In his hand are the depths of the earth; the heights of the mountains are his also." Try to imagine God's almighty hand. In that almighty hand are "the depths of the earth."[49] Go down as deep as you possibly can, and you can never escape God's almighty hand. Go as high as you can, to the highest mountains. There, too, you will find God's almighty hand.[50] God holds in his almighty hand everything on earth, from the depths of the earth to the heights of the mountains and everything in between.

In ancient times people believed that other powers controlled the depths of the earth.[51] No, the psalm declares: that is God's territory! People also believed that their gods lived on the mountain heights, close to heaven.[52] Wrong again, the psalm says. "The heights of the mountains are his also." The psalm declares "that nothing is beyond the reach of God. Whether one descends to the Dead Sea or ascends to Mount Hermon, God is still king there. . . . God's sovereignty knows no geographical limitations."[53]

From the vertical dimensions of depths and heights, verse 5 moves to the horizontal dimensions[54] of the sea and the dry land: "The sea is his, for he made it, and the dry land, which his hands have formed." In the beginning God made the sea and the dry land (Gen 1:9–10). Therefore both sea and dry land are his. God is King of the universe because he made all things.

Notice that verse 4 begins with God's hand, "In his *hand* are the depths of the earth," and verse 5 ends with God's hands, "the dry land, which his *hands*

---

existed, and it was one way for faith to reason in that culture (see Exod 15:11; Pss 96:4; 97:9; 136:2). In the pantheons of the ancient Near East, one god was believed to be supreme and to rule over others. His superiority and kingship were based on his actions as creator (see 24:1–2)." Mays, *Psalms*, 305.

47. Stek, *NIV Study Bible n.* 95:3–5.

48. "God is here *'ēl,* a term the Canaanites used to describe the top god in their pantheon, whom they would not identify with Yhwh, but Israel knows Yhwh *is* the great God." Goldingay, *Psalms,* III, 92.

49. "The Hebrew for 'depths' is not the ordinary *tǝhōmōt* but the more unusual *meḥqərê,* which by etymology means 'the utmost reaches that can be searched out.'" Alter, *Book of Psalms,* 336 n. 4.

50. Cf. Psalm 139:8, "If I ascend to heaven, you are there; if I make my bed in Sheol, you are there."

51. Cf. Weiser, *The Psalms,* 626, with references to Pss 6:5; 30:9; 88:10f.; 115:17; and Amos 9:2.

52. Ibid., with references to Pss 68:15f.; 89:12.

53. Massouh, "Psalm 95," *TrinJ* 4 (1983): 85.

54. Ibid.

have formed." The whole world — from the depths of the earth to the heights of the mountains, and from the sea to the dry land — the whole world is enclosed by God's hands.[55] Long before we learned the popular song, the psalmist was singing, "He's got the *whole* world in his hands!" That explains why the LORD is called "a great God, and a great King above all gods" (v 3). And that is why we have to "come into his presence with thanksgiving" and "make a joyful noise to him with songs of praise!" (v 2).

The second stanza of this psalm begins at verse 6. It opens with a second call to worship. It assumes that the pilgrims have now come to the gate of the Court of Women and the Court of Israel (men). Gentiles were forbidden to enter that gate. Archeologists have discovered a sign dating to about 31 A.D. that warns Gentiles: "Whoever is caught [going beyond the barrier] will have himself to blame that his death ensues."[56] But Israelite men and women were allowed to come closer to the Holy Place of God's presence by entering the Court of Women and the Court of Israel (see diagram below).

COURT OF THE GENTILES

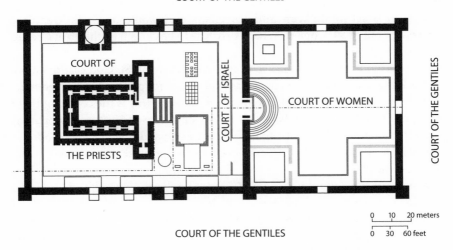

COURT OF THE GENTILES

Verse 6, "O come, let us worship and bow down, let us kneel before the LORD, our Maker!" The "O come" here is literally "enter"[57] — enter the gate leading to

55. "The repetition of 'his hand(s)', in vv 4a, 5b has the literary effect of surrounding the elements of the cosmos with references to God's hands. Structure reinforces content; that is, the whole world is in God's hands (see Pss 24:1–2; 138:7–8)." McCann, "Psalms," 1061. Cf. Psalm 139:7–12, "Where can I go from your spirit? . . ."

56. www.bible-archeology.com/2012/12.

57. "'Come in' is now the verb *bô'*, which in contrast to 'come on' [v 1] is an exhortation that

God's presence! Like verses 1–2, this "O come" is followed by three things to do. But whereas verses 1–2 called for "let us *sing* to the LORD; let us *make a joyful noise* to the rock of our salvation! Let us come into his presence *with thanksgiving*," verse 6 calls for quite different actions: "let us *worship* and *bow down*, let us *kneel* before the LORD, our Maker!" "All three verbs in verse 6, 'worship . . . bow down . . . kneel,' point to the physical act of submission."[58] This is not a time for a joyful noise but a time for humble submission. "Instead of rejoicing, the worshiper[s] [are] now reverent. Instead of using vocal and musical instruments, the believer[s] [are] using body language — kneeling, bowing — to convey reverence."[59]

Why should we show such humble submission before God? Verse 6 already answers that question when it calls the LORD "our Maker." Of course we should show reverence when we meet no one less than our *Maker*. Verse 7 expands even more on that answer: "For he is our God, and we are the people of his pasture, and the sheep of his hand." This is covenant language.[60] At Mount Sinai God told Israel, "You have seen what I did to the Egyptians, and how I bore you on eagles' wings and brought you to myself. Now therefore, if you *obey my voice and keep my covenant,* you shall be my treasured possession out of all the peoples" (Exod 19:4–5). If Israel would keep God's covenant, they would be God's "treasured possession out of all peoples." What a privilege to be chosen by the great Creator God as his special people!

Unfortunately, Israel failed to keep God's covenant. So God cast them out of the Promised Land into exile in Babylon. But through the prophet Jeremiah God promised to make a new covenant with Israel: "This is the covenant that I will make with the house of Israel after those days, says the LORD: I will put my law within them, and I will write it on their hearts; and *I will be their God, and they shall be my people*" (Jer 31:33). Notice how this promise is reflected in Psalm 95:7, "For he is our God, and we are the people of his pasture." Notice also how personal is this relationship between God and us: "*he* is *our* God, and *we* are the people of *his* pasture, and the sheep of *his* hand."

At the end of verse 7 God's "hand" is mentioned again. Verse 4 began with God's hand: "In his *hand* are the depths of the earth." Verse 5 ended with God's hands: "the dry land, which his *hands* have formed." The whole world is in his

---

suggests movement, and specifically movement into a sanctuary (96:8; 100:2, 4; Joel 1:13; Amos 4:4)." Goldingay, *Psalms,* III, 93. Cf. Hossfeld, *Psalms 2,* 461, "In the second section (vv 6–7b) the event of entry into the Temple is described."

58. Davidson, *Vitality of Worship,* 315. Although church architecture, following that of the synagogue, does not always allow for the physical act of kneeling, instead of literally kneeling it is more important that our attitude be one of humble submission.

59. Massouh, "Psalm 95," *TrinJ* 4 (1983): 85.

60. "This verse is a variation of the Covenant formula." A. Anderson, *Psalms 73–150,* 679.

hands. Now verse 7 adds that we are also in "his hand." We are "the sheep of his hand." The Creator of the universe holds us in his almighty hand. There is no safer place in the universe. God the Creator is our great Shepherd. God is sovereign over us. He is our King.[61] That's why we humbly submit ourselves to our great Shepherd and worship him with awe and reverence.

In the New Testament, Jesus calls himself "the good shepherd." Jesus said, "The good shepherd lays down his life for the sheep" (John 10:11). Jesus laid down his life on Good Friday. He died so that we might become God's people. When we come together for worship, therefore, we humbly submit ourselves not only to God the Father but also to his Son Jesus Christ, our good Shepherd and King. Jesus said, "My sheep hear my voice. I know them, and they follow me. I give them eternal life, and they will never perish. No one will snatch them out of my *hand*. What my Father has given me is greater than all else, and no one can snatch it out of the *Father's hand*. The Father and I are one" (John 10:27–30).

So in our worship we make a joyful noise and submit ourselves to the Father and his Son who are one. Paul confirms this when he writes to the Ephesians, "Be filled with the Spirit, as you sing psalms and hymns and spiritual songs among yourselves, singing and making melody to the Lord in your hearts, giving thanks to *God the Father* at all times and for everything in the name of our *Lord Jesus Christ*" (5:18–20).[62]

As we come together, then, to worship God in his sanctuary, Psalm 95 encourages us in the first two stanzas to make a joyful noise to God and to humbly submit ourselves to God.[63] Notice that "our worship is not centered in what we get out of church (edification or inspiration). Our worship is centered in what we give to God. Worship is the turning of our lives over to Him, nothing less. A service of worship, therefore, is a service of surrender."[64]

61. Cf. Mays, *Psalms*, 306, "The shepherd image . . . is a royal image of the relation of a king to those he rules and portrays his role as leader, provider, and protector."

62. Cf. Rev 5:11–14, "Then I looked, and I heard the voice of many angels . . . singing with full voice, 'Worthy is the Lamb that was slaughtered to receive power and wealth and wisdom and might and honor and glory and blessing!' Then I heard every creature in heaven and on earth and under the earth and in the sea, and all that is in them, singing, 'To the one seated on the throne and to the Lamb be blessing and honor and glory and might forever and ever!' And the four living creatures said, 'Amen!' And the elders fell down and worshiped."

63. "The first half of Ps 95 [vv 1–7c] displays balance and symmetry. God is both the great king and the good shepherd. He is the transcendent Creator and the immanent redeemer. He works in the vast world and among his people. He deserves to be worshiped in rejoicing and in reverence, with jubilation and with submission. The two styles of and reasons for worship complement each other very well." Massouh, "Psalm 95," *TrinJ* 4 (1983): 86.

64. Williams, *Psalms 73–150*, 183

The third stanza assumes that the pilgrims are still kneeling in the temple court, as close to the Holy Place as allowed. Suddenly a priest[65] begins to speak to them. The priest says, verse 7, last line, "O that today you would listen to his [God's] voice!" The priest asks for more than mere listening, of course. The pilgrims are to listen in order to *obey* God's voice.[66] The word "today" "stresses the urgency of hearing the message"[67] and giving an immediate response.[68]

Then the priest speaks the Word of the LORD. It's a warning! Verses 8–9, "Do not harden your hearts, as at Meribah, as on the day at Massah in the wilderness, when your ancestors tested me, and put me to the proof, though they had seen my work." The LORD reminds the pilgrims of their ancestors' journey from Egypt to the Promised Land.

Exodus 17:1–7 provides the background for the LORD's warning:[69]

From the wilderness of Sin the whole congregation of the Israelites journeyed by stages, *as the LORD commanded.* They camped at Rephidim [presumably at the LORD's command], but there was no water for the people to drink. The people quarreled with Moses, and said, "Give us water to drink." Moses said to them, "Why do you quarrel with me? Why do you *test the LORD*?" But the people thirsted there for water; and the people complained against Moses and said, "Why did you bring us out of Egypt, to kill us and our children and livestock with thirst?" So Moses cried out to the LORD, "What shall I do with this people? They are almost ready to stone me." The LORD said to Moses, "Go on ahead of the people, and take some of the elders of Israel with you; take in your hand the staff with which you struck the Nile, and go. I will be standing there in front of you on the rock at Horeb. Strike the rock, and water will come out of it, so that the people may drink." Moses did so, in the sight of the elders of Israel. He called the place *Massah* [testing] and *Meribah* [contention], because the Israelites *quarreled and tested the LORD, saying, "Is the LORD among us or not?"*[70]

65. Or "cultic prophet." Cf. Davies, "Psalm 95," *ZAW* 85, no. 2 (1973): 192–93, and Massouh, "Psalm 95," *TrinJ* 4 (1983): 87.

66. "'Hear' . . . has often the added dimension in Hebrew of 'obey,' for which the Old Testament has virtually no other word (cf. 'obeying' and 'obey' in 1 Sam 15:22)." Kidner, *Psalms 73–150*, 345.

67. Tate, *Psalms 51–100*, 502.

68. Cf. VanGemeren, *Psalms,* 721, "'Today' is reminiscent of Moses' insistence that 'the moment' of hearing the word evokes a response (cf. Deut 4:40; 5:3; 6:6; 7:11; 9:3; 11:20)."

69. It would be well to have the congregation read along either in the pew Bibles or by way of PowerPoint.

70. Some forty years later a similar incident happened at Kadesh: Israel quarreling with Moses about their thirst and the LORD providing water from a rock (Num 20:1–13). See Enns,

Back to Psalm 95:8–9, "Do not harden your hearts, as at Meribah, as on the day[71] at Massah[72] in the wilderness when your ancestors tested me, and put me to the proof, though they had seen my work."[73] Israel's ancestors had hardened their hearts.[74] They had failed to trust the LORD who was leading them by stages through the wilderness. The LORD was like a Shepherd for them: protecting them from danger and providing food and drink. But when there was no water at Meribah, Israel immediately started to quarrel with Moses and to complain against him, the servant of the LORD. Moses warned them of serious consequences. He asked, "Why do you *test the LORD*?" It was not Israel's place to put their Shepherd King to the test.[75] Testing the LORD was a self-centered demand for signs and wonders as if God's signs and wonders in the exodus from Egypt were not sufficient. Testing the LORD was a refusal to take the LORD at his word.[76] They went even farther than testing the LORD. They questioned, "Is the LORD among us or not?" They doubted that their covenant LORD was in their midst.[77] They implied that the LORD had forsaken them, left his sheep on their own in the wilderness. With their question, "Is the LORD among us or not?" they expressed their *dis*belief that the LORD was still shepherding his sheep.[78]

This third stanza reminds the pilgrims who are in the presence of the LORD at the temple that their ancestors questioned the presence of the LORD with them

"Creation and Re-Creation," *WTJ* 55 (1993; pp. 255–80): 264–67, for a discussion on whether Exodus 17 is the background of Psalm 95 or Numbers 20 or "everything in between."

71. "By reintroducing the word 'day' here in v 8 from the previous verse more of a contrast is effected between 'today' when they must listen to the Lord and the past when they hardened their hearts and would not listen to the Lord." Prinsloo, "Psalm 95," 403.

72. "At these historical places Israel had acted wantonly against the Lord (cf. Exod 17:1–7; Num 20:1–13; 27:14; Deut 6:16; 9:22; 32:51; 33:8; Ps 81:7). These places also symbolize a whole generation of faithless Israelites (cf. 78:18, 41, 56; Heb 3:7–11) who dared to challenge ('test') the Lord." VanGemeren, *Psalms*, 721.

73. "The three verbs that are strung together here [in verse 9 with 'your ancestors' as subject] emphasize the disobedience to Yahweh in the past and stand in sharp contrast to the three verbs in v 6 . . . where it is emphasized that Yahweh should be worshipped." Prinsloo, "Psalm 95," 404.

74. "The 'hardened' heart is one . . . no longer hearing, attentive, trusting, centred on his [the Lord's] will, but rather awake only to immediate desires and impulses." Eaton, *The Psalms*, 338.

75. "When finitude questions the motivation of Yahweh, it erects itself as the judge of divinity." Terrien, *The Psalms*, 671.

76. Kidner, *Psalms 73–150*, 346.

77. "The oracular warning is saying not only 'Do not be rebellious as your fathers were about the waters of Meribah,' but it is also saying 'Do not question the presence of God here today, as your fathers questioned it at Massah." Davies, "Psalm 95," *ZAW* 85, no. 2 (1973): 194. Cf. W. Dennis Tucker, Jr., "Psalm 95: Text, Context and Intertext," *Bib* 81, no. 4 (2000; pp. 533–41): 539–40.

78. "The problem is not merely one of thirst but of *dis*belief that Yahweh would continue to provide for the people he liberated." Broyles, *Psalms*, 374.

in the wilderness. Even though they had seen the LORD's work, the signs and wonders with which he delivered them from Egypt, his provisions of manna and quail in the wilderness, they questioned God's presence. The LORD here warns the pilgrims in the temple, "Do not harden your hearts, as at Meribah, as on the day at Massah in the wilderness, when your ancestors tested *me,* and put *me* to the proof, though they had seen *my* work." "The line's point is that there should have been no need for Israel to test or try . . . [the LORD], because they had been given ample indication of what . . . [the LORD] was like."[79]

Verse 10, "For forty years I loathed that generation and said, 'They are a people whose hearts go astray, and they do not regard my ways.'" "I *loathed* that generation" are strong words. "So great was Israel's sin, unbelief, and rebellion, that it aroused a feeling of revulsion in the heart and mind of God."[80] The LORD said, "They are a people whose hearts go astray, and they do not regard my ways." In verse 8 we heard that they had hardened their "hearts," the core of their being. Here the LORD says concerning this core, "their hearts go astray." As a result, "they do not regard my [the LORD's] ways." They are like sheep determined to go their own way instead of following their Shepherd.

Hence the LORD determined to cut them loose. Verse 11, "Therefore in my anger I swore, 'They shall not enter my rest.'" They shall not enter the Promised Land where God had promised to give them rest from their enemies and safety (see Deut 12:10). "They shall not enter my rest," God said to Israel when it was on the edge of the Promised Land. When the spies brought back a report that Canaan's people were powerful and its cities well fortified, Israel refused to enter the land. Instead, "all the Israelites complained against Moses and Aaron . . . , 'Would that we had died in the land of Egypt! Or would that we had died in this wilderness!'" They did not trust the LORD to lead them into the Promised Land. That's when the LORD said, "None of the people who have seen my glory and the signs that I did in Egypt and in the wilderness, and yet have *tested* me these ten times and *have not obeyed my voice,* shall see the land that I swore to give to their ancestors; *none of those who despised me shall see it*" (Num 14:2, 22-23). And they didn't. In the forty years of wandering in the wilderness that whole generation that escaped from Egypt died off. Their journey in the wilderness was marked by graves. They did not enter the LORD's rest in the Promised Land.

But for the pilgrims in Jerusalem, God's rest is more than the Promised Land. God's rest is to be in God's presence in the temple.[81] This final stanza of

79. Goldingay, *Psalms,* III, 96.

80. Stott, *Favorite Psalms,* 77.

81. "The poetic structure of Ps 95 sets up a tension between joyful worship / praise in the temple and fear of loss of God's rest (implying both the promised land and temple worship)." Renz, "Come, Let Us Listen," *Worship* 70, no. 2 (1996): 148. See pp. 146-52. Cf. Tucker, "Psalm 95,"

Psalm 95 warns the pilgrims, "O that today you would listen to his voice!" Do not harden your hearts and follow your own ways. Follow your great Shepherd. As you submit yourselves to God in his sanctuary by worshiping, bowing down and kneeling, so you should submit yourselves to the LORD in your whole life. If you do not obey the LORD in every area of life, you cannot be in his presence.[82]

In the New Testament Jesus issues us the same warning. In his Sermon on the Mount Jesus spelled out God's will for us. We are to listen to him, obey him, and follow our good Shepherd. If we harden our hearts and follow our own ways, we will not enter into God's rest. Jesus concludes his Sermon as follows,

> Not everyone who says to me, 'Lord, Lord,' will *enter the kingdom of heaven,* but only the one who *does the will of my Father in heaven.* On that day [of judgment] many will say to me, 'Lord, Lord, did we not prophesy in your name, and cast out demons in your name, and do many deeds of power in your name?' Then I will declare to them, 'I never knew you; *go away from me, you evildoers.'* Everyone then who hears these words of mine and *acts on them* will be like *a wise man* who built his house on rock. The rain fell, the floods came, and the winds blew and beat on that house, but it did not fall, because it had been founded on rock. And everyone who hears these words of mine and *does not act on them* will be like *a foolish man* who built his house on sand. The rain fell, and the floods came, and the winds blew and beat against that house, and it fell—and *great was its fall!* (Matt 7:21–27).

The season of Lent traditionally calls for self-examination and renewed commitment. We come to church regularly to make "a joyful noise to the rock of our salvation," to humbly submit ourselves to our good Shepherd, and to listen to his Word. Today is a good time to ask ourselves, As we leave church, do we leave that Word behind as well? Do we fail to act on that Word in the week ahead? Could Jesus accuse us of hardening our hearts and going our own way?

Bib 81, no. 4 (2000): 540, "In Ps 95:11 the threat of the oracle, 'they shall not enter into my rest,' is not really whether a worshiper can enter the temple of God, but whether they will remain in the presence of God." Cf. Hossfeld, *Psalms 2,* 461, "The goal is YHWH's rest, with all its rich connotations ranging from the land as heritage, to the Temple, to peace with God." Cf. Rogerson and McKay, *Psalms 51–100,* 218, "Rest denotes perhaps not only the resting-place for Israel after the wilderness wanderings, but God's final 'resting-place' in Jerusalem (Ps 132:8)." See also Massouh, "Psalm 95," *TrinJ* 4 (1983): 87.

82. "What is clear from this psalm is that there can be no truly joyful celebration of God which does not lead to moral responsibility and urgency." Davidson, *Vitality of Worship,* 316. Cf. Massouh, "Psalm 95," *TrinJ* 4 (1983): 88, "All worship must come from a sincere, obedient heart. Performing external gestures without inner conviction is both dangerous and hypocritical."

I think most of us will admit that we often fail to act on God's Word. We are born with a sinful human nature and cannot escape this on our own. The good news is that Jesus came for sinners. Jesus said, "I have come to call not the righteous but sinners" (Mark 2:17). He invited people, "Come to me, all you that are weary and are carrying heavy burdens, and I will give you *rest*. Take my yoke upon you, and learn from me; for I am gentle and humble in heart, and you will find *rest* for your souls" (Matt 11:28–29). Jesus promised, "Very truly, I tell you, anyone who hears my word and believes him who sent me has *eternal life*, and does not come under judgment, but has passed from death to *life*" (John 5:24). If we believe in Jesus and follow our good Shepherd, at the end of our journey on earth eternal rest awaits.[83]

Prayer[84]

O God, fountain of life,
to a humanity parched with thirst
you offer the living water of your grace
which springs from the rock, our Savior, Jesus Christ.
Grant us the gift of your Spirit, we pray,
that we may learn to profess our faith with courage
and announce with joy the wonder of your love.
We ask this through our Lord Jesus Christ,
who lives and reigns with you in the unity of the Holy Spirit,
one God, forever and ever. Amen.

Song[85]

1Now with joyful exultation
    let us sing to God our praise;
to the Rock of our salvation
    loud hosannas let us raise.
Thankful tribute gladly bringing,
    let us come before him now,
and, with psalms his praises singing,
    joyful in his presence bow.

---

83. See, e.g., Hebrews 4:9, 11, "So then, a sabbath rest still remains for the people of God. . . . Let us therefore make every effort to enter that rest, so that no one may fall through such disobedience as theirs."

84. *Book of Common Worship*, 246–47.

85. Public Domain. *Psalter Hymnal* (1987), # 95; *Psalms for All Seasons*, # 95D; *Lift Up Your Hearts*, # 512.

₂For how great a God, and glorious,
　　is the LORD of whom we sing;
over idol gods victorious,
　　great is he, our God and King.
In his hand are earth's deep places,
　　also his are all the hills;
his the sea whose bounds he traces,
　　his the land his bounty fills.

₃To the LORD, such might revealing,
　　let us come with reverence meet,
and, before our Maker kneeling,
　　let us worship at his feet.
He is our own God who leads us,
　　we the people of his care;
with a shepherd's hand he feeds us
　　as his flock in pastures fair.

₄While he offers peace and pardon
　　let us hear his voice today,
lest, if we our hearts should harden,
　　we should perish in the way,
lest to us, so unbelieving,
　　he in judgment should declare:
"You, so long my Spirit grieving,
　　never in my rest will share."

CHAPTER 15

"The LORD Is My Shepherd"

Psalm 23 (22)

Psalm 23 is the best-known and most popular psalm in the Psalter. *The Revised Common Lectionary* assigns the reading of Psalm 23 no less than four times in three years for Easter and Lent: the Fourth Sunday of Easter for Years A, B, and C, as well as the Fourth Sunday in Lent (Year A). The reading in Lent is intended as a response to the "First Lesson: 1 Sam 16:1–13," David anointed as king of Israel.

Although Psalm 23 is well known, it is surprisingly difficult to interpret and preach this popular psalm. There are at least three reasons for this problem. First, precisely because it is so well known and "owned" by people, it is difficult to preach it from a new angle and in a fresh way. James Mays, an expert on the psalms, writes, "During a long career of speaking and writing about psalms I have always before now turned away from it [Psalm 23]. Any interpretation seems presumptuous. The Twenty-third is poetically so precious and so owned by all who know it that it ought not be blurred by the comments and glosses of an interpreter."[1]

Second, because this psalm is frequently read at funeral services, it has many emotional associations for the hearers. Since the hearers often understand the psalm in the context of death and dying, preachers have to work hard to reverse this preconception so that the psalm can be heard as intended — a message for the living. Clinton McCann rightly points out that "it may be more important . . . that this psalm be read and heard as a psalm about living, for it puts daily activ-

---

1. Mays, *Preaching and Teaching the Psalms,* 118. Cf. Brueggemann, *Message of the Psalms,* "It is almost pretentious to comment on this psalm. The grip it has on biblical spirituality is deep and genuine. It is such a simple statement that it can bear its own witness without comment." See my meditation in Appendix 3, pp. 553–55, which reflects the impact of Psalm 23 on a twenty-year-old who had not yet studied the intricacies of biblical hermeneutics and Hebrew poetry.

ities, such as eating, drinking, and seeking security, in a radically God-centered perspective that challenges our usual way of thinking."[2]

Third, "the oriental imagery found in this well-beloved poem makes it difficult to separate facts from verbal images."[3] Biblical scholars have proposed a multitude of contradictory interpretations. Our favorite psalm has been sliced, diced, and cubed into so many parts that its unity and appeal are hardly discernible.[4] If preachers were to follow all the rabbit trails laid out by some commentators, they would never get around to preaching Psalm 23. Although we still have to make interpretive choices, in our presentation we shall not seek to counter the many possible interpretations but aim to get as quickly as possible to the points made by the psalm.

Text and Context

The entire Psalm 23 is a good preaching text since it is not only an individual psalm but also deliberately marked as a literary unit with an inclusio: the name of Yahweh is used only twice, once as the very first word (v 1) and again in the last line (v 6).[5]

The editors of the Psalter may deliberately have placed Psalm 23 next to Psalm 22. Psalm 22 emphasizes David's cry for help ("My God, my God, why have you forsaken me?") and stresses the enemies circling and threatening him (22:6–7, 11–13, 16–18, 20–21). Even though David, in Psalm 23, still has to "walk through the darkest valley" and is threatened by enemies (23:4–5), he responds with the confident trust, "The LORD is my shepherd, I shall not want" (23:1). "Psalm 22 ends with the psalmist in the 'congregation' (vv 22, 25)"; Psalm 23 ends with the psalmist in "the house of the LORD" (23:6) where the congregation was found.[6]

More important for discerning the specific point of Psalm 23 is to compare it with other psalms that speak of the LORD as shepherd (e.g., Pss 28:9; 80:1; 100:3). This investigation leads to a remarkable conclusion. As Mays puts it, "No other psalm says, 'My shepherd.' In all the other psalms where 'shepherd' is used as a metaphor for the deity, the relationship is to the community. Indeed, in all the many uses of the metaphor in the entire Old Testament, it is always '*our* shep-

---

2. McCann, "Psalms," 767.

3. A. Anderson, *Psalms 1–72*, 195. See also Weiser, quoted on p. 344 below.

4. Leupold, for one, *Exposition of the Psalms*, 208, bemoans the fact that because of various proposals regarding the images in Psalm 23 (shepherd, guide, host, pursuer) "one is compelled to admit that the beautiful little psalm has been pretty sadly fragmentized."

5. The inclusio is further strengthened by the use of two lamedh words, *lō'* (v 1) and *lǝ'orek* (v 6).

6. McCann, "Psalms," 769.

herd.'"[7] This insight provides a valuable clue for formulating the unique theme of Psalm 23: "The LORD is *my* shepherd."

This emphasis on the LORD as my personal shepherd, however, also confronts the modern preacher with a challenge. Mays reports that "W. L. Holladay, after a lot of research, found that this general popularity of Psalm 23 is quite recent and a distinctly American phenomenon. The shepherd psalm had no particular status in the liturgy and devotions practiced during most of Christian history, until the late nineteenth century, and then primarily in America. Why? Holladay thinks the first-person-singular idiom of the psalm fitted the individualism emerging in America."[8] The American preacher, therefore, will have to walk the fine line between encouraging hearers to confess the LORD as their personal shepherd while steering clear of promoting American individualism.

Mays escapes the horns of this dilemma as follows: "You cannot have the 'my' without the 'our.' You must not say 'my shepherd' without also first saying 'our shepherd.' Sheep by nature belong to a flock, and a sheep off by itself is lost and in danger (think of the parable!). The privilege and wonders of being able to say 'my shepherd' are a benefit that comes with belonging to the congregation."[9]

The psalm also reflects a broader historical context. Broyles notes that "while Psalm 23 is an intensely personal psalm, it may also echo Israel's corporate experience of God. . . . If so, the richness of the psalm is enhanced because we now see the individual's experience of Yahweh as part of a larger whole."[10] Certainly, the heart of Psalm 23, "for you are with me" (v 4), reflects God's many promises to Israel's patriarchs, Abram, Isaac, Jacob, and Joseph, "I will be with you." (See "Longitudinal Themes," pp. 349–51 below.)

---

7. Mays, *Preaching and Teaching the Psalms,* 120 (my emphasis). Cf. Craigie, *Psalms 1–50,* 206, "The distinctiveness in the opening words of this psalm lies in the use of the pronoun, *my* shepherd; the shepherd theme, traditionally interpreted communally of the 'flock' (or nation), is here given its most personal interpretation in the entire biblical tradition." Cf. Eaton, *Psalms,* 76, "Elsewhere in the Old Testament God is described as shepherd only of the nation, except for one reference to his shepherding of the nation's ancestors (Gen 48:15 . . .). So there is something remarkable here in the extended application of the theme in such a personal way."

8. Mays, *Preaching and Teaching the Psalms,* 121. See William L. Holladay, *The Psalms Through Three Thousand Years: Prayerbook of a Cloud of Witnesses* (Minneapolis: Fortress, 1993), 365.

9. Ibid., 120. Cf. McCann, "Psalms," 769, "To be in 'the house of the LORD' [v 6], literally or metaphorically, provides a communal dimension to this psalm that is usually heard exclusively individualistically."

10. Broyles, *Psalms,* 124–25, with credit to Craigie, *Psalms 1–50,* 206–7, in listing the same words of Psalm 23 used in other scriptures. Cf. Mays, *Preaching and Teaching the Psalms,* 120, "This psalmist was drawing on Israel's memory of what God had done for the people of God in the past. . . . Psalm 23 is woven with allusions to the memories recorded at other places in the Old Testament [with specific references to Deut 2:7; Exod 15:3; and Ps 78:19]."

Literary Interpretation

Although some identify Psalm 23 as a thanksgiving psalm or a royal psalm, it is usually identified as a song of trust or confidence.[11] The psalmist first addresses Israel, next God, then Israel again. He begins by declaring to Israel, "The LORD is my shepherd, I shall not want" (v 1). He continues in the third person by enumerating what the LORD does for him: "He makes me lie down . . . ; he leads me . . . ; he restores my soul [me]. He leads me . . ." (vv 2–3). In the verses 4–5 he switches to the second person by addressing the LORD directly: "Even though I walk through the darkest valley, I fear no evil; for *you* are with me; *your* rod and *your* staff — they comfort me. *You* prepare a table before me . . . ; *you* anoint my head with oil; my cup overflows." In verse 6 he switches back to addressing Israel again: "Surely goodness and mercy shall follow me all the days of my life, and I shall dwell in the house of the LORD my whole life long."

As we work our way into understanding the psalm, we shall discuss in turn its parallelisms, imagery, repetition of keywords, and its structure.

Parallelisms

The psalmist begins Psalm 23 with an impressive climactic parallelism describing the benefits of the LORD being his shepherd (vv 1–3). He follows this up with another climactic parallelism of these benefits when he walks through the darkest valley (v 4), and again when he is in the presence of his enemies (v 5). He concludes with "goodness and mercy" following him all the days of his life, advancing in the last line to the more specific dwelling "in the house of the LORD" (v 6).

A Psalm of David.

1The LORD is my shepherd,	A
I shall not want.	+ A'
2He makes me lie down in green pastures;	+ A''
he leads me beside still waters;	+ A'''
3he restores my soul.	+ A''''
He leads me in right paths for his name's sake.	+ A'''''

11. See Craigie, *Psalms 1–50*, 204. Cf. B. Anderson, *Out of the Depths*, 173, "Song of trust."

₄Even though I walk through the darkest valley,	A
I fear no evil;	+ A'
for you are with me;	+ A''
your rod and your staff — they comfort me.	+ A'''

₅You prepare a table before me in the presence of my enemies;	A
you anoint my head with oil;	+ A'
my cup overflows.	+ A''
₆Surely goodness and mercy shall follow me all the days of my life,[12]	B
and I shall dwell in the house of the LORD my whole life long.	+ B'

Imagery

The amount of imagery in Psalm 23 makes its interpretation contentious. As Weiser puts it, "The fact that the interpretation of the psalm is . . . so difficult is to be accounted for by the wealth of oriental imagery in its language and thoughts. For this abundance makes it more difficult to state precisely, point by point, what has to be regarded as a mere figure of speech and what can be accepted as actual fact, since both of them, image and fact, often blend in the poetical, allegorical style of the psalm."[13]

Some commentators opt for a single, controlling metaphor, the shepherd, which determines the meaning of all the figures of speech. This works well for verses 1–4 but unfortunately leads to forcing an interpretation on verse 5: somehow "a table" is prepared for a sheep, its head is anointed with oil, and its cup overflows.[14] Others opt for two controlling metaphors, the shepherd and the host. Still others opt for three metaphors, the shepherd (vv 1–3), the guardian (v 4), and the host (vv 5–6), or even four: the shepherd (vv 1–3), the guardian (v 4), the host (v 5), and the pursuer (v 6).[15] This splinters the psalm into so many shards

---

12. I have marked verse 6 with a B to indicate a new topic: "all the days of my life." But if one views this verse as continuing to list the LORD's benefits, it would be part of the final climactic parallelism: +A''', +A''''.

13. Weiser, *The Psalms,* 227.

14. "The table is simply a table — it is not a 'tableland' for sheep (the word is never used that way in the Old Testament). The ancients put oil on the heads of their guests, not of their sheep. . . . People, not sheep, drink from cups." Duane A. Garrett, "Preaching from the Psalms and Proverbs," in *Preaching the Old Testament,* ed. Scott M. Gibson (Grand Rapids: Baker, 2006; pp. 101–14), 112.

15. For a list of commentators defending the different positions, see, e.g., Andrew E. Arterbury and William H. Bellinger, Jr., "'Returning' to the Hospitality of the Lord: A Reconsideration of Psalm 23:5–6," *Bib* 86, no. 3 (2005; pp. 387–95): 387 nn. 5–8.

it can no longer communicate effectively. I think the most natural interpretation is that of two controlling metaphors, the shepherd (vv 1–4) and the host (vv 5–6).

Psalm 23 begins with a major, powerful metaphor, "The LORD is my *shepherd*." It follows through on this image with pictures of what a good shepherd does for his sheep: "He makes me lie down [a typical shepherd term[16]] in green pastures [an abundance of food]; he leads [an eastern shepherd "leads" his sheep] me beside still waters [which sheep can drink without danger of drowning];[17] he restores my soul [that is, my life]. He leads me in right paths [when the hills are crisscrossed by many paths] for his name's sake [a good shepherd has to protect his reputation]. Even though I walk through the darkest valley [literally, there are many dark valleys in Israel that cannot be avoided as the shepherd leads his sheep; metaphorically, God's people on earth walk through many dark valleys], I fear no evil; for you [my shepherd] are with me; your rod and your staff [tools of the shepherd's trade; also "symbolic equipment of a king"[18]] they comfort me" (vv 1–4).

With verse 5 the metaphor changes from a shepherd to an eastern (Bedouin) *host*,[19] perhaps "in order to connect the psalmist's message to the human audience explicitly."[20] "You prepare a table [a banquet table] before me in the presence of my enemies [good hosts offer protection from enemies; cf. Lot protecting his angel guests in Sodom (Gen 19:5–8)]; you anoint my head with oil [what a good host does; cf. Jesus' comment, 'You did not anoint my head with oil' (Luke 7:46)]; my cup overflows [with wine].[21] Surely goodness and mercy shall follow me [pursue me; not enemies but the LORD's goodness and mercy shall pursue me][22] all the days of my life, and I shall dwell [as his guest] in the house of the LORD

16. "The verb used here, *hirbits*, is a specialized one for making animals lie down; hence the sheep-shepherd metaphor is carefully sustained." Alter, *Book of Psalms*, 78 n. 2.

17. "The green pastures and still waters image the divine blessing of food and drink to sustain life. But the act of lying down is also a symbol of peace and tranquility (Isa 11:6–7; 14:30; Jer 33:12; Ezek 34:14–15)." Miller, *Interpreting the Psalms*, 114.

18. Mays, *Preaching and Teaching the Psalms*, 119.

19. "The metaphor of God as host in Ps 23:5–6 drew upon the common Israelite custom of hospitality. The metaphor of God as host would have likely evoked a picture of this custom in the minds of the hearers that was as vivid as the metaphor of God as shepherd (Ps 23:1–4)." Arterbury and Bellinger, "'Returning' to the Hospitality of the Lord," *Bib* 86, no. 3 (2005): 391. Cf. p 395, "The key to interpreting Ps 23:5–6 is found in ancient Israel's custom of hospitality. This ancient Israelite cultural expression would have most certainly provided the angle of vision from which the ancient Israelites heard or read and interpreted these verses."

20. Wilson, *Psalms*, I, 436.

21. "In a banquet hall the cup would be filled with choice wine." Ross, *Commentary on the Psalms*, I, 568.

22. "Instead of his enemies, only 'goodness (*ṭôb*) and kindness (*ḥesed*)' are in hot pursuit to hunt him down, as it were, from which there is no escape (v 6). Avenging enemies give way to personified blessings." Brown, *Seeing the Psalms*, 40.

[literally, the temple; metaphorically, continual fellowship with the LORD; cf. Ps 27:4–5] my whole life long" (vv 5–6).

These two major metaphors do not destroy the unity of the psalm, as some claim.[23] On the contrary, they establish the unity even as they create meaningful movement from the shepherd to the host. For, as B. Anderson explains, the shepherd and the host are the same person: the shepherd "is the protector of the sheep as they wander in search of grazing land. Yet he is also the protector of the traveler who finds hospitality in his tent from the dangers and enemies of the desert. . . . According to the Bedouin law of hospitality, once a traveler is received into the shepherd's tent, and especially once his host has spread food before him, he is guaranteed immunity from enemies who may be attempting to overtake him."[24]

The movement from shepherd to host adds a depth dimension of personal intimacy. "A sheep may delight in the security of being provided for, guided, and protected by its shepherd, but a guest may enjoy full rapport with his or her host. Thus the metaphors of host and guest complement and add a significant dimension to the metaphor of shepherd and sheep."[25]

Repetition of Keywords

We have already noted the repetition of the keyword Yahweh at the beginning (v 1) and end of the psalm (v 6). This inclusio not only marks the literary unit but also speaks powerfully to the thrust of this psalm. As Brueggemann observes, "The poem, like this trustful life, is lived fully in the presence of this name [Yahweh] which sets the parameters for both life and speech."[26]

The other important repetition noted by Brueggemann is "the repeated and pervasive first person pronoun, which abounds everywhere in the psalm. . . . The 'I' statements are filled with gratitude, yielding, trust, and thanksgiving. The 'I' here knows that in every case, life is fully cared for and resolved by this thou who responds to and anticipates every need."[27]

Structure

The major metaphors outlined above guide us in determining the structure of Psalm 23. Contrary to the NRSV divisions (vv 1–3, 4, 5–6), according to contents

23. E.g., Leupold, *Exposition of the Psalms*, 208.
24. B. Anderson, *Out of the Depths*, 181, 183.
25. Gene Rice, "An Exposition of Psalm 23," *JRT* 52, no. 1 (1995; pp. 71–78): 75–76.
26. Brueggemann, *Message of the Psalms*, 154.
27. Ibid., 155.

the natural break in the psalm comes at the switch from shepherd to host, from verse 4 to 5. The psalm, therefore, consists of two stanzas, vv 1–4 and 5–6 (so the NIV).[28]

But verse 4 is exceptional nevertheless, which may be why the NRSV and other versions centered it as they did. The words "for you [are] with me" (v 4) not only show a grammatical shift from the third person (vv 1–3) to the second person ("you"), they are also at the very center of Psalm 23, with twenty-six Hebrew words before them and twenty-six after them.[29] With the inclusio of Yahweh in verses 1 and 6 and this direct reference to Yahweh with the pronoun "you" [Yahweh] at the very center, scholars were bound to propose several interesting chiastic structures.[30] But for preaching purposes, I would stick with the two-part division, explaining in turn the metaphors of the LORD as shepherd and as host. Goldingay captures this two-part division in an interesting grammatical chiastic structure:

A   Yhwh is my shepherd (third person; vv 1–3)

 B   You are my shepherd (second person; v 4)

 B'   You are my host (second person; v 5)

A'   Yahweh is my host (third person; v 6).[31]

Theocentric Interpretation

Psalm 23 is obviously God-centered. As we have seen, it begins and ends with Yahweh (vv 1, 6). Moreover, in verse 3 the psalmist states, "He leads me in right

---

28. So also Craigie, *Psalms 1–50,* 205; Fokkelman, *Major Poems of the Hebrew Bible,* III, 38; Jacobson in deClaissé-Walford, Jacobson, and Tanner, *The Book of Psalms,* 238; Stek, *NIV Study Bible,* Ps 23 n. Stek argues for "two balanced stanzas, each having four couplets (a couplet is one line of Hebrew poetry): (1) stanza one: vv 1–2a, 2b–3a, 3b–c, 4a–c (v 4a–b is metrically a half-couplet); (2) stanza two: vv 5a–b, 5c–d, 6a–b, 6c–d. The triplet in the middle (v 4d–f) is then a centering line . . . focusing on the Shepherd-King's reassuring presence with his people. It serves as a transition between the two stanzas. . . ." On this centering device, see Stek, *NIV Study Bible,* Ps 6:6 n.

29. "Not counting 'A Psalm of David,' which was the work of later editors. . . . Was the writer of the psalm using this centering technique to emphasize these words, which are at the heart of what the psalm has to say? (The number twenty-six is itself of interest because the numerical value of the Hebrew letters in the word YHWH . . . is 10 + 5 + 6 + 5 = 26.)" Limburg, *Psalms,* 74.

30. See, e.g., C. M. Foley, "Pursuit of the Inscrutable: A Literary Analysis of Psalm 23," in *Ascribe to the LORD* (ed. Lyle Eslinger and Glen Taylor; Sheffield: JSOT Press [Supplement Series 67], 1988), 363–83; and W. Creighton Marlowe, "David's I-Thou Discourse: Verbal Chiastic Patterns in Psalm 23," *SJOT* 25, no. 1 (2011): 105–15.

31. Goldingay, *Psalms,* I, 347.

paths for *his name's sake*": the LORD leads him in the right paths because of his reputation as Yahweh. In verse 4, right at the center of the psalm, the psalmist confesses, "*you* [are] with me." Even the frequent pronouns "I" do not center so much on the psalmist as on what *the* LORD is doing for him.

One can also see the theocentricity of this psalm grammatically. As Broyles puts it, "The opening (vv 1–3) and closing (v 6) verses refer to Yahweh in the third person while the middle verses (vv 4–5), which overlap the images of him as shepherd and host, are praise addressed to him. Thus, the psalm opens and closes with testimony about God, and the praise to God in the middle ties together the two roles Yahweh plays."[32]

Textual Theme and Goal

How can we best formulate the theme of this rich psalm? It should certainly contain the vivid images of the LORD as shepherd and host. It should also contain the opening thematic statement, "I lack nothing" (NIV). And it should include its message at the exact center of the psalm, "You with me" (v 4). Putting all these ideas together, we can formulate the theme of Psalm 23 as follows: *Because the* LORD, *my Shepherd and Host, is with me, I lack nothing.*[33]

The specific goal is more difficult to determine since the psalm does not clearly indicate its original historical setting. This has led to proposals for many different settings: from a pilgrimage to Jerusalem to a thanksgiving setting at the temple and many others.[34] In view of all the speculation, it would be well to keep in mind Sigmund Mowinckel's words: "One would like to be able to say something about the occasion for this pearl among the psalms; but perhaps, what gives it a priceless value to all ages may be the very fact that it stands there as a pure expression of confidence in God, unhindered by all special historical circumstances."[35]

What is clear from the psalm, however, is that the psalmist faces danger. He

---

32. Broyles, *Psalms,* 124.

33. Cf. Waltke, *Psalms as Christian Worship,* 435, "The psalm's thesis: As one who trusts and follows *I Am,* I do not lack any good thing." Cf. Limburg, *Psalms for Sojourners,* 52, "The movement of the psalm as a whole can be summarized by considering the first, the middle, and the last words: 'The Lord . . . with me . . . forever.'"

34. For various proposals, see, e.g., Craigie, *Psalms 1–50,* 205; Ross, *Commentary on the Psalms,* I, 555–57; and Arterbury and Bellinger, "'Returning' to the Hospitality of the Lord," *Bib* 86, no. 3 (2005): 387–88.

35. Sigmund Mowinckel, *The Psalms in Israel's Worship,* II, trans. D. R. Ap-Thomas (Oxford: Blackwell, 1962), 41. Cf. Arterbury and Bellinger, "'Returning' to the Hospitality of the Lord," *Bib* 86, no. 3 (2005): 394, "It may be best to envision the psalm as being read in multiple contexts."

has to "walk through the darkest valley"; "evil" threatens him (v 4); "enemies" pursue him (v 5). Rolf Jacobson explains helpfully: "The rhetoric of the psalms of trust assumes that the psalmist has passed through a time of crisis or is perhaps in the midst of or about to enter such a crisis. . . . *It is the crisis that generates the words of trust* (compare Pss 27:1–3; 46:1–7; 62:1–7; etc.). Thus, the genre teaches us that danger, evil, and crisis are *part of the life of faith*. . . . Psalm 23 does not specify the exact crisis its author faced; rather, its metaphorical language can adapt to and speak to as wide a range of crises as there are people to pray the psalm."[36] Against the background of the dangers facing God's people, we can therefore formulate the goal of Psalm 23 as follows: *to encourage God's people with the good news that on their dangerous journey through life the* LORD *is with them so that they will lack nothing.*[37]

Ways to Preach Christ

There is no promise nor a clear type of Christ in Psalm 23.[38] Yet there are at least four ways to move from the psalm to Christ in the New Testament: redemptive-historical progression, analogy, longitudinal themes, and New Testament references, or a combination of these. I will demonstrate here the way of longitudinal themes and in "Sermon Exposition" below the way of redemptive-historical progression supported by analogies and New Testament references.

Longitudinal Themes

One can trace several longitudinal themes from Psalm 23 through the Old Testament to Christ in the New Testament. First, one can trace the major metaphors

36. Jacobson, "Psalm 23," in *Psalms for Preaching and Worship*, ed. Roger E. Van Harn and Brent A. Strawn (Grand Rapids: Eerdmans, 2009; 100–105), 101 (his italics). Cf. Kraus, *Psalms 1–59*, 309, "The background of the psalm of trust represents a definite danger. The petitioner has enemies (v 5), his life is threatened and persecuted."

37. Cf. Goldingay, *Psalms*, I, 347, "The lines [vv 1–3] may be addressing the community of the faithful, implicitly encouraging them to live by the same trust that the worshipper expresses."

38. Some may see the LORD my Shepherd as a type of Christ. But since typology involves analogy *and escalation*, the LORD cannot be a type of Christ since this would make Christ greater than the LORD.

If David was indeed the author of this psalm, King David could be considered a type of Christ who also expressed his confidence in God when going through the darkest valley. Jesus prayed in Gethsemane, "My Father, if it is possible, let this cup pass from me; yet not what I want but what you want" (Matt 26:39).

of God as shepherd and as host through the Old Testament to Christ in the New Testament. Beginning with the picture of God as shepherd, one can start with Genesis 48:15 (Jacob's confession, "the God who has been my shepherd all my life"), move on to Isaiah 40:10–11 and Ezekiel 34:30–31, and end up in the New Testament where Jesus called himself "the good shepherd" (John 10:11, 14) and was called, after his resurrection, "the great shepherd of the sheep" (Heb 13:20), "the shepherd and guardian of your souls" (1 Pet 2:25) and "the chief shepherd" (1 Pet 5:4). The book of Revelation projects this shepherd image to the distant future: "the Lamb at the center of the throne will be their shepherd, and he will guide them to springs of the water of life, and God will wipe away every tear from their eyes" (Rev 7:17), and the male child will come again "to shepherd all the nations with a rod of iron" (Rev 12:5). As the sermon progresses, one can trace the longitudinal theme of the LORD as host.[39]

Second, one can trace the central theme of Psalm 23, "You [are] with me" (v 4) through the Old Testament to Jesus Christ in the New Testament. "I will be with you," God promised Isaac (Gen 26:3), Jacob (Gen 28:15), Joseph (Gen 48:21), Moses (Exod 3:12), and others. At his birth, Jesus was identified as "Emmanuel," that is, "God is with us" (Matt 1:23). After his resurrection, Jesus sent his followers on a dangerous mission to "make disciples of all nations" with the promise, "Remember, I am with you always, to the end of the age" (Matt 28:19–20). Later, Paul received the same promise: "One night the Lord said to Paul in a vision, 'Do not be afraid, but speak and do not be silent; for I am with you, and no one will lay a hand on you to harm you, for there are many in this city who are my people" (Acts 18:9–10). Jesus will be with his people "to the end of the age," and then the new age will begin when "the tabernacle of God is among mortals. He will dwell with them as their God; they will be his peoples, and God himself will be with them" (Rev 21:3).

Third, one can perhaps[40] trace the longitudinal theme of dwelling "in the house of the LORD my whole life long" (Ps 23:6) from dwelling in the temple on a pilgrimage for a few days for fellowship with God, to Jesus who was God with us (see above) and who at Pentecost sent the Holy Spirit to fill us (Acts 2:4), to his promise when he was about to die, "Do not let your hearts be troubled. Believe

39. For example, on their journey through the wilderness, the LORD served as host for Israel by providing water, manna, and quail. Jesus also served as host on many occasions: when he fed the five thousand (Mark 6:30–44), when he fed about four thousand (Mark 8:1–9), when he served his disciples the Passover and turned it into the Lord's Supper (Mark 14:12–25), when we celebrate the Lord's Supper today, and in the future when he hosts us at "the marriage supper of the Lamb" (Rev 19:9).

40. This is the weakest of the three longitudinal themes since it is not directly part of the theme.

in God, believe also in me. In my Father's house there are many dwelling places. If it were not so, would I have told you that I go to prepare a place for you? And if I go and prepare a place for you, I will come again and will take you to myself, so that where I am, there you may be also" (John 14:1–3).

Redemptive-Historical Progression, Analogies, and New Testament References

Tracing one or more longitudinal themes may be a little cumbersome in a sermon. A better option is redemptive-historical progression supported by analogies and New Testament references. This way allows the preacher to move from the Old Testament dispensation of Psalm 23 directly to that of the New Testament. In its Old Testament context the message of Psalm 23 is, "Because the LORD, my Shepherd and Host, is with me, I lack nothing." In New Testament times Jesus is this Shepherd and Host who is with us so that we lack nothing. To support this claim we can use many analogies and New Testament references (see "Sermon Exposition" below).

Sermon Theme, Goal, and Need

Since the New Testament affirms the theme of Psalm 23, the textual theme can become the sermon theme with the understanding that "LORD" refers to both Yahweh and the Lord Jesus: *Because the LORD, my Shepherd and Host, is with me, I lack nothing.* The textual goal can also become the sermon goal: *to encourage God's people with the good news that on their dangerous journey through life the LORD is with them so that they will lack nothing.* This goal points to the need addressed in this sermon: the dangers and crises God's people face in life can leave them discouraged.

Liturgy, PowerPoint, and Sermon Outline

If Psalm 23 is the preaching text during Lent, verse 1, "The LORD is my shepherd, I shall not want," could be used as the communal Confession of Faith. Then the liturgist could encourage the congregation to say these words every morning during Lent as a "daily declaration of who we are, and to whom we belong."[41]

41. Mays, *Preaching and Teaching the Psalms,* 121.

PowerPoint can aid communication with slides of the sermon outline and the verses from Psalm 23 as well as the New Testament. Slides can also help Western hearers better understand the text with pictures of an eastern shepherd *leading* his sheep, "still waters" in contrast to raging rivers, the hills crisscrossed with paths, the dark ravines, the rod and staff, a Bedouin tent, a banqueting table, and anointing a head with oil. A slide will also help explain 26 as the numerical value of the name *Yahweh*.[42]

The sermon outline can follow the two textual images, concluding each with a move to Christ in the New Testament. Thus we will have a four-point sermon outline:

I. What the LORD as shepherd does for his sheep (Ps 23:1–4)
II. What the Lord Jesus as shepherd does for us his sheep (NT)
III. What the LORD as host does for his guests (Ps 23:5–6)
IV. What the Lord Jesus as host does for us his guests (NT)

Sermon Exposition

Psalm 23 is one of my favorite psalms. I suspect it is the favorite psalm of many people because it paints such a vivid picture of the LORD caring for us as a shepherd cares for his sheep. Life looks tranquil and calm. Verse 1 says, "I shall not want," that is, "I lack nothing" (NIV). Verse 4 says, "I fear no evil." Verse 6 says, "Surely goodness and mercy shall follow me all the days of my life." Life is good, right?

But that is to misunderstand the background of this psalm. The superscription says, "A Psalm of David."[43] For David, life was not that good. Many times King Saul tried to kill him. The Philistines pursued him. They killed his best friend, Jonathan. He lost the child he had with Bathsheba. His favorite son Absalom usurped his throne and David had to flee for his life. Then Absalom was killed and David mourned deeply for him. He cried out, "O my son Absalom, my son, my son Absalom! Would I had died instead of you, O Absalom, my son, my son!" (2 Sam 18:33). Life for David was hard, filled with crises and losses.

---

42. See pp. 355–56 below.

43. For the sermon we shall assume that David was indeed the author of this psalm. He is the most plausible author, "not simply because the editorial superscription associates it with him. . . . The shepherd theme and mention of 'enemies' in Psalm 23 are strong Davidic features." W. Creighton Marlowe, "David's I-Thou Discourse," *SJOT* 25, no. 1 (2011): 105. Even if David was not the actual author, he could still be the implied author, so that we can simply speak of "David" instead of the more impersonal "author," "psalmist," etc.

Psalm 23 reflects some of these trials. Verse 4 speaks of walking "through the darkest valley." Those of us who have suffered from depression can relate to this walking "through the darkest valley." The King James Version spoke of this as walking "through the valley of death." Not one of us can escape this last enemy, death. Verse 4 also speaks of "evil" and verse 5 of "the presence of my enemies." We have many enemies in our life on earth: physical diseases, mental illnesses, accidents, tornadoes, floods, terrorists, killers, kidnappers, thieves, hackers, angry neighbors. . . . Life on earth is hard! It's tough!

For David, too, life was hard. And yet, in spite of all the hardship he suffered, David begins, "The LORD is my shepherd, I shall not want." I lack nothing. The LORD provides for all my needs.

Interestingly, Psalm 23 is the only psalm that teaches us to call the LORD "*my* shepherd." The other psalms that speak of the LORD as shepherd all speak of "*our* shepherd" or "Shepherd of Israel."[44] But this psalm teaches each of us also to call the LORD "*my* shepherd." That makes the relationship very personal and intimate. It is not that the LORD is *my* shepherd and not yours. Rather, because the LORD is *our* shepherd communally, we can each confess that this LORD is also my personal shepherd.

"In the ancient world, kings were known as shepherds of their people. Thus to profess 'The LORD is my shepherd' is to declare one's loyalty to God and intention to live under God's reign."[45] Not just any god is my king. The LORD is my Shepherd-King. I am subject to him. I depend utterly on him. I wish to obey his will and live totally for him.

Because the LORD is his personal shepherd, David concludes, "I shall not want," that is, "I shall not be in want," or, as the NIV translates, "I lack nothing." David uses a word here that Moses used to describe God's care for Israel in the wilderness. Moses said, "Surely the LORD your God has blessed you in all your undertakings; he knows your going through this great wilderness. These forty years the LORD your God has been with you; *you have lacked nothing*" (Deut 2:7; cf. Neh 9:21). Like a shepherd leading his sheep through the wilderness, so the LORD led his people Israel through the difficult journey of the wilderness and they lacked nothing. The LORD provided for all their basic needs: protection from their

44. See pp. 341–42 above.
45. McCann, "Psalms," 767. Cf. Jacobson in deClaissé-Walford, Jacobson, and Tanner, *The Book of Psalms*, 240, "Kings were portrayed as shepherds (cf. 1 Kings 22:17; Jer 23:1–4; Ezek 34:1–10), and to portray God as shepherd is to portray God as a royal figure (cf. Ezek 34:10–16)." Cf. Carl J. Bosma, "Discerning the Voices in the Psalms," *CTJ* 43, no. 2 (2008; pp. 183–212): 208–9, "The label 'shepherd' was a conventional ancient Near Eastern metaphor for a king. . . . In like manner, this stock royal epithet was also used in the Psalter as an epithet for the Lord as the Shepherd-King." See there for many references.

enemies, food (manna and quail), and water. Nothing luxurious, but the LORD provided the basic necessities for life.

David uses the same word, "I lack nothing." Given the hardships David had faced in his life, this is still an amazing statement. Losing his best friend Jonathan, losing a baby son, losing his throne, losing his favorite son Absalom: "I lack nothing." How can David say this? How can we possibly say this when hardships strike?

In the following verses David mentions seven things the LORD as shepherd does for him and us. First, the shepherd gives us rest. Verse 2, "He makes me lie down in green pastures." Lying down means to rest. "So the first prospect held before the eyes of the faithful followers of the good Lord is that, when rest becomes imperative, He will supply it."[46] Jesus also gives us rest. He invites us, "Come to me, all you that are weary and are carrying heavy burdens, and I will give you rest" (Matt 11:28). A good shepherd will see to it that his sheep receive rest when they need it.[47]

Second, a good shepherd provides plenty of food. "He makes me lie down [not just anywhere but] in *green* pastures." Green pastures mean lots of food. In the wilderness, green pastures are few and far between. But a good shepherd leads his sheep to green pastures where they can eat their fill and then lie down. "Causing the flock to lie down there rather than simply feed suggests ample provision. It implies that they have eaten, are satisfied, and have no need to move on to look for further grass: this pasture will provide the next meal, too."[48]

Third, the shepherd leads his sheep to safe water. Verse 2, "he leads me beside still waters." Eastern shepherds *lead*[49] their sheep. They walk ahead of the flock and the sheep follow. "He leads me beside still waters." "Still waters" are not stagnant waters but waters of rest — quiet, restful waters. Rivers rushing down the wadis would be dangerous for sheep. They could fall in and be carried along and drown. So shepherds would sometimes make "a small dam in the rocky wadi, forming a pool of still waters where the flock may come down easily from the burning hillsides."[50] Or the shepherd may know of a spring flowing with still water.

---

46. Leupold, *Exposition of the Psalms*, 211.

47. "*Rest* means more than mere bodily repose. *Rest* connotes protection from enemies, the environment in which life might thrive, and indeed, the lifting of any threat of divine punishment (see Gen 6–9)." Jacobson in deClaissé-Walford, Jacobson, and Tanner, *The Book of Psalms*, 241.

48. Goldingay, *Psalms*, I, 349. Goldingay adds, "Lying down after feeding also hints at security (Ezek 34:14–15; Zeph 3:13; also Job 11:19; Isa 17:2)."

49. "Guiding (*nāhal*) is the act of a powerful but caring party toward a weaker and needy party ([Ps] 31:3 [4]; Gen 33:14; 2 Chron 28:15; Isa 40:11; 49:10; 51:18), just as Yhwh took Israel through the wilderness and into the promised land (Exod 15:13)." Ibid.

50. Eaton, *Psalms*, 77.

Fourth, the shepherd provides life, vitality. Verse 3, "he restores my soul," that is, he restores my life; he restores me.[51] The shepherd provides us with rest as well as sufficient food and water so that our life is restored. Note that a sheep can do none of these things for itself. Neither David nor we can do any of these things for ourselves. But our shepherd provides rest, food, water, and vitality so that we can go on living in spite of hardships.

Fifth, the shepherd leads us in right[52] paths. Verse 3, "He leads me in right paths for his name's sake." If ever you get to Jericho, look back to the hills in the west. You will see the hillside crisscrossed with many paths. Over the years flocks of sheep and goats have worn these paths into the hillside. Many paths to choose from. Which is the right path that will lead most directly to green pastures and still waters? Sheep have no idea, but the shepherd does.

The shepherd "leads me in right paths for his *name's sake*."[53] The good shepherd has a name to protect, a reputation to live up to. The shepherd's name is Yahweh, "I am that I am," the faithful God who made a covenant with Israel and promised to protect them and provide for all their needs. For his name's sake,[54] for his reputation,[55] he has to lead his flock in the right paths. It is unthinkable that he would select the wrong path and get lost with his sheep.

Sixth, the shepherd is personally *with us*. Verse 4, "Even though I walk through the darkest valley, I fear no evil; for you are with me." "You [are] with me" is the very center of Psalm 23. The Hebrew phrase "you with me" has 26 Hebrew words before it and 26 words after it. Interestingly, 26 is the numerical value of the name *Yahweh* with which the psalm begins (v 1) and ends (v 6). The name YHWH has four consonants, *yod*, the tenth letter of the Hebrew alphabet,

---

51. "The word 'soul' is not here the spiritual dimension of humankind but denotes the same as 'me,' repeated twice in v. 2, i.e., 'he restores me.'" VanGemeren, *Psalms*, 254.

52. "'Righteousness' (*sedeq*) here signifies in the most basic sense 'right,' namely, the paths that bring the sheep most directly to their destination (in contrast to 'crooked paths'; cf. 125:5; Pr 2:15; 5:6; 10:9)." Ibid. Cf. Terrien, *The Psalms*, 240, "The word 'righteousness' suggests moral or religious rectitude, but it originally possessed a physical meaning of directness and simplicity."

53. Cf. Ezek 36:22, "Say to the house of Israel, 'Thus says the Lord GOD: It is not for your sake, O house of Israel, that I am about to act, but for the sake of my holy name, which you have profaned among the nations to which you came.'" Cf. Ps 79:9, "Help us, O God of our salvation, for the glory of your name; deliver us, and forgive our sins, for your name's sake."

54. "'For the sake of his name' is a claim on God's promise and on God's character. It is a statement expressing the psalmist's trust that God is completely committed to maintaining the relationship that God has established." Jacobson in deClaissé-Walford, Jacobson, and Tanner, *The Book of Psalms*, 243.

55. Cf. Numbers 14:15–16, "Now if you kill this people all at one time, then the nations who have heard about you will say, 'It is because the LORD was not able to bring this people into the land he swore to give them that he has slaughtered them in the wilderness.'"

he, the fifth, *waw,* the sixth, and another *he,* the fifth. 10+5+6+5=26. Yahweh, the faithful covenant God, is with us. That is the center of Psalm 23 as well as its central message: "You are with me."[56] Yahweh is with us even when we walk through the darkest valleys. Better, *especially* when we walk through the darkest valleys.[57] The LORD is with us to protect us.[58]

Sometimes the right paths do indeed run through "the darkest valley."[59] In Israel, shepherds would often have to lead their flock through dark ravines. That is where dangers lurked: wild animals looking for a good meal or robbers seeking to enrich themselves (think of the Parable of the Good Samaritan where "A man was going down from Jerusalem [through a ravine] to Jericho, and fell into the hands of robbers" [Luke 10:30]). The good news is that our Shepherd is with us in these dark valleys. Just as he was with Israel earlier when they walked through dark valleys in the wilderness. Moses exclaimed, "Surely the LORD your God . . . knows your going through this great wilderness. These forty years *the LORD your God has been with you;* you have lacked nothing" (Deut 2:7). So Psalm 23 proclaims that God still does for us what he did for his people in the wilderness.

Because the LORD our Shepherd is with us as we walk through these dark valleys, we need not fear evil; we need not fear evil wild animals nor evil human beings. We need not fear coming to harm. Notice that we do not walk *into* the darkest valley but *through* it. Our Shepherd "will be there to meet us, to take our hand in his, and see us safely home. The believer need have no ultimate fear of evil, not even of the last enemy, death."[60]

Seventh, the shepherd provides comfort, that is encouragement, when we go through these dark valleys. Verse 4, "your rod and your staff — they comfort me." Shepherds carried a rod, a club, to fight off wild animals. That weapon encouraged sheep to go through dangerous, dark valleys. With his club the shepherd would protect them. Shepherds also carried a staff, a shepherd's crook, to support

---

56. See n. 29 above. Cf. McCann, "Psalms," 768, "The central affirmation, 'you are with me,' is made even more emphatic by the shift from third to second person in referring to God and by the presence of the Hebrew pronoun for 'you.' The direct address heightens the expression of the intimacy of God's presence."

57. "It is noteworthy that it is precisely in the middle of the crisis ('the darkest valley') that the psalm shifts from creedal affirmations about God to trusting prayer to God." Jacobson in deClaissé-Walford, Jacobson, and Tanner, *The Book of Psalms,* 243.

58. "Having Yhwh 'with' us is not merely a feeling. It does not signify mere presence but also action (e.g., Isa 41:10). This presence expresses itself by aggressive action to defeat enemies and thus protect the one to whom Yhwh is committed." Goldingay, *Psalms,* I, 351.

59. For literature and details on this translation, see Walter L. Michel, "ṢLMWT, 'Deep Darkness' or 'Shadow of Death'?" *Biblical Research* 29 (1984): 5–13.

60. Alton H. McEachern, "Preaching from the Psalms," *RevExp* 81, no. 3 (1984; pp. 457–58): 457.

themselves and to prod the sheep if needed.[61] The fact that the shepherd carried a staff encouraged the sheep to keep walking,[62] even through the darkest valley.[63]

So the LORD is our Shepherd. He provides us with rest, food, water, and vitality; he leads us in the right paths, is with us, and encourages us. That is what a good shepherd does.

In the New Testament Jesus called himself "the good shepherd" (John 10:11, 14). Like a good shepherd Jesus provides rest for his flock. He said, "Come to me, all you that are weary and are carrying heavy burdens, and I will give you rest" (Matt 11:28). Jesus also fed his flock. Jesus said, "I am the gate. Whoever enters by me will be saved, and will come in and go out and find *pasture*" (John 10:9).

During his life on earth, Jesus literally gave rest to and fed people. As Mark 6 tells the story of Jesus feeding the five thousand, you can hear echoes of Psalm 23. The story begins in Mark 6:30:[64]

> The apostles gathered around Jesus, and told him all that they had done and taught. He said to them, "Come away to a deserted place all by yourselves and *rest a while.*" For many were coming and going, and they had *no leisure even to eat.* And they went away in the boat to a deserted place by themselves. [So Jesus provides rest for his disciples.] Now many saw them going and recognized them, and they hurried there on foot from all the towns and arrived ahead of them. As he went ashore, he saw a great crowd; and he had *compassion* for them, because they were like *sheep without a shepherd* [Jesus will be their shepherd]; and he began to teach them many things. [Here the feeding begins: teaching them many things about the kingdom of God (Luke 9:11)]. When it grew late, his disciples came to him and said, "This is a deserted place, and the hour is now very late; send them away so that they may go into the surrounding country and villages and buy something for

61. See, e.g., Ross, *Commentary on the Psalms,* I, 566, and Vos, *Theopoetry of the Psalms,* 118–19.

62. David J. A. Clines, "Translating Psalm 23," in *Reflection and Refraction* (Leiden: Brill, 2006; pp. 67–80), 77, observes that the many versions that use "comfort" "are poor translations today, for it is hard to see how two lumps of wood could comfort or soothe a sheep. . . . 'Comfort' is fine if one is speaking Elizabethan English, where it usually meant 'encourage'. . . . The shepherd's rod and staff . . . encourage the sheep to keep on walking."

63. Calvin comments, David "compares the care which God takes in governing true believers to a shepherd's staff and crook, declaring that he is satisfied with this as all-sufficient for the protection of his life. . . . David now declares that as often as he shall be exposed to any danger, he will have sufficient defense and protection in being under the pastoral care of God." *Commentary on the Book of Psalms,* I, 394–95.

64. It would be helpful for the congregation to read along in their pew Bibles or with PowerPoint.

themselves to eat." But he answered them, "You give them something to eat." They said to him, "Are we to go and buy two hundred denarii worth of bread, and give it to them to eat?" [Two hundred denarii was about eight months' wages; thousands of dollars!] And he said to them, "How many loaves have you? Go and see." When they had found out, they said, "Five, and two fish." Then he ordered them to get all the people *to sit down* in groups on the *green* grass. [Mark here echoes Psalm 23:2, "He makes me *lie down* in *green* pastures. The crowd, too, needs to rest and be fed for the journey home.] So they sat down in groups of hundreds and of fifties. Taking the five loaves and the two fish, he looked up to heaven, and blessed and broke the loaves, and gave them to his disciples to set before the people; and he divided the two fish among them all. And *all ate and were filled;* and they *took up twelve baskets full of broken pieces and of the fish.* Those who had eaten the loaves numbered *five thousand men* (Mark 6:30–44).

Talk about lying down in green pastures. Jesus provided rest for his sheep and plenty of food.

Jesus also provided water for his sheep, but much more than "still waters." Jesus provided his sheep with "living water." He said to the Samaritan woman at the well, "Everyone who drinks of this water will be thirsty again, but those who drink of the water that I will give them will never be thirsty. The water that I will give will become in them a spring of water gushing up to eternal life" (John 4:13–14). Jesus offered "living water" so that his followers would receive eternal life.[65]

By providing rest, food, and living water, Jesus also provided life, vitality: "he restores my soul" (Ps 23:3). Jesus said, "I came that they [my sheep] may have *life,* and have it *abundantly*" (John 10:10).

In verse 3 David said of his shepherd, "He leads me in right paths." Jesus led his flock "in right paths" by modeling obedience to his Father's will and teaching them to do likewise (e.g., the Sermon on the Mount, Matt 5–7).

In verse 4 David said, "Even though I walk through the darkest valley, I fear no evil; for *you are with me.*" Jesus, the good shepherd, promised, *I am with you always,* to the end of the age" (Matt 28:20).[66]

---

65. Cf. John 6:35, 40, "Jesus said to them, 'I am the bread of life. Whoever comes to me will never be hungry, and whoever believes in me will never be thirsty. . . . This is indeed the will of my Father, that all who see the Son and believe in him may have eternal life; and I will raise them up at the last day.'" Cf. Rev 7:16–17, "They will hunger no more, and thirst no more . . . ; for the Lamb at the center of the throne will be their shepherd, and he will guide them to springs of the water of life, and God will wipe away every tear from their eyes."

66. Cf. Acts 18:9–10, "One night the Lord said to Paul in a vision, 'Do not be afraid, but speak and do not be silent; for *I am with you,* and no one will lay a hand on you to harm you.'"

Jesus will protect his flock from any and all enemies. In contrast to the hired hand who runs away when he sees a wolf coming, Jesus said, "I am the good shepherd. . . . I lay down my life for the sheep" (John 10:14–15). By laying down his life, Jesus would offer his sheep total security. Jesus said, "I give them *eternal* life, and they will *never* perish. No one will snatch them out of my hand" (John 10:28–29). So even though we walk through the darkest valley, we need fear no evil. Jesus said, "Do not be afraid, little flock, for it is your Father's good pleasure to give you the kingdom" (Luke 12:32). Jesus, the good shepherd, is with us providing total protection.

How is Jesus able to be as good a shepherd for us as the LORD was for his flock Israel? Matthew explains the miracle that happened when Jesus took on human flesh. Writes Matthew, "All this took place to fulfill what had been spoken by the Lord through the prophet: 'Look, the virgin shall conceive and bear a son, and they shall name him Emmanuel,' which means, '*God is with us*'" (Matt 1:22–23). In Jesus, God is with us. As God as shepherd was with Israel of old, so now in Jesus God is with us. God in Jesus is our good shepherd.

In Psalm 23:5 the image of the LORD being a shepherd for his sheep switches to the LORD being a host for his guest. From the shepherd being out in the fields with his sheep we move to the shepherd being in his tent hosting a guest. The relationship between a host and his guest is even more personal and intimate than that between a shepherd and his sheep.

Verse 5 lists four things the LORD as host does for his guest. Some are the same as what a shepherd does for his sheep, but host-guest is person to person. First, protection from enemies: "You prepare a table before me *in the presence of my enemies.*" Although enemies are still around, a good host will protect his guests from their enemies. "According to the Bedouin law of hospitality, once a traveler is received into the shepherd's tent, and especially once his host has spread food before him, he is guaranteed immunity from enemies who may be attempting to overtake him."[67] Think of Lot in Sodom hosting two angels. The citizens of Sodom wished to harm these guests but Lot insisted on keeping them safe even at the cost of his two daughters. Lot said, "Do nothing to these men, for they have come under the *shelter* of my roof" (Gen 19:8). A good host would protect his guests at all costs. Such a host is the LORD for David and us. The LORD protects us from our enemies even at the cost of his only Son. "God so loved the

---

67. B. Anderson, *Out of the Depths*, 183. Kidner, *Psalms 1–72*, 112, on the other hand, thinks that this feast in the presence of enemies "probably anticipates a victory celebration, where the enemies are present as captives; or an accession feast with defeated rivals as reluctant guests." On "the custom of hospitality in ancient Israel," see Arterbury and Bellinger, "'Returning' to the Hospitality of the Lord," *Bib* 86, no. 3 (2005): 388–92.

world that he gave his only Son, so that everyone who believes in him may not perish but may have eternal life" (John 3:16).

Second, as host the LORD provides abundant food: "*You prepare a table before me* in the presence of my enemies." The table is a banqueting table.

Third, as host the LORD provides respect for his guest: "you anoint my head with oil." In the days before sun-screen and moisture lotions, it was customary for hosts to show esteem for their guests by anointing their head with oil.[68] Recall Jesus' complaint when he was a guest of a Pharisee: "You did not anoint my head with oil" (Luke 7:46).

Fourth, the LORD provides plenty of wine: "my cup overflows."[69] "The overflowing cup or the abundant cup appears to be a commentary on the extravagance of God's provisions for guests. . . . The LORD, as a host, has vast resources upon which to draw."[70]

According to the New Testament, Jesus provides these things for his followers. In this time of Lent, we can think of the Last Supper. The night before he died, Jesus hosted the celebration of the Passover with his disciples. Here they remembered that the LORD saved their lives from "the destroyer" (Exod 12:23) through the blood of the lamb. During that meal, Jesus changed the Old Testament Passover to the New Testament Lord's Supper.

Jesus began by showing respect for his disciples: he washed their feet (John 13:1–5). Then, "while they were eating, Jesus took a loaf of bread, and after blessing it he broke it, gave it to the disciples, and said, 'Take, eat; this is my body.' Then he took a cup, and after giving thanks he gave it to them, saying, 'Drink from it, all of you; for this is my blood of the covenant, which is poured out for many for the forgiveness of sins'" (Matt 26:26–28).

The bread Jesus provided for his guests represented his own body. And the cup of wine represented his own blood of the covenant which would be "poured out for many *for the forgiveness of sins.*" Jesus would offer himself for his guests to pay for their sins, to protect them from their last enemy, death, and to save their lives. Then Jesus said, "I tell you, I will never again drink of this fruit of the vine until that day when I drink it new with you in my Father's kingdom" (Matt 26:29).

---

68. "The pouring of olive oil on the guest's head [connotes] the wealth, generosity, and care of the host to promote the renewal, joy, and healing of his weary and wounded guest." Waltke, *Psalms as Christian Worship,* 442. Davidson, *Vitality of Worship,* 85, with references to Ps 104:15 and 2 Sam 14:2, suggests that "oil was also used more generally on head and face as a sign of joy on festive occasions."

69. "Lit., 'My cup is a satiation.' LXX and Jerome rightly infer that the cup fills and gives great enjoyment to the person . . . rather than that the cup itself overflows." Goldingay, *Psalms,* I, 345 n. d.

70. Arterbury and Bellinger, "'Returning' to the Hospitality of the Lord," *Bib* 86, no. 3 (2005): 392.

It was a promise that in the future, Jesus would host a banquet for his followers in his Father's kingdom.[71]

Psalm 23:6 also shifts to the future: "Surely goodness and mercy shall follow me all the days of my life, and I shall dwell in the house of the LORD my whole life long." David had been pursued by his enemies: King Saul, the Philistines, even his own son Absalom. But now, he writes, as guest of the LORD, the LORD's "goodness and mercy"[72] shall follow me [pursue me][73] all the days of my life."

David started Psalm 23 with the LORD *before* him: verse 2, "he leads me." In the very center of the psalm he exclaims that the LORD is *with* him: verse 4, "you are *with* me." And now he concludes the psalm with the statement that the LORD *follows* him: verse 6, "goodness and mercy shall follow me."[74] In this respect Psalm 23 is like Psalm 139:5 which declared, "You hem me in, behind and before, and lay your hand upon me."

"Surely goodness and mercy[75] shall follow me *all the days of my life.*" "Usually, a guest may partake of traditional Arab hospitality for a maximum of three days. After that, it is good grace on the part of the guest to make an excuse to leave. . . . When God is our host, we are invited to stay not just for three days but 'all the days' of our lives."[76] Psalm 23 concludes, "and I shall dwell[77] in the house

71. Cf. Rev 19:9, "Blessed are those who are invited to the marriage supper of the Lamb."

72. "Goodness and mercy" are attributes of God. "The 'goodness' (*ṭôb*) of God is demonstrated in his abundant care and promises. . . . The 'love' (*ḥesed;* KJV, 'mercy') of God is the covenantal commitment to bless his people with his goodness, i.e., his promises." VanGemeren, *Psalms,* 256.

73. "NRSV's 'shall follow me' is a very weak translation. The Hebrew verb here clearly means 'pursue,' and John Goldingay uses the word 'chase,' which even better captures God's active, even frantic, attempt to reach us with the gift of life and the resources which sustain life." McCann, "Preaching the Psalms: Psalm 23," *JPr* 31, no. 2 (2008; 43–48): 46. Cf. Brown, *Psalms,* 35, David "joyously declares being the target not of enemies but of God's love, from which there is no escape. In dogged pursuit, God's benevolence will track down to secure and bless the speaker."

74. Mark S. Smith, "Setting and Rhetoric in Psalm 23," *JSOT* 41 (1988; pp. 61–66): 62–63.

75. "The final vignette abstracts God's attributes conveyed by the two images of Shepherd and Host: his goodness and *ḥesed*. In addition, the poet transmutes the implied tent into God's abode." Waltke, *Psalms as Christian Worship,* 436.

76. Larry G. Herr, "An Off-Duty Archaeologist Looks at Psalm 23," *BR* 8, no. 2 (1992; pp. 45–51): 50, with a reference to Judges 19:4–5.

77. Arterbury and Bellinger, "'Returning' to the Hospitality of the Lord," *Bib* 86, no. 3 (2005): 394, prefer "I will return" since it is the more literal translation of the verb and also "fits the context of hospitality far better than 'dwell' does. . . . Once a long-term relationship has been established, the guest returns to their host's house and hospitality whenever they are in the region again." Cf. Craigie, *Psalms 1–50,* 208; Davidson, *Vitality of Worship,* 85; and Clines, "Translating Psalm 23," 79. Goldingay, *Psalms,* I, 353, maintains that "both 'return to' and 'dwell in' make partial sense but also raise problems, and it finally makes little difference which we follow." Certainly in a sermon we should not make this an issue but simply follow the pew Bibles.

of the Lord my whole life long." Because he is being pursued by the Lord's goodness and mercy, David is convinced that he will dwell in the house of the Lord his whole life long. David here "leaves the realm of the imaginary and returns to the real world, a world as good as and even better than imagined. The sheepfold and banqueting table are transmuted into the house of God, which, in David's day, was a royal tent."[78] He expects to have fellowship with the Lord his whole life long.[79] This does not mean, however, that he will no longer have to walk through dark valleys. Instead it means, as he said in verse 4, that the Lord will be *with him* in those dark valleys. In other words, he will have continual fellowship with God.[80]

Some of you may recall that the King James version had, "I will dwell in the house of the Lord *forever*." That is probably saying too much.[81] In the Old Testament people could only envision dwelling in the house of the Lord for a long, long time: therefore, "my whole life long." But the King James Version is not entirely wrong. When Jesus had finished his saving work on earth and was about to ascend into heaven, he told his disciples, "Do not let your hearts be troubled. Believe in God, believe also in me. In my Father's house there are many dwelling places. If it were not so, would I have told you that I go to prepare a place for you? And if I go and prepare a place for you, I will come again and will take you to myself, *so that where I am, there you may be also*" (John 14:1–3). Because of the work of Jesus, our good shepherd, we will dwell in the house of the Lord forever.[82] That good news should encourage us even as we walk through the darkest valleys. Jesus promised to be with us always.

---

78. Waltke, *Psalms as Christian Worship*, 443, with a reference to Ps 15:1, "O Lord, who may abide in your tent?"

79. "The theme of continually abiding in God's house is a constant note in the psalms, for example, 27:4–6; 36:7–9; 52:8–9; 61:4. Whether or not the house or tent of the Lord is specifically the sanctuary, the expressed intent and desire at the conclusion of the psalm is to remain always in the sphere of God's presence and deliverance." Miller, *Interpreting the Psalms*, 117.

80. "We must not take this as implying persistent optimism. The speaker here knows that he must still often walk through a dark valley, but he also knows that no exposure to danger can separate him from God. . . . What is meant is continual fellowship with God." Westermann, *The Living Psalms*, 131.

81. "The Hebrew is clear: *ləʾorek yāmîm* 'for length of days' cannot possibly mean 'forever.'" Clines, "Translating Psalm 23," 79. Cf. Gene Rice, "An Exposition of Psalm 23," *JRT* 52, no. 1 (1995): 77.

82. Cf. Romans 8:38–39, "I am convinced that neither death, nor life . . . nor anything else in all creation, will be able to separate us from the love of God in Christ Jesus our Lord."

Prayer[83]

O God, our Shepherd and King,
    who brought again your Son Jesus from the valley of death.
Encourage us with your protecting presence,
    both when we skip through fresh pastures,
    and when we walk through the darkest valleys.
Encourage us at all times with your promise
    that we will dwell in the house of the LORD forever.
We pray in Jesus' name. Amen.

Song[84]

1My Shepherd will supply my need;
    the Lord God is his name.
In pastures fresh he makes me feed,
    beside the living stream.
He brings my wandering spirit back
    when I forsake his ways,
and leads me for his mercy's sake
    in paths of truth and grace.

2When I walk through the shades of death,
    your presence is my stay;
one word of your supporting breath
    drives all my fears away.
Your hand, in sight of all my foes,
    shall still my table spread;
my cup with blessings overflows,
    your oil anoints my head.

3The sure provisions of my God
    attend me all my days;
O may your house be my abode
    and all my work be praise.
There would I find a settled rest,
    while others go and come,
no more a stranger or a guest,
    but like a child at home.

83. Adapted from J. H. Eaton, *The Psalms*, 125.
84. Isaac Watts, 1719. Public Domain. *Psalter Hymnal* (1987), # 550; *Psalms for All Seasons*, # 23A; *Lift Up Your Hearts*, # 369.

CHAPTER 16

"Out of the Depths I Cry to You, O LORD"

Psalm 130 (129)

This well-known psalm is known as *De Profundis* — Latin for its opening words, "Out of the depths." By the fifth century Psalm 130 had become one of the church's seven "penitential psalms" along with Psalms 6, 32, 38, 51, 102, and 143.[1] Because of its emphasis on sin and grace, Luther designated this psalm as one of the "Pauline psalms," along with Psalms 32, 51, and 143.[2] *The Revised Common Lectionary* assigns Psalm 130 for reading on the fifth Sunday in Lent, Year A,[3] as a response to the reading of Ezekiel 37:1–14, the valley of the dry bones.

Text and Context

Although some have argued that verses 7 and 8 are a later addition addressed to Israel,[4] Psalm 130:1–8 is a complete literary unit. The verses 7–8 are "linked to verses 1–6 by the repetition of 'iniquities' (vv 3, 8) and 'hope' (vv 5, 7), as well as by similar syntactical uses of the preposition 'with' (vv 4, 7), each occurrence of which communicates a crucial aspect of God's character."[5] As a literary unit the whole psalm makes for a solid preaching text.

1. McCann, "Psalms," 1206. See there for its influence on Martin Luther, Theodore Beza, and John Wesley.
2. Weiser, *The Psalms*, 773.
3. It also assigns Psalm 130 for the sixth and twelfth Sunday after Pentecost in Year B.
4. E.g., Westermann, *The Living Psalms*, 117, 120.
5. McCann, "Psalms," 1205. McCann adds, "Furthermore, the movement from individual to communal perspectives is characteristic of the Songs of Ascents (see Psalms 121–124; 129; 131)." Cf. B. Anderson, *Out of the Depths*, 87–88, "The likelihood is that here, as in other laments (e.g., Psalm 22), the suppliant, speaking out of experience, teaches the community what this divine grace means in a larger sense."

As to its context, the editors of the Psalter may have placed this psalm right before Psalm 131 because both psalms conclude with the same admonition: "O Israel, hope in the LORD!" (Pss 130:7; 131:3). But for understanding the specific message of Psalm 130 it is more important to compare Psalm 130 with the other so-called penitential psalms. Leupold observes, "No other psalm expresses quite so well what an evil sin itself is. At the same time . . . the psalm has a distinct gospel emphasis."[6] This observation may help us in formulating the specific theme of this psalm.

Psalm 130 should also be understood, of course, in the context of the whole Old Testament. For example, passages from Exodus substantiate its message. McCann notes, "The vocabulary of Psalm 130 recalls God's self-revelation in Exodus 34. With God there is 'forgiveness' (Ps 130:4; Exod 34:9; NRSV 'pardon') of 'iniquities' (Ps 130:3, 8; Exod 34:7, 9, although the word is singular), which is manifestation of God's 'steadfast love' (Ps 130:7; Exod 34:6–7)."[7] The prophets also corroborate the psalm's message of forgiveness. For example, Amos writes, "I said, 'O Lord GOD, forgive, I beg you! How can Jacob stand? He is so small!' The LORD relented concerning this; 'It shall not be,' said the LORD" (Amos 7:2–3).

Literary Interpretation

Psalm 130 may seem rather straightforward, but the shifts in the person(s) addressed show its complexity. In verses 1–4 the psalmist addresses God directly. He shifts in verses 5–6 with his personal testimony to an unidentified audience. And finally, in verses 7–8, he addresses Israel directly.[8]

Although some identify the form of Psalm 130 as a thanksgiving song,[9] most label this psalm an individual lament.[10] In Chapter 1, pp. 10–11, we noted that the structure of lament psalms present some or all of these elements:

6. Leupold, *Exposition of the Psalms*, 902. See Zenger, *Psalms 3*, 439, for details on the context of Psalms 130–134.

7. McCann, *Theological Introduction*, 87.

8. John H. Hayes, *Preaching the New Common Lectionary, Year A: Lent . . .* , 26.

9. Understanding the perfect verbs in verses 1 and 5–6 as the past tense ("Out of the depths I cried to you, O LORD. . . . I waited for the LORD. . . .") instead of the iterative present as the NRSV translates. For a detailed discussion of form critics seeking to identify the form of Psalm 130, see Harry P. Nasuti, "Plumbing the Depths: Genre Ambiguity and Theological Creativity in the Interpretation of Psalm 130," in *The Idea of Biblical Interpretation* (Leiden: Brill, 2003; pp. 95–124), 96–101 and 120–24.

10. Note that, because of verses 7–8, Gerstenberger, *Psalms*, II, 357, calls it "an individual and communal complaint song." "The formal structure of individual complaint has . . . been modified

1) Introductory petition for God's help
2) Description of the trouble or complaint
3) Petitions for God's help
4) Reasons why God should hear or confidence that God will hear and save
5) Examples of God's saving acts in history
6) A vow to praise

Psalm 130 combines the first three elements in verses 1–2, "Out of the depths I cry to you, O LORD. . . ." Verses 3–6 express the confidence that God will hear and save: "If you, O LORD, should mark iniquities, Lord, who could stand? But there is forgiveness with you, so that you may be revered. I wait for the LORD, my soul waits, and in his word I hope. . . ." Instead of recalling God's saving acts in history and a vow to praise, the psalm concludes with a call to Israel to hope in the LORD and again the confidence that the LORD will hear and save Israel: "O Israel, hope in the LORD! For with the LORD there is steadfast love, and with him is great power to redeem. It is he who will redeem Israel from all its iniquities" (130:7–8).

We shall explore in some detail the psalm's parallelisms, its imagery, repetition of keywords, and structure.

Parallelisms

Like the other Songs of Ascents, Psalm 130 exhibits step parallelisms,[11] where one word or phrase in a verse is repeated in the next line or verse. This device links verses 2a and 2b ("voice"); 2 and 3 (*'ădonāy*), 5 and 6, and 7 and 8 (see the italicized words below). In addition, verses 1–2 show climactic parallelism. Verse 3b completes the thought of 3a and therefore shows advancing parallelism. Verse 4a with its "But" (*kî*) exhibits antithetic parallelism which verse 4b advances. Verses 5–6 return to climactic parallelism with the last line (v 6c) being synonymous parallelism. Verses 7b–8 again use climactic parallelism. We can sketch the parallelisms as follows:

₁Out of the depths I cry to you, O LORD.	A
₂*Lord,* hear my *voice!*	+ A′
Let your ears be attentive to the *voice* of my supplications!	+ A″

---

to fit the requirements of a communal setting" (p. 358). Waltke, *Psalms as Christian Lament,* 248, concludes, "In sum, Psalm 130 transforms a lament psalm (vv 1–2) into a song of trust." See also Zenger, *Psalms 3,* 426–27.

11. See deClaissé-Walford in deClaissé-Walford, Jacobson, and Tanner, *The Book of Psalms,* 887–90.

₃If you, O LORD, should mark iniquities,	A
Lord, who could stand?	+ A′
₄But there is forgiveness with you,	− B
so that you may be revered.¹²	+− B′

₅I wait for the LORD,	A
my soul waits,	+ A′
and in his word I hope;	+ A″
₆*my soul* waits for the Lord	+ A‴
more than those who watch for the morning,	+ A″″
more than those who watch for the morning.	A‴″

₇O Israel, hope in the LORD!	A
For with the LORD there is steadfast love,	B
and with him is great power to *redeem.*	+ B′
₈It is he who *will redeem* Israel from all its iniquities.	+ B″

Imagery

The psalm begins with the powerful metaphor of "the depths." "The 'depths' of the sea come with literal reference in Isa 51:10 and Ezek 27:34 and with metaphorical reference (as here) to overwhelming personal devastation in Ps 69:2, 14 [3, 15], where it denotes the effect of the assault of human attackers. . . . It indicates the objective fact of being engulfed in a 'sea of troubles,' which might include illness as well as the attacks of enemies. The more general image of deep waters indicates the waters of death or of Sheol. . . . Thus the psalmist is praying as from the dead."¹³

The psalmist cries to the LORD, "Let your ears [anthropomorphism] be attentive to the voice of my supplications!" (v 2). In verse 6 he uses a simile comparing his eager waiting with that of watchmen in the night: "my soul waits for the Lord more than those who watch for the morning." And he concludes in verses 7 and 8 with a vivid metaphor, "For with the LORD there is . . . great power to *redeem.* It is he who will *redeem* Israel from all its iniquities." To "redeem" is literally to buy off, to pay ransom to free those enslaved.

12. V 4b completes the antithetic thought of 4a; therefore +−B′: it advances (+) the antithetic parallelism of 4a (−B′).

13. Goldingay, *Psalms,* III, 524–25. Cf. Kraus, *Psalms 60–150,* 466, "The 'deep waters' are the kingdom of death, the place of separation from God and of God forsakenness." Cf. Mays, *Psalms,* 406, "It represents drowning in distress, being overwhelmed and sucked down by the bottomless waters of troubles."

Repetition of Keywords

Each of the first three stanzas alternates the names *Yahweh* or *Yah* ("I AM") and *Adonai* ("My Sovereign"). This focuses attention not only on Israel's covenant God but also on the fact that he is the sovereign Owner of all. The final stanza mentions the name of *Yahweh* twice so that God is named a total of eight times.

The problem addressed in this psalm is named once as "the depths" (v 1) and twice as "iniquities" (*'ăwônôt;* vv 3, 8). But the psalmist also testifies twice, "*I wait* for the Lord, *my soul waits,*" and adds the synonym "in his word *I hope*" (v 5). "The two verbs [wait / hope] are synonymous (Isa 51:5) [and are] used to speak of trust as an activity that must and does reckon with time, a stance of enduring the present in anticipation of vindication in the future."[14] The "hope" of verse 5 is picked up again in verse 7 when the psalmist exhorts Israel, "O Israel, hope in the Lord!"

Three times the psalm uses the unusual expression "with you": "*But (kî) with you* there is forgiveness" (v 4), and "*For (kî) with the Lord* there is steadfast love, and *with him* is great power to redeem" (v 7). Finally the "redeem" of verse 7 is repeated in verse 8 together with the "iniquities" of verse 3, "It is he who *will redeem* Israel from all its iniquities."

Structure

As can be seen in the NRSV, NIV, and ESV breaks, Psalm 130 consists of four stanzas, which are related in an ABA'B' pattern:[15]

   I. Address to God (vv 1–4)
      A. I cry out to God for mercy (v 1–2)
      B. With God is forgiveness (vv 3–4)
  II. Address to the congregation (vv 5–8)
      A'. I wait for God (vv 5–6)
      B'. With God is complete redemption (vv 7–8)

Overall, the structure of the psalm reveals a movement from the depths of despair, to a cry to the Lord for help, to confidence in the Lord's forgiveness,

---

14. Mays, *Psalms,* 407.

15. Waltke, *Psalms as Christian Lament,* 249. So also VanGemeren, *Psalms,* 920, and Zenger, *Psalms 3,* 425. In contrast, Allen, *Psalms 101–150,* 194, argues for an "overall chiastic structure," ABB'A', from v 3, "iniquities," v 4, "for with you," v 7, "for with Yahweh" and v 8, "its iniquities."

to hope in the LORD's word, to an exhortation to Israel to hope in the LORD. As Kidner puts it, "There is a steady climb towards assurance, and at the end there is encouragement for the many from the experience of the one."[16]

We can outline the structure of the psalm as follows:

I. Out of the depths I cry to the LORD (vv 1–2)
II. With the LORD there is forgiveness for iniquities (vv 3–4)
III. I wait for the LORD, hoping in his word (vv 5–6)
IV. Israel, hope in the LORD; he will redeem you from all your iniquities (vv 7–8)

Theocentric Interpretation

The eight references to God (*Yahweh, Adonai*) in eight verses are a clear indication that Psalm 130 is theocentric. Note specifically that in verses 1–2 the psalmist cries out directly to the LORD. Verses 3–4 continue the conversation with the LORD, concluding with, "But there is forgiveness with you [LORD], so that you may be revered." In verse 5 the psalmist acknowledges, "I wait for the LORD, my soul waits, and in his word I hope." Finally he admonishes Israel to hope in the LORD and provides two solid reasons for doing so: "For with the LORD there is steadfast love, and with him is great power to redeem" (v 7). He concludes with the firm assurance, "It is he [he himself] who will redeem Israel from all its iniquities" (v 8).

Textual Theme and Goal

The textual theme, its message for Israel, is rather easy to detect. The thrust of Psalm 130 is found in its final exhortation to Israel: "O Israel, hope in the LORD! For with the LORD there is steadfast love, and with him is great power to redeem. It is he who will redeem Israel from all its iniquities" (vv 7–8). We can therefore formulate the textual theme as follows: *Hope in the LORD, Israel, for he will redeem you from all your iniquities.*[17]

For discerning the textual goal, it would be helpful to know the psalm's historical setting. Most biblical scholars agree that Psalm 130 was composed after

16. Kidner, *Psalms 73–150,* 446.
17. Cf. Mays, *Psalms,* 406, "The theme of the song is hope for forgiveness that the LORD will bestow by showing steadfast love in the redemption of Israel from all its iniquities."

Israel returned from the Babylonian exile.[18] It may have "belonged to the pilgrimage festival of the autumn. In deepest sorrow and penitence the people are waiting and watching, perhaps at night, looking for the Lord and his word which was sometimes given at break of morning."[19] In any event, the imperative in verse 7, "O Israel, hope in the LORD!" indicates that the goal of this psalm is *to urge Israel to hope in the LORD for redemption from all their iniquities.*

Ways to Preach Christ

One could possibly trace the longitudinal theme of redemption from all iniquities from the Old Testament to Jesus Christ in the New Testament. But the most direct way to preach Christ from this psalm is the way of promise-fulfillment supported by New Testament references.

Promise-Fulfillment and New Testament References

Although there is no direct promise of the coming Messiah in this psalm, there is the promise of redemption from all iniquities. In fact, this is the central message of Psalm 130: "Hope in the LORD, Israel, for *he will redeem you from all your iniquities!*" This hope is directed towards the future when God will redeem his people from all their iniquities. The psalmist himself said, "I wait for the LORD, my soul waits, and *in his word I hope*" (v 5). The "word" in which he hopes is especially God's covenant promises.[20] The waiting, waiting, indicates that the fulfillment of these promises lies in the future.[21]

---

18. "The words *qaššubôt* [v 2] and *səlîḥâ* (v 4) are late Hebrew and help to establish the postexilic date of the psalm." Leupold, *Exposition of the Psalms,* 906-7. Cf. Allen, *Psalms 101-150,* 195; Broyles, *Psalms,* 468; and Waltke, *Psalms as Christian Lament,* 247 n. 53. For more detailed arguments, see Gerstenberger, *Psalms,* II, 356-57; Harry P. Nasuti, "Plumbing the Depths: Genre Ambiguity and Theological Creativity in the Interpretation of Psalm 130," in *The Idea of Biblical Interpretation* (Leiden: Brill, 2003), 107-10; and Thijs Booij, "Psalm 130:34: The Words and Their Context," in *Unless Some One Guide Me* (Maastricht: Shaker Pub., 2000; pp. 237-45), 242-43.

19. Eaton, *The Psalms,* 440.

20. "In plain terms, he speaks of a promise (*his word*) to cling to." Kidner, *Psalms 73-150,* 446. Cf. Waltke, *Psalms as Christian Lament,* 255, "'His word' refers to his covenant promises of salvation, not to a theorized priestly oracle of salvation." Cf. Mays, *Psalms,* 407, and Stek, *NIV Study Bible,* 926, Ps 130:5 n.

21. "From the concern with waiting like a watchman and from the concluding assurance that the Lord will redeem his people from their sins, I deduce that the 'word' denotes a new act of salvation by which the godly person is upheld in faith." VanGemeren, *Psalms,* 922.

These promises were fulfilled in Jesus Christ. He was the Word made flesh. John testifies, "In the beginning was the Word, and the Word was with God, and the Word was God. . . . And the Word became flesh and lived among us, and we have seen his glory, the glory as of a father's only son, full of grace and truth" (John 1:1, 14). Through the death and resurrection of his Son Jesus, God redeems his people from all their iniquities. This claim can be backed up by many New Testament references (see "Sermon Exposition" below).

Sermon Theme, Goal, and Need

We formulated the textual theme as, "Hope in the LORD, Israel, for he will redeem you from all your iniquities." Since the New Testament expands this promise to all people, with a slight change the textual theme can become the sermon theme: *Hope in the LORD, people, for he will redeem you from all your iniquities.*

With a similar change, the textual goal can become the sermon goal: *to urge people to hope in the LORD for redemption from all their iniquities.* This goal points to the need addressed: some people are in deep despair because of their iniquities.[22] The sermon introduction can illustrate this need, thus creating a hunger for the good news that follows.

Liturgy, Scripture Reading, and Sermon Outline

In the liturgy, Psalm 130:1–4 could be used as a prayer for forgiveness while the verses 7–8 could be used as the assurance of pardon. Alternatively, one could use verses 7–8 as a call to confession, verses 1–3 as the confession itself, and verse 4 as the assurance of pardon.[23] For Scripture reading it would be fitting that a good reader reads the whole psalm, pausing after verse 6, then addressing the congregation directly with the verses 7–8.

The sermon outline can follow the four points of the text, with moves to Christ in appropriate places, especially at the end. The sermon outline, then, would look as follows:

22. "The psalmist cries out of a situation of deep distress, here poetically likened to being engulfed by the mythical waters of chaos (as in Ps 69:2, 14–15). Commentators as early as Chrysostom associated this perilous situation with despair. Despair was viewed as a severe threat to salvation because it eliminated hope and trust in God." B. Anderson, *Out of the Depths*, 87.

23. Suggested by my proofreader Ryan Faber.

I. The cry to the LORD out of the depths (vv 1–2)
II. With the LORD there is forgiveness (vv 3–4)
III. Waiting for the LORD, hoping in his word (vv 5–6)
IV. Hope in the LORD; he will redeem his people from their iniquities (vv 7–8)
V. Through Jesus, the LORD redeems his people from their iniquities (NT)

Sermon Exposition

For the sermon introduction one might use a personal or contemporary illustration of being in "the depths," of being in absolute darkness, of being in utter despair. Many people today feel this way. They feel trapped in the darkness. Their life is utter chaos. They see no way out. Life is not worth living.

This is how the psalmist felt. He begins, "Out of the depths I cry to you, O LORD." He is in deep trouble. He is in "the depths" — that is short for "the depths of the sea."[24] He is in a sea of troubles. He is like the psalmist who cried out in Psalm 69, "Save me, O God, for the waters have come up to my neck. I sink in deep mire, where there is no foothold; I have come into deep waters, and the flood sweeps over me" (69:1–2). He is "drowning in distress, . . . overwhelmed and sucked down by the bottomless waters of troubles."[25]

What makes it worse is that it's his own fault. In verse 3 he speaks of "iniquities." Somehow his suffering in the depths is the result of his own sins.[26] That adds the burden of guilt to his pain.

Many years ago I had a parishioner who was dying of lung cancer. His greatest burden was not the pain and the dying; his greatest burden was that he had brought this affliction on himself by smoking cigarettes.

So the psalmist struggles in the depths, blaming himself for his terrible suffering. Humanly speaking there seems to be no way out. He should be giving up all hope. But he knows Israel's covenant God, the LORD. It was the LORD who redeemed Israel from their enslavement and suffering in Egypt. He may have known the words of Isaiah, "Was it not you [O LORD] who *dried up the sea,* the waters of the great deep; who made *the depths of the sea a way* for the redeemed

---

24. "The Hebrew *ma‘ămaqqîm* refers to the depths of the seas (see on 69:2; cf. Isa 51:10; Ezek 27:34), but here it is used figuratively of troubles and misfortunes. This symbolism is very apposite, because the deep or the seas can often represent Sheol or its sphere of influence (cf. Jon 2:2f.)." A. Anderson, *Psalms 73–150,* 875.

25. Mays, *Psalms,* 406.

26. "His present suffering, as so often in the OT, is assumed to be due to his personal wrongdoing." Allen, *Psalms 101–150,* 195.

to cross over?" (Isa 51:10). When one is in the depths, there is only One who can help. That is the LORD who is Master also of the depths.

The psalmist, therefore, turns to the LORD: "Out of the depths I cry to you, O LORD." Notice that the last three letters in LORD are printed in small capital letters. That indicates that the Hebrew here has the name *Yahweh*, the God who revealed himself to Moses as "I Am Who I Am," Israel's faithful covenant God, the God who was with them as they suffered in Egypt, the God who redeemed them from their enslavement.

The psalmist continues in verse 2, "Lord, hear my voice! Let your ears be attentive to the voice of my supplications!" Notice here that except for the first letter the name Lord is not capitalized. That indicates that the Hebrew here has the name *Adonai*. *Adonai* is the God who is "enthroned in the heavens" (Ps 129); the God who is sovereign over all things. *Adonai* is Lord of all, Master, Owner of all. *Adonai* is our Master; we are his servants.[27]

Urgently the psalmist pleads with his Master, "Lord, hear my voice!"[28] Let your ears be attentive to the voice of my supplications!" The NIV translates, "Let your ears be attentive to my cry for mercy."[29] Suffering as he does in the depths, and having himself to blame, he needs his Master's mercy, his grace.[30]

Verse 3, "If you, O LORD, should mark iniquities, Lord, who could stand?" The word "iniquities" denotes "going astray," deliberate "deviation from the right path."[31] "Iniquities" stands for the sinful acts and the resultant guilt. If the LORD should mark iniquities, if he should "keep careful watch over"[32] our sins, no one could stand.[33] We would all be condemned. For, as Paul puts it

27. "In this form of address the Lord-servant relationship and the proper bearing of the fear of God are indicated." Kraus, *Psalms 60–150, 467.* Cf. Allen, *Psalms 101–150,* 193 n. 2a.

28. "An imperative ['Hear my voice!'] from an inferior to a superior becomes an urgent request, not a command." Waltke, *Psalms as Christian Lament,* 253.

29. *Supplications* "comes from the same verbal root as the word translated in Psalms 111, 112, and 123 as 'showing favor' (*ḥānan*)." DeClaissé-Walford in deClaissé-Walford, Jacobson, and Tanner, *The Book of Psalms,* 928. Cf. A. Anderson, *Psalms 73–150,* 875, "The voice of my supplications, that is, my loud entreaties for favor."

30. "Release from the depths of despair and the abyss of sin and guilt comes not from the self-help of the one caught in that condition. It is to be found in the God whose nature is to forgive." Miller, *Interpreting the Psalms,* 140.

31. A. Anderson, *Psalms 1–72,* 255, 393.

32. "In speaking of keeping [marking] waywardness, the psalm utilizes the common verb *šāmar,* used to refer to guarding a city (127:1) or guarding people from danger (121:3–8); compare 130:6. . . . The psalm envisages the possibility that Yhwh might keep careful watch over our waywardness and make sure none of it escapes." Goldingay, *Psalms,* III, 526.

33. The rhetorical question expects a negative answer. "What the text means to say is that no one who has sinned can, as a creature, stand his ground when YHWH watches him." Booij, "Psalm 130:34: The Words and Their Context," 238. Cf. Pss 32:3–4; 51:3–5, 9.

in the New Testament, we "all have sinned and fall short of the glory of God" (Rom 3:23).

"But," verse 4, "there is forgiveness with you, so that you may be revered." That is the turning point in this psalm: "But there is *forgiveness* with you." This is the only time the Psalter uses the noun *forgiveness*.[34] It uses the verb "forgive" many times but here it uses the noun: "There is *forgiveness with you* [the LORD]." Forgiveness accompanies the LORD. Wherever the LORD goes, forgiveness comes along. It is part of the LORD's character. "The authority to forgive and the disposition to forgive belong to the LORD."[35] This means "that the character of God is neither bent against us, nor neutral in God's justice and righteousness, but is bent toward us in grace and mercy."[36]

We can see this clearly in God's sending his Son Jesus to earth to pay the penalty for our sins. As John puts it in John 3:16, "God *so loved* the world that he gave his only Son, so that everyone who believes in him may not perish but may have eternal life." Or, as Paul puts it in Romans 8, "If God is for us, who is against us? He who did not withhold his own Son, but gave him up for all of us, will he not with him also give us everything else?" (Rom 8:31–32). There is forgiveness with the LORD. The LORD is *for* us.

Verse 4 concludes, "But there is forgiveness with you, *so that you may be revered*." How can God's forgiveness result in his being revered? We could understand it better if the verse concluded, "But there is forgiveness with you, so that we may be saved, or so that we may rejoice." But now it reads, "There is forgiveness with you, so that you may be *revered*."[37] How does God's forgiveness lead to God's being revered?

The Bible tells us that without God's forgiveness we would suffer everlasting punishment. So when the LORD forgives us, we will *revere* the LORD for who he is and for what he has done.[38] As the NIV translates, we will "with reverence, serve" the LORD.

With Bernhard Anderson we can also think of it this way: "Forgiveness is the expression of God's grace, of God's freedom to 'be gracious to whom I will be gracious' and to 'show mercy upon whom I will show mercy' (Ex 33:19; see Rom 9:15). God's forgiveness, then, is a wonderful gift, the appropriate response to

---

34. Westermann, *The Living Psalms*, 118, and Davidson, *Vitality of Worship*, 425.

35. Mays, *Psalms*, 406.

36. Miller, *Interpreting the Psalms*, 141.

37. For seven different interpretations of these words, see Booij, "Psalm 130:34: The Words and Their Context," 239–41.

38. "They can live as 'God-fearers,' that is, as people who take the authority and disposition of the LORD as the greatest reality of all and base their living on God without reservation." Mays, *Psalms*, 407.

which is wonder and praise."[39] In short, our gratitude to God for his forgiveness will lead to our serving God with reverence.[40] "There is forgiveness with you, so that you may be revered."

The psalmist is so sure that "there is forgiveness with" the LORD, that he continues in verse 5, "I wait for the LORD, my soul waits, and in his word I hope." "I wait for the LORD," he says, that is, "I look expectantly" for the LORD.[41] He waits patiently, expecting the LORD to act. For emphasis he repeats "my soul waits." He will wait in anticipation for the LORD to act.[42]

"In his word I hope," he adds. This "word" could perhaps be God's word of pardon[43] but more likely it is God's covenant word of promise.[44] For example, God had promised Israel, "Though your sins are like scarlet, they shall be like snow; though they are red like crimson, they shall become like wool" (Isa 1:18). The psalmist responds: "I wait for the LORD [to act], my soul waits, and in his word I hope." The synonyms "wait" and "hope" "both bespeak active, eager anticipation that God will bring a newness that is well beyond anything known in the present tense."[45]

In verse 6 he repeats again, "my soul waits for the Lord." But here he adds, "more than those who watch for the morning." For emphasis he repeats again, "more than those who watch for the morning." "Those who watch for the morning" refers to the watchmen or sentries who stand guard during the night. It is a lonesome, tedious job. But also dangerous as they peer into the darkness for any sign of trouble. They eagerly wait for morning light so they can go to the safety of their homes and get some much-needed rest. Compared to those watchmen yearning for the morning, the psalmist is even more eager for God's new morning to arrive. He may have been thinking of Isaiah's words, "Those who *wait for the LORD* shall renew their strength, they shall mount up with wings like eagles,

---

39. B. Anderson, *Out of the Depths*, 88–89.

40. See the structure of the Heidelberg Catechism: guilt, grace, gratitude. Cf. Miller, *Interpreting the Psalms*, 142–43, "The forgiveness of God that delivers from the depths of despair, guilt and anxiety is not an end in itself but makes possible that glorification of God that is the primary end of all human life."

41. Waltke, *Psalms as Christian Lament*, 255.

42. "The verb *qāwâ* (piel) suggests an attitude of expectancy or waiting, looking for something to happen, looking for Yhwh to act." Goldingay, *Psalms*, III, 528–29.

43. Kraus, *Psalms 60–150*, 467, "He is waiting for the word [which] is here the oracle of salvation." So also Westermann, *The Living Psalms*, 120; Allen, *Psalms 101–150*, 194; Goldingay, *Psalms*, III, 529, and Davidson, *Vitality of Worship*, 425. Unfortunately, this interpretation seems to limit the meaning of "word" to the oracle that may (or may not) have been spoken in the temple.

44. See n. 20 above.

45. James D. Newsome, "Fifth Sunday in Lent," *Texts for Preaching*, 222.

they shall run and not be weary, they shall walk and not faint" (Isa 40:31). What a morning to wait for!

But right now the psalmist is still in "the depths." It is night for him. He is surrounded by darkness. But out of the depths he has cried to the LORD, the one with whom there is forgiveness. Now he eagerly waits for the Lord to come through for him, to fulfill his word of promise. He waits for the LORD "more than those who watch for the morning." And like those watchmen, he also knows that morning will surely come. For forgiveness is with the LORD. And the LORD will be true to his word.

After this personal testimony that he hopes in God's word and eagerly waits for God to act on his word, the psalmist turns to Israel. By this time Israel has probably suffered through the exile in Babylon. They returned to a devastated Palestine inhabited by foreign peoples who opposed them. The nation of Israel is in "the depths" as the psalmist was. So he turns to Israel and exhorts them in verse 7, "O Israel, hope in the LORD! For with the LORD there is steadfast love, and with him is great power to redeem." The psalmist hoped in the LORD's word because there is *forgiveness with the LORD*. Here he urges *Israel* also to hope in the LORD. And he adds two solid reasons for hoping in the LORD. "O Israel, hope in the LORD! *For* [because] *with the LORD there is steadfast love,* and *with him is great power to redeem.*" Two reasons for hoping in the LORD: "with the LORD there is steadfast love, and with him is great power to redeem."

The LORD's "steadfast love" is his covenant faithfulness. It is the LORD's love that never gives up on his people. It is "the sort of love that keeps on loving, no matter what. The same Hebrew word (*ḥesed*) is used for the love that young Hosea had for his wife, even after her unfaithfulness (Hosea 1–3). This is the kind of love that never gives up, like that of the father [in Jesus' parable] who never gave up on his rebellious son and kept hoping, waiting, watching for his return (Luke 15)."[46]

Patrick Miller observes that in this psalm "three fundamental characteristics — forgiveness, steadfast love or grace, and redemption — are set forth almost as intimate friends and companions of God. Wherever the Lord goes, they are there accompanying and going with God. To encounter this God is also to meet with grace and forgiveness and abundant redemption."[47] For this reason the psalm

---

46. Limburg, *Psalms*, 448. Cf. McCann, "Psalms," 1206, "The focus is on God's character. Israel's future does not depend on its own worthiness or ability to save itself but on God's faithful love and ability to redeem."

47. Miller, *Interpreting the Psalms*, 142. Cf. Westermann, *The Living Psalms*, 120, "'Steadfast love' and 'redemption' . . . are here in parallel; God's steadfast love, *ḥesed*, brings about 'plenteous redemption,' compare Psalm 103." Cf. Exodus 34:6–7, "The LORD passed before him [Moses], and proclaimed, 'The LORD, the LORD, a God merciful and gracious, slow to anger, and abounding

can conclude with the firm assurance of verse 8, "It is he[48] [the LORD] who will redeem Israel from all its iniquities." The LORD "will redeem Israel from *all its iniquities.*"

To redeem is to ransom. In Israel slaves could be set free if someone paid the ransom. Psalm 130 declares that the LORD will set Israel free. He will pay the ransom for each and every iniquity and the misery they have caused. "The psalm declares the certainty of a comprehensive and final redemption. . . . The declaration has an eschatological reach unusual in the Old Testament. . . . Redemption includes liberation not only from guilt but also from the whole imprisoning network of sin's effects on life."[49] The LORD will set his people free from every enslavement.

This promise began to be fulfilled in Jesus Christ. The psalmist said in verse 5, "I wait for the LORD, my soul waits, and in *his word* I hope." Jesus was the final Word of God, the Word made flesh. John testifies, "In the beginning was the Word, and the Word was with God, and the Word was God. . . . And the Word became flesh and lived among us, and we have seen his glory, the glory as of a father's only son, full of grace and truth" (John 1:1, 14). Through the death and resurrection of his Son, Jesus, God paid the ransom for all our iniquities.

Before Jesus was born, the angel instructed Joseph concerning Mary, "She will bear a son, and you are to name him Jesus, for he will save his people from their sins" (Matt 1:21) — an allusion to Psalm 130:8, "It is he who will redeem Israel from all its iniquities." Later, Jesus himself claimed that he had "authority on earth to forgive sins" (Matt 9:6). Still later, when Jesus instituted the Lord's Supper in remembrance of his death, he said, "this is my blood of the covenant, which is poured out for many for the forgiveness of sins" (Matt 26:28).

Paul writes in Romans 3, "Since all have sinned and fall short of the glory of God; they are now *justified by his grace* as a gift, through the *redemption* that is in *Christ Jesus, whom God put forward as a sacrifice of atonement* by his blood, effective through faith" (Rom 3:23-25). Again, in Ephesians 1 Paul writes, "In

---

in steadfast love and faithfulness, keeping steadfast love for the thousandth generation, forgiving iniquity and transgression and sin, yet by no means clearing the guilty. . . ."

48. "'He alone': The Hebrew is emphatic that God alone can deliver Israel. Thus the psalmist and the community must wait and trust, not turning to any substitute that will have no power to set men free." Rogerson and McKay, *Psalms 101-150,* 133.

49. Mays, *Psalms,* 407. Cf. A. Anderson, *Psalms 73-150,* 877, "The redemption from sins is a rather unique expression in the OT, at least in this explicit form, and it is tantamount to forgiveness which involves deliverance from the afflictions caused by the sins." Cf. Eaton, *Psalms,* 290, "He will put away the sin of his people, freeing them from the misery that it has brought upon them."

him [Jesus Christ] we have *redemption* through his blood, the *forgiveness* of our trespasses, according to the riches of his *grace*" (Eph 1:7).[50]

The parishioner who blamed himself for contracting lung-cancer experienced that forgiveness. I had left him a booklet that evening with some popular Bible verses. Among them, I believe, was Isaiah 1:18, "Though your sins are like scarlet, they shall be like snow; though they are red like crimson, they shall become like wool." And Jesus' words in Matthew 11:28, "Come to me, all you that are weary and are carrying heavy burdens, and I will give you rest." And 1 John 2:1–2, "My little children, I am writing these things to you so that you may not sin. But if anyone does sin, we have an advocate with the Father, Jesus Christ the righteous; and *he is the atoning sacrifice for our sins,* and not for ours only but also for the sins of the whole world." The next morning when I returned he showed me that little booklet, stained with tears. He had read through the verses and experienced that with the LORD is forgiveness. A few days later he died, at peace with God.

Psalm 130 encourages Israel and all people to hope in the LORD, for he will redeem us from all our iniquities. In fact, the LORD has already redeemed us through the death and resurrection of his Son, Jesus Christ.

Prayer[51]

Father, we commend to your steadfast love
    those who are crying from the depths.
Help them to watch and pray through their time of darkness,
    in sure hope of the dawn of your forgiveness and complete redemption.
In Jesus' name. Amen.

Song[52]

1Out of the depths I cry to you on high;
    Lord, hear my call.
Bend down your ear and listen to my sigh,
    forgiving all.
If you should mark our sins, who then could stand?
    But grace and mercy dwell at your right hand.

---

50. Cf. Romans 8:22–25, "We know that the whole creation has been groaning in labor pains until now; and not only the creation, but we ourselves, who have the first fruits of the Spirit, groan inwardly while we wait for adoption, the redemption of our bodies. For in hope we were saved. Now hope that is seen is not hope. For who hopes for what is seen? But *if we hope for what we do not see, we wait for it with patience.*"

51. Adapted from J. H. Eaton, *The Psalms,* 441.

52. Public Domain. *Psalter Hymnal* (1987), # 256; *Psalms for All Seasons,* # 130C; *Lift Up Your Hearts,* # 655.

₂I wait for God, I trust his holy word;
 he hears my sighs.
My soul still waits and looks unto the Lord;
 my prayers arise.
I look for him to drive away my night,
 yes, more than those who watch for morning light.

₃Hope in the Lord: unfailing is his love;
 in him confide.
Mercy and full redemption from above
 he does provide.
From sin and evil, mighty though they seem,
 his arm almighty will his saints redeem.

CHAPTER 17

"O Give Thanks to the LORD!"

Psalm 118 (117)

The Revised Common Lectionary assigns the reading of Psalm 118:1–2, 19–29 for Palm Sunday in Year A, B, and C[1] as a response to the reading of Isaiah 50:4–9a, "The Servant's Humiliation and Vindication." According to John Hayes, "Psalm 118 is appropriate for Palm Sunday reading for three reasons: (1) it is a psalm originally used by a leader (probably a king) entering the city and sanctuary triumphantly; (2) it is a psalm deeply rooted in the Jewish celebration of Passover, a festival around which much of the Christian passion narrative revolves; and (3) according to the gospel tradition (Mark 11:9–10; Matt 21:1–10; Luke 19:37–38; [John 12:12–13]), the psalm was sung by pilgrims accompanying Jesus as they entered Jerusalem on Palm Sunday."[2] These three reasons also indicate that *preaching* Psalm 118 will probably be a good fit for Palm Sunday.

Text and Context

The entire Psalm 118 makes for a lengthy but proper preaching text.[3] The author has marked it as a literary unit with the inclusio of the first and last verse (vv 1 and 29): "O give thanks to the LORD, for he is good; his steadfast love endures forever!"

As to its context, Psalm 118 is the last one in a group of psalms (113–118) called the Egyptian Hallel — so-called because they celebrate Israel's deliverance from Egypt (cf. Psalm 114:1, "When Israel went out from Egypt. . . ."). Richard Belcher

---

1. And Psalm 118:1–2, 14–24 for Easter, all three years. See p. 436 below.

2. Hayes, *Preaching the New Common Lectionary, Year A, Lent . . .* , 71.

3. One can, of course, also use as preaching text smaller sections of a lengthy psalm (see, e.g., pp. 436–45 on Psalm 118:10–24), but we have set as our goal to preach the whole psalm assigned by the lectionary.

remarks, "They seem to have been grouped together because of their deliverance and Exodus emphases. The psalms in this group focus mainly on the power of the LORD to deliver, as he delivered his people from Egypt."[4] It is no coincidence, therefore, that Psalm 118:14 quotes the Song of Moses sung after the LORD brought his people safely through the Red Sea: "The LORD is my strength and my might; he has become my salvation" (Exod 15:2a, b). Like the Song of Moses, the psalm also speaks of the LORD's "steadfast love" (Ps 118:1–4, 29; cf. Exod 15:13), of his "right hand" (Ps 118:15–16; cf. Exod 15:6, 12), of "my God . . . I will extol you" (Ps 118:28; cf. Exod 15:2c, d), and of enemy nations that can be faced without fear because of the LORD's power (Ps 118:10–12; cf. Exod 15:14–16). James Mays summarizes, "All these repetitions and relationships can be taken as directives that Psalm 118 is to be read and understood in light of the situation of Israel and of Israel's song and story in Exodus 14–15."[5]

Literary Interpretation

Psalm 118 is complex because sections alternate between different speakers who are not identified. A priest (probably) calls on Israel to "give thanks to the LORD" and to say, "His steadfast love endures forever" (vv 1–4). This is followed by a single person (the "I") relating his experience of deliverance from the nations surrounding him and his testimony (vv 5–14). After someone observes that "there are glad songs of victory in the tents of the righteous" (vv 15–16), the "I" returns (vv 17–19). A priest says, "This is the gate of the LORD" (v 20) and the "I" responds with thanksgiving (v 21). After the proverb about the rejected stone (v 22), the psalm turns to the plural ("our," "us," "we"), blessing "the one who comes in the name of the LORD" (vv 23–27). At the conclusion the "I" speaks once more, thanking and extolling his God (v 28), and a priest closes the psalm by encouraging Israel again to "give thanks to the LORD."

A major question for solid interpretation and sound preaching is, Who is the "I"? In contrast to some commentators who contend that the "I" is Israel personified, I think there is sufficient evidence that the "I" is a Davidic king.[6] First, the

---

4. Belcher, *The Messiah and the Psalms*, 190.

5. Mays, "Psalm 118 in the Light of Canonical Analysis," in *Canon, Theology, and Old Testament Interpretation* (Philadelphia: Fortress, 1988; pp. 299–311), 305. On p. 304 Mays lists words that appear in Exodus 14 as well as Psalm 118. Cf. Zenger, *Psalms 3*, 234–35, 239–40.

6. "The speaker seems to be the King or a representative of the nation, and consequently the whole Psalm concerns essentially the fortunes of the entire community. This accounts for the mixture of individuals and congregational experiences and acts of worship." A. Anderson, *Psalms 73–150*, 797. Cf. ibid., 798, "Johnson and many other scholars think that the speaker of these verses is the King. This is more likely than the suggestion that the subject of these verses is the personified Israel, or some ordinary worshipper."

editors of the Psalter have used the royal Psalm 2, which has several similarities with Psalm 118, as introduction to all the following psalms. Second, the editors placed Psalm 118 in Book V which "seeks a king like David."[7] Third, and most important, the psalm itself echoes the military tone of the Song of Moses and shows that this king, whoever he was, was in severe "distress" (v 5), "surrounded" by "all nations" (cf. Ps. 2:1–3) "on every side." But "in the name of the LORD" he "cut them off" (vv 10–12; cf. Ps. 2:8–9). This is followed by "glad songs of victory in the tents of the righteous [Israel's soldiers]" (v 15). The king (and his army) then march to the temple in Jerusalem where he requests, "Open to me the gates of righteousness, that I may enter through them and give thanks to the LORD" (v 19). John Stek sums up this position, "A Davidic king leads the nation in a liturgy of thanksgiving for deliverance and victory after a hard-fought battle with a powerful confederacy of nations (cf. 2 Chron 20:27–28)."[8]

There is no agreement on the form of the psalm either.[9] Because the "I" is identified as a king, some scholars have called it a "royal psalm." Others, however, call it an individual song of thanksgiving because the main character gives thanks to the LORD (vv 19, 21, 28). Bernhard Anderson combines the two, identifying this psalm as an "individual song of thanksgiving (royal)."[10] Still others, because the psalm calls on *Israel* to give thanks to the LORD (vv 1, 29), identify it as a communal song of thanksgiving. To cover all the bases of this complex psalm it seems best to identify it as an individual, communal song of thanksgiving (royal).

Within this broader category, the author makes use of different literary forms such as hymnic elements (vv 1–4, 29), wisdom sayings (vv 8–9), song of victory (vv 15–16), thanksgiving by the king (vv 21, 28), a proverb (v 22), praise of the LORD (vv 23–24), a prayer (v 25), and a priestly blessing and instruction (vv 26–27).[11]

To move gradually into discerning the message of this psalm we shall first examine its parallelisms, next its imagery, its repetition of keywords, and finally its structure.

---

7. Belcher, *The Messiah and the Psalms*, 191.

8. Stek, *NIV Study Bible*, Ps 118 n. Cf. Terrien, *The Psalms*, 784, "He also claims, in royal terms, that he escaped from a military entrapment by foreign nations. The style is that of the royal psalms. A threefold refrain, 'In the name of the Lord I cut them to pieces,' clinches the validity of this interpretation." So also, e.g., Davidson, *Vitality of Worship*, 384–85; and Eaton, *The Psalms*, 404–5.

9. "This psalm uniquely combines corporate hymnic praise (vv 1–4, 22–24, 29), individual thanksgiving (vv 5–18, 21, 28; which includes a victory song [vv 14–16]), a petition (v 25), and a processional liturgy of entering the temple gates and processing to the altar (vv 19–20, 26–27)." Broyles, *Psalms*, 438.

10. B. Anderson, *Out of the Depths*, 223. Cf. Allen, *Psalms 101–150*, 124, "Like Ps 18, this psalm was evidently composed as a royal song of thanksgiving for military victory; but it is set in the context of a processional liturgy."

11. See A. Anderson, *Psalms 73–150*, 797; and Allen, *Psalms 101–150*, 122.

Parallelisms

The author has marked Psalm 118 with a large number of repeated words and phrases, many of which signal poetic parallelisms. The psalm exhibits a rich variety of combinations of parallelism: synonymous parallelism (vv 8a, 9a; 10b, 11b, 12c) with an interesting combination of synonymous and advancing parallelism (vv 15b–16), climactic synonymous parallelism (vv 2b, 3b, 4b; 15b–16, mixed), climactic advancing parallelism (vv 6–7; 19), antithetic parallelism (vv 5b, 8b, 9b, 22), climactic antithetic (vv 13b–14), but mostly advancing parallelisms. Here is a snapshot of the psalm's parallelisms:

1O give thanks to the LORD, for he is good;	A
his steadfast love endures forever!	+ A'
2Let Israel say,	A
"His steadfast love endures forever."	B
3Let the house of Aaron say,	+ A'
"His steadfast love endures forever."	B'
4Let those who fear the LORD say,	+ A''
"His steadfast love endures forever."	B''
5Out of my distress I called on the LORD;	A
the LORD answered me and set me in a broad place.[12]	– A'
6With the LORD on my side I do not fear.	B
What can mortals do to me?[13]	+ B'
7The LORD is on my side to help me;[14]	+ B''
I shall look in triumph on those who hate me.[15]	+ B'''
8It is better to take refuge in the LORD	C
than to put confidence in mortals.[16]	– D
9It is better to take refuge in the LORD[17]	C'
than to put confidence in princes.	+– D'

12. The contrast in verse 5b shows antithetic parallelism: "Out of my distress [Heb. *a narrow place*] I called on the LORD [A]; the LORD answered me and set me in *a broad place* [–A']."

13. Completes the thought of v 6a, no fear, therefore advancing (+).

14. Verse 7a advances from v 6a, "the LORD is on my side," to "on my side to help me."

15. Advances from the LORD's help to, "I shall look in triumph on those who hate me."

16. Antithetic parallelism which advances in verse 9b to the more specific "princes"; hence +–D' for v 9b.

17. Synonymous parallelism with v 8a. A. Anderson, *Psalms 73–150*, 799, calls this "an external, repetitive parallelism," that is, "where the correspondence occurs between repetitive verses" (see his *Psalms 1–72*, 42).

₁₀All nations surrounded me;	A
in the name of the Lord I cut them off!	B
₁₁They surrounded me, surrounded me on every side;	+ A'
in the name of the Lord I cut them off!	B'
₁₂They surrounded me like bees;	+ A''
they blazed like a fire of thorns;	+ A'''
in the name of the Lord I cut them off![18]	B''
₁₃I was pushed hard, so that I was falling,	C
but the Lord helped me.[19]	– C
₁₄The Lord is my strength and my might;	+– C'
he has become my salvation.	+– C''
₁₅There are glad songs of victory in the tents of the righteous:	A
"The right hand of the Lord does valiantly;	B
₁₆the right hand of the Lord is exalted;	+ B'
the right hand of the Lord does valiantly."	B''
₁₇I shall not die, but I shall live,	C
and recount the deeds of the Lord.	+ C'
₁₈The Lord has punished me severely,	D
but he did not give me over to death.	+ D'
₁₉Open to me the gates of righteousness,	A
that I may enter through them	+ A'
and give thanks to the Lord.	+ A''
₂₀This is the gate of the Lord;	A
the righteous shall enter through it.	+ A'

18. The verses 10–12 build up a string of three advancing parallelisms in lines A while lines B are exactly the same and therefore synonymous.

19. Antithetic parallelism which advances with v 14a and b into climactic antithetic parallelism.

21I thank you that you have answered me	A
and have become my salvation.	+ A′
22The stone that the builders rejected	B
has become the chief cornerstone.[20]	– B′
23This is the LORD's doing;	C
it is marvelous in our eyes.	+ C′
24This is the day that the LORD has made;[21]	D
let us rejoice and be glad in it.	+ D′
25Save us, we beseech you, O LORD!	E
O LORD, we beseech you, give us success!	+ E′
26Blessed is the one who comes in the name of the LORD.	A
We bless you from the house of the LORD.	+ A′
27The LORD is God,	B
and he has given us light.	+ B′
Bind the festal procession with branches,	C
up to the horns of the altar.	+ C′
28You are my God, and I will give thanks to you;	A
you are my God, I will extol you.	+ A′
29O give thanks to the LORD, for he is good,	A
for his steadfast love endures forever.[22]	+ A′

Imagery

Psalm 118 is also filled with various types of imagery. As mentioned in n. 12 above, verse 5 presents the image of the king being in a narrow place ("distress")

20. In contrast to being "rejected," the stone has become "chief cornerstone": antithetic parallelism.

21. Adele Berlin, "Psalm 118:24," *JBL* 96, no. 4 (1977): 567–68, argues that because of the parallelism between verses 23–24,

> This (*zo't*) is the Lord's doing; it is marvelous in our sight.
> This (*zê*) is what the Lord has done today; let us exult and rejoice in it.

"It is not a day, even a special day, that is the subject of this psalm; it is God's actions." Therefore she proposes to translate verse 24 as, "This (thing), today, the Lord has done . . ." or "This is what the Lord has done today. . . ." Zenger, *Psalms 3,* 230 n. s, suggests that the verb "'do, act,' should be applied to YHWH's working as narrated in the psalm (cf. the keyword links to vv 15–17)." See also p. 242.

22. Inclusio with verse 1.

and the LORD setting him "in a broad place." In the verses 6 and 7 the LORD is on the king's "side." The verses 8 and 9 use the metaphor of taking "refuge" in the LORD.

The verses 10–11 picture the king "surrounded" by the nations, which could be understood literally,[23] on which verse 12 expands with two similes: "They surrounded me like bees [cf. Deut 1:44]; they blazed like a fire of thorns." A fire of thorns or brushwood "blazes up quickly and sweeps across the countryside with devastating effect."[24] In verse 13 the king follows up with the metaphors of being "pushed hard" and "falling."

The verses 15–16 three times use the anthropomorphic metaphor of "the right hand of the LORD." Gerstenberger remarks, "No doubt, the 'right hand of Yahweh' can be his powerful weapon against enemies (cf. 18:35; 44:3; 74:10–11; Exod 15:6). But the range of meaning is much wider; God's 'right (hand, arm)' is a metaphor for creative power, fatherly care, love, guidance, etc."[25]

Verse 22 uses the proverb of the rejected stone becoming the chief cornerstone as a metaphor for the king, rejected by the nations, returning as the victor. Verse 27 exclaims, "The LORD is God, and he has given us light." "Whereas darkness and gloom are symbols for disaster and defeat, light is a symbol of triumph, victory, and blessing. The light has shone on 'us.' The leader's victory is the people's, not just his."[26]

Repetition of Keywords

The psalmist mentions the full name of *Yahweh* 23 times plus 5 times the short form *Yah* for a total of 28 times (4×7). In addition verse 27 asserts, "The LORD is *God*," and the king closes his testimony by twice confessing, "You are *my God*" (v 28).

The problem faced by the king is highlighted in verses 10–12 with the four-fold repetition of being "surrounded" by all nations (further emphasized with

---

23. "This verb suggests being hemmed in, and links with the expression in v 5a. It might suggest a city besieged or an army encircled, or point to a less literal sense of being surrounded such as that applying to Nehemiah." Goldingay, *Psalms*, III, 358.

24. Davidson, *Vitality of Worship*, 384. Davidson adds, "The translation 'blazed' assumes a slight alteration to the Hebrew text and follows the Greek (LXX) interpretation. The Hebrew says 'extinguished' [see NIV, 'were consumed'], which presumably stresses that a fire of thorns, although it burns fiercely, soon dies away. In context this is less likely, since both similes seem to refer to the aggressive ferocity of those who surround the king."

25. Gerstenberger, *Psalms*, II, 305.

26. Goldingay, *Psalms*, III, 364.

advancing parallelisms and imagery (see above). The solution to the problem is highlighted in the same verses with the threefold repetition, "in the name of the LORD I cut them off!" and, in the verses 15–16, with the threefold repetition of "the right hand of the LORD."[27] The threefold "in the name of the LORD" in verses 10–12 is picked up again in verse 26: "Blessed is the one who comes in the name of the LORD."

Israel's required response to the message of the psalmist is also underlined with repetition: five times the psalmist uses the verb "give thanks" (vv 1, 19, 21, 28, 29). Though the opening, "O give thanks to the LORD," is also used in Psalms 105, 106, and 107, "no other chapter gives it [giving thanks] such prominence"[28] — another clue for formulating the specific textual theme of Psalm 118.

Structure

Aside from the obvious frame of verses 1–4 and 29, there is little agreement on the structure of Psalm 118. Note the different structures proposed by popular English versions.

Verse Divisions						*Versions*
1 / 2–4 / 5 – 9 / 10 – 14 / 15 – 18 / 19 / 20 / 21 – 25 / 26–27 / 28 / 29						NRSV
1 / 2–4 / 5–7 / 8 – 14 / 15–16 / 17 – 21 / 22–24 / 25 / 26–27 / 28 / 29						NIV
1 / 2–4 / 5–7 / 8–9 / 10–13 / 14 – 16 / 17–18 / 19 – 24 / 25 / 26–27 / 28 – 29						ESV
1 – 4 / 5 – 9 / 10 – 14 / 15 – 18 / 19 – 21 / 22 – 29						NASB

We can best get a handle on the structure by noticing two major sections within the frame, the first taking place outside the temple and the second in the temple complex.

A. The king's recital of the LORD delivering him from his enemies (vv 5–18). This first part is framed by the king's opening and closing summary of his experience: "Out of my distress I called on the LORD; the LORD answered me and set me in a broad place" (v 5), and "The LORD has punished me severely, but he did not give me over to death" (v 18).

---

27. "The three occurrences of 'right hand' (*yāmîn*) in vv 15b–16 recall the three occurrences in Exod 15:6, 12 (see also Isa 41:10 in the context of God's returning the exiles)." McCann, "Psalms," 1154.

28. Goldingay, *Psalms*, III, 356.

B. The second part describes the celebration of that deliverance in the temple (vv 19–28). It is framed by the king's intent to give thanks to the LORD: "Open to me the gates of righteousness, that I may enter through them and give thanks to the LORD" (v 19), and "You are my God, and I will give thanks to you; you are my God, I will extol you" (v 28).[29]

For further divisions into stanzas we can follow the breaks provided by the NRSV for the first part: verses 5–9, 10–14, 15–18. The second part is more challenging. The NRSV lists five shorter sections by different speakers: verses 19, 20, 21–25, 26–27, and 28. But this ignores the switch from singulars to plurals (our, us, we) in vv 23–27. Taking into account the plurals in verses 23–27, we can outline the structure of this psalm as a four-point chiasm:[30]

A. A priest urges Israel to give thanks to the LORD (vv 1–4)
B. The king's recital of being delivered by the LORD from his enemies (vv 5–18)
   1. The king's distress and the LORD's deliverance (vv 5–9)
   2. The king surrounded by all nations and the LORD's salvation (vv 10–14)
   3. The songs of victory and the king's reflection (vv 15–18)
B'. The celebration of that deliverance in the temple (vv 19–28)
   1. The king requests entry into the temple to thank the LORD (v 19)
   2. A priest responds with, "This is the gate of the LORD" (v 20)
   3. The king thanks the LORD (v 21)
   4. Priests or a choir rejoice over the LORD's doing (vv 22–27)
      a. Proverb about rejected stone being exalted (v 22)
      b. "This is the LORD's doing" (v 23)
      c. "Let us rejoice" in this day "the LORD has made" (v 24)
      d. Prayer: "Save us . . . O LORD" (v 25)
      e. Blessings for "the one who comes in the name of the LORD" (v 26)
      f. The LORD has given us light; start the festal procession (v 27)
   5. The king thanks and extols "my God" (v 28)
A'. The priest again urges Israel to give thanks to the LORD (v 29)

---

29. See McCann, "Psalms," 1154–55, and Belcher, *The Messiah and the Psalms*, 186–88.
30. Some scholars, such as Terrien, *The Psalms*, 783, have proposed a nine-point chiastic structure for the whole psalm. But their proposal is neither compelling nor helpful for preachers.

Theocentric Interpretation

The fact that the author names God (*'El*) 3 times and LORD (*Yahweh* / *Yah*) 28 times in 29 verses indicates that Psalm 118 is thoroughly centered on God. Although the king is another major character in this psalm, the king calls on God for help and testifies to the fact that the LORD answered him and was on his side and his refuge (vv 5–9). Also, it was "in the name of the LORD" that he cut off his enemies (vv 10–12). Next the king again testifies that the LORD helped him and was his strength, might, and salvation (vv 13–14, 21). The songs of victory credit "the right hand of the LORD," while the king pledges to "recount the deeds of the LORD" and "give thanks to the LORD" (vv 15–19). Even the king's exaltation to "chief cornerstone" is declared to be "the LORD's doing" (vv 22–23). The king's final words are his confession, "You are my God, and I will give thanks to you; you are my God, I will extol you" (v 28).

Another character in this psalm is the priest. Even when he blesses the king, the choir immediately credits the LORD: "The LORD is God, and he has given us light" (vv 26–27). The most important indication of the psalm's theocentric focus, however, is its frame (inclusio) which commands Israel at the beginning and end, "O give thanks to the LORD, for he is good; his steadfast love endures forever!" (vv 1, 29).

Textual Theme and Goal

Some have identified verse 17, "I shall not die, but I shall live, and recount the deeds of the LORD" as "the central thematic statement of the psalm."[31] But the author of the psalm has made his theme much more obvious. He has stated it twice, at the beginning and end of the psalm, urging Israel, "O give thanks to the LORD, for he is good; his steadfast love endures forever!" The LORD showed his steadfast love for the king by saving his life and in doing so he saved Israel.[32] Therefore, we can formulate the textual theme as: *Give thanks to the LORD, for in his steadfast love he saved Israel's king as well as his people.*[33]

---

31. E.g., Limburg, *Psalms,* 403.

32. Cf. Ps 118: 1–4, 15–16, 24–25, 27, 29. Cf. Weiser, *The Psalms,* 725, "Its content, testimony to the abiding goodness and grace of God is the theme of the psalm; in this theme the congregation and the king unite."

33. Cf. Williams, *Psalms 73–150,* 339, "His goodness is seen in His '*mercy,*' which '*endures forever.*' This mercy is the theme throughout. Divine mercy is seen as God answers our distress (v 5), granting us His presence (v 6), destroying our enemies (vv 10–12), helping us (v 13), and becoming our salvation (v 14)."

Even though we are not certain about the historical setting of this psalm — its author, date, occasion for writing,[34] and function in Israel's worship — formulating the goal of this psalm is not difficult. The verses 1 and 29 employ the imperative, second person plural: "O give thanks to the LORD!" The psalm's goal, therefore, is to urge Israel to give thanks to the LORD. Because verses 2-4 enjoin "Israel," "the house of Aaron," and "those who fear the LORD" to repeat, "His steadfast love endures forever," we can expand "Israel" to "all God's people." The goal of Psalm 118, then, is *to urge all God's people to give thanks to the LORD because in his steadfast love he saved Israel's king as well as his people.*

Ways to Preach Christ

The textual theme is "Give thanks to the LORD, for in his steadfast love he saved Israel's king as well as his people." To move to Christ in the New Testament we could use the way of redemptive-historical progression: If Israel was commanded to give thanks to the LORD for his good acts in saving their king from imminent death as well as his people, how much the more should we give thanks to the LORD for saving from certain death our King Jesus as well as us.

But there may be a more specific way. Although there is no promise of the coming Messiah in this psalm, the New Testament quotes or alludes to Psalm 118 some twenty-three times.[35] These references are possible because the Davidic king in the psalm functions as a type of King Jesus. A good way to preach Christ from this psalm, therefore, is typology supported by New Testament references.

Typology and New Testament References

Typology entails analogies and escalation between a type and its later antitype.[36] There are some obvious analogies and escalations between the Davidic king of

---

34. Though some commentators see this psalm as postexilic, Eaton, *Psalms*, 270-71, says flat out, "The view that the psalm is postexilic lacks firm grounds." Cf. Eaton, *The Psalms*, 405, "Post-exilic dating, based on the view that the 'fearers of the Lord' are proselytes in the late period and on supposed borrowing from other scripture, is not well founded." Cf. A. Anderson, *Psalms 73-150, 797,* "The Psalm dates, most likely, from the pre-Exilic times."

35. See Appendix IV in Nestle's *Novum Testamentum Graece,* 27th ed., 1993. Cf. Zenger, *Psalms 3,* 245, "Psalm 118 is the psalm most often cited or evoked in the New Testament. The number of the intertextually relevant passages varies from twenty to sixty, depending on the judgment of individual exegetes."

36. See my *Preaching Christ from the Old Testament,* 257-60.

Psalm 118 and King Jesus. As the king was in distress and called on the LORD (Ps 118:5), so Jesus was in even greater distress in Gethsemane and on the cross and called on the LORD. As the king was surrounded by enemies who wanted to kill him (Ps 118:10–12), so Jesus on the cross was surrounded by enemies who were in the process of killing him. As the king testified, "The LORD has punished me severely, but he did not give me over to death" (Ps 118:18), so King Jesus was being punished for "the sins of the whole world" (1 John 2:2) but was not given over to ultimate death: he rose again. As the king was rejected by his enemies but became the chief cornerstone (Ps 118:22), so Jesus was rejected by all, sentenced to death, and became the chief cornerstone (Mark 12:10).

We can list many analogies between the Davidic king of Psalm 118 and King Jesus, but for Jesus' triumphal entry into Jerusalem the New Testament finds these analogies especially in the verses 22–26. To avoid information overload, therefore, it seems best in this Palm Sunday sermon to make the moves to Jesus in the New Testament with these particular verses (see "Sermon Exposition" below). Many of the other verses we can highlight for the Easter Sunday sermon (see Chapter 19 below).

Sermon Theme, Goal, and Need

Since the New Testament sees the experiences of the Davidic king fulfilled in King Jesus, it does not alter the basic message and goal of the psalm. Therefore, with a slight change (Israel's king is the Davidic king then and King Jesus today), the textual theme can function as the sermon theme: *Give thanks to the LORD, for in his steadfast love he saved the Davidic king as well as us.*

Similarly, the textual goal can function as the sermon goal: *to urge all God's people to give thanks to the LORD because in his steadfast love he saved the Davidic king, Jesus, as well as his people.* This goal points to the need addressed in this sermon: we do not thank the LORD enough for saving our King, Jesus, as well as us.

Liturgy, Sermon Outline, and Scripture Reading

Psalm 118:24 has traditionally been used as a Call to Worship: "This is the day that the LORD has made; let us rejoice and be glad in it." It calls the church to joyful worship on Sunday because on that day the LORD raised Jesus from the dead. A combination of verses 5, 14, 17, and 29 can also be used for the Assurance of Pardon.

The sermon outline could follow the structure of the text (see p. 388 above), but I prefer more clearly to move from voice to voice (see below) since this will enhance the flow of the sermon and give it a kind of narrative quality.

Scripture reading is complicated because there may be many different voices for the various parts. To keep the reading fairly simple, I suggest three voices according to the characters we have identified. There is a priest who opens and closes the psalm and pronounces the blessing. There is the king who speaks the "I" parts. And there is a choir of some kind that communicates the plural ("we") parts. The liturgist can take the parts of the priest; another person the parts of the king; and two or more people or the congregation speaking in unison can take the parts of the choir.[37] I will lay out this proposal in detail so that we can see how noting these different parts enhances the meaning of Psalm 118.

PRIEST   1 O give thanks to the LORD, for he is good,
      for his steadfast love endures forever.[38]
      2 Let Israel say,

CHOIR   "His steadfast love endures forever."

PRIEST   3 Let the house of Aaron say,

CHOIR   "His steadfast love endures forever."

PRIEST   4 Let those who fear the LORD say,

CHOIR   "His steadfast love endures forever."

KING   5 Out of my distress I called on the LORD;
      the LORD answered me and set me in a broad place.
      6 With the LORD on my side I do not fear.
      What can mortals do to me?
      7 The LORD is on my side to help me;
      I shall look in triumph on those who hate me.
      8 It is better to take refuge in the LORD
      than to put confidence in mortals.
      9 It is better to take refuge in the LORD
      than to put confidence in princes.
      10 All nations surrounded me;
      in the name of the LORD I cut them off!
      11 They surrounded me, surrounded me on every side;
      in the name of the LORD I cut them off!
      12 They surrounded me like bees;
      they blazed like a fire of thorns;

37. If this seems too complicated, the liturgist can take the parts of both the priest and the choir.

38. Although Gerstenberger, *Psalms*, II, 301, argues that this second colon is the response of the community, I think it is more appropriate that the priest / liturgist introduces this colon and the community takes it over from there.

in the name of the LORD I cut them off!
13 I was pushed hard, so that I was falling,
    but the LORD helped me.
14 The LORD is my strength and my might;
    he has become my salvation.

PRIEST 15 There are glad songs of victory in the tents of the righteous:
CHOIR   "The right hand of the LORD does valiantly;
16 the right hand of the LORD is exalted;
    the right hand of the LORD does valiantly."

KING   17 I shall not die, but I shall live,
    and recount the deeds of the LORD.
18 The LORD has punished me severely,
    but he did not give me over to death.
19 Open to me the gates of righteousness,
    that I may enter through them
    and give thanks to the LORD.

PRIEST 20 This is the gate of the LORD;
    the righteous shall enter through it.

KING   21 I thank you that you have answered me
    and have become my salvation.

CHOIR 22 The stone that the builders rejected
    has become the chief cornerstone.[39]
23 This is the LORD's doing;
    it is marvelous in our eyes.
24 This is the day that the LORD has made;
    let us rejoice and be glad in it.
25 Save us, we beseech you, O LORD!
    O LORD, we beseech you, give us success!

PRIEST 26 Blessed is the one who comes in the name of the LORD.
CHOIR   We bless you from the house of the LORD.
27 The LORD is God,
    and he has given us light.

PRIEST   Bind the festal procession with branches,
    up to the horns of the altar.

KING   28 You are my God, and I will give thanks to you;
    you are my God, I will extol you.

PRIEST 29 O give thanks to the LORD, for he is good,
CHOIR   for his steadfast love endures forever.

---

39. Verse 22 could possibly be spoken by the king but this seems rather self-serving.

Sermon Exposition

The sermon introduction can illustrate the need addressed: How often do we thank God specifically for saving Jesus from death and, with him, for saving us from death?

The goal of Psalm 118 is to urge all God's people to give thanks to the LORD because in his steadfast love he saved the life of the Davidic king from imminent death and with him the lives of his people. The psalm begins with a command: "O give thanks to the LORD, for he is *good*." The LORD is not evil; he is good through and through. It's his nature to *be* good. It's his nature to *do* good. The LORD was good to Israel and is good to us today. That's why we should constantly thank him.

The next line explains God's goodness: "his steadfast love endures forever!" "His steadfast love" is a special word in Hebrew. It is often translated as "loving kindness," or "mercy." The word refers to God's covenant faithfulness. It is the LORD's love that never gives up on his people. He will never let us down. It is "the sort of love that keeps on loving, no matter what. The same Hebrew word (*ḥesed*) is used for the love that young Hosea had for his wife, even after her unfaithfulness (Hosea 1–3). This is the kind of love that never gives up, like that of the father [in Jesus' parable] who never gave up on his rebellious son and kept hoping, waiting, watching for his return (Luke 15)."[40] "His steadfast love endures *forever!*" This steadfast love is not here today and gone tomorrow. It endures *forever!*

This point is further emphasized in the next three verses. "Let Israel say, 'His steadfast love endures forever.' Let the house of Aaron say, 'His steadfast love endures forever.' Let those who fear the LORD say, 'His steadfast love endures forever.'" All of God's people must say, "His steadfast love endures forever!" "Israel" refers to the common Israelites; "the house of Aaron" is the priestly class; and "those who fear the LORD" are all who worship and revere the LORD. All these different groupings are to say about the goodness of the LORD, "his steadfast love endures forever!"

Next the psalm illustrates the goodness of the LORD with a personal experience. A king of David's line[41] begins to speak. He had been in terrible trouble. He was "hard pressed" (NIV), hemmed in, confined to a narrow place;[42] didn't know where to turn — but to the LORD. The king testifies in verse 5, "Out of my distress [this tight place] I called on the LORD; the LORD answered me and set

---

40. Limburg, *Psalms,* 448.

41. See nn. 6 and 8 above.

42. "The Hebrew behind 'distress' has the sense of being cramped or narrow." Limburg, *Psalms,* 403. So also, e.g., Kraus, *Psalms 60–150,* 397, and McCann, "Psalms," 1154.

me in a broad place." You see the goodness of the LORD? Out of this narrow place the king called on the LORD, and the LORD answered him and set him in a broad place. A complete reversal from being confined, hemmed in, to plenty of space, freedom.[43] And all because of the LORD's goodness, his steadfast love.

The king continues with his testimony in verses 6–7: "With the LORD on my side I do not fear. What can mortals do to me? The LORD is on my side to help me; I shall look in triumph on those who hate me." For emphasis he says twice that the LORD is on his side. When the LORD is on our side, we need not fear anything. What can mere mortals do to us? As Paul says in Romans 8, "If God is for us, who is against us?" (Rom 8:31; cf. Heb 13:6). No one! With the LORD on our side to help us, ultimate victory is certain.

From his own experience the king moves to a message for the people. Verses 8–9, "It is better to take refuge in the LORD than to put confidence in mortals. It is better to take refuge in the LORD than to put confidence in princes." Again for emphasis he says twice, "It is better to take refuge in the LORD." He pictures the LORD as a place of refuge when danger is all around.

Unfortunately, when we are faced with dangers we tend to look to our leaders for protection. We put our confidence in the Department of Homeland Security to protect us from terrorists; we put our trust in our physicians to heal diseases; we count on the police to protect our neighborhood. But placing our ultimate confidence in human beings is misplaced. The king says, "It is better to take refuge in the LORD than to put confidence in *mortals*. It is better to take refuge in the LORD than to put confidence in *princes*." No matter how low or how high,[44] no matter how powerful, to put our trust, our confidence, in human beings is wrong. Only the LORD is worthy of our confidence. "His steadfast love endures *forever*." No matter how great the danger, in his goodness the LORD will provide safety and security.

The king then doubles back to the distress he mentioned in verse 5. What was the problem exactly? Verses 10–12, "All nations surrounded me; in the name of the LORD I cut them off! They surrounded me, surrounded me on every side; in the name of the LORD I cut them off! They surrounded me like bees; they blazed like a fire of thorns; in the name of the LORD I cut them off!"

Notice the fourfold repetition of "surrounded." This was the king's "narrow

43. Perhaps a reminder of Israel's enslavement in Egypt, their cry for help and redemption. Cf. Exod 2:23–24, "The Israelites groaned under their slavery, and cried out. Out of the slavery their cry for help rose up to God. God heard their groaning, and God remembered his covenant with Abraham, Isaac, and Jacob."

44. "The mention of 'man' (*'ādām*) in parallelism with 'princes' (*nədîbîm*) is an example of merismus (cf 146:3), a literary manner of including all humankind, both lowly and exalted." VanGemeren, *Psalms*, 854.

place" of verse 5. He was surrounded, hemmed in, confined, in dire straights. The danger builds up to a climax: the king was "surrounded" by "*all nations*"; "surrounded," "surrounded *on every side*"; "they surrounded me like *bees.*" Thousands of them. Have you ever had a swarm of bees go after you? There is no escape. "They blazed like a fire of thorns." A fire of thorns or brushwood "blazes up quickly and sweeps across the countryside with devastating effect."[45] We see it on TV every time there is a drought. The fires consume brush, trees, homes. There is no escape.

That is how the king saw his enemies: a swarm of bees and a brush fire. No escape possible. But, he says, "in the name of the LORD I cut them off!" Three times, "in the name of the LORD I cut them off!" No matter how great the nations, "in the name of the LORD I cut them off!" "All nations . . . ," "surrounded on every side . . . ," like being "surrounded" by bees — "in the name of the LORD I cut them off!" Doing something in the name of the LORD means doing it "as the representative of the LORD and by the power of the LORD (see 54:1; 20:5, 7)."[46]

This is exactly what David did when he met Goliath. The mighty warrior Goliath taunted Israel and its God. But the young David went up against Goliath saying, "You come to me with sword and spear and javelin; but I come to you *in the name of the LORD of hosts,* the God of the armies of Israel, whom you have defied" (1 Sam 17:45). Then David slung a stone, struck Goliath on his forehead, and killed him. A youth gained the victory over a mighty, seasoned warrior because he came "in the name of the LORD." That shows the power of coming in the name of the LORD — the power of coming not in your own name or in the name of the nation but "in the name of the LORD."

This does not mean, however, that God's people will have an easy, victorious life on earth. The king admits in verse 13, "I was pushed hard, so that I was falling." He was pushed hard by his enemies, so that he "was falling." When soldiers fall on a battlefield they are about to die. So the king was about to die. But even at this crucial moment the goodness of the LORD came through for him. The king says, "but the LORD helped me."

In verse 14 the king adds: "The LORD is my strength and my might, and he has become my salvation." This is a direct quotation of the Song of Moses in Exodus 15. When God led Israel out of its enslavement in Egypt they were caught between Pharaoh's armies and the Red Sea. Israel was trapped, in a narrow place, surrounded. There was no way of escape. But the LORD opened a way through the sea. We read in Exodus, "Then Moses and the Israelites sang this song to the

---

45. Davidson, *Vitality of Worship,* 384. To explain or counter the NIV translation "they were consumed," see n. 24 above.
46. Mays, *Psalms,* 376.

LORD: 'I will sing to the LORD, for he has triumphed gloriously; horse and rider he has thrown into the sea. *The LORD is my strength and my might, and he has become my salvation*" (Exod 15:1–2).

The king quotes this last sentence word for word. Just as Israel long ago experienced the LORD's salvation from enslavement in Egypt, so the king had experienced the LORD's salvation from being encircled by evil nations. And he joyfully proclaims in the same words, "The LORD is my strength[47] and my might, and he has become my salvation." The LORD has given him the victory. Like Israel's victory long ago, the king's victory was not due to his own strength or military cunning. He gives all the credit to the LORD.

In response to the king's announcement of victory, the priest reports in verse 15, "There are glad songs of victory in the tents of the righteous." "The tents of the righteous" are the tents of those who are right with God. They are the soldiers who have the LORD on their side. You can see the soldiers in their tents singing their hearts out after this victory. And to whom do they give credit?

They sing, "The right hand of the LORD does valiantly;[48] the right hand of the LORD is exalted; the right hand of the LORD does valiantly." Three times "the right hand of the LORD," just as in the Song of Moses.[49] When the LORD delivered Israel from Egypt, Moses and the Israelites sang, "Your right hand, O LORD, glorious in power — your right hand, O LORD, shattered the enemy. . . . You stretched out your right hand, the earth swallowed them [the enemies]" (Exod 15:6, 12). It's all about the right hand of the LORD. "The right hand of the LORD does valiantly" is repeated twice. And between these two expressions, in the central, key position, "the right hand of the LORD is *exalted*." The LORD's right hand is lifted up in triumph.[50] It's the right hand of the LORD that gained the victory and signals the victory. The soldiers give all the credit to the LORD.

In verse 17 the king begins to speak again. In verse 13 he had said, "I was pushed hard, so that I was falling [he was near death], but the LORD helped me." Now he is certain that he will not die. He says, "I shall not die, but I shall live,

---

47. "The word 'strength' denotes his [the Lord's] power in saving (68:28; 86:16; 89:10; 132:8; Isa 51:9), while 'salvation' (*yəšûʿâ*; cf. v 15, 'victory' [*yəšûʿâ*]) suggests the whole process of his mighty acts, his judgments on the adversaries, and his help to his children, including the final climactic celebrations of victory." VanGemeren, *Psalms*, 854.

48. "Like the LORD's right hand, the word translated 'valiantly' . . . has strong associations with the battlefield and the power of the LORD there displayed (cf. 59:11); hence, the REB translates 'mighty deeds.'" Davidson, *Vitality of Worship*, 385.

49. "The three occurrences of 'right hand' (*yāmîn*) in vv 15b–16 recall the three occurrences in Exod 15:6, 12. . . . The word 'exalted' (*rômēmâ*, v 16a) again recalls Exod 15:2." McCann, "Psalms," 1154.

50. "The 'lifting of the right hand' could point back to an old gesture: after the battle the victor lifts his right hand and thereby attests his powerful superiority." Kraus, *Psalms 60–150*, 398.

and recount the deeds of the LORD. The LORD has punished me severely, but he did not give me over to death."

The king sees this whole experience of being in distress (v 5) and near death (v 13) as the LORD's discipline. The NRSV's "The LORD has *punished* me severely" is too strong.[51] The NIV translates verse 18 as, "The LORD has *chastened* me severely." The king does not mention a specific sin but sees his distress as the LORD's correction so that he would learn to put his full confidence in the LORD. And that he did, as we can see in this psalm. The king not only defeated his enemies "in the name of the LORD" (vv 10–12) but also taught others that "it is better to take refuge in the LORD than to put confidence in princes" (v 9).

The king said in verse 17, "I shall not die, but I shall live, and *recount the deeds of the LORD.*" And that is precisely what he is doing in this psalm. He recounts the saving deeds of the LORD for him. But he wants to do more than that: he wants to *thank* the LORD personally. So next we see him and his soldiers marching off to God's house, the temple. When they arrive at the gate of the temple, the king calls out, verse 19, "Open to me the gates of righteousness, that I may enter through them and give thanks to the LORD." "The gates of righteousness" are the gates to the temple's forecourt, close to the Holy Place, where the God of righteousness lives.

From within the forecourt, the gatekeeper priest responds, verse 20, "This is the gate of the LORD; the righteous shall enter through it." Normally, "the would-be worshippers were asked, at least formally, for a declaration of their faithfulness to the Covenant (see Pss 15, 24). Those who had been loyal to Yahweh's commands were accepted as righteous and were admitted to the temple precincts (cf. Isa 26:2)."[52] In this case, the gatekeeper need not ask for any declaration. He immediately allows the king "and (by implication) his entourage to enter: the victory is evidence enough of the covenant blessing that rests upon these men and makes them welcome to this place where conformity to the covenant is enshrined."[53] The

---

51. "English versions have Yah 'punishing,' giving a misleading impression. . . . Even when *yāsar* suggests a parent's or a teacher's chastisement, it does not denote retributive punishment but action designed to teach (cf. 16:7; 94:10, 12; LXX uses *paideuō,* but Jerome *arguo*). Yah put the leader under severe pressures to drive him to learn the lessons the psalm has referred to (e.g., vv 6–9; cf. 2 Cor 1:9). Goldingay, *Psalms,* III, 360. Cf. Davidson, *Vitality of Worship,* 385, "It was an experience which taught him more about what the LORD wanted him to be and to do, a needed corrective to keep him on course." Psalm 94 uses the same Hebrew word and translates it as "discipline": "Happy are those whom you *discipline,* O LORD, and whom you teach out of your law" (Ps 94:12).

52. A. Anderson, *Psalms 73–150,* 802. Cf. Kraus, *Psalms 60–150,* 395, 399. Cf. Zenger, *Psalms 3,* 241, "Only the 'righteous,' that is, those shown by YHWH (through their being saved) to be righteous, those who worship him alone (cf. v 28) may enter."

53. Allen, *Psalms 101–150,* 124–25.

king and his soldiers are righteous: "They are right and just in that they have been humbled by affliction and have learnt to put their trust in God."[54]

The king enters the temple forecourt and for the first time speaks directly to the LORD, v 21, "I thank you that you have answered me and have become my salvation." He thanks the LORD for answering his prayer when he was in such deep distress (v 5), surrounded by enemies (vv 10–12). The LORD helped him and became his "salvation."

Upon hearing the king's thanksgiving, a temple choir responds with a proverb about reversal of fortunes. Verse 22, "The stone that the builders rejected has become the chief cornerstone." The chief cornerstone was the most important stone in ancient buildings. Builders would carefully look for a stone that had perfect 90-degree angles and place it at the corner of the foundation.[55] This stone would not only support the corner but guide the direction of the walls. Builders would reject many stones as inferior and worthless. That is the way the king was rejected by his enemies: inferior and worthless — ready for the dump. But amazingly, somehow this rejected stone had become the chief cornerstone. The king who was rejected as worthless, as good as dead, was delivered by the LORD. He was victorious. And now in the LORD's temple, he is declared righteous. How could this be?

The choir[56] provides the answer in verse 23: "This is the LORD's doing; it is marvelous in our eyes." It is entirely the LORD's doing, the LORD's act. It's a miracle! "It is marvelous in our eyes." And they conclude, verse 24, "This is the day that the LORD has made; let us rejoice and be glad in it." The emphasis here is not so much on the day but on the fact that the LORD *acted* on this day. Consequently the REB translates, "This is the day on which the LORD *has acted*." And the NIV translates, "The LORD *has done* it this very day."[57] The LORD's saving acts call for joyful celebrations on that day:[58] "Let us rejoice and be glad in it."

But even as they celebrate their king's victory, the choir prays for all God's people, verse 25, "Save us, we beseech you, O LORD! O LORD, we beseech you, give us success!" They pray that they, the people, may also be saved, both now and in the future. They pray the LORD for success in their endeavors.[59]

---

54. Eaton, *The Palms*, 405.

55. "Lit. 'head of the corner' — either a capstone over a door (a large stone used as a lintel), or a large stone used to anchor and align the corner of a wall, or the keystone of an arch (see Zech 4:7; 10:4)." Stek, *NIV Study Bible*, Ps 118:22 n.

56. Note the first person, plural pronoun, "marvelous in *our* eyes."

57. See n. 21 above.

58. "The significance of the day is due to the event(s) celebrated on it." A. Anderson, *Psalms 73–150*, 803.

59. "The plea for 'success' is not a request for abundant material prosperity but an appeal to God to provide resources for life amid the current threat." McCann, "Psalms," 1155.

Then the priest blesses the king who cut off his enemies "in the name of the LORD." The priest says to him, verse 26, "Blessed is the one who comes in the name of the LORD." And the choir extends this blessing to all the king's followers: "We bless you [all (pl.)][60] from the house of the LORD."

Then they confess their faith. Verse 27: "The LORD is *God*, and he has given us light." They confess that the LORD, Israel's covenant God Yahweh, is *'ēl* , the highest God.[61] And, referring back to the blessing just received, they say, "he has given us light." "He has given us light" uses the same verb as the Aaronic blessing, "the LORD make his face *to shine upon* you" (Num 6:25). Basically they are saying, The LORD is the highest God and made his face to shine upon us.

The priest next orders, "Bind the festal procession with branches, up to the horns of the altar."[62] The celebration is about to begin. The NIV translates, "With boughs in hand, join the festal procession up to the horns of the altar." It was probably a victory dance around the altar in which people would place their willow and palm branches on the altar.[63]

The king speaks one final time in verse 28, "You are my God, and I will give thanks to you; you are my God, I will extol you." The king goes beyond the general confession of the choir in verse 27, "The LORD is *God*." The king makes a very personal confession. For emphasis he repeats twice, "You are *my* God . . . ; you are *my* God." And he promises to give thanks to God and extol him. In verse 16 the king's soldiers exclaimed, "the right hand of the LORD is exalted [lifted up in triumph]." Now the king himself promises to extol the LORD, that is, lift up his name in praise.[64]

---

60. Some commentators explain the plural "you" as a plural of majesty exalting the king. See Stek, *NIV Study Bible*, Ps 118:26 n.

61. "Verse 27a is a solemn confession which has its roots in the ancient festival of covenant renewal (cf. Josh 24:17ff.) and contests the deity of other powers (cf. 1 Kings 18:39)." Kraus, *Psalms 60–150*, 400.

62. This is a difficult sentence to translate. Are the people ordered to bind sacrifices or branches? Kidner, *Psalms 73–150*, 416, and others argue for "Bind the sacrifice with cords." Others argue for "Bind the festal procession with branches" (NRSV). A. Anderson, *Psalms 73–150*, 804, explains, "In recent years it has been customary to translate *ḥag* by 'procession' [instead of 'sacrifice'] . . . , or 'festal dance,' and to interpret the whole verse in the light of Mishnah (*Sukkah* iv:5f.), which describes how on the Feast of Tabernacles the procession of worshippers used to go round the altar. They also carried the *lulab*, a bundle of branches made up of myrtles, willows, and palms. . . . During the procession the altar was covered with the branches. . . ." Cf. Davidson, *Vitality of Worship*, 387.

63. "The interpretation of v 27b is far from easy; but the thrust is clear that they demonstrated their commitment in concrete acts, whether they came with 'boughs in hand' during the Feast of Tabernacles (*m. Sukkah* 3:4; based on Lev 23:40) or with 'festal sacrifices' (see NIV text note)." VanGemeren, *Psalms*, 857. See also Zenger, *Psalms 3*, 243.

64. A final reminder of the Song of Moses, "The LORD is my strength and my might, and he

The priest concludes the psalm in verse 29 by urging everyone, "O give thanks to the LORD, for he is *good*," and the choir again explains how good the LORD is: "for his steadfast love endures forever."

In this psalm we have seen the LORD's steadfast love in action many times. In his steadfast love the LORD responded to the king's call from deep distress and set him in a broad place (v 5). In his steadfast love the LORD enabled the king to cut off his enemies "in the name of the LORD" (vv 10–12). In his steadfast love the LORD helped the king and became his salvation when the king was falling and near death (vv 13–14).

Who was this king? We don't know other than that he was a king of the house of David. The king in this psalm was a type of Jesus the Messiah; he prefigured the later King Jesus. Jesus also was a stone rejected by people — inferior, worthless. As Isaiah prophesied, "He was despised and rejected by others; a man of suffering and acquainted with infirmity; and as one from whom others hide their faces he was despised, and we held him of no account" (Isa 53:3). Yet the LORD said, "I will allot him a portion with the great, and he shall divide the spoil with the strong" (Isa 53:12). A complete reversal from the rejected to the acclaimed. The rejected stone becomes the chief cornerstone.

Because this king in Psalm 118 prefigured King Jesus, the New Testament can quote this psalm when it tells the story of Jesus. On Palm Sunday as Jesus was approaching Jerusalem, he sent two of disciples ahead to get a colt. Mark tells the rest of the story in Mark 11:7–11:

> They brought the colt to Jesus and threw their cloaks on it; and he sat on it. Many people spread their cloaks on the road, and others spread leafy branches that they had cut in the fields. Then those who went ahead and those who followed were shouting, "Hosanna! Blessed is the one who comes in the name of the Lord! Blessed is the coming kingdom of our ancestor David! Hosanna in the highest heaven!" Then he entered Jerusalem and went into the temple; and when he had looked around at everything, as it was already late, he went out to Bethany with the twelve.

The people greeted Jesus by shouting "Hosanna!" This greeting comes from Psalm 118:25, "Save us." The Hebrew expression here is *hôšî'â nā'*. In time this was abbreviated to "Hosanna." And instead of a plea for salvation it "became more like a greeting or acclamation."[65]

---

has become my salvation; this is my God, and I will praise him, my father's God, and I will exalt him" (Exod 15:2).

65. McCann, *Theological Introduction*, 167. Cf. Leupold, *Exposition of the Psalms*, 819, Ho-

By this time Judaism understood Psalm 118 messianically, that is, it spoke to them of the coming Messiah.[66] So when the people saw Jesus entering Jerusalem riding a colt, they shouted the greeting, "Hosanna!"[67] And they cried out: "Blessed is the one who comes in the name of the Lord!" These are the very words the priest spoke to the king in Psalm 118:26: "Blessed is the one who comes in the name of the LORD." The people of Jerusalem greet Jesus as "the one who comes in the name of the LORD" — the one who represents the LORD and comes with his authority. They see Jesus as the Messiah who will bring in the kingdom of God. They add, "Blessed is the coming kingdom of our ancestor David! Hosanna in the highest heaven!'"

Mark adds, "Then he entered Jerusalem and went into the temple; and when he had looked around at everything, as it was already late, he went out to Bethany with the twelve." After his victory, the king of Psalm 118 had entered Jerusalem and gone into the temple to thank the LORD. So does Jesus. After his triumphal entry into Jerusalem he goes into the temple. Jesus is the king of David's house who will bring in the kingdom of God.

But it is not all joy that week. Later that week Jesus weeps over Jerusalem because of the hypocrisy of its leaders: "Jerusalem, Jerusalem, the city that kills the prophets and stones those who are sent to it! How often have I desired to gather your children together as a hen gathers her brood under her wings, and you were not willing! See, your house is left to you, desolate. For I tell you, you will not see me again until you say, 'Blessed is the one who comes in the name of the Lord'" (Matt 23:37-39). There is that phrase from Psalm 118 again.

Jesus is headed to the cross. Unlike the king of Psalm 118 (see v 18), Jesus is actually going to die. But he also trusts that he will rise from the dead, ascend into heaven, and come again on the last day. Jesus says, "I tell you, you will not see me again until you say, 'Blessed is the one who comes in the name of the Lord'" (Matt 23:39). When Jesus comes again on the clouds of heaven, people will greet him as

---

sanna "became a prominent factor in the celebration of the festival of Tabernacles, where especially on the seventh day, which was called the 'Great Hosanna,' palm branches, called *lulab*, were waved, and these branches, too, were called Hosannas."

66. "The special attention accorded Psalm 118 in the New Testament can primarily be explained by the fact that this psalm had great significance in Judaism. The petition 'hosanna,' 'save us,' (Ps 118:25) was a cultic formula used in the Feast of Tabernacles. Moreover, Psalms 113-118, known as the 'Hallel,' were a fixed part of the Jewish cycle of autumn feasts and of Passover (cf. Matt 26:30; Mark 14:26). Finally, it should be mentioned that in Judaism Ps 118:22-23 was interpreted as referring to Abraham, David, and the Messiah." Kraus, *Theology of the Psalms*, 193.

67. "The use of Psalm 118 at this point in the story of Jesus is not really surprising. After all, Jesus enters Jerusalem during the week of Passover; and Psalm 118 is the concluding psalm of the Hallel collection (Psalms 113-118) which were (and are) traditionally used at Passover." McCann, *Theological Introduction*, 167.

the victorious king: "Blessed is the one who comes in the name of the Lord." Then it will be evident to all that "the stone that the builders rejected has become the chief cornerstone," and that "this is the LORD's doing; it is marvelous in our eyes."

God's saving of Jesus even from death itself is the ultimate display of God's goodness, of his steadfast love. That is why we celebrate Jesus' resurrection every Sunday: "This is the day that the LORD has made; let us rejoice and be glad in it" (Ps 118:24). Because of Jesus' resurrection, all who believe in him will conquer death itself.[68] How we ought to give thanks to the LORD because in his steadfast love he raised Jesus from the dead. How we ought to give thanks to the LORD because in his steadfast love he will raise us also from the dead.

Prayer[69]

Faithful Father in heaven,
From the bottom of our hearts we thank you for your goodness;
    we thank you for your steadfast love which endures forever.
We thank you for your great love for us — a love so great
    that you were willing to send even your only Son to earth to save us.
Thank you for raising Jesus from the dead.
Thank you for the hope we now have that we, too,
    will be raised from the dead and live with you forever.
Thank you, Lord Jesus, for leaving your heavenly home to be with us.
Thank you for your willingness to die for us
    so that we might live with you forever.
May we ever praise you "with heart and life and voice,
    and in . . . [your] blissful presence eternally rejoice." Amen.

Song[70]

1Hosanna, loud hosanna
    the little children sang;
through pillared court and temple
    the lovely anthem rang.
To Jesus, who had blessed them,
    close folded to his breast,
the children sang their praises,
    the simplest and the best.

---

68. "But in fact Christ has been raised from the dead, the first fruits of those who have died. . . . Christ the first fruits, then at his coming those who belong to Christ" (1 Cor 15:20–23).
69. S.G.
70. Jennette Threlfall, 1873. Public Domain. *Psalter Hymnal* (1987), # 378; *Lift Up Your Hearts*, # 145.

₂From Olivet they followed
    mid an exultant crowd,
the victory palm branch waving,
    and chanting clear and loud.
The Lord of earth and heaven
    rode on in lowly state,
nor scorned that little children
    should on his bidding wait.

₃"Hosanna in the highest!"
    That ancient song we sing,
for Christ is our Redeemer,
    the Lord of heaven, our King.
O may we ever praise him
    with heart and life and voice,
and in his blissful presence
    eternally rejoice.

CHAPTER 18

"My God, My God, Why Have You Forsaken Me?"

Psalm 22 (21)

In response to the reading of Isaiah 52:13–53:12 (The Suffering Servant) the *Revised Common Lectionary* assigns the reading of Psalm 22 for Good Friday in all three years. Psalm 22 is quoted more frequently in the New Testament than any other psalm. On the cross, Jesus himself cried out the opening line of this psalm, "'*Elōi, elōi, lema sabachthani?*' which means, 'My God, my God, why have you forsaken me?'" (Mark 15:34; Matt 27:46). The Gospel writers used five other verses from Psalm 22 to describe Jesus' intense suffering on the cross: verses 7, "All who see me mock at me; they make mouths at me, they shake their heads"; 8, "Commit your cause to the Lord; let him deliver—let him rescue the one in whom he delights!"; 15, "My mouth is dried up like a potsherd, and my tongue sticks to my jaws"; 18, "They divide my clothes among themselves, and for my clothing they cast lots"; and 31, "He has done it."[1]

Because of the many New Testament references to Jesus' suffering on the cross and since the sermon is for Good Friday, preachers may be tempted to preach Psalm 22 focusing solely on Jesus' suffering and death. But that would not do justice to this psalm, and the church would miss out on a lot of good news. For when Jesus quotes the first line of this psalm, "My God, my God, why have you forsaken me?" he has the whole psalm in mind.[2] And this psalm offers

---

1. Verse references are the numbers in the English versions. V 7 appears in Mark 15:29 and Matt 27:39; v 8 in Matt 27:43; v 15 in John 19:28; v 18 in all four Gospels: Mark 15:24; Matt 27:35; Luke 23:34; John 19:23–24; and v 31 in John 19:30 ("It is finished" echoes the last word of Psalm 22, *'āśâ*, "he has done it." See Patterson, "Psalm 22," *JETS* 47, no. 2 (2004; pp. 213–33): 228, with discussion of the issues on pp. 226–27 n. 74.

2. "Citing the first words of a text was, in the tradition of the time, a way of identifying the entire passage." Mays, *Psalms*, 105. Cf. his *Preaching and Teaching the Psalms*, 108, "Sometimes brief quotes from the Old Testament are directives to the reader to reflect on the text so identified. I believe that

much more than lament: it moves from extended lament to exuberant praise and thanksgiving, concluding with the eschatological vision of the arrival of the kingdom of God with "all the families of the nations" (v 27) worshiping God. A sermon on Psalm 22 could well be entitled, "Through Suffering to Victory," or, "Through Trouble to Triumph." What a wonderful message for *Good* Friday. Jesus does indeed cry out in agony but he also has Easter in sight.

Text and Context

Because Psalm 22 has two distinct parts, lament in verses 1–21 and praise and thanksgiving in verses 22–31, some commentators suggest that this psalm originally consisted of two psalms.[3] But since all laments, except Psalm 88, move from lament to praise there seems to be little reason to deny the unity of this psalm. Today, therefore, most scholars agree on the literary unity of Psalm 22.[4] Since the psalm is a literary unit, the whole psalm is a lengthy but good preaching text.[5]

As to literary context, the neighboring psalms may shed some light on the meaning of Psalm 22. The editors of the Psalter have placed Psalm 22 between Psalms 21 and 23. Clinton McCann observes, "In Psalms 20–21, there is the certainty that the sovereign God will answer and help the king, who lives by his trust in God. Thus the canonical sequence emphasizes the sharp contrast [with Psalm 22]; there is no help and no answer for the psalmist,"[6] at least not initially.

---

is the case here. The entire psalm is viewed as though it were the libretto for our Lord's dying." Cf. Westermann, *The Living Psalms,* 298, "When the evangelists employ Psalm 22 to interpret Christ's passion, they have in view the entire psalm where suffering and deliverance from suffering together make up the whole." Cf. Ellen F. Davis, "Exploding the Limits," *JSOT* 53 (1992; pp. 93–105): 103 n. 1, with a reference to "C. H. Dodd's persuasive argument that the early Christian writers regarded this psalm as a source of 'testimonies' to the Passion, and that citation of a single expression should be treated in the context of the whole (*According to the Scriptures* [New York : Charles Scribner's Sons, 1953], pp. 57–59, 96–98)."

3. E.g., Broyles, *Psalms,* 115.

4. John S. Kselman, "'Why Have You Abandoned Me': A Rhetorical Study of Psalm 22," in *Art and Meaning* (ed. David Clines, David M. Gunn, and Alan J. Hauser; Sheffield: JSOT, 1982; pp. 172–98), 188, calls the view of two psalms "an opinion that is deservedly out of favor now, given the form-critical evaluation of the praise and thanksgiving section as integral to the lament form." Cf. VanGemeren, *Psalms,* 235, Compared to scholars in the past, "contemporary scholars are in greater agreement over the literary unity of Psalm 22."

5. For preaching Psalm 22 as a series of two or three sermons, see pp. 582–83 below.

6. McCann, "Psalms," 762. See there for "three key words from Psalms 20–21" that recur in 22:1–5: "helping," "answer," and "trust." Cf. VanGemeren, *Psalms,* 236, "Psalm 22 arrests the

But then comes the turn in the psalm: "From the horns of the wild oxen you have rescued me," "you have *answered* me" (v 21).[7] And the psalmist turns directly to God to praise him because the LORD "did not hide his face from me, but heard when I cried to him" (v 24). The praise conclusion of Psalm 22 (vv 22–31) "seems to anticipate and prepare for the ending of Psalm 23:5–6. Psalm 22 ends with the psalmist in the 'congregation' (22:22, 25), which would have been found in 'the house of the LORD' (23:6). Perhaps also the meal mentioned in both psalms would have taken place in 'the house of the LORD' (22:26; 23:5)."[8]

We can also compare Psalm 22 with other individual laments such as Psalms 70–71. Gerald Wilson has noted some similarities: "(1) the plea that Yahweh 'be not far' from the narrator (22:11, 19, 71:12); (2) reference to divine support from the psalmist's birth (22:9–10; 71:6); and (3) the plea for quick relief (22:19; 70:1, 5; 71:12)."[9] More important for preaching Psalm 22 is to see how it differs from other individual laments. This difference is found primarily in its intricate double lament form with ferocious animals in the second panel (vv 12–21) followed by an expanded praise section (vv 22–31; see "Structure," p. 416 below).[10]

Psalm 22 should also be understood in the context of the prophets, especially Isaiah's depictions of the Servant of the LORD (Isa 49 and 53). Compare, for example, Psalm 22:9, "Yet it was you who took me from the womb; you kept me safe on my mother's breast," with Isaiah 49:1, "The LORD called me before I was born, while I was in my mother's womb he named me"; and 22:6, "I am . . . scorned by others, and despised by the people," with Isaiah 53:3, "He was despised and rejected by others; a man of suffering and acquainted with infirmity." Compare 22:16, "They pierce my hands and my feet" (NIV), with Isaiah 53:5, "He was pierced for our transgressions" (NIV); and 22:15, "you lay me in the dust of death," with Isaiah 53:10, "Yet it was the will of the LORD to crush him with pain." Finally compare 22:27, "All the ends of the earth shall remember and turn to the LORD," with Isaiah 49:6, "I will give you as a light to the nations, that my salvation may reach to the end of the earth." In many ways the psalmist resembles the Servant of the LORD.

---

expressions of commitment to integrity and the confidence in Yahweh's victories of the psalmists in Psalms 20–21. David's anguish is a cry of loneliness and divine abandonment in Psalm 22."

7. See NRSV footnote z., "Heb *answered.*" See n. 91 below.

8. McCann, *Theological Introduction,* 132.

9. Wilson, *Psalms,* I, 412.

10. "Where the vow of praise would normally be we have the main features of a declarative praise psalm." Ross, *Commentary on the Psalms,* I, 528. Cf. Davis, "Exploding the Limits," *JSOT* 53 (1992): 97, "Rather than departing from the standard form of the lament, this final section vastly expands and varies one of its characteristic elements, the vow of praise."

Literary Interpretation

In the superscription the editors of the Psalter call Psalm 22, "A Psalm of David," as they do with all but four of the psalms in Book I (Pss 1–41).[11] It is an invitation to read the psalm from the perspective of David.[12] Many times in his life, David may have felt forsaken by God and beset by enemies, especially when King Saul tried to kill him (1 Sam 20–31) and his own son Absalom usurped the throne (2 Sam 15–18). But, as Allen Ross puts it, "We know of no time in the life of David that even comes close to the event that is described here; if it came from his experiences, the language of the psalm must be poetic and somewhat hyperbolic in places."[13]

From the psalm itself J. H. Eaton makes a good case for at least a royal speaker from David's line: "A special bond with the Lord is indicated at the outset in the threefold 'my God' (also v 10) and more vividly in the appeal to God as the one who, as father, had drawn him from the womb and committed him to his mother's breast. The mocking of enemies has its point in the psalmist's having been supposed to be the chosen of the Lord, the one in whom he 'delighted' (v 8). . . . The speaker is best regarded as the Lord's Anointed."[14] For convenience, we shall simply call the psalmist, David.

David uses the form of an individual lament but expands the vow to praise into a lengthy praise and thanksgiving section. He also uses a few other literary devices such as merism in verse 2, "by day" "by night," to communicate his continuous cry to God for an answer. In verse 14 he uses hyperbole to convey his intense suffering, "I am poured out like water, and all my bones are out of joint; my heart is like wax; it is melted within my breast."

As we explore the psalm in detail, we shall again begin with a snapshot of the psalm's parallelisms, next its imagery, its repetition of keywords, and finally its structure.

Parallelisms

This psalm exhibits mostly advancing parallelisms.[15] When advancing over three or more lines, this results in regular climactic parallelism.[16] But the psalm also has

---

11. The four exceptions are Pss 1 and 2, which introduce the Psalter, and 10, and 33 (possibly originally linked to Pss 9 and 32).

12. See pp. 28–30 above, "The Psalm's Original Historical Setting."

13. Ross, *Commentary on the Psalms*, I, 527.

14. Eaton, *The Psalms*, 118–19.

15. Note again that the difference between synonymous and advancing parallelism is not always clear cut. I will mark as advancing parallelism (+) wherever I think that one or more elements in the second line move beyond the first line.

16. See verses 1–2, 4–5, 9–10, 12–13, 14–15, 16–18, 22–23, 24, 26, 29, 30–31.

antithetic parallelism advancing over three or more lines. This results in climactic antithetic parallelism in verses 6–7, 11, 19–21. Both forms of climactic parallelism can express agonizing laments or powerful praise.

₁My God, my God, why have you forsaken me?	A
Why are you so far from helping me,	+ A′
from the words of my groaning?	+ A″
₂O my God, I cry by day, but you do not answer;	+ A‴
and by night, but find no rest.	+ A⁗
₃Yet you are holy,	A
enthroned on the praises of Israel.	+ A′
₄In you our ancestors trusted;	B
they trusted, and you delivered them.	+ B′
₅To you they cried, and were saved;	+ B″
in you they trusted, and were not put to shame.	+ B‴
₆But I am a worm, and not human;¹⁷	– A
scorned by others, and despised by the people.	+– A′
₇All who see me mock at me;	+– A″
they make mouths at me, they shake their heads;	+– A‴
₈"Commit your cause to the LORD; let him deliver —	B
let him rescue the one in whom he delights!"	+ B′
₉Yet it was you who took me from the womb;	A
you kept me safe on my mother's breast.	+ A′
₁₀On you I was cast from my birth,	+ A″
and since my mother bore me you have been my God.	+ A‴
₁₁Do not be far from me,¹⁸	– B
for trouble is near	+– B′
and there is no one to help.	+– B″
₁₂Many bulls encircle me,	A
strong bulls of Bashan surround me;	+ A′
₁₃they open wide their mouths at me,	+ A″
like a ravening and roaring lion.	+ A‴

17. In contrast to verse 5, they "were not put to shame," this self-description of being despised is antithetic parallelism, followed by three more lines of advancing antithetic parallelism resulting in climactic antithetic parallelism.

18. In contrast to verse 10, God being far from him makes verse 11a antithetic parallelism supported by two following advancing lines for climactic antithetic parallelism.

14I am poured out like water,	A
and all my bones are out of joint;	+ A′
my heart is like wax;	+ A″
it is melted within my breast;	+ A‴
15my mouth is dried up like a potsherd,	+ A⁗
and my tongue sticks to my jaws;	+ A‴″
you lay me in the dust of death.	+ A‴‴

16For dogs are all around me;	A
a company of evildoers encircles me.	+ A′
My hands and feet have shriveled;	B
17I can count all my bones.	+ B′
They stare and gloat over me;	+ A″
18they divide my clothes among themselves,	+ A‴
and for my clothing they cast lots.	+ A⁗

19But you, O LORD, do not be far away![19]	− A
O my help, come quickly to my aid!	+− A′
20Deliver my soul from the sword,	+− A″
my life from the power of the dog!	+− A‴
21Save me from the mouth of the lion!	+− A⁗

From the horns of the wild oxen you have rescued me.[20]	A
22I will tell of your name to my brothers and sisters;	B
in the midst of the congregation I will praise you:	+ B′
23You who fear the LORD, praise him!	+ B″
All you offspring of Jacob, glorify him;	+ B‴
stand in awe of him, all you offspring of Israel!	+ B⁗
24For he did not despise or abhor the affliction of the afflicted;	C
he did not hide his face from me,	+ C′
but heard when I cried to him.	+ C″

19. The "but" signals the contrast of antithetic parallelism supported by the next four advancing lines resulting in climactic antithetic parallelism.

20. I am following the paragraphs in the NRSV, though I think there are good reasons for beginning the new stanza with verse 22 (cf. the NIV and ESV; see pp. 414–15 below). In that case verse 21a, b would be marked +−A⁗, B, and v 22 would be A, +A′, etc.

₂₅From you comes my praise in the great congregation;	A
my vows I will pay before those who fear him.	+ A′
₂₆The poor shall eat and be satisfied;	B
those who seek him shall praise the LORD.	+ B′
May your hearts live forever!	+ B″
₂₇All the ends of the earth shall remember and turn to the LORD;	A
and all the families of the nations shall worship before him.	+ A′
₂₈For dominion belongs to the LORD,	B
and he rules over the nations.	+ B′
₂₉To him, indeed, shall all who sleep in the earth bow down;	A
before him shall bow all who go down to the dust,	+ A′
and I shall live for him.	+ A″
₃₀Posterity will serve him;	B
future generations will be told about the Lord,	+ B′
₃₁and proclaim his deliverance to a people yet unborn,	+ B″
saying that he has done it.	+ B‴

Imagery

Psalm 22 is filled with imagery. A few commentators think of "the dawn" in the superscription as "the metaphorical occasion for deliverance from danger,"[21] but "The Deer of the Dawn" is probably no more than a musical tune for singing the psalm.[22] "The words of my *groaning*" in verse 1b is literally "the words of my roaring": "The 'roaring' is that of a lion [cf. v 13] and is metaphorical for a loud and constant cry for help (32:3; 38:8)."[23] God being *"enthroned on the praises of Israel"* is a metaphor for God being lifted up, exalted, on the praises of Israel as he was enthroned in the tabernacle and temple on the ark of the covenant between the cherubim (cf. Ps 80:1). In verse 6 David compares himself to *"a worm"* — a lowly creature that is often stepped upon and associated with decay and death. "They *make mouths* at me" in verse 7 is "literally, 'they separate with a lip'; the idiom refers to sneering."[24] *"Commit* your cause to the LORD" (v 8) is literally "'to roll' — viz. 'He rolled [his burden] to the Lord.'"[25]

21. E.g., Brown, *Psalms*, 101.

22. Craigie, *Psalms 1–50*, 196 n. 1.a. Cf. Calvin, *Commentary on the Book of Psalms*, I, 357, "I think it highly probable that it was the beginning of some common song."

23. VanGemeren, *Psalms*, 238 n. 1.

24. Craigie, *Psalms 1–50*, 196 n. 8.a.

25. Ibid., n. 9.a.

Verse 9 presents the tender image of the LORD acting as a midwife: "Yet it was you *who took me from the womb*." "Yahweh acted as midwife, first pulling the child out, then immediately setting it at its mother's breast with the instinctive trusting expectancy of finding milk there."[26] In contrast, David uses the metaphors of violent animals to describe his enemies who have him cornered: "*Many bulls* encircle me, *strong bulls* of Bashan surround me; they *open wide their mouths* at me, *like a ravening and roaring lion* [simile]" (vv 12–13).[27] "Lion and ox are conventional pairs to represent the epitome of power."[28]

More similes and metaphors follow each other in quick succession in verses 14–16: "I am *poured out like water* [simile], and *all my bones are out of joint* [hyperbole and metaphor]; my heart is *like wax*[29] [simile]; it is *melted* [metaphor] within my breast; my mouth is dried up *like a potsherd*[30] [simile] and my tongue sticks to my jaws; you lay me in *the dust of death* [metaphor]. For *dogs*[31] [metaphor] are all around me; a company of evildoers encircles me." Verses 20–21 continue, "Deliver my soul from *the sword* ['a metaphor for violent death'[32]], my life from *the power of the dog* [metaphor; literally, 'the hand of the dog']! Save me from *the mouth of the lion* [metaphor]! From *the horns of the wild oxen* [metaphor] you have rescued me."

James Mays comments on the animal imagery: "The identity of these evil doers is hidden behind the animal masks they wear. Perhaps the metaphors give these enemies a demonic cast; in the ancient Near Eastern religions, demons and divine figures often appear as animals. The metaphors render them as bestial, powerful, dramatizing intensely the mortal overwhelming plight of the figure."[33]

---

26. Goldingay, *Psalms,* I, 330.

27. "The lion in particular is noted for its ravenous appetite and roar (v 13), as well as its distinctive weapon of destruction, the mouth (v 21a), comparable to the deadly horns of the wild ox (v 21b)." Brown, *Seeing the Psalms,* 138.

28. Mays, *Psalms,* 110.

29. "'Water' and 'wax,' expressive of formlessness, bring out the inner feeling of the anguished [cf. Josh 7:5]. . . . Great fear is likened to 'water' (cf. Josh 7:5; Ezek 7:17; 21:7) and to 'wax' (v 14; cf. 2 Sam 17:10)." VanGemeren, *Psalms,* 243.

30. "Lack of resilience and inability to cope any longer with the trauma of life is brought out in the image of the dried-out and useless 'potsherd.'" Ibid.

31. "In the ancient Near East, dogs were not 'man's best friend.' They prowled about, snarling and looking for food (Ps 59:14–15). They licked the blood of those killed or unable to fend for themselves (Ps 68:23; cf. 1 Kings 14:11; 16:4; 21:19, 23–24; 2 Kings 9:10, 36; and Luke 16:21)." Ibid., 244. Cf. Brown, *Seeing the Psalms,* 140, "Associated with filth and death, 'dog' (*keleb*) typically serves as a term of contempt in biblical tradition. . . . Dogs were half wild in ancient times, flourishing as scavengers on the margins of human civilization. . . . 'Dogs' are noted for their deadly mouth, specifically their bark and bite."

32. Goldingay, *Psalms,* I, 334.

33. Mays, *Psalms,* 110. Mays also notes that "the extended metaphor is unique to the psalms"

The animals in the animal metaphors are listed twice but in reverse order and with greater specificity on their lethal weapons, thus moving to a climax:

Verses 12–13, 16	Verses 20–21
a. bulls	d. (sword)
b. lion	c. power of the dog
c. dogs	b. mouth of the lion
d. (company of evildoers)	a. horns of the wild oxen

The praise section has fewer metaphors: "I will tell of *your name* [metaphor] to my *brothers and sisters* [metaphor]" (v 22). "He *did not hide his face* [anthropomorphic metaphor for withholding favor] from me" (v 24). "May your *hearts* [metaphor] live forever!" (v 26). "To him, indeed, shall all *who sleep* [metaphor for death] in the earth bow down; before him shall bow all who *go down to the dust* [metaphor]" (v 29).

Repetition of Keywords

The important, intimate keyword, "my God," is repeated three times (vv 1 [2×] and 10). In addition, David uses the name of *Yahweh* five times (vv 8, 23, 26, 27, 28), *Adonay* once (v 30) and "your name" once (v 22), so that God is named a full ten times.

David describes his trouble three times with the word "far": "why are you so far" (v 1) and "do not be far" (vv 11 and 19). He piles up five different phrases to show how his enemies mistreat him: "scorned," "despised," "all mock me," "they make mouths at me," "shake their heads" (vv 6–7). Three times he repeats that "our ancestors trusted" and God saved them (vv 4–5). Why does God not save *him?* He complains bitterly, "O my God, I cry . . . , but you do not answer" (v 2).

But finally, at the end of the lament section, David can say, "you have answered me" (v 21b) and in the praise section he proclaims, "he heard when I cried to him" (v 24), and "he has done it" (v 31). Therefore David himself begins to praise the God who sits "enthroned on the praises of Israel" (v 3): he praises the LORD in the midst of the congregation (v 22), urges others to "praise him" and adds synonyms, "glorify him," "stand in awe of him" (v 23), gives God credit for his praise (v 25) and concludes that "those who seek him shall praise the LORD" (v 26) — a fivefold repetition in the psalm of the word "praise." To highlight the universal extent of God's

---

(p. 110). Cf. McCann, "Psalms," 763, "In some ancient Near Eastern texts . . . animals are used to represent demonic forces; this dimension of the metaphor should be considered here as well." Cf. Kraus, *Psalms 1–59,* 297, and Westermann, *The Living Psalms,* 86.

praise he repeats "all" four times in verses 27–29: "All the ends of the earth"; "all the families of the nations"; "all who sleep in the earth"; "all who go down to the dust."

Structure

Commentators suggest different structures for Psalm 22. It will be helpful to begin again by considering the typical lament form. In Chapter 1, pp. 10–11, we noted the usual structure of lament psalms. Let's see how Psalm 22 fits that structure:

1) Introductory petition for God's help	22:1–2
2) Description of the trouble or complaint	22:6–8, 12–18
3) Petitions for God's help	22:11, 19–21
4) Reasons why God should hear	22:9–10
5) Examples of God's saving acts in history	22:3–5
6) A vow to praise	22:22, 25

As can be seen, Psalm 22 fits quite well into this mold but also has extras. The psalm shows a doubling of the complaint (vv 6–8 and 12–18) and a doubling of petitions for God's help (vv 11 and 19–21). More importantly, David has expanded the final vow to praise into a lengthy section on praise:

7) Encouragement for others to praise the LORD	22:23
8) Reasons to praise the LORD	22:24–26
9) The ends of the earth shall praise the LORD	22:27–29
10) Future generations will praise the LORD	22:30–31

While many commentators argue for two main sections, the lament (vv 1–21) and the praise (vv 22–31),[34] on the basis of the psalm's strophic structure (with a similar number of lines in each strophe) Samuel Terrien argues convincingly for three main sections: verses 1–11, 12–21, 22–29, plus an envoi[35] in 30–31. Each main section is introduced by a two-verse exordium which is followed by three major strophes. He diagrams this intricate structure as follows:[36]

---

34. E.g., Craigie, *Psalms 1–50*, 197; Davidson, *Vitality of Worship*, 79; Goldingay, *Psalms*, I, 323; VanGemeren, *Psalms*, 236; and Westermann, *The Living Psalms*, 82–83.

35. "Envoy, envoi: 'a short stanza concluding a poem in certain archaic metrical forms.'" "Exordium: 'the introductory part of an oration, treatise, etc.'" *Webster's Unabridged Dictionary*.

36. Terrien, *The Psalms*, 229. I have changed his Hebrew verse numbers to those of the English versions and have not reproduced the number of lines in each strophe. A few others who argue for a threefold structure are Kselman, "'Why Have You Abandoned Me': A Rhetorical Study of Psalm

I	II	III
vv 1–2	vv 12–13	vv 22–23
(i)	(i)	(i)
vv 3–5	vv 14–15	vv 24–25
(ii)	(ii)	(ii)
vv 6–8	vv 16–18	vv 26–27
(iii)	(iii)	(iii)
vv 9–11	vv 19–21	vv 28–29
		envoi
		vv 30–31

For sections I and II, this strophic structure fits well with the general lament structure, each section having a complaint followed by petitions for God's help. For section III we can combine some strophes based on the contents of the verses. There is only one point of disagreement among major English versions:

Verse Division	Versions
21b–24 / 25–26 / 27–28 / 29–31	NRSV
22 – 24 / 25–26 / 27–28 / 29–31	NIV, ESV

The issue is where to place verse 21b, the turn of the psalm, "From the horns of the wild oxen you have rescued me."

The NRSV's placing verse 21b with the following paragraph creates an inclusio between verses 21b ("answered") and 24c ("heard"). But the NIV's and ESV's placing verse 21b with the prior paragraph is supported by three even better arguments: this keeps all the animals, including the wild oxen, in section II; section II will have the same number of syllables as section I, 189;[37] and section III is marked as a unit by its own inclusio "I will tell" (v 22) and "will be told" (v 30).[38] Therefore, we can outline the structure of Psalm 22 as three stanzas[39] (the italicized words indicate inclusios):

22," 172–98; Mark Heinemann, "An Exposition of Psalm 22," *BSac* 147, #587 (1990): 286–308; and Fokkelman, *Major Poems of the Hebrew Bible,* II, 104–10.

37. Fokkelman, *Major Poems of the Hebrew Bible,* II, 104: "Sections I and II not only have exactly the same number of strophes (2+2 each) and verses (5+6 each), but also the same number of syllables: 189, down to the last point."

38. "I will tell" (*'spr*) v 22 and "future generations will be told" (*yspr*) v 30. Kselman, "'Why Have You Abandoned Me': A Rhetorical Study of Psalm 22," 192. So also Fokkelman, *Major Poems of the Hebrew Bible,* II, 106. On pp. 190–91 Kselman suggests chiastic structures in vv 22–26a and vv 26c–29.

39. Cf. Waltke, *Psalms as Christian Worship,* 397, "In sum, the psalm consists of three stanzas

I. Lament (I): God is *far from* helping David (vv 1–11)
    A. Complaint: *"My God, my God,* why have you forsaken me?
                 Why are you *so far* from helping me?" (vv 1–2)
    B. Confidence: Yet ancestors who trusted God "were saved" (vv 3–5)
    C. Complaint: "All who see me mock at me" (vv 6–8)
    D. Confidence: Yet "since my mother bore me you have been *my God*"[40]
        (vv 9–10)
    E. Prayer: *"Do not be far from* me" (v 11; inclusio, *far,* vv 1–11)
II. Lament (II): David is surrounded by beastly enemies (vv 12–21)
    A. Complaint: "Strong bulls . . . surround me" (vv 12–13)
    B. Complaint: "You lay me in the dust of death" (vv 14–15)
    C. Complaint: "They divide my clothes among themselves" (vv 16–18)
    D. Prayer: "O LORD, *do not be far away*" (vv 19–21; inclusio, *far,* vv 1–21)
III. Praise and thanksgiving for rescue (vv 22–31)
    A. *"I will tell* your name" (praise) and encourage others to do so
        (vv 22–24)
    B. "My vows I will pay before those who fear him" (vv 25–26)
    C. "All the families of the nations shall worship before the LORD"
        (vv 27–28)
    D. "Future generations *will be told*" and proclaim God's deliverance
        (vv 29–31; inclusio, *tell/told,* vv 22–31)

Theocentric Interpretation

The opening, "My God, my God," sets the stage for theocentric interpretation. "Notice that in declaring his right to say 'my God,' the figure speaks not of his own acts or character or status but only of God and what God has done."[41] Though David is suffering, he focuses our attention on God from beginning to end: "My God" (v 1), and "He has done it" (v 31). Ten times he names God. He feels abandoned by God; he cries out to God for help. He even says to God: "You lay me in the dust of death" (v 15). When God finally comes to his aid, David praises God and urges all God's people to do so. In fact, he predicts that "all the families of the nations shall worship . . . [the LORD]. For dominion belongs to the LORD, and he rules over the nations" (vv 27–28).

---

of ten verses each: 1–10, 12–21, 22–31, moving from torment to turmoil to triumph. Verse 11 stands apart, functioning as a janus linking the first two stanzas by the key word 'far off' (vv 1, 11, 19)."
    40. An inclusio between verse 1 "my God, my God" and verse 10 "my God."
    41. Mays, *Psalms,* 109.

Textual Theme and Goal

After this preliminary work we should be ready to formulate the theme and goal of Psalm 22. Still, we face some hard choices. Some commentators see verse 24 as the key verse: "For he did not despise or abhor the affliction of the afflicted; he did not hide his face from me, but heard when I cried to him." Consequently, they formulate themes like Heinemann's proposal: "The lesson comes through clearly that God hears the prayers of the faithful and answers according to his own perfect plan."[42] Aside from the fact that this formulation consists of two themes, these themes do not convey the lament nor cover the whole praise and eschatological sections.

Ellen Davis offers a better alternative by emphasizing lament as well as praise: "Psalm 22 is an individual lament whose theme is praise. The psalm's subject is the possibility, efficacy and necessity of giving praise to God *in extremis.*"[43] But we still need to include the eschatological section in the theme. I think we can cover the whole psalm with the following theme: *Praise the LORD who guided Israel's king through intense suffering to a victory which will eventually lead to all nations worshiping the LORD.*

The imperative "praise!" in the theme makes the goal rather obvious. This imperative is based on the three imperatives in verse 23: "You who fear the LORD, *praise* him! All you offspring of Jacob, *glorify* him; *stand in awe* of him, all you offspring of Israel!" The goal of the psalm, therefore, is *to urge Israel to praise the LORD for delivering their king from the brink of death.*

Ways to Preach Christ

Although there is no promise of the coming Messiah in this psalm, the eschatological conclusion of the psalm (vv 27–31) predicts the end-time kingdom of God when all nations will worship the LORD. Instead of making the move to Christ

---

42. Heinemann, "Exposition of Psalm 22," *BSac* 147, #587 (1990): 308. Nowell, *Sing a New Song,* 17, similarly suggests, "No matter how deep the suffering, God does deliver the one who cries out." In the same vein, Ross, *Commentary on the Psalms,* I, 548, suggests, "Those who suffer persecution and scorn for their faith must persevere in praying to God to deliver them, knowing that he does not abandon his afflicted people but will hear their prayer and give them reason to praise in the congregation." Cf. Waltke, *Psalms as Christian Worship,* 398, "The song's essential message is summarized in verse 24. In a word, in spite of God's awful delay in answering prayer, he answers and upholds ultimate justice."

43. Davis, "Exploding the Limits," *JSOT* 53 (1992): 96.

from that section alone, however, we can utilize the whole psalm because New Testament references make use of most of the psalm (see below).

Also, since Jesus on the cross quoted the first line of Psalm 22, "My God, my God, why have you forsaken me?" it is clear that Jesus identified with King David. Moreover, by Jesus' time King David was considered a type of the coming Messiah King. The best way to preach Christ from Psalm 22 therefore is typology supported by New Testament references. Jesus himself had taught his disciples, "Everything written about me in the law of Moses, the prophets, and *the psalms* must be fulfilled" (Luke 24:44). The New Testament writers followed up by quoting or alluding to Psalm 22 some twenty times.

Typology and New Testament References

As we saw in Chapter 17 above (pp. 390–91, 401–3), typology entails analogies between a type and its later antitype, plus escalation. There are many obvious analogies and escalations between King David's lament and praise in Psalm 22 and King Jesus' lament and praise on Good Friday and beyond. Some of the New Testament references that could be used to move to Christ in the New Testament are the following[44] (for details see the "Sermon Exposition" section below):

Psalm 22:1   "My God, my God, why have you forsaken me?"
Mark 15:34; Matt 27:46.

Psalm 22:6   "I am . . . scorned by others, and despised by the people."
Matt 27:29.

Psalm 22:7   "They shake their heads."
Mark 15:29; Matt 27:39.

Psalm 22:8   "Commit your cause to the LORD; let him deliver."
Mark 15:29–32; Matt 27:40–43; Luke 23:35.

Psalm 22:15   "My mouth is dried up like a potsherd."
John 19:28.

Psalm 22:16   "They pierce my hands and my feet" (NIV).
Mark 15:25; John 20:25.

Psalm 22:18   "They divide my clothes among themselves,
and for my clothing they cast lots."
Mark 15:24; Matt 27:35; Luke 23:34; John 19:23–24.

44. See Appendix IV, Nestle's *Novum Testamentum Graece,* 27th ed., 1993. In this listing I have omitted some of Nestle's references because they did not support typology and have added a few others.

Psalm 22:22   "I will tell your name to my brothers."
               John 20:17; Heb 2:12.
Psalm 22:23   ""You who fear the LORD, praise him!"
               Rev 19:5.
Psalm 22:24   The LORD "did not hide his face from me, but heard when I
               cried to him."
               Heb 5:7.
Psalm 22:27   "All the ends of the earth shall . . . turn to the LORD."
               Acts 1:8.
Psalm 22:28   "For dominion belongs to the LORD."
               Rev 11:15.
Psalm 22:31   "He has done it."
               John 19:30.[45]

Sermon Theme, Goal, and Need

We formulated the theme of Psalm 22 as follows: "Praise the LORD who guided Israel's king through intense suffering to a victory which will eventually lead to all nations worshiping the LORD." The New Testament shows that Jesus, as antitype, fulfilled the type of Israel's Davidic king. In preaching Psalm 22 in the context of the New Testament, therefore, the sermon theme will have to encompass both David and Jesus. We can accomplish this by changing "Israel's king" to "his anointed king." The sermon theme, then, becomes, *Praise the LORD who guided his anointed king through intense suffering to a victory which will eventually lead to all nations worshiping the LORD.*

We formulated the goal of the psalm as, "to urge Israel to praise the LORD for delivering their king from the brink of death." Since the sermon is addressed to God's people today, we can relate its goal directly to Jesus: *to urge God's people to praise the LORD for delivering Jesus from death.* This goal points to the need addressed: we do not praise the LORD enough for delivering Jesus from death.

Scripture Reading and Sermon Outline

Psalm 22 can best be read by a single, sorrowful voice reading the lament of verses 1–21a. Then a pause at the turn of the psalm and continue with a joyful, thankful

---

45. "It is finished" echoes the last word of Psalm 22, *'āśâ*, "he has done it." See Patterson, "Psalm 22," *JETS* 47, no. 2 (2004): 228, with discussion of the issues on pp. 226–27 n. 74.

voice through the verses 21b–26. At that point the congregation can respond in unison with verses 27–31.[46]

The sermon outline can follow the structure of the text we detected earlier, suspended at appropriate times for moves to Christ in the New Testament, concluding with a final move to Christ's resurrection and Second Coming.

I. Lament (I): God is far from helping David (vv 1–11)
II. Lament (II): David is surrounded by beastly enemies (vv 12–21)
III. Praise and thanksgiving for rescue (vv 22–31)
IV. Christ's resurrection and Second Coming (NT)

Sermon Exposition

First Lament: God Is Far from Helping David (verses 1–11)[47]

Psalm 22 begins with the familiar words, "My God, my God, why have you forsaken me?" These words are probably familiar to us because Jesus used these very words when he was hanging on the cross: "My God, my God, why have you forsaken me?" But these words were first spoken by King David or one of his descendants.[48] When the editors of the Psalter introduced the psalm with the words, "A Psalm of David," they intended that we should understand this psalm from the perspective of King David. David was mercilessly hunted by King Saul who wanted to kill him. Much later David had to flee for his life from his own son Absalom. There could have been many occasions where he felt forsaken by God.

But even in his greatest suffering, David does not give up on God. Even in the deepest darkness he cries out to God. And he calls God, "my God,"[49] my

---

46. "The individual worshiper twice makes reference to the congregation (vv 22, 25) that forms the larger context of the liturgical proceedings. The change of person and of tone in the final section (vv 27–31) indicates the congregational response and conclusion to the liturgy." Craigie, *Psalms 1–50*, 198.

47. At the suggestion of my proofreader Howard Vanderwell I have added four captions "to make it easier for a reader to find the section needed." In the sermon itself, which would be much shorter than this exposition, I would not use these captions lest they break up the flow of the sermon.

48. See pp. 28–30 above, "The Psalm's Original Historical Setting."

49. "'My God,' is rare and seems to represent an especially intimate form of address based on close personal attachment." McCann, "Psalms," 762. Cf. VanGemeren, *Psalms*, 237, "In the Psalter, 'my God' is equivalent to 'my Father.'" Cf. A. Anderson, *Psalms 1–72*, 186, "As a member of the Covenant people he recalls Yahweh's promise to be their God (cf. Deut 26:17ff.; Jer 7:23), and therefore also *his* God."

God" — twice for emphasis: *'Ēlî, 'Ēlî.*[50] He uses the name *'El,* which in Canaan referred to the highest God, the transcendent, sovereign God. This almighty God can help, no matter how great the peril. But God is not helping David out of his distress. And so he cries out, "My God, my God, why have you forsaken me?" Why have you left me?[51]

David does not expect an answer to his question of "why"? It's a rhetorical question.[52] He does not want God to give him reasons why he has forsaken him. He wants action. He wants God to come back and rescue him.

For emphasis he raises the question again, "Why are you so far from helping me, from the words of my groaning?"[53] His God has not only left him, he is far distant. So far, it seems, that he cannot help David. So far, in fact, that God does not seem to hear the words of his groaning. The word for "groaning" is literally the "roaring" of a lion.[54] One can hear the roar of a lion from a long distance. But God is so far away, it seems that he cannot hear David's loud groaning.

In verse 2 David continues his complaint, "O my God, I cry by day, but you do not answer; and by night, but find no rest." Again he addresses God as "my God."[55] Day and night he cries to his God but God does not answer. Is God too far away to answer?

Psalm 20 had virtually promised David, "The Lord *answer you* in the day of trouble! The name of the God of Jacob *protect you!*" (Ps 20:1). How is it possible that God now, in his day of trouble, does not answer him? For what a "day of trouble" it is for David. As we'll soon find out, his enemies are surrounding him, closing in for the kill. He cries out to God day and night, that is, continuously.

---

50. "In calling God twice his own God, and depositing his groanings into his bosom, he makes a very distinct confession of his faith." Calvin, *Commentary on the Book of Psalms,* I, 357. Cf. Miller, *Interpreting the Psalms,* 101, "In a situation where all evidence speaks against any claim on a relationship, the psalmist holds on to it, presupposes it, and indeed seems to stake everything on it."

51. "The verb means more literally 'to leave' (*'āzab*)." McCann, "Psalms," 762.

52. "The question is rhetorical and implies, 'You should not have abandoned me, and I appeal to you to come back now.'" Goldingay, *Psalms,* I, 325. Cf. Leupold, *Exposition of the Psalms,* 196–97, "The 'why' is not so much an attempt to find the deepest reason for it all as it is a complaint as to the incomprehensibility of it all." Cf. Ross, *Commentary on the Psalms,* I, 531.

53. The Hebrew does not have the words, "Why are you," but with ellipsis in the second parallel line, these words can be supplied from the first line.

54. "The Hebrew word (*šā'ag*) and its root basically connote the idea of a roar that is characteristic of a lion (Judg 14:5; Amos 3:4; Zech 11:3)." Patterson, Psalm 22," *JETS* 47, no. 2 (2004): 220. Cf. Ps 22:13, "roaring lion." Cf. Tanner in deClaissé-Walford, Jacobson, and Tanner, *The Book of Psalms,* 233, "This is not groaning or complaining or whining. These words are expressed in the raspy scream of one in deep distress."

55. Instead of *'ēlî,* twice in verse 1, this is *'ĕlohay,* "The One to be feared by me." Leupold, *Exposition of the Psalms,* 197.

He constantly cries out to God but finds no rest from his anxiety. He cannot understand why God would allow this calamity to happen to him.

In the next three verses David reminds God that God always came through for David's ancestors. He begins in verse 3, "Yet you are holy, enthroned on the praises of Israel." "You are holy" means that God is set apart, unique, separate from sinful human beings. As the holy God, God cannot "be untrue to his promises."[56] This holy God had his throne in the temple on the ark of the covenant between the cherubim. This holy God is also "enthroned on the praises of Israel." God is lifted up, exalted by the praises of Israel. The reason for these praises is that this holy God answered their prayers and saved them.

David continues in verses 4–5, "In you our ancestors *trusted*; they *trusted*, and you delivered them. To you they cried, and were saved; in you they *trusted*, and were not put to shame." "The word 'trusted' tolls like a bell three times. In a situation of great danger, the psalmist speaks to God about the effectiveness of trust. Following the second tolling of the bell a new verb is used, 'to cry,' which pushes the sense of trust beyond an inward, passive state — in which sense it is often understood today — into active trust, faith in action."[57] If we trust God, we may indeed cry out to God when we are in despair. If we trust God, we *will* cry out to him.[58] Trust is the basis, the reason, for crying out to God. If we did not trust God, there would be no point in crying out to him. But since we trust that God is a sovereign God who can help us, we can, we *should* cry out to him.

Notice what God did in response to that cry for help of David's ancestors: "In you our ancestors trusted; they trusted, and you *delivered* them. To you they cried, and *were saved*; in you they trusted, and *were not put to shame*."[59] To be

56. "Holiness characterizes God as the one apart from and above the limitations and imperfections of [hu]mankind, 'the wholly other,' and also as the pure, righteous and exalted one who cannot therefore be untrue to his promises." Rogerson and McKay, *Psalms 1–50*, 99. Cf. Ross, *Commentary on the Psalms*, I, 532, "To say that God is holy in the midst of a lament about unanswered prayer means that God is not indifferent or impotent like the pagan gods — he is different; he has power; and he has a history of answering prayers." Cf. Goldingay, *Psalms*, I, 327, "The reminder that Yhwh is the holy one is a reminder that Yhwh is the powerful, transcendent, divine God. It underlines the fact that Yhwh has the power to deliver the suppliant but is not doing so."

57. B. Anderson, *Out of the Depths*, 25.

58. "The parallelism of vv 4–5 is instructive as it suggests that trust and outcry are identical. . . . The context reveals that to cry out to God is possible because of the trust in God and the trustworthiness of God. Indeed trust in the Lord is manifest in the cry to God in questioning, seeking, anguish." Miller, *Interpreting the Psalms*, 102.

59. "David used this figurative language ['ashamed'] (metonymy of effect and understatement) instead of simply repeating 'deliver' again so that he could more directly contrast the faith-victories of his forefathers with the shame he presently felt as he was mocked for trusting God in the face of his own apparent faith-defeat." Heinemann, "Exposition of Psalm 22," *BSac* 147, #587 (1990): 290.

put to shame in Eastern cultures was (and is) the ultimate humiliation. David's ancestors "were not put to shame." But David is put to shame. He is put to shame for trusting a God who does not deliver him.[60]

In fact, he considers himself no more than a lowly worm, subhuman. Verse 6, "But I am a worm, and not human; scorned by others, and despised by the people." People step on worms. Worms are associated with decay and death. He is "scorned by others," that is, insulted and ridiculed by cutting remarks. He is "despised by the people," that is, he is held in contempt, "looked down upon and treated as worthless."[61]

David continues in verse 7, "All who see me mock at me; they make mouths at me, they shake their heads." They sneer at him, hurling insults and shaking their heads in scorn and rejection.[62] And then come their pious, irritating words, verse 8, "Commit your cause to the LORD; let him deliver — let him rescue the one in whom he delights!" They dare to quote the words of Psalm 37:5, "Commit your way to the LORD; trust in him, and he will act." "Commit your cause to the LORD," they say. Cast your burden on the LORD; trust him.[63] "Let him deliver"[64] the way he delivered our ancestors who trusted him. They accuse David of lacking trust in the LORD. That is why the LORD is punishing him so harshly.

They conclude sarcastically, "Let him rescue the one in whom he delights!" They know that David was the man after God's own heart. God had made a special covenant with David and his house (2 Sam 7:8-16). They imply here that God really does not delight in David anymore — witness his terrible suffering.[65]

In response, David again reminds God of how faithful God was in the past, this time in David's personal past. Notice the emphasis on God in the "you's" in verses 9 and 10, "Yet it was *you* who took me from the womb; *you* kept me safe

---

60. "In trust the psalmist cries out to God in order to be rescued and not experience the shame of trusting in an impotent or indifferent God." B. Anderson, *Out of the Depths*, 26.

61. Ross, *Commentary on the Psalms*, I, 534-35.

62. "'They shake their heads' expresses disparaging derision (2 Kings 19:21 = Isa 37:22; Job 16:4; Ps 109:25; Lam 2:15)." Waltke, *Psalms as Christian Worship*, 402.

63. "The first verb in their taunt is the imperative 'trust' ('cast yourself,' *gôl*, from the verb *gālal*, 'to roll'). . . . The meaning 'trust' must have in it the idea of rolling or casting burdens on the LORD." Ross, *Commentary on the Psalms*, I, 535-36.

64. "Deliver" is the same Hebrew word as in verse 4b, "they trusted and you delivered them."

65. "Their taunting plays on his former status, as the one so close in bond with the Lord, the one in whom the Lord 'delighted,' his Chosen One." Eaton, *The Psalms*, 120, with a reference to Psalm 18:19, "He brought me out into a broad place; he delivered me, because he delighted in me." These words are also found in David's song in 2 Sam 22:20. Cf. Westermann, *The Living Psalms*, 85, "God has abandoned him without help or pity . . . because in their view he is the object of God's just punishment."

on my mother's breast. *On you* I was cast from my birth, and since my mother bore me *you* have been my God." He uses the tender image of the LORD acting as a midwife. The LORD had pulled him from his mother's womb and gently placed him on her breast. There he found milk and was safe. Right from his very beginning God had looked after him and been his God.[66] The words of verse 9b, "you kept me safe on my mother's breast" can also be translated, "You made me *trust* in you, even at my mother's breast" (NIV).[67] Right from his very beginning God had made him trust his God.

This reflection gives David the confidence to cry out again to the God he trusts.[68] Verse 11, "Do not be far from me, for trouble is near and there is no one to help." In verse 1 he had said, "Why are you so *far* from helping me?" Now he asks God directly, "Do not be far from me, for trouble is near." God is *far* away but trouble[69] is *near*. "And there is no one to help."

Second Lament: David Is Surrounded by Beastly Enemies (verses 12–21)

David next describes his plight with images of ferocious animals surrounding him. Verses 12–13, "Many bulls encircle me, strong bulls of Bashan surround me; they open wide their mouths at me, like a ravening and roaring lion." The bulls of Bashan were known to be especially large and strong. They "surrounded" him, David says. There was no way of escape. They were about to be victorious.[70]

He likens his enemies not only to strong, killer bulls but also to hungry lions.[71]

---

66. "The idea that this relationship was of the longest possible standing is strongly emphasized by the fourfold repetition of birth images ('out of the womb,' 'upon my mother's breasts,' 'from birth,' and 'from my mother's womb')." Heinemann, "Exposition of Psalm 22," *BSac* 147, #587 (1990): 292.

67. "The words 'you kept me safe' (v 9) are a translation of a form of the verb 'to trust' (cf. v 5)." Davidson, *Vitality of Worship*, 80.

68. "As he recalls what God has done for him from birth, the suppliant finds in his despairing lament a firm foothold that enables him to step from lament to petition, 'Be not far from me!'" Westermann, *The Living Psalms*, 85.

69. "The word 'trouble' is the word that means a bind, a strait, some kind of distress (*ṣārâ* from *ṣārar*)." Ross, *Commentary on the Psalms*, I, 538.

70. "There were no bulls present of course; but by calling his enemies bulls the psalmist was saying that they were powerful, brutish, senseless, and dangerous. They surrounded him victoriously, as the word 'encircled' . . . suggests, for it is related to the word for 'crown.'" Ross, *Commentary on the Psalms*, I, 538.

71. "In the ancient Near East, these images of bulls and lions represent images of power and strength, indicating these are no ordinary enemies but are menacing and powerful enemies that would discourage others from getting involved." Tanner in deClaissé-Walford, Jacobson, and Tanner, *The Book of Psalms*, 234.

He says in verse 13, "they [his enemies][72] open wide their mouths at me, like a ravening and roaring lion." They could attack him any time and kill him.

David is terrified. He graphically describes himself in verses 14–15, "I am poured out like water, and all my bones are out of joint; my heart is like wax; it is melted within my breast; my mouth is dried up like a potsherd, and my tongue sticks to my jaws; you lay me in the dust of death." He says, "I am poured out like water." "I am drained," we would say today. "I am all washed up." No more energy. "And all my bones are out of joint." He is racked with pain and can no longer run to escape. He is "paralyzed with fear."[73] "My heart [the core of his being] is like wax; it is melted within my breast." "Just as under heat or pressure wax will melt, so under the pressure of the attacks of these people David's spirit has almost completely melted away — he has no will left to fight."[74] "My mouth is dried up like a potsherd, and my tongue sticks to my jaws." People who are dying often have such a dry mouth that relatives moisten their lips and tongue with water. David is on the brink of death.

The last line of verse 15 comes as a surprise. "You lay me in the dust of death." It's another "you." "*You* [God] lay me in the dust of death." "The dust of death" reminds us of Genesis 3:19, "You are dust, and to dust you shall return." David may be threatened with death by his enemies, but behind these he sees the hand of God. The sovereign God is in control, also of his enemies.[75]

In verse 16 he returns again to his enemies, "For dogs are all around me; a company of evildoers encircles me." In the ancient Near East dogs were not pets. Dogs were scavengers looking for dead meat.[76] When the evil queen Jezebel was thrown from her palace window she was eaten by dogs (2 Kings 9:30–36). David is surrounded by dogs. He is near death, otherwise dogs would not circle him. In the next line he explains who the dogs are: "a company of evildoers encircles me." He is surrounded by evildoers and cannot escape.

At the end of verse 16 David says, "My hands and feet have shriveled." The NIV has the better translation here: "they pierce my hands and my feet."[77] "The

72. "The enemies (and not the bulls) appear to the sufferer like ravenous lions." A. Anderson, *Psalms 1–72*, 189.
The NIV solves the ambiguity by translating verse 13, "Roaring lions that tear their prey open their mouths wide against me."

73. A. Anderson, *Psalms 1–72*, 190.

74. Ross, *Commentary on the Psalms*, I, 539. Cf. A. Anderson, *Psalms 1–72*, 190, "The psalmist has become greatly afraid and fainthearted (as in Deut 20:8; Josh 2:11)."

75. "Either God uses the adversaries as instruments of the perplexing punishment or he has given them a free hand by forsaking the psalmist (cf. vv 1–2)." A. Anderson, *Psalms 1–72*, 190.

76. See n. 31 above.

77. See NIV textual note about the Dead Sea Scrolls. A scroll found near Qumran at Naḥal Ḥever known as 5/6ḤevPsalms reads, "They have pierced my hands and my feet." This scroll, which is over 1,000 years older than the standard Hebrew Masoretic text, was not published until 1999. See

image in the Psalmist's mind was probably of dogs nipping at his hands and feet and puncturing them."[78] The image of dogs nipping at his hands and feet indicates that he was on the brink of death. Otherwise dogs would not come near.[79]

Verse 17, "I can count all my bones [he is a walking skeleton]. They stare and gloat over me." With smug satisfaction his enemies see him dying. For they can profit from his death. Verse 18, "They divide my clothes among themselves, and for my clothing they cast lots." A song from Mesopotamia says, "The coffin lay open, and people already helped themselves to my valuables; before I was even dead, the mourning was already done."[80] So David sees himself being killed by his enemies who gloat over him because they can divide the spoil.

The writers of the New Testament saw King David as a type of Christ: David prefigured Jesus Christ. What happened to David would happen to Christ, only on a more severe scale. So when the Gospel writers told the story of Jesus' suffering and death, they frequently quoted the words of David in Psalm 22. In fact, as Jesus hung on the cross, he himself identified with David and used the opening line of Psalm 22. Mark tells us, "At three o'clock Jesus cried out with a loud voice, 'Eloi, Eloi, lema sabachthani?'[81] which means, 'My God, my God, why have you forsaken me?'" (Mark 15:34; cf. Matt 27:46). But whereas David was only threatened by death, Jesus actually tasted death. Jesus was abandoned by God to a certain death on the cross, carrying the sins of the world.

In verse 9 David claimed to have had a close relationship with God from his birth: "It was you who took me from the womb; you kept me safe on my mother's breast." But Jesus had an even closer relationship with God from the day of his birth. The angel told Mary, "The Holy Spirit will come upon you, and the power of the Most High will overshadow you; therefore the child to be born will be holy; he will be called Son of God" (Luke 1:35). Moreover, Jesus was the Son of God not only from birth but from eternity. As John 1:1 puts it, "In the beginning was the Word [Jesus], and the Word was with God, and the Word was God."

In verse 6 David says that he was "scorned by others, and despised by the people."[82] When Jesus was judged by Pilate, Matthew reports that "the soldiers of

---

Conrad Gren, "Piercing the Ambiguities of Psalm 22:16 and the Messiah's Mission," *JETS* 48, no. 2 (2005; pp. 283–99), esp. pp. 283, 287–88, and 297–99. See also Tanner in deClaissé-Walford, Jacobson, and Tanner, *The Book of Psalms*, 230 n. 26, and Waltke, *Psalms as Christian Worship*, pp. 393–94 n. 66.

78. Ross, *Commentary on the Psalms*, I, 524 n. 9.

79. "To describe his enemies as dogs was to portray them as nasty predators and scavengers; but it also indicated that he was as good as dead, or appearing lifeless, for the 'dogs' would not come around otherwise." Ross, ibid., 540.

80. Kraus, *Psalms 1–59*, 298.

81. Aramaic for the Hebrew clause.

82. This picture reminds us of the Servant of the Lord in Isaiah 53: "He was despised and

the governor . . . stripped him and put a scarlet robe on him, and after twisting some thorns into a crown, they put it on his head. They put a reed in his right hand and knelt before him and *mocked* him, saying, 'Hail, King of the Jews!' They spat on him, and took the reed and struck him on the head" (Matt 27:27–30).

David emphasized that he was *surrounded* by enemies who threatened to kill him (Ps 22:12–13, 16, and 20–21). As he hung on the cross, Jesus was also surrounded by enemies — chief priests, scribes, elders, Roman soldiers — but they were in the very process of killing him.

According to verses 7–8, David was mocked, people shaking their heads, "Commit your cause to the LORD; let him deliver — let him rescue the one in whom he delights!" Jesus was similarly mocked. According to Matthew, "Those who passed by derided him, shaking their heads and saying . . . , 'Save yourself! If you are the Son of God, come down from the cross.' In the same way the chief priests also, along with the scribes and elders, were mocking him, saying, 'He saved others; he cannot save himself. He is the King of Israel; let him come down from the cross now, and we will believe in him. He trusts in God; let God deliver him now, if he wants to; for he said, 'I am God's Son'" (Matt 27:39–43; cf. Mark 15:29–32).

In verse 15 David cried out "My mouth is dried up like a potsherd, and my tongue sticks to my jaws." We read in John 19:28, "When Jesus knew that all was now finished, he said (in order to fulfill the scripture), 'I am thirsty.'"

At the end of verse 15 David said that God was the ultimate cause of his death: "You lay me in the dust of death." Jesus knew this also as he prayed in the Garden of Gethsemane, "My Father, if it is possible, let this cup pass from me; yet not what I want but what *you* want" (Matt 26:39).

In verse 16 David complained, "They pierce my hands and my feet" (NIV). Jesus' hands and feet were actually pierced as he was nailed to the cross.[83]

According to verse 18 David said, "They divide my clothes among themselves, and for my clothing they cast lots." All four Gospels report that the Roman soldiers divided his garments. Mark writes, "They crucified him, and divided his clothes among them, casting lots to decide what each should take" (Mark 15:24).[84]

Even the final words of David in Psalm 22, "he has done it," were echoed by Jesus on the cross. John reports, "When Jesus had received the wine, he said, 'It is finished' ['he has done it'].[85] Then he bowed his head and gave up his spirit" (John 19:30). Luke tells us that Jesus died, entrusting himself to his Father's care:

---

rejected by others; a man of suffering and acquainted with infirmity; and as one from whom others hide their faces he was despised, and we held him of no account" (Isa 53:3; cf. 52:14).

83. Cf. John 20:25, Thomas's comment, "Unless I see the mark of the nails in his hands, and put my finger in the mark of the nails and my hand in his side, I will not believe."

84. Cf. Matt 27:35; Luke 23:34; John 19:23–24.

85. A translation of *'āśâ*, "he has done it." See n. 1 above.

"'Father, into your hands I commend my spirit.' Having said this, he breathed his last" (Luke 23:46).

When Jesus on the cross quoted the beginning of Psalm 22, he had the whole psalm in mind.[86] Jesus anticipated that what happened to David would happen to him. Let's see, therefore, what happened to David in the rest of the psalm.

When David is so close to death that he sees his enemies dividing his clothes, he addresses God directly. He begs God for the second time (see v 11) in verse 19, "But you, O LORD, *do not be far away!* O my help, come quickly to my aid!" This is the first time he names God by the covenant name LORD. It's a reminder that God had made a special covenant with David. God had promised, "I will give you rest from all your enemies," and, "Your house and your kingdom shall be made sure forever before me; your throne shall be established forever" (2 Sam 7:11, 16). David reminds the LORD of his covenant obligations. "Do not be far away! O my help, come quickly to my aid!" He now calls God "my help" or "my strength" (NIV). In addressing God as "my help," he is growing more confident that God will still help him.[87]

Verses 20–21, "Deliver my soul from the sword, my life from the power of the dog! Save me from the mouth of the lion! From the horns of the wild oxen you have rescued me." He had earlier described his enemies as these savage animals. Now he zeroes in on what they use to kill. "Deliver my soul from *the sword*[88] [a symbol of a violent death], my life from *the power of the dog* [which crunches even bones]! Save me from *the mouth of the lion* [which rips flesh apart]! From *the horns of the wild oxen* [which gore people to death]."[89] At the same time his pleas to God become more urgent: "Deliver my soul!" "Save me!" The final line in verse 21 is the climax: "From the horns of the wild oxen *you have rescued me.*"[90] At the last moment, as he was about to be killed, God rescued him.[91] Saved at last!

---

86. See n. 2 above.

87. "Whereas the psalmist had concluded that there was no one to help (v 11), here the psalmist addresses God as 'my help' or 'my strength.'" McCann, "Psalms," 763.

88. The sword "refers to the most important weapon of warfare in the ancient Near East, consisting of a hilt and blade, ranging from sixteen inches to three feet in length. One or both edges of the blade were sharpened or whetted so as to slay effectively." Waltke, *Psalms as Christian Worship*, 407.

89. "The main idea is his concern with the things about his enemies that will cause him harm; from these he wants to be delivered." Ross, *Commentary on the Psalms*, I, 542.

90. "Strangely, the assurance of the demand also grows in strength. The first petition is formulated negatively: 'Do not be far away.' Then the psalmist switches to positive imperatives — 'save me, deliver me' — and finally to a perfect verb ('*ănîtānî*, 'you have rescued me,' v 21), indicating that rescue is a certainty." Davis, "Exploding the Limits," *JSOT* 53 (1992): 99.

91. Or "answered me." The verb *'ānâ* is the same verb as the one used in v 2, "but you do not answer." Cf. Tanner in deClaissé-Walford, Jacobson, and Tanner, *The Book of Psalms*, 236, "Verse

Praise and Thanksgiving for Rescue (verses 22–31)

David now breaks into praise. He tells God in verse 22, "I will tell of your name to my brothers and sisters; in the midst of the congregation I will praise you." To "tell of *your name* to my brothers and sisters" is to tell of God's saving deeds.[92] "In the midst of the congregation I will praise you." David's situation has been completely turned around. Whereas God did not answer him before, now God has answered him. Whereas he was surrounded by his enemies, now he is surrounded by his brothers and sisters in the congregation. In the midst of this congregation he promises to praise God. But he wants an ever larger circle of people to praise God.[93]

He turns to the congregation, verse 23, "You who fear the LORD, praise him! All you offspring of Jacob, glorify him; stand in awe of him, all you offspring of Israel!" He brings his message home by using three synonyms as commands: "praise him!" "glorify him!" and "stand in awe of him!" "Praise, honor, and awe. The first [praise] suggests a wordless enthusiasm, the second [glorify] a recognition of . . . the LORD's splendor; the third [awe] a sense of reverence, almost dread, and submission."[94]

David gives the reason for encouraging all Israel to praise, glorify, and revere the LORD in verse 24, "For he did not despise or abhor the affliction of the afflicted; he did not hide his face from me, but heard when I cried to him." It seemed that God despised David's affliction (v 1), but now it is clear that "he did not despise" his affliction. It seemed that God hid his face from David by not answering him (v 2), but now it is clear that "he did not hide his face" from David. Instead, he "heard when I cried to him." Just as God heard and saved his ancestors when they cried to him (v 5), so God heard and saved David.

And then David breaks out into praise again. Verse 25, "From you comes my praise in the great congregation; my vows I will pay before those who fear him." David gives God the credit for his praise: "From *you* comes my praise." It is because God rescued him that he can now praise God in the great congregation. David's voice now joins the praises of Israel upon which God is enthroned (v 3).

David continues in verse 25, "my vows I will pay before those who fear him." Apparently he had promised God that he would offer a sacrifice if God would save

---

21 begins with an imperative verb, *save me,* and ends with a perfect verb meaning *you answered me.* . . . The whole psalm pivots on this one word (at least in Hebrew), *'ănîtānî* ('you answered me')." Cf. Kraus, *Psalms 1–59,* 292 n. 21l.

92. "The 'name' stands for what God has done." Westermann, *The Living Psalms,* 88.

93. Ibid., 90. So also Miller, *Interpreting the Psalms,* 108, "The praise of the lamenting petitioner is public praise and can and should elicit an astonishingly wide echo of praise (cf. Ps 117:1)."

94. Goldingay, *Psalms,* I, 336.

him. God *had* saved him and now David follows through by sacrificing a peace offering in the temple.[95] "The sacrifice would actually become a communal meal. While the animal was roasting on the altar, the one who brought it would stand beside the altar and tell people what God had done. Then, all the people would eat together (it was the only sacrifice that Israelites could eat in the sanctuary). They would eat because God had blessed this person."[96]

Consequently David continues in verse 26, "The poor shall eat and be satisfied; those who seek him shall praise the LORD." The circle of praise is expanding from David to his family and now to the poor. They have eaten from David's sacrifice and are satisfied. Now "those who seek him shall praise the LORD." Then David turns to all partaking of this meal and offers a toast: "May your hearts live forever!" "A significant toast from one who stood so recently on the threshold of death."[97]

The circle of praise widens even more with verse 27: "All the ends of the earth shall remember and turn to the LORD; and all the families of the nations shall worship before him." To highlight the universal scope David repeats twice the word "all." "*All* the ends of the earth shall remember[98] and turn to the LORD; and *all* the families of the nations shall worship before him." God's praise moves from Israel to all the nations of the world. The Gentiles are now included. The whole world will turn to the LORD and worship him. What a vision!

Verse 28 gives the reasons for this universal praise: "For dominion belongs to the LORD, and he rules over the nations." Since the LORD is King of the entire world, universal praise is his due.

Verse 29 stretches the circle of praise still wider, far beyond the traditional Israelite view: "To him, indeed, shall *all* who sleep in the earth bow down; before him shall bow *all* who go down to the dust, and I shall live for him." Two more "all's." "*All* who sleep in the earth" are those who have died[99] as are "*all* who go

---

95. God had instructed Israel to eat their peace offering in the temple, "in the presence of the LORD your God . . . together with your son and your daughter, your male and female slaves, and the Levites resident in your towns, rejoicing in the presence of the LORD your God in all your undertakings" (Deut 12:18).

96. Ross, *Commentary on the Psalms,* I, 545. Cf. Broyles, *Psalms,* 119, "Thanksgiving in the OT often included a thanksgiving sacrifice, which was to be shared, as it were, as a communal meal with Yahweh, the priests, and the worshipper's family (Lev 7:15-16; Deut 12:5-7; 1 Sam 1:3-4; 9:12-13). Deuteronomy 16:10-17 implies that society's poor may also share in the offerings of those especially blessed."

97. Craigie, *Psalms 1–50,* 201.

98. That is, call the LORD to mind.

99. The NRSV has strengthened the parallelism by changing *dišnê,* "the rich, the fat ones" to *yašēnê,* "those who sleep." See VanGemeren, *Psalms,* 249 n. The NIV follows the MT and renders verse 29, "All the rich of the earth will feast and worship; all who go down to the dust will kneel before him — those who cannot keep themselves alive." If the pew Bible is the NIV, I would just

down to the dust" (cf. v 15 and Gen 3:19).[100] This verse states boldly that all the dead will bow down before the LORD; the dead *"shall live* for him."[101] This is astounding news for the Old Testament.[102] Only in Daniel 12:2 and Isaiah 26:19 do we find a similar, clear teaching of the resurrection from the dead. Daniel writes, "Many of those who sleep in the dust of the earth shall awake, some to everlasting life, and some to shame and everlasting contempt" (Dan 12:2).

God's praise will be extended not only in space from David and Israel to all the nations of the world. It will also be extended in time: not only into the past (the dead) but also into the future. Verses 30–31, "Posterity will serve him; future generations will be told about the Lord, and proclaim his deliverance to a people yet unborn, saying that he has done it." That's a missionary mandate. "Posterity will serve him; future generations will be told about the Lord." And then they, in turn, will "proclaim his deliverance[103] to a people yet unborn."[104]

What is the core of their preaching? They will "proclaim his *deliverance* to a people yet unborn, saying that *he has done it.*" Their message is that God has delivered; God has acted.[105] God can rescue his people even from certain death.[106]

---

go with its translation: the poor were praising the LORD (v 26); now the rich join them, as well as those who have died, and "those who cannot keep themselves alive," that is, all human beings. "The purpose is to indicate that all humanity — Israelite or non-Israelite, rich or poor — will acknowledge the rulership of Yahweh and bow to it." Wilson, *Psalms*, I, 422.

100. "The phrase 'go down to the dust' indicates that death is almost a certainty in view of v 15, which mentions 'the dust of death.'" McCann, "Psalms," 764–65.

101. "Emerging suddenly out of a deathlike loss of meaning, the psalmist's joyful confidence that God is responsive to his plea demands that the dead above all may not be excluded from celebration and worship." Davis, "Exploding the Limits," *JSOT* 53 (1992): 103. See her whole discussion on this verse (pp. 101–3).

102. "In the OT the dead have no connection to Yahweh, and they do not praise him (cf. Pss 6:5; 88:10–12 [30:9; 115:17]). *Sheol* is a place far removed from the cultus. But now the barrier is broken down. Also those who sleep in the earth (Dan 12:2) are drawn into the homage to Yahweh." Kraus, *Psalms 1–59*, 300.

103. The NIV translates, "They will proclaim his righteousness." VanGemeren, *Psalms*, 249, explains, "The object of the proclamation is God's 'righteousness' (ṣədāqâ), i.e., his acts of deliverance, whereby he demonstrates his sovereign, gracious, and victorious rule (cf. *TWOT* 2:754–55)." Cf. Stek, *NIV Study Bible*, Ps 4:1 n., "Very often the 'righteousness' of God in the Psalms (and frequently elsewhere in the OT) refers to the faithfulness with which he acts."

104. "No psalm or prophecy contains a grander vision of the scope of the throng of worshipers who will join in the praise of God's saving acts." Stek, *NIV Study Bible*, Ps 22:22–31 n.

105. "This is what provides the motive force to power the movement of the whole psalm: God has acted." Westermann, *The Living Psalms*, 90–91. Cf. Mays, *Preaching and Teaching the Psalms*, 115, "It is a formula that occurs in the Old Testament in a quite specific context and function — always as a testimony that a deliverance from dying (for an individual or the people) is the work of God. It is a revelatory code word from the history of salvation."

106. "In the context of this psalm, it refers to God's answering the cry of the suffering psalmist

Christ's Resurrection and Second Coming

When Jesus on the cross quoted the first line of this psalm, he had the whole psalm in mind. "My God, my God, why have you forsaken me?" Yes, God abandoned him to death. But Jesus also knew that the rest of the psalm proclaims that God can rescue even from certain death. In fact, Jesus had told his disciples several times about his suffering, death, and resurrection. He had said, "See, we are going up to Jerusalem, and the Son of Man will be handed over to the chief priests and the scribes, and they will condemn him to death; then they will hand him over to the Gentiles; they will mock him, and spit upon him, and flog him, and kill him; and *after three days he will rise again.*"[107]

Jesus knew the whole psalm. Even as he was dying on the cross, the light of Easter began to break through. For the God who rescued David from certain death ("From the horns of the wild oxen you have rescued me" [v 21]), would also rescue Jesus from certain death.[108] On Easter morning Jesus began to fulfill the amazing prediction, "To him [the LORD], indeed, shall all who sleep in the earth bow down; before him shall bow all who go down to the dust" (v 29). Jesus was the first to be raised from the dead. The rest of humanity will follow when Jesus comes again. "For the trumpet will sound, and the dead will be raised imperishable, and we will be changed" (1 Cor 15:52).[109]

David predicted[110] this universal praise of God in verse 27, "*All the ends of the earth* shall remember and turn to the LORD; and all the families of the nations shall worship before him."[111] After his resurrection Jesus began the movement to fulfill this universal praise of God. Jesus told his disciples, "You will be my witnesses in Je-

---

and saving him from certain death. When people hear that the one true and living God actually answers prayers and saves people from death, they will turn to him in faith and become his witnesses to their generations." Ross, *Commentary on the Psalms,* I, 547.

107. Mark 10:33–34. Cf. Mark 8:31 and 9:31.

108. Cf. Heb 5:7, "In the days of his flesh, Jesus offered up prayers and supplications, with loud cries and tears, to the one who was able to save him from death, and he was heard because of his reverent submission."

109. Cf. 1 Cor 15:20–23, "Christ has been raised from the dead, the first fruits of those who have died. For since death came through a human being, the resurrection of the dead has also come through a human being; for as all die in Adam, so all will be made alive in Christ. But each in his own order: Christ the first fruits, then at his coming those who belong to Christ."

110. "The vision of this hymn is prophetic in character and eschatological in scope." Mays, *Psalms,* 113.

111. Countering commentators who "suggest that the psalm envisages 'the conversion of all peoples,'" Gordon Wenham rightly points out that "they are suggesting a universalism that conflicts with other passages in the Psalms, for example, 2:9 and 149:6–9. The scope of salvation may be universal: it is open to all nations. But not all nations, and certainly not every member of every nation, will accept the terms of that salvation." *The Psalter Reclaimed,* 171.

rusalem, in all Judea and Samaria, and to *the ends of the earth*" (Acts 1:8). When Jesus comes again this universal praise will become a reality. For when Jesus comes again, as Paul put it, "at the name of Jesus *every knee* . . . [will] bend . . . , and *every tongue* . . . confess that Jesus Christ is Lord, to the glory of God the Father" (Phil 2:10–11).

David writes in verses 30–31, "Future generations will be told about the Lord, and proclaim his deliverance to a people yet unborn." This is the church's mission mandate until Jesus comes again: to proclaim the Lord's deliverance. And what is the heart of that message? Verse 31, "He has done it." God has done it! God has done it in Jesus. Jesus echoed this word "he has done it" when he cried out from the cross, "It is finished" (John 19:30). "This was not a cry of defeat but of victory — a realization that the purpose of God for the creation was made whole in the work of his faithful Son."[112] Jesus had finished his redemptive work. He paid the penalty for our sin and would defeat death and Satan on Easter Sunday. He ushered in the new creation where there will be no more sin, death, mourning, and crying (Rev 21:4). Then, as John put it in Revelation 11:15, "The kingdom of the world has become the kingdom of our Lord and of his Messiah, and he will reign forever and ever."

Conclusion

While we look forward to that perfect kingdom of God, we still live in a sinful, broken world. Sometimes we also may need to cry out, "My God, my God, why have you forsaken me?" As long as we begin with "*my* God, *my* God," our faith in God is still intact even in our suffering.[113] Would God ever forsake his own? In Psalm 37 the psalmist says, "I have been young, and now am old, yet I have not seen the righteous forsaken. . . . For the LORD loves justice; he will not forsake his faithful ones" (Ps 37:25, 28). Psalm 94:14 assures us, "For the LORD will not forsake his people; he will not abandon his heritage." Because Jesus was forsaken by God, we will never be forsaken by him.[114]

As I was writing this chapter, I was sitting in our sun-porch watching goldfinches feeding on our upside-down feeder. A young goldfinch sat nearby fluttering its wings. It could not manage the upside-down feeder. Somehow it would have to be fed by its mother. As I watched, the mother flew back to her young and deposited in its beak the thistle seeds she had harvested. Then the mother flew

---

112. Wilson, *Psalms,* I, 429.

113. "In calling God twice his own God, and depositing his groanings into his bosom, he makes a very distinct confession of faith." Calvin, *Commentary on the Book of Psalms,* I, 357.

114. "I am convinced that neither death, nor life, nor angels, nor rulers, nor things present, nor things to come, nor powers, nor height, nor depth, nor anything else in all creation, will be able to separate us from the love of God in Christ Jesus our Lord." Rom 8:38–39.

away. I sat there for ten minutes waiting for the mother to return, but she didn't. It looked as if she had forsaken her young one. I did not dare to get up for fear I would spook the young bird and separate it from its mother. But after ten minutes I had to get back to work. I stood up and the young bird flew away to a distant tree. My heart sank: How would it find its mother again? But as it was flying to the distant tree, I saw another bird join the young one. Apparently the mother bird had landed on a nearby roof and watched her young one so she could join it whenever it took off. Forsaken — yet *not* forsaken!

Ellen Davis writes perceptively in her sermon on Psalm 22, "The psalmist shows us the moment of astonished discovery to which faithful suffering leads: the moment when, cast down into the depths, cast down even by God's own hand, there we discover, beyond all logic and imagining, that the bottom of despair is solid. And suddenly we know, with strange but unshakable certainty, that we cannot fall — in life or in death, we cannot fall beyond the reach of God's love and power to save. It is out of that certainty that we discover our own boundless capacity for praise."[115] We cannot praise God enough for what he did for us in the death and resurrection of his Son Jesus Christ.

Prayer[116]

Merciful God, some of your children are joyfully singing your praise.
    Others are languishing in despair.
Through Jesus you are acquainted with our grief
    and in him we have resurrection hope.
Bind up those who are broken,
    bless those who are dying,
    shield those who are joyous,
and lead us all to your house,
    where we may feast together at your table.
Amen.

Song[117]

1Man of sorrows what a name
    for the Son of God, who came
ruined sinners to reclaim:
    Hallelujah, what a Savior!

---

115. Davis, *Wondrous Depth*, 154.
116. *Psalms for All Seasons*, 116.
117. Philip P. Bliss, 1875. Public Domain. *Psalter Hymnal* (1987), # 482; *Lift Up Your Hearts,* # 170.

2Bearing shame and scoffing rude,
 In my place condemned he stood,
sealed my pardon with his blood:
 Hallelujah, what a Savior!

3Guilty, helpless, lost were we;
 blameless Lamb of God was he,
sacrificed to set us free:
 Hallelujah, what a Savior!

4He was lifted up to die;
 "It is finished" was his cry;
now in heaven exalted high:
 Hallelujah, what a Savior!

5When he comes, our glorious King,
 all his ransomed home to bring,
then anew this song we'll sing:
 Hallelujah, what a Savior!

CHAPTER 19

"This Is the Day That the LORD Has Made"

Psalm 118:10–24 (117:10–24)

The Revised Common Lectionary assigns the reading of Psalm 118:1–2, 14–24 for Easter, Year A, B, and C, and Psalm 118:14–29 for the Second Sunday of Easter, Year C. Since Easter is one of the most important Christian feast days, during the main worship service, I think, people should hear the astounding message of Easter from one of the Gospels. But we could preach Psalm 118:10–24 during the Easter evening service, or, if there is no evening service, the following Sunday. If we have already preached on the whole psalm on Palm Sunday, preaching on a section of it on Easter Sunday evening or the following Sunday would make for a good series of two sermons on this psalm.

Since we examined every verse of this psalm in Chapter 17 above, we need not repeat the results here. Instead, after covering some necessary issues, we can move rather quickly to the "Sermon Exposition" section.

Text and Context

Although the Lectionary selects the reading of Psalm 118:1–2, 14–24, verse 14 is the conclusion of the section that begins at verse 10 with the king explaining the "distress" (v 5) he was in. For selecting a literary unit, therefore, we begin the preaching text at verse 10. And we end the text at verse 24, since the prayer of verse 25 changes the topic (see the NIV and ESV divisions listed on p. 387 above).

The immediate context, of course, is the whole of Psalm 118, with the broader contexts consisting of the Old Testament, especially Exodus 14–15, and the New Testament.

Textual Theme and Goal

In the selected preaching unit, the king begins to detail his "distress": "All nations surrounded me . . ." (v 10). But "in the name of the LORD I cut them off" (3×, vv 10–12). "The LORD helped me" (v 13). "The LORD . . . has become my salvation" (v 14, repeated in v 21). Next we hear about "the right hand of the LORD" doing valiantly (2×) and being exalted (vv 15–16). Because of the actions of the LORD, the king can cry out triumphantly, "I shall not die, but I shall live" (v 17). The king goes to the temple and thanks the LORD: "I thank you that you have answered me and have become my salvation" (v 21). A choir responds that the king's victory "is the LORD's doing" (v 23). And the section ends with the climax addressed to Israel, "This is the day that the LORD has made; let us rejoice and be glad in it" (v 24).

We can summarize the message of this section for Israel as follows, *Rejoice in the day commemorating the LORD's acts to save the Davidic king from death.* The goal of this passage is *to urge Israel to rejoice in the day commemorating the LORD's acts to save the Davidic king from death.*

Ways to Preach Christ

In Chapter 17 above (pp. 390–91) we determined that a good way to preach Christ from this psalm is typology supported by New Testament references. That is also the best way to preach Christ from this sub-unit.

Typology and New Testament References

In Chapter 17 we noted some of the analogies and escalations between the Davidic king of Psalm 118 and King Jesus. As the king was in distress and called on the LORD (Ps 118:5), so Jesus was in even greater distress in Gethsemane and on the cross and called on the LORD. As the king was surrounded by enemies who wanted to kill him (Ps 118:10–12), so Jesus on the cross was surrounded by enemies who were about to kill him. As the king testified, "The LORD has punished me severely, but he did not give me over to death" (Ps 118:18), so King Jesus was not given over to ultimate death: he rose again. As the king was rejected by his enemies but became the chief cornerstone (Ps 118:22), so Jesus was rejected by all, sentenced to death, and became the chief corner stone (Mark 12:10; Acts 4:11; Eph 2:20; 1 Peter 2:7; see further "Sermon Exposition" below).

Sermon Theme, Goal, and Need

Since the New Testament does not change the message of this passage but focuses it on Christ and the Lord's day, the textual theme can become the sermon theme: *Rejoice in the day commemorating the LORD's acts to save the Davidic king from death.*

The goal of this passage can become the sermon goal by broadening "Israel" to "God's people" and focusing it more specifically on Jesus and the Lord's day: *to urge God's people to rejoice on the Lord's day commemorating the LORD's acts to save king Jesus from death.* This goal points to the need addressed in this sermon: our lack of joy in celebrating the Lord's day.

Scripture Reading

If the entire psalm was read on Palm Sunday, we can limit the reading on Easter Sunday to the selected preaching text. But it would also be good to include the larger context of Psalm 118. Therefore, we can read the verses 1–2, 5, 10–24, and 29. Again, it would be helpful for understanding the psalm to have two or more voices read the parts: the liturgist reads the parts of the priest (and possibly of the choir), another voice the parts of the king, and two or more voices read in unison the parts of the choir.

PRIEST   1 O give thanks to the LORD, for he is good,
            for his steadfast love endures forever.
         2 Let Israel say,
CHOIR   "His steadfast love endures forever. . . ."

KING   5 Out of my distress I called on the LORD;
            the LORD answered me and set me in a broad place. . . .

         10 All nations surrounded me;
            in the name of the LORD I cut them off!
         11 They surrounded me, surrounded me on every side;
            in the name of the LORD I cut them off!
         12 They surrounded me like bees;
            they blazed like a fire of thorns;
            in the name of the LORD I cut them off!
         13 I was pushed hard, so that I was falling,
            but the LORD helped me.

14 The LORD is my strength and my might;
    he has become my salvation.

PRIEST 15 There are glad songs of victory in the tents of the righteous:

CHOIR   "The right hand of the LORD does valiantly;
16 the right hand of the LORD is exalted;
    the right hand of the LORD does valiantly."

KING 17 I shall not die, but I shall live,
    and recount the deeds of the LORD.
18 The LORD has punished me severely,
    but he did not give me over to death.
19 Open to me the gates of righteousness,
    that I may enter through them
    and give thanks to the LORD.

PRIEST 20 This is the gate of the LORD;
    the righteous shall enter through it.

KING 21 I thank you that you have answered me
    and have become my salvation.

CHOIR 22 The stone that the builders rejected
    has become the chief cornerstone.
23 This is the LORD's doing;
    it is marvelous in our eyes.
24 This is the day that the LORD has made;
    let us rejoice and be glad in it. . . .

PRIEST 29 O give thanks to the LORD, for he is good,

CHOIR   for his steadfast love endures forever.

Sermon Exposition

On Palm Sunday we noted that the goal of Psalm 118 is "to urge all God's people to give thanks to the LORD because in his steadfast love he saved the Davidic king as well as his people." The psalm begins and ends with this call to thank the LORD: "O give thanks to the LORD, for he is good, for his steadfast love endures forever."

On Easter Sunday, it is also fitting that we pause to give thanks to God for the wonderful gift he has given us in his Son Jesus. God's steadfast love for us is clearly visible when he sent his only Son to die for us to pay for our sins. God's love for us is even more apparent on Easter Sunday when God raised Jesus from the dead. For Jesus' resurrection from the dead means that he conquered death for us. Paul calls Jesus' victory over death "the first fruits." After that first harvest, another harvest will follow. We shall all share in Jesus' victory over that last enemy, death. On the last day we shall all rise from the dead. "O give thanks to the LORD, for he is good; his steadfast love endures forever!" "O give thanks to the LORD" because he raised Jesus from the dead.

The more specific goal of our text is to urge us to *rejoice* on the Lord's day. Our Sunday observances may frequently be lethargic, listless, indifferent — it's just another day. Sure, we go to church, but where is the joy and gladness? Our text urges us to rejoice on the Lord's day because on that day God acted to save king Jesus from death.

The evening before he died, Jesus and his disciples celebrated the Passover. On this occasion Jesus instituted the Lord's Supper as a sacred memorial. Jesus said, "Do this in remembrance of me" (Luke 22:19). Matthew and Mark report that Jesus and his disciples then sang "the hymn."[1] This hymn was likely Psalm 118,[2] so that Jesus entered his road of suffering with this psalm in mind.

In telling the story of Jesus' death and resurrection, the Gospel writers quote Psalm 118 several times. They can do this because the Davidic king who tells his story in this psalm prefigures the later King Jesus. What the king experienced was similar to what Jesus would experience, though what Jesus went through was much more intense and significant.

This is how the king relates his experience. He had been in terrible trouble. He was in deep distress, "hard pressed" (NIV), confined to a narrow place.[3] The king reports in verse 5, "Out of my distress [this tight, cramped place] I called on the LORD; the LORD answered me and set me in a broad place." In the verses 10–12 the king describes the trouble he was in. He writes that he was surrounded by all nations, surrounded on every side. He says in verse 12, "They surrounded me like bees; they blazed like a fire of thorns." His enemies wanted him dead. In verse 13 he says, "I was pushed hard, so that I was falling." When a soldier falls on the battlefield he is either dead or near death. The king says, "I was pushed hard, so that I was falling." He was near death. "But," he says, "the LORD helped me." And in verse 14 he declares confidently, "The LORD is my strength and my might; he has become my salvation."

The king's soldiers celebrate the victory in their tents. Verse 15, "There are glad songs of victory in the tents of the righteous." They credit the LORD for this victory: "The right hand of the LORD does valiantly; the right hand of the LORD is

---

1. Mark 14:26 and Matthew 26:30: "When they had sung the hymn, they went out to the Mount of Olives."

2. According to rabbinic tradition (*m. Pesahim* 10:5–7) they would sing Psalm 118 at the Passover meal.

3. "The Hebrew behind 'distress' has the sense of being cramped or narrow." Limburg, *Psalms*, 403. So also, e.g., Kraus, *Psalms 60–150*, 397, and McCann, "Psalms," 1154.

exalted; the right hand of the LORD does valiantly." It is the powerful 'right hand of the LORD" that gained the victory. The king, out of the valley of the shadow of death, shouts triumphantly in verse 17, "I shall not die, but I shall live, and recount the deeds of the LORD."[4]

Jesus had the same experiences, only on a more intense and far-reaching scale. Jesus' distress, his narrow place, was hanging on a cross bearing the sins of the world. As he hung between heaven and earth he was rejected by his people and mocked by the Roman soldiers: "If you are the King of the Jews, save yourself!" (Luke 23:37). They wanted him dead.

In his distress Jesus also called on the LORD. In Gethsemane he pleaded, "My Father, if it is possible, let this cup pass from me; yet not what I want but what you want" (Matt 26:39). At Calvary he cried out with a loud voice, "My God, my God, why have you forsaken me?" (Matt 27:46). And at the end he said, "Father, into your hands I commend my spirit" (Luke 23:46). Then Jesus died. He actually *died.*

Would God come through for Jesus as he did for the Davidic king? Would Jesus be able to shout triumphantly, "I shall not die, but I shall live, and recount the deeds of the LORD"? But Jesus actually died and was buried. *Could* God come through for Jesus?

On Easter Sunday the most astounding miracle in world history took place. Jesus rose from the grave and appeared to many. Later he said to his disciples, "All authority in heaven and on earth has been given to me. Go therefore and make disciples of all nations, baptizing them in the name of the Father and of the Son and of the Holy Spirit, and teaching them to obey everything that I have commanded you. And remember, I am with you always, to the end of the age" (Matt 28:18–20).

In Psalm 118:17 the Davidic king says, "I shall not die, but I shall live, and recount the deeds of the LORD." We know, of course, that the king would eventually die. But when God raised Jesus from the dead, a more literal fulfillment took place than the psalmist could have imagined. "I shall not die, but I shall live." In contrast to the Davidic king, Jesus would never die again. He would live *forever.* Also in contrast to the king, Jesus would recount the deeds of the LORD on a much larger scale. Through his disciples Jesus recounted the deeds of the LORD to "all nations," "to the ends of the earth" (Acts 1:8).

After his victory, the Davidic king heads for the temple to thank the LORD for his salvation. In verse 19 the king cries out, "Open to me the gates of righteousness, that I may enter through them and give thanks to the LORD." From within

4. "In his conflict with all the nations and in the significance of his salvation for the people of the LORD, the celebrant in Psalm 118 resembles the anointed king of Psalms 2; 18; 20; 21; and 89." Mays, *Psalms,* 379.

the temple a priest cries out (v 20), "This is the gate of the LORD; the righteous shall enter through it," that is, those who are right with God may enter.

The king then enters the temple forecourt and speaks directly to the LORD, "I thank you that you have answered me and have become my salvation" (v 21). Upon hearing how this rejected king was saved, a temple choir responds with a proverb about reversal of fortunes. Verse 22, "The stone that the builders rejected has become the chief cornerstone." The chief cornerstone was the most important stone in ancient buildings. It supported the corner of the building and set the direction for the walls. Builders would reject many stones as inferior and worthless. That is the way the king was rejected by his enemies: inferior and worthless — ready for the dump. But, amazingly, somehow this rejected stone had become the chief cornerstone. How could this be? The choir answers in verse 23, "This is the LORD's doing; it is marvelous in our eyes." It is entirely the LORD's doing, the LORD's act, the LORD's miracle! "It is marvelous in our eyes."

Jesus quoted these two verses in his Parable of the Wicked Tenants — a parable that predicted his own death. At the end of the parable he applied the words of Psalm 118:22 to himself: "The stone that the builders rejected has become the chief cornerstone." Jesus told this parable the same week he rode triumphantly into Jerusalem, the same week he would die. We read this parable in Matthew 21:33–42 (cf. Mark 12:1–12 and Luke 20:9–19). Jesus said,

> Listen to another parable. There was a landowner who planted a vineyard, put a fence around it, dug a wine press in it, and built a watchtower. Then he leased it to tenants and went to another country. When the harvest time had come, he sent his slaves to the tenants to collect his produce. But the tenants seized his slaves and beat one, killed another, and stoned another. Again he sent other slaves, more than the first; and they treated them in the same way. Finally he sent his son to them, saying, "They will respect my son." But when the tenants saw the son, they said to themselves, "This is the heir; come, let us *kill him* and get his inheritance." So they seized him, threw him out of the vineyard, and *killed him.* Now when the owner of the vineyard comes, what will he do to those tenants? They said to him, "He will put those wretches to a miserable death, and lease the vineyard to other tenants who will give him the produce at the harvest time."
>
> Jesus said to them [and here he quotes Psalm 118:22–23], "Have you never read in the scriptures: 'The stone that the builders rejected has become the cornerstone; this was the Lord's doing, and it is amazing in our eyes'?"[5]

---

5. "In Judaism Ps 118:22–23 was interpreted as referring to Abraham, David, and the Messiah. A messianic interpretation of the psalm was in the air." Kraus, *Theology of the Psalms*, 193.

Jesus is the son the landowner finally sends to the tenants. But when the tenants see the son, they say, "Let's kill him." And they killed him. Jesus here speaks of his own death which will take place in a few days. But Jesus sees light at the end of this dark tunnel. He says, "The stone that the builders rejected has become the *cornerstone*." A complete reversal of fortunes. Like the king in Psalm 118, Jesus would be rejected by his enemies. But he would become the cornerstone. From being treated as worthless, he would become most worthy. From dying a cruel death, he would rise from the grave and live forever more. The rejected Savior would become the cornerstone of the church.[6] How is this possible?

Jesus himself answers this question with Psalm 118:23, "This is the LORD's doing; it is marvelous in our eyes" (Matt 21:42). It is entirely the LORD's doing, the LORD's act, the LORD's miracle! "It is marvelous in our eyes."

After Pentecost, Peter quoted the same verses from Psalm 118. Peter and John were questioned by the authorities who wanted to know by what power they healed a sick person. We read in Acts 4,

> Then Peter, filled with the Holy Spirit, said to them, "Rulers of the people and elders . . . , let it be known to all of you, and to all the people of Israel, that this man is standing before you in good health by the name of Jesus Christ of Nazareth, whom you *crucified,* whom God *raised from the dead.* This Jesus is 'the stone that was rejected by you, the builders; it has become the cornerstone.' There is salvation in no one else, for there is no other name under heaven given among mortals by which we must be saved" (Acts 4:8–12).[7]

"God raised [Jesus Christ] from the dead" on Easter Sunday. Because God acted, the rejected, crucified Jesus became "the cornerstone." And what a cornerstone! Peter says, "There is salvation in no one else, for there is no other name under heaven given among mortals by which we must be saved." Jesus Christ, the cornerstone, is indispensable, absolutely necessary, for salvation.

Later Paul will also call Jesus "the cornerstone" of the church. He writes in Ephesians 2:19–22:

> You are no longer strangers and aliens, but you are citizens with the saints and also members of the household of God, built upon the foundation of the

---

6. "If the people of God are regarded as the temple which God builds, as is often the case in the biblical tradition, this saying [about the cornerstone] means that the Messiah who was rejected and killed by his own people, carries and supports the whole house of God." Kraus, *ibid.,* 193–94.

7. Cf. 1 Pet 2:4–8.

apostles and prophets, with *Christ Jesus himself as the cornerstone*. In him the whole structure is joined together and grows into a holy temple in the Lord; in whom you also are built together spiritually into a dwelling place for God.

Christ Jesus himself is the cornerstone of the church. Through Christ we are all joined together as a holy temple in which God dwells. Jesus Christ is indispensable for the Christian church. It all began on Easter Sunday when God raised Jesus from the dead.

The day God acted so miraculously must not be forgotten. It must be celebrated as a special day to remember God's wonderful act. Psalm 118:24 says, "This is the day that the Lord has made; let us rejoice and be glad in it." "This is the day on which the Lord *has acted*" (REB). "The Lord *has done* it this very day" (NIV). On this, the first day of the week, the Lord raised his Son, Jesus, from the dead for our salvation. This saving act calls for joyful celebrations on Easter Sunday. And not only on Easter Sunday but every Sunday. The early church designated Sunday as "the Lord's day" so that on that day especially we can rejoice in Jesus' resurrection.[8]

Paul pictures Jesus' resurrection as "the first fruits" of a harvest. He writes in 1 Corinthians 15:20–23, "Christ has been raised from the dead, the first fruits of those who have died. . . . All will be made alive in Christ. But each in his own order: Christ the first fruits, then at his coming those who belong to Christ." Elsewhere he writes, "For if we have been united with him in a death like his, we will certainly be united with him in a resurrection like his"(Rom 6:5).[9]

Jesus' resurrection from the dead means that death has been conquered. On the last day we shall all rise from the dead. How joyfully we should celebrate the Lord's day! "O give thanks to the Lord, for he is good, for his steadfast love endures forever." "O give thanks to the Lord" because he raised Jesus from the dead. "O give thanks to the Lord," for he will raise us also from the dead.

---

8. The rejoicing will also be heard on the last day: "Then I heard what seemed to be the voice of a great multitude . . . crying out, 'Hallelujah! For the Lord our God the Almighty reigns. *Let us rejoice and exult* and give him the glory, for the marriage of the Lamb has come, and his bride has made herself ready" (Rev 19:6–7).

9. Cf. Rom 8:11, "If the Spirit of him who raised Jesus from the dead dwells in you, he who raised Christ from the dead will give life to your mortal bodies also through his Spirit that dwells in you." Cf. 1 Peter 1:3, "Blessed be the God and Father of our Lord Jesus Christ! By his great mercy he has given us a new birth into a living hope through the resurrection of Jesus Christ from the dead. . . ."

Prayer[10]

Let us give thanks to the Lord our God.
> It is right to give our thanks and praise.

We give you thanks, great God,
> for the hope we have in Jesus,
> who died but is risen and rules over all.

We praise you for his presence with us.
Because he lives, we look for eternal life,
> knowing that nothing past, present, or yet to come
> can separate us from your great love
> made known in Jesus Christ, our Lord. Amen.

Song[11]

1Alleluia, alleluia!
> Hearts to heaven and voices raise.

Sing to God a hymn of gladness,
> Sing to God a hymn of praise.

He who on the cross a victim
> for the world's salvation bled,

Jesus Christ, the King of Glory,
> Now is risen from the dead.

2Alleluia, Christ is risen!
> Death at last has met defeat.

See the ancient powers of evil
> in confusion and retreat.

Once he died and once was buried;
> now he lives forevermore —

Jesus Christ, the world's Redeemer,
> whom we worship and adore.

10. *Worship Sourcebook*, Edition Two, WBK, p. 148, PD.

11. Christopher Wordsworth, 1862. Public Domain. *Psalter Hymnal* (1987), # 387; *Lift Up Your Hearts*, # 179.

₃Christ is risen, Christ the firstfruits
    of the holy harvest field,
which will all its full abundance
    at his second coming yield.
Then the golden ears of harvest
    will their heads before him wave,
ripened by his glorious sunshine
    from the furrows of the grave.

₄Alleluia, alleluia!
    Glory be to God on high;
alleluia! to the Savior,
    who has won the victory;
alleluia! to the Spirit,
    fount of love and sanctity:
alleluia, alleluia!
    to the triune Majesty.

CHAPTER 20

"God Has Gone Up with a Shout . . . , with the Sound of a Trumpet"

Psalm 47 (46)[1]

For Ascension Day the *Revised Common Lectionary* assigns the reading of Psalm 47 for all three years as a response to the ascension story recorded in Acts 1:1–11. As an "enthronement psalm," Psalm 47 is in its own right a fitting preaching text for Ascension Day or the Sunday after Ascension Day. Traditionally associated with Jesus' ascension, preaching this psalm will provide a rich background on the meaning of Jesus' enthronement.

Text and Context

Psalm 47 is a proper preaching text because, as an individual psalm, it is a literary unit. Moreover, the author has signaled the literary unit with an inclusio: "the Most High" (v 2) and "highly exalted" (v 9).[2]

The immediate context of Psalm 47 is formed by two Songs of Zion, Psalms 46 and 48. The editors of the Psalter have probably placed these psalms together because all three emphasize the mighty works of God on earth. Psalm 46 concludes, "Be still, and know that I am God! I am exalted among the nations [*gôyim*]! I am exalted in the earth [*'āreṣ*] (46:10). Psalm 47 picks up this theme: "God is the king [*melek*] of all the earth [*'āreṣ*]" (v 7); "God is king [*mālak*] over the nations [*gôyim*]" (v 8); "he is highly exalted" (v 9, a different Hebrew word

---

1. Psalm 47 in our English versions is Psalm 46 in the Septuagint and the Vulgate. Since the Hebrew text numbers the superscription as verse 1, the English verses 1–9 are verses 2–10 in the Hebrew.

2. "The psalm concludes with an inclusio, thus tying the end to the beginning and center. God is 'exalted' (*'ālâ* GK 6590), as he has ascended (*'ālâ*) into his heavenly palace. Truly he is 'the LORD Most High' (*'Elyôn*, from the root *'ly*, v 2)." VanGemeren, *Psalms*, 414.

from 46:10). Psalm 48 continues this theme: "Great is the LORD and greatly to be praised in the city of our God. His holy mountain, beautiful in elevation, is the joy of all the earth [*'āreṣ*], Mount Zion, in the far north, the city of the great King [*melek*]. . . . Your name, O God, like your praise, reaches to the ends of the earth [*'ereṣ*]" (vv 1–2, 10). Having been placed between the two Songs of Zion, Psalm 47 clearly identifies the God of Zion as "a great king over all the earth" (v 2), "the king of all the earth" (v 7), and "king over the nations" (v 8).[3]

Since Psalm 47 is classified as an enthronement psalm, we can also compare it with the other enthronement psalms: Psalms 93, 96, 97, 98, and 99. All these enthronement psalms, except for 93, call for the praise of God's kingship. But Psalm 47 is unique in two ways: first, it is addressed to "all you peoples" (v 1): all peoples of the earth are called to praise the LORD, "for [*kî*] the LORD . . . is . . . a great king over all the earth" (v 2; cf. v 7).[4] Second, "whereas the other divine kingship psalms speak simply of a 'coming' of Yahweh (cf. 96:13; 97:3; 98:9), Psalm 47:6 [English v 5] says that God 'mounts his throne.'"[5] These unique emphases in Psalm 47 will help us later in formulating its specific theme.

In addition to these literary contexts, we should also consider the possible historical context of Psalm 47. Psalm 47:5 says, "God has gone up with a shout, the LORD with the sound of a trumpet." When David brought the ark of the LORD from the house of Obed-Edom to the city of David to make it God's dwelling place, we read the same words in 2 Samuel 6:15, "So David and all the house of Israel brought up the ark of the LORD *with shouting, and with the sound of the trumpet.*" "The two passages are identical in the Hebrew. So God is pictured here ascending his earthly throne, whether or not this was dramatized anew by a periodic procession with the ark."[6]

Literary Interpretation

As to its form, Psalm 47 is generally identified as a hymn, a song of praise to God. But, as noted above, it is also classified as an enthronement psalm, a subclassification of the hymns. As an enthronement psalm, it has often been interpreted

3. Stek, *NIV Study Bible*, Ps 47 n.

4. "The opening summons to *all peoples* sets the scene truly: the vision is world-wide. 'Peoples,' 'nations' and 'all the earth' are words that dominate the psalm." Kidner, *Psalms 1–72*, 177.

5. Sabourin, *The Psalms*, 198.

6. Kidner, *Psalms 1–72*, 177–78. Kidner, p. 178, adds, "The perfect tense, 'God has gone up,' may mean that the allusion is to a single great event in David's day." Cf. Grogan, *Psalms*, 101, "Some verbal links with 2 Samuel 6 suggest that it was perhaps written to commemorate the bringing up of the ark to Jerusalem under David."

exclusively in the light of Israel's cult — a supposed annual enthronement re-enacted in the worship at the temple in Jerusalem. Others have interpreted the psalm historically — in the light of a military victory or the restoration of the temple after the exile. Still others have interpreted the psalm eschatologically — as a prophecy of the end-time. Weiser states that these three approaches don't exclude each other but "all three interpretations contain some elements of truth which, if rightly related to each other, are able to promote our understanding the psalm."[7]

We shall work our way into understanding the psalm by examining in turn its parallelisms, images, repetition of keywords, and its structure.

Parallelisms

A quick survey of the psalm reveals advancing (synthetic) parallelism in verse 1 and climactic parallelism in verses 2–4 with an impressive listing of the greatness of the LORD and what he has done for Israel. Verse 5 exhibits advancing parallelism followed by another round of climactic parallelism consisting of five imperatives urging the peoples to "sing praises" (vv 6–7). Verse 8 shows advancing parallelism while verse 9 concludes the psalm with a burst of climactic parallelism.

₁Clap your hands, all you peoples;	A
shout to God with loud songs of joy.	+ A'
₂For the LORD, the Most High, is awesome,	B
a great king over all the earth.	+ B'
₃He subdued peoples under us,	+ B''
and nations under our feet.	+ B'''
₄He chose our heritage for us,	+ B''''
the pride of Jacob whom he loves. Selah	+ B'''''
₅God has gone up with a shout,	A
the LORD with the sound of a trumpet.	+ A'
₆Sing praises to God, sing praises;	B
sing praises to our King, sing praises.	+ B'
₇For God is the king of all the earth;	+ B''
sing praises with a psalm.	+ B'''

7. Weiser, *The Psalms,* 375.

8God is king over the nations;	A
God sits on his holy throne.	+ A'
9The princes of the peoples gather	B
as the people of the God of Abraham.	+ B'
For the shields of the earth[8] belong to God;	+ B''
he is highly exalted.	+ B'''

Images

Psalm 47 is filled with images drawn from the coronation of kings in Israel[9] but here applied to God, "the king of all the earth" (v 7). The psalm begins with, *"Clap your hands, all you peoples; shout to God with loud songs of joy."* In 2 Kings 11:12, for example, we read about the coronation of Joash: "Then he [the priest] brought out the king's son, put the crown on him, and gave him the covenant; they proclaimed him king, and anointed him; *they clapped their hands and shouted,* 'Long live the king!'" Psalm 47 urges all peoples of the earth to follow suit by clapping and shouting songs of joy *to God*. Why? "For the LORD, the Most High, is awesome, a great king over all the earth" (v 2).

The image "the Most High" (*'elyôn*) likely was the title given to the god El in the Canaanite pantheon where he ruled supreme. Psalm 47 counters this pagan notion: not El but Israel's God, Yahweh, is "the Most High . . . a great king over all the earth."

To prove the point verses 3 and 4 recount what happened early in Israel's history when they entered the Promised Land: "He subdued peoples under us, and nations under our feet." "Nations *under our feet*" could be taken literally (see Josh 10:24) as well as figuratively: "The metaphor of subjugation, 'beneath our feet,' arose from the practice and artistic symbolism of victory, wherein a victor stood with his foot on the neck of the conquered foe."[10]

"He chose our heritage for us, *the pride of Jacob* whom he loves." "The pride of Jacob" or "the rising of Jacob" could possibly be "a literal (but probably also a metaphorical) description of Israel's mountain heartland running from the Negeb to

---

8. "Shields of the earth" is a figurative expression for "the princes" (v 9a; see pp. 451–52 below); therefore this is advancing parallelism and the whole of verse 9 is climactic parallelism.

9. "The terminology and subject matter of the hymn is clearly drawn from the coronation ceremonies of the earthly king. The clapping of hands, the shout, and the sounding of trumpets are fully attested by the accounts of coronation which appear in the historical literature." James Muilenburg, "Psalm 47," *JBL* 63, no. 3 (1944; pp. 235–56): 250–51.

10. Craigie, *Psalms 1–50*, 349, with a reference to Keel, *The Symbolism of the Biblical World*, 297. See also Ps 110:1.

Galilee."[11] In any case, "the pride of Jacob" does not refer to human arrogance but to the delight and joy Israel experienced from the land God had provided for them.

Verse 5 introduces the key metaphor: "God has gone up with a shout, the LORD with the sound of a trumpet." We noted above the similarity of these words with the words of 2 Samuel 6:15 when David brought the ark of the LORD up to the temple mount: "So David and all the house of Israel brought up the ark of the LORD *with shouting*, and *with the sound of the trumpet*." Shouting "Long live the king!" was part of the coronation ceremonies of Israel's kings,[12] as was the sound of the trumpet. For example, when Solomon was anointed king over Israel, "the priest Zadok took the horn of oil from the tent and anointed Solomon. Then they blew the trumpet, and all the people said, 'Long live King Solomon!'" (1 Kings 1:39).[13] Therefore, when verse 5 says, "God has gone up with a shout, the LORD with the sound of a trumpet," it pictures the coronation of God as king.

Verses 6–8 next instruct the peoples, "Sing praises to God, sing praises; sing praises to our *King* [itself an anthropomorphic metaphor], sing praises. For God is the *king* of all the earth. . . . God is *king* over the nations; *God sits on his holy throne*." God sitting on his holy throne is another anthropomorphic metaphor. "Yahweh is pictured as an oriental monarch seated on his throne to grant audience and to judge."[14]

Verse 9 completes the picture: "The princes of the peoples gather as the people of the God of Abraham." James Muilenburg writes, "The gathering of the people from far and near on the occasion of the choice of a new king or the royal festival is clearly corroborated. The coming together of the sheiks of the clans or the leaders of the people was characteristic."[15] "The princes of the peoples gather as the people of the God of Abraham" to show their reverence for the God of Abraham and to declare their loyalty to him.

"For *the shields of the earth* belong to God." "Shields" can be "a figurative expression for the rulers or mighty ones of the earth."[16] The parallelism here with "the princes of the peoples" (v 9a) indicates that "shields" does indeed refer to "the

---

11. Goldingay, *Psalms*, II, 78, with a reference to Psalm 46:3, the sea "rising up."

12. Cf. 2 Kings 11:12 quoted on p. 450 above, 1 Kings 1:39 quoted on this page, 1 Sam 10:24, and 2 Sam 16:16.

13. See also 2 Sam 15:10; 2 Kings 9:13; 11:14.

14. Wilson, *Psalms*, I, 729.

15. Muilenburg, "Psalm 47," *JBL* 63, no. 3 (1944): 251, with references to 1 Sam 10:17ff.; 11:15; 2 Sam 2:4; 3:21; 5:1, 3; 1 Kings 12:1, 20; 2 Sam 5:3; and Deut 33:5.

16. James Barr, *Comparative Philology and the Text of the Old Testament: With Additions and Corrections* (Winona Lake, IN: Eisenbrauns, 1987), 241–42. Cf. Ross, *Commentary on the Psalms*, II, 115, "'Shields' should be understood figuratively (a metonymy of adjunct), referring to the people who carried the shields, the powerful warriors of the earth."

powerful of the earth," as the LXX translates, or "the kings of the earth," as the NIV translates. The point is that since "the shields of the earth belong to God," no earthly power can stand in the way of God's kingship: "he is highly exalted" (v 9d). Muilenburg rightly concludes, "A complete appreciation of the poem demands a constant recognition that language and imagery and form all serve the single purpose of proclaiming that Elohim [Yahweh] is King over all the peoples of the world."[17] These images give us a picture of the message of this psalm.

Repetition of Keywords

The repetition of keywords is another important clue for discerning the author's main message. Psalm 47 begins with a call for all peoples to praise God: "*Clap* your hands, all you peoples; *shout* to God with loud songs of joy," which is followed by a fivefold repetition of the command, "sing praises" to "the king of all the earth" (vv 6–7). Thus the psalm uses a perfect seven imperatives urging the peoples to praise the king of all the earth. By repeating the word *kî* ("for") at three key points, verses 2, 7, and 9, the author gives three reasons why the peoples should praise God.

The psalm names God eleven times, eight times *'ĕlohîm* (vv 1, 5, 6, 7, 8 [2×], 9 [2×]), twice *yhwh* (vv 2, 5), and once *'elyôn* (v 2). Although the author mentions Yahweh only twice, these references are most significant: in verse 2 he calls Yahweh "the Most High" and "a great king over all the earth," while in verse 5 he equates Elohim and Yahweh in ascending to the throne: "God has gone up with a shout, the LORD with the sound of a trumpet." The LORD / God is named "king" four times: twice "king over / of all the earth" (vv 2, 7), once "our King" (v 6) and once "king over the nations" (v 8).

The root of "Most High" (*'ly*) runs like a thread through the psalm. It is first mentioned in verse 2, "the LORD, the Most High" (*yhwh 'elyôn*), is picked up in the center of the psalm, "God has gone up" (*'ālâ*, v 5), and again at its conclusion, "he is highly exalted" (*na'ălâ*, v 9). "The consonantal similarity in these three cases serves to form a strong unifying connection between the beginning, middle and end of the psalm."[18]

Structure

The structure of Psalm 47 is a contested issue. English versions and commentators divide the nine verses of the psalm into at least six different divisions:

17. Muilenburg, "Psalm 47," *JBL* 63, no. 3 (1944): 251.
18. J. du Preez, "Interpreting Psalm 47," *Missionalia* 25, no. 3 (1997; pp. 308–23): 311.

Verse Divisions	Versions
1 / 2–4 / 5 – 7 / 8–9	NIV (2011)
1 – 4 / 5 – 7 / 8–9	NRSV and ESV
1 – 4 / 5–6 / 7 – 9[19]	*NIV Study Bible* (1985)
1 – 4 / 5 / 6 – 9[20]	At least one commentator
1 – 4 / 5 – 9[21]	NASB and a few commentators
1 – 5 / 6 – 9[22]	Most commentators

What's a preacher to do when the experts are so divided? The above chart demonstrates that one of the major issues is where to place verse 5, "God has gone up with a shout, the LORD with the sound of a trumpet."

Although determining the precise structure sounds like an extremely theoretical debate, clarity on the structure will help us to discern more clearly the meaning of the parts of the psalm and to convey this meaning through an expository sermon outline. The best way to move forward may again be to start with the typical structure of a hymn. We noted in Chapter 1 (p. 11) that this typical pattern consists of most of the following elements:

1) A call to praise the LORD
2) Transition (*kî*, for, because)
3) Reasons why the LORD is to be praised
4) Conclusion: Praise the LORD!

Except for the conclusion "Praise the LORD," Psalm 47 fits well into this typical structure.

1) A call to praise the LORD	vv 1, 6
2) Transition (*kî*, for, because)	vv 2, 7
3) Reasons why the LORD is to be praised	vv 2–4, 7–9
4) Conclusion: Praise the LORD!	

19. Stek, *NIV Study Bible*, Ps 47 n., "Structurally, vv 5–6 form a centered . . . couplet between two four-line stanzas (in Hebrew). This center may represent a different voice in the liturgy."

20. McCann, "Psalms," 869, "It is also possible to construe v 5 as a central panel surrounded by two hymnic sections (vv 1–4, 6–9)."

21. Two stanzas, each composed with virtually the same number of words or syllables. E.g., Joost Smit Sibinga, "Some Observations on the Composition of Psalm XLVII," *VT* 38, no. 4 (1988; 474–80): 474; and J. P. Fokkelman, *Major Poems of the Hebrew Bible*, III, 77–80.

22. Two stanzas, each composed of ten lines. E.g., A. Anderson, *Psalms 1–72*, 360; Davidson, *Vitality of Worship*, 154; deClaissé-Walford in deClaissé-Walford, Jacobson, and Tanner, *The Book of Psalms*, 430; Goldingay, *Psalms*, II, 75; Kraus, *Psalms 1–59*, 466; Muilenburg, "Psalm 47," *JBL* 63, no. 3 (1944): 243–44; Ross, *Commentary on the Psalms*, II, 107; Terrien, *The Psalms*, 377; and Wilson, *Psalms*, I, 725–26.

Interestingly, we clearly have two stanzas, verses 1–4 and 6–9, but there is no place for verse 5. Should it go with the first stanza? The editor's "Selah" (pause) after verse 4 argues against this.[23] Should it go with the second stanza? The second parallel call to praise at verse 6 argues against that. Although there is merit in a balanced structure of two stanzas each with ten lines, McCann is probably right in suggesting two hymnic sections surrounding a central verse 5. Mays seems to agree, "A 'selah' concludes verse 4; it may separate verse 5 as the climax and center of the whole."[24]

But why would the author place verse 5 at the center between the two stanzas calling for praise? The answer may be that verse 5 describes an event that was re-enacted in the worship in the temple. This was the high point in the service: "God has gone up with a shout, the LORD with the sound of a trumpet." This event in remembrance of the LORD's ascension to the throne was the very foundation of the required praise: God is King of all the earth.

This proposal leads us to the following structure (italics indicate parallels in other verses):

A. A call to praise the LORD:
  "Clap your hands, all you peoples;
  shout to God *with loud*[25] songs of joy." (v 1)
B. Reasons to praise the LORD:
  "For the LORD, the Most High, is awesome,
  a great *king over all the earth.*[26]
  He subdued *peoples*[27] under us,
  and nations under our feet.
  He chose our heritage for us,
  the pride of Jacob[28] whom he loves. Selah" (vv 2–4)
C. The coronation of God as King:
  "God *has gone up*[29] with a *shout,*
  the LORD *with the sound*[30] of a trumpet." (v 5)

---

23. See p. 289 above. For other reasons, see Fokkelman, *Major Poems of the Hebrew Bible*, III, 78.
24. Mays, *Psalms*, 186.
25. "Shout" and "sound" (*qôl*) paralleled in v 5.
26. Paralleled in v 7a.
27. Paralleled in v 9b.
28. Vv 3–4 recall what Yahweh did for Jacob, Israel. "The pride of Jacob" (v 4) is paralleled in the universal hymn (vv 6–9) with "the God of Abraham" (v 9) — Abraham who had received God's promise, "in you all the families of the earth shall be blessed" (Gen 12:3).
29. Hebrew *'ālâ* as in v 9 "exalted."
30. Hebrew *bəqôl* as in v 1 "loud."

A'   A second call to praise the LORD
      "Sing praises to God, sing praises;
      sing praises to our King, sing praises." (v 6)
B'   More reasons to praise the LORD
      "For God is the *king of all the earth;*
      sing praises with a psalm.
      God is king over the nations;
      God sits on his holy throne.
      The princes of the *peoples* gather
      as the people of *the God of Abraham.*
      For the shields of the earth belong to God;
      he is highly *exalted.*" (vv 7–9)

We have, therefore, an ABCA'B' structure centering on the coronation of God as King of all the earth. McCann argues, "The vocabulary of v 5 reinforces this conclusion. On the one hand, v 5 recalls v 1, repeating 'shout' and ['sound' / 'loud' v 1, *qôl*]. . . . On the other hand, v 5 anticipates v 9 by way of repetition of the key root 'gone up' / 'ascended' (*'ālâ*), which appears in v 9 as 'exalted.' Thus both the pattern of repetition and the structure of the psalm serve to highlight the liturgical enactment of God's enthronement."[31] Hence the central message of Psalm 47 is the enthronement of the LORD God as King of all the earth.

Theocentric Interpretation

For the theocentric emphasis of this psalm we need not look far — eleven references to God in nine verses[32] clinches it. The author declares that "the LORD, the Most High, is awesome" (v 2) and that God "our King" (v 6) is "king over/of all the earth" (vv 2, 7), "king over the nations" (v 8). He emphasizes further what God has done for Jacob/Israel: "He subdued peoples under us. . . . He chose our heritage for us" (vv 3–4). And he leaves no doubt what God expects of peoples in return: he uses the perfect number of seven imperatives to urge the peoples to praise God (vv 1, 6–7).[33]

31. McCann, "Psalms," 869.
32. Eight times *'ĕlōhîm* (vv 1, 5, 6, 7, 8 [2×], 9 [2×]), twice *yhwh* (vv 2 and 5), and once *'elyôn* (v 2).
33. "It is evidence of the theocentric perspective of the psalm, which is entirely absorbed by its enthusiasm for the majesty of God, that it regards all distinctions to be annulled in the sight of God and ungrudgingly classes the converted Gentiles with the people of the God of Abraham." Weiser, *The Psalms,* 378–79.

Textual Theme and Goal

Most commentators are agreed on the theme of Psalm 47. For example, Mays suggests that the theme is, "The LORD is king over all the earth (vv 2, 7 specifically)."[34] Although this is part of the theme, homiletically a theme is not merely a sentence about the topic but a sentence about the *message* the psalm carries to its readers. In other words, we cannot overlook the seven imperatives in verses 1 and 6–7 that urge all peoples to praise God. Therefore we can formulate the theme of this psalm as follows: *Since the LORD, the Most High, has ascended his throne, all you peoples sing praises to the King of all the earth.*

To determine the original goal of the psalm, it would be helpful to know for what occasion it was written. Mays points out that "the occasion for the hymn is an event. Something has happened to which the psalm is a response. The LORD has 'gone up' (v 5) and assumed his throne (v 8)."[35] We noted above (p. 448) that the words of verse 5 also occur in 2 Samuel 6:15 when David brought the ark of the LORD from the house of Obed-Edom up to the city of David to make it God's dwelling place: "So David and all the house of Israel brought up the ark of the LORD *with shouting,* and *with the sound of the trumpet.*" This similarity may suggest that the event was a cultic procession of the ark into the temple. Bernhard Anderson explains: "This passage seems to refer to the bearing of the ark of the covenant in procession to the Temple (Ps 24:7–10) where Yhwh 'sits enthroned upon the cherubim' (Ps 99:1), the winged figures that flanked the ark. Since, however, the earthly temple was regarded as a microcosmic copy of the heavenly one, as in Isaiah's vision, the drama symbolized God's entrance into the heavenly palace (temple) and the ascension to his celestial throne."[36] Although we have

---

34. Mays, *Psalms,* 186. Cf. Muilenburg, "Psalm 47," *JBL* 63, no. 3 (1944): 251, "Language and imagery and form all serve the single purpose of proclaiming that Elohim is King over the peoples of the world." Cf. Eaton, *Psalms,* 130, "The theme is almost exclusively the enthronement of God as the supreme, universal king, presupposing his conquest of rivals and processional ascent." Alter, *Book of Psalms,* 166 n. 3, observes that "the existence of an actual [New Year] ritual of this sort is mere conjecture, and the psalm could simply be a symbolic celebration through song of the idea that God reigns supreme over all. This is precisely how this psalm came to be used in subsequent Jewish tradition in the New Year Liturgy." Rogerson and McKay, *Psalms 1–50,* 222, add the eschatological expectation: "Its central message is that 'God is king of all the earth' (v 7) and in the strength of this assurance it invites the congregation to enter in anticipation into the jubilations of the great day when God finally ascends his throne to receive the homage of all mankind (vv 8–9)."

35. Mays, *Psalms,* 186. Cf. Kraus, *Psalms 1–59,* 467, "In Psalm 47 individual statements permit us to think of the course of a cultic enthronement: vv. 5, 8. The hymn looks back to the event of Yahweh's going up (*'ālâ* in v 5), proclaims the enthronement as completed (*mālak* in v 8a), and sees the God-king now sitting on the throne (*yāšab* in v 8b)."

36. B. Anderson, *Out of the Depths,* 157. Cf. A. Anderson, *Psalms 1–72,* 360.

no evidence that there was an actual, annual cultic procession of the ark into the temple,[37] it is clear that Psalm 47 celebrates God's enthronement as king of all the earth and that the seven imperatives in verses 1 and 6–7 call for the praise of all peoples. Therefore we can formulate the goal of this psalm as *to urge all peoples to sing praises to the* LORD, *the King of all the earth.*

Ways to Preach Christ

We cannot use promise-fulfillment to preach Christ since Psalm 47 is not a prophecy concerning the ascension of Jesus Christ. Nor can we use typology, though this is advocated by some.[38] We could use analogy between God's enthronement and that of Christ or trace the longitudinal theme of God's kingship through the Old Testament to Christ the King in the New Testament. But the clearest way to preach Christ from this psalm is redemptive-historical progression supported by New Testament references.

Redemptive-Historical Progression with New Testament References

A. Anderson comments, "In the Christian Church, Psalm 47 has been used for Ascension Day, not as a prophecy of this event, but as a realization that the life and work of Christ are both a continuation and a focal point of the *Heilsgeschichte,* or salvation-history."[39] Because of the unity of and progression in redemptive history, preachers can legitimately move from God's ascension to the throne in Psalm 47 to Christ's ascension in New Testament times. There are many New Testament references to support this move, beginning with the passages that speak of Jesus' actual ascension: Luke 24:50–53 or Acts 1:9–11. Next we can move to passages that explain the meaning of Jesus' ascension: Jesus' own words, "All authority in heaven and on earth has been given to me" (Matt 28:18), and Paul's words in Ephesians 1:20–23 and Philippians 2:9–11. Further, we can use allusions to Psalm 47 in Revelation 7:10, 17; 11:15, and possibly the return of Christ on the

---

37. As Sigmund Mowinckel conjectured. See B. Anderson, *Out of the Depths,* 157–58. A. Anderson, *Psalms 1–72,* 360, thinks it more likely that it was a yearly celebration of Yahweh's kingship, probably including "a re-presentation of the major events of the salvation history."

38. E.g., Kraus, *Psalms 1–59,* 470: "The kerygma of the hymn to Yahweh the king can rightfully be transferred typologically by the church to the ascension of Christ into heaven." But Yahweh cannot be a type of Christ since the antitype is always greater than the type and Christ is not greater than Yahweh.

39. A. Anderson, *Psalms 1–72,* 361.

last day "with the sound of God's trumpet," 1 Thessalonians 4:16. (See further "Sermon Exposition" below.)

Sermon Theme, Goal, and Need

We formulated the textual theme as, "Since the LORD, the Most High, has ascended his throne, all you peoples sing praises to the King of all the earth." In the sermon theme we will want to include also Christ ascending his throne. The textual theme can function as the sermon theme with the understanding that "the LORD" can refer to both Yahweh and the Lord Jesus. Therefore the sermon theme is, *Since the LORD, the Most High, has ascended his throne, all you peoples sing praises to the King of all the earth.*

With the same understanding, the textual goal can function as the sermon goal: *to urge all peoples to sing praises to the LORD, the King of all the earth.* This goal points to the need addressed in this sermon: we do not sufficiently praise the LORD and rejoice in the enthronement of the King of all the earth. The sermon introduction can explore this need by pointing to our inclination to have other gods beside the LORD our God in spite of the first commandment, or by highlighting our lack of excitement about Ascension Day.

Liturgy, Scripture Reading, and Sermon Outline

The liturgist can use Psalm 47:1–2, or 5–6, or 5–7 as a call to worship. To accentuate the movement in the psalm, the scripture reading can be done by three people. The liturgist can invite the people to praise the LORD (vv 1 and 6), while a second voice gives the reasons for praising the LORD (vv 2–4 and 7–9), and a third voice announces the glad tidings of the LORD's enthronement (v 5).

LITURGIST	1 Clap your hands, all you peoples;
	shout to God with loud songs of joy.
SECOND VOICE	2 For the LORD, the Most High, is awesome,
	a great king over all the earth.
	3 He subdued peoples under us,
	and nations under our feet.
	4 He chose our heritage for us,
	the pride of Jacob whom he loves. Selah
THIRD VOICE	5 God has gone up with a shout,
	the LORD with the sound of a trumpet.

LITURGIST ~ 6 Sing praises to God, sing praises;
sing praises to our King, sing praises.

SECOND VOICE ~ 7 For God is the king of all the earth;
sing praises with a psalm.

8 God is king over the nations;
God sits on his holy throne.

9 The princes of the peoples gather
as the people of the God of Abraham.
For the shields of the earth belong to God;
he is highly exalted.

The sermon outline can follow the structure of the text with a final move to the ascension of Christ:

   I. All you peoples, clap your hands for the LORD, the Most High (vv 1–4)
  II. The LORD has gone up with the sound of a trumpet (v 5)
 III. Sing praises to the LORD, the King of all the earth (vv 6–9)
 IV. Sing praises to Jesus, our ascended King (NT)

Sermon Exposition

Today is (Last Thursday was) Ascension Day. For many people in our culture Ascension Day is not an important day to remember. Christmas seems much more important as well as Easter. Yet Jesus' ascension to his heavenly throne was the high point of his life. After his resurrection, Jesus had said to his disciples, "All authority in heaven and on earth has been given to me" (Matt 28:18). He claimed to be King of the universe. His ascension to his heavenly throne proved his claim. On Ascension Day we celebrate that Jesus is indeed King of the universe.

Psalm 47 also speaks of ascension. It speaks of God's ascension to his throne. It celebrates the enthronement of the LORD as King of all the earth. So the psalm begins joyfully in verse 1,[40] "Clap your hands, all you peoples; shout to God with loud songs of joy." It's a giant party. If you've ever seen the coronation of a king or queen or the inauguration of a president and heard all the noise, you'll know the mood this psalm calls for. When Israel crowned a new king, they would clap their hands. For example, we read in 2 Kings that when Joash was crowned king, they put a crown on his head, "proclaimed him king, and anointed him; *they clapped*

---

40. Since the superscription, "To the leader. Of the Korahites. A Psalm," does not contribute much to the meaning of the psalm, I would skip over it in the sermon.

their hands and shouted, 'Long live the king!'" (2 Kings 11:12). But for Joash that was only a little party compared to what Psalm 47 demands: "Clap your hands, *all you peoples.*" Not only Israel but all peoples of the earth are invited, commanded even (imperative), to clap their hands. Clapping hands is "an expression of enthusiastic joy."[41] And all the peoples of the earth are invited, commanded (another imperative), to "shout to God with loud songs of joy."

Shouting also speaks of enthusiastic joy. But it is more than that. At the coronation of a new king in Israel, people would shout, "Long live the king!" People still do that at the coronation of a king or queen: "Long live the queen!" But this shouting is more than wishing the queen or king a long life. This shouting also means: I acclaim you as my sovereign ruler; I am your subject. Shouting to God with loud songs of joy is more than expressing enthusiastic joy. It's telling God: I am your subject; you are my king.[42] All the peoples of the earth are invited, commanded, to acknowledge God as their sovereign king.

Why should all peoples acknowledge Israel's God as their king? Verse 2 gives the answer, "For the LORD [that is Israel's God, Yahweh], the Most High, is awesome, a great king over all the earth." The psalm claims that Israel's God is "the Most High." The Canaanites believed in a hierarchy of gods. One of them, the god El, was considered higher than any other gods; he was "the Most High" (*'elyôn*). Psalm 47 counters this pagan notion:[43] not El but Israel's God, Yahweh, is "the Most High."[44]

Verse 2 goes on to say that Israel's God "is awesome," that is, he is "awe-inspiring."[45] He is "a great king over all the earth." The king of Assyria called himself "the great king" (2 Kings 18:19) because he ruled over many nations. Not so, says Psalm 47. The LORD is the "great king over all the earth."[46] If Israel's God

---

41. Kraus, *Psalms 1-59*, 467.

42. "The reason for shouting is not only a feeling of joy but also the intention to acclaim the divine king (cf. 98:4) with some such exclamation as 'Yahweh is (or "has become") king.'" A. Anderson, *Psalms 1-72*, 361-62.

43. "The acclamation of Yahweh as king may have had a polemical tone when we recall similar expressions attributed to Baal by the Canaanites; e.g., 'The victor is Baal our king, our judge, and one over whom there is none' (Driver, *CML*, p. 97a; *Baal* II, iv: 43f.)." A. Anderson, ibid., 364.

44. Cf. Psalm 97:9, "For you, O LORD, are most high over all the earth; you are exalted far above all gods." In the Bible "the Most High" is the "maker of heaven and earth" (Gen 14:19, 22).

45. Leupold, *Exposition of the Psalms*, 370. Cf. Wilson, *Psalms*, I, 727, "'Awesome' (lit., 'worthy of fear'), employing the common Israelite designation for the appropriate human relation to Yahweh — a relationship of humble awareness of absolute dependence on his merciful and sustaining power."

46. "The title 'Great King' . . . evokes specifically the covenant-treaty context of Israel's faith. Just as a Hittite monarch was addressed as *great king* in the introductory sections of vassal treaties (e.g. *ANET*, 201-03), so too God is here the 'Great King' in relation to all his vassals." Craigie, *Psalms 1-50*, 349.

is indeed the "great king over *all the earth*," then all the peoples of the earth are subject to him. They should welcome him enthusiastically and acknowledge him joyfully as their king.

As proof that God is the "great king over all the earth," the psalm reminds people of what God had done for Israel in the beginning of its history. Verse 3, "He subdued peoples under us, and nations under our feet."[47] When God brought Israel out of slavery in Egypt, he subdued under them the peoples living in the Promised Land.[48] The psalm repeats the "under" for emphasis, "peoples *under* us and nations *under* our feet." "In the ancient Near East it was customary for the victor to place his foot on the neck of him who was subdued."[49] For example, to demonstrate his victory over Canaanite kings, Joshua had the chiefs of his warriors put their feet on the necks of these kings (Josh 10:24). But the psalm makes clear that it was not Joshua that gained the victory. It was the LORD who "subdued peoples under" Israel.

The LORD also gave them the Promised Land. Verse 4, "He chose our heritage for us, the pride of Jacob whom he loves." The LORD chose the land of Canaan for Israel. He gave it to them as an inheritance.[50] It was "the pride of Jacob whom he loves." In the eyes of those who had been wandering in the wilderness for forty years, Canaan was a wonderful country, "a land flowing with milk and honey" (e.g., Lev 20:24). Jacob, that is Israel, was rightly proud of this treasure. It was a gift of God's love,[51] of God's faithfulness to his covenant promises.

At this point the ancient editor has added the pause, "Selah." He seems to say, "Stop here for a while and reflect on this history."[52] When Jacob's descendants, God's people, wandered in the desert, they had absolutely nothing. God had to provide their sustenance: manna, quail, and water. Then he brought them to the land of the Canaanites, the land "flowing with milk and honey." The LORD "sub-

47. "Perhaps the poet had the occupation of Canaan in mind, but the Hebrew tenses are difficult to translate and could equally refer to the future, to the final consummation of God's victory over the world." Rogerson and McKay, *Psalms 1–50,* 222–23.

48. "The reference seems to be to the conquest of Canaan, and possibly also to the victories of David." A. Anderson, *Psalms 1–72,* 362.

49. Kraus, *Psalms 1–59,* 468, with references to Josh 10:24, Ps 110:1, as well as Egyptian and Babylonian depictions.

50. Cf. Joshua 11:23, "Joshua took the whole land, according to all that the LORD had spoken to Moses; and Joshua gave it for an inheritance to Israel according to their tribal allotments."

51. "'Love' is to be understood in the sense the term had in ancient Near Eastern suzerainty covenants, the favor shown vassals dependent on the great king." Mays, *Psalms,* 186.

52. "A Selah at this point suggests a musical interlude which gives pause for reflection." Leupold, *Exposition of the Psalms,* 371. See p. 289 above. For various interpretations of "Selah," see A. Anderson, *Psalms 1–72,* 49.

dued peoples under us, and nations under our feet. He chose our heritage for us, the pride of Jacob whom he loves." Surely, "the LORD, the Most High, is awesome, a great king over all the earth."

After this time for reflection comes the highpoint in this psalm. A reminder of Ascension Day! Verse 5, "God has gone up with a shout, the LORD with the sound of a trumpet." The wording, "with a shout" and "with the sound of a trumpet," reflects the occasion when David brought the ark of the covenant in procession up Mount Zion and placed it in a tent. We read in 2 Samuel 6 that "David went and brought up the ark of God from the house of Obed-Edom to the city of David with rejoicing. . . . David and all the house of Israel brought up the ark of the LORD *with shouting,* and *with the sound of the trumpet* [notice the same words in Psalm 47:5]. . . . They brought in the ark of the LORD, and set it in its place, inside the tent that David had pitched for it; and David offered burnt offerings and offerings of well-being before the LORD" (2 Sam 6:12, 15, 17). The ark of the LORD was finally in the place where it belonged, Jerusalem, the capital of Israel. It symbolized that the LORD was king of Israel. Later the ark was placed in Solomon's temple in the Holy of Holies. The ark stood for the presence of God. It was God's earthly throne. God reigned over Israel; he was its king.

But Psalm 47 moves far beyond that. "God *has gone up* with a shout." The LORD is not only confessed as the "Most High": he "has gone up" on high.[53] Verse 5 adds, "The LORD with the sound of a trumpet." The sound of the trumpet accompanied the coronation of kings in Israel.[54] Thus this verse describes the enthronement of the LORD. The LORD is king not only of Israel. He is the "great king over all the earth" (v 2). The LORD has ascended his throne (see v 8) — not only his earthly throne but his heavenly throne.[55]

No wonder this reminder of God's ascension gives rise to another series of calls to praise. Verse 6, "Sing praises to God, sing praises; sing praises to our King, sing praises." Four times, "Sing praises." People need to express their joy and acclamation at God's ascension not just with individual shouting and with the trumpet. They are to join together in singing praises to God.[56]

---

53. "The word describing the ascent (*'ālâ*) is obviously related to the Elyon of the opening strophe [v 2]." Muilenburg, "Psalm 47," *JBL* 63, no. 3 (1944): 247.

54. See p. 451 above.

55. "The verb *'ālâ* can mean to ascend into heaven (cf. Gen 17:22, 35:13; Judg 13:20; etc.) but in this verse the primary meaning seems to be that of going up to the Temple. . . . But in so far as the Temple was the earthly counterpart of the heavenly dwelling of God — the place where heaven and earth meet one another — the former meaning of *'ālâ* ('to go up') may also be implied." A. Anderson, *Psalms 1–72,* 363.

56. "'Make music for our God. . . .' The beauty and form of music thus complements the unformed energy of cheering and clapping (v 1) in bringing glory to God." Goldingay, *Psalms,* II, 79.

God is now called "*our* King." Why sing praises to our King? Verse 7 answers, "For God is the king of all the earth; sing praises with a psalm." For the second time the psalm calls God "the king of all the earth" (see verse 2). And it specifies, "sing praises with a psalm."[57]

Verse 8 continues, "God is king over the nations; God sits on his holy throne." "God is king over the nations." Twice God has been called "king over all the earth" (vv 2 and 7). Now God is called "king over the nations."[58] "God sits on his holy throne" — "holy" because God is holy and his throne on earth, the ark of the covenant, is in the Most Holy Place in the temple.

The psalm pictures God as sitting on his holy throne much as a newly crowned human king would sit on his throne. In ancient times, at the coronation of a new king, the leaders of conquered nations would gather to show their subjection to the new king and their loyalty to him.[59] That happens here too.

Verse 9, "The princes of the peoples gather as the people of the God of Abraham." "The princes[60] of the peoples" are the leaders of the peoples of the earth. They gather at God's enthronement. But then follows an amazing statement for the Old Testament: they "gather *as the people of the God of Abraham.*"[61] These Gentile leaders gather as the people of the God of Abraham. They gather as Abraham's offspring! These Gentiles gather as one with Israel! This possibility was almost unheard of in the Old Testament, where Israel was to be separate from the nations.[62]

Yet it was a sign of God's covenant faithfulness. God had promised Abraham, "In you *all the families of the earth* shall be blessed" (Gen 12:3). And again God had said to Abraham, "This is my covenant with you: You shall be the *ancestor of a multitude of nations*" (Gen 17:4). Psalm 47 speaks of the fulfillment of these covenant promises: Gentiles "gather as the people of the God of Abraham."

---

57. "Instead of 'psalm,' most commentators prefer some such meaning as 'choice song' (Oesterley), 'efficacious song' (Mowinckel), 'skilful song' (McFadyen, etc.)." A. Anderson, *Psalms 1–72*, 364.

58. The only time *gôyim* is used in this psalm.

59. The verses 8b and 9a "reflect rites by which earthly rulers acceded to the throne and initiated their reign with the acclamation of the vassal princes. The wording is traditional and mirrors existing customs (. . . foreign princes and ambassadors, who gather together in Jerusalem: cf. 2 Sam 8:1off; 15:18ff; 1 Kings 8:65; Ps 2:1off; 2 Chron 32:23)." W. A. M. Beuken, "Psalm XLVII: Structure and Drama," in *Remembering All the Way* (Leiden: Brill, 1981; pp. 38–54), 45.

60. "The psalm here deliberately refrains from giving the title 'king' which befits only God." Weiser, *The Psalms*, 378.

61. For differences between the Masoretic Text and the LXX and Syriac, see, e.g., Muilenburg, "Psalm 47," *JBL* 63, no. 3 (1944): 242–43, 248–49.

62. But see also Psalms 87; 102:21–22; Isaiah 2:2–4; 19:25; 56:6–8; 60:3–7; Micah 4:1–3; Zech 2:11; 8:20–23.

Psalm 47 says in effect that the LORD had made a place for his people among the nations ("He subdued peoples under us," vv 3–4), "so that the nations may be included among his people."[63] Gentiles will no longer be outside God's covenant with Israel; they will be included.[64] They "gather as the people of the God of Abraham."[65]

How is it that all these Gentile people are included with God's people? The final line explains: "For the shields of the earth belong to God; he is highly exalted." "The shields of the earth" refers "to the people who carried the shields, the powerful warriors of the earth,"[66] those with military power on earth, "the kings of the earth" (NIV). Since "the shields of the earth belong to God," no military power, no nuclear power even, can stand in the way of God's kingship.[67] God is the King of kings. He is King over the nations. "He is highly exalted."[68]

What a marvelous vision: all peoples of the earth united as one to serve God, their sovereign King. To fulfill this vision, God, in the fullness of time, sent his only Son, Jesus, to this earth. Jesus' mission was to be "the Lamb of God who takes away the sin of the *world!*" (John 1:29). Jesus paid for "the sin of the world" when he died on the cross. On the third day he rose again. After his resurrection Jesus told his disciples, "*All authority* in heaven and on earth has been given to me" (Matt 28:18). "All authority!" Jesus claimed to be the King of kings.

According to Acts 1 Jesus next appeared to his disciples for forty days "speaking about *the kingdom of God*" (Acts 1:3). Then we read about Jesus' ascension in Acts 1:6–11,

63. Mays, *Psalms,* 186.

64. "The innumerable princes and peoples are to become one people; and they will no longer be outsiders but within the covenant." Kidner, *Psalms 1–72,* 178. Cf. Mays, *Psalms,* 187, "The people of God are constituted, not by ethnic or national identity, but by recognition of the rule of the LORD." Cf. Beuken, "Psalm XLVII," 46, "The surprising call upon the nations [to 'clap your hands' (v 1)] receives here its foundation. Because the foreign princes gather around God's throne and in this way accept his sovereignty, they end up becoming part of the people of Abraham's God."

65. "The peoples are summoned to clap their hands and shout for joy [v 1] *because* they have been defeated (v 3). . . . They have been converted. They recognize the lordship of the God of Israel, and this makes them and their leaders part of the people of the God of Abraham [v 9]." Gordon Wenham, *The Psalter Reclaimed,* 176.

66. Ross, *Commentary on the Psalms,* II, 115.

67. "The psalmist transposes the ancient image of God's ascent to heaven or to the temple into a rising above all mankind and its struggles for power. . . . When he rises on high as king of the world, the blessed people of Abraham come into being." Beuken, "Psalm XLVII," 49.

68. Since the word "exalted" is the same as the word "gone up" or "ascent" in verse 5, the psalm's conclusion could also be translated, "he has greatly ascended." Broyles, *Psalms,* 215. The NEB has, "he is raised above them all." Cf. Psalm 97:9, "For you, O LORD, are most high over all the earth; you are exalted far above all gods."

So when they had come together, they asked him, "Lord, is this the time when you will restore *the kingdom* to Israel?" He replied, "It is not for you to know the times or periods that the Father has set by his own authority. But you will receive power when the Holy Spirit has come upon you; and you will be my witnesses in Jerusalem, in all Judea and Samaria, and to the ends of the earth." When he had said this, as they were watching, *he was lifted up,* and a cloud took him out of their sight. While he was going and they were gazing up toward heaven, suddenly two men in white robes stood by them. They said, "Men of Galilee, why do you stand looking up toward heaven? This Jesus, who has been taken up from you into heaven, will come in the same way as you saw him go into heaven."

The disciples asked Jesus if this was the time when he would bring in the kingdom of God. Jesus answered that something else must happen first. Just like Psalm 47, Jesus claimed that the Gentile nations are part of the kingdom of God. The nations must first be invited into the kingdom. Jesus predicted the coming of Pentecost. The outpouring of the Holy Spirit would empower the disciples to spread the gospel of the kingdom "in Jerusalem, in all Judea and Samaria, and to the ends of the earth."

We read in Acts 1, "When he had said this, as they were watching, he was lifted up, and a cloud took him out of their sight." It's a picture of Jesus ascending to his heavenly throne. God acknowledged Jesus' work on earth and made him King of kings. As Paul puts it in Ephesians 1, "God put this power to work in Christ when he raised him from the dead and *seated him at his right hand in the heavenly places, far above all rule and authority and power and dominion* . . . not only in this age but also in the age to come" (Eph 1:20–21).[69]

"This age" is the age we live in right now. In this age Christ rules from his heavenly throne. But on the last day, Christ will return to earth to usher in "the age to come." Then the trumpet will sound again. Paul writes in 1 Corinthians, "Listen, I will tell you a mystery! We will not all die, but we will all be changed, in a moment, in the twinkling of an eye, at the last trumpet. For the trumpet will sound, and the dead will be raised imperishable, and we will be changed."[70]

"The age to come" will be the age when all peoples of the earth will be united

69. Cf. Rev 5:13, "Then I heard every creature in heaven and on earth and under the earth and in the sea, and all that is in them, singing, 'To the one seated on the throne and to the Lamb be blessing and honor and glory and might forever and ever!'" Cf. the early Christian hymn, Phil 2:9–11, "Therefore God also highly exalted him and gave him the name that is above every name, so that at the name of Jesus every knee should bend, in heaven and on earth and under the earth, and every tongue should confess that Jesus Christ is Lord, to the glory of God the Father."

70. 1 Cor 15:51–52; cf. Matt 24:31 and Rev 11:15.

as one to serve their sovereign King. It will be God's perfect kingdom on earth. As the book of Revelation puts it, people "will hunger no more, and thirst no more; the sun will not strike them, nor any scorching heat; for the Lamb at the center of the throne will be their shepherd, and he will guide them to springs of the water of life, and God will wipe away every tear from their eyes" (Rev 7:16–17).

Meanwhile, the church has work to do. As the angels said to the disciples, "Men of Galilee, why do you stand looking up toward heaven? This Jesus, who has been taken up from you into heaven, will come in the same way as you saw him go into heaven." Do not stand there "looking up toward heaven." Look to the ends of the earth! Look to the nations! Proclaim the gospel of the kingdom to the ends of the earth! As a result we will already experience in *this* age what will be fully here in the age to come. Paul calls this "the mystery of Christ." The "mystery of Christ," he says, is that "the Gentiles have become fellow heirs, *members of the same body,* and sharers in the promise in Christ Jesus through the gospel" (Eph 3:4, 6).[71]

Therefore, we are to proclaim the kingship of Jesus Christ to the nations. Jesus Christ is King of kings. He rules over the nations. He rules over everything. As the song rightly says, "Ev'ry inch of this universe belongs to You, O Christ."[72] We may claim every nation, every area of life for Jesus Christ.[73] This all began with Jesus' ascension to his heavenly throne.

How we should rejoice on Ascension Day![74] How we should praise God for what he accomplished through his Son, Jesus! How we should praise Jesus for his coronation as King of the universe! How we should express our loyalty to Jesus our King. With our praise we will be joining the universal choir whose song John heard: "Then I heard every creature in heaven and on earth and under the earth and in the sea, and all that is in them, singing, 'To the one seated on the throne and to the Lamb be blessing and honor and glory and might forever and ever!'" (Rev 5:13).

71. Cf. Gal 3:7–9, 29, "Those who believe are the descendants of Abraham. And the scripture, foreseeing that God would justify the Gentiles by faith, declared the gospel beforehand to Abraham, saying, 'All the Gentiles shall be blessed in you.' For this reason, those who believe are blessed with Abraham who believed. . . . And if you belong to Christ, then you are Abraham's offspring, heirs according to the promise."

72. Matthew Westerholm, 1999.

73. "Church, society, nature, history, culture, economics — everything is subject to the reign of the crucified and risen Christ. *He* is Kurios, Lord." du Preez, "Interpreting Psalm 47," *Missionalia* 25, no. 3 (1997): 319.

74. "Sometimes we tend to think it is a loss that Jesus is no longer with us. . . . But we should rejoice, as the psalm calls us to rejoice, for Christ has ascended to rule over all the earth — to mount his throne as King of the nations, to share his Father's universal reign." Elizabeth Achtemeier, *Preaching from the Old Testament,* 161.

Prayer[75]

King of all creation,
  we wait for the day when, with all the hosts of heaven, we will sing:
"The kingdom of this world has become the kingdom of our Lord
  and of his Christ, and he shall reign forever."
Until that day, receive the praise of our hearts
  and direct the pattern of our lives so that in word and action
we may exhibit your kingdom to a watching world. Amen.

Song[76]

1Rejoice, the Lord is King:
  Your Lord and King adore!
Rejoice, give thanks and sing,
  And triumph evermore.
Lift up your heart,
  Lift up your voice!
Rejoice, again I say, rejoice!

2Jesus, the Savior, reigns,
  The God of truth and love;
When He had purged our stains,
  He took his seat above;
Lift up your heart,
  Lift up your voice!
Rejoice, again I say, rejoice!

3His kingdom cannot fail,
  He rules o'er earth and heav'n;
The keys of death and hell
  Are to our Jesus giv'n:
Lift up your heart,
  Lift up your voice!
Rejoice, again I say, rejoice!

---

75. *Psalms for All Seasons,* 294.
76. Charles Wesley, 1744. Public Domain. *Psalter Hymnal* (1987), # 408; *Lift Up Your Hearts,* # 224.

4Rejoice in glorious hope!
    Our Lord and judge shall come
And take His servants up
    To their eternal home:
Lift up your heart,
    Lift up your voice!
Rejoice, again I say, rejoice!

CHAPTER 21

"Bless the LORD, O My Soul!"

Psalm 104 (103)

Psalm 104 has been called "one of the crown jewels of the Psalter."[1] It is indeed a carefully crafted poem with an amazing message. The *Revised Common Lectionary* assigns Psalm 104:24–34, 35b for the Day of Pentecost in years A, B, C, as a response to the reading of the Pentecost story in Acts 2:1–21.[2] Alert people will immediately wonder why the lectionary skips over verse 35a: "Let sinners be consumed from the earth, and let the wicked be no more." It could be because this imprecatory prayer does not seem to fit in this beautiful psalm, nor the feast of Pentecost for that matter. But omitting this prayer sends the wrong message to the congregation, as if we can just pick and choose what we like in Scripture and omit what we dislike. We must read and preach this imprecatory prayer in the context of the whole psalm and scripture. Happily, when our preaching text is the whole of Psalm 104, we can communicate to the congregation also the hopeful message that comes through in verse 35a (see "Sermon Exposition" below).

---

1. H. Darrell Lance, "Psalm 104:24–34," *No Other Foundation* 7 (1986): 42. Cf. Davidson, *Vitality of Worship*, 339, "This psalm contains some of the finest lyric poetry in the Old Testament, notably in the central section from verses 5–30."

2. "The selection of this lection for Pentecost Sunday is based on its emphasis on the role of God's Spirit in creation (see v. 30) and the psalm's universal perspectives." John Hayes, *Preaching Through the Christian Year*, 296.

Text and Context

Psalm 104 is a literary unit because it is a single psalm and it is framed by the inclusio, "Bless the LORD, O my soul" (vv 1, 35).[3] Therefore, although the psalm is rather long,[4] it makes for a good preaching text.

The immediate context of Psalm 104 is Psalm 103. These two psalms form a pair: each being framed by the inclusio, "Bless the LORD, O my soul" — the only psalms in the Psalter to use this self-exhortation. Both psalms celebrate the LORD's kingship. Psalm 103 concludes with, "The LORD has established his throne in the heavens, and his kingdom rules over all" (103:19) — which is where Psalm 104 begins, "O LORD my God, you are very great. You are clothed with honor and majesty" (104:1). Psalm 103 ends with, "Bless the LORD, all his works" (103:22), and Psalm 104 continues by exploring the LORD's works: "O LORD, how manifold are your works! In wisdom you have made them all; the earth is full of your creatures" (104:24).

While these two psalms have several similarities, the message of each is distinct. "The first [103] speaks of the abounding steadfast love of the LORD; the second [104] of the innumerable creatures made and sustained by the wisdom of the LORD. Together the pair praise the LORD as the savior who forgives and the creator who provides."[5] In preaching the specific message of Psalm 104, we need to concentrate on what makes it different from Psalm 103. John Goldingay notes that "the world's creation by Yhwh stands on its own ground, separate from the theme of Yhwh's involvement in salvation. The psalm is totally concerned with Yhwh's relationship to the world as its creator, in two interwoven aspects, Yhwh's original activity in bringing the world into being, and Yhwh's ongoing activity in making the world work."[6]

A broader context consists of other creation hymns such as Psalms 8, 33, 145, and 148. For example, we can compare Psalm 104 with Psalm 8. Both psalms declare the sovereignty and majesty of God. But a major difference is the position of human beings in God's creation. Psalm 8 states, "Yet you have made them a little lower than God, and crowned them with glory and honor. You have given them dominion over the works of your hands; you have put all things under their feet" (8:5-6). In contrast, Psalm 104 does not mention human beings till verse 14 and then side-by-side with cattle, and in verse 23 where they appear after the "young

---

3. Further hints of an inclusio are the repetition of "my God" in vv 1 and 33, the synonyms "honor and majesty" (v 1) and "glory" (v 31), "theophanic language in vv 3, 4, 32, the repetition of *'ôlām (l-)* 'forever,' vv 5, 31, and a repeated double use of *rûaḥ* 'wind, spirit, breath,' vv 3-4, 29-30." Allen, *Psalms 101–150*, 32.

4. See Appendix 6, p. 582 below, for a suggestion of a series of three sermons on this psalm.

5. Mays, *Psalms*, 331. For more connections between these two psalms, see McCann, "Psalms," 1096.

6. Goldingay, *Psalms*, III, 181.

lions" return to their dens (v 22).[7] In other words, Psalm 104 pictures human beings as part of God's creation almost on a par with other creatures, except for the provision of wine, oil, and bread (v 15).

Because Psalm 104 deals with God's works of creation, another context is given in the creation stories of Genesis. Commentators have noted that the psalm more or less follows the order of creation set forth in Genesis 1.[8] But in the sermon I would not go there since it would detract from the specific message of Psalm 104. Again, we should check how Psalm 104 is different from Genesis 1.

Genesis 1, like Psalm 8, presents human beings as special creatures, created in God's image and given dominion over all the other creatures (Gen 1:26–28). Psalm 104, on the other hand, views human beings much more on a par with all other creatures. "Human beings are interdependently linked with all the other creatures; indeed, dependence upon God is the great equalizer of all the animal species and even the trees (v 16). All that distinguishes the lion from the human is that the former takes the 'night shift' while the latter works during the day (104:21–23)."[9]

In comparing Psalm 104 with Genesis 1, Bernhard Anderson comments, "What a different world is presented in Psalm 104! Here we do not find statements *about* God, but statements *to* God. We do not find theology based on reflection but prayer based on experience of the goodness and wonder of God's creation."[10] James Mays adds, "The psalm is lyrical and exuberant. It reads as if it were a poetic version of God's repeated appraisal of his work in Genesis 1: 'And God saw that

7. "The distinctiveness of Psalm 104 rests in part on what it defers saying. For the first thirteen verses not a single syllable addresses humanity's place in the created order. Where they *are* mentioned in the following verses, human beings are considered at most coinhabitants with the onagers [wild asses] and the coneys." Brown, *Seeing the Psalms,* 158. See also pp. 159–60.

8. See the correspondences listed by Kidner, *Psalms 73–150,* 368. Wenham, *The Psalter Reclaimed,* 148, calls Psalm 104 "a poetic paraphrase of Genesis 1." Cf. Terrien, *The Psalms,* 718, "Minor differences aside, the order of the creative acts in the psalm is clearly that of the Genesis Yahwist myth." On p. 710, Terrien states that "the eight strophes [of the psalm] correspond to the eight acts of creation in the Yahwist myth (Gen 1:1–24)." Cf. B. Anderson, *Out of the Depths,* 138, "The elaboration of the grounds for praise is developed in seven strophes, which follow the sequence of the Genesis creation story." Adele Berlin, "The Wisdom of Creation in Psalm 104," in *Seeking Out the Wisdom of the Ancients* (Winona Lake, IN: Eisenbrauns, 2005; pp. 71–83), 75 n. 13, observes, "While Genesis 1 is the main basis for the psalm, it also knows the story of Genesis 2–3. Human working of the soil is reflected in v 14, and the creation of humans from dust and God's breath is alluded to in v 29." By contrast, David Barker, "The Waters of the Earth: An Exegetical Study of Psalm 104:1–9," *GTJ* 7, no. 1 (1986): 57–80, argues that Psalm 104:6–9 "clearly point to the Noahic deluge of Genesis 6–9 rather than the creation account of Genesis 1" (p. 80).

9. William P. Brown, "The Lion, the Wicked, and the Wonder of It All: Psalm 104 and the Playful God," *JPr* 29, no. 3 (2006; pp. 15–20): 19.

10. B. Anderson, *Out of the Depths,* 139. For correspondences and differences, see also Allen, *Psalms 101–150,* 30–31, and Berlin, "The Wisdom of Creation in Psalm 104," 76.

it was good.' The psalm is so full of wonder and joy at what God has made — the joy of the psalmist and the joy of God."[11]

John Goldingay helpfully alerts us to several other differences between Psalm 104 and Genesis: "Over against Genesis 1–3, the psalm speaks not of a task of creation that could be completed over a week, after which God could simply rest, but of a job of work that continues as long as the world exists. . . . Whereas Genesis portrays creation as effortless, the psalm portrays it as requiring expenditure of divine energy in constraining and harnessing other dynamic forces. Whereas Genesis sees God as creating light but not explicitly creating darkness, and as introducing death only as a consequence of human disobedience, the psalm sees both darkness and light and death and life as parts of the intrinsic pattern of God's sovereignty in the world. . . . Whereas Genesis recognizes tensions between the human and animal world and sees both as living with a curse, the psalm speaks of none of this. Whereas Genesis describes God as blessing creation and giving over to nature the capacity to reproduce, the psalm sees God as continually involved with creation in bringing about that capacity."[12] Finally, whereas after the Fall into sin God cursed "the ground" (*'ǎdāmâ;* Gen 3:17), in Psalm 104 God's spirit renews "the face of the ground" (*'ǎdāmâ;* Ps 104:30).[13]

Aside from the context of the New Testament with which we shall deal later, a final context we need to consider here is the ancient Near Eastern cultural context. During excavations at El Amarna, archeologists discovered an Egyptian hymn to the sun god. Psalm 104 has "some striking resemblances to the Egyptian Akhenaten's great Hymn to the Sun (14th century BC, text in *ANET,* pp. 370f.), especially in the depicting of creatures of night and day (20–23), of the provision of beasts and birds (10ff.), of the sea with its ships (25f.), and of the life-and-death dependence of all creatures on their creator (27–30)."[14] This hymn to the sun

11. Mays, *Psalms,* 331. Cf. Alter, *Book of Psalms,* 367, 25 n., "This poem reads distinctly like a poetic free improvisation on themes from the creation story at the beginning of Genesis, rendered from the perspective of a human observer rather than through the magisterial omniscience of the narrator of Genesis." Cf. Weiser, *The Psalms,* 666, "The relation of this nature-hymn to the story of creation in the first chapters of Genesis is like that of a coloured picture to the clear lines of a woodcut."

12. Goldingay, *Psalms,* III, 197–98. See also pp. 189–90 on day and night. Cf. Scott Ellington, "The Face of God as His Creating Spirit," in *Spirit Renews the Face of the Earth* (Eugene, OR: Pickwick, 2009; pp. 3–16), 16, "The association of *pānîm* with *rûaḥ* in the affirmation of *creatio continua* in Psalm 104 lends to the latter a sense of being an active agent in creation not found in the Genesis 1 account. The implied and potential participation of the *rûaḥ 'ĕlohîm* in creation becomes for the psalmist an intimate and direct involvement with each creature, breath by breath and heartbeat by heartbeat. Creation happens every moment of every day before the face and through the spirit of Yahweh."

13. Goldingay, *Psalms,* III, 194.

14. Kidner, *Psalms 73–150,* 367.

promoted monotheism in Egypt. However the psalmist became acquainted with ideas in this Egyptian hymn and other ancient concepts,[15] the point for preachers is the polemical thrust of Psalm 104: the sun is not god; Israel's God, Yahweh, is "very great" (v 1), "wrapped in light as with a garment" (v 2). Yahweh "made the moon to mark the seasons" (v 19a) while the sun dutifully obeys its Maker every day: "the sun knows its time for setting" (v 19b).

The polemical thrust of Psalm 104 applies not only to Egyptian but also to Canaanite beliefs. In Canaan people elevated their god Baal as "the Most High" (*'elyôn*)[16] among their gods and called him the "rider of the clouds."[17] Psalm 104 speaks of Yahweh as making "the clouds your chariot, you ride on the wings of the wind" (v 3). The Canaanites also believed that the creation was "the result of a battle among the gods and the subsequent ordering of the forces of a watery chaos. . . . In each case, these ideas have been adopted and stamped with Israel's faith in the exclusive sovereignty of Yahweh. The elements of the cosmos are objects of God's action, not gods themselves (see vv 2–9, 19, 26); it is clear throughout that God 'made them all' (v 24)."[18]

Literary Interpretation

As indicated by the inclusio, "Bless the LORD, O my soul" (vv 1, 35), Psalm 104 is a hymn of praise. Scholars debate whether it is a hymn of an individual (vv 1, 33, 35)[19] or communal, or both. It seems best to regard the psalm as both the meditation of an individual and a communal call to "praise the LORD."[20]

15. See Kraus, *Psalms 60–150*, 298–99, and 302.

16. See Psalm 47, p. 460 n. 43 above.

17. Hilber, *Psalms*, 409–10, provides this and other parallels between Psalm 104 and the Baal myth: "Baal builds his own palace, having arisen to supremacy after the defeat of the chaos waters of Yamm, the 'Sea.' The palace of Baal is constructed with choice timbers of Lebanon (cf. 104:3, 16), utilizing fire and flame (cf. 104:4), and with a thundering voice (cf. 104:7)." I would not overload the sermon with all these parallels but concentrate on the point of Psalm 104, which is, in Hilber's words, "Israel's God, not the gods of the Babylonians or the Canaanites, is the true King, who brings order to creation and regulates the life-giving waters that satisfy the earth."

18. McCann, "Psalms," 1096–97.

19. Kraus, *Psalms 60–150*, 297.

20. Gerstenberger, *Psalms*, II, 226, calls it "a personal and communal hymn." Goldingay, *Psalms*, III, 181, points out that the psalm "finally closes with the plural bidding to 'praise Yah.'" Because the psalm deals with the cosmos and the place of humans in it (a theme in wisdom literature) and because verse 24 states plainly, "In wisdom you have made them all," Berlin, "The Wisdom of Creation in Psalm 104," 71, considers calling it a "wisdom psalm" but then retracts because "its stated aim is to 'bless the Lord,' not to instruct." Brown, *Seeing the Psalms*, 158, prefers

We shall work our way into the meaning of the psalm by quickly scanning its parallelisms, next the psalm's imagery, the repetition of keywords, followed by its structure.

Parallelisms

Psalm 104 features advancing (synthetic) parallelism with the second line advancing in some way on the first.[21] This results in an intricate set of parallelisms, many expanding into climactic parallelisms,[22] some combined with antithetic parallelism (see vv 8b–9, 29, 35a, b).

1Bless the LORD, O my soul.	A
O LORD my God, you are very great.	+ A'
You are clothed with honor and majesty,	+ A''
2wrapped in light as with a garment.	+ A'''
You stretch out the heavens like a tent,	B
3you set the beams of your chambers on the waters,	+ B'
you make the clouds your chariot,	C
you ride on the wings of the wind,	+ C'
4you make the winds your messengers,	+ C''
fire and flame your ministers.	+ C'''
5You set the earth on its foundations,	A
so that it shall never be shaken.	+ A'
6You cover it with the deep as with a garment;	B
the waters stood above the mountains.	+ B'
7At your rebuke they flee;	C
at the sound of your thunder they take to flight.	+ C'
8They rose up to the mountains,	+ C''
ran down to the valleys[23]	– C'''
to the place that you appointed for them.	+– C''''
9You set a boundary that they may not pass,	+– C'''''
so that they might not again cover the earth.	+– C''''''

"a cosmic hymn of praise," while Jacobson in deClaissé-Walford, Jacobson, and Tanner, *Book of Psalms*, 780, prefers "a creation hymn."

21. Again, these classifications are not scientifically precise. As can be seen in this psalm, Hebrew poetry is too varied and flexible to be caught in four airtight compartments.

22. See verses 1–2a, 3b–4, 7–8a, 10–11, 14–15, 16–17, 19–23, 24, 25–26, 27–30, and 31–32.

23. In contrast to the waters rising (v 8a), these waters run down to the valleys; therefore v 8b is antithetic parallelism (–) followed by three advancing lines resulting in a climactic antithetic parallelism.

10You make springs gush forth in the valleys;	A
they flow between the hills,	+ A′
11giving drink to every wild animal;	+ A″
the wild asses quench their thirst.	+ A‴
12By the streams the birds of the air have their habitation;	B
they sing among the branches.	+ B′
13From your lofty abode you water the mountains;	C
the earth is satisfied with the fruit of your work.	+ C′
14You cause the grass to grow for the cattle,	A
and plants for people to use,	+ A′
to bring forth food from the earth,	+ A″
15and wine to gladden the human heart,	+ A‴
oil to make the face shine,	+ A″″
and bread to strengthen the human heart.	+ A‴″
16The trees of the LORD are watered abundantly,	B
the cedars of Lebanon that he planted.	+ B′
17In them the birds build their nests;	+ B″
the stork has its home in the fir trees.	+ B‴
18The high mountains are for the wild goats;	C
the rocks are a refuge for the coneys.	+ C′
19You have made the moon to mark the seasons;	D
the sun knows its time for setting.	+ D′
20You make darkness, and it is night,	+ D″
when all the animals of the forest come creeping out.	+ D‴
21The young lions roar for their prey,	+ D″″
seeking their food from God.	+ D‴″
22When the sun rises, they withdraw	+ D‴″′
and lie down in their dens.	+ D‴″″
23People go out to their work	+ D‴″‴
and to their labor until the evening.	+ D‴″‴′
24O LORD, how manifold are your works!	A
In wisdom you have made them all;	+ A′
the earth is full of your creatures.	+ A″
25Yonder is the sea, great and wide,	B
creeping things innumerable are there,	+ B′
living things both small and great.	+ B″
26There go the ships,	+ B‴
and Leviathan that you formed to sport in it.	+ B″″

27These all look to you	A
to give them their food in due season;	+ A′
28when you give to them, they gather it up;	+ A″
when you open your hand, they are filled with good things.[24]	+ A‴
29When you hide your face, they are dismayed;[25]	− A⁗
when you take away their breath, they die	+− A′′′′′
and return to their dust.	+− A′′′′′′
30When you send forth your spirit, they are created;[26]	+ A′′′′′′′
and you renew the face of the ground.[27]	+ A′′′′′′′′
31May the glory of the Lord endure forever;	A
may the Lord rejoice in his works—	+ A′
32who looks on the earth and it trembles,	+ A″
who touches the mountains and they smoke.	+ A‴
33I will sing to the Lord as long as I live;	B
I will sing praise to my God while I have being.	+ B′
34May my meditation be pleasing to him,	C
for I rejoice in the Lord.	+ C′
35Let sinners be consumed from the earth,[28]	− D
and let the wicked be no more.	+− D′
Bless the Lord, O my soul.	E
Praise the Lord![29]	+ E′

24. "The second colon in its parallelism at each point puts the point more strongly. Yhwh gives with an open hand, with generosity, and the recipients receive not merely a sufficient portion but eat their fill, and of good things (cf. vv 13, 16). Goldingay, *Psalms,* III, 192.

25. In contrast to the open hand (v 28b), the Lord hides his face; therefore antithetic parallelism (−) in v 29a. Verse 29b and c add to the dismay of v 29a, "they die," and "return to the ground"; therefore two advancing statements of antithetic parallelism resulting in climactic antithetic parallelism.

26. In contrast to taking away "their breath" (*rûaḥ,* v 29b) and returning to dust (v 29c), verse 30a reads, "When you send forth your spirit (*rûaḥ*), they are created"; therefore continuing the advancing parallelism of vv 27–28. Verse 30b builds on this, "and you renew the face of the ground"; therefore advancing parallelism.

27. Note further the chiasm in verses 29–30:
    A   When you hide your face, they are dismayed;
       B   when you take away their breath, they die
          C   and return to their dust.
       B′ When you send forth your spirit, they are created;
    A′ and you renew the face of the ground.

28. In contrast to the psalmist who rejoices in the Lord (v 34), he prays that "sinners be consumed from the earth" (v 35a); therefore antithetic parallelism (−). Verse 35b adds to this desire, "and let the wicked be no more"; therefore advancing antithetic parallelism (+−).

29. Advancing from the individual "my soul" to the plural bidding *halǝlû yāh.*

Imagery

Psalm 104 is filled with anthropomorphic language and images that reflect the ancient Near Eastern worldview (see pp. 472–73 above). It begins by describing the LORD's clothing as fit for a King: "You are clothed with honor and majesty ['the attributes of royalty'[30]], wrapped in light[31] as with a garment" (v 2a). Next it pictures the LORD's actions: "You stretch out the heavens like a tent" (v 2b). "The heavens are likened to a tent stretched out over the whole earth."[32] The "tent" is also a reminder of the tabernacle tent where God dwelt.[33]

Verse 3 goes on to describe how and where the LORD constructed his dwelling place: "You set the beams of your chambers[34] on the waters" (v 3a). "The waters" are the waters of the heavenly ocean above the tent or dome (see Gen 1:6–8). Yet the LORD is not far removed from this world: He uses the clouds as his chariot and rides "on the wings of the wind," making the winds his messengers, "fire and flame" (lightning) his ministers (vv 3b–4).

The psalmist next moves to the LORD creating the earth: "You set the earth on its foundations, so that it shall never be shaken. You cover it with the deep as with a garment; the waters stood above the mountains" (vv 5–6). The LORD clothed the earth "with the deep," so that the waters below the dome covered even the mountains. "The deep" in the Old Testament is associated with the waters of chaos. But the LORD is not intimidated by chaos. Using his voice of thunder, he set boundaries to the waters (which are personified): "At your rebuke they flee; at the sound of your thunder they take to flight. They rose up to the mountains, ran down to the valleys to the place that you appointed for them. You set a boundary that they may not pass, so that they might not again cover the earth" (vv 7–9).

Having harnessed chaos, the psalmist moves to the LORD's provision of water for his thirsty creatures on earth. The LORD makes "springs gush forth in the valleys . . . , giving drink to every wild animal. . . . By the streams the birds of the air have their habitation; they sing among the branches" (vv 10–12). The LORD, like a farmer, also provides food for domesticated cattle and people: "You cause the grass to grow for the cattle, and plants for people to use, to bring forth food

30. McCann, "Psalms," 1097, with references to Pss 21:5; 45:3; 96:6; and 145:5.
31. "Light is regularly associated with God's presence. . . . 'Light' also indicates the cosmic dimension of God's rule (see Gen 1:3)." Ibid.
32. A. Anderson, *Psalms 73–150*, 719.
33. McCann, "Psalms," 1097.
34. "Chambers" "is often used to denote either a room in the upper storey of a large house, or a room on the flat roof of a house (cf. 1 Kings 17:19; 2 Kings 1:2; 4:10). In this verse it probably refers to the royal palace of Yahweh, which is founded on the waters above the firmament (Gen 1:7)." A. Anderson, *Psalms 73–150*, 719.

from the earth" (v 14). The LORD, like a gardener, even planted the great "cedars of Lebanon" (v 16). The LORD wastes nothing in his creation: "The high mountains are for the wild goats; the rocks are a refuge for the coneys" (v 18).

The LORD also made the moon and the sun. These gods of the Canaanites, the psalmist says, were created by the LORD simply as instruments to mark time for his creatures: to "mark the seasons," the feast days on their lunar calendar, as well as night and day (v 19): night, when "all the animals of the forest come creeping out. . . . seeking their food from God" (vv 20–21), and day, when "people go out to their work and . . . labor until the evening" (v 23).

Finally, the psalmist turns to the sea — the supposedly dangerous, unpredictable sea with its sea monsters: "Yonder is the sea, great and wide, creeping things innumerable are there, living things both small and great. There go the ships, and Leviathan that you formed to sport in it" (vv 25–26). The menacing sea has been tamed, and even Leviathan, the ancient sea monster, is not a threat; it merely plays in the sea.

The psalmist summarizes with anthropomorphic metaphors of the LORD's "hand" and "face": "These all look to you to give them their food in due season . . . ; when you open your *hand,* they are filled with good things. When you hide your *face,* they are dismayed; when you take away their breath, they die and return to their dust" (vv 27–29). But death is not the end; there is a new generation being born: "When you send forth your spirit, they are created; and you renew the face [metaphor] of the ground" (v 30).

But what about the so-called "natural disasters" such as earthquakes and volcanic eruptions? Here, too, the LORD is involved. With the anthropomorphic verbs of looking and touching the psalmist pictures the LORD as the one "who looks on the earth and it trembles, who touches the mountains and they smoke" (v 32).

Together all these images portray the LORD as the sovereign King of the universe who controls chaos, who created all things, who provides for all his creatures, who also brings about death and so-called "natural disasters." Absolutely nothing is outside the LORD's control.[35]

Repetition of Keywords

We noted earlier the repetition of "Bless the LORD, O my soul" (vv 1, 35, inclusio). The psalmist uses the keyword "LORD" (*Yhwh*) a full ten times: verses 1 (2×), 16,

---

35. "The view of nature that emerges from all this is highly significant. Nature is a single, all-embracing organism, governed by God's providence. All aspects of nature are fellow dependents of God and of each other. Nature is orderly and purposeful, operating according to a divine plan that provides for the need of every part." Leland Ryken, *The Literature of the Bible* (Grand Rapids: Zondervan, 1974), 193.

24, 31 (2×), 33, 34, 35 (2×), and twice he calls the LORD, "my God" (vv 1 and 33). The LORD is involved with this earth: the earth (*'ereṣ*) is named a perfect seven times (vv 5, 9, 13, 14, 24, 32, and 35). Once the psalmist uses "the ground" (*'ădāmâ*), "you renew the face of the ground" (v 30), perhaps in contrast to Genesis 3:17 where God cursed "the ground" (*'ădāmâ*). The word *rûaḥ*, "wind, spirit, breath," is used four times (vv 3, 4, 29, 30).

Patrick Miller notes two other keywords: "The two words that stand out in the psalm are 'work(s) / made' (*ma'ăśê / 'āśâ*; vv 13, 19, 24, 31) and 'satisfy / fill' (*śāba'*; vv 13, 16, 28, and 11 in the Syriac). This is no accident, for they suggest that the psalm's chief subject matter is *the 'works' or creation of God and God's 'satisfy-ing' or providing for the creation*."[36] This combination of creation and providence leads to the topic of joy and pleasure in God's creation. Not only is there beauty "in the order of a carefully and intricately crafted universe. Its capacity to evoke pleasure is an even more marked outcome of the Creator's work. That is revealed in several ways: in the songs of the birds, in the sea as a place for Leviathan to play, and through wine to gladden the heart. The word for 'joy' and 'take pleasure in' (*śāmaḥ*) occurs frequently in the psalm. One of the goals of creation, in its details and as a whole, is to provide pleasure and delight."[37] The repetition of these keywords will enable us later to formulate the theme of this psalm. But first we need to consider its structure.

Structure

Many of the English versions show broad agreement on the stanzas but differ here and there on the details.

Verse Divisions								*Versions*
1–4 / 5–9 / 10–13 / 14	–		23 / 24–26 / 27–30 / 31	–	35			NRSV
1–4 / 5–9 / 10–13 / 14	–	17 / 18	– 23 / 24–26 / 27–30 / 31	–	35			NASB
1–4 / 5–9 / 10–13 / 14–15 / 16	–	18 /19–23 / 24–26 / 27–30 / 31		–	35			ESV
1–4 / 5–9 / 10	–		18 /19–23 / 24–26 / 27–30 / 31–32 / 33–35[38]					NIV

36. Patrick D. Miller, "The Poetry of Creation: Psalm 104," in *God Who Creates*, ed. William P. Brown and S. Dean McBride, Jr. (Grand Rapids: Eerdmans, 2000, pp. 87–103), 95. See also n. 84 below.

37. Miller, *Interpreting the Psalms*, 223. Cf. Limburg, *Psalms*, 355, "Joy, delight, and play are important in this psalm. The purpose of wine is to make people happy (v 15); the psalmist hopes that the Lord will be happy in his works (v 31) [and with the psalmist's meditation (v 34a)] and declares that he himself is happy in the Lord (v 34b)."

38. The NIV separates v 1a from vv 1–4 and also vv 35c and d from vv 33–35. Cf. John H. Stek,

To discern the structure of this psalm, we shall go back again to the usual structure of hymns noted in Chapter 1, p. 11, and see how Psalm 104 fits this typical structure:

1) A call to praise the LORD   v 1a
2) Transition (*kî*, for, because)
3) Reasons why the LORD is to be praised   vv 1b–30
4) Conclusion: Praise the LORD!   vv 35c, d

The psalm lacks the typical "because" transition but has more than the usual number of reasons for praising the LORD. In addition it adds,

5) Prayer for the glory of the LORD to endure forever   vv 31–34
6) Prayer for the removal of sinners from the earth   vv 35a, b

The addition of these two prayers together provides an interesting clue for interpreting the imprecatory prayer (see "Sermon Exposition" below).

Of the many different proposals by commentators for a more specific structure, that of Allen and McCann[39] is the most compelling, not least because several sections are marked by inclusios. McCann writes, "Attention to stylistic detail suggests division as follows":[40]

vv 1–4   God and the heavens
vv 5–13   God and the earth (see "earth" in vv 5, 13)[41]
vv 14–23   God and people ("people," "cultivate," and "labor" in vv 14, 23)[42]
vv 24–30   "all" God's works ("all" in 24, 27)[43]
vv 31–35   Conclusion: God's joy (v 31) and human joy (v 34)[44]

"When the Spirit Was Poetic," in *The NIV: The Making of a Contemporary Translation,* ed. Kenneth L. Barker (Grand Rapids: Zondervan, 1986; pp. 72–87, 158–61), 80, "Following a one-line introduction (v 1) that announces the main theme (and should have been set off by spacing), the author composed a hymn to the Creator with a concentric structure of 3–5–9–5–3 lines consecutively."

39. Allen, *Psalms 101–150,* 32–33; McCann, "Psalms," 1097.

40. McCann, "Psalms," 1097.

41. "The occurrence of 'earth' [also] in v 9 may mark a subdivision of the larger vv 5–13." Ibid., 1098.

42. "Human beings enter the picture for the first time in v 14, and the words 'people' (*'ādām*) and 'cultivate' / 'labor' (*'ăbodâ / pā'al*) in vv 14, 23 may form an envelope structure for this section." Ibid.

43. "The 'all' in v 27 refers to the 'all' in v 24." Ibid. Each "all" begins the two subdivisions of vv 24–26 and 27–30 as in the NRSV's structure and that of the other versions (p. 479).

44. Allen, *Psalms 101–150,* 32–33, has the same structure and argues that this makes for a

As foundation for an expository sermon outline, however, it would be well to have a structure of the psalm based on its contents. Terrien[45] neatly subdivides the five sections above into eight strophes with seven wonders and a conclusion:

I.	vv 2–4	Architect of Heaven
II.	vv 5–9	The Earth and the Abyss
III.	vv 10–13	Springs and Rains
IV.	vv 14–18	Green Pastures and High Peaks
V.	vv 19–23	The Moon and the Sun
VI.	vv 24–26	The Great Green Sea
VII.	vv 27–30	The Giver of Life and Joy
VIII.	vv 31–35a	Light and Glory[46]

Theocentric Interpretation

This is another psalm where the centrality of God can hardly be missed.[47] The psalm sets its theocentric tone right at the beginning: "Bless the LORD, O my soul. O LORD my God, you are very great. You are clothed with honor and majesty" (104:1).[48] Then the psalm speaks of the many works of the LORD, exclaiming in verse 24, "O LORD, how manifold are your works! In wisdom you have made them all; the earth is full of your creatures." Next it goes on to declare that the LORD through his spirit is the source of life for all creatures, even the source of

---

"concentric composition [A, B, C, B', A'], the first and last of its five strophes being half the size of the central one."

45. Terrien, *The Psalms,* 710–17. Fokkelman, *Major Poems of the Hebrew Bible,* II, 264, identifies the same stanzas but combines VI and VII, vv 24–30, for a total of seven stanzas.

46. Terrien, *The Psalms,* 711, proposes that "the themes of the coupled strophes . . . correspond to each other," resulting in a concentric structure of the stanzas:

I. Light	VIII. Glory
II. Earth	VII. Terrestrial Creatures
III. Spring and Rain	VI. The Great Sea
IV. Vegetation	V. Night and Day

47. "The Psalm, from first to last, hallows the name of God." Kidner, *Psalms 73–150,* 372. Cf. Mays, *Psalms,* 334, "There is not a hint of anthropocentric claim here. In the praise of the creator, the human being sees itself simply as one of the creatures sustained by the providence of God." As noted in "Repetition of Keywords" above, the psalm uses the keyword "LORD" (*Yahweh*) a full ten times: verses 1 (2×), 16, 24, 31 (2×), 33, 34, 35 (2×) and twice he calls the LORD, "my God" (vv 1 and 33).

48. "Praise begins with its eyes focused solely and fully on God known in greatness and majesty." Miller, "The Poetry of Creation: Psalm 104," 88.

their death when he turns his face,[49] but also of their re-creation (vv 27–30). The psalm concludes with the prayer "may the glory of the LORD endure forever; may the LORD rejoice in his works. . . . I rejoice in the LORD. . . . Bless the LORD, O my soul. Praise the LORD! " (vv 31, 34, 35). "The fact that the psalmist's look at the world issues in joy and praise has profound theological implications — namely, that every experience of the world is also an experience of God."[50]

Textual Theme and Goal

Psalm 104 develops several themes. McCann highlights God's providence: "Under God's rule, water becomes not a threat to but a sustainer of life (vv 11–13a). . . . God provides for animate and inanimate things alike; the earth has what it needs. This theme of God's providence will be echoed by the repetitions of 'satisfied' in v 16 ('watered abundantly') and v 28."[51] Rogerson and McKay highlight a related theme, the other side of the coin, "dependence": "The main theme of Ps 104 is that of *dependence* — the dependence of the created order upon God, not merely for its origin, but for its continued life."[52] It is also important to incorporate in the theme the means by which God creates and sustains this earth since the word *rûaḥ*, "wind, spirit, breath," is used four times (vv 3, 4, 29, 30). But most of all we need to include the main theme that comes to expression in the inclusio (the "ballast lines"), "Bless the LORD, O my soul" (vv 1, 35).[53]

How can we formulate in a single sentence these several themes? A good formulation of this psalm's theme is, *Praise the LORD for his manifold works in the creation, preservation, and re-creation of the world by his spirit.*[54]

---

49. "Yahweh is firmly made the author of the withholding of provision; if the harvest fails, it is because Yhwh's face has turned away. The psalm accepts the logic of double predestination. If God gets the credit for giving, God is also responsible when provision fails." Goldingay, *Psalms*, III, 193.

50. McCann, "Between Text and Sermon: Psalm 104," *Int* 66, no. 1 (2012; pp. 67–69): 68. Cf. Berlin, "The Wisdom of Creation in Psalm 104," 75, "Creation is a part of what God revealed of himself to humans, a revelation that is impossible not to see. The natural world is, as it were, an ongoing visual revelation, just as the Torah is an ongoing textual (or aural) revelation. That is [also] the sense of Psalm 19. . . . God is revealed to Israel both through creation and through Torah."

51. McCann, "Psalms," 1098. Cf. Williams, *Psalms 73–150*, 233, God "holds all things together in His governing, providential care. . . . This is the thesis of Psalm 104."

52. Rogerson and McKay, *Psalms 101–150*, 27.

53. Cf. Davidson, *Vitality of Worship*, 341, "The closing words 'Praise the LORD' . . . underline the theme of the whole psalm." Cf. Stek, "When the Spirit Was Poetic," 80, "Following a one-line introduction (v 1) that announces the main theme. . . ."

54. I first formulated the theme as, "Praise the LORD who through his spirit created all things,

The goal of this psalm is stated with the imperatives in the inclusio, "Bless the LORD, O my soul" (vv 1, 35) and the final, "Praise the LORD!" (v 35). Since "Bless the LORD" can also be translated "Praise the LORD" (NIV) and the final phrase is "Praise the LORD!" the goal of the psalm can be formulated simply as "to urge people to praise the LORD."[55] But the psalmist also seeks to motivate such praise with the extensive lists of the works of the LORD. Incorporating this thought, the goal of the psalmist can be formulated as *to persuade people to praise the LORD for his manifold works in the creation, preservation, and re-creation of the world by his spirit.*

Ways to Preach Christ

There is no promise of Christ in Psalm 104, nor is there a type of Christ. One could possibly use a single New Testament reference as a way to Christ on the assumption that Paul had Psalm 104 in mind when he wrote about Christ, "He is the image of the invisible God, the firstborn of all creation; for in him all things in heaven and on earth were created, things visible and invisible, whether thrones or dominions or rulers or powers — all things have been created through him and for him. He himself is before all things, and in him all things hold together" (Col 1:15-17).[56]

But since Psalm 104 is scheduled to be preached at Pentecost, we ought to check how we can move to Christ in New Testament via the spirit of God. One can trace the longitudinal theme of God's wind / spirit from creation ("the Spirit of God was hovering over the waters" [Gen 1:2, NIV]), through the spirit's work pictured in Psalm 104, to the spirit empowering Old Testament prophets and kings, and on into the New Testament (Jesus' conception, Luke 1:35, his teaching about the Spirit, John 3:5-8), Pentecost (Acts 2:1-4), to the new creation (Rev 22:17). But the most direct way to Christ in the New Testament is redemptive-historical progression supported by New Testament references.

---

provides for all his creatures, and even re-creates them." My proofreader Ryan Faber suggested the more succinct theme.

55. Cf. Berlin, "The Wisdom of Creation in Psalm 104," 71, "Its stated aim is to 'bless the Lord.'" Cf. Virgil P. Howard, "Psalm 104," *Int* 46, no. 2 (1992; pp. 176-80): 176, "That doxology is the aim of Psalm 104 is already made clear by the opening and concluding self-incitement formula: 'Bless the Lord, O my soul' (vv 1, 35)."

56. See Roy Berkenbosch's powerful sermon on this text in Appendix 5, pp. 570-78 below. Another link to Christ in the New Testament may be that the word "rebuke" in the Septuagint ("At your rebuke they [the waters] flee" [Psalm 104:7]) is used in Luke 8:24 for Christ "rebuking" "the wind and the raging waves."

Redemptive-Historical Progression and New Testament References

The theme of Psalm 104 is, "Praise the LORD for his manifold works in the creation, preservation, and re-creation of the world by his spirit." In the fullness of time Jesus was conceived by the Holy Spirit (Luke 1:35) and taught people about the Holy Spirit: first Nicodemus about being "born from above (John 3:3–8), next the apostles about being "baptized with the Holy Spirit" to equip the apostles for their task in spreading the kingdom of God (Acts 1:4–8). Next, move on to Acts 2, the day of Pentecost, possibly Paul's words about the new creation for which we wait patiently (Rom 8:22–25), and concluding with Rev 21:1–4, "a new heaven and a new earth" (for the outworking of this proposal, see "Sermon Exposition" below).

Sermon Theme, Goal, and Need

We formulated the textual theme as, "Praise the LORD for his manifold works in the creation, preservation, and re-creation of the world by his spirit." Since the New Testament does not contradict this theme but expands on it by more clearly revealing the person of the Holy Spirit as well as the resurrection from the dead and the new creation, the textual theme can function as the sermon theme if we capitalize "Spirit": *Praise the LORD for his manifold works in the creation, preservation, and re-creation of the world by his Spirit.*

By capitalizing "Spirit," the textual goal can also function as the sermon goal: *to persuade people to praise the LORD for his manifold works in the creation, preservation, and re-creation of the world by his Spirit.* This goal points to the need addressed in this sermon: we do not praise the LORD enough for his Spirit working in the creation, preservation, and re-creation of the world. The sermon introduction can illustrate this need in order to prepare people to hear this particular message.

Liturgy, Scripture Reading, and Sermon Outline

Psalm 104:35c–d can be used as the call to worship: the congregation reciting the personal, "Bless the LORD, O my soul" (v 35c), and the liturgist following with the communal, "Praise the LORD!" (v 35d).

To emphasize the personal nature of this psalm, a good reader could read the whole meditation (vv 1–35c) with the liturgist adding the last line, "Praise the LORD!" Or, one could read the psalm responsively, alternating paragraphs between the liturgist and the congregation: liturgist, vv 1–4; congregation, vv 5–9; liturgist, vv 10–13; congregation, vv 14–18; liturgist, vv 19–23; congregation, vv 24–26; liturgist, vv 27–30; congregation, vv 31–35.[57]

The sermon outline can follow the eight stanzas of the psalm (see p. 481 above) with additional move(s) to the New Testament. But since a nine-point sermon will seem overwhelming and stall the sermon, we can keep the sermon moving by compressing the six miracles of verses 5–30 into one main point. The result is the following sermon outline:

I. The great Creator of the Cosmos	vv 1–4
II. The LORD performs six miracles on earth	vv 5–30
A. The LORD created the earth and the deep	vv 5–9
B. The LORD provides water for all creatures	vv 10–13
C. The LORD provides food and shelter for all creatures	vv 14–18
D. The LORD made the moon and sun, darkness and light	vv 19–23
E. The LORD made the sea and its inhabitants	vv 24–26
F. The LORD's spirit controls life, death, and re-creation	vv 27–30
III. God's Spirit at work in New Testament times[58]	NT
IV. God's Spirit and the new creation	vv 31–35; NT

Sermon Exposition

When was the last time you praised God's Holy Spirit for a cool drink of water? When was the last time you praised the Holy Spirit for a nice warm shower?

The author of this psalm is concerned that he does not praise the LORD enough. Therefore he begins his meditation by encouraging himself and his fellow worshipers, "Bless the LORD, O my soul." To bless the LORD is to laud, to praise the LORD.[59] "My soul" is not just a part of me but refers to my whole being,[60] my

---

57. For a more complicated responsive reading involving three voices and the congregation, see *Psalms for All Seasons,* "Psalm 104," p. 653–55.

58. Tentative. Where the move(s) to the New Testament will be made is difficult to plot in advance; it will become clearer as one writes the sermon whether this move fits here or at the end of the sermon or both.

59. "To bless God is not to increase his power by the words of blessing, but it means to praise him and to give him glory for all his works of creation, as the following verses clearly show." A. Anderson, *Psalms 73–150,* 718. Cf. McCann, "Psalms," 1100, "Praise involves the acknowledgment of God's sovereignty and the commitment to live under God's rule (see vv 1–4, 33–34)."

60. "All the powers of one's being in their psychosomatic unity are invited to join in praising God." B. Anderson, *Out of the Depths,* 138.

life.[61] So he encourages himself and all the other worshipers[62] to praise the LORD with their whole being, with their whole life. He will end the psalm on the same note: "Bless the LORD, O my soul." This is followed by the command to all God's people, "Praise the LORD!"

Why do you suppose that the psalmist tells himself, "Bless the LORD, O my soul"? And why do you suppose he ends the psalm by commanding all God's people, "Praise the LORD!"? As will become clear in the psalm, he offers two basic reasons why we ought to praise the LORD more than we do: first, because of who the LORD is; and second, because of what the LORD through his Spirit has done, is doing, and will do in the future. He begins with who the LORD is.

The Great Creator of the Cosmos (vv 1–4)[63]

We ought to praise the LORD more than we do because of who the LORD is. Verse 1, "Bless the LORD, O my soul. O LORD my God, you are very great." "To say that God is great is to say, in effect, that God reigns supreme, for greatness is frequently associated with sovereignty."[64] Psalm 95:3 says, "The LORD is a great God, and a great King above all gods."

The LORD is so great that he cannot be described beyond being "very great."[65] He cannot be described in human terms. Therefore verses 1 and 2 move on to describe the LORD in picture language: "You are clothed with honor and majesty, wrapped in light as with a garment." "Honor and majesty" refer to royalty. Human kings were described with words like "honor and majesty."[66] The LORD, "clothed with honor and majesty," is king, but not an ordinary king. The LORD is King of the universe.[67]

61. "'My soul' . . . [will] have to be understood in the sense of 'my life': "O my life, praise Yahweh!'" Kraus, *Psalms 60–150*, 291.

62. "We interpret the first person not so much in individualistic terms, but as a signal indicating the state of affairs in the congregation. Every single member is called on to join in this hymn." Gerstenberger, *Psalms*, II, 225.

63. I insert the outline headings into the sermon exposition as a convenience to the reader. I don't think I would use these headings in preaching the sermon since they tend to interrupt the flow.

64. McCann, "Psalms," 1097, with references to Pss 47:2; 48:2; 95:3; and 96:4. Cf. Jacobson in deClaissé-Walford, Jacobson, and Tanner, *The Book of Psalms*, 774, "The themes of greatness, splendor, and majesty are also associated with God's fidelity, mercy, and passibility (cf. 34:4; 35:27; 40:17; 111:3; 145:5, etc.)."

65. "Very great" is a greatness which we as human beings "cannot comprehend or measure, which . . . [we] can only sense in action." Westermann, *The Living Psalms*, 249.

66. See Pss 21:5 and 45:4.

67. Cf. Ps 8:1, "O LORD, our Sovereign, how majestic is your name in all the earth! You have

Since the LORD is much greater than human kings, the psalmist continues his description of the LORD as being "wrapped in light as with a garment." This is the closest he can come to describing God: the picture of being "wrapped in light." No human being, no human king is "wrapped in light." But the LORD is "wrapped in light as with a garment."

The New Testament also uses this image of light. John writes, "God is light and in him there is no darkness at all" (1 John 1:5). And Paul says that God "dwells in unapproachable light, whom no one has ever seen or can see" (1 Tim 6:16). Though God is so great that he is and remains invisible, the radiant light reveals his glory.[68]

Verse 2 continues, "You stretch out the heavens like a tent." Seemingly without effort the LORD stretches out the heavens like a tent,[69] a canopy above the earth. The King of the universe, wrapped in light, dwells high above this canopy.

The ancients conceived of the universe as consisting of three levels: heaven above, the earth beneath heaven, and water under the earth. The Bible uses this worldview to proclaim its messages relevantly in that culture. For example, in the Ten Commandments we read: "You shall not make for yourself an idol, whether in the form of anything that is in heaven above, or that is on the earth beneath, or that is in the water under the earth" (Exod 20:4). Heaven above was considered to be the place where God dwells.

Verse 3 describes how and where the LORD constructed his dwelling place: "You set the beams of your chambers on the waters" (v 3a). "Chambers" in the Old Testament denoted an upper room,[70] a penthouse or loft we would say.[71] The great King constructed his own penthouse by setting its beams "on the waters" of the heavenly ocean above the dome of the sky (see Gen 1:6–8).[72] Those waters

---

set your glory above the heavens," and Ps 96:5–6, "All the gods of the peoples are idols, but the LORD made the heavens. Honor and majesty are before him. . . ."

68. "In comparing *the light*, with which he represents God as *arrayed*, to a garment, he [the psalmist] intimates, that though God is invisible, yet his glory is conspicuous enough." Calvin, *Commentary on the Book of Psalms*, IV, 145 (his emphases; I have added the first two commas).

69. "The word translated 'tent' (*yərî'â*) seems to mean more specifically the curtain of a tent, and by far the majority of its uses designate the curtain of the tabernacle (see Exod 26:2)." McCann, "Psalms," 1097.

70. "Chambers" "is often used to denote either a room in the upper storey of a large house, or a room on the flat roof of a house (cf. 1 Kings 17:19; 2 Kings 1:2; 4:10). In this verse it probably refers to the royal palace of Yahweh, which is founded on the waters above the firmament (Gen 1:7)." A. Anderson, *Psalms 73–150*, 719.

71. "Such chambers were atop Solomon's temple (1 Chron 28:11; 2 Chron 3:9) and are appropriate for God's heavenly dwelling." Williams, *Psalms 73–150*, 234.

72. "The modern scientific view of the world is different from that of the ancient Near East, which thought in quaint (to us) terms of an oil-rig structure miraculously fixed in the subterra-

provided the foundation for the beams of the Lord's dwelling. Thus the Lord's loft is above the chaotic waters. The message is that the King of the universe rules supreme over the menacing waters.

Though his dwelling place is far above the earth, the Lord himself is not considered to be far removed from the earth. Verse 3, "You make the clouds your chariot, you ride on the wings of the wind." The Canaanites called their god Baal the "rider of the clouds."[73] Not so, says our psalmist. The Lord is the one who makes the clouds his chariot, moving from place to place. "You ride on the wings of the wind." It's a way of saying that God is actively engaged with this world.

Verse 4 continues, "You make the winds your messengers, fire and flame your ministers." The winds and fire and flame describe a thunderstorm with lightning flashing forth. As King of the universe the Lord can use all so-called "natural forces" to accomplish his will. As Psalm 148:8 says, "Fire and hail, snow and frost, stormy wind fulfilling his command!"

What an awesome God we serve! He dwells high above the earth and yet is very much involved in this world. When mighty thunderstorms roll over us, we feel tiny and helpless. But the Lord can use those thunderstorms to fulfill his purposes. "Bless the Lord, O my soul. O Lord my God, you are very great."

The psalmist now moves to the second reason why we ought to praise the Lord more than we do. We ought to praise the Lord because of what the Lord through his Spirit has done, is doing, and will do in the future. The psalmist mentions six miracles the Lord performs on this earth.

The Lord Performs Six Miracles on Earth (vv 5–30)

The Lord Created the Earth and the Deep (vv 5–9)

The first of these miracles is that the Lord created this earth in such a way that it is stable and has plenty of water. Verses 5–6, "You set the earth on its foundations, so that it shall never be shaken. You cover it with the deep as with a garment; the waters stood above the mountains." The Lord set the earth firmly on its foun-

---

nean ocean. Yet modern man, to whom this psalm is ultimately given, is also meant to share in the psalmist's awe and trust as his response to the God who from his own viewpoint has fixed the planet earth in its orbit and made it capable of supporting life." Allen, *Psalms 101–150*, 33.

73. See p. 473 above. Berlin, "The Wisdom of Creation in Psalm 104," 77, observes that "similar imagery is in Deut 33:26; Isa 19:1; Ps 18:11 [10] = 2 Sam 22:11; and Ps 68:34, where God rides in the sky, on the clouds, or on the wind."

dations. It is stable. It shall never be moved or shaken.[74] Then he covered it with the deep, with the waters standing above the mountains. Genesis 1 tells us that in the beginning "the earth was formless and empty, darkness was over the surface of *the deep,* and the Spirit of God was hovering over the waters" (Gen 1:2, NIV). "The deep" (*təhôm*) is the chaotic ocean which covered the earth and prohibited any form of life. But the Spirit of God was also there in the beginning, "hovering over the waters."

The Canaanites believed that the deep was a god, Yamm. Not so, says our psalmist. It was the LORD who covered the earth with the deep. He was going to use the deep to bring forth life on earth. The LORD was in charge.

Verse 7, "At your rebuke they [the chaotic waters][75] flee; at the sound of your thunder they take to flight." God only has to speak a word and the deep waters flee in all directions. Verse 8, "They rose up to the mountains, ran down to the valleys to the place that you appointed for them." As the waters subsided "they flowed over the mountains" (NIV) and ran down the valleys as rivers heading for the seas, the place the LORD had assigned for them. Verse 9, "You set a boundary that they may not pass, so that they might not again cover the earth." The LORD is in complete control.[76] "The chaotic forces have been tamed . . . , and the earth is safe."[77] This is the first miracle for which we should praise the LORD. The LORD made the earth stable and supplied it with plenty of water which he controlled.

Today we can see even better the LORD's provision for a stable planet earth with plenty of water. The mean distance of the earth from the sun is about 93 million miles (150 million km). If the earth were closer to the sun, the oceans would boil off and there would be no water. If the earth were farther from the sun, the oceans would freeze. The LORD placed the orbit of planet earth at just the right distance from the sun so it can retain its water. "Praise the LORD, O my soul!"

74. "This is testimony to the trustworthiness of the creation that the Lord has wrought. Especially when this closing testimony is heard over against the earlier metaphorical language of the Lord establishing creation *on the waters* — that is, on a foundation that is inherently chaotic — the image emerges of the Lord taming the untrustworthy, random elements of chaos." Jacobson in deClaissé-Walford, Jacobson, and Tanner, *The Book of Psalms,* 775.

75. Bible versions and commentaries disagree on the subject of verse 7, the waters or the mountains and valleys. In context, the waters are clearly the subject. See, e.g., Fokkelman, *Major Poems of the Hebrew Bible,* II, 265, nn. 20, 21, and Hossfeld, *Psalms 3,* 51, with references to Ps 114:3, 5.

76. "He first made the waters cover the earth and then he made them recede; then he barred them from ever covering the earth again." Berlin, "The Wisdom of Creation in Psalm 104," 78. Cf. Alter, *Book of Psalms,* 363, "God is the agent controlling the waters, and His 'blast' (or 'rebuke') drives the waters back into their appointed bed."

77. McCann, "Psalms," 1098.

The LORD *Provides Water for All Creatures (vv 10–13)*

The second miracle for which we should praise the LORD is that he provides this water for all creatures.[78] Verses 10–11, "You make springs gush forth in the valleys; they flow between the hills, giving drink to every wild animal; the wild asses quench their thirst." The springs[79] that gush forth in the valleys result in "still waters" (Ps 23). Here every wild animal can drink its fill. The psalmist singles out the wild asses or donkeys.[80] They were "resistant to all domestication" and thus were "an image of unfettered freedom."[81] The LORD provides water for even the wildest creatures.

The LORD provides water also for birds. Verse 12, "By the streams the birds of the air have their habitation; they sing among the branches." Trees and shrubs grow along the banks of the streams. These trees provide habitation for the birds. "They sing among the branches" their praise to the great Creator.

The LORD provides water not only in the low-lying valleys but also in the hills and mountains. Verse 13, "From your lofty abode you water the mountains; the earth is satisfied with the fruit of your work." From his lofty "chambers on the waters" (v 3),[82] the LORD provides rain for the parched hills and mountains[83] until the earth is satisfied.[84] The hills in Israel are brown in the summer, but with the winter rains they turn a luscious green. Another miracle for which the LORD should be praised.[85]

When was the last time we praised the LORD for water? When we drank

78. "Instead of dominating the earth, these waters are now made to serve the creatures of God." A. Anderson, *Psalms 73–150,* 721.

79. "In Israelite thought, springs had their origin in the waters of the great abyss, so that the destructive chaos was utilized for the furthering of life." Ibid.

80. "Most of the wildlife mentioned by name is also found in Job 38–39. . . . It seems likely that this zoological taxonomy is part of a known list or catalog, of the type associated with scribal circles, that poets deployed for their own purposes." Berlin, "The Wisdom of Creation in Psalm 104," 78–79.

81. Alter, *Book of Psalms,* 364.

82. "From the celestial ocean flows the 'heavenly gift' of rain (v 13; on this conception cf. Gen 7:11; 8:2) and accomplishes the miracle of clothing the parched brown earth with welcome verdure." Weiser, *The Psalms,* 668.

83. "When the psalmist speaks here of 'the mountains,' he may have in mind, primarily, such things as the upland corn fields and the vineyards on the slopes." A. Anderson, *Psalms 73–150,* 721.

84. "The term *satisfied (śāba')* is a key term for the witness of this psalm (vv 13, 16, 28; reading it also in v 11 for *śābar;* cf. 103:5; 105:40). The word means to be full or sated, as after a feast." Jacobson in deClaissé-Walford, Jacobson, and Tanner, *The Book of Psalms,* 775.

85. "It is small wonder that in a land where drought, with consequent famine, was often a grim reality (cf. Jer 14:1–6), the provision of this life-giving water heads the list of the LORD's providential provision for his people." Davidson, *Vitality of Worship,* 340.

a glass of cool water? When we showered? When we washed our dishes or our clothes? When we watered our plants and gardens? Water keeps us alive on planet earth. "Praise the LORD, O my soul!"

The LORD Provides Food and Shelter for All Creatures (vv 14–18)

The psalm mentions a third miracle: the LORD provides food and shelter for all creatures. Verses 14–15, "You cause the grass to grow for the cattle, and plants for people to use, to bring forth food from the earth, and wine to gladden the human heart, oil to make the face shine, and bread to strengthen the human heart." The grass the LORD causes to grow is fodder for domestic animals. The plants the LORD causes to grow can be used by people to bring forth food from the earth. In contrast to animals, human beings can cultivate the earth and bring forth food. They can plant vineyards, olive trees, and wheat fields.[86] Thus they can produce "wine to gladden the human heart, oil to make the face shine, and bread to strengthen the human heart."[87]

Wine was used at mealtimes and feasts to "gladden the human heart." Olive oil (a moisturizer) was used both to protect the face and to make it shine. And bread was used to strengthen the human person. Even though these foods were the result of human cultivation, they were still gifts from God. And they covered more than the basic necessities of life. Calvin comments, "In these words we are taught that God not only provides for men's necessity, and bestows upon them as much as is sufficient for the ordinary purposes of life, but that in his goodness he deals still more bountifully with them by cheering their hearts with wine and oil."[88]

The psalmist then moves his sights north of Israel. Verses 16–18, "The trees

---

86. "It is not a picture of the beginning of the world but of the world as it exists for the psalmist in real time. So human agricultural products — wine, oil, and bread, signifying the three agricultural seasons and the basic provisions for life — are mentioned in the domain of the land." Berlin, "The Wisdom of Creation in Psalm 104," 80. Cf. v 21, "The young lions roar for their *prey*, seeking their food from God."

87. "The terms ['wine to gladden the human heart . . . , and bread to strengthen the human heart'] are parallel and so clearly brought into conjunction with each other. . . . These elements are presented as basic elements of life so that God's provision for human existence can be seen to incorporate both the daily sustenance of our lives and a more festive libation for our enjoyment and relaxation. When the Christian community later incorporated these same elements into its central ritual, it was not only because of their symbolic potential to represent body and blood but because they are what God had provided for human life. The elements of life become the elements of the church in its sacramental life." Miller, *Interpreting the Psalms*, 224. Miller's thought, though intriguing, is a bit of a stretch because Christ instituted the Lord's Supper in fulfillment of the Passover's unleavened bread and wine (Luke 22:19–20).

88. Calvin, *Commentary on the Book of Psalms*, IV, 155.

of the LORD are watered abundantly, the cedars of Lebanon that he planted [he likens the LORD to a gardener who planted the great cedars of Lebanon[89] and then watered them abundantly]. In them the birds build their nests; the stork has its home in the fir trees. The high mountains are for the wild goats; the rocks are a refuge for the coneys." Notice how the LORD provides space and shelter for all his creatures. "The birds build their *nests*" in the mighty cedars of Lebanon; "the stork has its *home* in the fir trees. The *high mountains*[90] are for the wild goats [the ibex]; the *rocks* are a refuge for the coneys [the rock badger]." Nothing is wasted. For every creature on earth the LORD provides food and shelter.[91] "Praise the LORD, O my soul!"

The LORD Made the Moon and Sun, Darkness and Light (vv 19–23)

The psalm moves on to a fourth miracle: the LORD made the moon and sun. The Canaanites worshiped the moon and sun as gods. Not so, says our psalmist. The LORD made the moon and sun to benefit both the wild animals and human beings. Verse 19, "You have made the moon to mark the seasons; the sun knows its time for setting." Israel used a lunar calendar in which the phases of the moon marked the months and holy days.[92] In Egypt the sun was revered as the creator god. The psalm mentions this so-called god not only in second place, after the moon, but also portrays the sun as an obedient servant of its Maker: "the sun knows its time for setting" (v 19).

Verses 20–23, "You make darkness, and it is night, when all the animals of the forest come creeping out. The young lions roar for their prey, seeking their food from God. When the sun rises, they withdraw and lie down in their dens. People go out to their work and to their labor until the evening." The LORD makes the darkness[93] as a time for the wild animals to hunt for their food. Strikingly, the

---

89. "The cedars of Lebanon especially are trees of the Lord, since it seemed such giants could have been planted only by him in the world's first days." Eaton, *Psalms*, 250.

90. "The high mountains: perhaps, the most inaccessible places which would normally be useless but God has made them the homes for wild goats, possibly the Nubian ibex. . . . This animal may rarely be seen by man but it is not beyond God's providential care." A. Anderson, *Psalms 73–150*, 722.

91. "The point of these verses [vv 14–18] lies in God's providence for these creatures, not on their creation as such (unlike Gen 1). . . . The OT doctrine of creation is not merely about the distant past (the 'beginning'); it is also about the Creator, who personally oversees the promotion of life and order." Broyles, *Psalms*, 399.

92. "The first day of each new month was considered holy. Thus the monthly 'new moon' was associated with the weekly Sabbath (see Isa 1:13; Col 2:16)." Williams, *Psalms 73–150*, 238.

93. "In the Egyptian hymn, by contrast, the night is the result of the god's departure with the sunset and is the hour of evil." Eaton, *Psalms*, 251.

young lions roaring for their prey is understood as their prayer to God: "seeking their food from God."[94]

When the sun rises, it is time for the lions to return to their dens and for people to go to their work. Lions and humans are natural enemies. In his wisdom God keeps them apart: the lions can do their hunting at night and people can do their work from morning "until evening." Then it's the turn of the lions again, followed the next day by humans. "There is plenty of room in God's 'house' for all God's creatures, humans and animals, to live together, sharing the hospitality of God's table."[95]

Finally the psalmist bursts into song. Verse 24, "O LORD, how manifold[96] are your works! In wisdom you have made them all; the earth is full of your creatures." The psalmist marvels at the variety and complexity of this world. The heavens, the earth, the sea, springs and streams, grass and plants, moon and sun, animals and people — "the LORD God made them all." And the LORD not only made all these creatures but he *sustains* them. "In *wisdom* you have made them all." "The psalm is not merely saying that the creator created well, but that the creator embedded a wise and trustworthy order into the very creation and creatures that God made."[97] "In *wisdom* you have made them all."

The New Testament echoes this theme but links this wisdom to Christ. John 1 says that all things came into being through Christ: "In the beginning was the Word, and the Word was with God, and the Word was God. He [Christ] was in the beginning with God. All things came into being through him, and without him not one thing came into being" (John 1:1–3). And Paul calls Christ "the power of God and the *wisdom of God*" (1 Cor 1:24). "The whole creation is a testimony to the wisdom of God, to the sensibility and order, to the skill and intelligence and practicality of the Lord."[98] "Praise the LORD, O my soul!"

The psalmist concludes verse 24 with "The *earth* is full of your creatures." But what about the *sea*? What about that menacing, chaotic sea with its sea monsters?

94. "The psalm understands the 'preying' of the lion as a kind of 'praying'. . . . The lion's kill is an answer to prayer in this portrayal of God's created order. . . . God's provision of food is extended throughout the natural world, but it incorporates the understanding of a food chain that pits animal against animal (cf. Job 38:39–41)." Miller, "The Poetry of Creation: Psalm 104," 98–99.

95. B. Anderson, *Out of the Depths*, 141.

96. "This does not mean an amount that can be reckoned numerically, though the adjective 'many' makes us think in terms of numbers. . . . What it means here is 'multifarious,' 'manifold' (as RSV): God's works in all their abundance are understood as having a potential beyond anything we can conceive." Westermann, *The Living Psalms*, 250.

97. Jacobson in deClaissé-Walford, Jacobson, and Tanner, *The Book of Psalms*, 776–77.

98. Miller, *Interpreting the Psalms*, 224.

The LORD Made the Sea and Its Inhabitants (vv 24–26)

This question brings our psalmist to his fifth miracle.[99] Verses 25–26, "Yonder is the sea, great and wide, creeping things innumerable are there, living things both small and great. There go the ships, and Leviathan that you formed to sport in it." The sea is filled with innumerable "living things both small and great," all created by the LORD. The sea is not chaotic. The LORD tamed the sea. "There go the ships" — merchant ships sailing the Mediterranean, perhaps also fishing boats.[100] Who could ask for a more peaceful picture? Yes, Leviathan, that great sea monster, is still there. But the LORD tamed it also. The LORD formed it merely to play in the sea.[101] Human vessels sailing on the sea and giant fish playing in it. The chaotic sea has become a picture of peaceful tranquility. "Praise the LORD, O my soul!"

The LORD's Spirit Controls Life, Death, and Re-Creation (vv 27–30)

But the sixth and final miracle is even more astounding. The LORD's spirit controls life, death, and re-creation. Verse 27, "These all [animals as well as humans; creatures on earth as well as creatures in the sea] look to you to give them their food in due season."[102] The "due season" indicates that God does not provide for his creatures continuously. "All earth's creatures . . . look in hope and expectation (*šābar*) to . . . [the LORD] for food as the lions do, at the time when it is due: grass in spring, grain in high summer, olives and grapes in the fall."[103]

---

99. "The poet weaves into his praise even the sea, traditional object of dread to the Israelite landlubber." Allen, *Psalms 101–150*, 34. Cf. McCann, "Psalms," 1098, "In the Canaanite view, the sea was a god who represented chaotic power. . . . The 'great' living thing (v 25) that resides in the sea is Leviathan (v 26), a version of the divine chaos-monster known in other ancient Near Eastern sources."

100. Fishing "would make a nice parallel with human agricultural endeavors. Human work and its products are celebrated in the psalm as part of creation." Berlin, "The Wisdom of Creation in Psalm 104," 80.

101. "Overturning the traditional depiction of Leviathan as an eminently fear-inspiring creature, the psalmist portrays God and Leviathan as playmates, rather than pitting them as mortal enemies, and in so doing has incorporated the sea monster into the fold of God's life-sustaining order." Brown, *Seeing the Psalms*, 161. Cf. Jacobson in deClaissé-Walford, Jacobson, and Tanner, *The Book of Psalms*, 777, "Leviathan is not a fearsome, mythic monster to be conquered, but is just another creature of the Lord — most likely understood here as the whale or the shark."

102. Cf. Psalm 145:15–16, "The eyes of all look to you, and you give them their food in due season. You open your hand, satisfying the desire of every living thing."

103. Goldingay, *Psalms*, III, 192. Cf. Brueggemann, *Texts for Preaching*, 331, "All creatures depend on God's generosity and live by a ration of God's daily bread. No creature has private resources for life, and none, not even humans, can store up power for life. Such power must be regularly and faithfully given by God's generosity."

Verses 28–29, "When you give[104] to them, they gather it up; when you open your hand, they are filled with good things. When you hide your face, they are dismayed; when you take away their breath, they die and return to their dust." Somehow the LORD is also involved in the death of his creatures. This is clear after the Fall into sin related in Genesis 3. God pronounced the death sentence on Adam and Eve: "You are dust, and to dust you shall return" (Gen 3:19).

When God's creatures die, he hides his face, as it were. He no longer turns his face toward them with blessing.[105] He hides his face. He is no longer present with them. This takes away "their breath," "their spirit," and they die, returning to dust. "God's presence let's life live. God's absence causes life to terminate."[106]

But then an astonishing miracle happens: verse 30, "When you send forth your spirit,[107] they are created; and you renew the face of the ground." When the LORD hides his face, his presence, he takes away his creatures' spirit. But when he sends forth his life-giving spirit,[108] "they are created." New creatures are created, a new generation is born. God's creating is a continuous process. It goes on even today when new generations of people and animals are born.[109] "All organic existence derives from the Creator's life force. In such simple language, even the birth of a lamb or the emergence of a butterfly is traced back directly to the Creator of all living things."[110]

---

104. "In the Hebrew text, the verbs refer to continuing actions. . . . ' When you give to them (not once but again and again), they gather it up (not one time but frequently)." B. Anderson, *Out of the Depths*, 143.

105. Cf. Numbers 6:24–26, "The LORD bless you and keep you; the LORD make his face to shine upon you. . . ."

106. Brueggemann, *Texts for Preaching*, 332. Brueggemann continues, "The theological claim expressed in this language is enormous. The world is not autonomous. Creation is not a self-starter. It depends always, daily, and immediately on God's attentive self-giving. . . . The text stands as a massive protest against all modernity, all mistaken autonomy, all the seductions of technical thinking that imagine we can have life on our own terms. . . . without reference to God's life-giving spirit."

107. Cf. Psalm 33:6, "By the word of the LORD the heavens were made, and all their host by the breath (*rûaḥ*) of his mouth."

108. "The rhythm of life and death and the appearance of new life is the relation between the 'breath' (*rûaḥ*) of creatures and the 'breath' (*rûaḥ*) of the LORD. The notion that what animates creatures is the life-bringing breath of God is behind these verses (see Gen 2:7)." Mays, *Psalms*, 335. Cf. McCann, "Psalms," 1099, "The breath of creatures is not identical to God's breath, but God is responsible for giving life to the creatures (see Gen 1:2; 2:7; Job 34:14–15; Ps 146:4)." For a detailed overview of the work of the LORD's spirit in the Old Testament, see Jiri Moskala, "The Holy Spirit in the Hebrew Scriptures," *JATS* 24, no. 2 (2013): 18–58.

109. "Creation is not just an event that occurred in the beginning, as in the Genesis creation story, but is God's continuing activity of sustaining creatures and holding everything in being. . . . The whole order of being is radically dependent on God, the Creator." B. Anderson, *Out of the Depths*, 143.

110. Westermann, *The Living Psalms*, 251.

Moreover, the psalmist adds, when the LORD sends forth his spirit, he renews "the face of the ground." After the summer drought, the LORD turns the brown hills around Jerusalem into a luscious green. He again causes "the grass to grow for the cattle, and plants for people to use, to bring forth food from the earth" (v 14). The LORD controls this annual cycle of vegetation dying and rising. And he controls the generational cycle of creatures dying and rising. It is all in the hands of the LORD.[111] There is a hint here that one day God through his Spirit will renew not just the "face of the ground" but the entire creation. Psalm 104 seeks to persuade all of us to praise the LORD who through his Spirit created all things, provides for all his creatures, and re-creates them. "Praise the LORD, O my soul!"

God's Spirit at Work in New Testament Times (NT)

In the fullness of time God's Holy Spirit worked an even greater miracle, the conception of God's Son in the womb of Mary. We read in Luke 1 that the angel said to Mary, "The Holy Spirit will come upon you, and the power of the Most High will overshadow you; therefore the child to be born will be holy; he will be called Son of God" (Luke 1:35).

When Jesus grew up he taught people about God's life-giving Spirit. Jesus said to Nicodemus, "Very truly, I tell you, no one can see the kingdom of God without being born from above." When Nicodemus questioned how anyone can be born after having grown old, Jesus explained, "Very truly, I tell you, no one can enter the kingdom of God without being born of water and *Spirit*. . . . The wind blows where it chooses, and you hear the sound of it, but you do not know where it comes from or where it goes. So it is with everyone who is born of the Spirit" (John 3:3-8). We can be born again through God's life-giving Spirit. When God sends forth his Spirit, we are re-created. When God sends forth his Spirit, the Spirit breathes new life into us: we enter the eternal kingdom of God.

In Acts 1 we read more about the work of God's Spirit. Luke writes, "After his suffering he [Jesus] presented himself alive[112] to them [the apostles] by many convincing proofs, appearing to them during forty days and speaking about the kingdom of God. While staying with them, he ordered them not to leave Jeru-

---

111. A Reformed confession, the Heidelberg Catechism, Lord's Day 10, calls this control of the LORD over all things "God's providence." It explains, "Providence is the almighty and ever present power of God by which he upholds, as with his hand, heaven and earth and all creatures, and so rules them that leaf and blade, rain and drought, fruitful and lean years, food and drink, health and sickness, prosperity and poverty — all things, in fact, come to us not by chance but from his fatherly hand."

112. One could perhaps add that God through his Spirit raised Jesus from the dead (e.g., Rom 8:11; Eph 1:20; Col 2:12), but the focus this Sunday is not on Easter but on Pentecost.

salem, but to wait there for the promise of the Father. 'This,' he said, 'is what you have heard from me; for John baptized with water, but you will be baptized with the Holy Spirit not many days from now'" (Acts 1:3–5). The Holy Spirit would equip the apostles for their task in and for the kingdom of God. As God's spirit had equipped prophets and kings for their task in the Old Testament, so God's Spirit would equip the apostles for their task. Jesus said, "You will receive power when the Holy Spirit has come upon you; and you will be my witnesses in Jerusalem, in all Judea and Samaria, and to the ends of the earth" (Acts 1:8).

That day arrived on Pentecost. We read in Acts 2: "When the day of Pentecost had come, they were all together in one place. And suddenly from heaven there came a sound like the rush of a violent wind, and it filled the entire house where they were sitting. Divided tongues, as of fire, appeared among them, and a tongue rested on each of them. All of them were filled with the Holy Spirit and began to speak in other languages, as the Spirit gave them ability" (Acts 2:1–4).

Today we celebrate Pentecost, the outpouring of the Holy Spirit, the birthday of the Christian church. The gift of the Holy Spirit enabled the apostles to turn "the world upside down" (Acts 17:6). Because of the outpouring of the Holy Spirit, we are members of the church today, members of God's household. God's Spirit not only gave us life and sustained that life. God's Spirit also re-created us as special children of God,[113] citizens of the kingdom of God. "Praise the LORD, O my soul!"

God's Spirit and the New Creation (vv 30–35; NT)

But the outpouring of the Holy Spirit assures us of another pinnacle still to come. Psalm 104:30 says, "When you send forth your spirit, they are created; and you renew the face of the *ground*." After the Fall into sin God cursed the ground: to the man God said, "Cursed is the ground because of you; in toil you shall eat of it all the days of your life; thorns and thistles it shall bring forth for you. . . . By the sweat of your face you shall eat bread until you return to the ground, for out of it you were taken; you are dust, and to dust you shall return" (Gen 3:17–19). But Psalm 104 declares that God's spirit can "*renew the face of the ground*."[114] The New

---

113. "The inspiration of the Holy Spirit consummates our life as creatures and brings us to the true existence for which we are created. We are the creation of God twice over. Note that Psalm 51:10 uses the verbs of verse 30, 'create/renew,' to speak of God's regeneration of the sinner. In Ezekiel's vision of the valley of the dry bones the restoration of the people of God is portrayed as re-creation by the Spirit of God (Ezek 37:1–14). The Spirit of God is the source of life in every sense that the word 'life' can have." Mays, *Psalms,* 337.

114. "The thought seems to be of the continuing acts of Creation seen in the new seasons and generations, but the words express at least the basis for the greater biblical hope of the New Creation (Isa 65:17; 66:22; 2 Pet 3:13; Rev 21:1)." Eaton, *Psalms,* 251. Cf. Virgil P. Howard, "Psalm

Testament confirms this on a grand scale. Paul writes in Romans 8, "We know that the whole creation has been groaning in labor pains until now; and not only the creation, but we ourselves, *who have the first fruits of the Spirit,* groan inwardly while we wait for adoption, the redemption of our bodies. For in hope we were saved. Now hope that is seen is not hope. For who hopes for what is seen? But if we hope for what we do not see, we wait for it with patience" (Rom 8:22–25). What is it that we wait for with patience?

God's Spirit (Rev 3:22) showed John how this Spirit will finally "renew the face of the ground": "Then I saw *a new heaven and a new earth;* for the first heaven and the first earth had passed away, and the sea [chaos] was no more. And I saw the holy city, the new Jerusalem, coming down out of heaven from God, prepared as a bride adorned for her husband. And I heard a loud voice from the throne saying, 'See, the home of God is among mortals. He will dwell with them as their God; they will be his peoples, and God himself will be with them; he will wipe every tear from their eyes. *Death will be no more;* mourning and crying and pain will be no more, for the first things have passed away" (Rev 21:1–4). That is how God's Spirit will finally "renew the face of the ground." What a glorious future awaits God's people! "Praise the LORD, O my soul!"

Psalm 104 concludes with a prayer. Verse 31, "May the glory of the LORD endure forever; may the LORD rejoice in his works."[115] The "glory of the LORD" is "the manifestation of the divine presence that fills the world. . . . The psalmist hopes that the divine presence will remain in the world and that God will continue to approve of his creation, thereby guaranteeing its continued existence."[116] The prayer that the LORD may "rejoice in his works" reflects the original creation account: "God saw everything that he had made, and indeed, it was very good" (Gen 1:31). God rejoiced in his creation then, and the prayer is that God may continue to rejoice in his creation.[117]

In verse 32 the psalmist describes a final time how awesome the LORD is. He is the one "who looks on the earth and it trembles, who touches the mountains

104," *Int* 46, no. 2 (1992): 179, "Because it is God's spirit-breath that goes forth, there can be creation and re-creation (v 30a, b), new creation, transformed creation. Because God rejoices in the divine works, the time can be envisioned when sin and wickedness will be no more (v 35)."

115. The "reference to Yhwh's 'works' (*ma'ăśê;* cf. v 24; also v 13; and the mother verb *'āśâ* in vv 4, 19, 24) suggest that the splendor is the way Yhwh's greatness and power are reflected and demonstrated in the acts the psalm has described, past and present (cf. 19:1 [2]), and the honor that should there be given to Yhwh." Goldingay, *Psalms,* III, 194.

116. Berlin, "The Wisdom of Creation in Psalm 104," 82. Cf. A. Anderson, *Psalms 73–150,* 724.

117. "We often egocentrically assume the earth is at our disposal for our enhancement, but here we learn that it gives God pleasure. God is not a detached divine clockmaker who winds up his handiwork and lets it go on its own." Broyles, *Psalms,* 400.

and they smoke." Just one look from the LORD and an earthquake takes place. Just one touch and a volcanic eruption occurs. It reminds one of Mount Sinai where the LORD revealed his amazing power to Israel: "Now Mount Sinai was wrapped in smoke, because the LORD had descended upon it in fire; the smoke went up like the smoke of a kiln, while the whole mountain shook violently." The so-called natural disasters such as earthquakes and volcanic eruptions reveal the LORD's "divine supremacy."[118]

For his part, the psalmist declares, verses 33–34, "I will sing to the LORD as long as I live; I will sing praise to my God while I have being. May my meditation be pleasing to him, for I rejoice in the LORD." "The psalmist who sought the Lord's rejoicing and celebration (*śāmah*) in all 'his works' now declares that he . . . will rejoice and celebrate (*śāmah*) in the Lord."[119]

Verse 35 may surprise us. The psalmist prays, "Let sinners be consumed from the earth, and let the wicked be no more." This imprecatory prayer seems to sound a jarring note in an otherwise joyful psalm. But this prayer fits right in. The psalmist is aware that not everything on earth is joyful and harmonious. There are human beings who do not fit into God's harmonious world, who do not praise him for his awesome creation.[120] "There are those who challenge the authority of the creator God, 'the sinners' and 'the wicked'. . . . They are the fly in the ointment of creation. They have no proper place in a world which exists to praise God."[121] As Psalm 1 concluded, "the way of the wicked will perish." Hitler with his concentration camps and final solution was a blight on God's harmonious creation. Today ISIS with its terror and glorification of beheadings is a blight on God's creation. In Nigeria, Boko Haram has kidnapped hundreds of children. As I write this, the Taliban has murdered 146 people, mostly school children, in Pakistan. Lord, "let sinners be consumed from the earth, and let the wicked be no more." Better yet, as you once turned the persecutor Saul into the missionary Paul, let your Spirit convert evildoers into followers of Jesus (Matt 5:44). Verse 35 is a prayer for a future without evil. "Here there radiates faith in a new creation, a world freed from guilt and failure."[122]

---

118. "V 32 continues the tribute to the manifested glory of the Creator; the quaking and smoking at his manifestation denote his divine supremacy (18:7f.; 97:2f.; 144:5)." Eaton, *Psalms*, 252. Cf. v 4, "You make the winds your messengers, fire and flame your ministers." See also Amos 9:5.

119. Miller, "The Poetry of Creation: Psalm 104," 94.

120. "For human beings who turn away from God, do not praise him, but live conscious only of self and in self-reliance there is no longer room in the vast realm of joy, order, and dependence directed to God." Kraus, *Psalms 60–150*, 304.

121. Davidson, *Vitality of Worship*, 341.

122. Kraus, *Psalms 60–150*, 304. Cf. Rev 21:26–27, "People will bring into it [the new Jerusalem] the glory and the honor of the nations. But nothing unclean will enter it, nor anyone who practices abomination or falsehood, but only those who are written in the Lamb's book of life."

The psalm ends as it began, "Bless the LORD, O my soul." For good measure it adds the command for all people, "Praise the LORD!" We are to praise the LORD in our whole life for the wonderful works we see in his creation. But even more we ought to praise the LORD himself for who he is: our Creator, our Sustainer, and our Re-Creator.[123]

Prayer[124]

God of majesty, we are constantly surrounded by your gifts
　　and touched by your grace;
our words of praise do not approach the wonders of your love.
Send forth your Holy Spirit, that came in fullness at Pentecost
　　that our lives may be refreshed
　　and the whole world may be renewed,
in Jesus Christ our Lord. Amen.

Song[125]

1O worship the King all glorious above,
　　O gratefully sing his power and his love:
our shield and defender, the Ancient of Days,
　　pavilioned in splendor and girded with praise.

2O tell of his might and sing of his grace,
　　whose robe is the light, whose canopy space.
His chariots of wrath the deep thunderclouds form,
　　and dark is his path on the wings of the storm.

3Your bountiful care, what tongue can recite?
　　It breathes in the air, it shines in the light;
it streams from the hills, it descends to the plain,
　　and sweetly distills in the dew and the rain.

4Frail children of dust, and feeble as frail,
　　In you do we trust, nor find you to fail.
Your mercies, how tender, how firm to the end,
　　our Maker, Defender, Redeemer, and Friend!

123. "It is significant that while the psalm takes considerable delight in Yahweh's creation, it prescribes the primary object of our rejoicing to be the LORD himself." Broyles, *Psalms*, 401.

124. John Witvliet, *The Biblical Psalms in Christian Worship*, 75–76.

125. Robert Grant, 1833. Public Domain. *Psalter Hymnal* (1987), # 428; *Psalms for All Seasons*, # 104F; *Lift Up Your Hearts*, # 2.

Psalm 104 (103)

5O measureless Might, unchangeable Love,
   whom angels delight to worship above!
Your ransomed creation, with glory ablaze,
   in true adoration shall sing to your praise!

CHAPTER 22

"O Lord . . . , How Majestic Is Your Name in All the Earth!"

Psalm 8[1]

The Revised Common Lectionary, Year A, assigns Psalm 8 for reading on Trinity Sunday in response to the "First Lesson: Genesis 1:1–2:2a." There is indeed a close connection between the creation hymn Psalm 8 and the creation narratives of Genesis 1 and 2. Samuel Terrien well describes this popular psalm: "In its concise style and compact prosody, Psalm 8 proves itself to be one of the greatest poems of the Hebrew hymnal. It is a song to be chanted by those who truly rejoice over the Creator of nature and humankind. Yet it is also a hymn that is aware of the enigma of evil in nature and history."[2] In preaching Christ from Psalm 8 we face the challenge of coming to terms with its original intention as a hymn in praise of God the Creator and the New Testament use of the Greek (LXX) translation which allows it to be understood as a hymn in praise of Christ.[3]

Text and Context

Psalm 8 is a literary unit as indicated by the inclusio of verses 1 and 9, "O Lord, our Sovereign, how majestic is your name in all the earth!" and a new superscription for Psalm 9. As a literary unit, therefore, Psalm 8 is a proper preaching text.

The context of Psalm 8 is first of all its neighboring psalms. For example,

---

1. I will be using the NRSV verse references. For the Hebrew verse references, add 1 since the Hebrew counts the superscription as verse 1.

2. Terrien, *The Psalms,* 132.

3. See the informative article by Susan Gillingham, "Psalm 8 Through the Looking Glass: Reception History of a Multi-Faceted Psalm," in *Diachronic and Synchronic: Reading the Psalms in Real Time: Proceedings of the Baylor Symposium on the Book of Psalms,* ed. Joel S. Burnett, W. H. Bellinger, Jr., and W. Dennis Tucker, Jr. (New York: T. & T. Clark, 2007), pp. 167–96.

Psalm 7:17 ends with, "I will . . . sing praise to *the name of the* LORD, the Most High," while Psalm 8 begins with, "O LORD, our Sovereign, how majestic is *your name* in all the earth!"[4] Interestingly, the editors of the Psalter have placed Psalm 8 exactly in the middle of ten laments, five laments (64 poetic lines) before it (Pss 3–7)[5] and five (64 poetic lines) after it (Pss 9–13).[6] With this central position of Psalm 8 in the midst of laments the editors underscore that even in the midst of our sufferings on this earth we can still praise the LORD: "O LORD, our Sovereign, how majestic is your name in all the earth!" (vv 1, 9).[7]

Moreover, as Marvin Tate points out, "Regardless of the exact locale of the psalm, it seems to presuppose a context of stress and is designed to bolster faith in God on the part of the community of those committed to Yahweh. . . . Psalms 3–7 reflect distress, oppression, and dependence upon Yahweh for help. The same is true of Psalms 11–14."[8] God's people can trust that their sovereign LORD is able to help them in their distress.

We should also observe that "Psalm 8 moves away from the individualism of 3–7 with the word *our* ['our sovereign'], while its cosmic, prophetic scope . . . hark back to Psalm 2, which displays the same features."[9] In other words, Psalm 8 is not so much about the LORD's relationship to an individual as it is to all human beings.

---

4. "The obvious link between Ps 7:18 and Ps 8:2 [MT verse references] is the term *šēm*, 'name,' which in Psalms 3–13 occurs in 5:12; 7:18; 8:2, 10; 9:3, 11 with reference to YHWH." Carl J. Bosma, "Beyond 'Singers and Syntax': Theological and Canonical Reflections on Psalm 8," in *Tradition and Innovation in Biblical Interpretation,* ed. W. Th. Van Peursen and J. W. Dyk (Leiden: Brill, 2011; pp. 69–91), 81.

5. "We cannot miss its [Psalm 8's] echoes of Psalms 3–7. The remembering, or 'being mindful,' of 6:5, the glory of 3:3, the avenger of 7:3–5, and the enemies in all five psalms, are here in this one as well." Wilcock, *Message of Psalms 1–72,* 38.

6. John H. Stek, *The NIV Study Bible,* 2011 ed., Psalm 8 n. This assumes that Psalm 11 is classified as a lament (see Ps 11:3). Cf. Miller, *The Way of the Lord,* 232, "Ps 8 belongs with a group of psalms that begins with Ps 3 — after the introduction to the Psalter in Pss 1 and 2 — and concludes with Ps 14." See further Bosma, "Beyond 'Singers and Syntax,'" 77–86.

7. Cf. McCann, "Psalms," 712–13, "The movement from Psalms 3–7 to Psalm 8 suggests at least that the royal status and vocation of humanity are not diminished by suffering." Cf. Miller, *The Way of the Lord,* 232, "Psalm 8 thus makes its claim about the royal nature of the human, the godlike character of human existence, in the midst of quite other voices who cry out in the face of oppression, sickness, and suffering."

8. Marvin E. Tate, "An Exposition of Psalm 8," *PRSt* 28, no. 4 (2001; pp. 343–59): 346. Cf. Hubert James Keener, *The Canonical Exegesis of the Eighth Psalm: YHWH's Maintenance of the Created Order through Divine Intervention* (Winona Lake, IN: Eisenbrauns, 2013), 71, "As the center of the triptych of Pss 7–9/10, Psalm 8 reminds the reader why she can expect God to intervene on her behalf: Because YHWH shows his name to be majestic in all the earth by maintaining the created order."

9. Wilcock, *Message of Psalms 1–72,* 38.

In its broadest Old Testament context, we note further that the author of this creation hymn was acquainted with the creation stories of Genesis 1 and 2. He acknowledges the LORD as the sovereign Creator of the heavens, specifically the moon and stars: "When I look at your heavens, the work of your fingers, the moon and the stars that you have established" (Ps 8:3; cf. Gen 1:16, which also includes the sun). As to human beings, he states, "You have given them dominion over the works of your hands" (Ps 8:6; cf. Gen 1:26, 28 for the same thought but a different Hebrew word for "dominion"). The dominion over "all sheep and oxen, and also the beasts of the field, the birds of the air, and the fish of the sea, whatever passes along the paths of the seas" (Ps 8:7-8) seems to follow more closely the taxonomy of animals listed in Genesis 2 than in Genesis 1.[10]

Finally, Psalm 8:2 speaks of the LORD's "foes" and "the enemy and the avenger." This reference may suggest that the author does not have in mind the pristine, pre-fall world of Genesis 1 and 2 but the post-fall world of Genesis 3 and following. The point is "that Psalm 8 emphasizes the fact that even in a corrupt and rebellious world YHWH still keeps humans in a position of responsible, delegated 'lordship' over the creation."[11]

Literary Interpretation

Psalm 8 is usually identified as a hymn, which makes it the first hymn of praise in the Psalter. But it is somewhat different from the other hymns in the Psalter in that it does not have the usual call to "Praise the LORD." Instead it begins and ends with the direct praise of the LORD: "O LORD, our Sovereign, how majestic is your name in all the earth!" In fact, "It is the only hymn in the Old Testament composed completely as direct address to God."[12] "More precisely, it may be classified as "a descriptive praise psalm,"[13] "a psalm of creation,"[14] or "a hymn of creation praise."[15]

---

10. See Richard Whitekettle, "Taming the Shrew, Shrike, and Shrimp: The Form and Function of Zoological Classification in Psalm 8," *JBL* 125, no. 4 (2006; pp. 749-95): 754-56.

11. Bosma, "Beyond 'Singers and Syntax,'" 76.

12. Mays, *Psalms,* 65.

13. Claus Westermann, *Praise of God in the Psalms,* trans. Keith R. Crim (Richmond, VA: John Knox, 1965), 123.

14. Craigie, *Psalms 1-50,* 106. Craigie adds that "a number of scholars have noted the apparent mixture of forms within the psalm, claiming the presence of hymnic material, wisdom material and portions similar to the lament." Cf. A. Anderson, *Psalms 1-72,* 100, "Psalm of Creation."

15. Van Gemeren, *Psalms,* 137.

We shall examine in turn this psalm's parallelisms, imagery, repetition of keywords, and its structure.

Parallelisms

To the leader: according to The Gittith. A Psalm of David.

₁O LORD, our Sovereign,	A
how majestic is your name in all the earth!	+ A'
You have set your glory above the heavens.	A
₂Out of the mouths of babes and infants	B
you have founded a bulwark because of your foes,	+ B'
to silence the enemy and the avenger.	+ B''
₃When I look at your heavens, the work of your fingers,	A
the moon and the stars that you have established;	+ A'
₄what are human beings that you are mindful of them,[16]	− B
mortals that you care for them?[17]	+− B'
₅Yet you have made them a little lower than God,	A
and crowned them with glory and honor.[18]	+ A'
₆You have given them dominion over the works of your hands;	+ A''
you have put all things under their feet,	+ A'''
₇all sheep and oxen,	+ A''''
and also the beasts of the field,	+ A'''''
₈the birds of the air, and the fish of the sea,	+ A''''''
whatever passes along the paths of the seas.	+ A'''''''
₉O LORD, our Sovereign,	A
how majestic is your name in all the earth!	+ A'

16. Compared to the heavens (v 3) the rhetorical question "what are human beings?" is antithetic parallelism which v 4b advances (+−B'). Cf. A. Anderson, *Psalms 1–72*, 102, "'What' (*mâ*) forms an antithesis to 'how' (*mâ*) in verse 1, and the point of contrast is the majesty and power of God, and the relative littleness of man (cf. 144:3)."

17. Cf. Goldingay, *Psalms*, I, 158. "There is little difference between the implications of 'mortal' and 'human being' ('*ĕnôš, ben-'ādām*); both hint at human beings in their weakness. But 'attend to' (*pāqad*) takes further 'be mindful of' (*zākar*). God first thinks, then acts." Therefore advancing antithetic parallelism.

18. "Parallelism of specification and sequentiality." Alter, *Art of Biblical Poetry*, 120.

Psalm 8 begins and ends with advancing parallelism (vv 1 and 9). Verse 2 shows three lines of advancing, therefore, climactic parallelism. Verse 3 exhibits advancing parallelism while verse 4 has advancing antithetic parallelism. Verses 5–8 contribute a lengthy climactic parallelism.

Imagery

Psalm 8 contains several possible metaphors that make proper interpretation difficult. At this point it is too early in our study to decide on the right interpretation, so we shall just list our options here and make decisions later.

Particularly difficult is verse 2, "Out of the mouths of *babes and infants* you have founded *a bulwark* because of your *foes*, to silence the *enemy* and the *avenger*." The "babes and infants" have been understood both literally and metaphorically, which opens the way to a variety of interpretations. Hubert Keener lists six identifications scholars have proposed: "1) the children of 'Tochter Zion,' 2) Israelite children . . . , 3) children in general, 4) the psalmist himself, or a poetic representation of either, 5) all human beings, or 6) weak and humble human beings."[19] Keener judges that "the last of these interpretations is the most compelling."[20]

The "babes and infants" silence "the enemy and the avenger." The enemies can be understood literally, for example, as the Babylonians who captured Israel.[21] But they can also be understood as metaphors. In contrast to the children who "symbolize human weakness and helplessness . . . , the enemies symbolize human strength and self assertiveness: they don't recognize the power of the Name of God."[22] Metaphorically, the enemy can also be understood as the chaos God battled in ordering the world in the beginning and its continuing attempt to sow disorder. For example, Eaton comments, "The context suggests that these 'babes' are the weak and humble worshippers, whose inadequate singing of God's glory is yet used by him to still the avenger. So long as they sing, the chaos is silenced, the meaninglessness repulsed."[23]

---

19. Keener, *Canonical Exegesis*, 55.

20. Ibid., 55–56. I think a good rule of thumb is to use literal rather than figurative interpretation unless the literal makes no sense.

21. E.g., Wenceslaus Mkeni Urassa, *Psalm 8 and Its Christological Re-Interpretations in the New Testament Context: An Inter-Contextual Study in Biblical Hermeneutics* (Frankfurt am Main: Peter Lang, 1998), 48: "These children . . . represent the ever growing future generations of Israel before whom their enemies' plans are confounded (cf. Isa 12:1–6, Jer 31:35, Dan 7–12)."

22. Ibid. Waltke, *Psalms as Christian Worship,* 257, calls "infants and children a hyperbolic metaphor for people who depend totally upon him [the LORD]."

23. Eaton, *The Psalms,* 81. Cf. Tate, "Exposition of Psalm 8," *PRSt* 28, no. 4 (2001): 351, "We

"When I look at your heavens" (v 3), "the *heavens (šāmāyim)* designates the space above the earth, specifically what the ancients thought of as a visual dome, *rāqiaʿ* (see Gen 1:6; Ps 19:1). In their phenomenal world they conceptualized the blue sky as water being held up by the *rāqiaʿ*."[24] The heavens as "the work of your fingers" is an anthropomorphic metaphor, even more fine-tuned than "the works of your hands" in verse 6.

In verse 5, "you have *crowned* them with glory and honor," "the governing Hebrew verb here means 'adorn,' a figurative usage derived from *ʿăṭārâ*, a 'coronet.' In biblical times, this was worn as a sign of distinction and high rank, an emblem of nobility."[25] "The picture is one familiar in the world of the psalmist, that of the installation of a vassal king by the ruler of an empire as regent over certain territory that belongs to the suzerain. The vassal's authority is delegated; his rule occurs within the reign of his Lord, whose policy guides his decision and whose purpose sets his goals."[26] Verse 6 uses two metaphors, "You have given them dominion over the works of your hands [anthropomorphism]; you have put all things under their feet [metaphor]." "To be 'put under foot' . . . signifies ownership and / or control."[27]

Repetition of Keywords

The first keyword we should mention is the little word "all" (*kol*), which occurs in verses 1, 6, 7, and 9. Robert Alter notes, "The Hebrew says specifically 'all' the earth [vv 1 and 9], thus framing the whole poem with two symmetrical 'all's,' and that monosyllable, a mere grammatical particle, becomes the chief thematic keyword of the psalm. His dominion is over all, heaven and earth, angels and men and creatures of the field and air and sea, and He places 'all' at the feet of man."[28]

The word "all" is also repeated in verses 6 and 7: "You have given them

---

may take 'babes and infants' . . . as a metaphor for the weak and inherently helpless condition of human beings and think of the powerful words that come through such weak channels of communication: words of petition for divine deliverance, praise, prophecy, and teaching."

24. Waltke, *Psalms as Christian Worship*, 261.

25. Sarna, *On the Book of Psalms*, 64.

26. Mays, *Preaching and Teaching the Psalms*, 103.

27. Tate, "Exposition of Psalm 8," *PRSt* 28, no. 4 (2001): 356. Cf. Craigie, *Psalms 1–50*, 349, "The metaphor of subjugation, 'beneath our feet,' arose from the practice and artistic symbolism of victory, wherein a victor stood with his foot on the neck of the conquered foe." See Josh 10:24 and Ps 110:1.

28. Alter, *Art of Biblical Poetry*, 119.

dominion over the works of your hands; you have put *all* things under their feet, *all* sheep and oxen. . . ." McCann comments, "The 'allness' of God's majesty is given by God to humanity (vv 6–7). The repetition of 'all' in verses 6–7 affects how we hear the refrain when it recurs in verse 9. Verse 9 is an exact verbal repetition of verse 1, but the sense now is different precisely because the psalmist has told us that the majesty of God in 'all the earth' includes the glory and dominion of humanity. The identity of God and the identity of humanity are inseparable. The boundaries of the psalm must be held together with the center."[29]

A second repeated keyword is "how" or "what" (*mâ*) in verses 1, 4, and 9.

How majestic is your name in all the earth! (v 1)
What are human beings that you are mindful of them? (v 4)
How majestic is your name in all the earth! (v 9)

The rhetorical question in verse 4, "'what' (*mâ*) forms an antithesis to 'how' (*mâ*) in verse 1, and the point of contrast is the majesty and power of God, and the relative littleness of man (cf. 144:3)."[30]

A third repetition we should note are the five synonyms for royal qualities: "glorious" (*'addîr;* vv 1a and 9); "majesty" (*hôd;* v 1b); "strength" (*'oz;* v 2a); "glory and honor" (*kābôd wəhādār;* v 5b). "All of these are strong words indicating strength, power, and glory associated with God as King, Creator, and Divine Warrior."[31] But God as King has seen fit to confer these royal qualities of glory and honor on human beings (v 5b).

Structure

To discern the structure of Psalm 8, we can begin by comparing this psalm with the typical pattern of biblical hymns. We noted in Chapter 1 above, p. 11, that hymns consist of most of the following elements:

1) A call to praise the LORD	Ps 8:1ab, direct praise
2) Transition (*kî,* for, because)	Ps 8:3, translated "when"
3) Reasons why the LORD is to be praised	Ps 8:1c–2, 3–8
4) Conclusion: Praise the LORD!	Ps 8:9, direct praise

29. McCann, *Theological Introduction,* 58.
30. A. Anderson, *Psalms 1–72,* 102.
31. Tate, "Exposition of Psalm 8," *PRSt* 28, no. 4 (2001): 348.

As can be seen, the psalm has the typical elements of hymns except for the opening and closing calls to praise which Psalm 8 offers directly to the LORD.

Biblical scholars are not agreed on the precise structure of this psalm. Most see it as an introduction, with four strophes, and a conclusion. For example, Terrien proposes:

> Prelude: The Marvel of the Name (v 1ab)
>   Strophe I: The Majesty of God (vv 1c–2)
>   Strophe II: The Fragility of Man (vv 3–4)
>   Strophe III: The Greatness of Man (vv 5–6)
>   Strophe IV: The Service of Animals (vv 7–8)
> Postlude: The Marvel of the Name (v 9)[32]

The very center of the psalm is verse 4, the question, "what are human beings . . . ?" "This literary device — of placing a key thematic line at the very center of the psalm — was frequently used."[33] In this case it introduces a main idea of the psalm. "Thus," as Tate points out, "vv 4 and 5 form the central point of the psalm. The balanced poetic lines in vv 4 and 5 stand out in the middle of the psalm. Verse 5 is connected to v 4 by the unusual appearance in poetry of the *waw*-conjunction with an imperfect verb form at the beginning of v 5, which emphasizes the verse. Further, the chiastic structure of v 5 tends to make it the focal point of the psalm:

> A 'you have made him lack'
> B 'a little from *'ĕlohîm*'
> B 'with glory and honor'
> A 'you have crowned him.'"[34]

Being aware of this center will help us later in formulating the theme.

32. Terrien, *The Psalms*, 126. I have adjusted the verse references from the MT to reflect the NRSV/NIV. Fokkelman, *Major Poems*, II, 69, suggests within the inclusio (vv 1ab, 9) the same four strophes (vv 1c–2; 3–4; 5–6; 7–8) forming a "concentric ABC–C'B'A' pattern." For more detailed structural analyses, see, e.g., Bosma, "Beyond 'Singers and Syntax,'" 69–77, and Keener, *Canonical Exegesis*, 47–59.

33. Stek, *NIV Study Bible*, Psalms 8:4 n. and 6:6 n.

34. Tate, "Exposition of Psalm 8," *PRSt* 28, no. 4 (2001): 348. Cf. Alter, *Art of Biblical Poetry*, 120, "At the exact thematic center and in the fifth of the poem's ten lines, semantic movement is slowed to allow for the strong, stately emphasis of virtual synonymity, noun for noun and verb for verb in the same syntactical order: 'What is man that You should note him, / human creature, that You pay him heed?'"

Theocentric Interpretation

Psalm 8 is best known for its question, "What is man?" Therefore it might be tempting to focus the sermon on the answer to that question. But the focus of this psalm is not humankind but God. It begins and ends with the LORD: "O LORD, our Sovereign, how majestic is your name in all the earth!" In between that beginning and ending it does indeed speak of the exalted position of human beings: crowned with "glory and honor." But who did the crowning? The LORD: "You have . . . crowned them with glory and honor" (v 5). In fact, the very question, "What are human beings?" focuses not on human beings but on the LORD: "What are human beings that you [LORD] are mindful of them . . . ?" (v 4). "Comparatively man is of little account, yet God has bestowed upon him kingship over the whole earth. This, too, is a glorification of Yahweh, for the greater man's status is, the more awestruck should be his attitude to God who is the source of man's glory."[35]

Textual Theme and Goal

We noted above that Psalm 8 lacks the "Praise the LORD" call to praise which hymns commonly use. Instead it begins and ends by praising God directly. This raises the question how we can justify turning a hymn addressed to the LORD into a sermon addressed to people. The answer is the same as the answer for preaching prayers addressed to God (see pp. 2–4 above): the psalm is now found in the Psalter and, as part of the canon, is addressed to Israel. Consequently, Israel is expected to take these words addressed to the LORD on its own lips, "O LORD, *our* Sovereign, how majestic is your name in all the earth!"

On p. 509 above we saw that the center of the psalm is the question "what are human beings?" and its answer, "you have made them a little lower than God . . ." (vv 4–5). But this center functions within the frame (inclusio) of "O LORD, our Sovereign, how majestic is your name in all the earth!" (vv 1 and 9).[36] Somehow,

---

35. A. Anderson, *Psalms 1–72,* 100. Belcher, *The Messiah and the Psalms,* 158, adds, "The psalm begins with God and ends with God. The point is that the role of human beings within this world cannot be understood apart from a correct understanding of God. As Calvin writes near the beginning of the *Institutes,* 'It is certain that man never achieves a clear knowledge of himself unless he has first looked upon God's face'" (*Institutes,* I, 1, 2).

36. "Two matters especially impressed him [the psalmist]: (1) the glory of God reflected in the starry heavens, and (2) the astonishing condescension of God to be mindful of puny man, to crown him with glory almost godlike and to grant him lordly power over his creatures." Stek, *NIV Study Bible,* Ps 8 n.

our formulation of the textual theme has to do justice to both of these ideas. As Brueggemann puts it, "The center (v 5) and the boundaries (vv 1, 9) must be read together; either taken alone will miss the point. Human power is always bounded and surrounded by divine praise. *Doxology* gives *dominion* its context and legitimacy."[37]

We can hold the center and boundaries together by formulating the psalm's theme as, *Praise the* LORD, *our sovereign King, for his majesty displayed in the heavens and in all the earth, especially in crowning human beings with glory and honor.*[38]

To determine the goal of this psalm for Israel it would be helpful to know under what historical circumstances it was composed. Unfortunately, we cannot date this psalm with any certainty.[39] But we know that the goal of hymns was to encourage Israel to praise. Combining this goal with the theme, we can formulate the goal of Psalm 8 as *to encourage Israel to praise the* LORD *for his majesty displayed in the heavens and in all the earth, especially in crowning human beings with glory and honor.*[40]

Ways to Preach Christ

There is no promise of the coming Messiah in this psalm, nor is there a type of Christ.[41] But still one can move to Christ in the New Testament in at least three ways: 1) tracing the longitudinal theme of God visiting his people, or 2) redemptive-historical progression supported by New Testament references, or 3) by just using New Testament references that quote Psalm 8 and link it to Christ.

---

37. Brueggemann, *Message of the Psalms*, 37–38 (his italics). Cf. McCann, *Theological Introduction*, 58, "The boundaries of the psalm must be held together with the center."

38. Cf. Leupold, *Exposition of the Psalms*, 100, "Jehovah's glory is being set forth primarily by a consideration of the dignity with which He has invested man." For a detailed discussion for detecting the psalm's theme, see Keener, *Canonical Exegesis*, 46–51.

39. "Scholars have posited dates for the origin of the composition of Psalm 8 ranging from the 12th to the 5th Centuries BC, and possibly beyond." Keener, *Canonical Exegesis*, 45.

40. Cf. Mays, *Psalms*, 68, "The experience [of contemplating the vast depths of the night sky] is not, however, that of being 'lost in the cosmos'; rather, it is of awe and wonder at the marvelous majesty of God, who can make and has made a royal regent of this mere mortal. The question ['what are human beings'] is asked in the psalm to serve the purpose of the hymn, praise the LORD."

41. In spite of Leupold's attempt to use typology by stressing the dignity of the first Adam who then is a type of Christ. *Exposition of the Psalms*, 101.

Longitudinal Theme

One could possibly trace the longitudinal theme of God visiting his people by moving from verse 4, "What are human beings that you are mindful of them, mortals that you care for [visit] them?" to Jesus Christ as Elizabeth Achtemeier does: "That care of God for us and his visitation of us is most tellingly set forth in the fact that God has so loved the world that he has given his only Son to walk in our midst in that man of Nazareth and to dwell always with us in his Holy Spirit."[42] This move could be further supported by references to John 3:16; 20:22; and Matthew 28:20.

Redemptive-Historical Progression and New Testament References

A stronger bridge to Christ, however, is to move from the *theme* of the psalm to Christ in the New Testament. The theme is, "Praise the LORD, our sovereign King, for his majesty displayed in the heavens and in all the earth, especially in crowning human beings with glory and honor." Jesus Christ is our sovereign King, the Word through whom all things were made (John 1:1–2). Jesus displays his majesty in the heavens and in all the earth. He crowned us with glory and honor not only when he made us but he will crown us with glory and honor especially in his new creation. Jesus promised his disciples, "You will sit on thrones judging the twelve tribes of Israel" (Luke 22:30). Paul expands this promise to all followers of Christ: "If we endure, we will also reign with him" (2 Tim 2:12). And John heard a new song for the Lamb: "You [the Lamb] have made them to be a kingdom and priests serving our God, and they will reign on earth" (Rev 5:10).

New Testament References

Since the New Testament cites Psalm 8 several times linking it to Christ, one can also explain certain New Testament references. One could possibly make use of Matthew 21:15–16 where Jesus applies the Hosanna cries of "the mouths of infants and nursing babies" (Ps 8:2, LXX) to himself, or 1 Corinthians 15:27 and Ephesians 1:22 where Paul cites Psalm 8:6, "you have put all things under their feet," or Hebrews 2:6–8 where the author quotes at length Psalm 8:4–6. We'll have to decide later, when we work on the sermon, which of these options will work best (see "Sermon Exposition" below).

42. Achtemeier, "Preaching the Praises and Laments," *CTJ* 36, no. 1 (2001): 112.

Sermon Theme, Goal, and Need

Since the New Testament does not contradict but affirms the psalm's theme while focusing it on Christ, the textual theme can become the sermon's theme with the understanding that "LORD" refers both to Yahweh and the Lord Jesus: *Praise the LORD, our sovereign King, for his majesty displayed in the heavens and in all the earth, especially in crowning human beings with glory and honor.*

With the same understanding about "LORD" and by changing "Israel" to "God's people," the goal of the psalm can also become the sermon goal: *to encourage God's people to praise the LORD for his majesty displayed in the heavens and in all the earth, especially in crowning human beings with glory and honor.*

This goal points to the need addressed in this sermon: we do not sufficiently praise the Lord Jesus for his majesty displayed in the heavens and in all the earth, especially in crowning human beings with glory and honor.

Scripture Reading and Sermon Outline

Scripture reading can highlight the voices in Psalm 8 which switch from the plural "our" in verse 1ab and 9 to the singular "I" in verses 3–8. Therefore the congregation could read the verses 1ab, a single voice verses 1c–8, and the congregation concludes the reading with verse 9.[43] Alternatively, one could highlight in the reading not only the voices but also the central question and answer: a chorus could read verses 1–2; a solo voice asks the key question (vv 3–4); the "chorus thunders in answer" (vv 5–9),[44] perhaps with the congregation repeating verse 9 "to express their assent to the Psalm."[45]

The sermon outline can follow the structure of the psalm, concluding with Christ. The sermon outline, then, would be:[46]

I. Our Sovereign's name, LORD, is majestic in all the earth (v 1ab)
II. The LORD's glory is above the heavens and in the mouths of babes (vv 1c–2)

---

43. "This song of praise of an individual is framed by a choral refrain (vv 1a and 9), so that a cultic antiphonal song may have been at the base of it." Kraus, *Psalms 1–59*, 179.

44. Calvin Seerveld, *Voicing God's Psalms* (Grand Rapids: Eerdmans, 2005), 5–6.

45. John Witvliet, *Biblical Psalms in Christian Worship*, 88.

46. I would not mention all these points in the sermon since they would interrupt the flow of the sermon. This sermon outline, in contrast to a didactic two- or three-point sermon outline, is merely intended as a guide to keep the sermon on track.

   III. Looking at your heavens, what are human beings that you care for them? (vv 3–4)

   IV. The LORD made human beings a little lower than God: dominion (vv 5–6)

    V. The LORD placed all animals under human dominion (vv 7–8)

   VI. Our Sovereign's name, LORD, is majestic in all the earth (v 9)

  VII. Our Sovereign's name, Jesus, is majestic in all the earth (NT)

Sermon Exposition

About twenty years ago we were camping in a state park in northern Wisconsin. The ranger offered to take a group for a night walk — no lights allowed. As we walked down a trail under the forest canopy our eyes soon adjusted to the darkness. Then we came to a clearing and were absolutely astonished at the light. It seemed almost like daylight, with thousands of stars beaming down on us. It was an unforgettable moment of observing and reflecting on the immenseness of space and the greatness of its Creator. "O LORD, our Sovereign, how majestic is your name!" You can probably recall moments like that too.

But all too soon we went back to the campground with its artificial lights and then back to the city flooded with streetlights. Unable to clearly observe the night sky, our praise of the great Creator God was soon a thing of the past. Our lives were busy with things other than praising God for his wondrous heavens.

Psalm 8 was written to encourage Israel and us to praise the LORD for his majesty displayed in the heavens and in all the earth. The psalm is attributed to David. As a shepherd boy, David tended his father's sheep in the fields around Bethlehem. The nights in ancient Palestine were pitch-black, except for the light emitted by the moon and the stars. Almost every night David would have observed God's wondrous heavens the way we did on that night walk in northern Wisconsin. And that set him to thinking — as he records in this psalm.

David begins with praising the LORD. Verse 1, "O LORD, our Sovereign, how majestic is your name in all the earth!" David addresses God as LORD, *Yahweh*, Israel's faithful covenant God. Then he adds, "our Sovereign," *'ādon*, "a name which stresses God's ability to govern."[47] Kings were addressed with this term "sovereign."[48] But the LORD is not only the King of David. David calls the LORD, "*our* Sovereign": Israel's Sovereign, the King of all God's people, *our* King.

"How majestic is your name in all the earth!" "Your name" stands for God's

---

47. Belcher, *Messiah and the Psalms,* 159
48. See 1 Kings 1:11, 43, 47.

presence, "God's revelation of himself."[49] "How majestic is your name." "'Majestic' (*'addîr*, 'mighty') is a royal attribute."[50] Even today a king or queen is still addressed as "Your Majesty." The LORD's revelation of himself is majestic. It reveals his royalty. It reveals that the LORD is our powerful, almighty King. And this revelation of the LORD is "majestic in all the earth." Wherever you look on earth, you will see the LORD's majestic revelation of himself.

From "all the earth," verse 1 next turns to the heavens:[51] "You have set your glory above the heavens" — "in the farthest reaches above the skies."[52] The "glory" of the LORD refers to the LORD's weight, his worth, his importance.[53] "Glory" speaks of the LORD's essence. "You have set your glory above the heavens" indicates that wherever we look at the heavens we see the LORD's glory. Psalm 19 declares, "The heavens are telling the glory of God; and the firmament proclaims his handiwork" (Ps 19:1). Psalm 148 encourages God's people, "Let them praise the name of the LORD, for his name alone is exalted; his glory is above earth and heaven" (Ps 148:13).

From God's "glory above the heavens," verse 2 returns to the earth again and to its weakest members: "Out of the mouths of babes and infants you have founded a bulwark because of your foes, to silence the enemy and the avenger."[54] Can you imagine anything more helpless than "babes and infants"?[55] Without

---

49. Craigie, *Psalms 1–50*, 107. Cf. Anderson, *Psalms 1–72*, 101, "In Hebrew thought the name and its bearer are inseparably associated." Cf. Stek, *NIV Study Bible*, Ps 5:11 n., "The name of the Lord is the manifestation of his character. . . . It . . . is synonymous with the Lord himself in his gracious manifestation and accessibility to his people."

50. VanGemeren, *Psalms*, 138. Cf. Waltke, *Psalms as Christian Worship*, 260, "The adjective denotes someone or something that commands respect through the excellence of power." Cf. Goldingay, *Psalms*, I, 155, "Splendid and majestic, 'usually with the implication of mighty or powerful' (e.g. 76:4 [5]; 93:4; 136:18)." See, e.g., Psalm 93:4, "More majestic than the thunders of mighty waters, more majestic than the waves of the sea, majestic on high is the LORD!"

51. "The result is a merism, in which 'earth' and 'heaven' mark out the two extremes of all that God has created and declare all to be permeated with the majestic name of Yahweh." Wilson, *Psalms*, I, 200.

52. Wallace, *Words to God*, 159.

53. In the Old Testament the word "glory" (*kābôd*) is literally "heavy," "weighty." For example, the cloud on Mount Sinai is described as "heavy" (*kābôd*) with rain (Exod 19:16). "When used of the Lord, *kābôd* denotes splendor, majesty, magnificence." Limburg, *Psalms*, 93. See also p. 167 above.

54. The RSV's translation of Psalm 8:1c–2, following the LXX, is easier to understand and preach: "Thou whose glory above the heavens is chanted by the mouths of babes and infants, thou hast founded a bulwark because of thy foes, to still the enemy and the avenger." But if the pew Bible is the NRSV, the NIV, or the ESV, I think preachers should explain how "the mouths of babes and infants" (or "the praise of children and infants" [NIV]) "silence the enemy and the avenger."

55. Instead of understanding "babes and infants" figuratively (see "Imagery," p. 506 above),

adults to feed and protect them, they would die. How can God use the mouths of babes and infants to silence the enemy?[56]

Babes and infants ("sucklings," KJV) use their mouths to stay alive. Gerald Wilson writes, "For children (and especially 'toddlers and nursing infants') the 'mouth' is the source of nourishment. The psalmist uses this image of vulnerability and dependence to create a dramatic contrast with the presumed power of those who oppose God and his faithful ones. Mighty Yahweh, whose majestic power and glory are displayed throughout the creation, is able to build the innocent weakness of these dependent babes into a powerful opposition to his enemies."[57]

But the question remains, How do the mouths of infants form a "bulwark" to silence the enemy? It would be good to first identify the enemy. Verse 2 mentions three synonyms for God's enemies: God's "foes," "the enemy," and "the avenger." These three words refer to one and the same enemy: God's enemies are the forces of chaos, elsewhere in the Bible called "the great deep," "the floods," "the sea monsters," and "Leviathan." "Defeated and banished at the Creation, these were ever seeking to 'avenge' themselves."[58] God's enemies are powerful indeed. Avengers kill people. How can the mouths of babes and infants silence the avenger?

I think we should understand these words literally if that makes any sense at all. And it does. As Kidner, *Psalms 1–72*, 66, points out, "The startling contrast of verse 2 makes the proper impact. With all earth and heaven proclaiming God in verse 1, the rising discord of *foes . . . enemy . . . avenger* presents a challenge which God meets with 'what is weak in the world,' the immaterial (*by the mouth*) and the immature."

56. Some commentators suggest that even with their inarticulate babbling, babes use their mouths to praise God. For example, Kraus, *Psalms 1–59*, 181, writes, "Out of the stammering praise of the children Yahweh builds a bulwark, erects a lasting power, that is directed against the enemies of God and puts an end to them." Cf. Urassa, *Psalm 8*, 48, "With the songs of children, God establishes his strength." Waltke, *Psalms as Christian Worship*, 261, thinks of "the speech of prayers, including both petition and praise to God." I don't think these arguments are very convincing. The question remains, How do the songs or prayers of children "silence" God's enemies?

57. Wilson, *Psalms*, I, 202. Cf. 1 Cor 1:27, "God chose what is foolish in the world to shame the wise; God chose what is weak in the world to shame the strong." Cf. Leupold, *Exposition of the Psalms*, 102, "So secure is the honor of the name of the Lord that in the full consciousness of His great glory He has let the defense of His honor be committed to babes."

58. Eaton, *Psalms*, 45. Cf. McCann, "Psalms," 711: "The 'foes' / 'enemy' / 'avenger' are probably the chaotic forces that God conquered and ordered in the sovereign act of creation. Understood this way, v 2 anticipates the assertion of vv 3–8 that God uses the weak and seemingly insignificant human creature as a partner in caring for a creation that is constantly threatened by its enemy, chaos (see Gen 1:1–2:4, to which Ps 8:6–8 is obviously related; see also Job 38:8–11; Pss 29:10; 74:12–17; 89:9–11; 104:5–9)." Tate, "Exposition of Psalm 8," *PRSt* 28, no. 4 (2001): 352, agrees that they may be "the forces that threaten the cosmic order of creation, such as Rahab (Ps 89:10; Job 26:12; Isa 51:10), the helpers of Rahab (Job 9:13), the sea (Job 26:12, Pss 74:13; 89:10; Isa 51:10), the great deep (Isa 51:10), the floods (Ps 93:3), the sea monsters (Ps 74:13; Isa 51:3), the Behemoth and Leviathan (Job 40:15–41:34), and Leviathan (Ps 74:14; Isa 27:1)."

Babes and nursing infants use their mouths to stay alive. Marvin Tate suggests, "The cry of a newborn baby and the concomitant breath of life testify to God's continuous acts of creation and the gift of life, acts which reduce the enemies of life to impotent silence."[59] Willem VanGemeren adds, "The sound of the children is concrete evidence of God's fortress on earth. The continuity of the human race is God's way of assuring the ultimate glorification of an earth populated with a new humanity (Hab 2:14)."[60] Thus the mouths of babes and infants used for keeping them alive are a sign of the continuation of God's orderly creation. Possibly a sign also of the coming new creation when chaos will be defeated once and for all.

Verses 3–4, "When I look at your[61] heavens, the work of your fingers, the moon and the stars that you have established; what are human beings that you are mindful of them, mortals that you care for them?" David calls God's heavens not the work of God's *hands,* but the work of God's *"fingers."* "The celestial vault is the work of God's *fingers,* not just *hands:* a task at once enormous and minute. It is comparable to the art of a sculptor whose fingers, even more than his hands, fashion and mold the intricate designs of the Milky Way."[62]

David cries out, "When *I* look at your heavens, . . . what are human beings that you are mindful of them, mortals that you care for them?" "The intrusion of the first person 'I' in the psalm at this one point is . . . not accidental. . . . The 'I'

59. Tate, "Exposition of Psalm 8," *PRSt* 28, no. 4 (2001): 352. Tate continues, "This approach can make use of a number of texts that combine God's creative activity with birth and the care of life (see Job 10:8–12; Ps 22:10–12; 71:5–8; 119:73; 139:13–16; Is 44:24)." Cf. Calvin, *Commentary on the Book of Psalms,* I, 96, "Whence is it that nourishment is ready for them [infants] as soon as they are born, but because God wonderfully changes blood into milk? Whence, also, have they the skill to suck, but because the same God has, by a mysterious instinct, fitted their tongues for doing this?" Cf. Barbara Pitkin, "Psalm 8:1–2," *Int* 55 (2001; pp. 177–80): 180, "In the psalm, it is by following instinct and nursing that babies proclaim God's goodness. Their lives are a powerful witness to God's fatherly benevolence, and without speech they can return thanks. . . . 'Babies at the breast' expresses in a nutshell children who are fed, cuddled, and sheltered in protective arms. When children's needs are met and their lives flourish, God truly has established a bulwark against God's enemies."

60. VanGemeren, *Psalms,* 139.

61. *"Your* heavens" and *"your* fingers" imply that the heavens belong to the LORD "because he created them. . . . Ownership by creation probably functions as a subtle polemic against the universal pagan worship of these brilliant bodies." Waltke, *Psalms as Christian Worship,* 265.

62. Terrien, *The Psalms,* 129. Cf. Alter, *Art of Biblical Poetry,* 120, "Since this particular construct form appears only here in the whole Bible, we may well be expected to hear in it the indication of especially delicate work as the speaker scans the exquisite tracery of the night sky." Cf. Craigie, *Psalms 1–50,* 108, "In contrast to God, the heavens are tiny, pushed and prodded into shape by the divine digits; but in contrast to the heavens, which seem so vast in the human perception, it is mankind that is tiny."

of this psalm is what makes us aware that the general question, 'What is a human being?' is fundamentally a question, 'What am *I?*' and what possible meaning and significance can *I* or any other human being have in the midst of this cosmos that seems to have no end in time or space?"[63] That is the question we may also have raised when overwhelmed by the starry heavens.

But more than asking about the significance of human beings, David cries out in amazement, "What[64] are human beings that you are mindful of them, mortals that you care for them?" The word he uses for "human beings," *'ĕnôš*, highlights the insignificance of humans. It "lays emphasis on human vulnerability, on the essentially finite nature of human power."[65] The second word, translated "mortals," *ben-'ādām*, literally "son of man," also highlights human insignificance: "an earthling," made of dust (cf. Gen 2:7; 3:19).[66] Why should the almighty Creator God be mindful of such tiny, frail creatures? Why should the eternal Creator God care[67] for mortals — mortals who are here today and gone tomorrow?[68] David is simply astonished that, in spite of the incredible distance between God and human beings, God is still mindful of these tiny specks of dust on earth in a seemingly infinite universe. He is astonished that the almighty, eternal Creator God personally *cares* for us.

When we are away from city lights and look at the starry heavens, we may well ask the same questions: Why is the almighty Creator God mindful of us, tiny humans? Why does the eternal Creator God care for us, mortal creatures? The short answer is that it is all God's grace. Frail human beings have not earned God's attention and care; it is all God's grace.[69]

---

63. Miller, *The Way of the Lord*, 229.

64. "The deprecating, scornful import of the questions is intensified by the use of the Hebrew interrogative pronoun *mâ*, that goes with an object, rather than *mî*, which refers to a person." Sarna, *On the Book of Psalms*, 62.

65. Ibid., "The stem means 'to be weak, frail." Cf. Wilson, *Psalms*, I, 204, "In poetic contexts (such as here in Ps 8), *'îš* normally represents individual humans in their strength. By contrast, *'ĕnôš* most often emphasizes human frailty, weakness, and mortality; thus, the use of that term here is no accident but intentionally stresses the distance the psalmist experiences, opening up between the glorious creator God, Yahweh, and his far less significant and less powerful human creatures." See Bosma, "Beyond 'Singers and Syntax,'" 74–75, on "the self-abasement formula."

66. "If *ben 'ādām* has any special thrust, it is probably to emphasize the fragile mortality of the human condition." Wilson, *Psalms*, I, 204. Mays, *Psalms*, 68, observes, "His question is not about Israel alone; it is about the entire race. He believes and assumes that God remembers and visits every human, that Israel's experience with God is the truth about God's way with all."

67. "Both verbs presuppose being moved to action, whether benevolently or punitively." Sarna, *On the Book of Psalms*, 63.

68. Cf. Psalm 144:3–4, "O LORD, what are human beings that you regard them, or mortals that you think of them? They are like a breath; their days are like a passing shadow."

69. "These two exclamations ['thou art mindful' and 'thou dost care'] highlight the divine

The long answer is found in verses 5–6: "Yet you have made them a little lower than God, and crowned them with glory and honor. You have given them dominion over the works of your hands; you have put all things under their feet." Belcher notes that "it is very significant that Psalm 8 first of all stresses God's role as king over his creation in verses 1–2."[70] Thereafter royal terms are also used of human beings. God cares for us frail humans because in his grace he has given us a position of authority in his creation. Every human being "is involved in the kingdom of God. Being human means being ordained and installed in a right and responsibility within the divine sovereignty."[71]

"You have made them a little lower than God, and crowned them with glory and honor." The phrase "crowned them" helps us understand immediately that God has made us kings and queens in his creation. In the beginning God gave human beings a commission: "Have dominion over the fish of the sea and over the birds of the air and over every living thing that moves upon the earth" (Gen 1:28). David says that God crowned us "with glory and honor." "These words convey notions of importance, splendor, honor, authority, and power."[72] In fact, these are the attributes of God himself.[73] In spite of the fall into sin, human beings still carry that crown and have that commission to rule over God's creatures on behalf of God.[74]

---

grace implicit in the four that follow (5f.), for all is of God's giving." Kidner, *Psalms 1–72*, 67. Cf. Eaton, *Psalms*, 45, regarding verses 5–8, "It is by the free decision of God that man is thus raised from insignificance; man's power over this earth is only a gift of grace, to be wielded in heed of the Creator's will." Cf. Brevard S. Childs, "Psalm 8 in the Context of the Christian Canon," *Int* 23 (1969; pp. 20–32): 22, "We speak at times as if only the New Testament understood the concept of grace, but it is clear that the psalmist realizes that his position stems from God's creative initiative and rests on the incomprehensible favor which God has lavished on him. He does not attempt to mount a case as to why God thought to establish man as head, but rather meditates on this great act of grace."

70. Belcher, *The Messiah and the Psalms*, 159–60.

71. Mays, *Psalms*, 69. Mays adds, "God didn't just make us; God made us both a representation and representatives of the reign of the LORD to the other creatures."

72. Tate, "Exposition of Psalm 8," *PRSt* 28, no. 4 (2001): 355.

73. "Within the Book of Psalms the 'glory (*kābôd*) and honour (*hādār*)' with which humans are crowned in Psalm 8 are attributes usually associated with God (e.g., Pss 19:1; 29:1–2, 9; 96:3–6; 104:1, 31; 145:5, 11, 12 etc.)." Wallace, *Words to God*, 160. Cf. Wilson, *Psalms*, I, 207, "These are characteristics of God himself that adorn the frail humans created in his image and allow his power to be displayed through those creatures he has graciously chosen to extend his authority into the world." Cf. Bosma, "Beyond 'Singers and Syntax,'" 85.

74. "The significance of human beings is not to be limited to their existence before sin came into the world. People are still 'crowned' . . . with glory. The sequence of verbs (vv 5–6) expresses poetically the status God, by divine decree, gave to humans. The verses could be rendered, 'You made [past tense] him a little lower than the heavenly beings and crown [present tense] him with glory and honor. You make [present tense] him ruler over the works of your hands; you put [past

In verse 5 David makes the amazing claim concerning human beings, "You have made them a little lower than God," "a little less than God." This is such an extravagant claim for the status of frail humans that those who translated the Hebrew Old Testament into Greek (LXX) made it, "You have made them a little lower than angels" (so also the NIV). While this is a possible translation (and used in the letter to the Hebrews),[75] Craigie, among others, claims that "the translation *God* is almost certainly correct, and the words contain an allusion to the image of God in mankind and the God-given role of dominion to be exercised by mankind within the created order."[76] In any case, whether it is God, angels, or heavenly beings, "humans have been catapulted far beyond their seeming weakness and insignificance — not by any value of their own but simply by the action of a free divine choice and grace that causes the human jaw to drop and the mind to reel."[77]

Verse 6 further explains the exalted position of human beings in God's creation: "You have given them dominion over the works of your hands; you have put all things under their feet." "The creation of humans and crowning them with glory and honor has a purpose, to make them have dominion over the works of God."[78] What an amazing position: "dominion over the works of your hands." But it is not a dominion to do whatever we please. This dominion "corresponds to and is subordinate to the reign of the creator. Human beings are to use their power over creatures in a way that serves the purposes and practices of their own sovereign."[79]

---

tense] everything under his feet." VanGemeren, *Psalms*, 140–41. Cf. Goldingay, *Psalms*, I, 159, and Ross, *Commentary on the Psalms*, I, 288 n. 8.

75. "The LXX takes *God* ('*ĕlohîm*) in its rarer, generic sense to mean supernatural beings, i.e. 'angels' (cf. 1 Sam 28:13; Ps 82:1, 6f.), and Hebrews 2:7, 9 follows that translation." Kidner, *Psalms 1–72*, 67.

76. Craigie, *Psalms 1–50*, 108. Cf. Judah Kraut, "The Birds and the Babes: The Structure and Meaning of Psalm 8," *The Jewish Quarterly Review* 100, no. 1 (2010; pp. 10–24): 23, "My thesis makes it abundantly clear that *elohim* in verse 6 refers to God himself and not to angels or members of the heavenly retinue. The entire structure of the psalm is built upon the juxtaposition of God's powers in the first part of the psalm, with the powers of man in the second portion of the psalm." Cf. Urassa, *Psalm 8*, 54, "The main point here is not an ontological comparison between man and God, but the glory bestowed on him . . . by God. The concept of glory . . . which dominates the psalm, is in relation to God as Ruler of the universe and to man as a co-ruler with him." So also Ross, *Commentary on the Psalms*, I, 296. But A. Anderson, *Psalms 1–72*, 103, argues that "a little lower than angels" "is more likely because the Psalmist has been at pains to stress the infinite greatness of God and the comparative insignificance of man." However, "the comparative insignificance of man" makes it all the more remarkable that God would raise human beings to such high stature.

77. Wilson, *Psalms*, I, 207. Cf. McCann, "Psalms," 712, "The phrase 'image of God' does not occur in Psalm 8, but the language and movement of Psalm 8 suggest that humans represent God in the world."

78. Ross, *Commentary on the Psalms*, I, 296.

79. Mays, *Psalms*, 69.

Note the repetition of the word "all" in verses 6–8: "You have given them dominion over the works of your hands; you have put *all* things under their feet, *all* sheep and oxen, and also the beasts of the field, the birds of the air, and the fish of the sea, whatever passes along the paths of the seas."[80] "You have put all things under their feet" is "a common ancient Near Eastern image of subjugation,"[81] to bring under control.

In verse 7, the dominion over "all sheep and oxen," refers to all domesticated animals, while "the beasts of the field" refers to wild animals. Claus Westermann observes, "We moderns can hardly understand how lordship over the animals is a sign of honor bestowed upon us, for here we have an echo of a feeling for life from a very ancient age, an age for which the domestication of animals was humanity's highest achievement."[82]

Verse 8 adds to "all sheep and oxen" and "the beasts of the field": "The birds of the air, and the fish of the sea, whatever passes along the paths of the seas."[83] The "whatever passes along the paths of the seas" "may simply be an all-embracing way of describing marine life, but it may indicate that even the monsters of the ocean (whales, and even mythological monsters), which were so much larger than tiny humans, were to fall under human control."[84]

Verse 9 concludes the psalm the way it began in verse 1ab:[85] "O LORD, our

---

80. "The twofold 'all' in vv 6–7 corresponds to the twofold 'all' in vv 1 and 9. They so rule when they stop predators from damaging their crops and herds: the statements imply a promise that the life of a farmer can work. But the horizon is larger than that and recalls the OT's vision of the animate world living in harmony (Isa 11). That suggests a larger commission. When the work of creation was finished, this did not mean it had reached its destiny; humanity's calling was to take it there. How extraordinary that God should want to use humanity thus!" Goldingay, *Psalms*, I, 160.

81. Alter, *Book of Psalms*, 23 n. v 6. Wilson, *Psalms*, I, 209, comments: "But here the prostration of the earth under the feet of the divinely elevated human, while a sign of likeness to God and distinction from the rest of creation, is *not* an indication of human strength, power, and unlimited authority. The earth is *placed* under human authority by God — not by human power. Any authority exercised by humans over the earth is distinctly limited, derived from God, and ultimately responsible to him."

82. Westermann, *The Psalms*, 97.

83. "The list of beasts submitted to human rule is comprehensive, naming the main classes of animals (vv 8–9 [7–8]). It certainly stems from wisdom enumerations of living beings (cf. Gen 1:26; 1 Kings 5:13 [RSV 4:33]; Dan 2:38)." Gerstenberger, *Psalms*, I, 70. Cf. Whitekettle, "Taming the Shrew," 761, "The sequence of taxa in Psalm 8 represented a progression from highly controlled to minimally controlled animals for the Israelite reader:
          human beings — domesticated land — wild land — aerial — aquatic
           most controllable   →   →   →   *least controllable*"

84. Craigie, *Psalms 1–50*, 108–9, who adds, "The words are reminiscent of the ships and the monstrous Leviathan (Ps 104:25–26) that ply the waterways of the world." See p. 494 above.

85. In response to the question why v 1 is not cited in its entirety, including "the heavens,"

Sovereign, how majestic is your name in all the earth!" Wilson observes, "Our psalm ends as it begins. . . . Yet subtly our understanding of the ground for praising Yahweh has shifted from the first verse to the last. At the beginning our praise began by affirming the magnificence of the creator. At the end, we stand in awe at the unexpected grace that has elevated his human works to unimaginable heights of glory, honor, and responsibility; sharing God's image, we are also called to share his loving care for all he has made."[86] "O LORD, our Sovereign, how majestic is your name in all the earth!" Thus ends the hymn in praise of God the Creator.

The New Testament uses Psalm 8 in praise of Jesus Christ. For, as John explains, Jesus was the Word through whom God created all things in the beginning: "In the beginning was the Word, and the Word was with God, and the Word was God. He was in the beginning with God. All things [another 'all'] came into being through him, and without him not one thing came into being" (John 1:1–3). Thus the psalm in praise of God the Creator can also be understood in praise of Jesus Christ.[87]

In his letter to the Ephesians Paul uses Psalm 8:6b, "You have put all things under their feet," to proclaim the authority of the risen Christ. Paul writes, "God put this power to work in Christ when he raised him from the dead and seated him at his right hand in the heavenly places, far above all rule and authority and power and dominion, and above every name that is named, not only in this age but also in the age to come. And *he has put all things under his feet* and has made him the head over all things for the church" (Eph 1:20–22).[88]

Kraus, *Psalms 1–59*, 185, cites E. Baumann's words that "The thoughts of the psalmist in vv 2–8 essentially deal only with the earth."

86. Wilson, *Psalms*, I, 209. Cf. McCann, *Theological Introduction*, 58, quoted on p. 508 above.

87. According to Matthew, when Jesus triumphantly entered Jerusalem he used Psalm 8:2 to silence the enemy, that is, the chief priests and the scribes. "When the chief priests and the scribes saw the amazing things that he did, and heard *the children crying out in the temple, 'Hosanna to the Son of David,'* they became angry and said to him, 'Do you hear what these are saying?' Jesus said to them, 'Yes; have you never read, "Out of the mouths of infants and nursing babies you have prepared praise for yourself"?'" (Matt 21:15–16). The psalm speaks about the children's praise (LXX) of the great Creator God. Jesus applies these words to himself: he accepts the praise coming out of the mouths of infants and silences the enemy. Cf. Gillingham, "Psalm 8 Through the Looking Glass," 177 and n. 25, "Its point is to contrast the cynicism of the scribes and chief priests with the simple psalm-like praises of the children. The psalm is thus read as a prophecy in the process of fulfillment in the life of Christ: the psalmist's praise to God is now being offered to Christ himself." Matthew "basically follows the LXX version by reading v 2c [1c] as a separate clause and by reading Ps 8:3 [2] as an independent unit, referring to the children's praise on earth, not in heaven — as the MT implies." Cf. Keener, *Canonical Exegesis*, 140–41, and Urassa, *Psalm 8*, 117–54.

88. Cf. 1 Corinthians 15:25–27, "For he must reign until he has put all his enemies under his feet. The last enemy to be destroyed is death. For '*God has put all things in subjection under his* [LXX] *feet.*'" See further, Keener, *Canonical Exegesis*, 145–69, and Urassa, *Psalm 8*, 155–93, 219–40.

The letter to the Hebrews contains the longest quotation of Psalm 8. The author quotes Psalm 8:5–6 from the Greek translation (the Septuagint), which is somewhat different from the Hebrew.[89] He writes, "But someone has testified somewhere, 'What are human beings that you are mindful of them, or mortals ['the son of man'],[90] that you care for them? You have made them for a little while[91] lower than the angels;[92] you have crowned them with glory and honor, *subjecting all things under their feet.*' Now in subjecting all things to them, God left nothing outside their control. As it is, we do not yet see everything in subjection to them, but we do see Jesus, who for a little while was made lower than the angels, now crowned with glory and honor because of the suffering of death, so that by the grace of God he might taste death for everyone" (Heb 2:6–9).

Psalm 8:5–8 said that God crowned humankind "with glory and honor. You have given them dominion over the works of your hands; you have put all things

89. The use of the Greek translation (LXX) by the New Testament authors aided this christo-centric reading. Psalm 8:5, *'ĕlohîm* was translated as *angeloi*, angels; *ben-'ādām* of v 4 became *huios anthropou*, "son of man," with "Messianic overtones of the term by the second century B.C.E. . . . Furthermore, also in v 6 [5] *mǝ'at* ('a little less [lower]') is read as *braxu*, which implies time ('in a little while') more than substance ('a little less') and indicates that the figure is not so much the universal Everyone as a particular Someone who will 'in a little while' (*braxu*) be given a special place close to the angels." Gillingham, "Psalm 8 Through the Looking Glass," 169–70.

90. NIV, 1984. Miller, *The Way of the Lord,* 235, notes, "The presence of the expression *ben 'ādām,* traditionally translated as 'son of man,' . . . has led inexorably to a hearing of this text as not simply about humanity in general but about the one who was known as the 'son of man.'" Cf. John Barton, *Reading the Old Testament: Method in Biblical Study* (Philadelphia: Westminster, 1984), 83–84, "This is not simply a misreading of the Psalm; rather, it plays back on to the original text a new level of meaning. The Psalm is both originally, and in its citation in Hebrews, about the 'glory of man'; but the Christian writer sees Jesus as the key to the doctrine of man, and by narrowing the reference of the Psalm from man in general to Jesus in particular he makes it possible for us to go back and reread the Psalm, within the context of the Christian Scriptures, as implying more profound ideas about human nature than the psalmist himself had in mind. Within this context, the Psalm speaks of a glorification of man's nature which is already actual in Jesus, and potential for all mankind." Cf. Craigie, *Psalms 1–50,* 110, "The dominion of which the psalmist spoke may have had theological reality, yet it did not always appear to have historical reality in the developing history of the human race. The historical reality, according to Paul and the author of the Epistle to the Hebrews, is — and will be — fulfilled in the risen Christ." See further, Keener, *Canonical Exegesis,* 176–82, and Urassa, *Psalm 8,* 195–218.

91. "The Hebrew preposition used in the phrase translated 'a little lower than God' can be used of degree, as implied in this NRSV translation, or of time, i.e. 'for a little while.' The ancient Greek translators of the Old Testament understood it in this second, temporal, way." Wallace, *Words to God,* 163. See also Kidner, in the following note.

92. "The LXX takes God (*'ĕlohîm*) in its rarer, generic sense to mean supernatural beings, i.e. 'angels' (cf. 1 Sam 28:13; Ps 82:1, 6f.), and Hebrews 2:7, 9 follows that translation. *Little* can some-times mean 'for a little while' in both Hebrew and Greek, which is the sense probably implied in the Epistle." Kidner, *Psalms 1–72,* 67.

under their feet, all sheep and oxen, and also the beasts of the field, the birds of the air, and the fish of the sea, whatever passes along the paths of the seas." Now the author of Hebrews observes that this is not yet the case. We may have control over domesticated animals but certainly not over "the beasts of the field" — wild animals such as lions, tigers, and rhinos. Nor do we have control over all "the birds of the air, and the fish of the sea."[93] He writes that "we do not yet see *everything* in subjection to them [humankind], but we do see Jesus."

What does Jesus have to do with seeing everything in subjection to human beings? The answer is that Jesus is the second Adam. Jesus represents redeemed humanity.[94] Listen again to how the author of Hebrews describes Jesus: "We do see Jesus, who for a little while was made lower than the angels, now crowned with glory and honor because of the suffering of death, so that by the grace of God he might taste death for everyone" (Heb 2:9). We do see Jesus, who suffered *"death, so that by the grace of God he might taste death for everyone."* Jesus died and, wonder of wonders, rose again. In doing so, Jesus defeated the last enemy of the human race; he defeated death. With his resurrection, Jesus showed that he had dominion even over death. In doing so, Hebrews adds, God used Jesus' sufferings "in bringing many children to glory" (Heb 2:10).[95] As if that were not enough, Hebrews adds that Jesus tasted death for everyone, "so that through death he might destroy the one who has the power of death, that is, the devil" (Heb 2:14).[96] Talk about silencing "the enemy and the avenger" (Ps 8:2). Jesus destroys even that arch-enemy of the human race, the devil. Finally we see Jesus, *"now crowned with glory and honor"* (Heb 2:9). We now see Jesus enthroned as King of the universe, having dominion over all things.[97]

---

93. "The writer of Hebrews makes the point that man in his actual state has not fulfilled the promise of the psalmist. Taking this then as his clue, he moves into his christological confession." Childs, "Psalm 8," *Int* 23 (1969): 25. On the interpretation of Hebrews 2:5-9, see further George H. Guthrie and Russell D. Quinn, "A Discourse Analysis of the Use of Psalm 8:4-6 in Hebrews 2:5-9," *JETS* 49 (2006): 235-46, and Simon Kistemaker, *The Psalm Citations in the Epistle to the Hebrews* (Amsterdam: van Soest, 1961), 102-8.

94. "This eschatological restoration of human rule is accomplished already in Jesus who represents all redeemed humanity in achieving this dominion." Belcher, *Messiah and the Psalms,* 162. Cf. VanGemeren, *Psalms,* 137, "In Jesus' victory, the Christian has received the glorious renewal the psalmist speaks of (Heb 2:10-11)."

95. Heb 2:10, "It was fitting that God, for whom and through whom all things exist, in bringing many children to glory, should make the pioneer of their salvation perfect through sufferings."

96. Hebrews continues, "Since, therefore, the children share flesh and blood, he himself likewise shared the same things, so that through death he might destroy the one who has the power of death, that is, the devil, and free those who all their lives were held in slavery by the fear of death" (Heb 2:14-15).

97. Cf. Eph 1:20-22 and 1 Cor 15:25-27 quoted above on p. 522 and n. 88.

Through Jesus' victory over death and the devil himself, we have with him in principle dominion over all things. Through Jesus' dominion as King of the universe, we his people in principle rule with him over all things. When Jesus comes again he will make all things new.[98] He will restore human beings to what God in the beginning intended them to be: kings and queens caring for the world under the sovereignty of God the Father and his Son, and guided by the Holy Spirit.

Isaiah envisions a time when the enemy will be defeated and the human race will be restored to their exalted position in God's creation. Isaiah writes, "The wolf shall live with the lamb, the leopard shall lie down with the kid, the calf and the lion and the fatling together, and a little child shall lead them."[99] "A little child shall lead them." Even a little child shall lead the wolf, the leopard, and the lion. Redeemed humanity will function again as responsible caregivers of God's good creation.

How we ought to praise our God and Savior not only for redeeming us but also for his promise to restore his entire creation when Jesus returns. That restoration will include restoring humanity to their exalted position in God's creation as special representatives of our great King. Paul writes, "I endure everything for the sake of the elect, so that they may also obtain the salvation that is in Christ Jesus, with eternal glory. The saying is sure: 'If we have died with him, we will also live with him; if we endure, we will also reign with him'" (2 Tim 2:10–12). Eternal glory awaits us. "We will also reign with" Jesus. Thanks be to God.

Prayer[100]

Our Father in Heaven,

"How majestic is your name in all the earth!" We thank you for the honor you have bestowed on the human race to take care of your world and all its creatures.

Please forgive us for the mess we have made of your world: depleting the ozone layer, global warming, violence and warfare, the threat of nuclear annihilation, polluted streams and oceans, eroding soil and vanishing rainforests, animal species being abused and becoming extinct, even people, made in your image, suffering in refugee camps while others are being enslaved.

Thank you for restoring us to our exalted position through your Son, Jesus Christ. We look forward to the day when Jesus will return to make all

---

98. "The answer to the question about who we are is finally eschatological, where tears are no longer part of the human reality, where joy is the order of eternity, and where our transience disappears in the disappearance of death. We cannot see that yet. But we do see Jesus. That will have to do." Miller, *The Way of the Lord*," 236. That will have to do for now, until Jesus comes again to make all things new.

99. Isa 11:6. Cf. Isa 65:17–25, and Rev 21:1–7.

100. S.G.

things new. In the meantime we pray that your Holy Spirit may work powerfully in the hearts and lives of peoples and cultures so that this sin-broken world may even now reflect some of the beauty of your coming kingdom.

We pray in the name of Jesus who has redeemed us and who will at your time restore your wonderful creation. Amen.

Song[101]

1Lord, our Lord, your glorious name
    all your wondrous works proclaim;
in the heavens with radiant signs
    evermore your glory shines.
How great your name!

Refrain:
Lord, our Lord, in all the earth,
    how great your name!
Yours the name of matchless worth,
    excellent in all the earth.
How great your name!

2Infant voices chant your praise,
    telling of your glorious ways;
weakest means work out your will,
    mighty enemies to still.
How great your name! [*Refrain*]

3Moon and stars in shining height
    nightly tell their Maker's might;
when I view the heavens afar,
    then I know how small we are.
How great your name! [*Refrain*]

4Who are we that we should share
    in your love and tender care
raised to an exalted height,
    crowned with honor in your sight!
How great your name! [*Refrain*]

---

101. Public Domain. *Psalter* Hymnal (1987) # 8; *Psalms for All Seasons*, # 8A; *Lift Up Your Hearts*, # 500.

5With dominion crowned, we stand
    o'er the creatures of your hand;
all to us subjection yield,
    in the sea and air and field.
How great your name! [*Refrain*]

CHAPTER 23

"Make a Joyful Noise to the LORD, All the Earth!"

Psalm 100 (99)

The Revised Common Lectionary, Year A, assigns the reading of Psalm 100 for Christ the King Sunday as a response to the reading of Ezekiel 34:11–16, 20–24, "God, the true Shepherd." This psalm turns out to be a remarkably good fit for Christ the King Sunday and for concluding a series of sermons on preaching Christ from Psalms in the Christian year.

"The psalm is widely known as 'the Jubilate'"[1] — to shout for joy. Walter Brueggemann writes, "This psalm is one of the best-known and best-loved in the entire repertoire of the Psalter. It breathes a faith of simple trust, glad surrender, and faithful responsiveness."[2] Clinton McCann calls Psalm 100 "the banner hymn of the Reformed tradition."[3]

Verse 2b, "Come (*bo'û*) into his presence with singing," and verse 4, "Enter (*bo'û*) his gates with thanksgiving, and his courts with praise" suggest that "this psalm was originally intended to be sung by worshippers as they entered the Jerusalem temple. For countless generations of Jews and Christians, it has been

1. Eaton, *The Psalms,* 350.
2. Brueggemann, "Psalm 100," *Int* 39, no. 1 (1985; pp. 65–69): 65. Cf. James L. Mays, "Worship, World, and Power: An Interpretation of Psalm 100," *Int* 23, no. 3 (1969; pp. 315–30): 316, "Were the statistics known, Psalm 100 would probably prove to be the song most often chanted from within the history that runs from the Israelite temple on Mount Zion to the synagogues and churches spread across the earth."
3. McCann, "Psalms," 1079. Cf. Knight, *Psalms,* II, 123, "'The Old Hundredth' is the name of the tune that is sung around the world to the metrical version of this favourite psalm: 'All people that on earth do dwell.' It was composed by William Kethe of Scotland, a friend of John Knox the Reformer, in 1560. . . . [The tune] was composed by Louis Bourgeois and appeared first in the French Genevan Psalter of 1551."

used to accompany the entrance in heart and mind to the presence of God, for worship and thanksgiving."[4]

Text and Context

As a complete psalm, Psalm 100 is a literary unit and as such is a proper preaching text. The author has further marked the psalm as a literary unit with a chiastic structure of a perfect seven imperatives:

> Triple imperative call to worship (vv 1–2)
> > Central call to *know that the* LORD, *he is the true God* (v 3)
> Triple imperative call to worship (vv 4–5)[5]

Starting with its nearest neighbors in the Psalter, biblical scholars have observed that Psalm 100 is very similar to Psalm 95. Compare: "For he is our God, and we are the people of his pasture, and the sheep of his hand" (Ps 95:7) and "Know that the LORD is God. It is he that made us, and we are his; we are his people, and the sheep of his pasture" (Ps 100:3). In addition, "Both psalms open with a cry for shouts of joy (95:1b, 2b; 100:1b). . . . Both call for *tôdâ* ('thanksgiving') to be given to Yahweh in his presence (95:2; 100:1–4)."[6] McCann suggests, "Given the similarity between Psalms 95 and 100 . . . , one can reasonably conclude that they are intended to form a frame around Psalms 96–99, which seem to form the core of the [enthronement] collection."[7]

In a slightly broader context, Psalm 100 functions as a doxology to the enthronement Psalms 93–99. As Rolf Jacobson puts it, "The hymn crowns a series of enthronement psalms (i.e., those psalms that celebrate the reign of the Lord [Hebrew *yhwh mālak*]) with a final paean of praise. Whereas those psalms emphasize that the Lord reigns over all peoples, nations, and lands (see Pss 95:3–4; 96:1–3; 97:1; 98:4; 99:1; etc.), Psalm 100 calls on 'all the earth' to praise the Lord of Israel."[8]

---

4. Rogerson and McKay, *Psalms 51–100*, 230. Cf. Mays, *Psalms*, 317, "It is a processional song for movement through the gates of the temple into its courts (v 4) where the LORD is present (v 2)." See also nn. 15, 32, and 54 below.

5. Jacobson in deClaissé-Walford, Jacobson, and Tanner, *The Book of Psalms*, 735. See p. 534 and n. 25 below.

6. Tate, *Psalms 51–100*, 535. See also the similar structure of other psalms in n. 21 below.

7. McCann, "Psalms," 1077.

8. Jacobson, "Psalm 100," in *Psalms for Preaching and Worship*, ed. Roger E. Van Harn and Brent A. Strawn (Grand Rapids: Eerdmans, 2009; pp. 265–67), 266. See, e.g., Psalm 97:1, "The LORD is king! Let the earth rejoice; let the many coastlands be glad!" Cf. Westermann, *Praise and Lament*,

This context can guide our interpretation of the psalm.[9] As the climax of the enthronement psalms, we can understand Psalm 100 as a hymn in praise of Yahweh, the King of all the earth, even though the psalm itself does not explicitly refer to Yahweh as King. But it does use royal imagery: it pictures the LORD as a shepherd, often an image for a king: "we are his people, and the sheep of his pasture" (100:3). Moreover, it commands people of all the earth to "*serve* the LORD" (100:2) as one would serve a king.[10]

The command to "*serve* the LORD" connects with the introductory Psalm 2: "Now therefore, O kings, be wise; be warned, O rulers of the earth. *Serve* the LORD with fear, with trembling" (Ps 2:10-11). And this command in Psalm 2, in turn, is based on the decalogue, "You shall have no other gods before me.... You shall not bow down to them or *worship* [*serve*, ESV] them" (Exod 20:3-5).

Psalm 100 can also be understood against the background of Exodus. Wilcock claims that the words "It is he that made us, and we are his" (100:3) "refer to the making, not of humanity, but of Israel, when God constituted his nation at Sinai. He guided his people through the desert as 'the sheep of his pasture.' He instructed them there to set up the courts of his tabernacle."[11] Another background may be Joshua 24 where Joshua made a covenant with the people at Shechem and the people responded, "The LORD our God we will *serve*, and him we will obey" (Josh 24:24).[12]

But verse 1 opens up an even broader possible background: "Make a joyful noise to the LORD, *all the earth*." Together with verse 3, "It is he that *made* us, and we are his," this seems to reach back to the creation account when God

---

255, "The next . . . grouping is Pss 93-99, the psalms of the kingdom of Yahweh (excluding Ps 94). Psalm 100 has been added as a concluding doxology." See also Wenham, *The Psalter Reclaimed*, 182-84; and Zenger, *Psalms 2*, 494-97.

9. "Decisive for the interpretation of Psalm 100 is that it is understood to be the climax and conclusion of the preceding 'YHWH is king' psalms." Zenger, *Psalms 2*, 494.

10. "The language of the psalm is shaped by 'royal theology.' For example, v 1, 'make a joyful noise to,' a 'royal shout' in reaction to the enthronement of a king or his 'appearing' [cf. 1 Sam 10:24; 2 Kings 11:12]; v 2: 'serve him,' namely as your 'LORD' and king [cf. Exod 8:1-6; 9:1, 13; 10:3; Josh 24:14-15, 18; Isa 19:23; Mal 3:14]; 'enter his courts,' that is, where his audiences are held; v 3: know that you are '*his* people,' that is, that he is your king; the metaphor 'shepherd-flock' is a royal metaphor; even the imperative 'know' has, in the perspective of 'acknowledge,' its political dimensions; v 4: likewise, the imperative 'praise his name' has connotations of reverence for a king." Zenger, ibid. (Scripture references taken from Zenger's p. 495 nn. 10 and 11).

11. Wilcock, *Message of Psalms 73-150*, 108.

12. "Joshua 24 and 2 Chron 30:1-12; 35:1-19 apparently outline the scenario presupposed in Psalm 100: the right service to Yahweh is contested by other religious opportunities. In their summons to worship, leaders of the congregation admonish all to dedicate themselves to Yahweh, performing the right service to him. . . . The liturgists urge people to 'enter' with thanks and praise." Gerstenberger, *Psalms*, II, 204.

said, "Let us *make* humankind in our image, according to our likeness" (Gen 1:26). McCann notes that "there is a rich ambiguity in the word 'made' (*'āśâ*); it could refer to God's creation of the world and all living things (see Pss 95:5; 104:24), or it could refer to God's 'making' or electing Israel as God's own people (see Deut 32:6, 15). The ambiguity is appropriate, for Israel could never tell the story of its election apart from an understanding of God's intention for 'all the earth.'"[13]

Literary Interpretation

The psalm is usually classified as a hymn, sometimes more precisely as an "imperative hymn,"[14] an "entry hymn,"[15] or a "hymn of procession."[16] We shall investigate in turn the psalm's parallelisms, imagery, repetition of keywords, and its structure.

Parallelisms

The parallelisms of Psalm 100 are fairly simple. The psalm consists of four strophes, each of which shows advancing parallelism of three lines. In other words, the psalm consists of four climactic parallelisms.

A Psalm of thanksgiving.

1Make a joyful noise to the LORD, all the earth.	A
2Worship the LORD with gladness;	+ A′
come into his presence with singing.	+ A″

3Know that the LORD is God.	A
It is he that made us, and we are his;	+ A′
we are his people, and the sheep of his pasture.	+ A″

---

13. McCann, "Psalms," 1078.

14. "A judgment which is sustained by the seven imperative verbs used in vv 1–4." Tate, *Psalms 51–100*, 534.

15. "The further classification of it as an entry hymn is rather popular (e.g., Gunkel, Oesterley, Kraus, Anderson, Weiser, Dahood). The setting is assumed to be that of a company of worshipers in front of the gates to the sanctuary summoned to enter the courts of the sanctuary with shouts and songs of praise." Ibid., 534–35.

16. A. Anderson, *Psalms 73–150*, 698, mentions G. Quell, *Das Kultische Problem der Psalmen* (1926), 71.

₄Enter his gates with thanksgiving,	A
and his courts with praise.	+ A'
Give thanks to him, bless his name.	+ A''

₅For the LORD is good;	A
his steadfast love endures forever,	+ A'
and his faithfulness to all generations.	+ A''

Imagery

Psalm 100 uses only a few metaphors. "Come into his presence" (v 2) is literally "come before his face" (*pānāyw*). "It is he that made us" (v 3) is the metaphor of a potter.[17] Mays writes that "'He made us' is an abbreviation of the salvation history of election, deliverance, and covenant by which Israel was brought into existence as the people of the LORD."[18] The potter metaphor is followed by the familiar pastoral metaphor, "we are . . . the sheep of his pasture" (v 3).[19] The "bless his *name*" in verse 4 could be called a metaphor for God himself since the name "is synonymous with the Lord himself in his gracious manifestation and accessibility to his people."[20]

Repetition of Keywords

The psalm uses the name "LORD" in each of its five verses except verse 4 where it substitutes "his name." In addition God (*'ĕlohîm*) is mentioned once in the central sentence, "Know that the LORD is God" (v 3). Twice the peoples of "all the earth" are enjoined to come: "Come (*bo'û*) into his presence" (v 2) and "Enter (*bo'û*) his gates" (v 4). The psalm highlights with several synonyms that they are

17. "The language of creation appeals to the metaphor of the potter." Brueggemann, "Psalm 100," *Int* 39, no. 1 (1985): 67. See, e.g., Isa 29:16; 45:9–11; 64:8; Jer 18:6.

18. Mays, *Psalms,* 319. Mays adds in "Worship, World, and Power," *Int* 23, no. 3 (1969): 324 n. 23, "For 'make' as a metaphor for Yahweh's election and salvation, cf. Ps. 95:6f.; Deut 32:6, 15; Isa 43:1, 21; 44:2.

19. Stott, *Favorite Psalms,* 83, "The potter who made them was the shepherd who tended them."

20. "The name of the Lord is the manifestation of his character. . . . It . . . is synonymous with the Lord himself in his gracious manifestation and accessibility to his people." Stek, *NIV Study Bible,* Ps 5:11 n. Cf. Anderson, *Psalms 1–72,* 101, "In Hebrew thought the name and its bearer are inseparably associated."

to come with joy: "joyful noise," "gladness," "singing," "thanksgiving," "praise," "give thanks," and "bless his name." Also notable in terms of repetition is that this short psalm has the perfect number of imperatives, seven. These repetitions will help us in formulating the theme of this psalm.

Structure

In Chapter 1, p. 11 above, we noted that the typical structure of a hymn has most of the following elements:

1) A call to praise the LORD
2) Transition (*kî*, for, because)
3) Reasons why the LORD is to be praised
4) Conclusion: Praise the LORD!

Psalm 100 lacks the conclusion but has three of these elements twice in succession:[21]

1) A call to praise the LORD	vv 1–2 and 4
2) Transition (*kî*, for, because)	v 3 (*kî*) "that"[22] and 5 "for"
3) Reason(s) why the LORD is to be praised	vv 3 and 5

The psalm, then, has two stanzas: verses 1–3 and 4–5. Zenger further observes that there is "linear progression" from stanza 1 to 2: "While the first tricolon [vv 1–2] speaks rather generally about the 'service' of the nations before and for their king, YHWH, the third tricolon [v 4] proposes the vision of common worship by the nations and Israel in the Temple."[23]

In addition to this twofold structure, McCann observes that of the seven imperatives, the central one, "Know that the LORD is God" (v 3) is of a different order than the others which require action. This central imperative enjoins "Know!" — "'know' something that will underlie all action."[24] This centering of

---

21. "As regards structure, the pattern is the same as that of 95:1–7: call to praise (vv 1–2) and reason (v 3); further call to praise (v 4) and reason (v 5; cf. also 96 and 98)." Eaton, *The Psalms,* 349. Cf. Stek, *NIV Study Bible,* "Ps 100" n., "The second main division (vv 4–5) parallels the structure of the first (vv 1–3), namely, a call to praise followed by a declaration of why the Lord is worthy of praise — the corresponding elements of the two divisions are complementary."

22. After an imperative, *kî* is translated as "that" rather than "for." See Fokkelman, *Major Poems,* II, 259. "Know that the LORD is God" still offers the reason for praising the LORD.

23. Zenger, *Psalms 2,* 494.

24. "The lone imperative in verse 3 is of a different order; it demands not that the reader act

the imperative "know" suggests the possibility of a chiastic structure. For example, Jacobson writes, "The centering structure of the whole psalm looks like this:

> Triple imperative call to worship (vv 1–2)
>   Central call to *know that the* LORD, *he is the true God* (v 3)
> Triple imperative call to worship (vv 4–5)

These contrasting structures do not compete with each other so as to pull the psalm apart, but coexist with each other in such a manner as to hold the psalm together as an elegant, concise composition."[25]

Theocentric Interpretation

Psalm 100 is so clearly focused on God, there is not much danger of a preacher falling into an anthropocentric interpretation. But to highlight its theocentric emphasis we note here not only that the LORD is obviously the object of praise and thanksgiving, but, as Jacobson suggests, we should "carefully observe the text's verbal redundancy that makes the Lord the object of every verb":[26] "Make a joyful noise to the LORD. . . . Worship the LORD. . . . Come into his presence. . . . Know that the LORD is God. . . . Enter his gates. . . . Give thanks to him, bless his name," ending with the creed that summarizes Israel's faith, "For the LORD is good; his steadfast love endures forever, and his faithfulness to all generations."

Perhaps Mays best articulates the God-centered nature of this psalm: "The psalmist has done everything within the capacity of art to rivet attention beyond all else upon the name [*Yahweh*]. In four poetic lines the name is uttered four times; and in every measure lacking the name it is represented by an echoing

---

but that the reader 'know' something that will underlie all action." McCann, *Theological Introduction*, 65–66.

25. Jacobson in deClaissé-Walford, Jacobson, and Tanner, *The Book of Psalms*, 735. Cf. Zenger, *Psalms 2*, 493, "The three tricola in vv 1–4 constitute a concentric structure. While the first and third tricola each contain three appeals to worship, the middle tricolon calls for an awareness of the uniqueness of YHWH and the relationship of YHWH to all who dwell on the earth. This concentric structure is underscored by the fact that immediately before and immediately after the middle tricolon (at v 2b and 4a) stands the appeal, in the same words, 'go into' (thus forming the internal frame), *and* that the calls to festive song in v 1b (imperative + dative particle *l*) and v 4c (imperative + dative particle *l*) establish an external frame (*inclusion*)." See also Edesio Sanchez, "Translation of Psalm 100 — taking account of its structure," *The Bible Translator* 46, no. 2 (1995; pp. 243–45): 243–44.

26. Jacobson in deClaissé-Walford, Jacobson, and Tanner, *The Book of Psalms*, 739.

pronoun — as if to say this identity is so urgently important that no sentence can be spoken without some word that represents it."[27]

Textual Theme and Goal

The psalm is addressed to "all the earth" (v 1), which we can understand as "all peoples on earth."[28] The seven imperatives indicate that all peoples should do something, that is, worship Israel's God, the LORD. They should worship Israel's God because he alone is the true God (v 3) and he is good (v 5). Moreover, they should worship the LORD with gladness (and its synonyms in vv 1–2) and thanksgiving (superscription and v 4). In the light of these givens we can formulate the psalm's theme as follows: *Worship the LORD, all peoples of the earth, with gladness and thanksgiving, because the LORD alone is God and good.*

As to the goal of this psalm, we cannot be sure of its original historical setting, but we do know that the goal of hymns in general was to encourage Israel to praise the LORD. In this psalm that goal is expanded to all peoples of the earth. Moreover, the imperatives indicate that this psalm not only encourages all peoples to worship the LORD but, more strongly, enjoins them, urges them to do so. Therefore we can formulate the goal as, *To urge all peoples of the earth to worship the LORD with gladness and thanksgiving because the LORD alone is God and good.*

Ways to Preach Christ

Psalm 100 contains no promise of the coming Christ nor a type. But we can still move forward to Jesus Christ in the New Testament by way of analogy supported by New Testament references and redemptive-historical progression supported by New Testament references.

Analogy and New Testament References

One could possibly use analogy by focusing on the image of the LORD as Shepherd: "We are his people, and the sheep of his pasture" (v 3). In the New Testament, Jesus claims to be the good shepherd: "I am the good shepherd. The good shepherd lays down his life for the sheep" (John 10:11).[29]

27. Mays, "Worship, World, and Power," *Int* 23/3 (1969) 320.
28. See n. 37 below.
29. Cf. Reardon, *Christ in the Psalms,* 197. Williams, *Psalms 73–150,* 209, also uses analogy

Redemptive-Historical Progression and New Testament References

But a stronger bridge to Christ in the New Testament is redemptive-historical progression supported by New Testament references, for this bridge can carry forward the theme of Psalm 100, "Worship the LORD, all peoples of the earth, with gladness and thanksgiving, because the LORD alone is God and good." This Old Testament call for all the earth to worship the LORD begins to be realized in New Testament times when Jesus is born (Matt 2:11 [the wise men] and John 1:29; 3:16) and when Jesus sends out his disciples to "make disciples of all nations" (Matt 28:19). And it will be completely realized on the last day when Jesus comes again (Phil 2:8–11; Rev 7:9–12; see "Sermon Exposition" below).

Sermon Theme, Goal, and Need

Because the New Testament context does not change the theme of the psalm, the textual theme can function as the sermon theme provided we understand "LORD" as referring not only to the Old Testament "I am" but also to the Lord Jesus, the New Testament "I am": *Worship the LORD, all peoples of the earth, with gladness and thanksgiving, because the LORD alone is God and good.* Likewise, the textual goal can become the sermon goal: *To urge all peoples of the earth to worship the LORD with gladness and thanksgiving because the LORD alone is God and good.* This goal points to the need addressed in this sermon: All peoples of the earth do not worship the LORD with gladness and thanksgiving. The sermon introduction could illustrate this need, thus providing a context for hearing the relevance of this message.

Liturgy, Scripture Reading, Sermon Outline, and PowerPoint

The whole of Psalm 100 could serve as a fitting call to worship. But since it will likely be read again prior to the preaching of the Word, it is better to select as call to worship either verse 2 or 4 or verses 2 and 4 together.

The psalm seems to trace the movement of pilgrims from approaching the temple (vv 1–2) to the invitation for the pilgrims to enter the temple gates and

---

but blends it with promise-fulfillment: "The metaphor of sheep assumes that God is the shepherd (see Ps 23). Therefore, Isaiah promises, 'He will feed His flock like a shepherd' (Isa 40:11). This picture is now fulfilled in Jesus."

courts with thanksgiving and praise (v 4).[30] The Scripture reading can highlight this movement as follows:

LITURGIST:
> A Psalm of thanksgiving.

LITURGIST OR CHOIR:
> ₁Make a joyful noise to the LORD, all the earth.
> ₂Worship the LORD with gladness;
> come into his presence with singing.
> ₃Know that the LORD is God.

CONGREGATION (note the "us" and "we"):[31]
> It is he that made us, and we are his;
> we are his people, and the sheep of his pasture.

LITURGIST OR CHOIR:[32]
> ₄Enter his gates with thanksgiving,
> and his courts with praise.
> Give thanks to him, bless his name.

CONGREGATION:[33]
> ₅For the LORD is good;
> his steadfast love endures forever,
> and his faithfulness to all generations.

The sermon outline can follow the movement through the four strophes with a final move to Christ's First and Second Coming.

I. All the earth, come into the LORD's presence with joyful singing (vv 1–2)
II. Know, acknowledge, that the LORD is God; we are his people (v 3)
III. Enter the temple's gates with thanksgiving and praise (v 4)
IV. For the LORD is good, faithful to all generations (v 5)
V. Fulfillment in Christ's First and Second Coming (NT)

---

30. "We should perhaps imagine a liturgist or Levitical choir calling the congregation, who are outside the temple gates, to enter by a procession." Broyles, *Psalms*, 386.

31. Cf. Gerstenberger, *Psalms*, II, 205, "According to our analysis only v 3bc is the response of the congregation ('we'), while v 3a is summons, remembrance, exhortation."

32. "The opening words of the second part of the psalm were probably sung by the choir of priests, before the festival congregation passed through the gates of the Temple and entered its forecourts." Weiser, *The Psalms*, 647.

33. "V 5 is clearly a standard hymn, introduced by the exclamatory *kî*, 'yes,' as found many times in praise contexts. The *kî* verse states a brief hymn to be repeatedly sung by choir or congregation (cf. 33:4; 96:4–5)." Gerstenberger, *Psalms*, II, 204. Cf. Terrien, *The Psalms*, 690, "The blessing [v 5] is sung by the congregation." Cf. Weiser, *The Psalms*, 647.

PowerPoint could be used again to highlight the verses being explained but also to demonstrate the Old Testament separation of Israel from the Gentiles in the temple courts.[34]

Sermon Exposition

When Psalm 100 was composed, only a small minority of people in the world worshiped Israel's God, the LORD. Israel had little interest in spreading news about its God to Gentile nations. Israel had to keep itself separate from the nations, lest they be tempted to follow pagan idols (e.g., Lev 20:26).[35] In fact, Gentiles were not allowed to worship the LORD together with Israel. The temple had a separate court for Gentiles, as far from the Holy Place as possible. There was a court for the priests (right next to the Holy Place where God dwelt), next a court for Israel, then a court for women, and finally a court for Gentiles.

It comes as a surprise, then, that Psalm 100 calls all peoples of the earth to worship the LORD — even, verse 4, to enter the temple's gates with thanksgiving and its courts with praise. But there it is, verse 1,[36] "Make a joyful noise to the LORD, *all the earth.*" The psalm is addressed to "all the earth," all peoples of the earth.[37] All the nations of the earth are invited, no, commanded,[38] to "make a joyful noise to the LORD."

---

34. See p. 331 above.

35. "You shall be holy to me; for I the LORD am holy, and I have separated you from the other peoples to be mine" (Lev 20:26). Cf. Psalm 106:35-38, "But they mingled with the nations and learned to do as they did. They served their idols, which became a snare to them. They sacrificed their sons and their daughters to the demons; they poured out innocent blood, the blood of their sons and daughters, whom they sacrificed to the idols of Canaan; and the land was polluted with blood."

36. In the sermon I would probably skip over the superscription, "A Psalm of thanksgiving," at this stage and perhaps come back to it with verse 4, "Enter his gates with thanksgiving."

37. "The imperatives are directed in v 1a at *all the earth (kol-hā'āreṣ).* The phrase is common in the Psalter, where it parallels terms such as 'all those who dwell in the world' (. . . ; 33:8), 'all peoples' (. . . ; 96:3; cf. 66:8), 'among the nations' (. . . ; 96:10), 'all the ends of the earth' (. . . ; 98:3), and 'over the heavens' (. . . ; 108:5). These parallels indicate that, at least rhetorically, the psalm has a universal audience in mind." Jacobson in deClaissé-Walford, Jacobson, and Tanner, *The Book of Psalms,* 736. Cf. Mays, "Worship, World, and Power," *Int* 23, no. 3 (1969): 320, "The command is meant to be universal. This is no choir calling only to Israelites within the sound of its voice; the sequence of imperatives reaches out to mankind. . . . Against all practicality or human expectation of being heard, they summon mankind."

38. The first of seven imperatives. "The imperative is somewhat admonitory; this fits the fact that it is addressed to all the earth, which does not at the moment acknowledge Yahweh." Goldingay, *Psalms,* III, 135.

The "joyful noise" is not just shouting anything. Israel would make a joyful noise when a new king was crowned. They would shout, "Long live the king!"[39] Even today at Buckingham Palace when the queen appears on the balcony, people will shout, "Long live the queen." It is a shout of acclamation. You are my queen. I am your subject. So all peoples of the earth are commanded when they approach the temple of the LORD to acknowledge that this is the palace where the King of all the earth resides. When they enter into the presence of the King, they ought to shout to the LORD: "Long live the King." You are our King. We are your subjects.

Verse 2, "Worship the LORD with gladness; come into his presence with singing." Two more commands: "Worship!" and "Come!" The command to "worship" actually has a deeper meaning than we usually imagine when we go to church to worship. The phrase could be translated, "Serve the LORD!" This ambiguity leads Jacobson to a profound insight into the meaning of worship: "The term, similar to the English word 'service' or the German [and Dutch] *Dienst,* can mean both 'work/serve' and 'worship.' Here the meaning is obviously to worship, but the double sense of the word indicates that an act of worship is part of a deeper relationship that one has with one's God. One serves one's God in the same way that a worker serves an employer, a slave serves a master."[40] McCann adds, "The word [serve, *'ābad*] means to orient one's whole life and existence to a sovereign master, to be the servant or slave of a monarch."[41]

In a sense verse 2 is similar to the admonition in the introductory Psalm 2, "Now therefore, O kings, be wise; be warned, O rulers of the earth. *Serve* the LORD with fear, with trembling" (Ps 2:10–11). But instead of fear and trembling, Psalm 100 urges the peoples of the earth, "Make a *joyful* noise to the LORD. . . . Worship the LORD with *gladness;* come into his presence with *singing.*" The peoples of the earth should not come reluctantly or under compulsion. They should not come sadly but *gladly.* Only joy can properly express what a privilege it is to belong to the LORD and to worship the King of the universe.

---

39. See, e.g., 1 Sam 10:24 and 2 Kings 11:12. "To 'make a joyful noise' is an appropriate way to acknowledge and to greet a monarch (see Pss 95:1–2; 98:4, 6)." McCann, "Psalms," 1078.

40. Jacobson in deClaissé-Walford, Jacobson, and Tanner, *The Book of Psalms,* 737.

41. McCann, "Psalms," 1078, with references to Pss 2:11; 18:43; 22:30; 72:11; 97:7; and 102:22. McCann continues, "The word always occurs in the Psalter in relation to a royal figure, either human or divine." Cf. Tate, *Psalms 51–100,* 536–37, "The verb *'ābad* conveys a range of meaning. On the one side it means to function as a servant or a slave. . . . On the other side, the verb is used for worship: serve a god, worship a god. . . . It is frequently used in Deuteronomy for worship of other gods than Yahweh . . . as well as of commitment to and worship of Yahweh. . . ." Cf. Mays, "Worship, World, and Power," *Int* 23, no. 3 (1969): 322, "To serve Yahweh is conduct which excludes slavery to human government or subjection to the power of the 'gods'. . . . The psalm belongs at the point where men publicly assemble to recognize the power to which they will submit their living."

Verse 2 commands, "Come into his presence[42] with singing." Just as the shouts of joy are not empty shouts but acclamations of our King, so the singing does not consist of just any song. The songs should praise the LORD, praise him for his mighty acts in saving, protecting, and providing for his people. Psalm 107 instructs Israel, "Let them thank the LORD for his steadfast love, for his wonderful works to humankind. And let them offer thanksgiving sacrifices, and *tell of his deeds with songs of joy*" (Ps 107:21–22).

And why should all peoples of the earth make a joyful noise to Israel's God and worship him with gladness and singing? Verse 3 provides the answer: "Know that the LORD is God. It is he that made us, and we are his; we are his people, and the sheep of his pasture."

The answer begins with, "Know that the LORD is God."[43] Another command, the fourth one. The first three were commands to actions: "Make a joyful noise!" "Worship the LORD!" "Come into his presence!" The people of all the earth can either obey or disobey commands to actions. Commands are a matter of the will. But *know* seems to be a matter of the mind. What are the people to do with the command, *Know!*?

The reason why we have a problem with the command "*Know* that the LORD is God" is that we tend to think of knowing as theoretical. But "ancient Hebrew knew no division between theoretical and practical knowledge. . . . To know the Lord is also to follow the Lord's commandments and to do the Lord's will."[44] "Know that the LORD is God!" The Hebrew is emphatic. "It might be better rendered, 'Know that the LORD *alone* is God.' This is a call to universal acknowledgment of the Lord's universal reign."[45] Acknowledge that the LORD alone is God and act on that knowledge!

In the ancient Near East people believed in many gods. The sun was thought to be a god, as well as the moon and the stars, the sea, the river, the desert. Wher-

---

42. "The spatial reference is to the temple, where God's presence is conceived to dwell, an idea that will be developed in verse 4." Alter, *Book of Psalms*, 348.

43. Cf. Deut 4:35, 39, "To you it was shown so that you would acknowledge that *the LORD is God*; there is no other besides him. . . . So acknowledge today and take to heart that *the LORD is God* in heaven above and on the earth beneath; there is no other." Cf. 1 Kings 18:39, "When all the people saw it [the LORD's lightning striking the drenched altar], they fell on their faces and said, '*The LORD indeed is God; the LORD indeed is God.*'"

44. Jacobson in deClaissé-Walford, Jacobson, and Tanner, *The Book of Psalms*, 738, with a reference to Hos 4:1–4. Cf. A. Anderson, *Psalms 73–150*, 699, "This is more than merely an intellectual exercise; in this context it implies the acknowledgement that Yahweh is God, and a self-involvement in all the demands and responsibilities which the lordship of Yahweh implies (cf. Deut 4:39; Isa 43:10; Jer 3:13; 14:20)."

45. Jacobson, "Psalm 100," in *Psalms for Preaching*, 266. Cf. Psalm 46:10, "Be still, and know that I am God! I am exalted among the nations, I am exalted in the earth."

ever one traveled one had to deal with different gods. In bold opposition to that popular view, Psalm 100 states unequivocally that Israel's God, the LORD, alone is God. There are no other gods worthy of worship and service.

Brueggemann comments, "An enormous claim is made in the text by the claim that *Yahweh* is *Elohim*. It is asserted that the God of the Exodus is the sovereign of all of life. The religion of Israel is not a private or tribal affair but in fact characterizes the truth about all of life."[46] That is why this psalm commands all peoples of the earth to "make a joyful noise to the LORD," to "worship the LORD with gladness," and to "come into his presence with singing." All these actions are based on the knowledge that the LORD alone is God.

Verse 3 continues, "It is he that made us, and we are his; we are his people, and the sheep of his pasture." These words apply first of all to God's people Israel.[47] He "made" them, shaping them carefully as a potter shapes the clay. He called their father Abraham out of Babylonia to the Promised Land. When drought threatened God's people there, he led them to well-watered Egypt. When the Pharaoh of Egypt enslaved them, the LORD ["I am who I am"] brought them out with "a mighty hand and an outstretched arm" (Deut 5:15). He made a covenant with them at Mount Sinai that he would be their God and they would be his people. He brought them into the Promised Land. "It is he that made us, and we are his."[48] Since the LORD made Israel, they are his special possession.

Even more, "we are his people, and the sheep of his pasture." As the worshipers ascended Mount Zion and "came streaming through the Temple doors," they gave "the impression that they were like a flock that was following the shepherd's call."[49]

---

46. Brueggemann, "Psalm 100," *Int* 39, no. 1 (1985): 66. He adds, "Conversely, it is asserted that the false *Elohim* of coercion, oppression, and exploitation are in this moment dethroned and need no longer be obeyed. Cf. Brueggemann, *The Psalms*, 119, "In our social context, some of the more seductive of these idolatries ['that want our loyalty and chase after our life commitment'] are consumerism, militarism, ageism, racism, sexism, and capitalism [socialism? communism?]. Praise [of Yahweh] is a dismissal of every such claim."

47. A. Anderson, *Psalms 73–150*, 699, limits the understanding to Israel: "The reference is not to the creation of man, but to the formation of the people of God (cf. Isa 29:23; 43:1, 21; 44:2; 60:21)." So also Jacobson in deClaissé-Walford, Jacobson, and Tanner, *The Book of Psalms*, 738, "The phrase 'he made us' should not be understood as referring to God's act of creation, but to the Lord's action of claiming Israel as God's priestly nation." But since the psalm is addressed to "all the earth," the context suggests that "he made them" also refers to the creation of human kind. See p. 531 above for the ambiguity of "made." See, e.g., Ps 86:9, "All the nations you have made shall come and bow down before you, O Lord, and shall glorify your name."

48. For discussion on the alternative reading of "and not we ourselves," see, e.g., Kidner, *Psalms 73–150*, 356–57, and Jacobson, "Psalm 100," in *Psalms for Preaching*, 267.

49. Leupold, *Exposition of the Psalms*, 700.

The LORD was their Shepherd. They were the sheep of his pasture. The LORD would lead Israel to green pastures and quiet waters.

But remember, this psalm is addressed not just to Israel but to peoples of "all the earth." According to Genesis, the LORD made not only Israel but he "made" all nations. Psalm 104 exclaims, "O LORD, how manifold are your works! In wisdom you have *made* them all; the earth is full of your creatures" (Ps 104:24). We see the divine Potter at work in all of creation, especially in making humankind. Genesis 2 pictures God as a Potter fashioning the first human from the dust of the earth and breathing into his nostrils "the breath of life" (Gen 2:7).[50]

So in a sense the LORD is Shepherd not only of Israel but of peoples of "all the earth." He made them; they are his. The LORD is King of all the earth. That is why this psalm can begin with, "Make a joyful noise to the LORD, all the earth." "The nations are to recognize and acknowledge their own createdness and, as a consequence, their belonging to the one God and creator, and this recognition opens for the nations the gate to an equal sharing in Israel's worship."[51] As McCann puts it, "Psalm 100 wants us to know that God is shepherd both of God's people and of the whole cosmos."[52] Therefore the peoples of "all the earth" are commanded, "Know, acknowledge, that the LORD alone is God!" Once they acknowledge this, they will want to come joyfully to God's temple to praise the LORD together with Israel.[53]

Verse 4 begins the second half of this psalm with three imperatives: "Enter!" "Give thanks!" and "Bless!" A choir of priests probably sang these words, inviting the worshipers to enter through the temple gates and into the courts.[54] Verse 4,

---

50. Cf. Gen 1:26, "Then God said, 'Let us *make* humankind in our image, according to our likeness; and let them have dominion . . . (Gen 1:26)." See also, e.g., Gen 2:21–23; 5:1–2; 10; 11; 12:1–2.

51. Zenger, *Psalms 2,* 496, quoting J. Jeremias, "Psalm 100," 614. Cf. Eaton, *The Psalms,* 349, "Although the expressions 'his people' and 'the flock of his pasture' focus on the covenant community, there is no break with the initial address to 'all the earth'; the representative character of the assembly is thus maintained throughout." Cf. Eaton, *Psalms,* 241, "The smaller circle of Israel worshiping at Zion has a representative character, maintaining on behalf of all the yearly and daily round of priestly service. . . . God's cosmic rule and his shepherding of Israel are but aspects of his one kingly work."

52. McCann, "Psalms," 1079. Cf. p. 1078, "The clustering of personal pronouns and pronominal suffixes in v 3 is striking, as is their sequence: 'he . . . he . . . us . . . we . . . his . . . his.' This arrangement dramatically suggests that the question of human identity must begin and end with God."

53. The LORD had promised Abraham, "In you all the families of the earth shall be blessed" (Gen 12:3; cf. 18:18; 22:18; 26:4). Later the LORD promised, "And the foreigners who join themselves to the LORD, to minister to him, to love the name of the LORD, and to be his servants . . . — these I will bring to my holy mountain, and make them joyful in my house of prayer . . . ; for my house shall be called a house of prayer for all peoples" (Isa 56:6–7).

54. See Weiser, *The Psalms,* 647, quoted in n. 32 above. Cf. Brueggemann, *Texts for Preaching,*

"Enter his gates with thanksgiving, and his courts with praise. Give thanks to him, bless his name." While the first stanza stressed joyful praise, the emphasis in the second stanza is more on giving thanks. Notice the call to thanksgiving twice: "Enter his gates with *thanksgiving*, and his courts with praise. Give *thanks* to him, bless his name." Because of this emphasis on thanksgiving, the ancient editors gave the psalm the heading, "A Psalm of Thanksgiving."[55]

The invitation to give thanks to the LORD went out to all worshipers: "Enter his gates with thanksgiving, and his courts with praise." Thanksgiving and praise are very similar.[56] "The aim in both praise and thanksgiving is 'to exalt and glorify God.'"[57] But thanksgiving focuses more on gratitude for the things God has done.[58] We'll hear more about what God has done at the end of the psalm. But first verse 4 commands again, "Give thanks to him,"[59] and adds, "bless his name." To bless God's name is to "praise God for his blessings,"[60] for what he has done.

Remember again, this psalm is addressed not just to Israel but to peoples of "all the earth." Amazingly, "'all those who dwell on earth' are invited, like the Israelites (or together with them), to pass through the gates of the walls surrounding the Temple precincts and, in the courts of the Temple, to join in singing . . . the traditional songs of praise to YHWH."[61] Or perhaps it is not so amazing. Had not God promised Abraham, "in you all the families of the earth shall be blessed" (Gen 12:3)? Psalm 96 also demanded, "Ascribe to the LORD, O families of the peoples, ascribe to the LORD glory and strength. Ascribe to the LORD the glory due

---

575, "'Enter,' 'give thanks,' 'bless.' The first verb is the same as the last verb in v 2, making clear that this is a liturgical procession."

55. Davidson, *Vitality of Worship,* 326, notes, "This is the only time the word 'thanksgiving' (Hebrew *tôdâ*) appears in the headings of the Psalms. The word can either refer to a type of sacrifice or to the attitude that gives rise to and accompanies such a sacrifice (see 50:14)." Cf. Gerstenberger, *Psalms,* II, 203.

56. As suggested by the parallelism of "thanksgiving" and "praise."

57. Tate, *Psalms 51–100,* 538.

58. Ibid., "Thanksgiving is more directly focused on what God has done and the experience of the one giving the thanksgiving, but praise also almost always arises from an awareness of what God has done, though it is more generalized and expresses what he *does.*"

59. Brueggemann, *Texts for Preaching,* 575, states that "'Give thanks,' suggests not only an act of gratitude, but also a public acknowledgment of belonging to Yahweh in loyalty, i.e., 'confessing Yahweh.'"

60. A. Anderson, *Psalms 73–150,* 699, with references to Pss 34:1, 16:7, and 104:1. Psalm 34:1 is clearest because of its parallelism: "I will bless the LORD at all times; his praise shall continually be in my mouth." See also, e.g., Psalm 135 which begins with "Praise the LORD," tells what the LORD has done for his people, and ends with, "O house of Israel, bless the LORD!" and a final "Praise the LORD!" Cf. Williams, *Psalms 73–150,* 209, "To bless God's name is to praise Him for who He is as He relates to us."

61. Zenger, *Psalms 2,* 496.

his name; bring an offering, and come into his courts" (Ps 96:7–8). Why were the nations ordered to come into the courts of the LORD's palace? Psalm 96 answers, "Say among the nations, 'The LORD is king!'" (Ps 96:10). The King of all the earth has a right to the devotion and praise of the whole world.

Psalm 100 has its own answer to the question why it enjoins "all the earth" to come to the temple to thank and bless the LORD. The answer is given in verse 5: "For the LORD is good; his steadfast love endures forever, and his faithfulness to all generations." This final verse offers three reasons for thanking and blessing the LORD: first, "the LORD is *good*"; second, "his *steadfast love* endures forever"; and third, "his *faithfulness* [endures] to all generations." These are three characteristics of the LORD: goodness, steadfast love, and faithfulness.[62]

The basic reason for all peoples to enter the temple courts to thank the LORD is that "the LORD is *good.*" "Goodness is of the very essence of God's nature."[63] The LORD is the source of all good things. The LORD is the one who gives us life, who provides our daily bread, who gives us joy and happiness, who surrounds us with family and friends, you name it.[64] The LORD is the one who offers us salvation. Psalm 34:8 declares, "O taste and see that the LORD is good; happy are those who take refuge in him." Psalm 100 commands us to give thanks to the LORD because he is good. All the good things we experience in life come from the LORD.[65] Therefore, come and give thanks to him.

But verse 5 presents two more reasons for giving thanks to the LORD: "his steadfast love endures forever, and his faithfulness to all generations." "His steadfast love" (*ḥesed*) or "loving kindness" (NASB) or "unfailing love" (NLT) is the love that keeps loving, no matter what.[66] His "steadfast love" is the basis for the

---

62. "Ps 100:5 contains the only form of this expression in the OT which brings together the three aspects of goodness, loyal-love, and faithfulness." Tate, *Psalms 51–100*, 538.

63. Weiser, *The Psalms*, 647, who continues, "and his acts of grace are not the product of a momentary friendly whim or manifestations of the arbitrary mood of a divine despot. That the cult community is capable of 'believing' in God and 'trusting' in him finds its justification in the constancy and, consequently, in the reliability of God's gracious purposes within the covenant relationship."

64. "That the Lord is 'good' implies that he is the source of all that gives life its rich positive and creative variety, and that says 'No' to all that is evil and threatens to destroy his creative purposes." Davidson, *Vitality of Worship*, 327. Cf. Tate, *Psalms 51–100*, 539, "Yahweh is 'good' because he does good things; acts which give life, which deliver from evil, and which empower the recipient with power."

65. Cf. Matt 7:11, "If you then, who are evil, know how to give good gifts to your children, how much more will your Father in heaven give good things to those who ask him!" Cf. James 1:17, "Every generous act of giving, with every perfect gift, is from above, coming down from the Father of lights, with whom there is no variation or shadow due to change."

66. See above pp. 257–58 and p. 376.

salvation of God's people.[67] "His steadfast love endures *forever*"; that is, as far into the future as we can imagine, and beyond. His steadfast love will never end. Forever we can count on the LORD's steadfast love. What a reason to give thanks to the LORD!

Verse 5 mentions a third reason for giving thanks to the LORD: "his faithfulness [endures] to all generations." "Faithfulness" is another crucial term in the Old Testament. Faithfulness means that the LORD is reliable, dependable.[68] You can count on the LORD to be there for you. What a reason to give thanks to the LORD!

As the LORD's "steadfast love endures *forever*," so "his faithfulness [endures] to *all generations*."[69] "These phrases reach out to include the furthest reaches of time so as to say that . . . [the LORD's steadfast love and faithfulness] will be coextensive with history. . . . The basis of praise [and thanks] is the confidence that the LORD's faithful favor in the past has already opened up the future as the sphere of his goodness."[70]

Summarizing our findings, the first stanza of the psalm calls upon the peoples of "all the earth" to do three things: to "make a joyful noise to the LORD," to "worship the LORD with gladness," and to "come into his presence with singing." Verse 3 offers three reasons for giving the LORD this joyful praise. The basic reason is that "the LORD is God." He alone is King of all the earth. From this follows a second reason for praising the LORD: "It is he that made us, and we are his." And a third reason: "We are his people, and the sheep of his pasture." Three reasons for the peoples of "all the earth" to bring joyful praise to the LORD for *who he is:* our King, our Maker, and our Shepherd.

The second stanza of the psalm also calls upon the peoples of "all the earth" to do three things: to "enter his gates with thanksgiving and his courts with praise," to "give thanks to him," and to "bless his name." Instead of joyful praise it calls more for thanksgiving. Verse 5 offers three reasons for thanking the LORD. First, "For the LORD is good." Second, "his steadfast love endures forever." And third, "his faithfulness [endures] to all generations." Three reasons for the peoples of all

---

67. "In the Psalter's vocabulary of praise, *ḥesed* is the characterizing term for Yahweh's salvation; for example, 'Yahweh has made known his salvation . . . he has remembered his *ḥesed* and faithfulness to the house of Israel'" (Ps 98:2f.). Mays, "Worship, World, and Power," *Int* 23, no. 3 (1969): 328.

68. "The sense of 'faithfulness' is reliable support; the same Hebrew root appears as the word for the sturdy pillars (NRSV 'supports') supporting the door frame in 2 Kings 18:16." Limburg, *Psalms*, 338.

69. "'Faithfulness' is used so often as a word-pair with 'loyalty' [steadfast love] in the phraseology of the Psalter that it functions as a hendiadys meaning 'faithful loyalty' [faithful steadfast love]." Mays, "Worship, World, and Power," *Int* 23, no. 3 (1969): 327.

70. Ibid., 329. Cf. Leupold, *Exposition of the Psalms*, 700, "It is for gifts that endure into the eternities that praise and thanksgiving in a special sense should be offered."

the earth to thank the LORD for what he is and *does for us:* he is good to us, loves us forever, and is faithful to all generations.

Thus Psalm 100 looks forward to peoples of "all the earth" worshiping Israel's God, the LORD, together with Israel.[71] But this wonderful event never took place in Old Testament times. Relatively few Gentiles joined Israel in worshiping the LORD. Yet the LORD remained faithful to "all generations." In the fullness of time, he sent his only Son to make it happen. When Jesus was born in Bethlehem, wise men came from the East to worship the newborn king and offer him rich gifts (Matt 2:11). These were the first Gentiles to worship Jesus. Many more would follow later. John wrote, "God so loved the *world* that he gave his only Son, so that *everyone* who believes in him may not perish but may have eternal life" (John 3:16). Jesus is "the Lamb of God who takes away the sin of the world!" (John 1:29; cf. 1 John 2:2). Jesus died and rose for the peoples of "all the earth." After his resurrection, Jesus sent out his disciples to spread the good news to "all the earth": "Go therefore and make disciples of *all nations,* baptizing them in the name of the Father and of the Son and of the Holy Spirit" (Matt 28:19). Then Jesus ascended to his throne in heaven where he rules as King of the universe.

Meanwhile, the church is still mandated to "make disciples of all nations." After 2000 years of mission work, 2.1 billion people identify themselves as Christians. That may seem like a lot, but there are more than 7 billion people in the world. This means that more than 2/3 of the people in the world do not worship the Lord. And God wishes for all nations to offer praise and thanksgiving to him.[72]

But Scripture gives us solid hope that one day all nations will worship the Lord. Psalm 86:9 declares confidently, "All the nations you have made shall come and bow down before you, O Lord, and shall glorify your name." Paul quotes an

---

71. Psalm 100 expressed "the hope that the 'confession' attested in v 3 will one day bring Israel and the nations together to what will then be a common worship service of thanksgiving and sacrifice.... [Verse 3] presents one of the most spectacular theological statements in the Hebrew Bible in that it takes the so-called covenant formula, which traditionally is a general expression of the special position of Israel in contrast to the nations, and now places it *also* on the lips of the nations as a confession of *their* relationship to YHWH." Zenger, *Psalms 2,* 495–96. Cf. Carl J. Bosma, "Discerning the Voices in the Psalms," *CTJ* 43 (2008; pp. 183–212): 212, "In Psalm 95:6–7, Israel is invited to come and submit herself to the Lord, the great Shepherd-King. Psalm 100:3 picks up the expanded covenant formula from Psalm 95:7 (cf. Ps 79:13) and boldly extends the invitation to come and serve the Lord to 'all the earth.' As a result, the foundational covenant formula has been universalized."

72. See, e.g., Psalm 67:1–3, "May God be gracious to us and bless us and make his face to shine upon us, that your way may be known upon earth, your saving power among all nations. Let the peoples praise you, O God; let all the peoples praise you." Cf. Ps 117:1, "Praise the Lord, all you nations! Extol him, all you peoples!"

early Christian hymn about Jesus: "God . . . highly exalted him and gave him the name that is above every name, so that at the name of Jesus *every knee* should bend, in heaven and on earth and under the earth, and *every tongue should confess that Jesus Christ is Lord,* to the glory of God the Father" (Phil 2:8–11).

When Jesus comes again, Gentile nations will indeed worship the LORD together with Israel,[73] as Psalm 100 urges and desires. In Revelation 7 John reports a marvelous vision of the time of the end, "After this I looked, and there was a great multitude that no one could count, *from every nation, from all tribes and peoples and languages,* standing before the throne and before the Lamb, robed in white, with palm branches in their hands. They cried out in a loud voice, saying, 'Salvation belongs to our God who is seated on the throne, and to the Lamb!' And all . . . fell on their faces before the throne and worshiped God, *singing,* 'Amen! *Blessing* and glory and wisdom and *thanksgiving* and honor and power and might be to our God forever and ever! Amen" (Rev 7:9–12).

What a picture, peoples of "all the earth" together worshiping God and the Lamb Jesus with gladness and thanksgiving. Pray for the church as it seeks to bring the good news of Jesus to the nations. Pray for all nations that, through the work of the Holy Spirit, they may join the church in praising God the Father and his Son Jesus Christ.

Prayer[74]

O God, our Maker and Shepherd, inspire in us the joy that is a genuine
response to your work of salvation.
Grant that with thankful hearts we may ever serve before your face.
Enable us to carry out Jesus' commission to "make disciples of all nations."
We pray that peoples of all nations may indeed offer you the praise and
thanksgiving you so richly deserve
because you alone are God and you are good.
We pray this in Jesus' name. Amen.

Song[75]

1All people that on earth do dwell,
 sing to the LORD with cheerful voice;
serve him with joy, his praises tell.
 Come now before him and rejoice.

---

73. See Romans 11.

74. S.G. The first two lines are adapted from J. H. Eaton, *The Psalms,* 350.

75. William Kethe, 1561, alt. Public Domain. *Psalter Hymnal* (1987), # 100; *Psalms for All Seasons,* # 100A; *Lift Up Your Hearts,* # 1.

2Know that the LORD is God indeed;
    he formed us all without our aid.
We are the flock he comes to feed,
    the sheep who by his hand were made.

3O enter then his gates with joy,
    within his courts his praise proclaim.
Let thankful songs your tongues employ,
    O bless and magnify his name.

4Because the LORD our God is good,
    his mercy is forever sure.
His faithfulness at all times stood
    and shall from age to age endure.

Ten Steps from Text to Sermon

---

1. Select the preaching text.
Select the preaching text with an eye to congregational needs. The text must be a literary unit and contain a vital theme.

2. Read the text in its literary context.
Read and reread the text in its context and jot down initial questions.

3. Outline the structure of the text.
In the Hebrew note the major affirmations, clausal flow, plot line, scenes, or other literary structures. Mark major units with headings and verse references.

4. Interpret the text in its own historical setting.
  a. Literary interpretation;
  b. Historical interpretation;[1]
  c. Theocentric interpretation.
Review your results with the help of some good commentaries.

5. Formulate the text's theme, goal, and need addressed.
  a. State the *textual theme* in a brief sentence that summarizes the *message* of the text for its original hearers: subject and predicate. What is the text saying?
  b. State the *goal* of the author for his original hearers. What is the text doing? Does the author aim to persuade, to motivate, to urge, to warn, to comfort? Be specific.
  c. State the *need* the author addressed — the question behind the text.

---

1. In order to avoid repetition, in the chapters above I combine historical interpretation with determining the author's goal in Step 5b.

6. Understand the message in the contexts of canon and redemptive history.

   a. Canonical interpretation: interpret the message in the context of the whole canon;

   b. Redemptive-historical interpretation: understand the message in the context of God's redemptive history from creation to new creation;

   c. Christocentric interpretation: explore the ways of 1) redemptive-historical progression, 2) promise-fulfillment, 3) typology, 4) analogy, 5) longitudinal themes, 6) New Testament references, and 7) contrast.

7. Formulate the sermon theme, goal, and need addressed.

   a. Ideally, your *sermon theme* will be the same as your textual theme (Step 5a). If Step 6 forces a change, stay as close as possible to the textual theme. Your theme will guide especially the development of the body of the sermon.

   b. Your *goal* must be in harmony with the author's goal (Step 5b) and match the sermon theme. Your goal will guide the style of the sermon as well as the content of its conclusion.

   c. State the *need* you are addressing. This need should be similar to the need addressed by the author. The need will inform the content of your sermon introduction.

8. Select a suitable sermon form.

Select a sermon form that respects the form of the text (didactic or narrative, deductive or inductive) and that achieves the goal of the sermon.

9. Prepare the sermon outline.

If possible, follow the flow of the text (Step 3) in the body of the sermon. Main points, derived from the text, support the theme. The introduction should expose the need. The conclusion should clinch your goal.

10. Write the sermon in oral style.

Say it out loud as you write it. Write in oral style, using short sentences, vivid words, strong nouns and verbs, active voice, present tense, images, and illustrations.

An Expository Sermon Model

A. Introduction (usually no more than ten percent of the sermon)
1. Normally, begin with an illustration of the *need* addressed (Step 7c).
2. Connect this illustration to the need of the present hearers.
3. *Transition:* Show that this need or a similar issue was also the question behind the biblical text.
4. State the *theme* of the text/sermon (Step 7a).

For the sake of maintaining suspense, you may postpone disclosing the theme at the beginning (inductive development), but by statement and restatement, you must make sure that the hearers catch the point of the sermon.

B. The Sermon Body
1. Expose the *structure of the text*. The main points, affirmations, moves, scenes of the text (Step 3) normally become your main points in the sermon.
2. The *main points* should usually support the theme and be of the same rank.
3. Follow the *textual sequence* of the points unless there is good reason to change it, such as climactic arrangement (Step 9).
4. Use simple, *clear transitions* that enable the hearers to sense the structure of and movement in the sermon. E.g., "Not only . . . but also. . . ." Or, "Let's first see. . . . Now we see secondly. . . ." Or, "Let's look at verse 8. . . . Now let's move to verse 12. . . ."
5. Use *verse references* before quoting the text so that the hearers can read along. Visual learning is nine times more effective than aural.
6. Use some personal observations to *illustrate* difficult concepts or to make the point. Personal observations are more natural and powerful than canned illustrations about Bishop Whately. Personal *experiences* are also helpful as long as you don't promote yourself but preach Christ.

C. Conclusion
1. Be brief.
2. Don't introduce new material. Narrow the focus; don't expand it.
3. Clinch *the goal* (Step 7b).
4. Be concrete. Can you offer some concrete suggestions of what the hearers can do in response to the Word preached?

A Meditation on Psalm 23[1]

Sidney Greidanus

Psalm 23 has been a beacon for me for most of my life. It became a guiding light when at age twenty I left my family and friends in Alberta to travel to far-off Ontario for training in the Royal Canadian Air Force. My parents gave me a little Bible in which my mom had inscribed on the first page, "From Mom and Dad. Psalm 23." Naturally I read Psalm 23, "The Lord is my shepherd." I had never seen an Eastern shepherd, but still I got the idea: on my journeys far from the safety of home, the Lord would care for me as a shepherd cares for his sheep.

After four months of officer training in Ontario, my class moved to southern Alberta for flight training. And this is where I ran into my first major obstacle: I could not take the loops, rolls, stalls, and tailspins. I suffered from severe air sickness, and, as the weeks went by, it did not get any better. Obviously, a pilot with his head in a barf bag is a disaster. I was about to be washed out — a failure. I remember one night as I lay on my cot that I earnestly begged the Lord to heal me of this air sickness. Suddenly I felt an indescribable peace and slept like a baby. The next morning my instructor had me do loops and rolls and tailspins and I did not get air sick. He took over and went through even more stomach-wrenching maneuvers. I never had to reach for the barf bag and have never been air sick since. The Lord is my shepherd.

My class moved to Manitoba for jet training, and I ran into another problem. We had to learn to land the jet at breakneck speed. I am the kind of person who likes to think things over before acting. But here there was no time to think:

---

1. In the mid–1990s our church in Grand Rapids asked each of its members to write a personal meditation on his or her favorite Bible passage. I wrote the following meditation, which I include here partly because it is biographical, but, more importantly, because it demonstrates the powerful impact of a psalm on the life of a young person.

approach the runway at high speed at a thousand feet; whip the plane into a downward spiral; release the airbrakes; put down flaps and landing gear, and nail the runway. The plane was down before my thinking could catch up. I was scared! Every time I went up solo, I thought that this would be my final flight; I would not survive the landing. But somehow I did not give in to the fear of death; I kept flying because I knew that the Lord was my shepherd.

When my training was completed, I joined the reserve squadron in Edmonton, and Marie and I decided to get married. The Rev. John Henry Piersma asked us to choose our wedding text. Psalm 23, of course! We did not hear much of the sermon that day, but my parents gave us a plaque with words of Psalm 23. This plaque now hangs in our bedroom. Every morning, when we wake up, the assurance is there, "The Lord is my shepherd, I shall not want. . . . Surely goodness and mercy shall follow me all the days of my life and I will dwell in the house of the Lord forever."

With a commercial flying license in hand, I applied for a position with Air Canada. But the Lord closed that door: no openings at that time. Within six months the Lord opened another door. Even though I had not completed high school, after an entrance exam, I was accepted as a student at Calvin College. From there, on to Calvin Seminary and graduate school, for I now hoped to become a Bible teacher.

With minimal income, the Lord provided enough for our family of four so I could complete six years of graduate study at the Free University in Amsterdam. I thought, "Now I am all set to be a Bible teacher at one of 'our' Christian colleges." But the Lord closed that door for the time being; there appeared to be no openings at these Christian colleges. Instead the Lord opened the door to serve as pastor of a Christian Reformed church. Nine years later the Lord opened the door to a teaching position, first at Calvin College, then at The King's College in our hometown Edmonton, and finally at Calvin Theological Seminary, which required pastoral experience for its preaching position.

As I now look back over my life, I can clearly see that the Lord was my shepherd every step of the way, closing many doors and opening many others. What about the future? Recently I learned something about shepherds and sheep from my brother-in-law who is a sheep rancher in Alberta. One evening, when the flock had come into the corrals for the night, he heard a sheep bleating in the pasture. The sheep was lost. She could not find home because she was blinded by a combination of pink-eye and foggy weather. My brother-in-law tried to chase her home, but she ran around him in large circles. Then he noticed that she responded to his voice by coming towards him. So he walked back to the safety of the corral, talking her in. Jesus said, "I am the good shepherd." The good shepherd "goes ahead of them, and the sheep follow him because they know his voice" (John 10:11, 4).

I encourage you to reflect on your life and observe the hand of the good Shepherd protecting you from danger, providing for all your needs, and guiding you by closing certain doors and opening others. And then decide that you will follow the voice of the good Shepherd no matter what difficulties you face.

But what about the future with its threats of unemployment, disease, weapons of mass destruction, and death? Can our Shepherd shield us from these future threats? Psalm 23 offers this final comfort, "Surely goodness and mercy shall follow me all the days of my life, and I shall dwell in the house of the LORD forever."

Sermons on Psalms 72 and 80

Ryan Faber[1]

While proofreading the chapters of this book, my outstanding former seminary student, the Reverend Ryan Faber, preached a series of sermons on these psalms for Advent and Lent. Together we decided to include two of his Advent sermons in this Appendix — sermons on Psalms 72 and 80. The sermon on Psalm 72 clearly demonstrates not only that this ancient psalm can be preached during the Advent season but that it can be done relevantly for this day and age. I was concerned about preaching the sad lament of Psalm 80 the Sunday before a joyous Christmas. Ryan solved this problem brilliantly by preparing a wonderfully pastoral sermon for a "Blue Christmas Service."

---

1. Ryan Faber is Pastor of Worship & Administration at Faith Christian Reformed Church, Pella, Iowa.

"Endow the King with Your Justice":
An Advent Sermon on Psalm 72[2]

In his instructions for public worship the Apostle Paul urged, "first of all, that petitions, prayers, intercessions and thanksgiving be made for all people, for kings and for all those in authority, that we may live peaceful and quiet lives in all godliness and holiness. This is good," he said, "and it pleases God" (1 Tim 2:1–3).

When it comes to praying for those in authority, there may be no better place to begin than Psalm 72. Its superscription describes it as a psalm "of Solomon." That could mean that Solomon wrote it. But it could also mean that this prayer was written, or offered, for Solomon.

Bible scholars agree that the prayer itself ends at verse 17. But that is not where the Psalm as we have it in our Bibles ends. It continues with a doxology, a word of praise to God — "Praised be the Lord our God, the God of Israel" (Ps 72:18) — and this note: "This concludes the prayers of David son of Jesse" (Ps 72:20). If you look in the pew Bible, the next thing you'll see is these words: "Book III. Psalms 73–89."

Those who compiled the psalter, those who gathered these ancient songs of Israel together into the book of Psalms, arranged them into five sections or books. At the end of each book, they added a doxology, a word of praise to God. And, at the end of Book II, they added this note: "This concludes the prayers of David son of Jesse" (Ps 72:20). That means they understood Psalm 72 to be a prayer of David, perhaps even David's last prayer.

It was written by David for Solomon, possibly, probably, for his coronation, when Solomon was crowned king of Israel. That's how it came to be used in Isra-

---

2. This sermon was preached on December 14, 2014 at Faith Christian Reformed Church, Pella, Iowa. Unless otherwise noted, Scripture quotations are from the New International Version (2011), which is the church's pew Bible.

elite history. Some scholars describe it as a "coronation hymn," a song or prayer the people would have sung or prayed whenever anyone was crowned king in Israel.[3] This was how God's ancient people prayed for their president.

They prayed primarily for one thing: That God would endow the king with justice. No, that God would endow the king with God's justice, with God's righteousness (Ps 72:1). The people believed that "the authorities that exist have been established by God," and that "there is no authority except that which God has established" — as the Bible says (Rom 13:1). Which means, as the Bible also says, that those in authority are "God's servants" (Rom 13:4, 6). It is their job to do justice, God's justice.

But what is that justice? Psalm 72 reflects what some theologians call "a preferential option for the poor." The king was to be especially concerned for the "afflicted," the "needy," the "weak," and all those who suffer "oppression and violence" (Ps 72:2–4, 12–14). Psalm 72 presents in poetic form a job description for Israel's king, and perhaps for political leaders today.[4] It was the king's job to "defend the afflicted among the people" and "to save the children of the needy" (Ps 72:4). The king should "take pity on the weak and helpless" and "rescue them from oppression and violence" (Ps 72:13–14).

According to Scripture, how just a society is, is not determined by how well the powerful fare, but by how well the weak are doing. "The test," writes Nicholas Wolterstorff, "is not whether the economically powerful have enough to eat — they almost always do; but whether the economically powerless have enough. Justice," he says, God's justice, "is society's charter of protection for its little ones," those for whom God has a special concern in Scripture.[5]

The Bible describes God as one "who shows no partiality and accepts no bribes. He defends the causes of the fatherless and the widow, and loves the foreigner residing among you" (Deut 10:17–18). If that's what God does, how can his servant, the king, do otherwise? He cannot. Certainly not if he has been endowed with God's justice and God's righteousness.

That's what David prayed for his son Solomon. It became the ancient Israelites' prayer for all their kings and those in authority over them: "Endow the king with your justice, O God" (Ps 72:1). But not even Solomon in all his splendor ever fulfilled the expectations of Psalm 72. Not fully.

The book of Kings uses the language and imagery of Psalm 72 to describe Solomon's rule. To some extent, Solomon lived into and up to the expectations

3. Beth LaNeel Tanner in *Psalms for Preaching and Worship,* ed. Roger E. Van Harn and Brent A. Strawn (Grand Rapids: Eerdmans, 2009), 197.

4. Nicholas Wolterstorff, *Hearing The Call: Liturgy, Justice, Church, and World,* ed. Mark R. Gornik and Gregory Thompson (Grand Rapids: Eerdmans, 2011), 107–8.

5. Ibid., 97.

of this prayer. His kingdom may not have extended "from the River to the ends of the earth," but he did rule from sea to shining sea. The book of Kings says that "Solomon ruled over all the kingdoms from the Euphrates River to the land of the Philistines, as far as the border of Egypt. These countries brought tribute and were Solomon's subjects all his life" (1 Kgs 4:21; see Ps 72:8, 10). The Psalm imagines the kings of Sheba and Seba presenting the king gifts. We know that the queen of Sheba visited Solomon and brought him gifts (Ps 72:10; 1 Kgs 10:1–10).

Solomon came closer than any other Israelite king in fulfilling the model of a true king sketched in Psalm 72, but in the end not even Solomon in all his splendor satisfied these expectations. When he died, "the whole assembly of Israel went to Rehoboam [his son] and said: 'Your father put a heavy yoke on us, but now lighten the harsh labor and the heavy yoke he put on us'" (1 Kgs 12:3–4). Hardly a king who rescued people from oppression (Ps 72:14).

One person said this seems to be "the best we can hope for" in this life from "any ruler, leader, or governor — partial fulfillment and eventual failure at fulfilling the ideal for his vocation."[6] God may answer this prayer and endow the king with his justice. And through his or her reign, life may even take on a bit more of the shape of the world to come.

But no human king can ever fully or finally bring us the kingdom of God. Psalm 146 reminds us: "Put no confidence in princes, nor on human help depend. They shall die, to dust returning; all their thoughts and plans shall end."[7]

Psalm 72 knows this. Its language — a king who endures as long as the sun does its successful journeys run (Ps 72:5, 17), one whose kingdom extends "to the ends of the earth" (Ps 72:8) — this language always pointed beyond any mere human king.

As one person writes: "Christians have always known that they can pray this Psalm in its fulness only for the heir of David who is Jesus of Nazareth. For them, the prayer is a form of petition for" the coming of Christ and "the consummation of the kingdom of God."[8]

As it was for the ancient Israelites. None of Solomon's successors ever came close to the splendor of Solomon. Eventually the Babylonians conquered Israel and the last Davidic king was carried off into exile. The temple was in ruins; the royal palace, reduced to rubble. And yet the people continued to pray Psalm 72. No longer as a prayer for the king, for there was no king on David's throne, but as a prayer for the king, the king who had been promised.

---

6. James L. Mays, *Psalms* (Louisville: John Knox Press, 1994), 238.

7. *Psalter,* 1887, "Praise the Lord, Sing Hallelujah," alt. *Psalter Hymnal* (Grand Rapids: CRC Publications, 1987), 146.

8. Mays, *Psalms,* 238.

The people never forgot God's promise to David. It distressed David that the ark of the Lord remained in a tent while he lived in a house of cedar. He wanted to build a house for God. Initially the prophet Nathan told him, "Whatever you have in mind, go ahead and do it." But that night the word of the LORD came to Nathan and told him to tell David that David was not to build God's house but that God would build David's house. "When your days are over," God said, "and you rest with your ancestors, I will raise up your offspring to succeed you, your own flesh and blood, and I will establish his kingdom. . . . I will establish the throne of his kingdom forever" (2 Sam 7:1-16).

There are only two verbal forms in Hebrew. The form of most of the verbs in Psalm 72 is ambiguous. They can be read more than one way. Most modern English versions translated them as prayers — may he, may he, may he. But the older King James Version translated them as prophecies — he will, he will, he will.

Psalm 72 was probably first written as a prayer, but when the house of David collapsed with the Babylonian captivity, the people came to read it as prophecy. This was probably how the Psalm was understood when the book of Psalms was put together, as prophecy. Its earliest Jewish interpreters understood the Psalm as a messianic psalm.

So did several Old Testament prophets. They pick up the language of this prayer as they write about the coming Messiah. Isaiah 11: "A shoot will come up from the stump of Jesse, from his roots a Branch will bear fruit. . . . with righteousness he will judge the needy, with justice he will give decisions for the poor [the afflicted] of the earth" (vv. 1, 4). Zechariah 9: "See, your king comes to you, righteous and victorious, lowly and riding on a donkey. . . . His rule will extend from sea to sea and from the River to the ends of the earth" (vv. 9-10). An exact quotation of Psalm 72.

The New Testament sees these promises fulfilled in Jesus Christ. About Jesus' triumphal entry on Palm Sunday, Matthew says that "this took place to fulfill what was spoken through the prophet" (Matt 21:4-5), that prophecy of Zechariah.

When the angel Gabriel appeared to Mary, he told her: "You will conceive and give birth to a son, and you are to call him Jesus. . . . The Lord God will give him the throne of his father David, and he will reign over Jacob's descendants forever; his kingdom will never end" (Luke 1:31-33).

In the story of Epiphany, when those three kings of orient are, bearing gifts traversed afar, following yonder star, the kings of distant shores brought tribute, they presented him gifts, they bowed down to him and worshiped him — as Psalm 72 says (Ps 72:10-11; Matt 2:1-12).

Psalm 72 prays that the king might be endowed with God's justice, that he might "defend the afflicted among the people and save the children of the needy," and "crush the oppressor," rescuing the weak and needy "from oppression and violence" (Ps 72:1, 4, 13–14). In his inaugural address, Jesus claimed to be endowed, anointed, with God's Spirit "to proclaim good news to the poor," the afflicted, and "to set the oppressed free" (Luke 4:18–19).

Ultimately Jesus is the one for whom Psalm 72 prays. Only Jesus fully and finally fulfills the expectations of this prayer. He came down, he will come down, to bring us justice — to defend the afflicted and to rescue them from oppression.

After he had risen victorious from the grave, Jesus appeared to his disciples "over a period of forty days and spoke about the kingdom of God." One time, when they were gathered together, the disciples asked Jesus: When, Lord, when are you going to restore the kingdom? Jesus answered: "It is not for you to know the dates or times the Father has set by his own authority" (Acts 1:3–7). In the gospels that is always a reference to the return of Christ (see Matt 24:36; Mark 13:32). That's when the kingdom will be fully and finally restored.

But in the meanwhile, as you wait, "you will receive power when the Holy Spirit comes on you, and you will be my witnesses," Jesus said, "in Jerusalem, and in all Judea and Samaria, and to the ends of the earth" (Acts 1:8).

Psalm 72 can certainly guide us as we make "petitions, prayers, intercessions and thanksgiving" "for kings and all those in authority" (1 Tim 2:1–2). We should want those in authority over us to do justice, God's justice. But we know that our hope for a new creation cannot finally be tied to what people can do.[9] In this life, the best we can hope for is partial fulfillment and eventual failure. And so, with the ancient people of God, we keep praying for the king, for the long-expected king to come.

Advent is a season of "watching and waiting, looking above."[10] But it is more than that. It is also a time for working, because Jesus said that, in the meanwhile, "you will be my witnesses, in Jerusalem, and in all Judea and Samaria, and to the ends of the earth" (Acts 1:8). As we wait the kingdom's final consummation, we are its witnesses — people who work for God's justice, the justice of God's kingdom in this world.

So one person concludes: The job description of Psalm 72 — to defend the afflicted, to deliver the needy, and to have pity on the weak — the job description of Psalm 72 is not only for the kings of Israel, nor is it only for political leaders today. "It is for all of us who claim to serve in God's kingdom. Psalm 72 shows us the way we should structure our lives and order our relationships"[11] as we watch

---

9. "Our World Belongs to God" (Grand Rapids: Christian Reformed Church in North America, 1987), para. 56.

10. Fanny J. Crosby, 1873, "Blessed Assurance: Jesus Is Mine."

11. Beth LaNeel Tanner in *Psalms for Preaching and Worship*, ed. Roger E. Van Harn and Brent A. Strawn, 199.

and wait and work for the coming of the One who came, who will come, to bring us justice. Amen.

Let us pray:

We pray, O God, for kings and all those in authority.
We pray for our president and members of congress.
We pray for our governor and state legislators.
We pray for county supervisors and city council members.

Endow them with your justice, O God,
that they might defend the afflicted
and save the children of the needy.
May they deliver the needy who cry out,
the afflicted who have no one to help.
May they take pity on the weak and needy,
rescuing them from oppression and violence.

Endow us, O God, with your justice,
that we might serve all people in righteousness,
defending the afflicted and saving the children of the needy.

We long, O God, for that day when every challenge to your rule
and every resistance to your will shall be crushed.
Our hope for that day and for a new creation
is not tied to what people can do,
and so we pray for the coming king who will bring us justice,
who will finally and forever set things right in our world.

May he rule from sea to sea and from the River to the ends of the earth.
May his name endure forever;
and may your promise to Abraham be forever realized in him,
that through him all nations will be blessed,
and they will call him blessed.
In his name we pray — Amen.

"Restore Us, O God":
An Advent Sermon on Psalm 80[12]

This morning's Scripture reading forces us to face the facts. It has been said that facts are stubborn things. We may not like them, but we are powerless to change them. The sad fact we face this morning is this: For some of us, this is not the most wonderful time of the year. In many of our worlds, all is not calm; all is not bright.

We're listening this Advent season to various Psalms assigned by the Revised Common Lectionary. The lectionary is a schedule of Scripture readings for public worship used in many Christian denominations. Among the Psalms assigned for Advent is this plaintive plea of God's ancient people. John Calvin called it "a sorrowful prayer."[13] "Restore us, O God"; "restore us, Lord God Almighty; make your face shine on us, that we may be saved" (Ps 80:3, 19).

It is an Advent prayer. It "presents the situation of need to which the coming of Jesus responds."[14] The angel told Joseph to give Mary's child the name Jesus, "because he will save his people from their sins" (Matt 1:21). No doubt that is good news of great joy for all God's people (Luke 2:10). It is, in fact, God's answer to the prayer of Psalm 80. But behind it stands a sad admission: God's people need saving; God's world needs restoration.

Some of us know that all too well. For some of us, this is not the most won-

---

12. This sermon was preached on December 7, 2014 at Faith Christian Reformed Church, Pella, Iowa. Unless otherwise noted, Scripture quotations are from the New International Version (2011), which is the church's pew Bible.

13. John Calvin, *Commentary on the Psalms*, trans. James Anderson (Grand Rapids: Baker, n.d.), III:295.

14. Fred B. Craddock et al., *Preaching Through the Christian Year A* (Harrisburg: Trinity Press International, 1992), 23.

derful time of the year. It brings with it painful memories. We came to a church decorated like this one. Ribbons and wreaths. Evergreens. Candles. And a casket. It was a Christmas funeral. We remember that last time, years ago, that our family got together for Christmas. It ended with a fight that began a feud. We haven't spoken to some of our siblings since.

No, in some of our worlds all is not calm; all is decidedly not bright. Some of us aren't sure how we'll make it through this first Christmas since a loved one passed away; another Christmas that a child refuses to come home. Things have gotten so complicated since our daughter's divorce last year. We're not sure we'll see our grandchildren at all this holiday season.

For many of us, these could be our words. These *are* our words: "How long, Lord God Almighty," how long "will your anger smolder against the prayers of your people? You have fed them with the bread of tears; you have made them drink tears by the bowlful" (Ps 80:4–5). "I am worn out from my groaning," another psalmist cried. "All day long I flood my bed with weeping and drench my couch with tears" (Ps 6:6). "Tears have been my food day and night" (Ps 42:3).

So great is the people's grief, so long the continuance of their calamities. John Calvin said they were so filled with sorrow that they could not contain any more.[15]

Psalm 80 was probably written not long after the Assyrians decimated the northern kingdom. They destroyed Israel's homes and farms, plundered whole towns and set them on fire, and, in the end, destroyed their capital city (see 2 Kgs 17:1–6). As a result, the people became "an object of derision to their neighbors, and their enemies mocked them" (Ps 80:6). Their walls were broken down so that all who passed by could plunder them (Ps 80:12).

The people felt abandoned by God. It felt like his face was turned away from them. Nothing was more devastating in the Old Testament. Another psalmist extolled God's care of creation: "All creatures look to you to give them their food at the proper time," he wrote. "When you give it to them, they gather it up; when you open your hand, they are satisfied with good things." But "when you hide your face, they are terrified; when you take away their breath, they die and return to the dust" (Ps 104:27–29). When you hide your face, we are terrified.

Nothing was more necessary in the Old Testament than that God's face shine upon his people. This was how God had instructed the priests to bless the people: "The Lord make his face shine upon you and be gracious to you; the Lord turn his face toward you and give you peace" (Num 6:25–26).

But when you hide your face, we are terrified. "How long, O Lord, how long will you hide your face from me? Will you forget me forever?" (Ps 13:1). "How long will your anger smolder against the prayers of your people?" (Ps 80:4).

15. Calvin, *Commentary on the Psalms,* III:299.

Central to the Old Testament's psalms of lament is the people's complaint against God. Whatever hardship they experience, whatever suffering they endure — they believe that God did this to them. One person describes it as "a vigorous, nearly accusatory address" against God.[16] You fed us the bread of tears; you made us drink tears by the bowlful. You made us an object of derision. You broke down our wall (Ps 80:5-6, 12).

These psalms assume that God is responsible and has caused, or at least permitted, the people's trouble. But, as one person writes, "even when such an accusatory tone is employed, it is clear that lament is [always] an act of faith," because it testifies that "only God, who caused the trouble can right the wrong."[17] If these horrible events are not outside God's control, if they did not catch him off guard as they may have caught us off guard, then surely he has the power to change them.

Another person explains: "Throughout the psalm appeal is made to God's power," which means his ability, not only to judge, but also to save; not only to kill, also to make alive again. The Psalm addressed God as "the shepherd who leads the flock from danger to safety," and as the one who sits "enthroned between the cherubim" (Ps 80:1). That phrase "evokes the image of God as King," as do later references to God's "right hand" (Ps 80:17).[18]

There is a refrain throughout the Psalm: "Restore us, O God; make your face shine on us, that we may be saved." Throughout the Psalm it builds. It begins by addressing God as God (Ps 80:3); then, as God Almighty (Ps 80:7), the Lord of hosts, or literally the God of angel armies. The title "reflects the power of God to direct battles." If God's people survive, if they are saved, "it will [only] be through God's power and not their own."[19]

When the Psalm's refrain reaches its crescendo, God is called "the Lord God Almighty" (Ps 80:19). Not only is he God; he is Almighty. That means that he is able "to provide whatever I need for body and soul," and that he is able to "turn to my good whatever adversity he sends me in this sad world." But not only is he able to do this, he desires to do it, because he is not only God Almighty; he is the Lord God Almighty.[20] The Lord — that's God's covenant name, a reminder of his commitment to his people.

---

16. Walter Brueggemann, *The Psalms and the Life of Faith*, ed. Patrick D. Miller (Minneapolis: Fortress, 1995), 76.

17. Ibid.

18. Nancy R. Bowen in *Psalms for Preaching and Worship*, ed. Roger E. Van Harn and Brent A. Strawn (Grand Rapids: Eerdmans, 2009), 211.

19. Ibid.

20. Heidelberg Catechism, Question & Answer 26, in *Ecumenical Creeds and Reformed Confessions* (Grand Rapids: Faith Alive Christian Resources, 1988), 22.

That's why John Calvin described the people's present situation as "unbecoming" of God.[21] At the heart of the people's lament stands this conviction: Their present circumstance is not consistent with what they know to be the character of their covenant God. That means it cannot last forever. This too shall pass, because this is *not* who God is. This is not who they have experienced God to be. As one person writes, the people's prayer is dominated by this tension: "Of old thou hast done thus — [but] now?"[22]

The people remember God's mighty deeds for them and for their salvation. "You transplanted a vine from Egypt; you drove out the nations and planted it. You cleared the ground for it, and it took root and filled the land. The mountains were covered with its shade, the mighty cedars with its branches. Its branches reached as far as the Sea, its roots as far as the River" (Ps 80:8-11).

This is "the story of Israel from exodus and conquest through possession of the land up to the Davidic empire whose boundaries reached from sea to river."[23] The image of Israel as a vine, carefully and lovingly tended by its God, is not uncommon in the Old Testament.[24] Here the image "introduces the anguish and bewilderment of the people over the contrast and contradiction between what God began and what he has now done, leaving them exposed for strangers to gather the fruit of the vine and for wild animals [foreign nations] to ravage."[25]

Calvin writes: "Nothing seems more inconsistent than that God should abandon the vine which he had planted with his own hand, to be rooted up by wild beasts."[26] "It is unbecoming that God should now suffer the vine which he has planted and cultivated so carefully with his own hand to be wasted by wild beasts. God's covenant was not made to last only for a few days, or for a short time; when he adopted the children of Abraham, he took them under his keeping forever."[27]

The people may not understand, they may never understand why God allowed their walls to be broken down. They may not understand, they may never understand why God allowed them to be plundered by those who passed by. We may not understand, we may never understand why God allows us to experience the pains, the betrayals, the disease, the deaths we face in this sad world.

With the ancient people, we can only cling to our God. At the heart of their

---

21. John Calvin, *Commentary on the Psalms,* III:302.
22. Claus Westermann, *Praise and Lament in the Psalms,* trans. Keith R. Crim and Richard N. Soulen (Atlanta: John Knox, 1981), 55.
23. James L. Mays, *Psalms* (Louisville: John Knox, 1994), 263.
24. See Isa 5:1-7; 27:2-6; Ezek 15:1-8; 17:6-8; 19:10-14.
25. Mays, *Psalms,* 263.
26. Calvin, *Psalms,* III:303.
27. Ibid., 302.

lament stands this conviction: God was our help in ages past, he remains our hope for years to come. We don't know how long his anger will smolder against the prayers of his people. We don't know how long he might hide his face from us. But this we do know: It cannot last forever. The Shepherd of Israel will hear us. He will awaken his might and come and save us (Ps 80:1–2).

As the prayer ends, that hope is concentrated in a particular person. This is how God will make his face shine on us, that we may be saved: "Let your hand rest on the man at your right hand, the son of man you have raised up for yourself" (Ps 80:17). Later Jewish tradition understood this to be a reference to the Messiah.[28]

Jesus Christ is God's answer to the prayer of Psalm 80. In Jesus Christ, God came down from heaven to visit his people. In Jesus Christ, God acted to restore us and our world. In Jesus Christ, God's face shines upon us, that we might be saved. As Paul wrote: The God who said, "Let light shine out of darkness," has made his light shine in our hearts, that we might see the glory of God in the face of Jesus Christ (2 Cor 4:6).

And yet in this sad world it can still feel like God has turned his face away. There are nights that we flood our bed with weeping and drench our couch with tears (Ps 6:6). Sometimes it feels like tears have been our only food day and night (Ps 42:3), and the darkness is our closest friend (Ps 88:18).

God had done amazing things for his ancient people. He rescued them from slavery in Egypt and brought them up into a good and spacious land. Yet they still experienced broken walls. In the same way, God has done amazing things for us in Jesus Christ. By the death and resurrection of Jesus Christ, he has rescued us from slavery to sin and death. He has opened to us the way of eternal life. He has guaranteed our glorious resurrection. Yet we still experience broken walls, betrayal, abandonment, abuse, disease, depression, and death.

The Bible describes Jesus as "the firstfruits of those who have fallen asleep." It promises that "as in Adam all die, so in Christ all will be made alive." Restored. Renewed. Redeemed. But — "but each in turn: Christ, the firstfruits; then, when he comes, those who belong to him" (1 Cor 15:20–23).

Jesus Christ is God's answer to the prayer of Psalm 80. The angel told Joseph to name Mary's child Jesus, "because he will save his people from their sins" (Matt 1:21). In Jesus Christ, God makes his face shine on us, that we may be saved. Jesus Christ is "the son of man" that God "has raised up for himself" (Ps 80:17).

The prophet Daniel also spoke about this son of man. Daniel saw him "coming with the clouds of heaven." "He was given authority, glory and sovereign power; all nations and peoples of every language worshiped him," Daniel said.

---

28. Nancy R. Bowen in *Psalms for Preaching and Worship*, ed. Roger E. Van Harn and Brent A. Strawn, 211.

"His dominion is an everlasting dominion that will not pass away, and his kingdom is one that will never be destroyed" (Dan 7:13–14).

This is the hope of Psalm 80: When God awakens his might to come and save us (Ps 80:2). He has come in Jesus Christ. And he will — fully, finally and forever — when Christ comes again. Jesus promised that we would one day "see the Son of Man coming in a cloud with power and great glory." When that happens, he said, "stand up and lift your heads, because your redemption is drawing near" (Luke 21:27–28). The Bible promises that not only will God cause his face to shine on us, but that we will see him face to face and his name will be written on our foreheads (Rev 22:4).

This Advent season, as we look and long for that day, while living in this vale of tears, we pray with God's ancient people: Awaken your might, great Shepherd God, come and save us. Restore us, Lord God Almighty; make your face shine on us, that we may be saved. Amen.

Let us pray.

Around us, O God, the singing can be heard: "Joy to the world . . . let heaven and nature sing." This season is to be one when hope eases our minds, when peace soothes our hearts, when love warms our souls, and when joy comes each morning.

But there are many who do not feel this joy. Some might try, others have given up trying. "Where is this joy for us?" they ask. The world has found joy but some feel as if it has passed them by. Our minds are not at ease . . . we feel too much doubt. Our hearts are not at peace . . . there is too much to do. Our souls are not warmed . . . the chill of death is too troubling. Where, O God, can joy be found?

As the nights have been growing longer, so has the darkness wrapped itself around our hearts. In this season of our longest nights, we offer to you the pain in our hearts, the traumas that some of us cannot put into words. There are those among us who are grieving over what might have been. A death or loss has changed our experience of Christmas. Once it was a special day for us too, but someone has died or moved away. Or we have lost a job, or a cause. We find ourselves adrift, alone, lost.

For others the Christmas season reminds us of all that used to be and cannot be anymore. The memories of what was, the fears of what may be, stifle us. All around us we hear the sounds of celebration. But all we experience is a sense of feeling blue.

We pray for the lonely, that they might find comfort in another's touch.
We pray for the downtrodden, that they might find relief from their burdens.

We pray for those wrestling with depression, that a light of calm might bring
  them peace.
We pray for those dealing with stress, that they might find the courage to let
  go.
We pray for the grief-stricken, that they might experience the newness of life
  that you bring.

May joy come to the world, O God, and may we grasp some of that. We
do not pray for joy that is temporary or fleeting, but a joy that runs deep and
sustains us even in moments of despair. We seek this joy in a season that can
be less than joyful.

Restore us, Lord God Almighty; make your face shine upon us, that we
may be saved. Amen.[29]

---

29. Adapted from All Saints Episcopal Church, Atlanta, "Blue Christmas Service," December
2008 and http://philosophyovercoffee.blogspot.ca/2005/12/blue-christmas-prayer.html (accessed
on December 4, 2014).

A Sermon on Colossians 1:15–20

Roy Berkenbosch

Roy Berkenbosch was an excellent, mature student in my first class of the new Christian college we started in Edmonton, Alberta, in 1979 (The King's College; now The King's University). He went on to Calvin Theological Seminary for his M.Div., served as missionary in Bangladesh, next as senior pastor in a church in Grand Rapids, and in 1995 became Campus Minister / Director of Interdisciplinary Studies at The King's University. In 2014 I attended the 35th homecoming of The King's University where Roy preached on Colossians 1:15–20. His sermon blew me away for its vividness, power, and especially its depiction of the cosmic Christ and his relevance for our culture.

In this series on Preaching Christ from Psalms, *my focus has been on connecting the message of each psalm with Jesus Christ in the New Testament. Usually this was accomplished by linking the psalm with Jesus' First and/or Second Coming. Roy's sermon on Colossians 1 goes far beyond this to reveal the cosmic Christ and his relevance for our world, culture, and Christian living. With his permission I have included his sermon in this Appendix to fill in the picture of Christ from the New Testament perspective. This sermon not only adds another reason for the importance of preaching Christ from the Old Testament but it will also function as a model sermon (provided credit is given) that can be used to start or conclude any series of sermons on preaching Christ from the Old Testament.*

Paul's Preaching of Christ:

A Sermon on Colossians 1:15–20

Sisters and Brothers, friends of the Lord Jesus Christ.

As it turns out, Fellowship church also celebrates its 35th anniversary this year. Fellowship and King's, like twins, born of common stock. Please understand, we have a rule here at Fellowship that every sermon must cite Walter Brueggemann at least once — so let me begin by offering you a delectable quote (for which, unfortunately, I cannot find a proper citation, but I believe it is in *The Prophetic Imagination*). He once said that the whole purpose of education is to teach our youth how to sing the doxology.

Imagine that: students lifted out of their seats: "Fill thou my life, O Lord my God, in every part with praise, that my whole being may proclaim thy being and thy ways."

Imagine: students plump with uncontainable praise so that at the very slightest provocation they burst into song — "joyful, joyful we adore thee", "Holy, Holy, Holy" . . . "Praise God from whom all blessings flow."

Class, please consider that the square of the length of the hypotenuse is equal to the sum of the square of the lengths of the two perpendicular sides. And their eyes widen with wonder and they proclaim, "Hallelujah. Indescribable Majesty. Our God is an awesome God."

Class, please turn to page 92 in your reader where we are reminded that a synecdoche is a figure of speech in which a term for a part of something refers to the whole and, instead of the fog that usually clouds their eyes, bright voices chant in unison, "With every breath I take I will praise thee." As if their very lungs were filled with song so that to breathe was to praise, to speak was to sing, to live was to glory. A bit of a stretch? Perhaps.

But, I believe that it was the intention of the Apostle Paul, when he wrote Colossians 1, to teach us to sing the doxology and, to that end, he offers doxology.

Colossians 1:15–20 is one of the first Hymns to Christ. It is a remarkable passage, not least for its sheer verbal density. These verses are two run-on sentences containing, as if they were on steroids, a whopping 218 words. It's as if Paul can't get the words out fast enough, piling on one exuberant subordinate clause after the next, constructing a cascade of breathless exaltation that reaches higher and higher as he strives to speak the unspeakable wisdom and power of God made known in Jesus.

But listen, the enthusiastic Apostle is not simply about rhetoric.

He is about theology and mission, and in the sweeping claims made about Jesus, Paul aims to accomplish at least two things for Christian believers. In the first place I think Paul wants to radicalize our understanding of who Jesus is. He wants to stretch our imaginations and deepen our confession by expanding our idea of Jesus into cosmic proportions. Secondly, he wants to radicalize our sense of mission by showing us how subversive these claims about Jesus really are.

First, the Cosmic Christ. I wonder if you have ever heard of the icosadodecahedron. I didn't think so. (I practiced saying that word all week so I could sound as brainy as Brian Martin, our resident physicist.) Maybe you know it as the Hoberman sphere? It's a ball made up of hundreds of rods, each of which is multi-jointed to others. There is one in the Liberty Science Museum that you can see on-line that spans 30–40 feet when it is extended — it is huge. But the whole thing can be compacted into a little ball that you can carry around in your pocket. (see http://www.youtube.com/watch?v=xRLotMaNgjQ)[1]

Jesus, as Paul understands him, is like that. He is the "immensity of Glory cloistered in the dark womb" of Mary, as John Donne put it. A child born in Bethlehem, one who wore the features of a particular person born in space and time; he lived and breathed and died. He did ordinary human things like we do them. He was God in flesh, one of us, accessible, approachable.

He collapsed himself into human proportions so that we could look him in the eye . . . but there is more to him than meets the eye. He is the very image of the invisible God in whom the FULLNESS of the godhead dwells; he is the firstborn over all creation — no Johnny come lately on the scene of history, but he is the one by whom and for whom all things were created, things visible and invisible, all thrones and rulers and authorities; in him all things are reconciled and in him all things hold together. Over and over Paul uses the little word *panta,* "all" things, to describe the all-encompassing, cosmos-filling power and glory of Jesus.

1. I owe this illustration to my former seminary colleague, Scott Hoezee, Director of the Centre for Excellence in Preaching at Calvin Theological Seminary, although in personal correspondence he claims no memory of it. I, on the other hand, seem to recall being well-instructed by Scott on this particular passage, although I too can find no record of it. John Vriend once said that preachers were hunter-gatherers who should plunder at will — perhaps I took his advice?

It is hard to exaggerate the claims that Paul makes here:

Jesus is nothing less than the image of the invisible God,
    a partner in creation and the ruler of it all:
The whole wide and wonderful world that a good education helps us explore
        and discover is a world
made by Christ,
    held together by Christ and
        reconciled by Christ;
every metaphor and molecule,
every finch and every freckle,
every octave and octopus,
every kind kin and kelp cracker,
every formula, every friend,
every logger and legislator,
the whole ball of wax, fallen and jaded and dysfunctional though it may be,
      ALL OF IT belongs to Christ;
    and its residual glory either shouts out his praise
      or its brokenness cries out for his reconciling mercies,
but NONE of it falls outside the reach of his redemptive renewing concern.

But not only that; Paul adds that Christ is the one in whom all things hold together.

Christ is the cohesive center who keeps this fractured and fragmented world from chaos.

Paul picks up all the strands of human knowledge, the world as we know it, in fact he picks up even the threads of invisible realities — powers and principalities, ideologies and cultural authorities — he picks up every thread he can lay his hands on and "braids it into a thick strong cord, and then lashes the entire spiritual rope to the heart of Christ Jesus alone."[2]

This is the gospel that Paul proclaims — it is exhaustive, expansive, and all-encompassing, and it makes me want to sing the doxology.

And it makes me want to celebrate a Christian university too, because King's University exists for the exact purpose of leading students on an exploration of the heights and depths, the length and breadth of the creation that God loves, and which God claims, and which God makes new.

We need a Colossians-sized vision of the cosmic King, because anything less

2. Again I believe I owe also this rhetorical conclusion to Scott Hoezee. I wish it was original with me!

than that is inadequate to bring our students into the full glory of their humanity, into the full stature they inherit as children of God called to be salt and light; anything less than that is certainly inadequate to inflame their hearts to meet the missional calling to engage the world and to render all things new in Christ.

Several years ago I read a little poem by Tim Hansel that made such an impression on me that I have never forgotten it — my version goes like this:

> I would like to buy $3 worth of God, please
> Not enough to explode my soul or disturb my sleep, Just $3.00 worth
> Just enough to equal a cup of warm milk or a snooze in the sunshine
> I don't want so much of God that it will make me love the vagrant on the
>   street who threatens my middle-class sensibilities,
> or the inconvenient Indian who exposes my hypocrisy,
> or the emotionally demanding neighbor who will devour my precious time
> Not so much of God that I must stand in solidarity with the wretched of the
>   earth.
> Just $3 worth of God please,
> enough to snack on for two Sunday morning hours of bliss
> I want ecstasy, not transformation
> I want the warmth of the womb, not new birth
> I'd like a pound of the eternal in a paper sack
> I would like $3 worth of God please.[3]

Compare that with Paul's prayer for the Colossians: I pray that God may fill you so you may please him in every way, in every good work, strengthened with ALL the power. Over and over Paul names God in ways that embrace the whole cosmos. In Ephesians 3 he offers a similar tongue-twisting prayer that if we were to translate it literally it would read, "May you be fully filled with the ever-filling fullness of God."

We might be able to fit $3 worth of God into morning prayers and even a daily chapel, but as our vision of Christ expands, like a Hoberman sphere, it gradually must fill up and overwhelm the whole curriculum, and more than that, the whole character of the learning community. Because Jesus is the cosmic Christ, we look for his fingerprints everywhere, in economic theory and in world history, in the social sciences as well as the natural sciences; we listen for his voice across centuries of literature and poetry, we discern his traces through the annals of history. Our quest is to discover the mind of Christ so that we may discern the spirits

---

3. This comes from an essay in Tim Hansel's collection of essays titled, "When I Relax I Feel Guilty."

of our age, learning to recognize both the seductive lies of the "Gods That Fail," as well as the quiet but persistent cadences of truth that endure, so that we may speak wisdom to our students, help them to discover the will of the paradigm-shifting Lord in the midst of the complex and confusing world that they inhabit.

Christian education is about placing all learning under the lordship of Jesus: if he is creator of all things, the one in whom all things cohere, and if his life and death somehow aim to reconcile all things, including all paradigms and ideologies, then what a tragedy it would be if we were to limit the doxology to morning prayers and Bible readings, without sounding out the deeper claims, without intentionally embodying in our classroom practices, our curricular design and our community life, the implications of life in Christ. What a tragedy if, in the face of such mind-bending claims, we were to remain impotently stuck in the hopeless dualisms that want to confine Jesus to the private spaces of personal spirituality; "preoccupied," as Wendell Berry puts it, "with incanting anemic souls into heaven" while the rest of life is left to what Paul names in 2:8 as "hollow and deceptive philosophies which depend on human tradition and the base principles of this world."

The trivialization of God suggested by the phrase "$3 worth of God," as if God could be reduced to small manageable bits that easily fit into my self-interested life without disturbance, is an expression of the dualistic worldview that always threatens to diminish the gospel and render Christian education impotent.

A split-vision worldview carves the world up into spiritual and secular spaces, splitting faith from life, church from culture, theology from economics, prayer from politics, and worship from work. That is precisely what the culture wants — a pleasant and undemanding private faith, buried deep in the folds of the interior life, but never transgressing into the public sphere. In the public sphere there is no Lord and everyone does what is right in one's own eyes. By all means allow religion and religious education to shape the private imagination, but leave the rest of life to the public and dominant disenchanted imagination, the one that shapes public policy, the one that makes law, the one that sponsors armies and manages resources — leave all of that to the secular powers.

When we fail to recognize the cosmic lordship of Jesus, we abandon the world to lesser gods with tragic consequence. In his wise essay, "Christianity and the Survival of Creation," Wendell Berry comments, and I quote at length:

> The church has for the most part stood silently by while a predatory economy has ravaged the world, destroyed its natural beauty and health, divided and plundered its human communities and households. It has flown the flag and chanted the slogans of empire. It has assumed with the economists that "economic forces" automatically work for the good; and has assumed

with industrialists and militarists that technolog ,etermines history. It has assumed with almost everyone that progres ,ood, that it is good to be modern and "with the times"; it has admired ᴗaesar and comforted him in his depredations and defaults. But in its alliance with Caesar, Christianity connives directly in the murder of creation.

It is here that we begin to get a whiff of the subversive power of Paul's hymn to Christ. Because the claims of Jesus are so sweeping, so absolute, so extravagant, his followers necessarily find themselves at odds with the claims of other powers.

In their book, *Colossians Remixed,* Brian Walsh and Sylvia Keesmaat point out that the language Paul uses to describe Christ in this hymn is a deliberate and intentional borrowing of language that the early church would have recognized because it was language used to describe empire.

In the imperial cult and throughout the empire it was proclaimed that "Caesar was equal to the beginning of things." It was the emperor who "restored order" and who was called "the beginning of life and vitality." Moreover Caesar was named the "savior" who had put an end to war and in whom "all things now were held together." Caesar was therefore deified as the one in whom God was made manifest; he is "the image of the invisible God." Furthermore, putting together language of "head and body" as Paul does, would immediately bring to mind Greek ideas of Zeus as the sovereign head of the body of the cosmos and images of Caesar, or Rome, as the head of the body politic of the empire.

So what does Paul do with this iconic language of empire? He turns them all on their head and replaces Zeus, Caesar, and Rome and any other pretender to sovereignty with Jesus Christ and names Him as the head of all things. Jesus, not Caesar, holds all things together. Jesus, not Pax Romana, makes peace, not through violent conquest or military conquest, but by his blood shed on a cross.

Who has supremacy? Not Rome, not Ottawa, not Moscow, not the Toronto Stock Exchange, not Microsoft, not Disney, not the inviolable ideologies of individual rights, personal fulfillment and self-rule, nor the myths of progress. Jesus! That's right. The immensity once "cloistered in her dark womb." The One who says, love your enemies, forgive your offender, turn the cheek, blessed are the poor in spirit, blessed are the hungry and thirsty for justice. This one, who seems so small, so insignificant in the presence of the assembly of global authorities, this one expands like a Hoberman sphere — no, better yet, expands like the rock not hewn by human hands (Daniel), that rolls through the dreams of empires and emperors, dashing them to pieces, rolling on through Babylon, rolling on through Rome, rolling on through time, gaining speed and gaining size until it fills the whole earth.

The early Christian confession was subversion that bordered on treason.

The hymn to Christ, as cosmic doxology, is a refusal to be compromised to the seductive but hollow promises of the gods who cannot deliver. In Caesar's day his image was plastered everywhere: on coins, on buildings, in public stadiums, in order to so thoroughly capture the public imagination that there would always be consent for whatever Caesar wanted and did. Today the claims of empire have different faces, but they are equally ubiquitous and they have similar powers to shape our imagination and thus to shape our actions.

The point is that we live and teach in an environment not unlike the early church, where the public imagination is made captive to the reigning powers — of market place, of nationhood, of ethnic identity. The power of the Christ hymn lies in its Holy Spirit–given capacity to reshape the Christian imagination — it does not simply give us more information about Jesus — it aims to take hold of our imagination so that we come to see the world differently — as Paul says it in 2 Corinthians 5:16 — we no longer see the world from a merely human point of view but now we see all things in Christ in whom all things are reconciled.

Every story in Scripture is an invitation to reimagine the world, not simply as we would have it, but as God would have it. The gift of God is the possibility of a future that we could not envision, but which God makes real in Jesus Christ — it is called the kingdom of God and it is described by the signs and wonders of the gospels:

the poor have plenty, the fallen are lifted up,
the empty are filled, eunuchs have kids,
the blind see, the lame walk, sinners are forgiven,
the marginalized are embraced and the powerful eat humble pie.

Biblical hope is the capacity to see beyond appearances to grasp what God is doing in the world. And faith is the courage to live today as if that future was already a reality, allowing every thought, action, and decision to be shaped not by the "pretenders of this world" but by the new reality of Jesus Christ, in whom all of God's promises are "Yes!"

The King's University was founded as a place, no, rather, a community where teachers and students, guided by a cosmic and subversive vision of Christ, are able to dream dreams and see visions and together make ready the highway for our God.

Does that seem too audacious? Too triumphalist? Too big a dream for this small enterprise called King's? If you've seen our financial records you might think so. And after all we are only 700 students, not 35,000, like the university down the street.

Let me leave you with just one more idea. In C. S. Lewis's Chronicles of

Narnia there is a poignant moment when the children walk into what appears from the outside to be no more than a shabby little building. But once they step into it, they discover a vastness they could not have guessed at before. "Why," Lucy exclaims, "it's bigger on the inside than the outside." "Yes," comes the reply, "something like that happened once on earth. In a place called Bethlehem there was a tiny stable whose inside was bigger than its outside because that stable contained the whole world."

And that is why a relatively small and unlikely enterprise like Christian-imagination-forming education, Christian-world-renewing education is possible. It's why we dream dreams of our students as world reconcilers and culture changers — because at the heart of who we are and what we must do is Jesus the Christ, and he makes us bigger on the inside than we may appear on the outside.

And that makes me feel like singing the doxology!

Series of Sermons on Psalms

This book will help preachers to preach several series of sermons on Psalms. Psalms 1 and 2, which introduce the Psalter, can serve to start any series of sermons on psalms (see Chapters 2, pp. 46–75, and 10, pp. 214–39 above).

A Series of Sermons on the Christian Year

Since the psalms selected for this book follow the recommended readings for the Christian year of *The Revised Common Lectionary, Year A*, it provides guidance for preaching a series of twenty-two sermons on psalms covering the entire Christian year from the first Sunday of Advent to Christ the King Sunday (Chapters 2–23).[1] If desired, it will also provide help with shorter series of sermons on psalms such as Advent (Chapters 3–6, pp. 76–156) and Lent (Chapters 12–18, pp. 272–379).

A Series of Sermons on Creation–Fall–Redemption–New Creation

For "ordinary time" preachers can use this book to prepare a series of four or more sermons on psalms reinforcing the foundational biblical theme: Creation–Fall–Redemption–New Creation.[2] Preachers can select one or more psalms from each of the four categories (most psalms cover more than one category).

1. This and the following sermon series can be reinforced with congregational singing of each preached psalm as provided in *Psalms for All Seasons: A Complete Psalter for Worship*.
2. This sermon series can be reinforced with congregational singing not only from *Psalms for All Seasons* (n. 1 above) but especially from *Lift Up Your Hearts: Psalms, Hymns, and Spiritual*

Creation

Psalm 8: "O Lord . . . , How Majestic Is Your Name in All the Earth."
(Chapter 22)
Psalm 29: "The Voice of the Lord Is Powerful." (Chapter 9)
Psalm 104: "Bless the Lord, O My Soul." (Chapter 21)

Fall

Psalms 22: "My God, My God, Why Have You Forsaken Me?" (Chapter 18)
Psalm 51: "Create in Me a Clean Heart, O God." (Chapter 11)
Psalm 80: "Restore Us, O Lord God of Hosts." (Chapter 6)
Psalm 130: "Out of the Depths I Cry to You, O Lord." (Chapter 16)

Redemption[3]

Psalm 1, "Happy Are Those Whose Delight Is in the Law of the Lord."
(Chapter 2)
Psalm 2: "I Will Make the Nations Your Heritage." (Chapter 10)
Psalm 23: "The Lord Is My Shepherd." (Chapter 15)
Psalm 32: "Happy Are Those Whose Transgression Is Forgiven." (Chapter 12)
Psalm 47: "God Has Gone Up with a Shout . . . , with the Sound of a Trumpet."
(Chapter 20)
Psalm 72: "Give the King Your Justice, O God." (Chapter 4)
Psalm 100: "Make a Joyful Noise to the Lord, All the Earth." (Chapter 23)
Psalm 118: "O Give Thanks to the Lord." (Chapter 17)
Psalm 121: "The Lord Is Your Keeper." (Chapter 13)
Psalm 122: "Pray for the Peace of Jerusalem." (Chapter 3)
Psalm 146: "Happy Are Those Whose Help Is the God of Jacob." (Chapter 5)

Songs. The first part of *Lift Up Your Hearts* traces in its selected songs "The Story of Creation and Redemption: Old Testament Life and Witness, Advent Expectation, Christ's Life, Christ's Passion and Exaltation, Joining in the Spirit's Work, Trusting in the Triune God, and Hope for Things to Come" (p. v, Contents).

3. Since Psalms 47, 72, 122, and 146 reach beyond "Redemption" to the "New Creation," I have listed them under both categories.

New Creation

Psalm 47: "God Has Gone Up with a Shout . . . , with the Sound of a Trumpet." (Chapter 20)
Psalm 72: "Give the King Your Justice, O God." (Chapter 4)
Psalm 95: "Let Us Make a Joyful Noise to the Rock of Our Salvation." (Chapter 14)
Psalm 96: "Sing to the LORD a New Song." (Chapter 7)
Psalm 104: "Bless the LORD, O My Soul." (Chapter 21)
Psalm 122: "Pray for the Peace of Jerusalem." (Chapter 3)
Psalm 146: "Happy Are Those Whose Help Is the God of Jacob." (Chapter 5)

A Series of Sermons on "Beatitude" Psalms

In a series on "beatitude" psalms, one needs to be especially careful to understand the preaching text in the light of the whole psalm. From the psalms covered in this volume, one can select any of the following:

Psalm 1: "Happy Are Those Whose Delight Is in the Law of the LORD." (Chapter 2)
Psalm 2: "Happy Are All Who Take Refuge in Him." (Chapter 10)
Psalm 32: "Happy Are Those Whose Transgression Is Forgiven." (Chapter 12)
Psalm 146: "Happy Are Those Whose Help Is the God of Jacob." (Chapter 5)[4]

A Series of Two or More Sermons on a Lengthy Psalm

Preachers can also preach a series of two or more sermons on a lengthy psalm, as long as the preaching text is understood in the context of the whole psalm. We have already seen how this can be done above in Chapters 4 and 8 (Psalm 72) and 17 and 19 (Psalm 118). Since the structure of Psalm 72 divides into two sections with similar contents (see pp. 102–3 above), one could also preach a series of two sermons on Psalm 72:

---

4. Other psalms with "Happy," "Blessed" that might work in a "happy series" are Psalms 33:12; 34:8; 40:4; 41:1; 65:4; 84:4, 5, 12; 89:15; 94:12; 106:3; 112:1; 119:1, 2; 127:5; 128:1–2; and 144:15. For a happiness series on Book I, consider Pss 1:1; 2:11 (inclusio); 40:4; 41:1 (bookends around Book I); 32:1–2; 33:12; and 34:8. See Carl J. Bosma, "Discerning the Voices in the Psalms," *CTJ* 44 (2009): 165–66.

I. Prayer for the King and his Kingdom, I (vv 1–11)
II. Prayer for the King and his Kingdom, II (vv 12–20)

Psalm 51, also, consisting of two halves (see p. 249 above), offers more than enough material for two sermons:

I. Prayer to blot out our transgressions (vv 1–9)
    A. Prayer for God to blot out our sins (Ps 51:1–2)
    B. Acknowledgment that we are born sinners (Ps 51:3–5)
    C. Prayer for God to cleanse our "inward being" (Ps 51:6–9)
II. Prayer for a right spirit and vows (vv 10–19)
    A. Prayer for God to create "a clean heart" in us (Ps 51:10–12)
    B. Vow to spread the good news of God's "ways" (Ps 51:13–17)
    C. Prayer for Zion and a vow of "right sacrifices" (Ps 51:18–19)

Psalm 95, consisting of two distinct messages (see p. 323 above), could also be preached as a series of two sermons:

I. Make a joyful noise to the rock of our salvation, the great Creator God, submitting to him (vv 1–7c)
II. If you do not listen to (obey) the LORD's voice, you shall not enter his rest (vv 7d–11)

Other lengthy psalms we have presented can easily be turned into a series of two or three sermons. For example, Psalm 104 (pp. 469–501) has enough material for three sermons:

I. Praise the LORD, the great Creator (vv 1–9)
II. Praise the LORD, the great Provider (vv 10–30)
III. May the LORD rejoice in his works (vv 31–35)

Psalm 22 (pp. 405–35) can be preached in two or three sermons.

Two sermons:

I. David's lament: "My God, my God, why have you forsaken me?" (vv 1–21)
II. David's praise: "In the midst of the congregation I will praise you." (vv 22–31)

Three sermons:

I.   David, forsaken by God, pleads, "Do not be far from me" (vv 1–11)
II. David, on the brink of death, begs God, "Do not be far from me" (vv 12–21)
III. David praises and thanks God for his deliverance (vv 22–31)

A Series of Sermons on Editorially Connected Psalms

One can also preach series on the psalms the editor(s) of the Psalter intentionally linked together. For example, one can preach a two-sermon series on Psalms 1 and 2 which together introduce the Psalter, Psalms 9 and 10, Psalms 18 and 19, Psalms 32 and 33, Psalms 42 and 43,[5] Psalms 103 and 104,[6] Psalms 105 and 106, as well as Psalms 111 and 112, or a three-sermon series on Psalms 134, 135, and 136[7] (see Chapter 1, pp. 23–24, "The Context of Neighboring Psalms").

A Series of Sermons on Psalms with the Same Form

One can also prepare a series of sermons on psalms that have the same form. For example, since many of the Hymns of Praise "seek to enhance our awareness of God," one could preach a series of sermons on Hymns "which deal with various attributes and activities of God." Or one could preach a series of sermons on the Laments "which dissect with probing candor the anatomy of doubt, guilt, grief, and despair at both the individual and corporate levels."[8] Or one could

---

5. Psalms 42 and 43 are often identified as a single psalm and Psalms 32 and 33 as "a conjoined set." Miller, *The Way of the Lord,* 169.

6. Psalms 103 and 104 are clearly connected by their shared inclusios: each begins and ends with "Bless the LORD, O my soul" — a phrase that occurs only here in the Psalter. "The topic of the first is God as savior, who forgives sinners, and of the second is God as creator, who sustains all life. Together they provide a meditation on the two typical works of the LORD." Mays, *The Lord Reigns,* 121. Mays, "The Place of the Torah-Psalms," *JBL* 106, no. 1 (1987; pp. 3–12): 10–11, identifies Psalms 111 and 112, 105 and 106, 9 and 10, 18 and 19, and 118 and 119 as arranged "in pairs to bring topics together to create a more comprehensive theological statement."

7. "Psalm 135 picks up the emphases on praise and ministry in the house of the Lord expressed in Psalm 134 (cf. Ps 134:1 with 135:1–2). In turn, Psalm 135 prepares the reader for Psalm 136 with its emphasis on God's goodness (cf. Ps 135:3 with Ps 136:1)." Köstenberger and Patterson, *Invitation to Biblical Interpretation* (Grand Rapids: Kregel, 2011), 282.

8. William E. Hull, "Preaching on the Psalms," *RevExp* 81, no. 3 (1984): 451.

preach a series of sermons on the Songs of Thanksgiving,[9] or the Salvation History Psalms,[10] or the Psalms of Ascents (Pss 120–134), or a short series on the so-called imprecatory psalms.[11]

A Series of Sermons on Psalms with Similar Topics

- God's coming kingdom, Ps 2 (pp. 214–39 above), Ps 22 (405–35), Ps 72 (94–118, 177–89, 557–62), Ps 96 (157–76)
- God's creation, Ps 8 (502–27), Ps 29 (190–213), Ps 104 (469–501)
- God's forgiveness, Ps 32 (272–95), Ps 47 (447–68), Ps 51 (240–71), Ps 130 (364–79)
- God's justice, Ps 72 (94–118, 557–62), Ps 96 (157–76), Ps 146 (119–37)
- God's law, Ps 1 (46–75), Ps 32 (272–95), Ps 95 (316–39)
- God's providence, Ps 23 (340–63, 553–55), Ps 100 (528–48), Ps 104 (469–500), Ps 121 (296–315)
- God's salvation, Ps 22 (405–35), Ps 80 (138–56, 563–69), Ps 95 (316–39), Ps 118 (380–404, 436–46), Ps 130 (364–79)
- God's sovereignty, Ps 8 (502–27), Ps 29 (190–213), Ps 47 (447–68), Ps 100 (528–48)
- God's steadfast love, Ps 32 (272–95), Ps 51 (240–71), Ps 100 (528–48), Ps 118 (380–404)
- Prayer, Ps 32 (272–95), Ps 51 (240–71), Ps 72 (94–118, 177–89, 557–62), Ps 80 (138–56, 563–69), Ps 122 (76–93)
- Trust God, Ps 23 (340–63, 553–55), Ps 121 (296–315), Ps 146 (119–37)
- Worship / Praise / Thanks, Ps 8 (502–27), Ps 22 (405–35), Ps 47 (447–68), Ps 95 (316–39), Ps 96 (157–76), Ps 100 (528–48), Ps 104 (469–501), Ps 118 (380–404, 436–46), Ps 122 (76–93), Ps 146 (119–37)

A Series of Sermons on Favorite Psalms

William Hull offers the excellent suggestion "to introduce the congregation to the entire sweep of the Psalter by preaching a series on its best-known chapters" —

9. Bernhard Anderson, *Out of the Depths*, 214-15, lists as "Community Songs of Thanksgiving" Pss 65, 67, 75, 107, 124, and 136, and as "Individual Songs of Thanksgiving," Pss 18, 21, 30, 32, 34, 40:1-11, 66:13-20, 92, 103, 108, 116, 118, and 138.

10. Pss 78, 105, 106, 135, and 136. Anderson calls these "Narrative or Storytelling Psalms." Ibid., 213.

11. Select from Pss 12, 35, 52, 57-59, 69, 70, 83, 109, 137, and 140.

psalms that the congregation could select by popular vote. He himself offers a list of possible "classics": Pss 1, 8, 15, 19, 22, 23, 32, 46, 51, 73, 84, 90, 91, 103, and 139.[12] We have covered six of these. For Ps 1, see above pp. 46–75; Ps 8, pp. 502–27; Ps 22, pp. 405–35; Ps 23, pp. 340–63; Ps 32, pp. 272–95; and Ps 51, pp. 240–71.

12. Hull, "Preaching on the Psalms," *RevExp* 81, no. 3 (1984): 452.

Select Bibliography[1]

Achtemeier, Elizabeth. *Preaching from the Old Testament*. Louisville: Westminster / John Knox, 1989.

Allen, Leslie C. *Psalms 101–150*. Waco, TX: Word Books, 1983.

————. *Psalms: Word Biblical Themes*. Waco, TX: Word Books, 1987.

Alter, Robert. *The Art of Biblical Poetry*. New York: Basic Books, 1985.

————. *The Book of Psalms: A Translation with Commentary*. New York: Norton & Company, 2007.

Anderson, A. A. *Psalms 1–72* (The New Century Bible Commentary). Grand Rapids: Eerdmans, 1972.

————. *Psalms 73–150* (The New Century Bible Commentary). Grand Rapids: Eerdmans, 1981.

Anderson, Bernhard W. *Out of the Depths: The Psalms Speak for Us Today*. 3rd ed., rev. and expanded. Louisville: Westminster / John Knox, 2000.

Arthurs, Jeffrey D. *Preaching with Variety: How to Re-create the Dynamics of Biblical Genres*. Grand Rapids: Kregel, 2007.

Belcher, Richard P., Jr. *The Messiah and the Psalms: Preaching Christ from All the Psalms*. Fearn, Scotland: Mentor, 2006.

Bellinger, W. H., Jr. *Psalms: Reading and Studying the Book of Praises*. Peabody, MA: Hendrickson, 1990.

Berlin, Adele. *The Dynamics of Biblical Parallelism*. Bloomington: Indiana University Press, 1985.

Book of Common Worship. Louisville: Westminster/John Knox, 1993.

Brown, William P. *Seeing the Psalms: A Theology of Metaphor*. Louisville: Westminster / John Knox, 2002.

---

1. In order to keep the bibliography within reasonable limits, only books and a few articles frequently quoted are included in this bibliography. All other books, articles, and essays are fully referenced when first mentioned in each chapter and in shorter form thereafter.

————. *Psalms.* Nashville: Abingdon, 2010.

Broyles, C. *Psalms.* Peabody, MA: Hendrickson, 1999.

Brueggemann, Walter. *The Message of the Psalms: A Theological Commentary.* Minneapolis: Augsburg, 1984.

————. *The Psalms and the Life of Faith.* Minneapolis: Fortress, 1995.

————. *Texts for Preaching: A Lectionary Commentary Based on the NRSV — Year A.* Louisville: Westminster / John Knox, 1995.

Calvin, John. *Commentary on the Book of Psalms.* Vols I–V. Trans. James Anderson. Grand Rapids: Eerdmans, 1949.

Childs, Brevard S. *Introduction to the Old Testament as Scripture.* Philadelphia: Fortress, 1979.

Craigie, Peter C. *The Old Testament: Its Background, Growth, and Content.* Nashville: Abingdon, 1986.

————. *Psalms 1–50* (Word Biblical Commentary, Vol. 19, with a 2004 supplement by Marvin E. Tate). Dallas: Thomas Nelson, 2004.

Davidson, Robert. *The Vitality of Worship: A Commentary on the Book of Psalms.* Grand Rapids: Eerdmans, 1998.

Davis, Ellen F. *Wondrous Depth: Preaching the Old Testament.* Louisville: Westminster / John Knox, 2005.

DeClaissé-Walford, Nancy L., Rolf A. Jacobson, and Beth Laneel Tanner. *The Book of Psalms.* Grand Rapids: Eerdmans, 2014.

Delitzsch, Franz. *Biblical Commentary on the Psalms.* Vols. I–III. Trans. Francis Bolton. Grand Rapids: Eerdmans, 1959.

Dillard, Raymond B., and Tremper Longman, III. *An Introduction to the Old Testament.* Grand Rapids: Zondervan, 1994.

Eaton, J. H. *Psalms: Introduction and Commentary.* London: S.C.M., 1967.

————. *The Psalms: A Historical and Spiritual Commentary.* London: T&T Clark, 2003.

ESV Study Bible: English Standard Version. Wheaton, IL: Crossway, 2008.

Fokkelman, J. P. *Major Poems of the Hebrew Bible: At the Interface of Hermeneutics and Structural Analysis.* Vols. II and III. Assen: Van Gorcum, 1998.

Futato, Mark David. *Transformed by Praise: The Purpose and Message of the Psalms.* Phillipsburg, NJ: P & R, 2002.

————. *Interpreting the Psalms: An Exegetical Handbook* (Handbooks for Old Testament Exegesis). Grand Rapids: Kregel, 2007.

Gerstenberger, Erhard S. *Psalms: Part 1, With an Introduction to Cultic Poetry.* Grand Rapids: Eerdmans, 1988.

————. *Psalms: Part 2, and Lamentations.* Grand Rapids: Eerdmans, 2001.

Goldingay, John. *Songs from a Strange Land: Psalms 42–51.* Downers Grove, IL: InterVarsity, 1978.

————. *Psalms.* Vols. I–III (Baker Commentary on the Old Testament Wisdom and Psalms). Grand Rapids: Baker Academic, 2006.

Greidanus, Sidney. *The Modern Preacher and the Ancient Text: Interpreting and Preaching Biblical Literature.* Grand Rapids: Eerdmans, 1988.

————. *Preaching Christ from the Old Testament: A Contemporary Hermeneutical Method.* Grand Rapids: Eerdmans, 1999.

Grogan, Geoffrey W. *Psalms: The Two Horizons Old Testament Commentary.* Grand Rapids: Eerdmans, 2008.

Hayes, John H., et al. *Preaching the New Common Lectionary, Year A, Advent, Christmas, Epiphany.* Nashville: Abingdon, 1986.

————. *Preaching the New Common Lectionary, Year A, Lent, Holy Week, Easter.* Nashville: Abingdon, 1986.

————. *Preaching the New Common Lectionary, Year B, Advent, Christmas, Epiphany.* Nashville: Abingdon, 1987.

————. *Preaching Through the Christian Year, Year A: A Comprehensive Commentary on the Lectionary.* Philadelphia: Trinity, 1992.

Hilber, John Walter. *Psalms* (Zondervan Illustrated Bible Backgrounds Commentary: Old Testament). Grand Rapids: Zondervan, 2013.

Hossfeld, Frank-Lothar, and Erich Zenger. *Psalms 2: A Commentary on Psalms 51–100.* Trans. Linda M. Maloney. Minneapolis: Augsburg Fortress, 2005.

————. *Psalms 3: A Commentary on Psalms 101–150.* Trans. Linda M. Maloney. Minneapolis: Augsburg Fortress, 2011.

Kidner, Derek. *Psalms 1–72: An Introduction and Commentary on Books I and II of the Psalms.* London: InterVarsity, 1973.

————. *Psalms 73–150: A Commentary on Books III–V of the Psalms.* London: InterVarsity, 1975.

Knight, George A. F. *Psalms.* Vols. I and II. Philadelphia: Westminster, 1982 and 1983.

Kraus, Hans-Joachim. *Theology of the Psalms.* Trans. Keith Crim. Minneapolis: Augsburg, 1986.

————. *Psalms 1–59: A Commentary.* Trans. Hilton C. Oswald. Minneapolis: Augsburg, 1988.

————. *Psalms 60–150: A Continental Commentary.* Trans. Hilton C. Oswald. Minneapolis: Fortress, 1993.

Leupold, Herbert Carl. *Exposition of the Psalms.* Columbus, OH: Wartburg, 1959.

Lift Up Your Hearts: Psalms, Hymns, and Spiritual Songs. Ed. Joyce Borger, Martin Tel, and John D. Witvliet. Grand Rapids: Faith Alive Resources, 2013.

Limburg, James. *Psalms for Sojourners.* Minneapolis: Augsburg, 1986.

————. *Psalms* (Westminster Bible Companion). Louisville: Westminster/John Knox, 2000.

Longman, Tremper III. *Literary Approaches to Biblical Interpretation.* Grand Rapids: Baker, 1987.

————. "Psalms." In *A Complete Literary Guide to the Bible.* Ed. Leland Ryken and Tremper Longman III. Grand Rapids: Zondervan, 1993. Pp. 245–55.

McCann, J. Clinton, Jr. *A Theological Introduction to the Book of Psalms: The Psalms as Torah.* Nashville: Abingdon, 1993.

————. "Psalms." In *The New Interpreter's Bible.* Vol. 4. Nashville: Abingdon, 1994.

Magonet, Jonathan. *A Rabbi Reads the Psalms.* London: SCM, 1994.

Mays, James Luther. *Psalms* (Interpretation Commentary). Louisville: John Knox, 1994.

———. *The Lord Reigns: A Theological Handbook to the Psalms*. Louisville: Westminster, 1994.

———. *Preaching and Teaching the Psalms*. Ed. Patrick D. Miller and Gene M. Tucker. Louisville: Westminster / John Knox, 2006.

Miller, Patrick D. *Interpreting the Psalms*. Philadelphia: Fortress, 1986.

———. *They Cried to the Lord: The Form and Theology of Biblical Prayer*. Minneapolis: Fortress, 1994.

———. *The Way of the Lord: Essays in Old Testament Theology*. Grand Rapids: Eerdmans, 2007.

Newsome, James. *Texts for Preaching: A Lectionary Commentary Based on the NRSV —Year A*. Louisville: Westminster John Knox, 1995.

The NIV Study Bible. Ed. Kenneth Barker. Grand Rapids: Zondervan, 1985.

Nowell, Irene. *Sing a New Song: The Psalms in the Sunday Lectionary*. Collegeville, MN: Liturgical, 1993.

Petersen, David L., and Kent Harold Richards. *Interpreting Hebrew Poetry*. Minneapolis: Fortress, 1992.

Psalms for All Seasons: A Complete Psalter for Worship. Ed. Martin Tel, Joyce Borger, and John D. Witvliet. Grand Rapids: Calvin Institute of Christian Worship, Faith Alive Resources, Brazos, 2012.

Psalter Hymnal. Ed. Emily R. Brink. Grand Rapids: CRC Publications, 1987.

Rad, Gerhard von. *Old Testament Theology, Vol. 1: The Theology of Israel's Historical Traditions*. Trans. D. M. G. Stalker. Edinburgh and London: Oliver and Boyd, 1962.

———. *Biblical Interpretations in Preaching*. Trans. John E. Steely. Nashville: Abingdon, 1977.

Reardon, Patrick Henry. *Christ in the Psalms*. Ben Lomond, CA: Conciliar, 2000.

Rogerson, J. W., and J. W. McKay. *Psalms*. Vols. I–III. Cambridge: Cambridge University Press, 1977.

Ross, Allen P. *A Commentary on the Psalms*. Vol. I (1–41). Grand Rapids: Kregel, 2011.

———. *A Commentary on the Psalms*. Vol. II (42–89). Grand Rapids: Kregel, 2013.

Sabourin, Leopold. *The Psalms: Their Origin and Meaning*. New York: Alba House, 1974.

Sarna, Nahum M. *On the Book of Psalms: Exploring the Prayers of Ancient Israel*. New York: Schocken, 1993.

Stek, John H. "Psalms: Introduction and Notes." In *The NIV Study Bible*. Ed. Kenneth Barker. Grand Rapids: Zondervan, 1985.

Stott, John. *Favorite Psalms: Growing Closer to God*. Grand Rapids: Baker, 2003.

Tate, Marvin E. *Psalms 51–100* (Word Biblical Commentary, Vol. 20). Dallas: Word, 1990.

Terrien, Samuel. *The Psalms: Strophic Structure and Theological Commentary*. Grand Rapids: Eerdmans, 2003.

VanGemeren, Willem A. *Psalms* (The Expositor's Bible Commentary, Vol. 5; Rev. ed.). Ed. Tremper Longman III and David E. Garland. Grand Rapids: Zondervan, 2008.

Van Harn, Roger E., and Brent A. Strawn, *Psalms for Preaching and Worship: A Lectionary Commentary*. Grand Rapids: Eerdmans, 2009.

Vos, Cas J. A. *Theopoetry of the Psalms*. London: T & T Clark, 2005.

Wallace, Howard N. *Words to God, Words from God: The Psalms in the Prayer and Preaching of the Church*. Aldershot, Hampshire, England: Ashgate, 2005.

Waltke, Bruce K., and James M. Houston with Erika Moore. *The Psalms as Christian Worship: A Historical Commentary*. Grand Rapids: Eerdmans, 2010.

————. *The Psalms as Christian Lament: A Historical Commentary*. Grand Rapids: Eerdmans, 2014. (Waltke wrote the exegetical sections.)

Webster, Brian, and David R. Beach. *The Essential Bible Companion to the Psalms: Key Insights for Reading God's Word*. Grand Rapids: Zondervan, 2010.

Weiser, Arthur. *The Psalms: A Commentary*. Trans. Herbert Hartwell. Philadelphia: Westminster, 1962.

Wenham, Gordon J. *The Psalter Reclaimed: Praying and Praising with the* Psalms. Wheaton, IL: Crossway, 2013.

Westermann, Claus. *The Psalms: Structure, Content and Message*. Trans. Ralph D. Gehrke. Minneapolis: Augsburg, 1980.

————. *Praise and Lament in the Psalms*. Trans. Keith R. Crim and Richard N. Soulen. Atlanta: John Knox, 1981.

————. *The Living Psalms*. Trans. J. R. Porter. Grand Rapids: Eerdmans, 1989.

Whybray, R. N. *Reading the Psalms as a Book*. Sheffield: Sheffield Academic, 1996.

Wilcock, Michael. *The Message of Psalms 1–72: Songs for the People of God*. Downers Grove, IL: InterVarsity, 2001.

————. *The Message of Psalms 73–150: Songs for the People of God*. Downers Grove, IL: InterVarsity, 2001.

Williams, Donald M. *Psalms 1–72* (The Preacher's Commentary, Vol. 13). Nashville: Thomas Nelson, 1986.

————. *Psalms 73–150* (The Preacher's Commentary, Vol. 14). Nashville: Thomas Nelson, 1989.

Wilson, Gerald H. *Psalms*. Vol. I (The NIV Application Commentary: From Biblical Text . . . to Contemporary Life). Grand Rapids: Zondervan, 2002.

Witvliet, John D. *The Biblical Psalms in Christian Worship: A Brief Introduction and Guide to Resources*. Grand Rapids: Eerdmans, 2007.

Zenger, Erich, and Frank-Lothar Hossfeld. *Psalms 2: A Commentary on Psalms 51–100*. Trans. Linda M. Maloney. Minneapolis: Augsburg Fortress, 2005.

————. *Psalms 3: A Commentary on Psalms 101–150*. Trans. Linda M. Maloney. Minneapolis: Augsburg Fortress, 2011.

Subject Index

Select Scripture Index

Select Scripture Index